Routledge Handbook of Sport for Development and Peace

Sport and physical activity are now regularly used to promote social and economic development, peacebuilding and conflict resolution, on an international scale. The emergence of the 'Sport for Development and Peace' (SDP) sector, comprised of governments, NGOs, sport organizations and others, reveals a high level of institutionalization of this activity, while SDP now constitutes an important element of the scholarly analysis of sport.

This volume analyses and critically discusses the central elements of, and research issues within, the field of SDP and also provides a series of case studies (substantive and geographic) of key research. It is the most holistic and far-reaching text published on this topic to date. Featuring multidisciplinary perspectives from world-leading researchers and practitioners from around the world, the book covers a wide range of topics, including SDP structures, policies and funding streams, how SDP relates to human rights, social exclusion and corporate social responsibility, SDP and gender, SDP and disability, SDP and health, SDP and homelessness, and SDP and the environment.

The Handbook of Sport for Development and Peace is a vital resource for researchers, students and educators in the fields of sports studies, physical education, sport for development and peace, sport-based youth development, sport and politics, sociology of sport, and sport policy.

Holly Collison is Lecturer at the Institute of Sport Business, Loughborough University London, United Kingdom.

Simon C. Darnell is Assistant Professor at the Faculty of Kinesiology and Physical Education, University of Toronto, Canada.

Richard Giulianotti is Professor at the School of Sport, Exercise and Health Sciences, Loughborough University, United Kingdom and Professor II in the Department of Sports, Physical Education and Outdoor Studies, University of Southeast Norway, Norway.

P. David Howe is Associate Professor at the School of Kinesiology, Western University, Canada.

Routledge Studies in Sport Development

Series Editors

Richard Giulianotti
Loughborough University and University of Southeast Norway

B. Christine Green
University of Illinois at Urbana-Champaign

The *Routledge Studies in Sport Development* series showcases high-calibre work within the vibrant, diverse and rapidly expanding field of sport and development. It includes books in two broad areas. First, the *development of sport*, focusing on the various ways in which sport is delivered, for example through building sport facilities, training coaches and athletes, improving sport performance, increasing public participation in sport, and strengthening the governance, management, marketing and delivery of sport. Second, *sport for development and peace* (SDP), examining how sport is used for different non-sporting social benefits, such as peacebuilding and conflict reduction, health education, gender empowerment, community development, tackling crime, improving education, promoting 'positive youth development', and advancing the social inclusion of marginal populations. The series is committed to diversity in theory and method, is multidisciplinary in approach, and includes work centring on local, national and transnational issues and processes, and on the global North and/or South.

Available in this series:

Routledge Handbook of Sport for Development and Peace
Edited by Holly Collison, Simon C. Darnell, Richard Giulianotti and P. David Howe

Routledge Handbook of Sport for Development and Peace

Edited by Holly Collison, Simon C. Darnell,
Richard Giulianotti and P. David Howe

LONDON AND NEW YORK

First published 2019 by Routledge

2 Park Square, Milton Park, Abingdon, Oxfordshire OX14 4RN

52 Vanderbilt Avenue, New York, NY 10017

Routledge is an imprint of the Taylor & Francis Group, an informa business

First issued in paperback 2020

British Library Cataloguing-in-Publication Data
A catalogue record for this book is available from the British Library

Library of Congress Cataloging-in-Publication Data
A catalog record has been requested for this book

ISBN: 978-1-138-21048-6 (hbk)
ISBN: 978-0-367-52016-8 (pbk)

Typeset in Bembo
by Out of House Publishing

Contents

Contents

Contents

Contributors

Nida Ahmad is a PhD student, Faculty of Health, Sport and Human Performance, University of Waikato, New Zealand

Gary Armstrong is Senior Lecturer, Department of Sociology, City University, London, UK

Davies Banda is Senior Teaching Fellow, Moray House School of Education, University of Edinburgh, United Kingdom

Chris Barkley is Senior Business Development Advisor, Grassroot Soccer, South Africa

Pete Beeley is Partnerships Manager, Sport for Social Change, Comic Relief, United Kingdom

Bella Bello Bitugu is Director of Sports, University of Ghana, Ghana

David Black is Professor and Department Chair, Department of Political Science, Dalhousie University, Canada

Andrew Bloodworth is Senior Lecturer, Sport Science, College of Engineering, Swansea University, United Kingdom

Veerle De Bosscher is Professor, Department of Sports Policy and Management, Vrije Universiteit Brussel (VUB), Belgium

Evi Buelens is Pedagogical Mentor, Sport Coaches School, Flemish Sport Administration, Brussels, Belgium

Cora Burnett is Professor, Department of Sport and Movement Studies and Director of the Olympic Studies Centre, Faculty of Health Sciences, University of Johannesburg, South Africa

Hikabwa Chipande is Lecturer, Department of History, University of Zambia

Paul Darby is Reader, School of Sport, Ulster University, Northern Ireland

Colin Deal is a PhD student, Faculty of Kinesiology, Sport, and Recreation, University of Alberta, Canada

Pieter Debognies is a PhD student, Sport and Society and Voicing Youth, Vrije Universiteit Brussel (VUB), Belgium

Inge Derom is Assistant Professor, Department of Movement and Sport Sciences, Vrije Universiteit Brussel (VUB), Belgium

Peter Donnelly is Professor, Faculty of Kinesiology and Physical Education, University of Toronto, Canada

Henry Dorling is Senior Lecturer, School of Sport, Health and Social Science, Southampton Solent University, United Kingdom

Oliver Dudfield is Head of Sport for Development and Peace, Commonwealth Secretariat, United Kingdom

Jutta Engelhardt is Research Development Expert, Department of Health and Integration, Swiss Red Cross, Switzerland

James Esson is Lecturer, Department of Geography, Loughborough University, United Kingdom

Shawn Forde is a PhD student, School of Human Kinesiology, University of British Columbia, Canada

Audrey Giles is Professor, Faculty of Health Sciences, University of Ottawa, Canada

Andrew M. Guest is Associate Professor, Psychological Sciences, University of Portland, USA

Reinhard Haudenhuyse is Post-doctoral researcher, Sport and Society and Voicing Youth, Vrije Universiteit Brussel (VUB), Belgium

Lyndsay Hayhurst is Assistant Professor, School of Kinesiology and Health Science, York University, Canada

Ian Henry is Professor Emeritus, School of Sport, Exercise and Health Sciences, Loughborough University, United Kingdom

Sarah J. Hillyer is Director and Assistant Professor, Centre for Sport, Peace, and Society, University of Tennessee, USA

Hans Hognestad is Associate Professor, Department of Sports, Physical Education and Outdoor Studies, University of Southeast Norway, Norway

Nick Holt is Professor, Faculty of Kinesiology, Sport, and Recreation, University of Alberta, Canada

Ashleigh M. Huffman is Assistant Director and Assistant Professor, Center for Sport, Peace, and Society, The University of Tennessee, USA

Robert Huish is Associate Professor, Department of International Development Studies, Dalhousie University, Canada

Bora Hwang is a PhD student, School of Sport, Exercise and Health Sciences, Loughborough University, United Kingdom

Ruth Jeanes is Senior Lecturer, Faculty of Education, Monash University, Australia

Helene Jørgensen is a PhD student, Faculty of Kinesiology, Sport, and Recreation, University of Alberta, Canada

Tess Kay is Professor, College of Health and Life Sciences, Brunel University, United Kingdom

Laura Kelly is Research Fellow, Third Sector Research Centre, School of Social Policy, University of Birmingham, United Kingdom

Bruce Kidd is Vice President of the University of Toronto, Principal of University of Toronto-Scarborough, and Professor, Faculty of Kinesiology and Physical Education, University of Toronto, Canada

Friederike Kroner is Programme Coordinator, SCORE Namibia, Windhoek, Namibia

Roger Levermore is Associate Professor, Department of Management, Hong Kong University of Science and Technology, Hong Kong

Iain Lindsey is Associate Professor, Department of Sociology, Durham University, United Kingdom

Mary G. McDonald is Professor, Georgia Institute of Technology, USA

Mike McNamee is Professor, Applied Ethics in the College of Engineering, Swansea University, United Kingdom

Jonathan Magee is Research Officer, Institute of Sport, Exercise and Active Living, Victoria University, Australia

Alicia Malnati is Associate Research and Media Coordinator, Centre for Sport, Peace, and Society, University of Tennessee, USA

Will Massey is Assistant Professor, College of Public Health and Human Sciences, Oregon State University, USA

Rob Millington is Post-doctoral research fellow, School of Kinesiology and Health Science, York University, Canada

Arthur Milroy is Coaches Programme Coordinator at the International Olympic Committee, Lausanne, Switzerland

Oscar Mwaanga is Associate Professor, School of Sport, Health and Social Science, Southampton Solent University, United Kingdom

Zeno Nols is a PhD student, Sport and Society and Voicing Youth, Vrije Universiteit Brussel (VUB), Belgium

Steve Olivier is Vice Principal and Deputy Vice-Chancellor, University of the West of Scotland, United Kingdom

Angela Osborne is Researcher, Centre for Sport and Social Impact, La Trobe University, Australia

Sarah Oxford is Lecturer, Institute for Health and Sport, Victoria University, Australia

Kurtis Pankow is a PhD student, Faculty of Kinesiology, Sport, and Recreation, University of Alberta, Canada

Karen Petry is Deputy Head, Institute of European Sport Development and Leisure Studies, Deutschen Sporthochschule Köln, Germany

Shannon Pynn is a PhD student, Faculty of Kinesiology, Sport, and Recreation, University of Alberta, Canada

Dean M. Ravizza is Associate Professor and Senior Research Practitioner, Bosserman Centre for Conflict Resolution, Salisbury University, USA

James Rosbrook-Thompson is Senior Lecturer, Faculty of Arts, Law and Social Sciences, Anglia Ruskin University, United Kingdom

Anthony Rossi is Associate Professor, School of Exercise and Nutrition Sciences, Queensland University of Technology, Australia

Steven Rynne is Senior Lecturer, School of Human Movement and Nutrition Sciences, University of Queensland, Australia

Martha Saavedra is Associate Director, Center for African Studies, University of California, Berkeley, USA

Ben Sanders is an Independent Consultant in sport for development and peace

Nico Schulenkorf is Associate Professor, Sport Management, University of Technology Sydney, Australia

Emma Sherry is Associate Professor and Department Chair, Management and Marketing, Swinburne University, Australia

Katja Siefken is Lecturer, School of Health Sciences, University of South Australia, Australia

James Skinner is Professor, Institute of Sport Business, Loughborough University London, United Kingdom

Ramón Spaaij is Professor, Institute for Health and Sport at Victoria University, Australia, and Special Chair, Department of Sociology, University of Amsterdam, the Netherlands

Carolyn Spellings is Monitoring and Evaluation Coordinator, Center for Sport, Peace, and Society, University of Tennessee, USA

Max Stephenson Jr is Professor, and Director of the Institute for Policy and Governance, Virginia Tech, USA

Solveig Straume is Associate Professor, Faculty of Business Administration and Social Sciences, Molde University College, Norway

Naofumi Suzuki is Professor, Graduate School of Social Sciences, Hitotsubashi University, Japan

Holly Thorpe is Associate Professor, Faculty of Health, Sport and Human Performance. University of Waikato, New Zealand

Jasper Truyens is a PhD student, Sport and Society and Voicing Youth, Vrije Universiteit Brussel (VUB), Belgium

Christian Ungruhe is Post-doctoral fellow, Department of Public Health, Aarhus University, Denmark

Nicolien van Luijk is Post-doctoral fellow, School of Human Kinetics, University of Ottawa, Canada

Jikkemien Vertonghen is Post-doctoral researcher, Sport and Society and Voicing Youth, Vrije Universiteit Brussel (VUB), Belgium

Jon Welty Peachey is Associate Professor, College of Applied Health Sciences, University of Illinois, USA

Meredith Whitley is Assistant Professor, Exercise Science, Health Studies, Physical Education and Sport Management, Adelphi University, USA

Neftalie Williams is a PhD student, Faculty of Health, Sport and Human Performance. University of Waikato, New Zealand

Tom Woodhouse is Emeritus Professor, Department of Peace Studies and International Development, University of Bradford, United Kingdom

Geoffrey Woolcock is Research Fellow, Institute for Resilient Regions, University of Southern Queensland, Australia

Liv Yoon is a PhD student, School of Human Kinesiology, University of British Columbia, Canada

Kevin Young is Professor, Department of Sociology, University of Calgary, Canada

Laura Zanotti is Associate Professor, Department of Political Science, Virginia Tech, USA

Introduction

The focus of this handbook is 'Sport for Development and Peace' (SDP). SDP may be defined as a broad social field in which sport and related activities are used to pursue different types of non-sporting development and peacebuilding goals across the world (see Kidd 2008; Levermore 2008; Darnell 2012). These development goals are varied and centre, for example, on poverty reduction, education and training, conflict resolution, the empowering of women, the social inclusion of minorities, health promotion, and reducing urban crime and violence. SDP is also known by other titles, such as 'Sport for Development' (SFD), 'Sport for Change' and 'Sport for Good'. We also view SDP as encompassing other fields which use sport for development purposes, such as 'positive youth development' (PYD) in North America and 'sports-based interventions' in the UK (Kelly 2011; Holt 2016). As it is the best known of all these titles for such activities, we have elected to use SDP to capture the broad focus of this handbook.

Sport for development and peace: main features

We understand SDP to be a broad social field in which sport and related activities are utilized to pursue different types of non-sporting development and peacebuilding goals across the world (Kidd 2008; Levermore 2008; Darnell 2012). To elaborate on this definition, we see SDP as having several basic features.

SDP has a diverse range of development and peacebuilding goals. As the chapters in this handbook serve to demonstrate, these goals include drawing young people into education, employment and training; promoting conflict resolution and peaceful relations in divided communities; empowering women and promoting gender equality; assisting the social inclusion of people with disabilities; promoting health education, such as in tackling HIV/AIDS, obesity and diabetes; working to cut homelessness; and, reducing gang activity, urban violence and crime. The choice of specific SDP goals will depend to a large extent on the perceived needs in local areas, and will also vary over time.

The 'sports' within SDP are also highly diverse. Modern sports are central, particularly the most popular sport of football ('soccer'), with others such as baseball, basketball, cricket and rugby also figuring prominently (cf. Schulenkorf et al. 2016). But SDP also involves much more varied types of play and physical culture, including water sports, e-sports, capoeira, parkour, chess and children's games (see, for example, Thorpe 2016). SDP initiatives primarily centre on intervention programmes intended to promote social development and peace. These programmes use sport activities as attractive hooks to draw young people into participating, and as pedagogical devices to promote – and to educate young participants on – specific development and peacebuilding themes (Hartmann and Kwauk 2011; Kelly 2011). Programmes usually feature some monitoring and evaluation of impacts, although it is relatively rare for longitudinal studies to be implemented long after the activities have ended.

Finally, SDP is almost entirely focused on working with young people who are understood to be 'at risk' or are otherwise living in marginalized social contexts (Collison 2016). Hence, most SDP work is undertaken with young people in low- and middle-income countries (the 'global South'), although a substantial volume of SDP activity is conducted in high-income countries with socially excluded groups such as the young unemployed (Coalter 2013). The age-range of these young people varies according to local and national contexts, the goals of the programmes, and the expertise of the non-governmental organizations (NGOs), with a particular focus tending to be on youths aged in their early teens through to early twenties. While many early programmes tended to have a heavy bias towards male participants, from the mid-2000s onwards the field of SDP has been more explicitly focused on a stronger gender balance by engaging girls and young women in activities and in organizational management (Chawansky 2011).

The background and organization of SDP

We recognize that modern sports have always been used to promote specific, favoured types of personal and social development among young people and as such SDP can be seen as having a long and a short history. For example, many sports originated in English schools in the late nineteenth century, when various games were created and institutionalized with the aim of securing social order and cultivating a specific ideal of 'muscular Christian gentlemen' among male pupils (Mangan 1986). However, it was in the early 1990s that SDP really began to crystallize as a distinctive international field of activity, becoming a new 'movement' (Kidd 2008). SDP officials and volunteers came to identify themselves within this field, and to be tied into different sets of relationships and partnerships with each other. This institutionalization occurred through the establishment of distinctive organizations, methods, funding systems, partnerships, policies and programmes. There are now many hundreds of SDP programmes across the world, and even more organizations that contribute to delivering these SDP activities.

SDP's development has been significantly guided by its various relationships with the United Nations (UN) (Beutler 2008). The UN's Millennium Development Goals (MDGs) and Sustainable Development Goals (SDGs), running respectively from 2000–2015 and 2015–2030, have heavily influenced the shaping of many SDP programme objectives (UN 2003; 2015). The UN has also formally advocated for the role of sport in promoting development and peacebuilding, as Article 37 of the SDGs states:

> Sport is also an important enabler of sustainable development. We recognize the growing contribution of sport to the realization of development and peace in its promotion of tolerance and respect and the contributions it makes to the empowerment of women and of young people, individuals and communities as well as to health, education and social inclusion objectives.
>
> *UN 2015: 37*

Despite the global reach of the UN, the most important stakeholders within the field of SDP are the user groups of young people and their wider communities. These user groups vary enormously in their demographic, social and cultural profile, ranging for example from children traumatized by war, rape and ethnic cleansing in the world's poorest nations through to young adults receiving employment guidance or health education in Western Europe or North America.

The field of SDP is also made up of a wide range of organizational partners or stakeholders (Giulianotti 2011). NGOs make up the greatest number of these stakeholders, playing a pivotal role in organizing and delivering sport programmes. The world of sport also contributes substantially through its many athletes, clubs, leagues and federations, which help to resource or to run programmes, often through their own charitable foundations. Intergovernmental bodies such as the UN and Commonwealth Secretariat play key roles in delivering policy and strategy, acting as advocates for SDP, and delivering resources to different programmes. Local and national governmental bodies provide important support for SDP activities, particularly as gatekeepers to schools, sport clubs and communities. Private businesses also tend to act largely as donors to NGOs, ranging from funding international programmes through to donating equipment, food or transport to help run specific SDP events. Increasingly, SDP also features social enterprises which combine development and business activities, such as employing young people to manufacture sport equipment for SDP usage and for sale.

Scale is a critical factor in most of these stakeholder categories. For example, in the case of NGOs, international agencies tend to play a coordinating and fund-raising role, while local and national agencies tend to undertake the implementation work on the ground. In addition, most stakeholders enter into diverse partnerships in order to deliver SDP programmes. A distinct realm of activity, SDP also has relatively close ties to the wider development and sport fields. Many SDP programmes are supported by national and international development funds, and rely on access to sport facilities and coaches to deliver their activities. Further links arise between the SDP, education and youth fields, for example as SDP NGOs work with relevant government ministries in these other areas.

History, emergence and institutionalization

While there are particular features that serve to define the SDP sector in its current form, it is important to acknowledge that SDP is the latest iteration of sport designed and organized to meet non-sport goals and support social development. In this sense, while the idea and practice of sport for development has gained significant international traction in recent years, it also has a meaningful history. As Kidd (2008: 371) has argued:

> To be sure, social development through sport has a long history. Its aspirations can be traced back to the 'rational recreation' interventions of the improving middle and working class in the late nineteenth century, the 'playground movement' of the early twentieth century, and the confessional and workers' sports movements of the interwar period, among other antecedents. A more recent incarnation has been the 'midnight basketball' interventions in the United States and Canada. International social development through sport dates back to nineteenth-century colonizing.

Similarly, Giulianotti (2011) has suggested that the current SDP sector can be contextualized within a three-stage historical model. In the first stage (late eighteenth to mid-twentieth century) sport was implicated in European colonial projects; in the second (1940s to 1990s), sport was a 'highly contested field in colonial and post-colonial contexts' (Giulianotti 2011: 210); the third stage (mid-1990s onward) has seen a fuller emergence of the sport for development philosophy and the establishment of the SDP sector.

Both summaries serve as reminders that the history of sport is socially and politically complex, and even fraught, as is the history of international development itself. For many historians, the modern notion and era of 'development' was effectively called into being when then United States President Harry Truman delivered his inauguration speech of 1949 in which he called for developed nations to support the advancement of the world's underdeveloped people and countries (see Rist 1997). This invocation sparked an intense interest in international development throughout the second half of the twentieth century, particularly policies and practices led and delivered from the global North to the global South. Crucially, while Truman's call for a renewed commitment to development marked something of a break from the traditional colonial project (in that it suggested a model based primarily on technical assistance rather than evolutionary thinking or racial hierarchies) it still maintained — and even solidified — the unequal power relations and geo-political structures that had been created by European empires. This has led scholars like Ruth Craggs (2014: 5) to contend that:

> Although development as a global project and academic discipline may have begun in this [post-Second World War-] period, many scholars now argue that the ideas and practices that underpinned post-war development had their origins earlier, in the late colonial period.

In this sense, the very notion of development is something of a product of colonial thinking, an insight that is in turn germane to SDP given that sport was part of the colonial project, as a way for European colonial powers to export their preferred vision of social development and to train their own citizens (especially young men) to be good colonial subjects (Mangan 1998). Thus, when modern SDP practitioners claim 'a range of wider individual and collective benefits presumed to be associated with participation in sport' (Coalter 2013: 18) they are often drawing, either implicitly or explicitly, on ideas with significant historical roots.

This said, even though the history of development and sport respectively are important for explaining and understanding the current SDP sector, it would be an oversimplification to suggest that SDP is merely a continuation of the same cultural, political or ideological processes of colonialism or colonial-era sport. Indeed, important shifts were necessary for the SDP sector to cohere in the ways that it did in the late twentieth century. For example, Coalter (2010) has shown that the move in the 1990s away from international development policy based heavily on economics and towards approaches that embraced 'softer' and more culturally focused development goals such as promoting social capital, provided a context in which champions of sport's social benefits could secure an ideological and political footing for their programmes. Similarly, the new threats and issues that shaped the international development landscape in the 1990s, notably the HIV/AIDS pandemic on the African continent, presented whole new types of development challenges, but also ones to which sports people and sport organizations were well positioned to respond (Mwaanga 2010). Finally, the historical connections between sport and peacebuilding, conflict resolution and reconciliation (Giulianotti and Armstrong 2011) meant that sport already had a departure point from which to enter into contemporary conflicts and propose peaceful solutions.

The result was the emerging institutionalization of the SDP sector at the turn of the millennium. In 2001, UN Secretary-General Kofi Annan named former Swiss President Adolf Ogi to the newly created position of Special Advisor on Sport for Development and Peace. A year later, the UN convened an Inter-Agency Task Force on Sport for Development and Peace to study the possibilities for SDP within the UN system. In 2003, the First International Conference on Sport and Development was held in Magglingen, Switzerland, sponsored by Ogi's office, the Swiss Agency for Development and Cooperation, and the Swiss Federal Office of Sport. It marked one of the first times that the international sport community *and* the international development community came together, and still stands as a landmark event in the institutionalization of SDP.

This momentum continued throughout the early 2000s. An international working group on SDP was created after the 2004 Olympics in Athens. The working group was intergovernmental and designed to convince and lobby national governments to take an interest in SDP. Originally led by SDP non-governmental organization *Right to Play* (the first secretariat of the working group) it was eventually steered by the newly formed UN Office on Sport for Development and Peace (UNOSDP). By 2013, the UN went so far as to proclaim 6 April to be the annual 'International Day of Sport for Development and Peace,' stating that:

> The adoption of this day signifies the increasing recognition by the United Nations of the positive influence that sport can have on the advancement of human rights, and social and economic development.
>
> *UN 2013*

Finally, the institutionalization of SDP reached new heights in 2015, when the United Nations announced the Sustainable Development Goals and the 2030 Agenda for Development. Sport's inclusion in the SDGs was a significant acknowledgement of the institutionalization of the SDP sector, and recognized SDP as a potentially powerful and useful tool in the fight to enhance global equality. However, with such lofty goals, the SDP sector is a ripe environment for critical reflection and a large part of this current volume is designed to aid both students and practitioners in the field to engage with these critical processes.

Critical issues

Academic inquiry has both advocated for the use of sport within development contexts while simultaneously exposing critical issues therein. Here we touch on a number of critical issues that stand as key points of debate and tension within the sector.

One such issue is the very notion of *development* itself, and in particular its ambiguity. Scholars have for some time challenged the idea of development and contested its various forms and definitions (Black 2010). For some, 'development' has become a term in vogue. Rist suggests 'the meaning of the term "development" remains vague, tending to refer to a set of beliefs and assumptions' about the nature of social progress rather than anything more precise' (2007: 485). Through the second half of the twentieth century, development was seen largely in terms of facilitating economic growth. However, in recent years there has been a much greater recognition of the diverse social aspects of human development, as reflected in both the MDGs and the SDGs. Such issues of ambiguity and contestation over definition are not uncommon within the SDP sector, as well as its broader connecting fields, which can lead to conflict but also opportunity.

In turn, as the practice of sport, physical activity and physical education has been connected to various development contexts, the spectrum of SDP models and approaches has also expanded. In 2007, Coalter proposed a classification of the different approaches to SDP based on the emphasis given to sport to achieve specific objectives. While acknowledging potential overlap between different approaches to programming, Coalter nonetheless identified *Sport Plus*, in which sports are adapted or augmented with development objectives, and *Plus Sport*, where sport is used to attract participants for the purpose of achieving development objectives. In its purest sense, *Plus Sport* programmes operate in the absence of any sport development agendas. However, the overlaps or blurred lines between these different styles of programing also create debate, and even provokes questions like: 'is that SDP?'. The issue of which comes first, sport or development, is also embedded in broader discussions about evaluation, impact, objectives, scale, professionalization, funding and partnerships. While this tension between *Sport Plus* and *Plus Sport* is not easily reconciled, we might argue that, as with many critical issues within the sector, it is healthy for fostering ongoing critical engagement and reflection.

In a somewhat similar manner, the SDP landscape is often organized and oriented with reference to a top down or a bottom-up approach (Black 2017). In the former, the main international development actors are considered to be the relatively powerful actors who have the authority and resources to direct or even impose their development agenda on less powerful others. This is contrasted by the latter, in which development is (and/or should be), locally defined and driven, and accompanied by policies and research that aim 'to privilege the perspective of historically subaltern groups, and to act in partnership or solidarity with them' (Black 2017: 9). The distinction and tension between top down and bottom up leads to a number of critical issues for the SDP sector, including connections (between decision-makers, implementers and recipients), contexts (power, transnational relationships and local-global politics) and inequalities (root causes, economic disparity, social capital). It also has implications for research and the approaches taken by SDP analysts. Some research, for example, is conducted from the standpoint of top-level policy-making (Hayhurst 2009), organizational practices (Giulianotti 2011) or global and emerging trends within the sector (Darnell *et al.* 2017), whereas others focus on grassroots-level community programming (Burnett 2014), local voices and perspectives (Collison 2016), and cultural or Indigenous practices (Mwaanga and Mwansa 2013). Many of the chapters in this collection demonstrate this diversity of approach, and therefore speak to the ongoing tension between top down and bottom up.

Sport is also popular and even culturally seductive, and this has increased its use as a tool to enhance global development. Political leaders, decision-makers, corporations, agencies, celebrities and, indeed, local groups and participants have all been drawn to the passion that the practice of sport can produce, and attempted to harness this within the SDP sector (Collison 2016). For some, this seductive power of sport can lead to forms of 'evangelism', in which 'unquestioned beliefs' emerge regarding the power of sport's ability to transform the world, largely through 'wishful thinking' (Giulianotti 2004; Coakley 2011: 307). It is also from this standpoint of unquestioned beliefs that Coalter draws attention to the need for critical assessments of SDP. As he concludes, in the SDP sector 'there is little space for sceptics, less for agnostics and atheists are beyond the pale' (Coalter 2013: 35). The issue of evangelism therefore has implications for the integrity of the sector, and the need for advocacy, growth, accountability, and monitoring and evaluation based on data and critical appraisals.

This leads to the final critical issue discussed here: monitoring and evaluation (M&E). The requirement and need for M&E has become one of the most significant challenges, and sites of critique, within the SDP sector in recent years. It is connected to knowledge production, as well as engagement with and between local organizations, the influence of external donors and even debates over methodologies (Kay 2012). Even the assumption that M&E is an appropriate tool for evidencing impact and assessing the worth of SDP has been questioned, especially as it is often aligned with the politics of legitimacy, accountability, sustainability and validation (Jeanes and Lindsey 2014). In turn, many social scientists have highlighted the importance of M&E in empowering local voices and have advocated for participatory methodologies within these processes (Burnett 2008; Nicholls *et al.* 2011). An additional point of contestation is whether conducting research and managing M&E are one and the same. We would argue that the assumption that research *necessarily* informs, guides, influences or even constructs M&E frameworks or evidence is misguided. Progressive research methodologies focused on M&E, for example participatory action research, may well serve the dual purpose of knowledge production while producing and assisting with the formal process of evidencing and reporting, but the relationship between these processes requires ongoing negotiation and reflexivity.

The structure of the handbook

The historical context and the critical issues outlined above run throughout this text. With this in mind, the handbook is organized into four parts: The SDP sector; The social study of SDP; Themes and issue in SDP; and SDP in national contexts. We submit that organizing the volume in this way will be useful for both academics and practitioners alike. Those new to the field of SDP, such as students and newly employed practitioners, will likely find part one informative while part two is designed to highlight how different theoretical positions and academic disciplines have contributed substantially to the sector. The critical issues section will be of use to all with an interest in the SDP sector, as it illuminates many of issues that are worthy of ongoing reflection. The final section offers important case studies focused on specific national and regional contexts. It is also important to state that given constraints of space and word count, we could not include a chapter focused on each and every national context in which SDP has an impact; instead we selected different types of locations to highlight the diversity of SDP on a global scale.

Part one begins with an analysis of the historical backdrop of SDP before discussing the distinctive nature and key characteristics of SDP as a field or 'sector'. We turn then to examine the global development of SDP, and to explore the structure and organization of the sector. The next chapters consider different organizational stakeholders within SDP; highlight the large numbers and pivotal roles of NGOs; assess the work of the International Olympic Committee (IOC) within the sector; and explore the role of the private sector by focusing on the realm of corporate social responsibility in SDP. Part one concludes with detailed discussions of the reoccurring and emerging themes of the UN's Sustainable Development Goals, Monitoring and Evaluation, Human Rights and Social Exclusion – and the influence that they are likely to have upon future developments within the sector.

The second part of the handbook addresses the social study of the SDP sector, and begins with a general introduction to the importance of social theory in the pursuit of robust academic accounts of the field. The chapters on research methods and ethics underline their importance for students and academics when studying and researching SDP, and also aim to inform practitioners on how scholars in the sector go about their work. This leads to discussion of two important theoretical approaches – feminist and post-colonial perspectives – which are adopted widely across the sector. We then provide three chapters that discuss the contributions of distinctive academic disciplines to the study of SDP. Anthropology, arguably the starting point for both development studies and colonial exploitation, has reinvented itself over the last three decades and now makes a major and critical contribution to the SDP sector. In turn, the disciplines of psychology and management, respectively, have also made important contributions to developing the sector, and to enabling students, academics and practitioners to make sense of SDP.

In part three of this handbook, we examine themes and issues that are central to much of the work in the SDP sector. The diversity of these themes and issues, and the range of contexts in which they arise, mean that this is the largest section of the handbook, featuring fifteen chapters. It starts by exploring important social issues including gender, peace, disability and volunteering, as well as issues of social capital and health. Education and understandings of positive youth development are also taken up in this part of the handbook. In turn, part three highlights the significance of diverse issues, from the role of actions sports and coaching to issues of homelessness and the plight of refugees. The importance of the environment is also discussed, before discussions turn to specific national and regional case study examples.

The final part of the handbook explores SDP in national and regional contexts, and includes chapters focused on locations across both the global South and North that are highly diverse in geographical, political, cultural, economic and social terms. It begins with an analysis of SDP work in the broader African context with specific reference to sports academies. What follows is an analysis of SDP in the Belgian context, specifically on the region of Flanders. We then turn to explore SDP work in five continents, in Cambodia, Canada, Australia, Cuba and Liberia, respectively. The focus on Norway examines the role of a leading donor nation with respect to SDP and its influence on Africa. The final three chapters also explore SDP in varied locations, with a focus on the African continent's most developed nation (South Africa), a relative newcomer to the sector (South Pacific), and a nation (Zambia) often regarded as the diamond in the SDP crown.

Overall, the handbook features a total of 46 chapters; given the rapid growth of the SDP sector in recent years it likely could have included many more. If, as we anticipate, the sector continues to expand, we are confident that the growing global community of scholars focused on SDP will continue to fill emerging knowledge gaps, and contribute to what is one of the most significant fields of study to have emerged in sport, and in development, over the past few decades.

References

Beutler, I. (2008). Sport serving development and peace: Achieving the goals of the united nations through sport. *Sport in Society*, *11*(4), 359–369.

Black, D. R. (2010). The ambiguities of development: Implications for 'development through sport'. *Sport in Society*, *13*(1), 121–129.

Black, D. R. (2017). The challenges of articulating 'top down' and 'bottom up' development through sport. *Third World Thematics: A TWQ Journal*, *2*(1), 7–22.

Burnett, C. (2014). The intersecting life worlds of sport for development (SfD) coaches in the Kiambiu slum of Nairobi, Kenya. *African Journal for Physical Health Education, Recreation and Dance*, *20*(3): 963–973.

Burnett, C. (2008). Participatory action research (PAR) in monitoring and evaluation of sport-for-development programmes: Sport and physical activity. *African Journal for Physical Health Education, Recreation and Dance*, *14*(3), 225–239.

Chawansky, M. (2011) New social movements, old gender games? Locating girls in the sport for development and peace movement. In A. Snyder and S. Stobbe (eds), *Critical Aspects of Gender in Conflict Resolution, Peace Building and Social Movements*. Bingley: Emerald.

Coakley, J. (2011). Youth sports: What counts as 'positive development?', *Journal of Sport and Social Issues*, *35*(3), 306–324.

Coalter, F. (2007). *A Wider Social Role for Sport: Who's Keeping the Score?* New York: Routledge.

Coalter, F. (2010). The politics of sport-for-development: Limited focus programmes and broad gauge problems? *International Review for the Sociology of Sport*, *45*(3), 295–314.

Coalter, F. (2013). *Sport for Development: What Game are we Playing?* London: Routledge.

Collison, H. (2016). *Youth and Sport for Development: The Seduction of Football in Liberia*. London: Palgrave Macmillan.

Craggs, R. (2014). Development in a global–historical context. In V. Desai and R. Potter (eds), *The Companion to Development Studies* (3rd edn). London: Routledge, pp. 5–10.

Darnell, S. C. (2012). *Sport for Development and Peace: A Critical Sociology*, London: Bloomsbury.

Darnell, S. C., Giulianotti, R., Howe, P. D. and Collison, H. (2017). Re-assembling sport for development and peace through actor network theory: Insights from Kingston, Jamaica. *Sociology of Sport Journal*, 1–34.

Giulianotti, R. (2004). Human rights, globalization and sentimental education: The case of sport. *Sport in Society*, 7(3), 355–369.

Giulianotti, R. (2011). Sport, peacemaking and conflict resolution: A contextual analysis and modelling of the sport, development and peace sector. *Ethnic and Racial Studies*, 34(2), 207–228.

Giulianotti R. (2011a). The sport, development and peace sector: A model of four social policy domains. *Journal of Social Policy, 40*: 757–776.

Giulianotti, R. and Armstrong, G. (2011). Sport, the military and peacemaking: History and possibilities. *Third World Quarterly*, 32(3): 379–394.

Hartmann, D. and C. Kwauk (2011). Sport and development: An overview, critique, and reconstruction. *Journal of Sport and Social Issues*, 35(3), 284–305.

Hayhurst, L. M. (2009). The power to shape policy: Charting sport for development and peace policy discourses. *International Journal of Sport Policy*, 1(2), 203–227.

Holt, N. (ed.) (2016) *Positive Youth Development Through Sport*. London: Routledge.

Jeanes, R. and Lindsey, I. (2014). Where's the 'evidence?' Reflecting on monitoring and evaluation within sport-for-development. *Sport, Social Development and Peace*. Bingley: Emerald. pp. 197–217.

Kay, T. (2012). Accounting for legacy: Monitoring and evaluation in sport in development relationships. *Sport in Society*, 15(6), 888–904.

Kelly, L. (2011). 'Social inclusion' through sports-based interventions? *Critical Social Policy*, 31(1), 126–150.

Kidd, B. (2008). A new social movement: Sport for development and peace. *Sport in Society*, 11(4), 370–380.

Levermore, R. (2008). Sport: A new engine of development? *Progress in Development Studies*, 8(2), 183–190.

Mangan, J. A. (1986) *The Games Ethic and Imperialism: Aspects of the Diffusion of an Ideal*. London: Viking.

Mangan, J. A. (1998). *The games Ethic And Imperialism: Aspects of the Diffusion of an Ideal*. London: Routledge.

Mwaanga, O. (2010). Sport for addressing HIV/AIDS: Explaining our convictions. *LSA Newsletter*, 85(March), 61–67.

Mwaanga, O. and Mwansa, K. (2013). Indigenous discourses in sport for development and peace: A case study of the Ubuntu cultural philosophy in Edusport Foundation, Zambia. *Global Sport-for-Development*. London: Palgrave Macmillan, pp. 115–133..

Nicholls, S., Giles, A. R. and Sethna, C. (2011). Perpetuating the 'lack of evidence' discourse in sport for development: Privileged voices, unheard stories and subjugated knowledge. *International Review for the Sociology of Sport*, 46(3), 249–264.

Rist, G. (1997). *The History of Development: From Western Origins to Global Faith* (3rd edn). London: Zed Books.

Rist, G. (2007). Development as a buzzword. *Development in Practice*, 17(4–5), 485–491.

Schulenkorf, N., Sherry, E. and Rowe, K. (2016). Sport for development: An integrated literature review. *Journal of Sport Management*, 30: 22–39.

Thorpe, H. (2016). Action sports for youth development: Critical insights for the SDP community. *International Journal of Sport Policy and Politics*, 8(1), 91–116.

United Nations (UN). (2003). Sport as a Tool for Development and Peace: Towards Achieving the United Nations Millennium Development Goals, Geneva: UN Inter-agency Task Force on Sport for Development and Peace.

UN. (2013). International Day of Sport for Development and Peace. Available at: www.un.org/sport/content/about-unosdp/international-day-sport-development-and-peace.

UN. (2015). Transforming our World: The 2030 Agenda for Sustainable Development. Available at: https://sustainabledevelopment.un.org/post2015/transformingourworld.

Part I
The SDP sector

1

The history of SDP

Rob Millington and Bruce Kidd

Introduction

Sport for development and peace (SDP) has been referred to as a 'new' social movement that has emerged as a strategy for realizing broad developmental objectives in the last three decades (Kidd 2008). Most of the articles in this *Handbook* place SDP in this period. Yet throughout recorded history, sport and physical activity (and their earlier variants) have regularly been associated with notions of promoting 'social good'. In classical Greek societies, athletics, and gymnastics (the antecedents to sport and physical education today[1]) were understood to offer an avenue to both personal and societal transformation. In Plato's *Republic*, Socrates and Glaucon reflect on the importance of gymnastic training for guardians of the city, and compare the similarities between athlete and soldier. In *Nicomachean Ethics*, Aristotle discusses athletics as an avenue for the maintenance of strength and self-worth in the absence of war, writing, 'a courageous action in war is pleasant, it is concealed in the same way that the pleasure of honour and victory felt by a boxer endures to obtain that honour' (cited in Giulianotti and Armstrong 2011: 380). The parallels drawn here between athlete and soldier, between athletics and war, were not unique to the philosophers of antiquity. Indeed, in many societies, both competitive and non-competitive forms of physical activity have been popularly associated with military prowess in the interests of promoting social good, however defined, from the celebrated mesomorphic bodies of gods, soldiers, and athletes in classical Greece and Rome to the use of sport in British imperialist expansion (Park 2007a; 2007b). In the twenty-first century, notions of 'sport for good', by which we mean sport initiated, organized and played for social purpose,[2] remain steadfast, underpinned by similar 'common-sense' understandings of sport's seemingly innate ability to spur social transformation.

Despite this history, it is only recently that sport has been institutionalized within the international development sector. Once seen by the development community as an indulgence, or even a distraction from more pressing matters (Holden 2008), sport is now directly connected to the achievement of major development policies, including the Sustainable Development Goals (SDGs), the United Nation's (UN) primary development mandate through 2030 (United Nations n.d.). Sport's rise within the development paradigm is visible in many spheres, from governmental agencies to non-governmental organizations, to corporate social responsibility endeavors. In the public sphere, government agencies have advocated for – and initiated – sport for development programs. Germany, for instance, has a governmental program dedicated to Sport for Development (see Federal Ministry of Economic Cooperation and Development n.d.), while the Government of Canada has listed sport for development as one of the five objectives of the current Canadian Sport Policy, and the Truth and Reconciliation Commission of Canada has made five recommendations as to how sport can be utilized in meeting the aims of reconciliation with Indigenous peoples (Truth and Reconciliation Commission of Canada 2015; Government of Canada 2016). Outside the global North, Ghana has been an advocate of SDP throughout the African Union, and Cuba has used sport and physical activity programs to promote development both at home and abroad (Huish, Carter and Darnell 2013). International sporting federations such as the International Olympic Committee (IOC) and the Fédération International de Football Association (FIFA) have also developed their own SDP programs, and sport mega-events like the Olympic Games and the FIFA World Cup are increasingly connected to development strategies for host nations in the global South. Non-governmental organizations such as the Kenya-based *Mathare Youth Sport Association* and the Canadian-based *Right to Play* have made sustained interventions, while corporate social responsibility endeavors, like Nike's *Girl Effect*, are increasingly popular and commonplace. The UN has also been an ardent advocate for SDP since the early 2000s, in not only connecting sport to development policies including the Millennium Development goals (MDGs) and Sustainable Development Goals (SDGs), but also in creating the UN Office on Sport for Development and Peace (operational from 2001–2017), the position of Special Advisor to the Secretary-General on Sport for Development (currently Wilfried Lemke), and in naming 2005 as the International Year for Sport and Physical Education.

This chapter discusses the emergence and growth of SDP within this trajectory. It begins by placing SDP in the longer history of 'sport for good' so as to feature the ideological and programmatic antecedents of SDP today. It then briefly discusses the early internationalization of 'sport for good' through nineteenth and early twentieth-century colonialism and imperialism, its incorporation in human rights discourses via the United Nations in the second half of the twentieth century, and the global spread of non-governmental organizations and social movements employing sport in the twenty-first century. The chapter then turns to the emergence of SDP in the early 1990s, identifying the features that distinguish it from earlier forms of 'sport for good' and the social and political conditions that enabled its growth and influence. The chapter concludes with a discussion of the political and social issues facing SDP today, and offers some pressing questions for future avenues of research.

History of 'sport for good'

SDP is the most recent expression of the long tradition of 'sport for good' that has shaped modern sports from their beginnings in the early nineteenth century. In fact, for most of the modern period, it was taken for granted that sport should be conducted for social purpose, especially individual and community development and improvement. Yet as older forms of 'sport for good' were marginalized by the late twentieth-century triumph of global capitalist sport (i.e. sport for commodity production, which developed sport for careers through professional sport) and 'sport for sport's sake' (i.e. sport for winning and 'bragging rights'), SDP has taken on a distinct identity with the renewal of 'sport for good' focused on the global South. We argue therefore that sport for development is not a new social movement per se, as much as a rather familiar expression of the ambition of 'sport for good'. This section traces the history of 'sport for good' from the idea of sport for education and nation-building that emerged from the game-playing curriculum of the nineteenth-century British public school through the age of imperialism and its use of sport as a colonizing tool, to the role of 'sport for good' in human rights movements in the second half of the twentieth century to SDP today.

Early examples: sport, character building, and colonialism

In their work on sport, militarism, and peacekeeping, Richard Giulianotti and Gary Armstrong (2011) detail three phases that demarcate sport's historical ties to social transformation and social good: 'colonialism and civilization' spanning from the late eighteenth to mid-twentieth centuries; 'nationalism, ideology and armed conflict' from the mid-twentieth to early twenty-first century; and contemporary SDP. In the first phase, sport was a key element in empire building and colonial expansion, particularly in Britain. The formative institution was the all-male, upper-class British 'public' school, where a succession of progressive headmasters transformed the once delinquent, rough-and-ready culture of game-playing, in the context of the early industrial revolution and rapid urbanization, into an approved curriculum of moral and leadership development organized around sports. Those reforms simultaneously provided the structure for modern sports. The Christian socialist Thomas Hughes dramatized the educational power of sport in his best-selling *Tom Brown's Schooldays*, and despite contemporary critics and satirists, who lampooned it as 'muscular Christianity', Hughes succeeded in legitimating sports as a force for education and social benefit throughout the globe. Hughes' joyous vision of sport as character- and nation-building influenced youth leaders, policy-makers and parents everywhere and can still be heard in athletic banquets and SDP fund-raisers to this day (MacAloon 2008).

The reality, though, was more complex. While many boys enjoyed rewarding experiences from sport, such as gaining habits of mind, confidence and friendship networks that stood them in good stead throughout their lives, others were damaged and embittered by the experience. Then, as now, the nature of opportunities varied widely and affected different boys in strikingly different ways. Moreover, despite the promotion of the now familiar values of a 'level playing field' and fair play for all, there was a decidedly upper-class and masculine bias to early modern sport. Few opportunities were extended to working-class boys and men – none for girls and women – and where they were, under the banner of 'rational recreation', it was as much a form of social control as humanitarian outreach. Sport for the 'lower classes' stressed 'civilized' behavior as an alternative to drinking, gambling, and idleness, and promoted self-improvement and the values of rationality, industry, purpose, and respectability (Donnelly 2011).

Yet the ideals of 'sport for good' were taken up by a wide array of organizations, including state schools, playgrounds, amateur sports clubs, and secular and faith-based youth groups such as the Boy Scouts, the YMCA, and the Young Hebrew Association. These quickly spread to other countries through emulation, trade, emigration, and imperialism. With the creation of the Dominion of Canada in 1867, for example, middle-class nationalists transformed the sports introduced by the British garrisons into a vehicle for citizenship education and Canadian nation-building (Kidd 2011). Such was the appeal that even those excluded groups who were forced to create their own opportunities and organizations to enjoy sport at all – in western societies this meant the organized working classes, girls and women, immigrants and Indigenous peoples – developed a strong sense of social purpose (Kidd 2006).

The belief in the moral and civilizing force of sport readily lent itself to the tasks of Empire in what is now the global South, in a way that eerily prefigures SDP today (Donnelly 2011; Donnelly *et al.* 2011). In both Britain and the United States, sport and physical education were seen as avenues to train soldiers for domestic and international policing. Physical education transformed colleges into 'theaters of organized physical combat', instilling enlightened cultural values within the nation and abroad (Park 2007b: 1641). The new codes of imperialist manliness – physical courage, strength, endurance, sportsmanship, and patriotism – were expanded in romanticized visions of the soldier, the pioneer, and the athlete in the colonial 'frontier' (Allen 2011).

Soldiers, missionaries, and educators played a prominent role in promoting the ideals of sport and social good, deploying them in the colonial *milieu* through what J. A. Mangan (2006) has called 'missionary muscularity'. These men, Mangan (2006: 780) argues, stood as 'striking testimony to the power of the uplifted Christ to draw to himself ... all that is noblest in strength and finest in culture'. Through sport, Empire and Christian mission were thus inextricably linked, in not only training of soldiers and missionaries, but also as a means of social control and cultural imperialism (Hokkanen and Mangan 2006). Teaching colonial subjects sports such as cricket was seen as part of the larger project of leading 'barbarous' nations and peoples along a teleological path to modernity and civilization that framed the colonizer as the possessor of knowledge to be benevolently bestowed upon the colonizers and in ways that justified colonial rule (Hokkanen and Mangan 2006). Near the end of the nineteenth century, more than 10,000 British missionaries had been sent overseas at the cost of two million pounds annually, a sum equal to the entire annual cost of British civil service salaries (Giulianotti and Armstrong 2011). Australia and Canada, white settler countries within the Empire, increasingly did the same. The British Empire was thus in part an enormous sports complex, driven institutionally by the military and the church; 'sport travelled the world with the bullet and the bible' (Hokkanen and Mangan 2006: 382).

Sport, human rights, and self-determination

To be sure, not all those on the receiving end accepted these efforts with deference. Within many colonized countries the enlightenment values of liberalism instilled through sport (i.e. rationality, free thought, equality) were turned toward anti-colonial purposes (Gidwani 2008). In the British West Indies, for example, cricket carved out a distinct space for independence movements and the subversion of colonial rule. In Barbados, Trinidad, Saint Lucia, and Jamaica, nationalist sentiment on the cricket pitch boiled over into mass mobilizations for independence (James 1969; Holden 2008; MacLean 2009). The same occurred in the American imperial setting. Although baseball was intended to provide teachers, military personnel, and missionaries with the comforts of home, while dissuading what were perceived to be uncivilized behaviors and local sporting practices, it unwittingly stimulated resistance to imperialism. Local teams in Japan, Cuba, and the Philippines challenged notions of white superiority and rule (Gems 2006). In each of these cases, the anti-colonial leaders employed arguments that drew upon the ideals of 'sport for good'.

After World War II, many of these anti-imperial movements gained legitimacy through the United Nations, referencing the 1948 United Nations Declaration of Human Rights. The Universal Declaration set out the UN's goal for international cooperation to achieve a common standard of freedoms and rights. Drawing upon the tradition of liberalism, the Declaration affirmed '"life, liberty and security of person", "equality before the law", and the freedoms of thought, expression and peaceful assembly and association; and [the] prohibition of "discrimination", "slavery or servitude", "arbitrary arrest", and "torture or cruel, inhuman or degrading treatment or punishment."' It also affirmed collective rights such as the rights to social security, education, a 'standard of well-being adequate to health and well-being' and 'rest and leisure' (United Nations 1948). Sport was a key avenue in actualizing the right to self-determination, through state membership in the UN and other international governing bodies, as well as international sporting federations like the IOC and FIFA (see Darby 2005; Millington 2015). This, of course, is not to say that membership for newly independent states within these groups was fully accepted. Within the Olympic movement, recognition as a National Olympic Committee did not automatically bring membership on the IOC itself, so, and despite their numbers, African and Asian nations often saw their interests ignored. It was this circumstance, in the context of broader efforts to create an independent bloc of 'third world' countries, that an effort was made in the 1960s to organize the Games of the New Emerging Forces (GANEFO), with a focus on solidarity and non-western sport. Although the games were held but once, in Jakarta in 1963, the idea of a global South-centric sporting event remained alive for many years. It is also worth noting that during the period between World War I and World War II, other excluded groups, notably the workers' sports associations and first-wave feminist sports organizations, held their own version of the Olympics (Kidd 2005).

There are many other examples where human rights activists used the well-known moral claims of sport associated with 'sport for good' to broaden their support. The international campaign against apartheid sport, led by exiled black South African sportspersons and supported by athletes and sport organizations around the world, eventually succeeded in stopping all international sporting exchanges with apartheid South Africa, effectively denying the white supremacist regime the legitimacy provided by international competition (Kidd and Donnelly 2000). In addition, while much of sport remains a bastion of hyper-masculinity, sport has also proven an effective arena for the struggle for women's rights. The first World Conference on Women in Sport, held in 1994, built upon the World Conference on Human Rights a year prior that affirmed the rights of women and girls as inalienable and integral parts of universal human rights. The Brighton Declaration of Women and Sport, which emerged from the 1994 conference, promises the provisions of human rights, equal opportunity to participate in sport, and the fair allocation of resources, power, and responsibility without discrimination on the basis of sex – notions recalled under Title IX in the US, and the Charter of Rights and Freedom in Canada (cited in Kidd and Donnelly 2000). Worker's rights movements have also targeted sport-manufacturing sweatshops operating in developing countries, including those of Nike, Umbro, and Adidas, for their working conditions and use of child labor (Kidd and Donnelly 2000).

The long tradition of 'sport for good' led the UN and other international forums to enshrine sport and physical actively in the Universal Declaration of Human Rights, the International Charter on Physical Education and Sport (1978, revised as the International Charter of Physical Education, Physical Activity and Sport in 2015), the International Convention of the Rights of the Child (1990), and most recently, in the International Convention on the Rights of Persons with Disabilities (2006) (Kidd 2008). These undertakings provided the backdrop for the growing support for SDP. To be sure, though, the story of sport and human rights is complex and contested. As Richard Giulianotti (2004) argues, while the Universal Declaration sets out both individual and collective rights, western governments largely ignore the collective rights they proclaim; they also largely ignore the histories of colonialism that necessitated such a declaration. This history is often overlooked in contemporary SDP practices. And yet, hegemonic notions of 'sport for good', enveloped in discourses of human rights and self-determination, continue to underpin the contemporary SDP movement.

The emergence of SDP

From the preceding it is clear that the history of sport and social good has informed and shaped the contemporary moment within which SDP has emerged. Yet it is also important to situate the SDP movement within the broader development history, *writ large*. It is only more recently that scholars have flagged this gap. Simon Darnell and David Black (2011) have noted that it is significant that most of the academic attention paid to SDP has been located within sport studies, rather than development studies. SDP needs to be integrated with all forms of development, including its history.

For many, this development history begins in 1949, with US President Harry Truman's inauguration, in which he called for a new, post-war program that made

> the benefits of [American] scientific advanced and industrial progress available for the improvement and growth of underdeveloped areas. [...] The old imperialism, exploitation for foreign profit [Truman continued,] has no place in our place. What we envisage is a program of development based on the concepts of democratic fair dealing.
>
> *quoted in Esteva 1992: 6*

The significance of Truman's speech rests in the reframing of global South countries from colonial appendages to autonomous, 'underdeveloped' nations that required the aid of the global North, thus de-linking development from colonial exploit – at least in theory. While not officially welcomed into the development fold until the early 2000s, sport played a prominent role in this new vision, albeit in an ad hoc manner. In the late 1940s, sport was used in reconstructive efforts of a post-World War II Europe by the United Nations Relief and Rehabilitation Administration for Reconstruction and Rehabilitation; in the 1950s and 1960s, it played a role in the political posturing of the Cold War and anti-colonial struggles; and the 1970s and 1980s saw early efforts to push for more social measures of development by UNESCO and the IOC's Olympic Solidarity commission (see Giulianotti and Armstrong 2011; Millington 2015).

The late 1980s and early 1990s saw a more formalized effort in implementing sport in the development context, through the reintroduction of the Olympic Truce and the UN's Declaration of 1994 as the 'International Year of Sport and the Olympic Ideal'. Whereas previously traditional 'sport for good' projects focused on the provision of basic sports coaching, equipment and infrastructure (for instance, the Norwegian Olympic Committee started to support sport-for-all projects in Tanzania in 1984 (Kidd 2008; Coalter 2010)), sport for development programs in the 1980s and 1990s began to focus on humanitarian assistance, particularly for refugees, and more broadly based endeavors, such as education and public health. With the decline of state-interventionist model and the rise in entrepreneurialism as a strategy of social development post-Cold war, the first early sport for development efforts were led by athletes and non-governmental organizations (NGOs). These groups responded to the appeals of post-apartheid southern African activists for sport-related international aid, and drew upon the increasing popularity of international aid campaigns like 'make poverty history'. As Kidd has noted:

> These efforts resonated with the growing use of sport in the developed world to address 'social problems', the increasing inclusion in human rights campaigns of the rights to sport, physical education and play, especially with the ratification of the International Convention on the Rights of the Child in 1990; the internationalization of feminist efforts to realize full opportunities for girls and women at the Brighton, Windhoek, Montreal and Kumamoto conferences; and ... the reassertion of the benefits of sport and physical activity through the World Health Organization, UNESCO and other international bodies.
>
> *Kidd 2008: 374*

Most prominent among these initiatives was that of Norwegian four-time Olympic speed skating champion, Johan Olav Koss. Seeking to give something back after the 1992 Lillehammer Olympics, Koss, with the aid of a range of NGOs including the Red Cross, Save the Children, and the Norwegian People's Council, created a sport-focused humanitarian program, *Olympic Aid*. *Olympic Aid*, which originally sought to raise funds for vaccinations and emergency goods to children in Sarajevo and Afghanistan (Kidd 2008). Over time, the program began to conduct its own programs for children in refugee camps, eventually growing into one of the more prominent SDP NGOs, *Right to Play*. *Right to Play* now operates in 20 countries, predominantly in the global South, and seeks to 'use play to educate and empower children and youth to overcome the effects of poverty, conflict and disease in disadvantaged communities' (Right to Play, n.d.).

Social and political conditions that enabled SDP

From these early efforts, SDP has emerged as one of the more celebrated and visible forms of international development. This rise to prominence continues to be informed by universal ideals attributed to sport, the transformative opening created by the end of the Cold War and fall of apartheid, and the do-it-yourself ideology spurred by neoliberal ideology. Further, the ascension of SDP is a response, at least in part, to the failings of traditional development policy and philosophy, and the persistence of underdevelopment in much of the world (Levermore and Beacom 2009). These failures have spurred the advance of a 'fourth pillar' of development aid – direct, multilateral, and private development aid being the other three pillars – that includes non-specialist development agencies and seeks to address the social and cultural components of development (Develtere and De Bruyn 2009; Darnell and Black 2011). SDP has been a natural avenue for these non-specialist agencies that include non-governmental and corporate organizations.

The UN has also advocated for the benefits of this fourth pillar and the role of sport therein. In 2005, the UN called upon ten stakeholders – including NGOs, corporation, sporting federations, and an emerging class of socially conscious athletes – to take up the sport for development cause (UNOSDP 2005). Thus, what distinguishes the SDP movement from previous manifestations of sport for good is its 'almost exclusive emphasis upon international development, its entrepreneurial youth leadership, its focus on individual empowerment as a strategy for social change [and] its insistence upon non-governmental organizations' (Kidd 2011: 608). Furthermore, whereas sport has been used for the purposes of 'development' since at least the 1940s, it was predominantly done so in an unofficial way (see Millington 2015); in the contemporary context, sport has become increasingly formalized and institutionalization within the development community. Indeed, that former UN Secretary-General Ban Ki-Moon heralded sport as a means to make the world a 'better, more tolerant place for all', and integrated sport into the highest levels of development policy, illustrates the rise of SDP (United Nations 2015).

Issues and research questions

Despite the fanfare with which SDP has been greeted by the international community, it faces many of the same pitfalls as conventional development: a proliferation of organizations that compete with each other for donors and beneficiaries; a lack of political, democratic, and regulatory accountability; a proclivity for relying upon and promoting neoliberal approaches to development (e.g. an underpinning belief in an individual responsibility for development, recalling the 'bootstraps' model of development that characterized the 1990s); and a reliance upon hegemonic power dynamics between the global North and South (see Darnell and Black 2011; Kidd 2011).

Indeed, as Simon Darnell (2007: 561) notes, the SDP paradigm remains dependent upon and operates through two overlapping frameworks: 'that of sport and play as universal and integrative social practices' that recall previous notions of sport for good, and that of 'international development as the benevolent deliverance of aid, goods and expertise from northern, "First World" to the southern, "Third World"'.

As noted above, 'mainstreaming' SDP within the broader development paradigm remains a central issue to scholars in both sport and development studies. Part of this effort rests in grappling with the notion of development itself. That the idea of development has been mobilized for a myriad of socially transformative ends – from imperialism, to colonialism, to humanitarianism – speaks to the draw of progress narratives, and the encompassing and amorphous nature of the term itself. As Douglas Hartmann and Christina Kwauk (2011) argue, 'the multiplicity and ambiguity around conceptions of development presents one of the most important initial challenges for understanding and theorizing the sport and development field' (p. 268). Indeed, while development has come to hold a broader set of political meanings (human rights, neoliberal, neocolonial), the underlying sentiment of 'helping the world's poor', combined with apolitical understandings of sport for social good, have come to perpetuate a priori understandings of sport's contribution to meeting development aims.

In practice, while there have been substantial successes in SDP interventions, development achievements remain difficult to sustain and apply across diverse social and cultural settings, and often fail to address systemic matters of underdevelopment. We also know that even the best interventions can have harmful effects. David Black (2010) has noted that Rwanda was portrayed as a development 'success story' until the 1994 genocide, and the neoliberal ideologies that defined development theory and policy in the 1980s and 1990s, despite some initial successes, have in many cases undermined development efforts. Further, the development industry has grown to such a degree that it is now marred by competing interests and ambiguity. These issues further illustrate the need to account for the history of sport and/in development. Given the relatively new institutionalization of SDP within the development sector, recognizing the broader development history affords SDP advocates an opportunity to learn from 'from some of the dangers and missteps that have befallen more "mainstream" development practitioners through the chequered post-Second World War history of this enterprise' (Black 2010: 122).

Highlighting the history of sport for development thus provides an opportunity to explore how sport might offer an alternative approach to development, while identifying future research questions. These questions pertain to the historical implications of sport for development, the SDP industry, and the notions of sport for good.

- Historically, since there are powerful continuities, both ideologically and organizationally (e.g. Right to Play began as Olympic Aid) what are the antecedents of other SDP programs and what are the historically determined power dynamics in which they operate?
- In its enthusiasms and blind spots, SDP is decidedly neoliberal. To what extent does it thus bear the DNA of the period in which it was developed (i.e. the end of the Cold War and apartheid and the hopeful phase of neoliberalism, along with its distrust of government and the welfare state)?
- Organizationally, how might SDP programs better address the need to compete for donors, volunteers, and participants? What forms of oversight can be established that ensure NGOs and SDP programs are accountable? And in terms of 'sport for good', how can SDP program ensure that human rights are protected?

Further, the promotion and protection of human rights remains a central concern within SDP research. While human rights discourses pervade the mission statements of SDP programs, there are few assurances that human rights are not being infringed upon, particularly in large-scale SDP initiatives, like those attached to the hosting of sport mega-events (see Zhang and Silk 2006; Millington and Darnell 2014). The case of the 2010 Olympics in Beijing offers a recent example, where development promises, including the protection of human rights, were attached to the Games. Yet *Amnesty International* and *Human Rights Watch* documented multiple human rights violations in the build up to, as well as during, the event and the freedom of speech of athletes was often stymied (Kidd, 2010).

The history sketched out in this chapter is not intended to depict the present as a 'necessary outcome of a necessarily continuous past' (Dean 2002: 21), but rather to chart some of the historical movements and maneuverings that have come to inform the emergence of SDP. While sport has long been seen as a force of social good, it has also reached what Fred Coalter (2010) calls an idealist, mythopoeic status – elements of truth are at play, but these truths become distorted and repeatable so as to evoke vague and generalized images regarding sport and development, rendering it apolitical, and erasing darker parts of its history. In this way, rather than purely a force of 'social good', SDP is best understood as an 'empty form' (see Hartmann and Kwauk 2011), its meaning derived by those who use it, and confined to the time and space in which it is used. Viewing SDP as an empty form may be productive in ensuring that sport for development programs are malleable and geared toward the specificities of local contexts. Importantly, however, such a construction does not remove the need to foreground the history of SDP so as to challenge what are often ahistorical, apolitical, and a priori understandings of sport and social good.

Notes

1 While it is commonplace to equate modern forms of sport with earlier game-forms and contests as a trans-historical category, we choose to distinguish them, accepting Norbert Elias' (1972) famous caution that the 'similarities outweigh the differences'. We do accept that there has been some sort of trans-historical effort to recruit forms of physical activity to contemporarily valued social purpose.
2 The term was coined by Donnelly (1982).

References

Allen, D. (2011). A man's game: Cricket, war and masculinity, South Africa, 1899–1902. *The International Journal of the History of Sport*, 28(1), 63–80.

Black, D. R. (2010). The ambiguities of development: Implications for 'development through sport'. *Sport in Society*, 13(1), 121–129.

Coalter, F. (2010). The politics of sport-for-development: Limited focus programmes and broad gauge problems? *International Review for the Sociology of Sport*, 45(3), 295–314.

Darby, P. (2005). The new scramble for Africa: The African football labour migration to Europe. In J. A. Mangan (ed.), *Europe, Sport, World: Shaping Global Societies*. Portland, OR: Frank Cass, pp. 217–244.

Darnell, S. C. (2007). Playing with race: Right to play and the production of whiteness in 'development through sport'. *Sport in Society*, 10(4), 560–579.

Darnell, S. C. and Black, D. R. (2011). Mainstreaming sport into international development studies. *Third World Quarterly*, 32(3), 367–378.

Dean, M. (2002). *Critical and effective histories: Foucault's methods and historical sociology*, XX: Routledge.

Develtere, P. and De Bruyn, T. (2009). The emergence of a fourth pillar in development aid. *Development in Practice*, 19(7), 912–922.

Donnelly, P. (1982). Social climbing: A case study of the changing class structure of rock climbing and mountaineering in Britain. In A. Dunleavy, A. Miracle and R. Rees (eds), *Studies in the Sociology of Sport*. Fort Worth, TX: Texas Christina University Press, pp. 13–28.

Donnelly, P. (2011). From war without weapons to sport for development and peace: The Janus-face of sport. *SAIS Review*, 31(1), 65–76.

Donnelly, P., Atkinson, M., Boyle, S. and Szto, C. (2011). Sport for development and peace: A public sociology perspective. *Third World Quarterly*, *32*(3), 589–601.

Elias, N. (1972). The Genesis of sport as a sociological problem. In E. Dunning (ed.), *The Sociology of Sport*. Toronto: University of Toronto Press.

Esteva, G. (1992). Development. In W. Sachs (ed.), *The Development Dictionary: A Guide to Knowledge as Power*. London & New York: Zed Books, pp. 6–25.

Federal Ministry of Economic Cooperation and Development (n.d.). Issue: Sport for Development. Available at: www.bmz.de/en/what_we_do/issues/sport-for-development/index.html.

Gems, G. R. (2006). Sport, colonialism, and United States imperialism. *Journal of Sport History*, *33*(1), 3–25.

Gidwani, V. (2008). *Capital, Interrupted: Agrarian Development and the Politics of Work in India*. Minneapolis: University of Minnesota Press.

Giulianotti, R. G. (2004). Human rights, globalization and sentimental education: The case of sport. *Sport in Society*, 7(3), 355–369.

Giulianotti, R. G. and Armstrong, G. (2011). Sport, the military and peacemaking: History and possibilities. *Third World Quarterly*, *32*(3), 379–394.

Government of Canada. (2016). Sport in Canada. Available at: http://canada.pch.gc.ca/eng/1414151906468.

Hartmann, D. and Kwauk, C. (2011). Sport and development: An overview, critique, and reconstruction. *Journal of Sport and Social Issues*, *35*(3), 284–305.

Hokkanen, M. and Mangan, J. A. (2006). Further variations on a theme: The games ethic further adapted – Scottish moral missionaries and muscular Christians in Malawi. *The International Journal of the History of Sport*, *23*(8): 1257–1274.

Holden, G. (2008). World cricket as a postcolonial international society: IR meets the history of sport. *Global Society*, *22*(3), 337–368.

Huish, R., Carter, T. F. and Darnell, S. C. (2013). The (soft) power of sport: The comprehensive and contradictory strategies of Cuba's sport-based internationalism. *International Journal of Cuban Studies*, *5*(1), 26–40.

James, C. L. R. (1969). *Beyond a Boundary*. London: Stanley Paul.

Kidd, B. (2005). Another world is possible: recapturing alternative Olympic histories, imagining different games. In K. Young and K. Wamsley (eds), *Global Olympics: Historical and Sociological Studies of the Modern Games*. Bangalore, India: Elsevier, pp. 145–160.

Kidd, B. (2006). Muscular Christianity and value-centred sport: the legacy of Tom Brown in Canada. *International Journal of the History of Sport*, *23* (5), 701–713.

Kidd, B. (2008). A new social movement: Sport for development and peace. *Sport in Society*, *11*(4), 370–380.

Kidd, B. (2010). Human Rights and the Olympic Movement after Beijing, *Sport in Society*, *13*(5), 901–910.

Kidd, B. (2011). Cautions, questions and opportunities in sport for development and peace. *Third World Quarterly*, *32*(3), 603–609.

Kidd, B. and Donnelly, P. (2000). Human rights in sports. *International Review for the Sociology of Sport*, *35*(2), 131–148.

Levermore, R. and Beacom, A. (2009). *Sport and International Development*. London: Palgrave MacMillan.

MacAloon, J. (ed.). (2008). *Muscular Christianity in Colonial and Post-colonial Worlds*. London: Routledge.

MacLean, M. (2009). A national(ist) line in postcolonizing cricket: Viv Richards, biographies and cricketing nationalism. *Sport in Society*, *12*(4–5), 537–550.

Mangan, J. A. (2006). Christ and the imperial playing fields: Thomas Hughes's ideological heirs in empire. *The International Journal of the History of Sport*, *23*(5), 777–804.

Millington, R. (2015). *The United Nations and Sport for Development and Peace: A Critical History* (Unpublished doctoral dissertation). Queen's University, Kingston, ON, Canada.

Millington, R. and Darnell, S. C. (2014). Constructing and contesting the Olympics online: The internet, Rio 2016 and the politics of Brazilian development. *International Review for the Sociology of Sport*, *49*(2), 190–210.

Park, R. J. (2007a). Biological thought, athletics and the formation of a 'man of character': 1830–1900. *The International Journal of the History of Sport*, *24*(12), 1543–1569.

Park, R. J. (2007b). Physiologists, physicians, and physical educators: Nineteenth century biology and exercise, hygienic and educative. *The International Journal of the History of Sport*, *24*(12), 1637–1673.

Right to Play. (n.d.). 'Where we work.' Available at: www.righttoplay.com/Learn/ourstory/Pages/Where-we-work.aspx.

Truth and Reconciliation Commission of Canada. (2015). *Summary of the Final Report of the Truth and Reconciliation Commission of Canada*. Winnipeg, MB: Truth and Reconciliation Commission of Canada.

United Nations. (1948). *Universal Declaration of Human Rights. UN General Assembly.*

United Nations. (2015). 'Ban calls on world's athletes to help bolster emerging new UN sustainability agenda.' *Sport for Development and Peace: The UN System in Action.* Retrieved from www.un.org/wcm/content/site/sport/home/template/news_item.jsp?cid=42802.

United Nations. (n.d.). Sport and Sustainable Development Goals. Available at: www.un.org/sport/content/why-sport/sport-and-sustainable-development-goals.

United Nations Office on Sport for Development and Peace. (2005). *The Magglingen Call to Action 2005.* Geneva: United Nations.

Zhang, T. and Silk, M. L. (2006). Recentering Beijing: Sport, space, and subjectivities. *Sociology of Sport Journal, 23*(4), 438–459.

2

The SDP sector

Richard Giulianotti

Introduction

Since its emergence in the early 1990s, the sport for development and peace (SDP) sector has rapidly established itself as a prominent site of activity within global sport, and as a familiar, if still seemingly quirky, component of the wider field of international development. In this chapter, I set out in detail the SDP sector with a particular focus on its organizational aspects and, through use of the concept of 'global civil society', its location within international development. The discussion is anchored by a relatively broad definition of the SDP sector, as encompassing many different agencies, communities, programmes, and campaigns which use sport to promote diverse kinds of non-sporting social development and peacemaking around the world. The majority of SDP activity is aimed at assisting young people who are marginalized or otherwise 'at risk', for example with regard to poverty, health, work, education, gender inequality, disability, or violent conflict. Building on prior studies of the SDP sector (Giulianotti 2011a; 2011b), the chapter responds in part to calls for social scientists to consider more fully how the development sector is organized and structured (Watkins *et al.* 2012; Viterna and Robertson 2015).

The scope and status of the SDP sector

To begin, it is important to confirm some key points on the status and scope of the SDP sector. I understand the field of SDP as constituting a distinctive *sector* for three main reasons: in terms of *identity*, officials who work with SDP organizations largely view themselves as part of a distinct field of activity, particularly vis-à-vis the broader development (or aid) and sport sectors; second, in terms of *institutionalization*, there is an increasing array of experts, knowledge systems (such as programme manuals), organizations, funding schemes, and career pathways that focus on SDP; and third, there are expanding matrices of *relationships* (contacts, links and partnerships), which occur across diverse actors within the SDP domain.

Turning to consider the scope of the SDP sector, this is broad in three main senses. First, the sector encompasses activities in both *the global North and the global South*. Most SDP work is undertaken by NGOs in low- and middle-income countries, particularly sub-Saharan Africa. At the same time, many leading SDP stakeholders – such as sport federations, national governments, and NGOs – are based in the global North, while several leading international NGOs such as Right to Play, streetfootballworld, and the Homeless World Cup support activities in high-income countries. Intervention programmes in the South and North also often share the same set of themes, such as gender empowerment, crime reduction, and improving youth employability. Thus, as in the development sector, we might query the extent to which we should differentiate between SDP work in the global North and South (cf. Lewis 2015).

Second, most SDP activities aim to have *pragmatic developmental benefits* for young people, such as in improving job prospects or changing health-related behaviours. However, the definition of SDP provided here – referring to sport-related activities that pursue wider non-sporting social benefits – is sufficiently broad for us to look beyond this technical focus, to include concern with *social justice* issues, for example on economic inequality, democratization, and human rights. Third, while the SDP sector refers by name to 'sport', its range of activities is much wider and includes *play, games, and physical culture*; for example, capoeira, parkour, hiking, fishing, snow and water activities, new and old children's games, and also e-sports.

Sport, development, and global civil society

The SDP sector has complex interrelationships with the respective sport and development sectors. First, there are significant and often unacknowledged ties between SDP and the *development of sport* sectors. Initially, they appear as mutually exclusive: 'development of sport' is concerned with sport per se, for example building sport facilities, promoting public participation in sport, and improving sport performance; conversely, SDP has specific *non*-sporting objectives. Yet, at everyday level, these two categories are often deeply interconnected: for example, SDP NGOs often rely on help from local and national sport authorities, and access to local sport coaches and facilities, in order to deliver programmes; and, elite athletes, sport clubs and governing bodies often have their own charitable foundations or social responsibility departments to support sport-based social interventions.

Second, the SDP sector has varied links with the *wider development and peacebuilding sectors*. Many key players within the development field – such as the Council of Europe, United Nations, and national development agencies like USAid or NORAD (Norway) – also contribute significantly to sport-related development work. SDP is a field of activity for mainstream development NGOs, but also a focus for public relations work by corporations, and for advancing the foreign policy interests of different nations and governments. Yet at local and national levels, one recurring weakness in SDP work by NGOs relates to a lack of coordination or integration within the wider development sector in these locations.

I have argued elsewhere that the SDP sector should be viewed as part of *global civil society* (Giulianotti 2011a). According to Kaldor (2003: 591), global civil society is a kind of competitive political space in which diverse groups and organizations contest 'the arrangements that shape global developments'. The field of international development per se is perhaps the most obvious and largest component of global civil society. Seen this way, the SDP sector appears as a complex field in which different groups and organizations – diverse NGOs, social movements, governmental bodies, corporations, sport bodies, and more – seek to advance their own philosophies, interests and agendas on development and peacebuilding, and on how sport should be marshalled to achieve their diverse aims and objectives. This picture of SDP provides the main theoretical context for my four-fold model of the SDP sector, to which I now turn.

The SDP sector: a four-fold model of policies and stakeholders

In prior work, I mapped out the SDP sector through an ideal-type model of four sets of social policies and philosophies that are associated with types of organizational or professional SDP stakeholder (Giulianotti 2011a). Like any other ideal type, this model is not intended to account for all empirical aspects of SDP; instead, the model seeks to capture and to categorize the underlying tendencies, properties, and logics of this specific field of social life (cf. Weber 1949: 90).

The four SDP policy and stakeholder categories are as follows:

1. *Neoliberal* social policies, which are particularly associated with the *corporate or private sector*, and thus with programme donors. In the wider policy context, neoliberalism generally centres on reducing welfare spending, privatizing state assets, and idealizing the free market and the individual consumer (Harvey 2005). The neoliberal approach to SDP and to social development leans towards private, choice-based acts of philanthropy, and towards the charitable foundations of corporations, particularly in the form of 'corporate social responsibility' (CSR) programmes, such as Nike's 'Lace Up Save Lives' programme to combat HIV/AIDS (Smith and Westerbeek 2007; Levermore 2011). Neoliberal values are also viewed as underpinning the strategies and messages of many SDP programmes, for example in seeking to turn highly marginalized young people in lower-middle-income countries into entrepreneurial, self-reliant market agents.

2. *Strategic developmentalist* social policies are associated particularly with *local, national and international governmental organizations*; here, we may also include *sport federations* which operate as governmental bodies within their sporting disciplines. Strategic developmentalism involves organizational and advocacy activity; for example in facilitating cross-sector networking and collaboration, helping other stakeholders to develop SDP policies and practices, promoting the importance of specific international issues (such as sport interventions with refugees), and providing some resource support (finance, personnel, expertise) for projects and campaigns. A crucial role has been played here by the United Nations (UN), as I discuss later; the Commonwealth Secretariat has also become very active in SDP policy strategy in recent years (Dudfield 2014). Other key actors include the diplomacy and development arms and foreign embassies of nation states such as the UK, United States, Germany, Netherlands and the Nordic countries; local municipalities which provide sport venues and access to schools to recruit participants and volunteers; and, sport federations such as the IOC, FIFA, UEFA, ICC and FIVB.[1]

3. *Developmental interventionist policies* are primarily associated with *non-governmental organizations* (NGOs) which represent the greatest number of organizations within the overall SDP sector. Their activities centre on facilitating and implementing SDP programmes in different locations. SDP NGOs come in many shapes and sizes. The largest international NGOs within the SDP sector – such as Right to Play and streetfootballworld – often operate as umbrella organizations that support their networks of local and national affiliates or partners, for example by providing funding, training, expert advice, and 'toolkits' to guide intervention practices. Some NGOs were established in other fields of social development but later added sport to their portfolios. The development goals of SDP NGOs vary, from classic SDP programmes with young people that promote peacebuilding or reduce crime, through to consciousness-raising campaign work on diversity issues around racism, sexism, and homophobia in sport.

4. *Social justice policies* are advocated by a mix of *advocacy and radical NGOs, campaign groups, social movements and investigative journalists and academics*. This 'fourth estate' of development activity is typically underpinned by critiques of neoliberalism and the advocacy of structural changes. In SDP, these activities include promoting freedom of speech across sports governance, advancing the rights of workers in merchandise factories or sports infrastructure projects, protection of the environment, and anti-corruption initiatives around sport governance. Most actors here

are already engaged in wider political and development work, and utilize sport to promote their messages, often through critiques of other SDP stakeholders, for example by protesting against the practices of specific corporate sponsors or the governments of competing nations at sport mega-events, or by exposing corruption within sport federations (Giulianotti *et al.* 2015; Jennings 2015). These social justice stakeholders may be more widely located among 'alter-globalization' and other movements that hold transformative visions of global civil society, rooted in ideals of egalitarianism, environmentalism, and participatory democracy (Keane 2003; Harvey 2005; Pleyers 2010).

The SDP sector: elaborating the model

The United Nations

If we turn to elaborate this four-fold model, we should begin by considering the key strategic developmentalist role that has been played by the United Nations (UN). At its peak involvement with SDP in the 2000s, the UN acted as the sector's *chief global advocate*, had its own specialist SDP office (the UNOSDP), and enabled at least twenty associate agencies such as the United Nations Development Programme (UNDP) and UNICEF to be engaged in SDP programmes and campaigns (Beutler 2008). Key milestones for UN involvement in SDP included the foundation of the UN's Inter-Agency Task Force on SDP in 2001; the 2003 resolution passed by the United Nations' General Assembly which asserted sport's global social role; the crucial step of marking the year 2005 as the UN's International Year of Sport and Physical Education, which approved the founding of the UNOSDP; giving the IOC observer status within the UN in 2009; in 2013, establishing 6 April as the UN's annual international day of sport for development and peace; and, in 2015, through Article 37 in the UN's Sustainable Development Goals (SDGs), which argues explicitly for sport's social role, as 'an important enabler of sustainable development', in making a 'growing contribution … to the realization of development and peace in its promotion of tolerance and respect' (UN 2015: 37).

According to Coalter (2013: 28–30), the UN's involvement in SDP has been underpinned by two factors: a *rights-based focus*, such as in advancing the rights of all to sports participation; and, an *evangelical belief* in the inherent capacity of sport to transform lives. In policy terms, UN SDP activity has been directed towards pursuing the Millennium and subsequent Sustainable Development Goals (MDGs, SDGs); these goals have come to influence and to shape the objectives of many SDP programmes that are run by NGOs across the world (UN 2010; 2015).

Subsequently, there have been distinct reductions or restrictions in UN involvement within the SDP sector. Crucially, the UNOSDP was closed in May 2017, while many organizational stakeholders across the SDP sector had believed that, up to that point, the office itself could have offered stronger leadership and advocacy. In addition, outside of Article 37, the SDGs provide no further reference to sport's social role. Overall, the UN's disengagement with SDP left a large vacuum to be filled within the sector with regard to leadership, advocacy and strategic development at transnational level.

Stakeholder involvements within the SDP sector

If we look more broadly at the four-fold model, we find that each organizational stakeholder will have at least some *external motives and interests* for their involvement with the SDP sector. To safeguard commercial interests, corporations may view SDP and corporate social responsibility activities as good domains for public relations and promotional work, and oppose the extension of SDP to include rights-based issues. Reflecting the wider politicization of international aid, governmental departments and agencies may view the SDP sector as an effective cultural field in which to exercise or to accumulate 'soft power'; thus, their choice of locations for conducting SDP activity will be at least partly determined by their diplomatic, political, and commercial interests (cf. Lancaster 2006). Sport governing bodies may view SDP as a Trojan horse for spreading their sports into new territories, for example by parachuting coaches and equipment into communities that have little or no experience of these specific sporting disciplines. Some NGOs might implement programmes in inflexible rather than locally sensitive ways and may avoid sharing their expertise with other 'competitor' NGOs that are also on the lookout for funding. Overall, these extraneous factors may lurk behind the activities of these SDP stakeholders, and at least complicate any potential collaborative work across these agencies.

The four-fold model also enables us to see how different stakeholders may enter into activities that extend *beyond their natural 'homes'*. A noteworthy trait in recent years has been the entry of commercial or neoliberal organizations and logics into other categories within the model. Three key observations follow from this point.

First, *social enterprises* have grown substantially in number across the sector since the mid-2000s and feature different mixtures of social intervention work and commercial activity. For example, some SDP NGOs also undertake commercial activity – such as private sport coaching, production of sport balls and other equipment, and sport-related tourism – which helps to provide jobs for local people and to keep the organization financially afloat. Second, some *private companies* have moved into the territory normally occupied by governmental bodies, by taking on 'strategic developmentalist' roles while still seeking to pursue profitable commercial returns for their endeavours. For example, some of these companies stage major international SDP conferences and networking events that charge high registration fees from speakers and delegates and which build profitable ties with corporate donors within the sector. Third, allegations sometimes surface that key figures within governmental organizations, NGOs, and sport federations have engaged with the SDP sector for their *personal enrichment*, including in some cases through criminal activity. Some of the most egregious allegations centre on sport leaders and officials; for example FIFA Vice-President Jack Warner who allegedly siphoned off a US$10 million payment from South Africa's football authorities that was officially earmarked for an 'African diaspora' legacy project (*The Telegraph*, 28 May 2015).

I turn now to consider NGOs, who provide by far the greatest number of stakeholders within the SDP sector largely due to their critical function in planning and delivering intervention programmes. One important issue centres on the potential danger of *NGO-ization* occurring within the SDP sector and the broader development sectors. NGO-ization refers to how essentially public issues – relating, for example, to health, education, gender equality, crime and conflict resolution – are depoliticized, and turned into technical problems to be solved, when they are dealt with by NGOs rather than by communities or governmental bodies. The point here is that NGOs have no democratic mandate, are unelected and therefore are potentially unaccountable to local populations. In some contexts, the role of NGOs may have neocolonial features, particularly when global North donors identify a 'social problem' within a global South location, and then fund a global North NGO to enter and to fix that problem. In addition, NGOs have been criticized for pursuing technical, piecemeal and pragmatic social welfare programmes when deeper, structural changes are necessary (Choudry and Kapoor 2013). Yet, we may recognize that NGO-ization is not an inevitable aspect of NGO work or of the SDP sector in general: many NGO officials argue that they are highly sensitive to engaging with local communities, including in recruiting employees and volunteers; and, that they help to strengthen underdeveloped public spheres, for example by developing young people into effective social and political actors.

Additional possible stakeholders

An important issue to consider is how the four-fold model of the SDP sector might be augmented with further stakeholder categories. Four additional possibilities might be raised here. First, I noted at the outset that the model refers to organizational or professional SDP stakeholders. If we look beyond this domain, then one crucial additional set of SDP stakeholders to consider would be the *young user groups of SDP programmes and their wider communities*. Importantly, these user groups and communities are neither uniform nor homogeneous. Instead, they experience different levels and forms of marginality and social exclusion. In relation to the model, their policy classification is also likely to be somewhat blurred, as many young user groups hold largely pragmatic views on SDP, the development sector, and global civil society *tout court*. A second category to consider might be *sport celebrities, athletes, and clubs*. A third category, noted earlier, would be *social enterprises* which combine aspects of social intervention and commercial work. Finally, a fourth category might include diverse *religious organizations* which may play key social and political roles in different communities.

The existing four-fold model might accommodate all these categories, depending on the nature of the specific example or case. For example, social enterprises may fall into neoliberal or development interventionist categories depending on where their emphasis lies, as NGOs or as businesses); religious organizations might appear as strategic governmental or development interventionist organizations; and, the richest sport clubs and athletes may fit the neoliberal category by running private foundations, while local sport clubs might fit the 'strategic developmental' or 'developmental interventionist' categories depending on the roles that they play within SDP programmes.

SDP sector interrelations: fragmentation, competition, partnerships

I turn now to consider the interrelations between different organizational stakeholders across the SDP sector. Three main types of interrelation – fragmentation, competition, and partnership – are prominent and outlined below, with the last of these being of particular significance for discussion.

To begin, a recurring concern among SDP stakeholders and researchers is that there is too much *fragmentation* across the sector. Fragmentation may occur when, for example, different SDP stakeholders located in the same community fail to communicate or collaborate with each other; national government does not recognize SDP as a legitimate or distinct field of activity; SDP programmes are short-term and run by poorly funded NGOs; and, NGOs operate under the radar of government, sports federations and international development agencies. Fragmentation may be counteracted in a variety of ways, notably through the advocacy work of intergovernmental organizations; production of SDP national action plans by governments; establishment of sustainable national networks or coalitions involving different SDP stakeholders; and, securing long-term funding for SDP NGOs to undertake their work.

In addition, *competition* may occur across the diverse stakeholders within the SDP sector, in line with Kaldor's earlier envisaging of global civil society as a contested space (or 'field'). Thus, for example, SDP stakeholders may seek to protect their 'turf' from potential rivals, particularly in competitive funding environments. Competition might be manifested in various ways: lack of communication with other SDP agencies; building networks that exclude potential rivals; and, even in seeking to rename or rebrand SDP, for example as 'sport for change', 'sport for development', and 'sport for good'. Competitive relationships and forms of social closure may also be unintended consequences of how the SDP sector has evolved. For example, as the largest NGOs establish strong partnerships with donors and other key stakeholders, and are able to hoover up funding, so that small and new NGOs struggle increasingly to 'break into' the sector and gain funding for their innovative development work. That said, given that funding opportunities can be very scarce, it is surprising that there is not substantially more competition between SDP agencies particularly NGOs.

Finally, *partnership* activity has grown very rapidly within the SDP sector over the past two decades, engaging multiple stakeholders, and typically being focused on the implementation of intervention programmes or, less usually, the conducting of public campaigns. The prominence of partnerships points to a potential weakness in Kaldor's (2003) analysis of global civil society, in terms of placing excessive emphasis on the competitive aspects between stakeholders, and saying too little on the interdependencies, partnerships, cooperation, and networking that occurs across these agencies. The centrality of partnerships within SDP requires their consideration in some more detail.

Partnerships

In any service delivery, partnerships are at their most effective when the different participants have shared goals, cultural fit, complementary (but not identical) skills, and can bring specific 'added value' to their particular areas of work (cf. Child and Faulkner 1998). In SDP, partnerships are strongest when they deliver complementary inputs and overall added value for the different contributors. Consider, for example, the case of an SDP programme that is focused on crime reduction within a community: the programme may be delivered by local NGO officials; be funded by corporate and international governmental donors; make use of sport coaches provided by local sport clubs; run activities in schools provided by local and national education departments; employ sport equipment provided by sport governing bodies; and, benefit from transport, food and other refreshments paid for by a local UN office.

Partnership-building can be significantly enhanced by usage of *multi-media platforms and technologies*, such as online social media sites and mobile telephony. For example, Facebook, twitter, Instagram, WhatsApp, Viber and other social media platforms enable NGOs to communicate with their volunteers, potential user groups, donors, and other stakeholders. Online communication channels are also used by local NGOs to access 'toolkits' for implementing programmes, and by social justice organizations to share information, resources, and advice, and to disseminate messages to wider audiences (Castells 2012).

NGOs are in the best position to develop effective partnerships when they have maintained a long-term presence in particular nations or regions and have thereby established strong social networks and relatively high levels of social capital across different SDP organizations, programme user groups, and local communities. In Kosovo, for example, we found that the long-term co-presence of influential 'international community' organizations – especially NGOs, national embassy officials and development funds, and intergovernmental organizations like the Council of Europe – helps substantially to build social capital across potential partners, and to secure consistent funding streams between NGOs and donors (Giulianotti *et al.* 2016).

The funding set-up of the SDP and wider development sectors can place NGOs in relatively *weak partnership positions* with financial donors and other stakeholders. NGOs may experience development as a competitive marketplace in which they must commodify their work and adapt practices and goals to suit the interests of prospective benefactors.

One potential concern is that, within the SDP sector, NGO aims and objectives may be influenced by the specific development ideologies and interests of corporate and governmental donors from the global North. The result may be the proliferation of programmes that promote neoliberal mores of 'self-help' and 'responsibilization' among marginalized young people, while lacking the scope to pursue deeper structural changes which would otherwise challenge global North state and corporate interests. An additional, ironic side-effect may be a perverse incentive, which helps NGOs to secure funding while undermining their social impacts. The point here is that, to impress current and future donors, NGOs usually offer evidence that their work has real impacts, for example in moving young people into education, employment and training, or out of crime and gang activity. To obtain this evidence, NGOs may prefer to fill their programmes with 'safe-bet' young people who are almost certain to produce successful 'results' rather than engage with 'risky' user groups who actually have the most acute need for help (Krause 2014).

Some scholars have indicated that one potential solution to these problems within the development sector lies with corporate partners, who should stop viewing NGOs as mere tools for gaining a stronger market or public relations position, and instead cultivate the critical independence and autonomy of these agencies (Baur and Schmitz 2012). Certainly, some funding organizations do purposefully seek out and offer support to new, small, innovative NGOs. However, such fundamental changes would require a radical shift in corporate strategy, and the probable introduction of some kind of global concordat for reshaping future NGO-corporate partnerships within SDP and beyond.

A further, double-edged partnership relates to *NGO ties with governmental organizations*, particularly the different departments and foreign embassies of nation states. Many NGOs benefit strongly from ties with state bodies that deliver resources, open doors, and gaining advocates for the SDP sector. More problematically, these relationships may see NGOs acting as 'state-financed development diplomats', in terms of implementing programmes that fit with the particular political interests of their paymasters (Tvedt 1998). A related issue concerns how the international aid sector has become markedly more dangerous for NGO workers following the 9/11 attacks and the 'War on Terror' led by the American Bush administration from 2001 onwards (Gill 2016). Thus, in the context of SDP's continued growth and the stronger involvement of governmental organizations, NGOs need to be careful about their partnerships or the types of funding that they receive from particular states, in part to protect their security and any claims that they might have in regard to political neutrality.

Finally, a further partnership strongly evident in the wider development sector involves international NGOs and the mass media, which combine to portray and to frame the poor and destitute in specific ways in news programmes and humanitarian appeals that are directed at global North audiences (Boltanski 1999; Chouliaraki 2013). Chouliaraki (2013: 180–184) argues that these mediated portrayals of human need and suffering are rooted in what she calls *neoliberal post-humanitarianism*, and which has two main aspects: 'pragmatism', which centres on 'artful story-telling' that ultimately marginalizes politics and social change; and 'privatism', which situates acts of solidarity (with those 'in need') within the private realm and aims at empowering consumers, rather than cultivating dispositions of other-oriented care' (Chouliaraki 2013: 180). The overall effect is to marketize rather than to politicize humanitarianism, to reach out to consumers rather than citizens, and thereby to fail to germinate real social change.

The ways in which SDP stakeholders represent human need and suffering, including through the potential prism of neoliberal post-humanitarianism, have been relatively unexplored by researchers. However, we might argue that these stakeholders often present their marginalized programmes user groups through *spectacles of suffering and joy*. The websites, brochures, and presentations of NGOs, sport organizations, governmental agencies, and other SDP partners tend to mix images of poor-but-happy young people playing sports, to demonstrate to audiences 'what can be done' through charitable donations to support such work. These images also serve to buttress the rather essentialist narratives of many SDP stakeholders on the 'power of sport' to transform lives.

Social justice issues: partnerships and strategies

I argued earlier that a 'fourth estate' of campaign groups, social movements and other social justice groups tends to be relatively marginal to the partnerships and networks of the SDP sector, for example in participation on SDP programmes or in attending major SDP conferences. In this final section, I explore some of the ways in which these social justice groups may and do enhance their influence, networks and partnerships within the sector.

First, social justice groups may continue to take the lead in *highlighting public issues and campaigning for responses* from more powerful organizations. This type of activism predates the establishment of the SDP sector; for example, in struggles by athletes and campaign groups to tackle sexism, racism, and homophobia in different sports. In the SDP context, one strong illustration is found in how FIFA's award of the 2022 World Cup finals to Qatar generated a variety of international campaigns and investigative reports on the abuse of migrant workers and the suppression of LGBTQ people in that country. In turn, many international governmental organizations and nation states voiced their concerns about the reports. Pressed to act, FIFA established a unit to monitor working conditions in Qatar, and commissioned a Harvard University law professor to recommend future human rights policy for the governing body (Brannagan and Giulianotti 2015; Ruggie 2016).

Second, social justice organizations may seek to *establish their own partnerships and networks* that draw in other stakeholders, depending on the relevant issue. One recent network has been the Sport and Rights Alliance (SRA), founded in 2015, whose members include Amnesty International, Greenpeace, Human Rights Watch, Terre des Hommes, and Transparency International Germany; trade unions such as the International Trade Union Confederation and FIFPro (the world football players' union); and fan organizations such as Football Supporters Europe and Supporters Direct Europe. SRA has pressed sport federations to ensure that mega-events such as the Olympics and World Cup finals are allocated, organized, and delivered in ways that meet environmental, human rights, and anti-corruption standards. The SRA's foundation followed FIFA's award of the World Cup finals to Russia (2018) and Qatar.

A third approach to partnerships and networking involves these social justice organizations *taking on some NGO features* in order to operate 'inside' the wider SDP, sport and development sectors. For example, the Swiss NGO *Terre des Hommes* maintained their critical campaigning on human rights issues in sport, particularly around sport mega-events, while also seeking to secure influence 'from within' through dialogue with powerful stakeholders within governmental organizations and sport federations, and through participating at major sport conferences.

Finally, some participants within social justice movements may move into *working within mainstream SDP agencies*, or may *convert their organizations into NGOs*. These transitions may gain political influence within the SDP sector, secure more resilient organizational structures, and improve employment security for leading members. Yet questions remain over whether new

NGOs may deliver deeper social and political changes. Some research in relatively extreme contexts suggests that such an influence is possible, for example, when NGOs become involved in political mobilizations where democratic processes are weak (Boulding 2014). However, alongside the risk of 'NGO-ization' discussed earlier, NGOs may themselves be poorly placed to pursue deep social change, partly due to pressure to hit funding-body 'performance targets' (Banks *et al.* 2015).

Concluding comments

To sum up, the SDP sector has been a rapidly growing field of international development activity since the early 1990s, comprising a wide diversity of stakeholders operating at local, national and transnational levels in the global South and North. While critical roles are played by NGOs in delivering programmes and driving partnerships across the sector, the UN and other governmental agencies, along with sport organizations, and corporate and other donors, all make highly influential contributions, particularly in resourcing and shaping intervention strategies and activities.

There is scope for the sector to undergo *some changes* in pursuit of its social goals. First, stronger and more sustainable work would be achieved through *better coordination and integration* of stakeholders throughout the sector, and through closer ties with the wider field of international development. Second, development issues relating to the *environment and climate change* have tended to be ignored by SDP programmes; this oversight is no longer possible in light of the centrality of these issues to at least eight of the seventeen UN SDGs. Third, NGOs and other SDP organizations, along with higher and further education institutions, should look closely at *further professionalizing the sector*, through the development of specialist degree programmes and other advanced qualifications for those seeking to work in this area. Such training should help to improve further the expertise and quality of work that is undertaken by NGOs and other SDP stakeholders. Finally, there is a danger that, over the long term, mainstream SDP will be dominated by the *same cluster of stakeholders* with a set outlook and culture. The sector's social relevance, sustainability and vitality would benefit greatly from a fresh infusion of new ideas and agencies. The best way forward in this regard is to enable *new and grassroots NGOs, and social justice groups*, to enter into the mainstream realm of SDP, by gaining funding, undertaking work, joining networks, and contributing to the development of future strategies, policies and programmes across the sector.

Note

1 International Olympic Committee (IOC), Fédération Internationale de Football Association (FIFA), UEFA (Union of European Football Associations), ICC (International Cricket Council), and Fédération Internationale de Volleyball (FIVB).

References

Banks, N., Hulme, D. and Edwards, M. (2015). NGOs, states, and donors revisited: Still too close for comfort? *World Development*, 66(February), 707–18.

Baur, D. and Schmitz, H. P. (2012). Corporations and NGOs: When accountability leads to co-optation. *Journal of Business Ethics*, *106*(1), 9–21.

Beutler, I. (2008). Sport serving development and peace: Achieving the goals of the United Nations through sport. *Sport in Society*, *11*(4), 359–369.

Boltanski, L. (1999) *Distant Suffering: Morality, Media and Politics*. Cambridge: Cambridge University Press.

Boulding, C. (2014). *NGOs, Political Protest and Civil Society*. Cambridge: Cambridge University Press.

Brannagan, P. and Giulianotti, R. (2015). Soft power and soft disempowerment: Qatar, global sport, and football's 2022 World Cup finals. *Leisure Studies 34*(6), 703–719.

Castells, M. (2012). *Networks of Outrage and Hope*. Cambridge: Polity.

Child, J. and Faulkner, D. (1998). *Strategies of Co-operation: Managing Alliances, Networks, and Joint Ventures*. New York: Oxford University Press.

Choudry, A. and Kapoor, D. (2013). *NGOization: Complicity, Contradictions and Prospects*. New York: Zed Books.

Chouliaraki, L. (2013). *The Ironic Spectator: Solidarity in the Age of Post-Humanitarianism*. Cambridge: Polity.

Dudfield, O. (ed.) (2014). *Strengthening Sport for Development and Peace*. London: Commonwealth Secretariat/CABOS.

Gill, P. (2016). *Today We Drop Bombs, Tomorrow We Build Bridges: How Foreign Aid Became a Casualty of War*. London: Zed Books.

Giulianotti, R. (2011a). The sport, development and peace sector: A model of four social policy domains. *Journal of Social Policy, 40*(4), 757–776.

Giulianotti, R. (2011b). Sport, peacemaking and conflict resolution: A contextual analysis and modelling of the sport, development and peace sector. *Ethnic and Racial Studies, 34*(2), 207–228.

Giulianotti, R., Armstrong, Hales, G. G. and Hobbs, R. (2015). Sport mega-events and public opposition: A sociological study of the London 2012 Olympics. *Journal of Sport and Social Issues, 39*(2), 99–119.

Giulianotti, R., Collison, H., Darnell, S. and Howe, D. (2016). Contested states and the politics of sport: The case of Kosovo – division, development and recognition. *International Journal of Sport Policy and Politics, 9*(1), 121–136.

Harvey, D. (2005). *A Brief History of Neoliberalism*. Oxford: Oxford University Press.

Jennings, A. (2015). *The Dirty Game: Uncovering the Scandal at FIFA*. London: Century.

Kaldor, M. (2003). *Global Civil Society: An Answer to War*. Cambridge: Polity.

Keane, J. (2003). *Global Civil Society?*, Cambridge: Cambridge University Press.

Krause, M. (2014). *The Good Project: Humanitarian Relief NGOs and the Fragmentation of Reason*, Chicago: University of Chicago Press.

Lancaster, C. (2006). *Foreign Aid: Diplomacy, Development, Domestic Politics*. Chicago: University of Chicago Press.

Levermore, R. (2011). CSR for development through sport: Examining its potential and limitations. *Third World Quarterly, 31*(2), 223–241.

Lewis, D. (2015). Contesting parallel worlds: Time to abandon the distinction between the 'international' and 'domestic' contexts of third sector scholarship? *Voluntas, 26*(5), 2084–2103.

Pleyers, G. (2010). *Alter-Globalization: Becoming Actors in the Global Age*. Cambridge: Polity.

Ruggie, J. (2016). 'For the Game, For the World': FIFA and Human Rights. Research Report, Harvard Kennedy School.

Smith, A. C. T. and Westerbeek, H. M. (2007). Sport as a vehicle for deploying corporate social responsibility. *Journal of Corporate Citizenship, 7*(25), 43–54.

Tvedt, T. (1998). *Angels of Mercy or Development Diplomats*. Oxford: James Currey.

United Nations (UN) (2010). *Contribution of Sport to the Millennium Development Goals*. New York: United Nations.

United Nations (UN) (2015). *Transforming our World: The 2030 Agenda for Sustainable Development*. New York: United Nations.

Viterna, J. and Robertson, C. (2015). New directions for the sociology of development. *Annual Review of Sociology, 41*: 243–269.

Watkins, S. C., Swidler, A. and Hannan, T. (2012). Outsourcing social transformation: Development NGOs as organizations. *Annual Review of Sociology, 38*(1), 285–315.

Weber, M. (1949). *The Methodology of the Social Sciences*. Glencoe, IL: Free Press.

3

SDP and global development

David Black

Introduction

How do sport and global development relate to each other? Though sport is often portrayed as a new entrant to the field of global development, this portrayal is increasingly untenable. Leaving aside the much longer history of sport as an instrument of personal, social, community, and national development, stretching back to the nineteenth century (Kidd 2008), the contemporary upsurge of intentional interventions in development through sport is now roughly a generation old. A growing array of organizations, varying in shape, size, and type, have demonstrated staying power in the competitive landscape of global development (see www.sportanddev.org; www. beyondsport.org/Network), while a robust body of scholarship has emerged to critically analyse this phenomenon (e.g. Burnett 2009; Darnell 2012; Coalter 2013; Hayhurst 2015). It is therefore time to take stock of some of the key characteristics of sport for development (SFD) praxis in relation to the broader field of global development.

This chapter:

1) Sketches the broad contours and recent trajectory of global development theory and practice, emphasizing the long-standing distinction between 'top-down' and 'bottom-up' orientations, and more recent efforts to transcend these orientations through 'multi-stakeholder partnerships'.
2) Situates SFD in relation to these dynamics, arguing that while SFD may be a relatively 'new' field in relation to the post-Second World War history of global development, it has been in the *forefront* of the new, multi-stakeholder politics of 'partnership'.
3) Discusses the ways in which top-down and bottom-up manifestations of SFD have been connected, giving particular attention to the example of sports mega-events.
4) Explores the potential for more equitable forms of engagement between top-down and bottom-up orientations in SFD.

I will argue that, more than most forms of development praxis, SFD has been characterized by relatively close – indeed co-dependent – connections between top-down and bottom-up dynamics. The challenge faced by scholars and practitioners is not the *lack* of connections, but rather their *form* and *effects*. The relationship between top-down and bottom-up manifestations of SFD can be described as an inequitable symbiosis. While there have been clear advantages to actors from both 'sides' as a result of this situation, it has also limited the role and relevance of sport in addressing the structural inequities, or 'root causes' that underpin persistent poverty, inequality, and marginalization. SFD actors need to develop a better understanding of the structural differences between these orientations, a higher level of critical distance between top-down and bottom-up SFD actors, and a closer relationship between bottom-up SFD and actors in other development domains (e.g. health, education, disability, or anti-poverty).

Understanding the dynamics of global development praxis

In order to make this argument, we must briefly enter the murky waters of development theory and practice. To be sure, the meanings of development are diverse and contested. To make sense of this confusing mélange, the idea of top-down versus bottom-up development helps capture two broad orientations that have consistently co-existed throughout the post-Second World War history of the modern 'development project'. This project is distinguished from earlier eras by the emergence of an extensive network of national, international, and civil society organizations with the expressed intent of instigating, enabling, or supporting development in the 'global South' (see Black 2010; Payne and Phillips 2010).

The ideas of top-down and bottom-up development have been used in a variety of ways. Most obviously, they refer to the *actors and the levels of analysis* emphasized in development thought and practice, distinguishing the priorities of national, intergovernmental, and corporate development actors from those of local communities and grassroots, small-scale, or 'community-based' organizations in civil society. A variation on this spatial sense of the term derives from the distinction between the global North and South, or colonizer and post-colonial. In this context, developing country governments have often taken on the mantle of the 'sub-altern' to challenge the entrenched privileges of rich countries in the global North. This spatial or agential distinction has been closely related to a *methodological distinction* between large-scale quantitative and/or theoretical trends and approaches to development, on the one hand, and small-scale qualitative and participatory methods, on the other.

In addition, however, the top-down/bottom-up distinction can be understood as a normative and prescriptive division concerning the *process and objectives* of development, and the actions required to enable these processes and objectives. In other words, development can be seen in a fundamentally liberal or 'problem solving' sense of enabling people, communities, and/or countries to adapt, succeed, and prosper in the world *as it is*. Alternatively, it can be understood in a more radical or 'critical' sense of addressing the structural roots of poverty, inequality, and marginalization, emphasizing the need to restructure or *transform* the current order. This latter orientation can be understood as 'bottom-up' in the sense that it aims to see the world from the perspective of historically marginalized groups, and to act in partnership or solidarity with them.[1]

Two caveats need to be entered about these broad orientations. First, *neither* orientation assumes the viability of the status quo. *Both* understand development as a process of far-reaching social change. The key difference concerns the question of social change *how, and for whom?* In other words, who are the principle architects and beneficiaries of the development process?

Second, beyond the bottom-up orientation I have sketched, there is a well-known 'hyper-critical' orientation that sees 'development' as irredeemably colonial and exploitative. From this perspective, development praxis cannot be rescued, but must be transcended. In development studies, this is typically characterized as a 'post' or 'anti-development' orientation (e.g. Escobar

1995; Rist 2014). Because the prescriptions that flow from it tend to be vague and impractical, as well as hostile to the very idea of development, it cannot be easily accommodated within development praxis. But this hyper-critical orientation has significantly influenced 'bottom-up' development thinking, through its critique of existing development practices and its efforts to address the problems highlighted by these critiques. It has sharpened understanding of social power, inequity, and marginalization in development, and thus helped 'bottom-up' approaches understand what needs to change.

How have these differences played out in the 'real world'? Since the early 1980s, much attention has focused on the ongoing distinction between market-oriented, rational choice, or neoliberal development approaches on the one hand, and more interventionist and participatory, 'alternative' or 'human development' perspectives on the other (Pieterse 2010). Some time ago, Jean-Philippe Thérien (1999) neatly captured these alternative perspectives as 'two tales of world poverty', which he termed the Bretton Woods and the UN paradigms respectively. Of course, neither of these perspectives has remained static. For example, the harshly neoliberal 'Washington consensus' of the 1990s became the softer, gentler but still neoliberal 'post-Washington consensus' of the 2000s (Onis and Senses 2005). But debates and practices concerning global development were more or less aligned with one or the other of these orientations.

As I have already suggested, these orientations have been evident ever since 'development' was institutionalized as a global priority in the late 1940s and early 1950s. In the first development decades, top-down development was mostly reflected in modernization approaches, ranging from an emphasis on infrastructure and 'big push' interventions, up to and including the Basic Human Needs approach promoted by the World Bank in the 1970s. Modernization approaches have never really gone away, as reflected in the renewed emphasis on large-scale infrastructure projects.

The bottom-up orientation was more diverse, including structuralist, dependency, and other neo-Marxist approaches emphasizing (and seeking to change) entrenched divisions of wealth and class, but also small-scale and grassroots approaches like the Buddhist economics of E. F. Schumacher (1973) emphasizing that 'Small is Beautiful'. Taken together, however, they stressed the need to challenge the structural roots of poverty and inequality, and the importance of solidarity with those who were exploited by prevailing global structures of power, wealth, and knowledge.

In the new millennium, however, global development praxis has been complicated by a concerted effort by various development actors, both state and non-state, to promote a grand, pragmatic synthesis between these two orientations. This is consistent with the 'Third Way' politics that rose to prominence in the 'developed' countries of Western Europe and North America during the 1990s and 2000s (see also Kapur 1999). It can be loosely characterized as 'big tent' development. The general argument is that development is 'too important' to politicize, and that there is a need for new and intensified 'multi-stakeholder partnerships' to enhance coordination, exploit complementarities, and unlock new sources of development finance. Development can, and should, be 'rendered technical' (Li 2007) – a set of interlinked problems to be solved through the application of technical knowledge. This attempt to depoliticize development is, ironically, deeply political.

There are many factors that have contributed to this dynamic. They include a proliferation of 'new' development actors in the post-Cold War era, including a dramatic expansion in the number of non-governmental development organizations (or 'tamed social movements' – Kaldor 2003); the rise of new donors from both an expanded EU and the 'rising states' of the global South, such as the BRICS[2] states; and the rising salience of corporations, corporate social responsibility, and 'new philanthropists' like the Gates Foundation, leading to a dramatic growth in public–private partnerships (Black and O'Bright 2016). They also include an increasingly assertive 'global South', emboldened by the rise of the BRICs and others, and by their recovery from the debt crisis and structural adjustment conditionalities of the 1980s and 1990s. The growing range of development actors has underpinned the push towards big tent development in several ways: by intensifying challenges of competition and coordination; by introducing new development agendas; and by broadening the sources of development finance in ways that greatly appeal to traditional development actors in an era of fiscal restraint.

This new global politics of development partnership has been anchored by a series of landmark international agreements, including the Millennium Development Goals (2000), the Paris Declaration and the Accra Agenda for Action on Aid Effectiveness (2005 and 2008), and the Busan Partnership for Effective Development Cooperation (2011) (Picciotto 2011). Most recently, this process has led to the United Nations Sustainable Development Goals (SDGs), adopted in September 2015. The SDGs are unprecedented in their breadth and ambition, combining the UN's Sustainable Development and Social Development agendas to arrive at a set of 17 Goals and 169 targets (in contrast with the 8 goals and 18 targets of the MDGs). They are also unprecedented in their objective of encompassing *all* countries, North and South, rather than just 'low-income countries'. Their supporters stress these as virtues, whereas their detractors see the breadth and ambition of the SDGs as 'Senseless, Dreamy, and Garbled' (Easterly 2015). To be at all feasible, they will require development finance on a scale far beyond even the most optimistic projections for traditional foreign aid. In this sense, they strongly reinforce the assumed need for multi-stakeholder partnerships, since they will depend on new sources of development finance, largely from corporations and private philanthropists. Finally, and most relevant to this chapter, they encompass an improbable combination of traditional, top-down (or neoliberal) development through dramatically accelerated growth, and a bottom-up emphasis on 'no one left behind', along with the need for decisive action on the climate crisis in ways that cannot be easily imagined without dramatically curtailing global growth.

SFD in global development

It is in this ambiguous context, marked by the continued co-existence of top-down and bottom-up orientations along with a concerted effort to foster a grand development synthesis, that SFD has risen to prominence. How are we to situate the groups concerned with sport's role in development in relation to the broader politics of global development?

A first key observation is that, like other fields of development praxis, the hundreds of non-governmental SFD organizations and initiatives run the ideological, institutional, organizational, and financial gamut from small, informal, loosely organized and/or highly radical to large, formal, hierarchically structured and/or richly financed, with sophisticated public relations machines and celebrity 'athlete ambassadors'. They also vary in their closeness to SFD actors in governmental, intergovernmental, and international sport organizations (notably the IOC and FIFA) on the one hand, and multinational corporations and private philanthropists, on the other. Richard Giulianotti (2011) distinguishes four 'domains' of Sport for Development and Peace (SDP) actors: a neoliberal domain, closely linked to transnational corporations and their corporate social responsibility activities; developmental interventionist actors, consisting of mainstream non-governmental and community-based organizations; strategic developmental actors associated with national governments, intergovernmental organizations like the UN and the Commonwealth, and international sports federations like the IOC, FIFA, and FIBA; and finally new social movements and radical non-governmental organizations (NGOs) that gravitate towards confrontation and social mobilization to challenge corporate, international sport organization (ISO), and governmental authority and priorities. These categories, or domains, sit on a fluid continuum. Organizations often operate closely across these boundaries, sometimes within 'multi-stakeholder partnerships'. But only the fourth category of new social movements and radical NGOs consistently adopts a bottom-up orientation, with some developmental interventionist actors leaning this way, both ideologically and in practice.

Second, the distinction between top-down and bottom-up orientations tends to be less clear-cut in SFD than in other domains of development praxis. This is partly because sport-oriented groups are, on the whole, less self-consciously *political*. In this sense, the 'myth of autonomy' (Allison 1993: 5–6) concerning sport and politics remains influential, with sport still widely seen as a space for 'escape from' politics. This helps to explain the attraction of SFD to states and corporations, since it is consistent with the idea that development is something that can be 'rendered technical' and to which all right-thinking people should be able to agree. But the general point is that, on the whole, there is a fluid and permeable boundary between grassroots and community-based groups, on the one hand, and high-powered corporate, governmental, and sporting organizations, on the other. Even those groups that are not at all linked to elite athletes, sport organizations, or corporate sponsors are often *inspired by* the sporting heroes who have frequently risen from humble beginnings, and the wealthy franchises, supporters, and corporate sponsors they are aligned with. Thus, top-down and bottom-up manifestations of SFD are often closely connected, even though top-down tendencies typically predominate.

Third, and building on the permeability between top-down and bottom-up orientations in SFD, this domain of development praxis is particularly well suited to the new landscape of 'big tent' development partnerships. SFD has often been thought of as somehow immature or underdeveloped in relation to the development field as a whole. Yet in its pervasive co-mingling of top-down and bottom-up orientations, it has been in the *forefront* of development actors, modelling the sort of multi-stakeholder partnerships between 'grassroots' organizations, private sector sponsors, elite sports leagues and federations, and governmental and intergovernmental organizations in ways that mainstream development thinkers and practitioners are increasingly advocating.

Why has this been the case? As noted above, many SFD actors have been less attuned to the political nature of development work than actors in other sectors. Traditional development organizations in civil society are often explicitly motivated by theoretical, ideological and/or normative viewpoints that lead them to 'keep their distance' from top-down development actors, and/or to pursue some variation of 'insider' vs 'outsider' strategies of engagement and advocacy with the latter (Nelson 2006). These decisions usually reflect considerable self-reflection. SFD organizations and practitioners, on the other hand, are typically less preoccupied with these strategic calculations, and more with 'getting on with the work'. Many SFD leaders are less well schooled in the structural origins of poverty and inequality, but deeply invested in the redemptive appeal of sport, particularly for those who have been immersed in it.

The timing of the rise of the SFD sector is also important. Most contemporary SFD organizations are post-Cold War inventions. They were products of the period when Francis Fukuyama (1992) famously declared that history had 'ended', with the big ideological cleavages resolved in favour of liberalism. This view was always controversial, and now seems extraordinarily naïve, but unlike earlier development decades marked by sharp divisions among alternative designs for human improvement, the 'era of SFD' has lacked this clarity of ideological and practical alternatives.

Finally, the new grassroots push in SFD has come at the same time as leading top-down actors, particularly in the international sport and corporate worlds, have recognized the appeal of development as the latest manifestation of the long-standing emphasis on 'sport for good'. In this sense, ISOs and their major corporate sponsors have embraced inclusive social and sustainable development as the latest adaptation in their ongoing need to sustain the social legitimacy of sport and, by extension, themselves (Peacock 2011). As these increasingly rich and powerful top-down actors take up the 'cause' of SFD, many SFD 'start-ups' find their offers of publicity, capacity, and financial support irresistible.

The 'unequal symbiosis' between top-down and bottom-up orientations in SFD

As noted above, there is a diverse array of SFD actors. Scholars still need to better understand the full range of these actors and their activities, while tracking the way in which the sector is growing and changing (see Donnelly *et al.* 2011, 592). In doing so, they need to be mindful of the degree to which SFD scholarship has been heavily concentrated in a narrow range of countries, mostly in Europe, North America, and Australasia (Schulenkorf *et al.* 2016), and thus encompasses a relatively narrow range of perspectives. In general, however, top-down and bottom-up (or grassroots) actors in SFD seem to be more co-dependent than actors in other sectors of global development.

From the perspective of bottom-up or community-based actors, we need to recognize that SFD organizations are still 'late adopters' – late into the complex and multi-dimensional politics of global development, and the diverse and competitive arena of development actors. As relative newcomers, frequently with limited networks and sources of public funding (Kidd 2008: 376), they have felt compelled to lean on their greatest assets, which are often the profile and resources provided by their links to high-performance sports organizations, clubs, and celebrity athletes. It is no accident, for example, that one of the best known and most successful SFD organizations, the Mathare Youth Sports Association (MYSA), was from the outset determined to attach itself to elite sport through the creation of a MYSA United side in the Kenyan Premier league – a measure which, in the view of founder Bob Munro, not only provided profile and role models, but a measure of financial and political security in the vulnerable conditions of urban slums.[3] Moreover, it can be argued that one of the strategic assets of new and relatively vulnerable SFD organizations is *precisely* that they are typically regarded as relatively *less* political, and therefore threatening, than more traditional development and human rights organizations, especially those supported by international 'partners'. This has become an increasingly important consideration as a wave of governments in the global South have imposed stringent regulations on the activities of internationally 'partnered' civil society organizations (CSOs), particularly when these activities are perceived as political advocacy and policy work (Clarke and Mehtta 2015). The universalistic and redemptive veneer of sport and play, in contrast, is a source of security and protection as SFD organizations seek to consolidate their programmes and presence, which they will be intuitively reluctant to surrender.

For top-down SFD actors on the other hand – notably leading ISOs and corporate sponsors – a close association with grassroots sport and development partially mitigates and obscures the growing wealth, elitism, entitlement, and corruption that has challenged their 'brand' and thus their legitimacy. ISOs, in particular, have become increasingly sought after as 'partners'. This is evident in their attractiveness to wealthy corporate sponsors, leading politicians pitching sports mega-events (SMEs), and UN and other international organizations seeking strategic relationships (e.g. www.olympic.org/cooperation-with-the-un). Yet they are also vulnerable, depending on the willingness of powerful state and corporate actors to acquiesce in their unique status as the governors of world sport. As noted above, their ability to navigate this distinctive combination of wealth, influence, and vulnerability depends on the legitimacy of their 'movements' – most obviously Olympism, but also, more broadly, the noble ideals associated with elite sports and sporting events (see Hoberman 1995: Peacock 2011). As a result, both bottom-up and top-down actors in SFD have a compelling interest in sustaining their complementarities and obscuring their differences. In short, their relationship is symbiotic; yet it is also deeply unequal, with top-down actors and interests routinely predominating.

The unequal symbiosis of SFD in practice: the case of SMEs

Nowhere is this unequal symbiosis more evident than in the dynamics surrounding contemporary SMEs. On the one hand, the neoliberal SME – ascendant since the Los Angeles Olympics of 1984 – has in many respects become the ultimate 'top-down' development device. It offers a strategic opportunity for national, regional, and urban development that attracts a confluence of elite and tenuously accountable ISOs, ambitious politicians, and private sector interests in powerful 'booster coalitions'. These events institutionalize 'states of exception' – virtual peacetime states of emergency – that enable dramatic acceleration of the preferred development schemes of local and national elites, through exceptional governance arrangements and their extraordinary capacity for capital mobilization (Gaffney 2014; Pentifallo 2015). On the other hand, these bids and hosts, particularly in the 'rising states' that have aggressively pursued them (e.g. Brazil, South Africa, India, South Korea, China, Mexico, Malaysia), have increasingly stressed their 'sustainable' and 'inclusive' development benefits for the society as a whole. It has become virtually impossible to justify hosting these events in the global South without invoking their 'bottom-up' benefits. Moreover, they have been associated with rapid growth in the number of 'grassroots' organizations and initiatives seeking to use the SME 'space' to advance community-based programmes and projects. Some of these bottom-up actors and initiatives are the direct result of elite ISO sponsorship (e.g. Football for Hope); others are local initiatives seeking to exploit the opportunities triggered by the SME-linked state of exception (e.g. the Football Foundation of South Africa in Gansbaai). But either way, they have sought to activate the bottom-up potential of top-down sport (e.g. Cornelissen 2011; Swart *et al.* 2011).

These tendencies are by no means confined to hosts from the global South; both the London and Vancouver Olympic Games featured urban renewal, social inclusion, and sustainable development initiatives, for example. Nevertheless, SMEs in rising states both promote and confront heightened developmental claims and expectations (e.g. Carey *et al.* 2011; Millington and Darnell 2014). To justify the extraordinary costs and efforts associated with SME hosting in the global South, it has become necessary to claim that the poor majority will be major, if not principal, beneficiaries.

What can we say about the *actual* developmental impacts of SMEs in 'rising states'? The question is not easily answered, as such events always generate 'multiple narratives' (Kidd 2009/10), and enable many small-scale SFD activities and initiatives. However, if we were to try to summarize their 'bottom-up' developmental impacts, we would have to conclude that:

- the emphasis and expenditures on 'grassroots' and inclusionary undertakings are dwarfed by the effort required to achieve 'top-down' objectives (Cornelissen 2011);
- the more 'pro-poor' infrastructural priorities articulated in the bid stage are regularly displaced or downgraded in favour of the urgent need to complete elite sporting venues and the broader infrastructural developments required by local and international elites who are the primary consumers of the event; and

- no 'actually existing' SME has contributed decisively to the reduction of socio-economic inequalities, and sustained poverty alleviation, in host cities and countries.

The last point requires some qualification. Cleary, the overall developmental record of SMEs in rising states is mixed. Some, such as the 1988 Olympics in South Korea, are widely seen as a 'qualified success' (Bairner and Cho 2014), marking the country's 'graduation' from developing country status and acting as a stimulus to political liberalization. Others, such as South Africa (2010), have a more ambiguous balance sheet, with some advances in urban renewal and transportation infrastructure along with the symbolic victory of succeeding where failure was widely anticipated, but with a classic legacy of 'white elephant' venues and major opportunity costs relative to acute social needs. Still others, such as Mexico (1968), Delhi (2010), and Brazil (2016), have been widely associated with setbacks in the developmental ambitions of their political and economic backers (Zolov 2004; Baviskar 2010; Wade 2017). In no case, however, can these events be seen to have successfully generated inclusive, redistributive effects, to the benefit of the relatively disadvantaged majority.[4] In short, what 'bottom-up' successes may have been associated with these events are hard not to see as decorative 'window dressing' to their fundamentally top-down developmental consequences (Black and Northam 2015).

Towards more socially inclusive and sustainable SFD?

Despite the tendency of SFD initiatives towards a symbiosis that favours top-down interests and priorities, there are some contemporary dynamics that *could* shift the balance towards more bottom-up, socially inclusive possibilities. There is nothing inevitable about this prospective re-balancing, but it is possible to identify some key *forces for* change, and dynamics among SFD actors that could have a bearing on the *direction of* change.

With regard to the forces of change, there are dynamics both within and beyond sport that have made the status quo of the past several decades increasingly untenable. Within sport, there is a growing crisis in the elite sport system and the ISOs that govern it (McAloon 2016). This is reflected in: the multiple crises accompanying the Rio Games cycle; the sharp decline in SME bidders, particularly (though not only) from the global South; the new wave of evidence concerning pervasive doping; and the deep corruption and leadership crises within FIFA, to cite only the most obvious examples. Taken together, these multiple challenges clearly undermine the legitimacy of elite sport. They also undermine the value of ISO 'brands', and thus their appeal to corporate sponsors. Leading ISOs – above all, the IOC and FIFA – must respond and, based on historic patterns, are likely to gravitate towards an emphasis on the latest normative currents of world society, including more socially and environmentally inclusive initiatives and 'legacies'. The current crisis therefore opens up the possibility, at least, of more truly developmental SMEs, concerned from the ground up with issues of social equity, inclusion, and poverty alleviation (Black and Northam 2015). ISOs must, of course, be held to account if such reforms are to be meaningful and sustainable. The role of bottom-up SFD organizations could be vital in doing so, as could elite 'athlete activists' who have been crucial to the rise of SFD but muted in their criticism of the bodies that govern their sports.

These sport-based crises are embedded within a much wider set of fissures and challenges in the global political economy, and a growing sense that existing structures, institutions, and social practices are increasingly unsustainable – ecologically, economically, socially, and politically. National and regional institutions are under strain (witness Brexit and the tremors within the EU); regional and global economies teeter on the brink of renewed crisis, while grappling with widening inequalities; unprecedented migrations of people are met by growing manifestations of xenophobic intolerance; and the old 'solutions' to global crises of renewed growth and intensified resource exploitation deepen environmental stresses. The degree to which sport and sport-based organizations can, and should, play a meaningful role in addressing these kinds of 'broad gauge problems' (Coalter 2010) should not be overstated, but it is increasingly clear that these challenges cannot be adequately addressed on the strictly palliative basis that has characterized much SFD work. Sports people, like citizens everywhere, must become more attuned to these deep challenges, and the role their organizations and initiatives play in sustaining and/or challenging them.

Concerning the *direction of* change, In part because small-scale or grassroots SFD organizations have been relatively closely connected with top-down organizations within and beyond sport (Hayhurst and Frisby 2010), they have tended to be weakly connected with each other. Given both the sport-based and broader social challenges they confront, SFD organizations should give more attention to building coalitions of 'like-minded' groups in the sector, and in doing so, establish a greater degree of 'critical distance' from the top-down organizations (state, non-state, and corporate) with which they have been aligned (see Sanders 2016). By concerting their learning, analysis, and advocacy on a more systematic basis, these organizations' ability to hold 'top-down' actors to account and to push for change – concerning the developmental implications of SMEs for example, or the need for more socially inclusive and transformative SFD programming – will be enhanced.

Finally, SFD organizations tend to be weakly connected with well-developed coalitions of non-state development actors in civil society more broadly. To cite just one example, there are no SFD organizations among the more than 80 development CSOs that compose the long-standing Canadian Council for International Cooperation.[5] Weak articulation with bottom-up actors in the wider development community militates against a better understanding of the nature of the challenges faced in other, co-related dimensions of global development work; a clearer appraisal of the role sport can play in relation to other development actors and challenges; and an enhanced profile for SFD beyond the realm of sport and popular culture. As SFD praxis matures therefore, it should aim for a fuller integration with the wider community of development CSOs, and a creative tension between bottom-up and top-down orientations in its own work and relationships.

Notes

1   On the distinction between 'problem solving' and 'critical' theory, see Cox 1996.
2   Brazil, Russia, India, China, and South Africa.
3   I am indebted to Owen Willis for highlighting this point.
4   Space does not allow this point to be elaborated. On widening inequalities in post-apartheid South Africa, see Southall 2018. For contrasting assessments of the developmental legacies of the Rio Games, see Nolen 2016, and Wade 2017.
5   Though in fairness, it should be acknowledged that some CCIC members engage in some sport-based programming.

References

Allison, L. (1993) (ed.). The changing context of sporting life. *The Changing Politics of Sport*. Manchester: Manchester University Press.
Bairner, A. and Cho, J-H. (2014). The legacy of the 1988 Seoul Olympic Games: A qualified success? In J. Grix (ed.). *Leveraging Legacies from Sports Mega-Events*. Palgrave Macmillan.
Baviskar, A. (2010). Spectacular events, city spaces and citizenship: The Commonwealth Games in Delhi. In J. Shapiro *et al.* (eds), *Urban Navigations: Politics, Space and the City in South Asia*. New Delhi: Routledge.

Black, D. (2010). The ambiguities of development: implications for 'development through sport'. *Sport in Society*, *13*(1), 121–129.

Black, D. and Northam, K. (2015). Mega-events and 'bottom-up' development: beyond window dressing'. In G. Anderson and C. J. Kukucha (eds), *International Political Economy*. Don Mills: Oxford University Press Canada.

Black, D. and O'Bright, B. International development and the private sector: The ambiguities of 'partner-ship'. *International Journal*, *71*(1), 144–166.

Borger, J. (2007). 'Olympics blamed for forcible removal of 2m over 20 years'. *The Guardian*, 6 June. www.theguardian.com/world/2007/jun/06/sport.china.

Burnett, C. (2009). Engaging sport for development for social impact in the South African context. *Sport in Society*, *12*(9), 1192–1205.

Carey, M., Mason, D. and Misener, L. (2011). Social responsibility and the competitive bid process for major sport events. *Journal of Sport and Social Issues*, *35*(3), 246–263.

Clarke, R. and Mehtta, A. (2015). Five trends that explain why civil society space is under assault around the world. *From Poverty to Power* (Oxfam-GB Blog), 25 August. https://oxfamblogs.org/fp2p/5-trends-that-explain-why-civil-society-space-is-under-assault-around-the-world/.

Coalter, F. (2010). The politics of sport-for-development: limited focus programmes and broad gauge problems? *International Review for the Sociology of Sport*, *45*(3), 295–314.

Coalter, F. (2013). *Sport for Development: what game are we playing?* Abingdon, Oxon: Routledge.

Cornelissen, S. (2011). More than a sporting chance? Appraising the sport for development legacy of the 2010 FIFA World Cup. *Third World Quarterly*, *32*(3), 503–529.

Cox, R. (1996). Social forces, states, and world orders: Beyond international relations theory (1981). In R. Cox with T. Sinclair, *Approaches to World Order*. Cambridge: Cambridge University Press.

Darnell, S. (2012). *Sport for Development and Peace: A Critical Sociology*. London: Bloomsbury Academic.

Donnelly, P., Atkinson, M., Boyle, S. and Szto, C. (2011). Sport for development and peace: A public soci-ology perspective. *Third World Quarterly*, *32*(3), 589–601.

Easterly, W. (2015). The SDGs should stand for 'senseless, dreamy and garbled'. *Foreign Affairs*, 28 September. http://foreignpolicy.com/2015/09/28/the-sdgs-are-utopian-and-worthless-mdgs-development-rise-of-the-rest/.

Escobar, A. (1995). *Encountering Development: the Making and Unmaking of the Third World*. Princeton, NJ: Princeton University Press.

Fukuyama, F. (1992). *The End of History and the Last Man*. New York: Avon Books.

Gaffney, C. (2014). The mega-event city as neo-liberal laboratory: The case of Rio de Janeiro'. *Percurso Academico*, Bella Horizonte, *4*(8), 217–237.

Giulianotti, R. (2011). The sport, development and peace sector: A model of four social policy domains. *Journal of Social Policy*, *40*(4), 757–776.

Hayhurst, L. (2015). Sport for development and peace: A call for transnational, multi-sited, post-colonial feminist research. *Qualitative Research in Sport, Exercise and Health*. Published online, 17 November.

Hayhurst, L, and Frisby, W. (2010). Inevitable tensions: Swiss and Canadian sport for development NGO perspectives on partnerships with high performance sport. *European Sport Management Quarterly*, *10*(1), 75–96.

Hoberman, J. (1995). Toward a theory of Olympic internationalism. *Journal of Sport History*, *22*(1), 1–37.

Kaldor, M. (2003). The idea of global civil society. *International Affairs*, *79*(3), 583–593.

Kapur, A. (1999). A third way for the third world. *Atlantic Monthy*, December. www.theatlantic.com/maga-zine/archive/1999/12/a-third-way-for-the-third-world/377927/.

Kidd, B. (2008). A new social movement: Sport for development and peace. *Sport in Society*, *11*(4), 370–380.

Kidd, B. (2009/10). Canada needs a two-track strategy for hosting international games. *Policy Options/Options Politiques*, December–January.

Li, T. (2007). *The Will to Improve: Governmentality, Development, and the Practice of Politics*. Durham, NC: Duke University Press.

McAloon, J. (2016). Agenda 2020 and the Olympic movement. *Sport in Society*, *19*:(6), 767–785.

Millington, R. and Darnell, S. (2014). Constructing and contesting the Olympics online: The internet, Rio 2016, and the politics of Brazilian development. *International Review for the Sociology of Sport*, *49*(2), 190–210.

Nelson, P. (2006). The varied and conditional integration of NGOs in the aid system: NGOs and the World Bank. *Journal of International Development*, *18*(5), 701–13.

Nolen, S. (2016). 'The Party in Rio is over. Now what?' *The Globe and Mail*, 27 August, www.theglobeandmail.com/news/world/the-party-in-rio-is-over-now-what/article31586139/.

Onis, Z. and Senses, F. (2005). Rethinking the emerging post-Washington consensus. *Development and Change*, *36*(2), 263–290.

Payne, A. and Phillips, N. (2010). *Development*. Cambridge: Polity.

Peacock, B. (2011). 'A secret instinct of social preservation': Legitimacy and the dynamic (re)constitution of Olympic conceptions of the 'good'. *Third World Quarterly*, *32*(3), 477–502.

Pentifallo, C. (2015). The City and the Spectacle: Homelessness, Social Housing, and Vancouver 2010. PhD dissertation, University of British Columbia.

Picciotto, R. (2011). *Multilateral Development Cooperation and the Paris Process: the road to Busan*. Ottawa: the North-South Institute, June, www.nsi-ins.ca/content/download/Picciotto2011.pdf.

Pieterse, J. N. (ed.) (2010). *Development Theory: Deconstructions/Reconstructions, (2nd edn)*. London: SAGE, pp. 182–202.

Rist, G. (2014). *The History of Development: From Western Origins to Global Faith*, (4th edn). London: Zed Books.

Sanders, B. (2016). An own goal for sport for development: Time to change the playing field. *Journal of Sport for Development*, *4*(6), 1–5.

Schumacher, E. F. (1973). *Small is Beautiful: A Study Of Economics as if People Mattered*. London: Blond & Briggs.

Schurlenkorf, N., Sherry, E. and Rowe, K. (2016). Sport for development: An integrated literature review. *Journal of Sport Management*, *30*(1), 22–39.

Southall, R. (2018). Inequality in South Africa: The immediate enemy. In D. Pillay, G. M. Khadiagala, R. Southall and S. Mosoetsa (eds), *New South African Review 6: The Crisis of Inequality*. Johannesburg: Wits University Press.

Swart, K., Bob, U., Knott, B. and Salie, M. (2011). A sport and sociocultural legacy beyond 2010: A case study of the Football Foundation of South Africa. *Development Southern Africa*, *28*(3), 415–427.

Thérien, J-P. (1999). Beyond the north-south divide: The two tales of world poverty. *Third World Quarterly*, *20*(4), 723–742.

Wade, S. (2017). Olympic ghost town: Bills due, venues empty after Rio Games. *Associated Press*, 11 Feb. https://apnews.com/cb13cba9a71047e387097af9acfd2036.

Zolov, E. (2004). Showcasing the 'land of tomorrow': Mexico and the 1968 Olympics. *The Americas*, *61*(2), 159–188.

4

SDP structures, policies and funding streams

Solveig Straume

Introduction

In recent years, the Sport for Development and Peace (SDP) sector has gained significant prominence in terms of policy and practice, while also constituting an academic research field. The reasons for this growth are complex and stem from changes in international sports politics as well as shifts within the international aid system, which moved from emphasizing economic development to a broader focus on civil society, social development and culture (Levermore and Beacom 2009). These shifts paved the way for new actors in the international aid arena, including those initiating SDP programmes. Driven originally by sports organizations (Straume 2010), actors from outside of sports increasingly entered the arena, thus joining the so-called new social movement (Kidd 2008). These new actors embraced the idealized beliefs in sport that many sport organizations had preached for decades, particularly that sport could positively influence a range of individuals and groups and thus offer simple, low-cost and effective ways to pursue social change and development (Coalter 2007; Hayhurst 2009; Hasselgård and Straume 2011; Nicholls *et al.* 2011).

The SDP sector has continued to grow in recent years, and as Hasselgård (2015: 4) points out, it:

> has become an integrated part of the international development aid architecture, which is the structure of development agencies, institutions and systems that govern the delivery and management of aid (transfer of finance resources and expertise) from donors in the Global North to low-income recipient countries in the Global South.

Similarly, Giulianotti (2011b: 54) argues that SDP is now 'a significant component (or sub-field) of global civil society, which features a range of institutional actors with diverse political agendas'. Overall, this illustrates the institutionalization of the SDP sector. However, and as discussed in this chapter, the general SDP field is largely heterogeneous and involves a 'loose amalgam of organizations and stakeholders mobilizing sport for development on an international scale' (Darnell and Huish 2015: 6). These stakeholders illustrate the transnational complexity of the SDP sector (Giulianotti 2011b) as they come from public sector organizations, non-governmental organizations (NGOs) of different sizes, scopes and affiliations, and also from the commercial sector and corporations, as well as universities and schools and even smaller-scale private initiatives. As Guest (2009: 1336) argues, this diversity often means that SDP programmes must 'confront the bureaucratic challenges of implementing programmes with a wide variety of stakeholders across distinct communities'.

With this in mind, and drawing primarily on published literature, this chapter offers an overview of the structures, policies and funding streams that make up the SDP sector. The chapter also draws upon primary SDP research undertaken by the author, as well as examples gleaned from online sources. The main questions that frame the chapter are: What characterizes the diversity of structure and funding within the global SDP sector? And, on whose terms are SDP policies developed? The chapter is divided into two main parts. The first provides a description of SDP structures and funding streams. The second explores how SDP policies are developed, and discusses some implications of current SDP policies and funding. The conclusion discusses future directions in SDP policy research.

The complexity of SDP

In an attempt to thematically structure the SDP field, Levermore and Beacom (2009: 9–10) broadly grouped the programmes within the SDP sector into six major clusters: 'Conflict resolution and intercultural understanding; Building physical, social, sport and community infrastructure; Raising awareness, particularly through education; Empowerment; Direct impact on physical and psychological health as well as general welfare; and Economic development/poverty alleviation.' Similarly, the Sport and Development Platform groups various SDP approaches into the following eight categories: Education and child and youth development; Peacebuilding; Disability; Disaster response; Health; Gender; Economic development; and Child protection and safeguarding. At the basis of categorizations such as these lies a functionalist view of sport as a tool to meet development goals, to solve problems and challenges, and consequently to improve the lives of individuals and communities alike (Coalter 2007).

In reality, the various organizations that make up the field of SDP often focus on more than one of the above-mentioned categories, depending on their size, scale and scope. For instance, in an assessment of 50 different SDP organizations and initiatives in urban settings in the global South, Massao and Straume (2012) found that all of the organizations under study focused on more than one of the above-mentioned clusters.

Another method of conceptualizing the structure of the SDP sector is by analysing the role of organizations within the field and their connections with other stakeholders that deliver, or support the delivery of, SDP. Conceived in this way, the SDP sector is heterogeneous, multifaceted and varied in terms of size, scope, policy domain and funding, but essentially connected through a shared interest in mobilizing sport towards development, broadly defined. This understanding of the SDP sector is illustrated in Figure 4.1. The solid lines in Figure 4.1 indicate direct financial support, dialogue, negotiations and lobbying between different SDP stakeholders. The two-way arrows illustrate that relations and interactions between stakeholders on all levels are ambiguous and marked by agency on both the donor and recipient sides.

With this overview of SDP in mind, it is possible to identify 11 distinct but connected SDP stakeholder groups. Each is discussed below.

Governments and government agencies

Influenced by trends in international aid, public sector stakeholders such as governments and government development agencies from both the global North and the global South have been attracted to SDP, and have developed policies and strategies to guide the sector and influence other

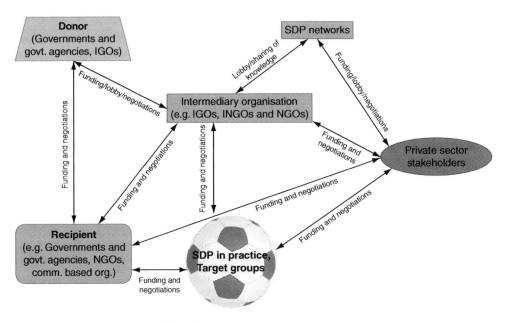

Figure 4.1   SDP structures and funding streams
Adapted from van Eekeren 2006 and Hasselgård 2015

SDP stakeholders. UK's Department for International development (DIFD), The Norwegian Agency for Development Cooperation (NORAD), The Swedish International Development Cooperation Agency (SIDA) and The Canadian International Development Agency (CIDA) are examples of government development agencies from the global North that have been involved in SDP in recent years. Their involvement in SDP often comes in the shape of financial and technical support and advice to other stakeholders such as intermediary organizations running SDP projects, (see Figure 4.1). For example, NORAD supports the Norwegian Olympic and Paralympic Committee and Confederation of Sports' (NIF) SDP initiatives with an annual sum of NOK 11.7 million (approx. €1,3 million) in the period 2016–2018 (Norwegian Olympic and Paralympic Committee and Confederation of Sports n.d.). Governments and government agencies from the global South also increasingly support SDP. For instance in Zimbabwe, the Ministry of Sports and Recreation's (n.d.) main vision is: 'A Zimbabwean society that fully exploits and utilises sport and recreation to foster development, social integration and empowerment', a vision that is enabled through cooperation with NIF and NORAD. Giulianotti *et al.* (2016) argue that sports governing bodies (such as NIF) could be classified as government organizations as they often play the same role as the state within the SDP sector. Essentially this illustrates that the lines between various SDP stakeholders are often intertwined.

Intergovernmental organizations

Intergovernmental organizations (IGOs) – traditional development organizations with a long history of aid provision – are also important SDP stakeholders. Their involvement in SDP is typically indirect, through supporting younger and less experienced stakeholders, such as smaller-scale or national NGOs, through technical, financial or ideational support. Institutions such as the International Labour Organization and the Inter-American Development Bank have supported SDP initiatives in their areas of operation.

Among IGOs, the UN have made a particular contribution to the legitimation of SDP, starting around the turn of the millennium and eventually leading to the establishment of the UN Office of Sport for Development and Peace (UNOSDP) in 2001. The UNOSDP was an active promoter of sport and its connections to the 17 Sustainable Development Goals (SDGs) announced in 2015 (United Nations Office on Sport for Development and Peace 2014). In May 2017, however, the UN dissolved the UNOSDP as it formed a direct partnership with the International Olympic Committee (IOC). The decision was justified on the basis that the UN would have access to the expertise of the IOC, its 206 National Olympic Committees and the International Sports Federations, which in turn would, according to the IOC President Thomas Bach:

> strengthen the position of sport even more in society and will help sport to fulfil its role as 'an important enabler of sustainable development', as outlined in the United Nations Sustainable Development Goals. The direct partnership is fully in line with the UN resolution, which 'supports the independence and autonomy of sport as well as the mission of the IOC in leading the Olympic Movement'.
>
> *Wickstrøm 2017*

It remains to be seen how this shift will influence the SDP sector.

International non-governmental organizations

As the name indicates, international non-governmental organizations (INGOs) are non-governmental organizations (NGOs) that are international in their scope and mission. Many large INGOs operate projects and support initiatives of other NGOs, while also working with individual governments and government agencies. INGOs from the world of sports have been involved in SDP for years. An example is found in Guest's work (2009), which illustrates the long and ambitious history of sport for development within the Olympic Movement. In addition, international sport federations such as FIFA, FIBA and UEFA are global supporters of a number of SDP projects worldwide. For instance, from 2005–2015, the *Football for Hope* programme has, according to FIFA, benefited 450 programmes run by 170 NGOs in 78 countries throughout the world (FIFA n.d.). Among INGOs, SDP organizations such as *Right to Play, Fight for Peace International, Peace Players International* and *Coaches across Continents (CAC)* also work on transnational levels. *Fight for Peace,* for example, was founded as an NGO in the favelas of Rio de Janeiro in 2000. The organization has now grown to become an INGO, supported by the likes of the IOC, operating in over 25 countries through their global network of partner organizations. (Fight for Peace n.d.) Similarly, *CAC,* a self-proclaimed global leader in the sport for social impact movement, provides consultancy resources to corporations, governments, foundations and NGOs to teach the skills necessary to organize sport as a social impact tool (Coaches across continents n.d.). INGOs are typically supported and funded by governments and government developing agencies, IGOs, other INGOs and foundations.

National non-governmental organizations

Together with IGOs and INGOS, NGOs are significant SDP stakeholders (Levermore and Beacom 2012). NGOs are important because they are often responsible for operating SDP programmes, and thus are involved with target groups or beneficiaries either directly or through close collaboration with other community-based organizations (Figure 4.1). Channelling aid funds through NGOs has also been a strategy for international donors, who often regard NGOs to be more effective than recipient government agencies, particularly in the global South (Spaaij 2009; Straume and Steen-Johnsen 2012; Banda 2013). According to Levermore and Beacom (2012), global North-led NGOs, together with INGOs, often play a formative role in SDP policy and programming. However, as Lindsey and Grattan (2012: 91) argue, SDP programmes are mostly delivered by SDP NGOs from the global South. Their assessment found that such NGOs often 'received limited international input and were more diverse than commonly identified in the existing literature'. An example of a global South SDP NGO (although supported by international partners) is the Kenyan NGO Mathare Youth Sports Association (MYSA) that was founded in 1987 as a self-help youth sports and community development project in Mathare, one of Africa's largest and poorest shanty towns on the outskirts of Nairobi. Today, MYSA has grown to include projects in Botswana, Tanzania, Sudan and Uganda as well as the Kakuma refugee camp in Kenya, and is, according to Giulianotti *et al.* (2016: 8), 'widely regarded as the greatest success story among sport and development projects in Africa'.

Private sector stakeholders

Private sector stakeholders in SDP range from local businesses to multinational corporations. Examples of the latter include Nike, Adidas, Vodafone and BP, each of which have entered the SDP arena as part of their corporate social responsibility (CSR) strategies (Levermore 2010). Breitbarth *et al.* (2015: 259) suggest that 'sport makes an ideal vehicle for deploying CSR', and consequently CSR through sport has gained momentum as an aspect of SDP. Indeed, a recent study has demonstrated the rising trend of multinational enterprises using CSR through sport, demonstrating 'that the corporate world has acknowledged – in practice – that the sporting context is a powerful vehicle for the employment of CSR' (Bason and Anagnostopoulos 2015: 233). According to Naish (2017), multinational corporations are one of the largest sources of revenue for SDP NGOs and thus play a significant role as SDP stakeholders. On a more critical note, Levermore (2013) argues that private sector stakeholders involved in SDP often have economic interests in low-income countries, and view SDP programmes, and improvements in development in general, as advantageous for their own profit ambitions. Such efforts are in turn often associated with a neoliberal approach to development, which, in the case of SDP, often translates into efforts to empower individuals in order to improve their self-control, employability skills and job-competitiveness and eventually become consumers of products.

Sport clubs and teams

Many sport clubs, teams and fan groups are also SDP stakeholders, either directly or indirectly through funding of SDP programmes or in-kind support. An example is the Manchester United Football Club and its 'United for UNICEF' scheme, which raises funds and advocates for UNICEF's work with vulnerable children worldwide. Similarly, when FC Barcelona set out on their 'Peace Tour' in 2013, they offered a football clinic for Jewish, Arab, Israeli and Palestinian children in cooperation with the Israeli NGO 'the Peres Center for Peace and Innovation' (Levermore 2013). Likewise, the *Football Club Social Alliance (FCSA)* was founded in 2007, and administered through the *Scort Foundation*. The main mission of the FCSA is to empower young women and men in their role as proactive community leaders, through 'The Young Coach Education Programme' which has been initiated in countries worldwide. Member clubs in the alliance include FC Basel 1893, SV Werder Bremen, Bayer 04 Leverkusen FK Austria Wien and Queens Park Rangers FC (The Football Club Social Alliance n.d.). Like the private sector stakeholders, the SDP engagement from sport clubs and teams are usually part of the clubs' CSR strategies, and is often administered through the club's official foundations.

Independent individuals

This stakeholder group ranges from individuals directly involved in the implementation of SDP projects, such as SDP participants and SDP practitioners, to those that are involved in SDP in a more indirect, and often symbolic, way. The latter group includes sports celebrities championing SDP NGOs and programmes. The campaign *Common Goal* is one such example. The initiative aims at encouraging professional football players to donate a minimum of 1 per cent of their wages to football charities and call attention to the power of sports in bringing communities together (Common Goal n.d.). As Naish (2017: 302) argues:

> SDP NGOs tend to hold professional sports people in high regard, and will recruit them as patrons, supporters and funders. SDP is especially vulnerable to being 'spun' in this way, as professional sports people can and do provide an easy route for PR messaging.

For instance, *Right to Play* have used more than 300 professional and Olympic athletes as ambassadors for their programs (Right to Play n.d.). Individuals have also initiated their own SDP projects; an example of this is the former Norwegian football player Tommy Nilsen, who founded the football project *Karanba* in a favela in Rio de Janeiro in 2006. Ten years later, with support from FIFAs *Football for Hope* programme and the Norwegian Ministry of Foreign Affairs, *Karanba* has grown to become an SDP organization with nearly 30 employees, helping over 1,000 children and youth in disadvantaged communities in the suburbs of Rio (Karanba n.d.).

Social movements and campaign groups

Social movements and campaign groups are highlighted by Giulianotti *et al.* (2016: 5) as one of four main stakeholder SDP groups which have increased their engagement in SDP in recent years. These groups emphasize social justice and human rights in sport and include organizations such as *Amnesty International* and the international conference and communication initiative *Play the Game*. However, despite an increasing and incredibly important engagement, this stakeholder group remains a relatively minor actor in the current SDP landscape.

Universities and schools

Universities and schools have marginal status in the SDP sector compared to INGOs, NGOs and private sector stakeholders. They do, however, play an important part in many SDP projects and programmes. Many SDP projects take place in-school, and cooperation with local schools are therefore crucial (illustrated in: Hasselgård and Straume 2015). In turn, many universities support SDP practices. For example, through the *Salud Escolar Integral* project, together with several other stakeholders, Brock University in Canada aims at teaching life skills for healthy development through active play, games, physical education and sport in El Salvador (Brock University n.d.). Similarly Darnell and Huish's (2015) study of a Cuban higher education institution providing scholarships for international students to obtain degrees in sports and physical education is an example of a South–South SDP partnership.

Further, some universities form research partnerships with SDP organizations worldwide (Welty Peachey and Cohen 2016). Third actors within this stakeholder category are children and youth academies in the global South. While such academies have traditionally had a clear 'sport development' agenda, (i.e. to identify, develop and acquire talented athletes, particularly in football), Hasselgård (2015) argues that many football academies now overlap with mainstream SDP initiatives, as they increasingly focus on providing academic or life skills education in addition to sport.

Foundations

Charities and foundations have been a relatively stable source of income for SDP over the years (Naish 2017). This may take the form of NGOs that distribute funds to other stakeholders based on applications, or through private sector donors, philanthropy and CSR initiatives from sport clubs (as discussed above). According to its website, the UK-based foundation *Laureus Sport for Good* has, since its inception in 2000, raised more than €100 million and supported over 150 SDP projects worldwide. Since 2003, *Comic Relief* has invested more than £30 million in funding SDP projects both in the UK and overseas (Wicks 2016). Both are high profile examples of charities that have contributed significantly to SDP in recent years.

SDP networks

The last stakeholder group in this overview are SDP networks, such as *Sport Plus Alliance* (previously Kicking Aids Out), *Youth Initiative Canada* and *streetfootballworld*. SDP networks are particularly important in helping SDP organizations achieve global visibility and recognition, share experiences and knowledge, and apply for financial support. The various SDP networks are supported by partners both from governments, IGOs, INGOs and private sector stakeholders.

As Figure 4.1 shows, and as discussed above, these 11 stakeholder groups are largely connected to and dependent on each other in terms of funding, publicity, legitimation and implementation. This has been pointed out by several SDP scholars, among them van Eekeren (2006) who speaks of the dynamic SDP arena, and Levermore (2013) who states that many SDP initiatives are characterized by a collection of different actors working together. Giulianotti *et al.* (2016) on the other hand, utilize a Bourdieusian approach, and argue that SDP is a contested field where different stakeholders struggle for influence and status. This argument, which also involves organizations competing for similar sources of funding, is increasingly relevant as more stakeholders enter the SDP sector (Spaaij 2009; Lindsey and Banda 2011).

Overall, scholars like Hasselgård (2015) argue that the architecture of SDP should be conceptualized along three interconnected levels; the international level, the national donor country level and the local level in the recipient country. To this, Naish (2017) adds the significance of the transnational level. Most stakeholders in SDP operate on one or more of these levels and this complexity characterizes the SDP sector and its shared institutions, policies and politics. Thus 'an understanding of the flow of SDP ideals (ideas, values) within and between the different levels of SDP is needed' (Hasselgård 2015: 21). Following this, and with the above stakeholders in mind, Figure 4.2 adds levels, politics, policies and strategies to the web of structures and funding outlined in Figure 4.1. The solid lines still point to the interactions that are going on between different SDP stakeholders but the dashed lines indicate influence in terms of policy, strategies and public opinions. This is discussed further in the next section.

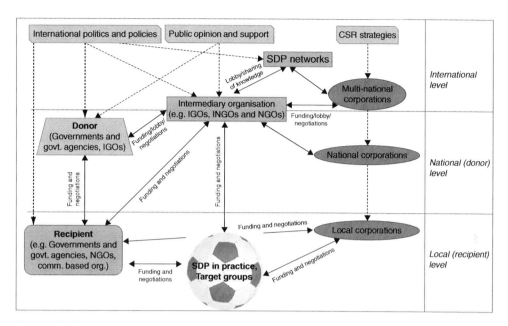

Figure 4.2 The complex web of SDP structures, policies and funding streams
Adapted from van Eekeren 2006 and Hasselgård 2015

SDP policy development and its implications

As illustrated in Figure 4.2, international politics and policies inform and influence different stakeholders in the SDP sector. This is demonstrated by Straume (2010), who studied Norwegian SDP programming in Tanzania in the early 1980s. Inspired by European and Norwegian sport politics of the time, the project took on 'sport for all' as an ideal. 'Sport for all' policies, first emerging in the 1960s, were built upon the idea that the health and well-being of citizens was a government concern, and needed to be emphasized in order to facilitate social development. This fit within a broader European society experiencing social challenges caused by post-industrialisation, and 'sport for all' was eventually adopted by a number of European governments whose heavy investments yielded increased sports participation in the 1960s and 1970s (Houlihan 1994). 'Sport for all' policies were further adopted by INGOs such as the Council of Europe and UNESCO, which emphasized that sport and physical education was a human right that should be encouraged in all levels of society. In turn, the Norwegian Olympic and Paralympic Committee and Confederation of Sports (NIF) followed this rhetoric of the time, and when initiating an SDP project in Tanzania, NIF worked to promote 'sport for all' through its programmes. Straume (2010) further argues that a most decisive argument for NIF to initiate an SDP project was that the political strategies of Norwegian development aid at the time made funds available for NGOs that had not traditionally been part of the aid system. This opened the door for sport organizations to enter the field of international development. However, as Lie (2005: 13) argues, 'development assistance always comes with certain strings attached', and so was the case of the *Sport for All* project. Public aid priorities were more or less fixed, and NIF had to comply with them, meaning prioritizing SDP programme delivery on recipients' terms and particularly for vulnerable groups.

This analysis corresponds with research on the general politics of international aid. Aid has traditionally reflected ideas and policies generated by powerful international organizations such as the World Bank and the International Monetary Fund (Nustad 2003). Critical analyses of such structures have been put forth by post-development scholars, who have criticized the development apparatus for being hegemonic, monolithic and homogenizing, and even conceptualized the idea of 'development' 'as a massive, superior discourse and an execution of power with the poor as victims' (Nustad 2003: 39). The rejoinder to the post-development approach has been that it lacks an actor-orientation, and draws 'a caricature of development discourses as almighty and totally dominating to the people exposed to them' (Nustad 2003: 44). Indeed, Grillo (1997: 20) has suggested that post-development literature sees development as 'a monolithic enterprise, heavily controlled from the top, convinced of the superiority of its own wisdom and impervious to local knowledge'. The key point here is that many development scholars now recognize the importance of studying the interplay between development discourse, policy and local agency, and the ways in which different stakeholders 'receive, translate, interpret, resist, manipulate, or embody development discourses' (Lie 2011: 75).

Such trends can be seen in recent SDP research. A recurring argument from SDP policy scholars has been that the sector is largely compatible with the neoliberal policy perspective (Hayhurst 2009; Levermore 2009; Giulianotti 2011a; Hartmann and Kwauk 2011; Hayhurst et al. 2011). Neoliberal paradigms are often characterized by a strong donor or interventionist approach, that claims to know what direction development should take in order to secure economic and consequently social progress. For instance, in a discourse analysis of six central SDP policy documents produced by the SDP International Working Group, Hayhurst (2009: 203) found that 'SDP policy models are wedded to the increasingly neoliberal character of international development'. Further, Hayhurst (2009: 221–222) argued that such an approach often 'places the onus on individuals to be responsible for their welfare, "healthify" and help the state to cut expenses by participating in these projects'. In so doing, she showed how an 'instrumentalisation of "policy-driven ideas" … continue to be leveraged through sport and sealed into the success stories of SDP'. Darnell (2012: 51) has similarly problematized the neoliberal aspects of SDP policy, arguing that it 'represents, facilitates and allows "some" manner of development change … but does so while eschewing significant and direct challenges to the structures that sustain inequality for vast populations'.

These perspectives join a trend in critical SDP research highlighting the strong dominance of Global North ideologies, agendas and input in SDP interventions. As Darnell and Huish (2015: 7) write:

> Within the structures that see SDP policy, aid, expertise and volunteer labour flow from the global North to South … tensions remain between Northern notions of development to be implemented trough SDP programmes and Southern demands for development in the face of global inequalities … relations of power in SDP often remain structured in a top-down or hegemonic manner due in large part to the access to resources governed by broader global economics.

Still, some scholars have challenged these critiques and called for research focused on local agency, in order to understand SDP from the perspectives of actors in the global South (i.e. Guest 2009; Lindsey and Grattan 2012; Jeanes and Magee 2014). As Lindsey and Grattan (2012: 92) state: 'organizations from the Global North may have less influence on local sport-for-development than has hitherto been acknowledged'. It is therefore important to understand the local, recipient level of SDP, in relation to policy formation and implementation. In a contribution to this debate, Hasselgård and Straume (2015: 101) highlight the interface between policy and practice in SDP, showing that different world views are often negotiated within SDP projects, as discourses and policy-driven ideas are 'translated and given meaning by recipient organization or local project staff in the social contexts where it is implemented'. These findings connect to those of Guest (2009) whose ethnography of an Olympic Aid (now Right to Play) project in Angola demonstrated that the recipients did not uncritically adopt discourses and solutions presented to them by the Northern donors, but 'participated in sport and play on their own terms and employed their own meanings' (Guest 2009: 1347).

As this discussion illustrates, SDP policy and research is diverse and has fostered important discussions regarding the functionalist notion of sport for development, relations of power, top-down programming and local agency. A further illustration of this is given in Straume and Steen-Johnsen (2012), who, in a study of Norwegian SDP to Tanzania in the 1980s, revealed multiple power relationships between Norwegian donors and Tanzanian recipients. The Norwegian governing body – NIF – that initiated the project had to conform to the guidelines of NORAD, which itself had to conform to current political guidelines. Similarly, on the Tanzanian side, the National Sport Council had to comply with the demands of NIF and NORAD while simultaneously conforming to their own political norms and strategies. This led Straume and Steen-Johnsen (2012: 109) to conclude that the aid system in SDP 'is one in which values are negotiated […] the relationship between donors and recipients is not unambiguous. Neither is the apparent donor and recipient only a donor and a recipient; nevertheless, their roles are defined by the aid relationship'.

Conclusion

This chapter has set out to address SDP structures, funding streams and policy development. It has done so by identifying 11 interconnected stakeholder groups that contribute to, and act upon, the SDP sector. At least two main points can be concluded from this discussion. First, the overall structure of the SDP sector is more or less dynamic, complex and interdependent, particularly as funding, knowledge, ideas and policies flow within and between various structures. Both Figure 4.1 and Figure 4.2 illustrate this complexity. Important in both figures are the two-way arrows indicating that relations and interactions between stakeholders on all levels are ambiguous and marked by agency on both the donor and recipient sides. Second, and despite these multiple flows, SDP policy scholars have also highlighted the strong dominance of global North ideologies, agendas and input within many SDP interventions. This criticism relates both to the development (and influence) of (neoliberal) global North-led policies as well as the flow of SDP funds which also tend to be dominated by global North actors.

That said, nuance is required in analysing such structures and processes. As Naish (2017: 305) argues, it is 'clearly a temptation to view the flow of money as an indication of how power functions in SDP'. However, this chapter has highlighted that the SDP system is one in which such structures, goals and resources are negotiated. As Giulianotti (2011b) found, SDP project officials often show a strong resistance to forsaking the philosophies of the organization in order to secure funding. Thus, power and its associated resources, are constantly negotiated within the SDP sector.

With these ideas in mind, future research should continue to strive for more and better understandings of how the interdependencies of the SDP sector work in practice. More knowledge of the way funds and policies influence different SDP stakeholders would also make an important contribution to the field, particularly in driving the sector towards policies that are increasingly based on development cooperation and equal partnership.

References

Banda, D. (2013). Young people, sex education and HIV/AIDS in Zambia. In B. Houlihan, and M. Green (eds), *Routledge Handbook of Sports Development*. London: Routledge.

Bason, T. and Anagnostopoulos, C. (2015). Corporate social responsibility through sport: A longitudinal study of the FTSE100 companies. *Sport, Business and Management: An International Journal*, 5(3), 218–241.

Breitbarth, T., Walzel, S., Anagnostopoulos, C. and Van Eekeren, F. (2015). Corporate social responsibility and governance in sport: 'Oh, the things you can find, if you don't stay behind!'. *Corporate Governance*, 15(2), 254–273.

Brock University. (n.d.). 'Brock and Central America: Collaborating on Education, Research and Development Goals'. Available at: https://brocku.ca/webfm_send/24348 (accessed 5 February 2017).

Coaches across Continents. (n.d.). 'Why does CAC exist?'. Available at: https://coachesacrosscontinents.org/about/ (accessed 8 August 2017).

Coalter, F. (2007). *A wider social role for sport: Who's keeping the score?*. London & New York: Routledge.

Common Goal. (n.d.). 'What we do'. Available at: www.common-goal.org/ (accessed 8 August 2017).

Darnell, S. (2012). *Sport for Development and Peace: A Critical Sociology*. London: Bloomsbury Academic.

Darnell, S. C. and Huish, R. (2015). Cuban sport policy and South–South development cooperation: An overview and analysis of the Escuela Internacional de Educación Física y Deporte. *International Journal of Sport Policy*, 7(1), 123–140.

Fifa. (n.d.). 'Football for hope'. Available at: www.fifa.com/sustainability/football-for-hope.html (accessed 8 August 2017).

Fight for Peace. (n.d.). 'Fight for Peace'. Available at: http://fightforpeace.net/ (accessed 8 August 2017).

Giulianotti, R. (2011a). The sport, development and peace sector: A model of four social policy domains. *Journal of Social Policy*, 40(4), 757–776.

Giulianotti, R. (2011b). Sport, transnational peacemaking, and global civil society: Exploring the reflective discourses of 'sport, development, and peace' project officials. *Journal of Sport and Social Issues*, 35(1), 50–71.

Giulianotti, R., Hognestad, H. and Spaaij, R. (2016). Sport for development and peace: power, politics, and patronage. *Journal of Global Sport Management*, 1(3–4), 129–141.

Grillo, R. D. (1997). Discourses of development: The view from anthropology. In R. D. Grillo and R. L. Stirrat (eds), *Discourses of Development: Anthropological Perspectives*. Oxford: Berg.

Guest, A. M. (2009). The diffusion of development-through-sport: Analysing the history and practice of the Olympic Movement's grassroots outreach to Africa. *Sport in Society*, 12(10), 1336–1352.

Hartmann, D. and Kwauk, C. (2011). Sport and development: An overview, critique, and reconstruction. *Journal of Sport and Social Issues*, 35(3), 284–305.

Hasselgård, A. (2015). Norwegian sport for development and peace: Donor discourse and local practice. PhD, Norwegian School of Sport Sciences.

Hasselgård, A. and S. Straume (2011). Utvikling til idrett eller idrett til utvikling? NIF som idrettsbistandsaktør. In D.V. Hanstad, G. Breivik, M. K. Sisjord, and H. B. Skaset (eds), *Norsk Idrett: Indre spenning og ytre press*. Oslo: Akilles.

Hasselgård, A. and Straume, S. (2015). Sport for development and peace policy discourse and local practice: Norwegian sport for development and peace to Zimbabwe. *International Journal of Sport Policy*, 7(1), 87–103.

Hayhurst, L. M. C. (2009). The power to shape policy: Charting sport for development and peace policy discourses. *International Journal of Sport Policy*, 1(2), 203–227.

Hayhurst, L. M. C., Wilson, B. and Frisby, W. (2011). Navigating neoliberal networks: Transnational Internet platforms in sport for development and peace. *International Review for the Sociology of Sport*, 46(3), 315–329.

Houlihan, B. (1994). *Sport and International Politics*, Upper Saddle River, NJ: Prentice Hall.

Jeanes, R. and Magee, J. (2014). Promoting gender empowerment through sport? Exploring the experiences of Zambian female footballers. In N. Schulenkorf, and D. Adair (eds), *Global Sport-For-Development: Critical Perspectives*. Basingstoke: Palgrave Macmillan.

Karanba. (n.d.). About Karanba. Available at: www.karanba.com/en/ (accessed 4 February 2017).

Kidd, B. (2008). A new social movement: Sport for development and peace. *Sport in Society, 11*(4), 370–380.

Laureus Sport for Good. (n.d.). 'Introduction to Laureus'. Available at: www.laureus.com/content/introduction-laureus (accessed 4 February 2017).

Levermore, R. (2008). Sport: A new engine of development. *Progress in Development Studies, 8*(2), 183–190.

Levermore, R. (2009). Sport-in-international development: Theoretical frameworks. *Sport and International Development*. Berlin: Springer.

Levermore, R. (2010). CSR for development through sport: Examining its potential and limitations. *Third World Quarterly, 31*, 223–241.

Levermore, R. (2013). Sport in international development: Facilitating improved standards of living? In B. Houlihan and M. Green (eds), *Routledge Handbook of Sports Development*. London: Routledge.

Levermore, R. and Beacom, A. (2009). Sport and development: Mapping the field. In R. Levermore and A. Beacom (eds), *Sport and International Development*. Basingstoke: Palgrave Macmillan.

Levermore, R. and Beacom, A. (2012). Reassessing sport-for-development: Moving beyond 'mapping the territory'. *International Journal of Sport Policy, 4*(1) 125–137.

Lie, J. H. S. (2005). Reproduction of Development's Trusteeship and Discursive Power. PhD course Globalization of Epistemologies and Epistemologies of Globalization. Course arranged by IMER, Department of Social Anthropology and Department of Sociology at the University of Bergen.

Lie, J. (2011). Developmentality. The New Aid Architecture and the Formation of Partnership Between the World Bank and Uganda. Unpublished PhD thesis. University of Bergen.

Lindsey, I. and Banda, D. (2011). Sport and the fight against HIV/AIDS in Zambia: A 'partnership approach'? *International Review for the Sociology Of Sport, 46*(1), 90–107.

Lindsey, I. and Grattan, A. (2012). An 'international movement'? Decentring sport-for-development within Zambian communities. *International Journal of Sport Policy and Politics, 4*(1), 91–110.

Massao, P. and Straume, S. (2012). Urban Youth and Sport for Development. Available at: www.youthpolicy.org/wp-content/uploads/library/2012_Urban_Youth_Sport_Development_Eng1.pdf (accessed 5 February 2017).

Naish, J. (2017). Sport for development and peace. Alignment, administration, power. In A. Bairner, J. Kelly and J. W. Lee (eds), *Routledge Handbook of Sport and Politics*. London: Routledge.

Nicholls, S., Giles, A. R. and Sethna, C. (2011). Perpetuating the 'lack of evidence' discourse in sport for development: Privileged voices, unheard stories and subjugated knowledge. *International Review for the Sociology of Sport, 46*(3) 249–264.

Norwegian Olympic and Paralympic Committee and Confederation of Sports. (n.d.). 'Idrettens utviklingssamarbeid'. Available at: www.idrettsforbundet.no/tema/idrettens-utviklingssamarbeid/ (accessed 2 February 2017).

Nustad, K. G. (2003). *Gavens Makt: Norsk Utviklingshjelp som Formynderskap*. Oslo: Pax Forlag.

Right to Play. (n.d.). Athlete Ambassadors. Available at: www.righttoplay.com/Learn/keyplayers/Pages/Athlete-Ambassadors.aspx (accessed 17 January 2017).

Spaaij, R. (2009). The social impact of sport: Diversities, complexities and contexts. *Sport in Society, 12*(9), 1109–1117.

Sport and Development Platform. (n.d.). Learn More. Available at: www.sportanddev.org/en/learn-more (accessed 2 February 2017).

Straume, S. (2010). Sport is in lack of everything here! Norwegian sport for all to Tanzania in the early 1980s. *Stadion, 36*(2)177–198.

Straume, S. and Steen-Johnsen, K. (2012). On the terms of the recipient? Norwegian sports development aid to Tanzania in the 1980s. *International Review for the Sociology of Sport, 47*(1), 95–112.

The Football Club Social Alliance. (n.d.). 'Alliance'. Available at: http://football-alliance.org/the-alliance/ (accessed 4 February 2017).

United Nations Office on Sport for Development and Peace. (2014). 'Sport and Sustainable Development Goals'. Available at: www.un.org/sport/content/why-sport/sport-and-sustainable-development-goals (accessed 15 December 2016).

Van Eekeren, F. (2006). Sport and Development: Challenges in a new era. In Y. Auweele, C. Malcolm and B. Meulders (eds), *Sport and Development*. Leuven: Lannoo Campus.

Welty Peachey, J. and Cohen, A. (2016). Research partnerships in sport for development and peace: Challenges, barriers, and strategies. *Journal of Sport Management, 30*(3), 282–297.

Wicks, S. (2016). Sport is a Powerful Vehicle for Change. Available at: www.comicrelief.com/news/blog-sport-powerful-vehicle-for-change (accessed 9 August 2017).

Wickstrøm, M. A. (2017). UN Secretary-General Closes UNOSDP. Available at: www.playthegame.org/news/news-articles/2017/0309_un-secretary-general-closes-unosdp/ (accessed 8 August 2017).

Zimbabwe Ministry of Sport and Recreation. (n.d.). Ministry of Sports and Recreation. Available at: www.zarnet.ac.zw/dev/govportal/government-ministries/ministry-sports-and-recreation (accessed 24 January 2017).

5

International governmental organizations in the SDP sector

Rob Millington

Introduction

In December of 2005, the United Nations (UN) hosted the second Magglingen Conference on Sport and Development. The conference was organized by Adolf Ogi (the then-Special Advisor to the UN Secretary-General on Sport for Development and Peace), the Federal Office of Sport (FOSPO, the Swiss national office of sport), and the Swiss Agency for Development and Cooperation (a faction of the Swiss Ministry of Foreign Affairs), with the express purpose of exploring how sport could be mobilized to meet the Millennium Development Goals (MDGs) (UNOSDP 2005). The summary report for the conference, the 'Magglingen Call to Action 2005', called upon ten stakeholders – including sport organizations and bilateral development agencies – to contribute to sport and development by integrating sustainable development principles into their policies, program and projects, and to raise awareness of the ideal of 'sport for all'. The Magglingen Conference was significant in that it advanced the trend of connecting sport to international development goals under the banner of sport for development and peace (SDP), and formally outlined the role of international governmental organizations (IGOs) in meeting these development aims.

Since the Magglingen Call, the SDP sector has seen continued growth, with sport gaining in both credibility and popularity as a tool of development within the international aid sector, thanks in large part to its championing by the UN. Over this period, SDP was formally integrated within the UN system via various initiatives including establishing the aforementioned Special Advisor position, opening the UN Office on Sport for Development and Peace, proclaiming 2005 as the International Year of Sport and Physical Education, and by being connected to the MDGs. The place of sport within the development sphere was further solidified in 2015 through the 17 Sustainable Development Goals (SDGs), that succeeded the MDGs to form the primary development agenda through 2030, and importantly, directly connected sport to the achievement of development goals for the first time via Article 37 (UN 2016).

In the years between the Magglingen Call and the SDGs, SDP programs and organizations have proliferated, with hundreds of organizations mobilizing sport in pursuit of development. While these organizations range in size and scope, and comprise a myriad of government-sponsored, non-governmental and corporate-based organizations,

IGOs have also emerged as among the most visible and influential. Here, IGO refers to supra-national organizational bodies that are composed of member states and operate as a governing body internationally. In this way, they differ from governmental organizations and non-governmental organizations that act as partners, intermediaries or a force of opposition to both state and corporate entities (Hayhurst *et al.* 2015). Given the range of institutional actors and diverse policy agendas of IGOs, the ways in which sport is employed in the development context is diverse. This chapter focuses on three most prominent IGOs promoting SDP: the UN, the International Olympic Committee (IOC), and the Fédération Internationale de Football Association (FIFA). In following the UN's lead, the IOC and FIFA have sought to position themselves as development agents via their own SDP programs, particularly by connecting the Olympic Games and World Cup of Football to broad-based development strategies for host nations. The chapter proceeds by providing a brief overview of each of these organizations' history in promoting sport as a tool of development, before offering insights into how the UN, the IOC and FIFA each view their role in the international development sphere. The chapter concludes by offering critical rejoinders to the SDP vision outlined by each of these three IGOs, and presenting some future areas of research in the field.

The United Nations: bringing SDP into the new millennium

The early 2000s were a watershed for the SDP paradigm. Seeking to reframe its approach to development issues from the strict economic measures of the 1970s and 1980s, and the structural adjustments of the 1990s, the UN sought to capitalize on the turn of the millennium as an opportunity to reframe its approach to development (see Millington 2015). This putative shift was manifest in the Millennium Development Goals, announced in 2000, that laid out the UN's primary development mandate through eight objectives to be achieved by 2015: eradicate extreme poverty and hunger; achieve universal primary education; promote gender equality and empower women; reduce child mortality; improve maternal health; combat pandemic illnesses such as HIV/AIDs; ensure environmental sustainability; and create a global partnership for development (UN 2015). Importantly, sport played a role in this shift, not only within the aforementioned institutionalization of SDP within the UN structure, but also in policy, with the UN detailing sport's contribution to each of the eight MDGs, via the United Nations Inter-Agency Task Force on Sport for Development and Peace (see Sport for Development and Peace International Working Group 2008).

Despite this framing of SDP as nascent and a novel approach to development in the new millennium, sport has a much longer history in the development context (see Millington and Kidd in this collection), a history that includes its use by the UN in the post-World War II era. For example, the International Labour Organization – an agency of the UN-precursor organization, the League of Nations – used sport as a means to promote 'social good', particularly in orphanages and refugee camps in Europe after World War II (Millington 2015). Upon its founding in 1945, the UN was primarily focused on post-war reconstruction, particularly through the provision of humanitarian aid in Europe. However, the organization's scope soon expanded to 'development' in the rest of the world (Millington 2015). Indeed, the UN Charter, signed in 1945, detailed the purpose of the UN and its subsidiary organizations, and made clear the role of the organization in supporting nation-building and development for once-dependent territories. Chapter XI of the Charter, for example, made explicit the UN's role in assisting former colonies in promoting self-determination by recognizing the 'political aspirations and stages of development and advancement of each territory' (UN n.d.a). Importantly sport was also included in various development and humanitarian declarations in the twentieth century: in 1959 the UN expanded the League of Nation's 1924 Declaration of the Rights of the Child to include 'the opportunity for play and recreation'; in 1978 the United Nations Educational, Scientific, and Cultural Organization's (UNESCO) International Charter of Physical Education and Sport declared sport and physical education a 'fundamental right for all'; and the 1990 Convention on the Rights of the Child outlined the right to rest, leisure, play and recreational activities (see Millington 2015).

Thus, the UN's formalization of SDP within its institutional structure in the early 2000s was not without precedent, although it certainly intensified over this period. As noted above, the UN capitalized on the new millennium to incorporate sport into international development policy, publishing a number of documents on the utility of sport in development. In 2003, the UN created the UN Inter-Agency Task Force on Sport for Development and Peace to explore how sport could be utilized in pursuit of the MDGs. The task force outlined three primary objectives for the SDP paradigm: first, to ameliorate social issues, such as underprivileged children, education, gender equality and refugees; second, to promote health, including HIV/AIDS prevention, drug prevention, immunization, and health for people living with disabilities; and third, to provide an economic stimulus through poverty alleviation, local economic development, job creation, and environmental protection (UN 2003). Throughout the rest of the decade, the UN continued to frame sport as a simple, low-cost, and effective means of achieving development goals through a myriad of publications, including 'Sport for Development and Peace: Towards achieving the Millennium Development Goals' (UN 2003); 'Sport for a Better World: Report on the International Year of Sport and Physical Education' (UN 2005); 'Women 2000 and Beyond: Women, Gender Equality and Sport' (UN 2007); and 'Achieving the Objectives of the United Nations through Sport' (UN 2008).

By the end of its mandate, the success of the MDGs – and the role of sport therein – were mixed at best. On the one hand, then UN Secretary-General Ban Ki-moon argued that the MDGs were successful in helping to 'lift more than one billion people out of extreme poverty, to make inroads against hunger, to enable more girls to attend school than ever before and to protect our planet' (UN 2015). On the other hand, the UN also recognized that development had been uneven, and inequalities persisted or even worsened. In October of 2015, the UN announced the Sustainable Development Goals (SDGs) as the successor to the MDGs to form the focus of global development through 2030. Expanding the development objectives from 8 to 17, the SDGs are designed as a 'universal call to action to end poverty, protect the planet and ensure that all people enjoy peace and prosperity' (UNDP n.d.). Significantly, the role of sport in meeting the SDGs has been explicitly outlined by the UN. In the document that accompanied the announcement of the SDGs, 'Transforming our world: The 2030 Agenda for sustainable development', Article 37 reads:

> Sport is also an important enabler of sustainable development. We recognize the growing contribution of sport to the realization of development and peace in its promotion of tolerance and respect and the contributions it makes to the empowerment of women and of young people, individuals and communities as well as to health, education and social inclusion objectives.
>
> *UN 2016*

In many ways, including sport within official development policy bespeaks the growth of the SDP sector since the early 2000s, and the regard with which sport is held by the international community.

The growth of the SDP sector has undoubtedly benefited from the credibility afforded to it through the UN. Indeed, the myriad of organizations now employing sport in pursuit of development speaks to the influence of the UN and the mandate it set out via the 2005 Magglingen call to action. It is also important to note that the benefits afforded to the SDP sector in this regard have been reciprocal: given the critiques the UN faced regarding its effectiveness as an IGO towards the end of the twentieth century, the UN has benefited from the visibility and popularity of the SDP paradigm as 'evidence' of its usefulness. For this reason, it was surprising to many when, in May of 2017, the UN established a direct partnership with the IOC to promote SDP, and announced its closure of the UNOSDP, to avoid parallel work (see IOC 2017a). The partnership is indicative for both the growth of the sector and the assent of the IOC as the most influential IGO promoting sport for development in the 2010s.

International Olympic Committee: promoting 'Olympics values' in developing regions

Of the hundreds of organizations that have taken up or initiated SDP programs since the UN's 2005 'call to action', the International Olympic Committee has been one of, if not the most visible. Indeed, the IOC has a long-standing relationship with the UN, a relationship that has been at times both contentious and mutually beneficial (Van Luijk 2015). For decades, the IOC has sought to assert its authority over global sport, and position itself as a leader in sporting and cultural matters on a global scale. It is perhaps unsurprising then, that the IOC would view the Magglingen Call as an opportunity to advance these dual goals, and leverage its relationship with the UN to do so. As the IOC asserts:

> By using sport as a tool, the IOC and its partners implement various activities across the globe in fields such as humanitarian assistance, peace-building, education, gender equality, the environment and the fight against HIV/AIDS, hence contributing to the achievement of the UN Millennium Development Goals. Last year's decision to grant the IOC UN observer status pays tribute to these efforts and is a sign of the strong bonds between the IOC and the UN, which share the same philosophy and values.
>
> *IOC 2010a*

In some ways, the UN's abdication of its leadership of SDP to the IOC with the formal closure of the UNOSDP, was a culminating moment for the relationship between the two organizations. While the IOC is often seen as a relative new-comer to the development paradigm, the groundwork for its development efforts can be traced back to the revival of the modern Olympics and the vision of Pierre de Coubertin. Indeed, Coubertin's vision was for the Games to be a force of education, social development and global harmony (Binder 2001): from the outset the aims of the Olympic Movement were to 'place sport at the service of the harmonious development of man with a view to promoting a peaceful society concerned with the preservation of human dignity' (IOC 2011: 3).

The antecedents of the IOC's SDP ambitions were slowly cultivated throughout the twentieth century. Under the presidency of Avery Brundage (1952–1972) in particular, the IOC sought to shift the vision of the Olympic Movement from one of individual and moral character building in the tradition of Coubertin, to one of global humanitarian rights and development, particularly within a post-colonial context (Chatziefstathiou and Henry 2012). Towards the end of the century, the UN sought to take a more active role in the global community, using sport to promote physical education and social good, under the banner of 'sport for all'. Fearing threats to its autonomy and international status, the IOC had largely resisted the overtures of the UN and other IGOs to collaborate on issues related to global sport. By the 1970s, however, the IOC sought to build a stronger relationship with the UN as a means of strengthening its international standing (Guest 2009). Such partnerships proved fruitful as, moving into the 1980s, the IOC had begun to solidify its leadership in the international sporting realm, increasing its commitment to global humanitarian issues through the Olympic Solidarity program. The 1981 Baden-Baden conference further committed the IOC to mobilizing the Olympic Movement in pursuit of social development. To these ends, the IOC expanded Olympic Solidarity to establish 'Olympafrica' that focused on development in Africa, and partnered with various UN agencies, particularly the United Nations High Commission on Refugees (UNHCR) to promote sporting activities, providing equipment and funds for facilities in refugee camps in Ghana, Kenya and Tanzania (Guest 2009).

By the early 2000s, amid broader developments in the SDP sector, the IOC's efforts to promote development intensified under the banner of 'Olympism in Action' (OIA). The IOC defines OIA as the manifestation of the three Olympic values − excellence, friendship, and respect − into 'six fields of activities': development through sport; peace through sport; education through sport; sport at a grassroots level; sport and the environment; and women in sport (IOC 2009). One example of OIA's work is the Osire refugee camp in Namibia, where the IOC teamed with the UN to implement sport programs aimed at alleviating illness, including HIV/AIDS, and promoting education. Through this project 'the IOC and UNHCR are looking to provide young people with meaningful recreational activities and the necessary tools to make informed decisions in life' (IOC 2010b). The IOC is also active in promoting education in developing countries through a branch of OIA, the Olympic Values Education Program (OVEP), that teaches 'Olympic values' in a network of 9000 associated schools in 180 countries, mostly in the global South (IOC 2010c).

More recently, in December 2014, the IOC released the Olympic Agenda 2020, outlining 40 recommendations for the Olympic Movement moving forward. The UN's SDGs feature prominently in the Agenda, with the IOC pledging to promote sustainable development through the Olympic Games, including in the bid process, hosting of the Games and in the Olympic Movement's daily operations. Further, the IOC also pledged to continue its work in the development context by spreading 'Olympic values-based education' in school curricula worldwide and to further the reach and impact of OIA (IOC 2014). Connecting the Olympic Games themselves to sustainable development in the Agenda highlights a broader trend where the IOC has sought not only to promote 'soft', social development through sport, but also 'hard', structural development for developing nations. This includes the construction of sporting infrastructure through a 'Sport for Hope Centre' in both Zambia and Haiti. The centres aim to 'provide young people and local communities with positive sports and development opportunities; offer state-of-the-art facilities to National Federations and athletes; and promote Olympic values of excellence, friendship and respect' so as to 'contribute to a better and more peaceful world through sport' (IOC 2017b). The centres also offer educational opportunities and health care options, with the educational programs focusing on the 'values of Olympism', environmental and social responsibilities, life skills development and health services including hygiene, sports medicine and health care services provided by the Red Cross (IOC 2017c).

The IOC has also cast the hosting of the Olympic Games themselves as a means for developing polities to unlock funds for infrastructural development − including such things as roads, airports, housing and sport facilities − while offering opportunities for foreign investment by projecting an image of modernity to a global audience (see Roche 2000; Black and Van Der Westhuizen 2004; Millington and Darnell 2014; Darnell and Millington 2016). The 2016 Olympic Games in Rio de Janeiro, Brazil offers the latest example of connecting sports mega-events (SMEs) to development strategies, continuing a trend established by the 2008 Olympics in Beijing, China, the 2010 Commonwealth Games in India, and the 2014 Olympics in Sochi, Russia. This trend is indicative of a broader shift in SDP programming that seeks to promote social good and capitalist accumulation in tandem, while allowing the IOC to use the Olympic platform to further assert its leadership in the SDP sector. Indeed, over the past few decades, the IOC has risen in both status and influence, informing how SDP is understood and implemented, and providing a model to other IGOs, perhaps most notably FIFA, who has also attached the hosting of the World Cup to development strategies for host nations including South Africa (2010), Brazil (2014) and Qatar (2022).

FIFA: sport for development through football for hope

Like the IOC, FIFA has sought to advance their standing in the international community through SDP initiatives, albeit on a smaller scale. In the early 2000s, and as part of broader corporate social responsibility endeavours, FIFA created its own SDP program, Football for Hope, that offers 'funding, equipment, training and more visibility, as well as a platform for discussion and collaboration', with the goal of promoting 'the use of the world's most popular sport to spark positive change for a better future' (FIFA, 2013). Over the past decade, the Football for Hope program has supported 450 programs run by 17 non-governmental organizations (NGOs) in 78 countries, mostly in the global South, and focuses on providing 'HIV/AIDS education, conflict resolution, gender equality, social integration of people with intellectual disabilities, peacebuilding, youth leadership and life skills' (FIFA, n.d.a). FIFA also has several other SDP programs, including the Forward Football Development Program, aimed at improving the way soccer is supported across the globe 'so that the sport can reach its potential in every nation and so that everyone that wants to take part can do so without barriers'; the Goal Program that builds facilities such as soccer fields, technical centres, and youth academies; and the Solitary Fund that grants emergency support to FIFA member associations that have been affected by humanitarian or natural disasters (FIFA n.d.b).

In contrast to the Olympic Games, the FIFA World Cup has always been more globally oriented, with the event often finding a home in Central and South America, and membership in FIFA long having symbolic meaning for nationalist independence movements, particularly in the decolonization era. Indeed, the 1950s and 1960s saw many newly dependent countries seek membership in FIFA as a means of affirming independence within the eyes of the international community (Darby 2005). More recently, however, FIFA has followed the precedent set by the IOC in connecting the World Cup to broad-based development strategies for host nations, particularly in the global South. FIFA has positioned the event as a catalyst to unlocking funds for structural developments, foreign investment, and environmental remediation and protection (see Gaffney 2010; 2013). In this regard, FIFA has made sustainable development plans a requirement for bid nations, and South Africa (2010), Brazil (2014) and Qatar (2022) all explicitly drew upon discourses of development in their successful bids for the World Cup (cf. Gaffney 2013).

As the first 'first-order' sport mega-event (see Black 2008) to be hosted in an African nation, the 2010 South African World Cup offers important insights into how IGOs like FIFA have mobilized sport and sports mega-events in pursuit of development. Perhaps more than any other 'developing' nation, South Africa has readily connected SMEs to its national development strategies, particularly in attempts to project a new, post-apartheid image of the country (Cornelissen and Swart 2006). As Scarlett Cornelissen (2004) argues, the first few years after apartheid were marked by efforts to forge a new, unified national identity and sense of loyalty for the government and nation: sport was an important element of this effort. The strategy of tying SMEs to development materialized most famously through South Africa's successful bid for the 1995 Rugby World Cup, led in large part by Nelson Mandela, that set both precedent and acted as a catalyst for future SME bids (Cornelissen 2004). A year after the Rugby World Cup, South Africa hosted and won the African Cup of Nations. In 1997 the country bid, unsuccessfully, for the 2004 Olympic Games, followed by a failed bid in 1998 for the 2006 FIFA World Cup. This pattern continued into the new millennium, albeit more fruitfully, with the successful bids for the 2003 Cricket World Cup, the 2003 President's Cup (Golf), the 2004 International Women's Golf Cup, and ultimately the 2010 World Cup (Cornelissen 2004; Cornelissen and Swart 2006). South Africa's successful bid for the 2010 World Cup thus marked a culminating point for the nation's efforts in the SDP realm, and for FIFA's ambitions as an IGO on the world stage. In bidding for the event, the South African government positioned the World Cup not only as a means to showcase the nation's democratic transition and stability in the post-Mandela era, but also as an opportunity to boost its economy and standing in the international community (Cornelissen 2004).

More recent events suggest that the development potential of SMEs remains a powerful and seductive discourse. In December of 2010, FIFA awarded the 2022 World Cup to Qatar, marking the first time the event will be held in the Middle East. Many saw Qatar as a curious selection, given that it is one of the world's smallest states, has little history with the sport, and is home to a less than optimal climate for a major and prolonged outdoor sporting event (Brannagan and Giulianotti 2015). Further, Qatar's vast wealth would seem to differentiate it from the development discourses attached to other recent SME bids in the global South. And yet, early narratives surrounding the 2022 World Cup have illustrated a common development thread. Like other SMEs in developing countries, the Qatar World Cup has been forecasted as a means to brand a new identity, both at home and abroad, by offering a vision of a modern, twenty-first-century state. Qatar has a history of using sporting events – including the Qatar Open Tennis Tournament, the Qatar Open Golf Masters, the 2006 Asian Games and the 2011 Asian Cup football tournament and two failed Olympic bids for 2016 and 2022 – to celebrate their national culture, while projecting an image of modernity, and challenging Orientalist stereotypes (Brannagan and Giulianotti 2015). Further, the event may be particularly attractive for Qatar in providing an opportunity to expand its influence, both regionally and globally. Indeed, SMEs hold potential as a form of 'soft power', in allowing host nations to exert a degree of influence by broadcasting a carefully manicured national image to a global audience, thus attracting tourists and investment, while boosting national pride (Grix and Houlihan, 2014; Brannagan and Giulianotti 2015).

Despite this trend connecting sport mega-events like the World Cup and Olympic Games to development strategies, the failures of the events to bring about social transformation have begun to disrupt some of these narratives. In many instances, the events exacerbate socioeconomic inequalities and often fail to meet sustainability goals, particularly in regard to stadium-use and environmental protection and remediation (see Gaffney 2010; 2013). The high costs for hosting the events have often been met with social unrest within host nations, as shifting public opinion has resulted in many prospective hosts from within drawing their bids. The 2022 Olympic Winter Games, for instance, has seen Sweden, Poland, Norway, Ukraine and Germany withdraw their bids after public polls revealed a lack of popular support, forcing both the IOC and FIFA to re-evaluate the requirements for hosting the Games. These changes are encapsulated in efforts like the IOC's 'Agenda 2020', that have been directed at lowering the cost and size of the Games, and allowing them to be held in more than one country; a notion potentially attractive to Gulf nations such as Qatar and regional powers like India (Darnell and Millington 2016).

Discussion and conclusion

The initiatives undertaken by IGOs in the development context are generally viewed in positive terms for the services they provide, their *ex officio* status outside governmental and corporate spheres, and ability to build transnational networks (Hayhurst *et al.* 2015). Indeed, IGOs hold an important position as intermediaries between public and private interests, that often work on behalf of marginalized and disenfranchised groups (see Hudson 2001). And yet, IGOs are not, and should not, be sheltered from critiques of global civil society. For instance, IGOs are not democratic institutions accountable to public will, and often operate with little oversight. As a result, the interests of IGOs may compete with those of the public sphere, and indeed, with one another. Further, IGOs do not exist outside the hegemonic power dynamics that have long defined the relationship between the global North and South. Following Peter Redfield's (2005) critique of the humanitarian NGO Doctors Without Borders, the problematic position of IGOs in the development landscape is a product of their operation within a climate of absent political authority that extend 'norms of power in an effort to effect the government of health, but without any certainty of control as responsibility for rule is ever deferred by humanitarian organizations' (Redfield, 2005: 330). Within the SDP sector, Roger Levermore (2010) echoes such sentiments in describing the corporate social responsibility tilt to SDP that has been 'largely driven by asymmetrical power relations, where initiatives are heavily influenced by aims infused with top-down, Northern, competitive, heterosexual and masculinist traits' (p. 230). From this perspective, IGOs, particularly those based in the global North, work alongside, and at times even perpetuate, (neo)colonial power dynamics, without borders, and outside the realm of government (Redfield 2005; Darnell 2007;).

As the IGO with the greatest influence on development policy, and given the number of organizations under its purview that utilize sport, the UN's role in promoting SDP has not escaped critical attention. These critiques centre on the UN's often ahistorical and apolitical framing of sport's role in promoting development that ignores the colonial histories of sport (see Millington 2015), and allows sport to be presented as a novel approach to addressing matters of underdevelopment through top-down and homogenizing development policies like the MDGs and SDGs (Ilcan and Phillips 2010). Indeed, the 'one size fits all' approach to development proffered through these policies have been criticized for their failure to account for the contextualities of under-development, and for downloading and individualizing the responsibility of development onto those who are meant to achieve these goals (see Millington 2015). In this regard, claims to the universal and transcendent nature of sport allow sport-based intervention projects and global North organizations to enter the global South for the purposes of development, while obscuring geo-political power dynamics (see Darnell 2010; Millington 2015).

These top-down approaches to development through sport are perhaps most visible within the development discourses attached to SMEs. Both the IOC and FIFA have been subject to critique for the tensions surrounding their promises of promoting 'sport for good' on the one hand and capitalist accumulation on the other (see Darnell 2012; Boykoff, 2015). In this sense, the merits and ethics of the IOC's and FIFA 'soft' SDP programs have been called in to question. Indeed, in his analysis of Olympism in Action, Simon Darnell (2012) argues that the development agenda advanced by the IOC remains secondary to the economic and growth oriented approaches to development, and one that subscribes to and promulgates neoliberal discourses. Despite the IOC and FIFA's positioning of SMEs as vehicles for structural and symbolic re-imaginings of host cities and nations, the social good that emerges from such events are regularly over-shadowed and overwhelmed by their deleterious social, economic and environmental effects (see Broudehoux 2007; Curi *et al.* 2011; Gaffney 2010; Millington *et al.* In press). For instance, Broudehoux (2007) argues that the cost of the Olympics, both social and financial, 'are generally borne by those at the bottom of the economic ladder who endure tax increases, inflation, soaring rents, and an enormous debt that undermines future welfare investments' (p.386). Others have argued that developing nations are in a much more precarious position to take on the economic burden of hosting a SME, and that such events create a 'winner's curse' that requires nations to seek bigger and better events on a continual basis (Cornelissen and Swart 2006; Black 2008; Cornelissen 2009). Further, while the IOC and FIFA mandated that prospective host nations include sustainability and legacy components in their bids for the events, there exist few, if any, mechanisms through which these promises are enforced, or required to be kept.

Given these critiques, it is important to note that other international organizations have emerged to challenge and disrupt the positive and apolitical understanding of SDP and SME (Millington and Darnell 2014). These groups, that include Amnesty International and Human Rights Watch, have sought to bring visibility to the deleterious and harmful effects of mega-event hosting, documenting such things as human rights abuses at the 2008 Beijing Olympics, that included forced evictions, media censorship and restrictions of civil society (Human Rights Watch 2013), or the human rights abuses of migrant works in the stadium construction of the Qatar World Cup (Brannagan and Giulianotti 2015). The work of these groups provides insights into future avenues of research regarding the neocolonial tendencies of IGO utilizing sport, the democratic accountability of IGOs in the development paradigm, and the need to explore the dual and competing mandates of sport for profit and sport for good often proffered by sport-related IGOs.

References

Binder, D. (2001). 'Olympism' revisited as context for global education: Implications for physical education. *Quest, 53*(1), 14–34.

Black, D. (2008). Dreaming big: The pursuit of "second order" games as a strategic response to globalization. *Sport in Society, 11*(4), 467–480.

Black, D. and Van Der Westhuizen, J. (2004). The allure of the global games for 'semi-peripheral' polities and spaces: A research agenda. *Third World Quarterly, 25*: 1195–1214.

Boykoff, J. (2015). *Celebration Capitalism and the Olympic Games*. New York: Routledge.

Brannagan, P. M. and Giulianotti, R. (2015). Soft power and soft disempowerment: Qatar, global sport and football's 2022 World Cup finals. *Leisure Studies, 34*(6), 703–719.

Broudehoux, A. (2007). Spectacular Beijing: The conspicuous construction of an Olympic Metropolis. *Journal of Urban Affairs, 29*(4), 383–399.

Chatziefstathiou, D. and Henry, I. (2012). *Discourses of Olympism: From the Sorbonne 1894 to London 2012*. Basingstoke: Palgrave Macmillan.

Cornelissen, S. (2004). Sport mega-events in Africa: Processes, impacts and prospects. *Tourism and Hospitality Planning and Development, 1*(1), 39–55.

Cornelissen, S. (2009). A delicate balance: Major sport events and development. In R. Levermore and A. Beacom (eds), *Sport and International Development*. London: Palgrave Macmillan.

Cornelissen, S. and Swart, K. (2006). The 2010 Football World Cup as a political construct: The challenge of making good on an African promise. *The Sociological Review, 54*(S2), 108–123.

Curi, M., Knijnik, J. and Mascarenhas, G. (2011). The Pan American Games in Rio de Janeiro 2007: Consequences of a sport mega-event on a BRIC country. *International Review for the Sociology of Sport, 46*(2), 140–156.

Darby, P. (2005). The new scramble for Africa: The African football labour migration to Europe. In J. A. Mangan (ed.), *Europe, Sport World: Shaping Global Societies*. Portland: Frank Cass, pp. 217–244.

Darnell, S. C. (2007). Playing with race: Right to play and the production of whiteness in 'development through sport'. *Sport in Society*, *10*(4), 560–579.

Darnell, S. C. (2010). Sport, race, and bio-politics: Encounters with difference in 'sport for development and peace' internships. *Journal of Sport and Social Issues*, *34*(4), 396–417.

Darnell, S. C. (2012). Olympism in action, Olympic hosting and the politics of 'Sport for Development and Peace': Investigating the development discourses of Rio 2016. *Sport in Society*, *15*(6), 869–887.

Darnell, S. C. and Millington, R. (2016). Modernization, neoliberalism, and sports mega-events: Evolving discourses in Latin America. In R. Gruneau and J. Horne (eds), *Mega-Events and Globalization: Capital, Cultures and Spectacle in a Changing World Order*. New York: Routledge, pp. 65–80.

FIFA. (n.d.a). *Sustainability*. Available at: www.fifa.com/sustainability/index.html.

FIFA. (n.d.b). *FIFA Forward Football Development Programme*. Available at: www.fifa.com/development/fifa-forward-programme/index.html.

FIFA. (2013). *Football for Hope Forum*. Bel Horizonte, Brazil: Fédération Internationale de Football Association.

Gaffney, C. (2010). Mega-events and socio-spatial dynamics in Rio de Janeiro 1919–2016. *Journal of Latin American Geography*, *9*(1), 7–29.

Gaffney, C. (2013). Between discourse and reality: The un-sustainability of mega-event planning. *Sustainability*, *5*(9), 3926–3940.

Giulianotti, R. (2011). Sport, transnational peacemaking, and global civil society: Exploring the reflective discourses of 'sport, development, and peace' project officials. *Journal of Sport and Social Issues*, *35*(1), 50–71.

Grix, J. and Houlihan, B. (2014). Sports mega-events as part of a nation's soft power strategy: The cases of Germany (2006) and the UK (2012). *The British Journal of Politics and International Relations*, *16*(4), 572–596.

Guest, A. (2009). The diffusion of development-through-sport: Analysing the history and practice of the Olympic Movement's grassroots outreach to Africa. *Sport in society*, *12*(10), 1336–1352.

Hayhurst, L., Millington, R. and Darnell, S. C. (2015). The non-governmental agencies perspective. In M. Parent and J. L. Chappelet (eds), *Routledge Handbook of Sports Events Management: A Stakeholder Approach*. New York: Routledge, pp. 397–416.

Hudson, A. (2001). NGOs' transnational advocacy networks: From 'legitimacy' to 'political responsibility'? *Global Networks*, *1*(4), 331–352.

Human Rights Watch. (2013). *Statement: Sports and Human Rights*. Available at: www.hrw.org/news/2012/02/27/statement-sports-and-human-rights-un-human-rights-council.

Ilcan, P. and Phillips, L. (2010). Developmentalities and calculative practices: The millennium development goals. *Antipode*, *42*(4), 844–874.

International Olympic Committee. (2007). *Teaching Values: An Olympic Education Toolkit*. Lausanne: International Olympic Committee.

International Olympic Committee. (2009). *Olympism in Action*. Available at: www.olympic.org/olympism-in-action.

International Olympic Committee. (2010a). *Sport officially recognized to Boost Millennium Development Goals*. Available at: www.olympic.org/news/sport-officially-recognised-to-boost-millennium-development-goals.

International Olympic Committee. (2010b). *IOC and UNHRC Launch Programme for refugees in Namibia*. Available at: www.olympic.org/education-through-sport/ioc-and-unhcr-launch-programme-for-refugees-in-namibia.

International Olympic Committee. (2010c). *OVEP Ready to go Global*. Available at: www.olympic.org/education-through-sport/ovep-ready-to-go-global.

International Olympic Committee. (2011). *Hope: When Sport can Change the World*. Lausanne: International Olympic Committee.

International Olympic Committee. (2014). *Olympic Agenda 2020: 20+20 Recommendations*. Lausanne: International Olympic Committee.

International Olympic Committee. (2017a). *IOC Welcomes Enhancement of Close Cooperation with the United Nations*. Available at: www.olympic.org/news/ioc-welcomes-enhancement-of-close-cooperation-with-the-united-nations.

International Olympic Committee. (2017b). *Sport for Hope*. International Olympic Committee. Available at: www.olympic.org/sport-for-hope.

International Olympic Committee. (2017c). *Sport for Hope: About the Programme.* International Olympic Committee. Available at: www.olympic.org/sport-for-hope/about-the-programme.

Levermore, R. (2010). CSR for development through sport: Examining its potential and limitations. *Third World Quarterly, 31*(7), 223–241.

Millington, R. (2015). The United Nations and Sport for Development and Peace: A Critical History. Unpublished doctoral dissertation. Queen's University, Kingston, ON, Canada.

Millington, R. and Darnell, S. C. (2014). Constructing and contesting the Olympics online: The internet, Rio 2016 and the politics of Brazilian development. *International Review for the Sociology of Sport, 49*(2), 190–210.

Millington, R., Darnell, S. C. and Millington, B. (in press). Ecological modernization and the Olympics: The case of golf and Rio's 'green' games. *Sociology of Sport Journal, 35*(1), 1–33.

Redfield, P. (2005). Doctors, borders, and life in crisis. *Cultural Anthropology, 20*(3), 328–361.

Roche, M. (2000). *Mega-Events and Modernity: Olympics and Expos in the Growth of Global Culture.* London: Routledge.

Sport for Development and Peace International Working Group. (2008). *Harnessing the Power of Sport for Development and Peace: Recommendations to Governments.* Toronto: Right to Play.

United Nations. (2003). Sport for Development and Peace: Towards achieving the Millennium Development Goals. *Report for the United Nations Inter-Agency Task Force on Sport for Development and Peace.* New York: United Nations.

United Nations. (2005). *Sport for a Better World: Report on the International Year of Sport and Physical Education.* New York: United Nations.

United Nations. (2007). *Women 2000 and Beyond: Women, Gender Equality and Sport.* New York: United Nations.

United Nations. (2008). Achieving the objectives of the United Nations through sport. *Report from the Special Adviser to the United Nations Secretary-General on Sport for Development and Peace.* Geneva: United Nations, pp. 1–26.

United Nations. (2015). *The Millennium Development Goals Report: Summary.* New York: United Nations.

United Nations. (2016). *Transforming our World: the 2030 Agenda for Sustainable Development.* Available at: sustainabledevelopment.un.org/post2015/transformingourworld.

UNDP. (n.d.). *Sustainable development Goals.* Available at: www.undp.org/content/undp/en/home/sustainable-development-goals/.

United Nations Office on Sport for Development and Peace. (2005). *The Magglingen Call to Action 2005.* Geneva: United Nations.

Van Luijk, N. (2015). (Post)political Power and International Sport: Examining the International Olympic Committee's Journey to Permanent Observer Status at the United Nations. Unpublished doctoral dissertation. University of British Colombia, Vancouver, BC, Canada.

6

Non-governmental organizations in the SDP system

Naofumi Suzuki

Introduction

The last few decades have seen a rapid growth of the Sport for Development and Peace (SDP) sector, of which non-governmental organizations (NGOs) constitute the core. The number of organizations working within the sector has exploded, particularly in the 2000s. The Swiss Academy for Development has managed a website called the International Platform on Sport and Development (the Platform, sportanddev.org) since 2003. The Platform has been dedicated to the development of the sector, by means of connecting people and organizations, accumulating knowledge, and disseminating the practice of SDP. Registered on the Platform are a range of organizations including international institutions, governmental agencies, private for-profit corporations, non-profit/NGOs, sports clubs and federations, universities, and research institutes. According to the author's record, the number of registered organizations was about 150 in 2008, 380 in March 2012, 430 in September 2012, and 555 in 2014. The number has reached 971 by February 2018. This chapter is based on the database constructed using the Platform. The data collection and refinement took several years ranging from 2012 to 2018. Of the 948 valid entries, 686 were in the category of 'Non-profit organization/charity/NGO/INGO' (Table 6.1).[1] This shows the magnitude of contribution that the non-profit/non-governmental sector has made to the practice of SDP. While much research has been done to study the processes in which some of those NGOs have made impacts on the local levels, only a few studies have been done to understand the global picture of the whole sector (Levermore and Beacom 2009; Svensson and Woods 2017). This chapter aims to provide the basis for such macroscopic studies in the future, by presenting the results of analysis in terms of geographical distribution of SDP practices, and of historical development of the sector.

Methodology

The database was constructed following the steps below. First, all organisations listed on the platform were imported to a spreadsheet. The information of each organisation was also imported to corresponding columns. Second, additional web searches were conducted for each of the organisations. The purpose was twofold: to validate the information on the platform, and to

Table 6.1 The number and type of organisations registered on sportanddev.org by February 2018

Organisational types	Count	Percentage (%)
Non-profit organisation/charity/NGO/INGO	686	72.4
Sports club/sports federation	91	9.6
Business/corporation	85	9.0
International organisation	38	4.0
University institute/research institute	37	3.9
Government agency	11	1.2
Total	948	100.0

Source: Author's database based on sportanddev.org

supplement the data concerned with geographical locations and years of establishment. Typically, additional sources were the websites and/or Facebook pages of the organisations. In so doing, duplicated entries were identified and excluded from the analyses. The analysis on geographical distribution contained: (1) the distribution of places of origin by region; and (2) a cross-tab analysis of places of origin against places of delivery. The latter step was applied to 611 NGOs, of which locations of delivery were identified. The analysis on historical development was done using 517 NGOs, after excluding the ones whose years of establishment could not be identified. It consisted of two steps: (1) a histogram was drawn according to the years of establishment; and (2) the accumulated number of NGOs by year were estimated by adding the number of NGOs established on a year to that of those established in the previous years. To examine the development process of the sector, density dependence theory of population ecology is applied (Hannan and Freeman 1989; Hannan *et al*. 2007).

Geographical distribution of SDP NGOs

This section sketches out the geographical distribution of SDP NGOs in terms of their places of origin as well as delivery. Generally, NGOs can take many different forms. They vary in size, missions, and scope of activities. Some are to raise global awareness about particular issues concerning development and human rights. Others focus on particular local contexts and deal with problems of the vulnerable group of people they meet day by day. SDP NGOs are the ones that use elements of sport to promote causes related to development and peace. Their forms are also diverse. Nevertheless, it is important to note that the SDP sector was founded on the early examples of localized NGOs that developed their practices over a long period of time keeping close relations with their direct beneficiaries (Coalter 2010). Arguably, the value of SDP lies in the innovative approaches that implementing NGOs deliver on the ground so as to complement the conventional practice of international development. Meanwhile, SDP shares a problem with its parental practice of international development in general. It is often accused of imposing the agenda of the North upon the communities in the South (Darnell, 2011; Welty Peachey *et al*., 2017). The geographical analysis of SDP NGOs is therefore purported to explore the distribution of actual programmes delivered on the ground, and to examine to what extent the North-South relationship is reflected in the distribution.

Table 6.2 shows the places of origin, i.e. the locations of the main contact, of SDP NGOs. Some 228 organisations – just about one third – were located in Africa, while 182 organisations – over a quarter – were based in Europe. The fact that they combined to constitute about 60 per cent of SDP NGOs conforms to the existing literature maintaining that SDP is predominantly a Euro-African phenomenon (Levermore and Beacom 2009; Svensson and Woods

Table 6.2 The places of origin of SDP NGOs

Region	Count	Percentage (%)
Africa	228	33.2
Europe	182	26.5
Asia	120	17.5
North America	90	13.1
Latin America and the Caribbean	50	7.3
Oceania	16	2.3
Total	686	100.0

Source: Author's database based on sportanddev.org

Table 6.3 The places of origin of SDP NGOs in Asia

Region	Count	Percentage (%)
Southern Asia	78	65.0
Western Asia	18	15.0
South-Eastern Asia	15	12.5
Eastern Asia	9	7.5
Total	120	100.0

Source: Author's database based on sportanddev.org

2017). Following these two regions were Asia with 120 organisations registered, North America with 90, Latin America and the Caribbean with 50, and Oceania with 16. Noticeably, Asia is underrepresented – only over 17 per cent – considering the population size. As Table 6.3 shows, of the 120 NGOs in Asia, almost one third are based in South Asia, leaving the other parts of Asia far behind.

Table 6.4 indicates the relationship between the place of origin and the places of delivery, i.e. the locations where SDP NGOs implement their programs. Seventy-five organisations were left out of the analysis, due to the lack of reliable information on the places of delivery. The remaining 611 organisations had delivered their programs in 1,779 locations in total. In spite of the concern over its reliability, this table helps to explore the overall tendency. At least six points can be noticed.

First: in terms of providers, the first column from the right of Table 6.4 shows that European NGOs constitute by far the largest majority with 43 per cent. It is followed by Africa with 17 per cent, North America 16, and Asia 12. Latin America and the Caribbean and Oceania constitute only around 4 per cent each. Although Africa constituted the largest majority in terms of the number of organisations (Table 6.2), it fell far behind Europe in this respect. This might be because the NGOs based in Europe tend to run their programs in a relatively large number of countries, whereas those based in Africa might be inclined to limit their activities to a much smaller number of locations. Thus, the practice of SDP may be characterized by the pattern that NGOs from the North expand their geographical scopes covering multiple countries in the South.

Second: in fact the patterns of delivery indicate the 'North-South' setups are very prevalent in the SDP sector. In terms of the distribution of the places of delivery, nearly 40 per cent of them

Table 6.4 The places of origin and delivery of SDP NGOs

Places of origin	No. of NGOs	Places of delivery (counted by country)						
		Africa	Asia	Europe	Latin America and the Caribbean	North America	Oceania	Total
Africa	203	270	4	3	4	1	2	309
(%)		(15.2)	(0.2)	(0.2)	(0.2)	(0.1)	(0.1)	(17.4)
Asia	111	31	149	19	11	1	0	220
(%)		(1.7)	(8.4)	(1.1)	(0.6)	(0.1)	(0.0)	(12.4)
Europe	166	254	150	313	68	10	16	827
(%)		(14.3)	(8.4)	(17.6)	(3.8)	(0.6)	(0.9)	(46.5)
Latin America and the Caribbean	45	4	6	3	54	1	0	73
(%)		(0.2)	(0.3)	(0.2)	(3.0)	(0.1)	(0.0)	(4.1)
North America	70	89	49	14	62	45	1	280
(%)		(5.0)	(2.8)	(0.8)	(3.5)	(2.5)	(0.1)	(15.7)
Oceania	16	15	17	2	6	0	30	70
(%)		(0.8)	(1.0)	(0.1)	(0.3)	(0.0)	(1.7)	(3.9)
Total	611	663	375	354	205	58	49	1779
(%)		(37.3)	(21.1)	(19.9)	(11.5)	(3.3)	(2.8)	(100.0)

Source: Author's database based on sportanddev.org

were concentrated in Africa. Asia and Europe follow with around 20 per cent. Latin America and the Caribbean represents over 10 per cent, and North America and Oceania around 3 per cent. Again, the practices of SDP seemed to be centred on Africa, reflecting the overall climate of international development in the 2000s, where the concentration of poverty in the region was considered to be one of the most pressing issues.

Third: there seems to be a tendency of the North providing programs in the South; Europe, North America and Oceania (14 out of 16 organisations based in Australia) are providers, while Africa, Asia, and Latin America and the Caribbean are recipients. European NGOs deliver nearly half of their programs in Africa and Asia combined. It might reflect the reality that the relationships between European countries and its former colonies are still strong. A country-by-country analysis would allow more accurate understanding on this point. Similarly, about two thirds of the programs provided by North American NGOs are in Africa, Asia, or Latin America and the Caribbean. The relatively strong relationship between North America and Latin America and the Caribbean is evident, reflecting the geopolitical and historical contexts. The same applies to Oceania, where a small number of Australian NGOs seem to provide programs in surrounding countries within the region.

Fourth: however, SDP might not be just a 'North-South', post-colonial phenomenon. Indeed, the most common pattern is the 'Europe-Europe', constituting nearly one third of the programs delivered by European NGOs, and about one sixth of all programs. Although the number is not as high, North American NGOs provide about one sixth of their programs in North America as well. The prevalence of Europe-Europe setups can be partly explained by the fact that an increasing number of networking NGOs and funding agencies have registered themselves on the Platform in the category of 'non-profit organisation/charity/NGO/INGO'. These organisations tend to cover tens of countries, and thus a small number of European, network-type organisations make a large impact statistically. Therefore, the number might not reflect the significance in terms of actual impact. That said, in the both regions, it is true that much effort has been made to address domestic issues concerned with urban deprivation, disability, or integration of immigrants and ethnic minorities. For instance, a significant number of programs have been dedicated to development and peacebuilding in Eastern Europe.

Fifth: there is also a significant overlap of the places of origin and those of delivery in the regions normally considered to be the 'recipients' of development assistance. When the places of origin are Africa, Asia, or Latin America and the Caribbean, the vast majority seemed to be delivered in the same regions. The proportions of the programs delivered within the same regions are 87 per cent in Africa, 68 per cent in Asia, and 74 per cent in Latin America and the Caribbean, respectively. These 'South-South' setups aggregate 487 cases, which constitute about 27 per cent of the total. This might suggest that a significant proportion of SDP practices might be composed of localized or endogenous programs. As discussed in the later sections, the conception of SDP practice is credited to early good practices that took endogenous, localized approaches.

Sixth: unlike Africa, the proportion of Asia is not considerably higher for the places of delivery, one fifth of the total, than for the places of origin (17.5 per cent, see Table 6.3). The number is still low compared to the gigantic population size of the region. This underrepresentation may be related to several factors. It might reflect Asia's standpoint in football, which is what the overwhelming majority of SDP NGOs employ (Levermore 2009). It might also be affected by the fact that Japan, the largest ODA donor for the region, has little presence in the SDP sector, with only four Japan-based organizations registered on the Platform as of February 2018. Or it may be because of the inevitable bias of the Platform itself given the geographical location of the operator.

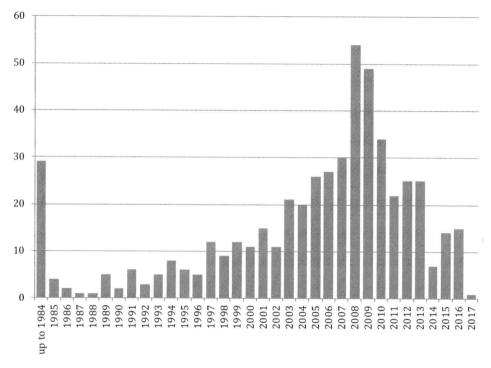

Figure 6.1   The founding year of SDP NGOs
Source: Author's database based on sportanddev.org

In summary, the analysis so far has reconfirmed that SDP has a highly Euro-African inclination, while other regions, especially Asia, are relatively underrepresented. The influence of international geopolitics seems evident in the relationship between the places of origin and those of
delivery, where European NGOs are delivering their programs in Africa and Asia, and North
American ones in Latin America and the Caribbean. Although these 'North-South' setups seem
to be the most common, it is also indicated that there are a significant number of 'South-South'
and 'North-North' setups. This suggests that endogenous practices have made a significant contribution to SDP.

Population ecology of SDP NGOs

This section looks at the historical growth of sector. Figure 6.1 shows the number of NGOs
established in each year since 1985. Of the 686 NGOs, 517 were included in the analysis.
For those left out, it was not possible to locate information concerning year of establishment.
Figure 6.2 shows the accumulated numbers by year, so as to estimate the total number of SDP
NGOs existing in a particular year. However, the estimates cannot be perfect, not only because of
the possible bias of the Platform itself, but also because some of the NGOs might have disbanded
at some point during this period. The analysis below is therefore directed to grasping the general
tendency.

The counts were few and far between before 1984, and thus the number of those established
before 1984 is shown as an aggregate. The origin of SDP is generally credited to Mathare Youth

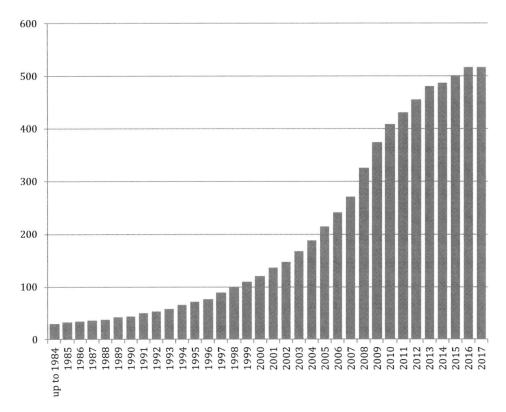

Figure 6.2 The cumulative number of SDP NGOs by year
Source: Author's database based on sportanddev.org

Sports Association (MYSA) established in 1987, and thus it is likely that those older NGOs entered the sector relatively recently after SDP became more established. Such NGOs would include the ones that had operated in the field of international development and recently started to incorporate elements of sport into their activities (plus sport), and the sport organisations that entered into international development with the belief in the ability of sport to contribute to the field (sport plus) (Coalter 2007; Burnett 2008; Levermore and Beacom 2009). The existence of these types of NGO indicates that not all SDP NGOs are newly established for the purpose of SDP, but existing NGOs are increasingly adopting the sport-based approaches developed by the earlier good practices. This indicates the necessity of distinguishing years of establishment from years of entry to the field of SDP to more accurately analyse its growth process, though it was technically not possible this time.

As shown in Figure 6.1, only a few SDP NGOs were established every year in the late 1980s and the early 1990s. It started to grow faster in the late 1990s, and around the 2000s the count constantly hit double digits. It peaked in 2008 at 54 and in 2009 at 49. The numbers started to dip after that, although this might be because in the last few years newer NGOs have probably not yet been connected to the Platform. Accordingly, the growth process of the sector can be divided into three stages. The first stage is from the late 1980s to the early 1990s, when the early examples of SDP NGO started their practices independently. The second stage is from the late 1990s to the early 2000s. This was the period of expansion when the speed of growth accelerated

Table 6.5 The 'second generation' of SDP NGOs

Organisation	Established year	Country of origin	Places of delivery	Themes
Hearts of Gold	1998-	Japan	Cambodia, East Timor etc.	Peacebuilding, Education
Sport Sans Frontières	1999-	France	Afghanistan, Burundi, Haiti, Kosovo etc.	Peacebuilding, Education
Magic Bus	1999–	India	India	Education
Football 4 Peace International	2000–	UK	Israel, Ireland	Peacebuilding
Moving the Goalposts Kilifi	2001–	Kenya	Kenya	Gender equality
Grassroots Soccer	2002–	USA	Africa	Health (HIV/AIDS)

Sources: Heart of Gold (www.hofg.org/jp/); Sport Sans Frontières (www.sportsansfrontieres.org/); Magic Bus (http://magicbusindia.org/magicbus/); Football 4 Peace International (www.football4peace.eu); Right to Play (www.righttoplay.com/International/Pages/Home.aspx); Moving the Goalposts (www.mtgk.org/); Grassrootsoccer (www.www.grassrootsoccer.org/)

as a number of SDP NGOs were established one after another in a short space of time. The third stage is from the mid-2000s and onwards. This period was characterized by mainstreaming of the sector, while the number of SDP NGOs steadily increased. The United Nations incrementally strengthened its advocacy of SDP during the 2000s and the UN Office for Sport for Development and Peace (UNOSDP) was established in 2008 (Kidd 2008). This was also the time when the sport's contribution gradually started being recognized by the mainstream of international development.

This process conforms to what density dependence theory of population ecology holds. Hannan and his colleagues developed an ecological approach to organisational studies, so as to explain the birth, growth, and death of particular types of organisation (Hannan and Freeman 1989; Hannan *et al.* 2007). According to density dependence theory, the growth of the population size remains slow after a certain organisational type is conceived. As the number of the same type of organisation increases, the type starts being recognized as legitimate and thus more resources become available to allow many more organisations to be born and survive. This improved environment leads to the acceleration of growth. However, the environment becomes saturated at some point, and the competition between organisations intensifies. As a result, the growth of the sector slows down to reach a plateau or even the population size may become to shrink. This process resembles the pattern that a particular biological species shows in a restricted environment, where the growth speed of population is dependent on its size.

The growth of the population of SDP NGO could be explained using this model. In the first stage, a few early good practices developed themselves largely unnoticed. Three of the best-known examples are MYSA (1987–), the Sport Coach Outreach (SCORE, 1991–) and the Olympic Aid (1992–, renamed Right to Play in 2000). While Olympic Aid was mainly a fundraising vehicle until 2000, MYSA and SCORE endogenously grew their programs in Nairobi, Kenya and in and around Cape Town, South Africa, respectively. Their models are not described here as they are well documented elsewhere. Importantly, though, Coalter (2010) argues that one of the factors contributing to the success of MYSA and SCORE was that they were largely unnoticed in the early stages. This allowed them to cautiously develop their programs by closely working with the local communities for a long period of time.

In the second stage, the growth spurt happened. A number of SDP NGOs were launched around the year 2000. Table 6.5 shows several examples of these 'second generation' NGOs. The diversity is evident in terms of geography and themes. The fact that they were explicitly targeted on specific development agendas suggests that sport became noticed as a tool to promote development and peace around this time. In the early 2000s, SDP started to promote itself as a sector, rather than just separate NGOs. The advocacy by the UN was sought after through the establishment of Sport for Development and Peace International Working Group in 2001, and networks of SDP NGOs were prompted by the launch of streetfootballworld (2002–) as well as the Platform (2003–). These could be seen as the start of the legitimation process.

In the third stage, the effort to gain recognition as a sector started to pay off. In addition to the UN's advocacy incrementally becoming more formalized, other stakeholders such as governmental agencies, private corporations, charitable foundations and sports federations began to show interest in the sector. This made more resources available for SDP NGOs, and thus the population size steadily increased during this period. Certainly, this could be seen as the legitimation of SDP NGOs. Although Figure 6.2 alone is not enough to conclude that the speed of growth had actually slowed, there are signs that the competition between SDP NGOs might have intensified recently. An increased level of interest by donors not only means an increase in available resources, but also stronger demands for accountability. This can lead to mission drift for the recipient NGOs. Coalter (2010) points out that even MYSA and SCORE are exposed to such risks these days. Consequently, the quality of programs delivered on the ground may well be compromised. The number of SDP NGOs registered on the Platform seems to still be increasing in 2017. Thus, if the density dependence theory holds in the case of SDP NGOs, the competitiveness of the sector must be more intensified now. This means that there is a higher risk for the program quality to deteriorate. A further analysis of the Platform, including estimation of disbanding years of past entries, would be necessary to examine if such a risk has become materialized.

Conclusion

This chapter has briefly examined the geographical distribution and historical development of SDP NGOs using a database the author compiled based on the Platform. Without doubt, the practice of SDP is heavily reliant on NGOs that carry the responsibility of delivering the programs on the ground to make an impact to the local communities. Historically, SDP was conceived when a few localized NGOs were created in the late 1980s and early 1990s. They nurtured themselves over a long period of time, deeply embedded in the contexts of vulnerable populations they served. The practice became noticed by the wider society around the beginning of the new millennium, and the number of SDP NGOs rapidly increased. The increase in number meant the increase in recognition, and SDP NGOs were legitimated as a population in the 2000s.

They have also expanded geographically; however, the practices of SDP are distributed predominantly in Europe and Africa, indicating a strong tie between the regions. Africa has been the main stage of SDP, with endogenous NGOs seemingly prevalent in the continent. Likewise, the geopolitics of international development seems to affect the patterns of SDP NGOs' distribution in other regions as well. The 'North-South' setups are very common, but the 'South-South' and 'North-North' setups are increasingly prevalent. The endogenous nature of SDP NGOs from the early days may have remained intact until now.

The recent rapid expansion, however, may pose some threats. Growing interest in the sector might mean that SDP NGOs are exposed to the risk of mission drift and short-termism.

Furthermore, the population growth might have resulted in more severe competition between SDP NGOs. Either way, there might be a risk that the quality of programs delivered for the beneficiaries by these implementing NGOs could be compromised. If this were the case, the value of the whole sector would be under threat. Further studies are needed to examine if such a concern has any substance.

Note

1   The Platform recently renewed the system of the database. Notably, there were two changes relevant to this study. First, some entries have multiple types, in which case the first one was selected for this study. Second, the new category of 'non-profit organisation' was added. In this study, it is merged with the category of 'non-profit organisation/charity/NGO/INGO'.

References

Burnett, C. (2008). Accounting for sports development. In V. Girginov (ed.), *Management of Sports Development*. Oxford: Elsevier.

Coalter, F. (2007). *A Wider Social Role for Sport: Who's Keeping the Score?* London: Routledge.

Coalter, F. (2010). The politics of sport-for-development: Limited focus programmes and broad gauge problems? *International Review for the Sociology of Sport. 45*(3), 295–314.

Darnell, S. (2011). *Sport for Development and Peace: a Critical Sociology*. London: Bloomsbury.

Hannan, M. T. and Freeman, J. (1989). *Organizational Ecology*. Cambridge, MA: Harvard University Press.

Hannan, M. T., Polos, L. and Carroll, G. R. (2007). *Logics of Organization Theory: Audiences, Code, and Ecologies.* Princeton, NJ: Princeton University Press.

Kidd, B. (2008). A new social movement: Sport for development and peace. *Sport in Society, 11*(4), 370–380.

Levermore, R. (2009). Sport-in-international development: Theoretical frameworks'. In R. Levermore and A. Beacom (eds), *Sport and International Development*. Hampshire: Palgrave Macmillan.

Levermore, R. and Beacom, A. (2009). Sport and development: Mapping the field. In R. Levermore and A. Beacom (eds), *Sport and International Development*. Basingstoke: Palgrave Macmillan.

Svensson, P. G. and Woods, H. A. (2017). Systematic overview of sport for development and peace organizations. *Journal of Sport for Development. 5*(9), 36–48.

Welty Peachey, J., Musser, A., Shin, N. R., & Cohen, A. (2017). Interrogating the motivations of sport for development and peace practitioners. *International Review for the Sociology of Sport*, 1012690216686856.

7

Partnerships in and around SDP

Iain Lindsey and Bella Bello Bitugu

Introduction

There has been strong, widespread and consistent recognition of the importance of partnerships to Sport for Development and Peace (SDP) policy and practice. For example, in one of their early SDP policy documents, the United Nations (2006: 61) advocated:

> Local development through sport particularly benefits from an integrated partnership approach to sport-in-development involving a full spectrum of actors in field-based community development including all levels of and various sectors of government, sports organizations, NGOs and the private sector.

Subsequently, the United Nations and other multinational institutions have continued to promote SDP partnerships, as exemplified in the following extract from the Commonwealth Secretariat's recent analysis of sport and the Sustainable Development Goals:

> Partnership working was identified as a critical component of most successful SDP policy and programmes across the Commonwealth – in particular, those that position sport-based approaches within a broader range of development interventions and that work to deliver on broader policy objectives (i.e. health, education, community development).
>
> *Dudfield and Dingwall-Smith, 2015: 76*

The focus on partnerships within SDP policy and practice is also representative of their prioritisation within wider global development policies and agendas. The eighth Millennium Development Goal specifically sought to 'Develop a Global Partnership for Development'. More recently, there has been reinforcement of the importance of partnerships to achieving the Sustainable Development Goals (SDGs). The seventeenth SDG gave particular priority to partnerships as a 'means of implementation' for all the other SDGs, and an underpinning target for SDG 17 is to:

> Enhance the Global Partnership for Sustainable Development, complemented by multi-stakeholder partnerships that mobilize and share knowledge, expertise, technology and

financial resources, to support the achievement of the Sustainable Development Goals in all countries, in particular developing countries.

United Nations, 2015: 26

The importance placed on partnerships has also been reflected in academic research. There is a long-standing wealth of development studies literature that provides theoretical and empirical insights into, and critiques of, partnerships across different levels from the global to local, in diverse contexts and settings, and involving a wide range of development organisations. Within the SDP literature, partnership has commonly been recognised and considered as an important issue, although studies that are solely and specifically focused on partnerships are somewhat rarer (for exceptions see: Hayhurst and Frisby 2010; Lindsey and Banda, 2011).

Nevertheless, an issue that is recognised across the SDP and development studies literature is the nebulous nature and lack of clarity as to what defines a 'partnership' – an issue that reflects the status of partnership as a development 'buzzword' (Black 2010: 125). Fowler (2000: 23) succinctly captures the way in which the terminology of partnership has been loosely and problematically applied: 'Relationships within and beyond institutions in the [development] aid system are dominated by the notion of 'partnership' between everyone, for everything, everywhere.'

Rather than impose a potentially arbitrary and ultimately narrowing definition, a more appropriate approach in a chapter such as this is to consider how different 'partnerships' may be classified and use such a classification as a basis for structuring and differentiating examination of varying issues that affect these different relationships. Unsurprisingly, given the level of ambiguity in usage of the term, there can be various ways to classify those relationships that have been labelled as 'partnerships'. One potential approach is to differentiate partnerships by the forms that they take – that is, by the number and types of 'partners' involved, by the degree of formality or informality in their relationships, and/or by their geographical scope across or within countries. While these aspects are considered throughout the chapter, sections of the review that follow will be structured according to an alternative categorisation based on three potential and differentiated purposes of SDP partnerships.

First, partnerships orientated towards the provision, or acquisition, of funding and resources for SDP organisations and their programmes will be examined. A second section will then consider partnerships associated with policy and strategic development within countries, typically in the global South, that have been the central focus of the SDP 'movement'. Partnerships that have been developed to enhance the local implementation and delivery of SDP programmes will be considered in the third section. This categorisation, while not necessarily offering a clear-cut distinction between different partnerships, does have the benefit of linking to a broad geographical progression – moving from largely international relationships in the first section, through a national orientation in the second, to the third section which is more localised in focus. The concluding section of the chapter will then provide a synthesis of issues from across the preceding sections, illuminating points of relevance to various SDP organisations and future SDP research in turn.

'Partnerships' for funding and resources

The term 'partnership' is commonly applied to relationships between organisations providing and receiving resources for SDP. Funding provided through such relationships is often vital to the delivery of SDP activities in global South contexts (Akindes and Kirwan 2009). It is also through similar relationships that additional human resources, commonly in the form of volunteers, are also made available to SDP organisations operating in such contexts (Darnell

2010). Partnership relationships may also be the conduit to a further form of resource, namely that of 'expertise', in which different knowledge, skills and capacities are brought to bear with the intention of improving SDP practice. Such an aspiration is, for example, central to the International Scientific Network for Sport for Development – a partnership including African and European academic institutions and SDP NGOs, which was initially instigated through funds provided by the German government.

As implicit in the previous paragraph, it is international and external donors that most commonly provide SDP funding and resources for their 'partner' organisations that operate within countries of the global South. Various international donors involved with SDP are well recognised in the literature (e.g. Akindes and Kirwan 2009; Giulianotti 2011a) and may be categorised as follows:

- *International non-governmental organisations (NGOs)*, such as Right to Play and Coaches Across Continents, have been at the forefront of SDP but vary significantly in purpose, histories and geographical reach;
- *Governments from the global North*, and their associated ministries and institutions such as the German development agency, GIZ, and UK Sport
- *International governing bodies for particular sports*, such as the International Olympic Committee and FIFA
- *Transnational corporations* have become increasingly engaged in providing resources for SDP, with NIKE and Barclays being examples.

SDP literature is, however, less comprehensive in considering the composition and characteristics of the in-country 'partner' organisations with which international donors work. Funding and resources have more commonly been provided to in-country NGOs rather than governments of the global South. Nevertheless, it is rare for SDP literature to differentiate the characteristics of in-country NGOs that may or may not receive funding, although there are some indications that it may be larger and longer-standing NGOs that primarily garner international support (Lindsey 2017; Lindsey *et al.* 2017).

Relationships associated with the provision of funding and resources for SDP have, nevertheless, been widely considered in the literature. In doing so, researchers have often used neocolonial or postcolonial theoretical lenses to identify that the conceptualisation and operation of SDP bears contemporary imprints of historic relations of colonialism and imperialism between countries of the global North and South (Hayhurst 2009; Darnell 2012). The context of long-standing and current global inequalities and power relations thus provide the context for international SDP partnerships (Nichols *et al.* 2011). As a consequence, a common and important critique in the SDP literature is that the application of the term 'partnership' to relationships between international and in-country organisations may serve to downplay or mask significant power imbalances that can often subjugate those in the global South (Hayhurst 2009; Coalter 2010; Straume and Hasselgård 2014).

If these power imbalances in 'partnerships' are primarily a consequence of the funding and resources held by international donors, they are constituted in SDP practice through a variety of different mechanisms. Wachter (2014) cites one representative of an international donor reflecting that they only 'gave lip service to a bilateral decision making processes', and such a perspective is representative of literature that critiques international donors' prescription of particular goals and approaches to be addressed through SDP projects (Coalter 2010; Hartmann and Kwauk 2011). Less attention has been paid, however, to how the processes by which donors identify and select in-country partners may prioritise those types of organisations which are more aligned with international norms (Lindsey 2017). Mechanisms of power may also operate somewhat more indirectly, as Forde (2014) demonstrates through analysis of Northern influence in defining and creating Right to Play's curricula for sport and HIV/AIDS education. Requirements for in-country organisations to monitor and evaluate the use and impact of SDP funds in particular ways also represents the enactment of systems of accountability that reinforce international donors' power over those who may receive or benefit from the resources that they provide (Hayhurst and Frisby 2010; Kay 2012).

The significant power imbalances that may underlie the rhetoric of international 'partnerships' does, therefore, have significant implications for SDP. Some internationally prescribed SDP projects may have little relevance within the communities in which they are delivered. Common discourses can portray members of local communities as 'deficient' (Coalter 2013) and thus serve to undermine and ignore the importance of locally based knowledge and skills to SDP (Blom et al. 2015). The sustainability of SDP projects (and the partnerships associated with them) is also often questioned, especially as support from international donors is commonly time-limited (Lindsey 2017; Reis et al. 2016). Some SDP research also identifies longer-term consequences of the prevalence of funding and resources from international donors. As theorised extensively by development scholars (see, for example, Preston 1996; Willis 2011), in-country SDP organisations may become increasingly dependent on funding and resources provided by international donors. There is also the accompanying danger of 'mission drift' as these in-country organisations adapt their aims and approaches to the availability of funding and resources available from different international donors (Coalter 2010; Reis et al. 2016). Development studies literature (e.g. Seckinelgin 2005) has further indicated that in-country organisations can, over time, 'internalize' practices implemented by their international 'partners' – a consequence recognised by Lindsey et al. (2017) among some SDP NGOs in Zambia.

The preceding critiques of international partnerships for funding and resources offer support to Akindes and Kirwan's (2009: 242) somewhat hyperbolic assertion that SDP 'can also be viewed as part of an external agenda with essentially no local design or input'. However, studies which empirically investigate the perspectives of in-country organisations on their relationships with international donors have remained relatively rare. Research by Guest (2009) and Hasselgård and Straume (2015) represent exceptions in this regard, and both of these studies indicate how local organisations and stakeholders in Angola and Zimbabwe respectively managed to reshape and resist agendas pursued by international donors. These possibilities are reinforced, in part, by Lindsey et al.'s (2017) long-standing research in Zambia that found increased possibilities for local adaptation as a result of the distant relationships and lack of localised expertise among international donors, and as a result of the development over time of skills in partnership management by staff from in-country NGOs. The findings from these relatively isolated studies point to the potential value of long-term research examining local and potentially changing perspectives on partnership, which may add further nuance to more generic suggestions that improved communication and personalised relationships may enable the development of more equitable partnerships (Blom et al. 2015; MacIntosh et al. 2016).

'Partnerships' for policy and strategic development

Following from the primarily international relationships considered in the preceding section, the chapter now turns to partnerships that may be orientated towards developing policy and strategy for SDP within specific countries. Policy and strategic development is a central concern of governments, and so the section particularly focuses on relationships between governments and those civil society organisations, such as NGOs, that are most prominent in the provision of SDP projects and activities. As yet, and in comparison to international partnerships, there is far more limited literature on policies for SDP and on relationships between government and civil society organisations within particular countries. The section begins, therefore, by offering a brief overview of key themes identified in literature on government-civil society relationships in other development sectors.

Impetus to improve government-civil society relationships in other development sectors increased from the mid-1990s in response to problems identified through the preceding decade when global development policies had primarily prioritised civil society organisations (Batley and Rose 2011). Having national governments centrally involved in partnerships for development policy was seen as a way of addressing problems of fragmentation, duplication and uneven provision by a diversity of, internationally supported, NGOs – a context that has distinct similarities with that currently found in SDP (Lindsey 2017). Development researchers responded to the increased prioritisation of partnerships for development policy through numerous studies of government-civil society relationships in different development sectors and by developing various conceptual models that support analysis and improvement of such relationships (see Teamey 2007; 2010, for reviews of such research).

Such models commonly identify a range of different forms of government–civil society relationships that may be associated with development policy and which may also be more or less akin to what could be considered as 'partnerships'. Relationships more akin to partnerships could be orientated towards, for example, increasing opportunities for policy dialogue among different stakeholders and/or greater mutual recognition of the different roles that government and civil society organisations may take in policy development and implementation (Batley and Mcloughlin 2010). Moving away from relationships based on partnerships, a number of models also identify the possibilities of increased or improved government regulation to ensure that civil society organisations contribute effectively to development policies (e.g. Sansom 2006). There is also recognition within development studies research and models of influential factors and significant complexities in partnerships for policy and strategy between governments and civil society organisations. In global South contexts, many governments and some civil society organisations may not have the capacity to engage effectively across their respective sectors (Batley and Mcloughlin 2011). Power imbalances, which may also be linked to the resource capacity of governments or civil society organisations, can again significantly influence the operation of partnerships (Batley 2006). A further, significant consideration is that the diverse array of civil society organisations and variation between different institutions or levels of government may mean that multiple forms of relationships, that are orientated to slightly different purposes, may exist concurrently even within individual countries (Teamey 2010).

These issues raised in the development studies literature are important for informing consideration of government-civil society partnerships for SDP policy and strategy. Frequent calls (e.g. Kidd 2008; Sanders *et al.* 2012; Commonwealth Secretariat 2014) for national governments to increase their involvement in SDP and associated partnerships are exemplified by the Sport for Development and Peace International Working Group:

> national governments can play an important role in convening key players to encourage knowledge exchange, networking, collaboration, partnerships, and coordinated participation in national Sport for Development and Peace policy and program development and implementation.

(SDPIWG 2008: 14)

At best, however, there is significant variation across different regions and countries in the extent to which such aspirations for greater governmental involvement in SDP have been realised. For example, from their in-depth comparative study of 10 sub-Saharan African countries, de Coning and Keim (2014: 158) concluded that, 'as necessary political commitment and leadership is not in place, very little impetus exists to drive [SDP] policy as a pillar for development'. Other research points, even more problematically, to relationships between governments and SDP NGOs being characterised by dislocation or even conflict. For example, research in Zambia (Lindsey *et al.* 2017), Ghana and Tanzania (Lindsey 2017) has identified historical mistrust between governments and particular SDP NGOs, similar to that long recognised in other development sectors (e.g. Batley 2006; Mundy *et al.* 2010).

Various reasons can be identified for the limitations of partnership working between governments and SDP NGOs. Capacity within government for engagement in SDP is limited in many countries, especially as high-performance sport is often a priority for governmental resources (Dudfield 2014). On the other hand, NGOs in different contexts have been found to be fearful of losing their independence if they seek to develop relationships with governmental institutions (Giulianotti 2011b; Sanders *et al.* 2012). More generally, Lindsey (2017) and Lindsey and Bitugu (2018) argue that aspirations portrayed in global SDP policies and by various in-country stakeholders lack clarity as to the different roles and competencies that governments and NGOs could each bring to bear in seeking improved partnerships for policy and strategic development. It is in this respect, in particular, that increased awareness and usage of models presented in the development studies literature may be beneficial to SDP.

Besides relationships between governments and NGOs that may be specifically related to SDP, attention should also be paid to the extent to which partnerships for policy and strategic development have emerged between SDP stakeholders and those in other development sectors. Enhanced policy dialogue and influence, for example, is one consequence of a partnership between Right to Play Ghana and the Ghanaian Education Service that initially focused on enabling SDP provision in schools. Wider research in this area does, however, remain relatively limited – although it does begin to point to significant constraints on the development of partnerships. A common theme in the available literature is the lack of interest in, and understanding of, SDP on behalf of policy-makers in other development sectors – as recognised by Chepyator-Thomson (2014) in respect of education policy across multiple African countries and also by Lindsey and Banda (2011) and Njelesani (2011) in respect of health and education policy-makers' views in Zambia in particular. Both Sanders *et al.* (2012) and Lindsey (2017) also point to the fragility of any support for SDP within other policy sectors with it being dependent on individual politicians and civil servants who may be quickly displaced following elections. From the alternate perspective, attempts from SDP stakeholders to engage or integrate with policy-makers in different sectors also appear to vary significantly in intensity, scope and effectiveness (as Lindsey and Banda 2011, identify in Zambia). Other researchers (e.g. Black 2010: 127; Giulianotti 2011b) also point to a 'myth of autonomy' among some SDP stakeholders who may view engagement with other development sectors as unnecessary. There obviously remains much work to do if partnerships orientated towards policy and strategic development for SDP are to be enhanced and become more effective.

'Partnerships' for implementation and delivery

The focus of this section moves further towards local and community contexts in which partnerships may specifically support the implementation and delivery of SDP by, and among, particular organisations. Svensson *et al.* (2016) accurately recognise that such partnerships are, as yet, even more infrequently examined in SDP research. In contrast to the preceding sections, theories and concepts from the development studies literature are also less readily applicable and applied to more localised forms of partnerships. Therefore, the section will strongly draw on, and consider the relevance of, specific examples of partnerships both among SDP organisations and between such organisations and those from other development sectors.

There have certainly been efforts to develop partnerships and relationships between SDP organisations delivering programmes in specific contexts. For example, a Youth Development through Sport (YDS) Network comprising a range of organisations involved in SDP was established in Ghana and similar groupings have been instigated, at various times, in Zambia and South Africa as well as in other countries (Lindsey 2017; Lindsey *et al.* 2017). Such networks may seek to fulfil different purposes. They may offer scope for information sharing and mutual capacity building among their members. Edging towards more strategic purposes, further aspiration within the YDS network was to act as an in-country hub for SDP that would provide collective advocacy and a forum for cooperative approaches to working with prospective donors (Lindsey 2017).

While the operation of such multi-organisational networks may serve to enhance subsequent SDP delivery by their individual member organisations, what appears to be even less common is different SDP organisations working closely together to implement particular programmes in partnership. This may be unsurprising as partnership-based implementation requires partners to bring and share *different* capacities, skills or resources that would not otherwise be available to single organisations (Lindsey 2011). That SDP organisations primarily share *similar* expertise in respect of sport mitigates against such partnerships. Significantly, and as also found across development sectors (Hulme and Edwards 1997; Webb 2004), the similarities between SDP organisations more often leads to them being in competition with each other, especially for limited (international) funding (Kidd 2008). In Zambia, for example, the breakdown of earlier SDP networks was as a result of such competition and the related absence of trust required between member organisations to sustain partnership working (Lindsey and Banda 2011).

Implementation and delivery partnerships between SDP organisations and those from other development sectors are more commonly recognised in the literature. Specific studies have most commonly identified and considered partnerships between SDP organisations and schools (e.g. Sanders *et al.* 2014; Sherry and Schulenkorf 2016; Svensson *et al.* 2016; Lindsey *et al.* 2017). Such partnerships are premised on the potential for mutual benefit – schools may be able to provide enhanced access to facilities and participants for SDP organisations who may, in turn, offer sport-based provision that adds to existing educational curricula as well as training to enable school teachers to deliver such provision in the future. In similar partnerships with local industries and stakeholders, Right to Play Ghana have also used sport-based activities to encourage enrolment in schools and address issues of child labour. Further variations of purpose and members in implementation and delivery partnerships involving SDP organisations identified in the literature include:

- building relationships with community leaders and political groups to gain local acceptance for SDP activities (Giulianotti 2011b);
- pooling resources to enhance the efficiency or scale of SDP provision (Hayhurst and Frisby 2010)
- linking with private sector organisations to enhance pathways to employment for SDP participants (Spaaij 2012);

- working with higher education institutions to gain student volunteers or academic expertise in monitoring and evaluation of SDP programmes (Svensson *et al.* 2016).

With SDP activities typically being focused or targeted within particular localities, partnerships for implementation and delivery of these activities can be very particular to their specific contexts (Svensson *et al.* 2016). Drawing generic conclusions on the forms that these partnerships take, factors affecting them and practices that may enable effective partnerships can, therefore, be problematic. Bearing this caveat in mind, benefit can still be derived from reflection on different features of partnerships for implementation and delivery. Lindsey (2013), for example, considers the number of members that may be involved in particular partnerships and tentatively suggests, 'the efficacy of information sharing may be enhanced within broader networks, while delivery of development activities may be least challenging in [partnerships] between a smaller number of organisations'.

Variation in the degree of formality or informality in partnerships can also have implications for their effectiveness. For example, and in contrast to the more formalised partnerships that may exist and be promoted to a greater extent in the global North, Lindsey *et al.* (2017) note how personal and informal relationships have been key to the formation of some partnerships in Zambia but also may serve to limit diversity among members of partnerships. The possibility of informal partnerships dissolving if key individuals are no longer involved (Lindsey *et al.* 2017) also links to a more widely recognised need for organisations to have sufficient capacity to undertake the requirements of working in partnership (e.g. Sanders *et al.* 2014; Sherry and Schulenkorf 2016). Developing sustainable partnerships may be especially challenging in contexts where member organisations' own circumstances may be changeable and uncertain and the chapter's second author has direct experience of partnerships between schools and local NGOs in Ghana disbanding after the withdrawal of international funding and support.

Conclusions

Sections throughout the chapter have only served to reinforce comments in the introduction regarding the extent to which partnership discourses and practices are pervasive across and within SDP. That the term 'partnership' can itself be widely, if nebulously, applied in respect of SDP is demonstrated through the diversity of relationships considered through the chapter – partnerships have been shown to have various and multiple purposes, to operate within SDP as well as across SDP and other sectors, to include different types and numbers of members, to have differing levels of formality, and to be of varying geographical scope. Individual SDP organisations will most commonly be involved in multiple, and perhaps many, different partnerships at any one time.

There is thus huge complexity associated with partnerships in and around SDP. The challenges of working in partnerships also means that, in some cases, they may detract from the potential impact of SDP as much as they may, in other instances, enhance it. For SDP organisations and practitioners, this means that partnerships should be approached with some caution as well as potential enthusiasm. SDP organisations must have the capacity to commit human and other resources if they are to build effective partnerships. Similarly, individual SDP practitioners need particular skills, of communication and relationship building for example, to work within and across partnerships. Rather than seeking partnerships 'for everything, everywhere' (c.f. Fowler 2000: 23), these issues and requirements indicate that SDP organisations should seek to be more discerning and prioritise the development of particular partnerships that may offer the greatest likelihood of productive benefit.

There also needs to be particular awareness of a recurring theme across the chapter, namely that power is an ever present issue within partnerships. Any suggestions that partnerships may have, share or develop 'equal power' or be based on a 'level playing field' may be more of an idealised wish than a reality. Rather, the fundamental basis of even the most effective partnerships is that members respectively bring different resources, skills and capacities and, as a result, have different degrees of power. It is therefore important to be able to manage and encourage open acknowledgement and discussion of power relations within partnerships. The scope and skills to resist uneven relations of power within partnerships may be just as vital.

In addition to such implications for SDP practice, a number of concluding points can be made that are of relevance to those interested in studying or researching partnerships in and around SDP. As considered across the chapter, examination of partnerships is more extensive within the more long-standing development studies literature and, as some scholars of SDP have experienced, significant benefit can be drawn from engaging with theories, concepts and frameworks that have previously been developed and applied within other development sectors. This is not to say that there is no room for further empirical studies of SDP partnerships – there is, as the chapter has identified, a particular need for research that engages with, and seeks to understand the perspectives of, stakeholders from the global South who are involved in various types of SDP partnerships. Optimism in this regard can be taken from the growing interest in, and enactment of, participatory methodologies that themselves involve partnership working between SDP researchers and practitioners (Whitley and Johnson 2015; Collison and Marchesseault 2016). As this chapter is itself an outcome of a partnership between the authors' universities[1] (c.f. Lindsey et al. 2016), we would also wish to advocate for further efforts to develop similar North–South academic partnerships in the future.

Note

1   As stated above, collaboration between the two authors on this chapter would not have been possible if it had not been for funding and support from a Leverhulme Trust International Networks grant (IN-050).

References

Akindes, G. and Kirwan, M. (2009). Sport as international aid: Assisting development or promoting under-development in sub-Saharan Africa?. In R. Levermore and A. Beacom (eds), *Sport and International Development*. Basingstoke: Macmillan.

Batley, R. (2006). Engaged or divorced? Cross-service findings on government relations with non-state service-provider. *Public Administration and Development, 26*(3), 241–251.

Batley, R. and Mcloughlin, C. (2010). Engagement with non-state service providers in fragile states: Reconciling state-building and service delivery. *Development Policy Review, 28*(2), 131–154.

Batley R. and Rose, P. (2011). Analysing collaboration between non-government service providers and governments. *Public Administration and Development, 30*(4), 230–239.

Black, D. R. (2010). The Ambiguities of development: Implications for development through sport. *Sport in Society, 13*(1), 121–129.

Blom, L. C., Judge, L., Whitley, M. A., Gerstein, L., Huffman, A. and Hillyer, S. (2015). Sport for development and peace: Experiences conducting US and international programs. *Journal of Sport Psychology in Action, 6*(1), 1–16.

Chepyator-Thomson, J. R. (2014). Public policy, physical education and sport in English-speaking Africa. *Physical Education and Sport Pedagogy, 19*(5), 512–521.

Coalter, F. (2010). The Politics of sport-for-development: Limited focus programmes and broad gauge problems? *International Review for the Sociology of Sport, 45*(3), 295–314.

Coalter, F. (2013). *Sport for Development: What Game Are We Playing?* Abingdon: Routledge.

Collison, H. and Marchesseault, D. (2016). Finding the missing voices of sport for development and peace (SDP): Using a 'participatory social interaction research' methodology and anthropological perspectives within African developing countries. *Sport in Society*, doi:10.1080/17430437.2016.1179732.

Commonwealth Secretariat. (2014). *Strengthening Sport for Development and Peace: National Policies and Strategies*. London: Commonwealth Secretariat.

Darnell, S. C. (2010). Sport, race, and bio-politics: Encounters with difference in 'sport for development and peace' internships. *Journal of Sport and Social Issues, 34*(4), 396–417.

Darnell, S. (2012). *Sport for Development and Peace: A Critical Sociology*. London: Bloomsbury Academic.

de Coning, C. and Keim, M. (2014). Findings on the status and standing of policy. In M. Keim and C. de Coning (eds), *Sport and Development Policy in Africa: Results of a Collaborative Study of Selected Country Cases*. Stellenbosch: African Sun Media.

Dudfield, O. (2014). Sport for development and peace: opportunities, challenges and the Commonwealth's response. In Commonwealth Secretariat, *Strengthening Sport for Development and Peace: National Policies and Strategies*. London: Commonwealth Secretariat.

Dudfield, O. and Dingwall-Smith, M. (2015). *Sport for Development and Peace and the 2030 Agenda for Sustainable Development: Commonwealth Analysis Report*. London: Commonwealth Secretariat.

Forde, S. D. (2014). Look after yourself, or look after one another? An Analysis of Life skills in sport for development and peace HIV prevention curriculum. *Sociology of Sport Journal, 31*(3), 287–303.

Fowler (2000). Partnerships: Negotiating Relationships. INTRAC Occasional Papers Series No. 32. Available at: http://cercle.lu/download/partenariats/INTRACPartnershipnegociatingrelationship.pdf (accessed 18 January 2017).

Giulianotti, R. (2011a). The sport, development and peace sector: A model of four social policy domains. *Journal of Social Policy, 40*(4), 757–776.

Giulianotti, R. (2011b). Sport, transnational peacemaking and global civil society: Exploring the reflective discourses of 'sport, development, and peace' project officials. *Journal of Sport and Social Issues, 35*(1), 50–71.

Hartmann, D. and Kwauk, C. (2011). Sport and development: An overview, critique and reconstruction. *Journal of Sport and Social Issues, 35* (3), 284–305.

Guest, A. (2009). The diffusion of development through sport: Analyzing the history and practice of the Olympic Movement's grassroots outreach to Africa. *Sport in Society, 12*(10), 1336–1352.

Hasselgård, A. and Straume, S. (2015). Sport for development and peace policy discourse and local practice: Norwegian sport for development and peace to Zimbabwe. *International Journal of Sport Policy and Politics, 7* (1), 87–103.

Hayhurst, L. (2009). The power to shape policy: Charting sport for development and peace policy discourses. *International Journal of Sports Policy and Politics, 1*(2), 203–227.

Hayhurst, L. M. C. and Frisby, W. (2010). Inevitable tensions: Swiss and Canadian sport for development NGO perspectives on partnerships with high performance sport. *European Sport Management Quarterly, 10*(1), 75–96.

Hulme, D. and Edwards, M. (1997). NGOs, states and donors: An overview. In D. Hulme and M. Edwards (eds), *NGOs, States and Donors: Too Close for Comfort?* Basingstoke: MacMillan.

Kay, T. (2012). Accounting for legacy: Monitoring and evaluation in sport in development relationships. *Sport in Society, 15*(6), 888–904.

Kidd, B. (2008). A new social movement: Sport for development and Peace. *Sport in Society, 11*(4), 370–380.

Lindsey, I. (2011). Partnership working and sport development. In B. Houlihan and M. Green (eds), *Handbook of Sport Development*. Abingdon: Routledge.

Lindsey, I. (2013). Community collaboration in development work with young people: Perspectives from Zambian communities. *Development in Practice, 23*(4), 481–495.

Lindsey, I. (2017). Governance in sport-for-development: Problems and possibilities of (not) learning from international development. *International Review for the Sociology of Sport, 52*(7), 801–818.

Lindsey, I. and Banda, D. (2011). Sport and the fight against HIV/AIDS in Zambia: A 'partnership' approach? *International Review of Sociology of Sport, 46*(1), 90–107.

Lindsey, I. and Bitugu, B. (2018). Distinctive Patterns, Processes and Actors of Policy Diffusion: Drawing Implications From The Case of Sport in International Development. *Policy Studies*, doi: 10.1080/01442872.2018.1479521.

Lindsey, I., Kay, T., Jeanes, R. and Banda, D. (2017). *Localizing Global Sport for Development*. Manchester: Manchester University Press.

Lindsey, I., Zakariah, A. B. T., Owusu-Ansah, E., Ndee, H. and Jeanes, R. (2016). Researching 'sustainable development in African sport': A case study of a North-South academic collaboration. In L.

M. C. Hayhurst, T. Kay and M. Chawansky (eds), *Beyond Sport for Development and Peace: Transnational Perspectives on Theory, Policy and Practice*. Abingdon: Routledge.

MacIntosh, E., Arellano, A. and Forneris, T. (2016). Exploring the community and external-agency partnership in sport-for-development programming. *European Sport Management Quarterly, 16*(1), 38–57.

Mundy, K., Haggerty, M., Sivasubramaniam, M., Cherry, S. and Maclure, R. (2010). Civil society, basic education, and sector-wide aid: insights from Sub-Saharan Africa. *Development in Practice, 20*(4–5), 484–497.

Nicholls, S., Giles, A. R. and Sethna, C. (2011). Privileged voices, unheard stories and subjugated knowledge: Perpetuating the 'lack of evidence' discourse in sport for development. *International Review for the Sociology of Sport, 46*(3), 249–264.

Njelesani, D. (2011). Preventive HIV/AIDS education through physical education: Reflections from Zambia. *Third World Quarterly, 32*(3), 435–452.

Preston, P. (1996). *Development Theory: An Introduction*. Oxford: Blackwell.

Reis, A. C., Vieira, M. C. and de Sousa-Mast, F. R. (2016). 'Sport for Development' in developing countries: The case of the Vilas Olímpicas do Rio de Janeiro. *Sport Management Review, 19*(2), 107–119.

Sanders, B., Phillips, J. and Vanreusel, B. (2014). Opportunities and challenges facing NGOs using sport as a vehicle for development in post-apartheid South Africa. *Sport, Education and Society, 19*(6), 789–805.

Sansom, K. (2006). Government engagement with non-state providers of water and sanitation services. *Public Administration and Development, 26*(3), 207–217.

Seckinelgin, H. (2005). A global disease and its governance: HIV/AIDS in sub-Saharan Africa and the agency of NGOs. *Global Governance: A Review of Multilateralism and International Organizations, 11*(3), 351–368.

Sherry, E. and Schulenkorf, N. (2016). League Bilong Laif: Rugby, education and sport-for-development partnerships in Papua New Guinea. *Sport, Education and Society, 21*(4), 513–530.

Spaaij, R. (2012). Building social and cultural capital among young people in disadvantaged communities: Lessons from a Brazilian sport-based intervention program. *Sport, Education and Society, 17*(1), 77–95.

Sport for Development and Peace International Working Group (SDPIWG). (2008). Harnessing the Power of Sport for Development and Peace: Recommendations to Governments. Available at: www.un.org/wcm/content/site/sport/home/unplayers/memberstates/sdpiwg_keydocs (accessed 21 April 2015).

Straume, S. and Hasselgård, A. (2014). 'They need to get the feeling that these are their ideas': Trusteeship in Norwegian sport for development and peace to Zimbabwe. *International Journal of Sport Policy and Politics, 6*(1), 1–18.

Svensson, P. G., Hancock, M. G. and Hums, M. A. (2016). Examining the educative aims and practices of decision-makers in sport for development and peace organizations. *Sport, Education and Society, 21*(4), 495–512.

Teamey, K. (2007). Literature Review on Relationships between Government and Non-state Providers of Services. Available at: www.idd.bham.ac.uk/research/pdfs/Literature_Review.pdf (accessed 27 July 2015).

Teamey, K. (2010). Research on relationships between government agencies and non-state providers of basic services: A discussion on the methods, theories and typologies used and ways forward. Whose Public Action? Analysing Inter-sectoral Collaboration for Service Delivery. NGPA Research Paper 38. Available at: www.lse.ac.uk/internationalDevelopment/research/NGPA/publications/WP38_Teamey_Web_final.pdf (accessed 18 January 2017).

United Nations. (2006). *Report on the International Year of Sport and Physical Education 2005*. Geneva: United Nations.

United Nations General Assembly (UNGA). (2015). Transforming our world: The 2030 Agenda for Sustainable Development, United Nations General Assembly Resolution 70/1. Available at: https://sustainabledevelopment.un.org/post2015/transformingourworld/publication (accessed 26 January 2017).

Wachter, K. (2014). North-South Partnerships and Power Relations in sport for Development: The case of Mathare Youth Sports Association. Unpublished MA Thesis, Southampton Solent University.

Webb, D. (2004). Legitimate actors? The future roles for NGOs against HIV/AIDS in sub-Saharan Africa. In N. Poku and A. Whiteside (eds), *The Political Economy of AIDS in Africa*. Aldershot: Ashgate.

Whitley, M. A. and Johnson, A. J. (2015). Using a community-based participatory approach to research and programming in Northern Uganda: Two researchers' confessional tales. *Qualitative Research in Sport, Exercise and Health, 7*(5), 620–641.

Willis, K. (2011). *Theories and Practices of Development (2nd edn)*. Abingdon: Routledge.

8

SDP and Olympism

Ian Henry and Bora Hwang

Introduction: Olympism and SDP

The links between the Olympic Movement and the philosophy of sport for development and peace, are perhaps fairly obvious in the current context within which the Olympic Movement operates. Strands of Sport for Development and Peace (SDP) thinking are readily identified in, for example, the current version of the Olympic Charter and its character-isation of Olympism, and in a number of recent initiatives. These include activities such as the promotion of the Olympic Truce since 1992 (IOC 2015) and the IOC's promotion of gender equity in leadership and participation in Olympic sport (Henry and Robinson 2010), as well as funding initiatives to promote sport and its benefits among refugees from war-affected areas such as Syria and Iraq introduced in 2012 and consolidated in the establishing of the Olympic Refuge initiative in 2017, and in the IOC's teaming up with the United Nations (UN) and its Office for SDP between 2001 and 2017 (IOC 2017; 2014). However, this nevertheless represents a relatively recent set of policy emphases for the movement, and one which has been subject to criticism in particular from two different types of source. The first might be broadly described as the application of critical theories and/or post-colonial theory, which cast the global North as donor and the global South in a subservient position as 'grateful' beneficiaries of such activities. The second type of critique is derived from what might broadly be described as a development theory perspective, which contests the con-tribution of sport to development goals, and the rigour of the evidence gathered to support positive development claims.

The structure of this chapter will be focused around three elements. The first is briefly to trace the development of the sport aid movement within the Olympic domain, and the evolution of the policy of development through sport. The second element relates how both development of sport and to a lesser extent development through sport, became a battleground in the Cold War struggle between East and West to secure the support of the newly independent decolonising nations of Africa and Asia. The third section of the chapter will address strengths and limitations in the maturing of the policy thinking behind SDP within the Olympic Movement in the early part of the twenty-first century, and identify the critiques emanating from post-colonial/critical studies on the one hand and policy monitoring and evaluation on the other.

The historical construction of Olympism as an idea/'philosophy'

In the Olympic context, the SDP movement took its most visible initial form in 1992 with the inauguration of the organisation Olympic Aid, which was established by the Organising Committee for the Lillehammer Winter Olympics. Olympic Aid was promoted in particular by the four-time gold medallist speed skater, Johann Olav Koss. Koss donated his medal winning bonuses to the work of Olympic Aid, and persuaded a number of other medal winners to do the same, raising a significant sum, reported as $18 million (Canadian Encyclopedia 2016). Olympic Aid as an organisation was subsequently effectively 'rebranded' Right to Play in 2000 with Koss as its CEO.

The mission of Olympic Aid was to raise money for humanitarian purposes in regions that had been subject to violent conflict and other forms of disaster. While this involved sourcing money from sport, either directly by sporting individuals or bodies, or by influencing others, when the organisation transformed into Right to Play it specifically articulated its priorities as working with young people through sport and education to enhance their lives, defining itself as 'a global charitable organisation that uses the power of sport and play to educate children who are facing adversity, poverty and conflict'. (Right to Play n.d.) and thus having a clear Sport for Development agenda.

While Olympic Aid and subsequently Right to Play clearly associated the Olympic community with what has become known as the SDP movement, the promotion of the modern Olympics since their inception has been bound up with arguments about the use of sport for ethical purposes. The revival of the Olympic Games was the product of the political energies of Coubertin, and from the outset Coubertin had a (multi-faceted) moral agenda, the themes of which can be traced in his prodigious output of writings and speeches promoting and sustaining the establishing of the Modern Olympics (Muller 2000). However, while these themes evolved both in some of Coubertin's later writings (Chatziefstathiou 2005; 2012) and in the subsequent development of his ideas by Olympic scholars and policy-makers, these themes were not always consistent with a progressive ideology of personal development at the individual level, or of international peace at the global level, which would reflect the ideology of SDP. For example, Coubertin's recognition of the role which sport could play in developing moral and physical character was originally to be employed for nationalistic purposes in terms of the need to develop the potential of France's (male) youth to provide effective national defence in the light of the country's defeat in the Franco-Prussian War (Guttman 1992: 8). Even when Coubertin's concern with internationalist interests subsequently overtook his concern with national decline, his form of internationalism was clearly Eurocentric and would even be described in contemporary terms as racist. He referred, for example, to 'the natural indolence of the Oriental' (Coubertin 1896: 359), and to the Olympic Games exercising 'that necessary and beneficent influence for which I look – an influence which shall make them the means of bringing to perfection the strong and hopeful youth of *our white race*', (Coubertin 1908: 545), emphasis added). In addition, Coubertin's (1928) well-known views on gender were hardly progressive, and he remained explicitly opposed to the participation of women in the Olympic Games as reflected in his published views across the period from the inception of the Modern Games to the period shortly before his death. Even though women's participation in the Games had grown modestly from a relatively insignificant start in the early editions, Coubertin rejected arguments for women's inclusion on the basis that there would be little public interest in female performance, and that spectating at such contests would amount to a form of voyeurism rather than an interest in the 'pure' (and morally appropriate) form of competition which male Olympic sport incorporated. After the Amsterdam Games where a women's track race of 800 meters allegedly ended with a number of female competitors collapsing, media commented on this episode as unseemly and unfeminine (Coubertin 1928).

Though views expressed by Coubertin would clearly be at odds with an SDP perspective, some of his later views and their interpretation by Olympic scholars and policy-makers reflected a more progressive perspective. The wording of the definition of Olympism given in the Charter from 1993 reflects such an interpretation of Coubertin's view of Olympic values. In addition to providing a definition of the nature of Olympism the 1993 version of the Olympic Charter, and those versions that followed, claim that 'Modern Olympism was conceived by Pierre de Coubertin'. This seems to imply that the principles of Olympism were those introduced by Coubertin in his accounts of the philosophical ideas underpinning the modern Olympic Movement. However a number of Coubertin's proclamations are clearly inconsistent with contemporary thinking reflected in the principles of SDP, making any claim that the principles of Olympism were immutable (unchanged that is since their introduction by Coubertin), and universal (applying to all cultures at all times) difficult to sustain (Parry 1988; 2006).

A modern account of Olympism and thus of Olympic values is given expression in the Olympic Charter. Versions of the Olympic Charter (formerly referred to as *l'Annuaire*) have been in existence from 1908 and have sought to define the role and mission of the IOC. However, it was only in the 1991 December version of the Olympic Charter that the place of Olympism in the philosophy of the Olympic Movement was explicitly stated in the form largely incorporated in the current version. The preamble to the 2016 Charter asserts that 'Modern Olympism was conceived by Pierre de Coubertin' and in the subsequent opening section of the Charter the 'Fundamental Principles of Olympism' are outlined as follows:

1. Olympism is a philosophy of life, exalting and combining in a balanced whole the qualities of body, will and mind. Blending sport with culture and education, Olympism seeks to create a way of life based on the joy of effort, the educational value of good example, social responsibility and respect for universal fundamental ethical principles.
2. The goal of Olympism is to place sport at the service of the harmonious development of humankind, with a view to promoting a peaceful society concerned with the preservation of human dignity.

International Olympic Committee 2017: 3

These principles emphasise the role of sport as a *means* in the context of education, and of the development of social responsibility, to achieve the *ends* of harmonious development of human kind, and of a peaceful society which seeks to preserve human dignity. These means, and ends are synonymous with many of those for sport for development and peace, as for example cited by Right to Play in its on-line tool kit:

Sport for Development and Peace refers to the intentional use of sport, physical activity and play to attain specific development and peace objectives, including, most notably, the Millennium Development Goals (MDGs). Successful Sport for Development and Peace programs work to realize the rights of all members of society to participate in sport and leisure activities. …. Effective programs intentionally give priority to development objectives and are carefully designed to be inclusive.

Sport in the context of its purported usefulness in achieving the UN's MDGs, and subsequently the Sustainable Development Goals (SDGs) of the UNs 2030 Strategy, has been at the core of the deepening of the relationship between the IOC and the United Nations, which has taken place since the early 1990s. However, the often-problematic use of sport for development purposes and its hidden agendas are illustrated in an earlier period within the history of the development of Olympic Solidarity.

The birth and evolution of Olympic Solidarity: funding the development of Olympic sport in newly independent states

The role of Olympic Solidarity has evolved considerably since the inception of its predecessor, the Commission for International Olympic Aid (Al Tauqi 2003), not least with the arrival of significant commercial funding sources. Olympic Solidarity as an organisation currently administers and distributes the proportion of income allocated to the National Olympic Committees (NOCs) from the sale of television rights of the Olympic Games, and promotes sport aid programmes to meet the specific needs of NOCs (Zammit and Henry 2014). Its primary role is thus as a vehicle of solidarity of the developed and developing world in the Olympic Movement through the redistribution of funds. However, its role is very different today from that which was originally the case both in terms of the volume of funds distributed and the nature of activities supported. In particular there has been a shift from what was seen as primarily aid for sport to a more general concern for aid through sport; an approach that is related, or complementary, to the goals of SDP.

Olympic Solidarity emerged in the 1960s stimulated initially by a draft resolution proposed by two Russian IOC members, Adrianov and Romanov, and presented to the 58th IOC session in 1961, which proposed establishing a system of aid for Asian and African countries. The response to this proposal was the establishing of the International Olympic Aid Commission under the leadership of Count Jean de Beaumont which he described as having the following aims:

> to further the *moral action* of the IOC in a more practical and direct manner by offering help to all the countries who need help; to explain how one gets organised, how one trains, how one follows the rules and by-laws of the IOC. Particularly how one helps oneself, and also how one enters into the large family of amateur Olympic sport, by avoiding any discrimination on racial, religious or political grounds, *aiming only (at) the development of the human being towards a harmonious accomplishment of the individual,* being quite understood that it is the best man (sic) who wins and who gets applauded.
>
> de Beaumont 5 April 5 1963: speech in Dakar, emphases added

Although this policy response might, at one level, appear to be motivated by altruistic and progressive concerns, private correspondence from at least one key IOC member (the Briton, Lord Luke) illustrates the suspicion of Russian motives on the part of Western observers during a period in which the decolonisation of Asian and African nations was having a major impact on the balance of power in both the UN and the IOC.

> There is another confidential point, which needs to be watched (but not mentioned in public) – it is my private opinion that the *USSR are only keen about this effort in so far as it is part of their political objective of extending their influence in Africa,* and they see in the IOC a means to that end. We must not forget that the overwhelming influence of the USSR in the United Nations affairs has been accentuated by their support of the African states, and *we have to beware that too much influence on the IOC of increased African*

membership could have the same effect. In the same way the *USSR is jealous of the effort the USA is making in Africa through various forms of aid.* Therefore, to sum up, we are fairly close to political issues in our new-found African venture and we must therefore treat them carefully.

Lord Luke, 28 August 1962: Letter to Jean de Beaumont, emphases added

Not only was there suspicion of the Russians' motives on the part of some senior members of the IOC, there is evidence that the President and the Chancellor also held particularly right wing views about the suitability of some African and Asian groups to be provided with financial support.

Can you imagine non-organized people, knowing practically nothing – or not much – about sport, receiving suddenly money for what? What those people should receive … are: educators in sport, trainers and material … That money should be used for that only: material sent from Europe and Instructors sent from Europe or USA, *but certainly not cash money which will disappear in the pocket of some clever negroes*!

Otto Mayer, IOC Chancellor (Chief Exec) 25 January 1962: Letter to Avery Brundage: emphasis added

The then IOC president, Avery Brundage himself, resisted support for black and coloured South Africans during the anti-apartheid struggle, and sought to render de Beaumont's Commission for International Olympic Aid relatively powerless by denying the right to raise or administer funds and the right to use the term 'Olympic' in its organisational title (Henry and Al-Tauqi, 2008).

This was hardly an indication that the Olympic Movement might move in the direction of promoting Sport for Development. Three principal factors made a difference to the IOC's position. The first was the inauguration of the GANEFO Games (the Games of the Newly Emerging Forces) held in Indonesia in 1963. GANEFO was a movement established to challenge the dominance of the IOC, and the West more generally, on world sport, and had 32 nations as members (Lutan and Fan 2005). Although this threat passed (as the second edition of the GANEFO Games planned to be held in Egypt in 1967 failed to materialise ostensibly for economic reasons) nevertheless the potential costs of any rift between the NOCs and the IOC had been made apparent promoting a taste for compromise on the part of the IOC (Connolly 2012). The second factor was that the NOCs, bolstered by the arrival of new NOCs from newly liberated Asian and African nations, began to organise to press for recognition of their interests on a reluctant IOC. They set up their own global body in 1969, the Permanent General Assembly of NOCs, whose demands included the establishing of an Olympic Solidarity Commission with funding to support nations which were weaker in economic and sporting terms.

The third factor was the attraction of serious funding by the Organising Committee for the 1984 Los Angeles Games, in the form of lucrative broadcasting contracts which significantly enhanced the level of income at the disposal of the IOC. This meant that the IOC was no longer able to argue that it did not have funds to support the activities of the NOC sector including those that fell under the auspices of Olympic Solidarity. Thus as the strength of the Soviet bloc began to crumble in the late 1980s, Olympic Aid, at this stage largely in the form of 'development of sport' rather than 'development through sport', increased considerably from one quadrennial to the next (Zammit and Henry 2014).

The Olympic Movement, sport for development and international relations

From the end of the 1980s there was a growing emphasis on the part of the Olympic Movement to stress the role which sport could play, not only in physical health and positive social development, but also more explicitly in addressing some of the negative consequences, particularly on youth, of exposure to violence, civil conflict and war. As we have noted the organisation Olympic Aid (later to become Right to Play) was established in 1992 specifically targeting aid through sport for those affected by conflict. This focus on sport and the promotion of just, peaceful and inclusive societies was, however, expanded to take in a wide range of social, economic, physical and environmental ambitions – in particular those associated with the UN's MDGs.

The IOC dates cooperation between itself and the UN back to 1922 when an institutional cooperation between the IOC and the International Labour Organisation was established (IOC 2015). In the period from the early 1990s the IOC intensified efforts to work in partnership with the UN. In 1992 the IOC renewed the 'tradition' of the Olympic Truce, with the UN adopting a resolution calling on its members to observe the truce in 1993. In addition, the United Nations opened its Office for Sport Development and Peace in 2005, and in 2009 the UN General Assembly granted the IOC Permanent Observer status, giving the IOC the right to attend meetings of the Assembly and thus access to the UN Agenda.

In April 2014, the UN and the IOC signed a formal cooperation agreement designed to strengthen collaboration between the two organisations at the highest level (IOC 2009) and the IOC Honorary President Jacques Rogge was appointed as the Special Envoy of the Secretary-General for Youth, Refugees and Sport to the United Nations (UN 2014a). These measures while reflecting the joint efforts to cooperate in the field of sport, dovetailed the strategic thinking of the two organisations such that Ban Ki Moon, the UN Secretary-General, could claim in a speech at the 2009 IOC Congress that 'Olympic principles are United Nations principles' (International Olympic Committee 2009) and subsequently, the IOC could announce,

> In 2015, in a historic moment for sport and the Olympic Movement, sport was officially recognised by the UN as an 'important enabler' of sustainable development, and included in the UN's Agenda 2030. The IOC believes in the potential of sport to help achieve 11 of the 17 Sustainable Development Goals (SGDs) established by UN Agenda 2030.
>
> *International Olympic Committee, n.d.*

The outcomes claimed by the IOC for sport's contribution to the achievement of the SDGs are of course contingent on circumstances. Detractors claim that in some circumstances sport is often responsible for negative outcomes in respect of the SDGs. To give just a few examples, whether one is referring to: achieving gender equality and empowering all women and girls (SDG 5); promoting inclusive and sustainable economic growth, employment and decent work for all (SDG 8); or conserving and promoting use of terrestrial ecosystems (SDG 14), negative examples abound of failure to achieve or even address these goals in the field of sport.

In May 2017 the UN made a surprise announcement that

> The Secretary-General has agreed with the President of the International Olympic Committee (IOC), Thomas Bach, to establish a direct partnership between the UN and the International Olympic Committee. Accordingly, it was decided to close the UN Office on Sport for Development and Peace (UNOSDP), effective 30 April of this year.
>
> *(United Nations 2017).*

Several commentators and significant stakeholders expressed surprise and disappointment at this turn of events. The Council of Europe's Consultative Committee of the Enlarged Partial Agreement on Sport (EPAS CC),[1] for example, adopted a resolution at its meeting on 9 May, expressing concern over the closure:

> Given that this decision is very recent and very little information has been given to make a balanced assessment of its impact, the EPAS CC considers nevertheless that this decision might send a problematic message, at a point in time where the awareness about the societal role of sport is growing in general, and where in particular the UN, several governments and numerous organisations from civil society is wishing to focus on how sport can contribute to achieving the 2030 Sustainable Development Goals (SDG)

Perhaps the major benefit of the UN establishing its Office for SDP was that it gave official recognition and thus political legitimacy to the significance of the role which sport could play in achieving social goals such as the MDGs. The closure of the Office, however, notwithstanding the 'direct partnership' in this area with the IOC, seemed to send out the message that this was a marginal policy concern and thus susceptible to efforts to achieve economies. Such a move may lead governments of member states and other bodies to come to similar conclusions.

Critiques of the UN/IOC relationship and its activities in relation to SDP

In this section we will critically evaluate the contribution UN/IOC relationship with the SDP sector at a broad strategic level. The most significant critiques might be described as falling under the two poles of Gordon, Lewis and Young's (1999) classic typology, namely 'analysis of policy' and 'analysis for policy'. Analysis of policy generally relates to analysis of how policy is determined, who it benefits and how; while 'analysis for policy' incorporates policy advocacy and monitoring and evaluation.

In terms of analysis for policy in relation to sport for development and peace in the Olympic context, the most prominent work is a set of accounts developed generally in the domain of critical theory(ies), predominantly relating to the field of post-colonial studies. In terms of analysis for policy, the most prominent work relates to monitoring and evaluation which falls broadly within the field of development studies, and is more closely associated with consideration of whether 'practical' development outcomes sought are being achieved. One of these branches may be more heavily theory oriented, while the other is principally located in practice. However, neither is bereft of theoretical insights or practical implications.

However, reconciling these two types of account is problematic. McEwan suggests that there is a little exchange of ideas between postcolonialism and development because of their differing disciplinary traditions and politics and thus divergences in the languages and concepts used to articulate core issues. She quotes Sharp and Briggs (2006: 6 in MacEwan 2009: 77)

> For many who have spent a professional lifetime working in 'development', either as theorists or practitioners, postcolonialism is seen to offer overly complex theories which are largely ignorant of the real problems characterising everyday life in the global South. Alternatively, many postcolonial theorists consider development studies still to be mired in Eurocentric, modernist, and/or neo-colonialist mindsets.

This implies that postcolonial critiques representing 'analysis of policy' are riven with overt and/ or implicit ideological assumptions, while development approaches representing 'analysis for policy' incorporate lessons for practice, which purport to be rational and objective but which are implicitly, and problematically, riven with unacknowledged epistemological and political assumptions.

A powerful example of post-colonial work is Darnell's (2007) research on motives and experiences of workers and volunteers delivering programmes on the part of the IOC's key delivery agency, Right to Play, which provides illustrative evidence of the nature of the global North's patronage in terms of the perspectives of these individuals. Although the study is broadly theoretically inspired and deeply critical of the North-South relations reflected in the responses of interviewees, there are important practical implications, if only, for example, in terms of training and sensitising volunteers that can be taken from such studies. The difference between Darnell's critical studies of SDP in action and the general critique of the IOC and its activities by authors such as Helen Lenskyj (2000; 2002; 2008) is that Lenskyj's critique appears to admit of no circumstance in which the holding of an Olympic Games will provide net benefits, and thus it is often difficult to see the implications of this type of approach for improving practice.

In terms of analysis for policy, there is a growing body of work that is associated with defining and measuring development, in an evaluative and prescriptive manner. We will comment here briefly on evaluation in relation to one high profile SDP policy intervention developed by an Olympic bidding group, namely London 2012's International Inspiration programme. Within the Olympic Movement, sport for development and peace initiatives have begun to achieve considerable prominence in the bidding and hosting strategies of host cities (and nations) for the Games. International Inspiration represents perhaps the most spectacular of these proposals. This was a programme delivered through three key partners, UK Sport, the British Council and UNICEF. The UN resolution of October 2014 (United Nations 2014b) describes International Inspiration as 'the first [international] legacy initiative ever linked to the Olympic and Paralympic Games, which has reached over 25 million children in 20 countries around the world through the power of high-quality and inclusive physical education, sport and play'. This offer to promote sport aid internationally has been emulated in subsequent bids for hosting the Summer Games such as the SDP elements of Tokyo 2020's 'Sport for Tomorrow' programme, its popularity with the IOC reflecting both its focus on young people in particular, and the direct relationship between the SDP initiatives incorporated and the goals of the IOC as expressed in the Charter's definition of Olympism.

The first stage of the International Inspiration programme delivered in the first five of the 20 nations selected for the programme, namely Azerbaijan, Brazil, India, Palau and Zambia was evaluated by a research group commissioned by the Board of International Inspiration (Henry et al. 2011). The programme was both diverse and complex and the approach adopted by the evaluation team was analogous to a form of *metaevaluation* of the various project evaluations adopted or undertaken by the core partners and/or their delivery agencies (Chen et al. 2014). Metaevaluation incorporates two principal elements, namely evaluation synthesis which focuses on reporting a synthesis of outcomes in terms of the range, scope and depth of results; and an evaluation of evaluations which focuses on *process*, i.e. the appropriateness of evaluation approaches adopted, the rigour of their application, and the soundness of conclusions drawn.

Leaving aside the detailed nature of the evaluation, many of the technical difficulties associated with legitimating claims through monitoring and evaluations systems can be illustrated by focusing on the broad strategic goal of the programme to 'reach' the lives of 12 million children in 20 countries through sport, and the difficulties associated in measuring achievement of such a goal.

In seeking to assess the impact of interventions such as those promoted by International Inspiration, it is important to estimate additionality, i.e. to distinguish what is additional activity[2] and what is activity which would have occurred anyway but which for example is simply rebranded under in this case the International Inspiration banner

A significant concern with the data collected and the conceptualisation of impact also related to the operationalisation of participants 'reached', and those 'engaged'. The following shared definitions were adopted:

ENGAGED Regularly engaged – more than 12 times per year – in high quality and inclusive PE, Sport and Play in schools and communities

REACHED With opportunity to participate in high quality PE, sport and play, or to access other rights or entitlements through such participation

The principal concern here was that the population 'reached' would include individuals who had perhaps attended only one event, on a single occasion and thus whose involvement was limited and who were likely to be little affected by the experience. Yet data for this type of potentially marginal participation was incorporated into the gross figure provided to assess the number of young people whose lives had been 'enriched by the power of sport'. The method of calculating 'reach' thus appears to have been potentially influenced by a wish to meet the hugely ambitious target of 12 million for the programme as a whole (and was the basis for the subsequent claims that more than double the target number had been reached).

Measuring impact in this way by reference to 'reach' data might be argued to represent a fairly unhelpful measure. Measures of engagement, by contrast, offered a much more meaningful indicator of positive impact. Where individuals had been counted as engaged they would have participated in an International Inspiration activity on at least 12 occasions. Even though these are still only output rather than outcome measures, the opportunity of achieving desired outcomes such as social inclusion of children with disabilities, or of increased understanding leading to the adoption of safe and healthy behaviours, would seem to be much more likely to be effected given this type of regular exposure.

Conclusion

This brief discussion of the above critical perspectives on Olympic involvement in SDP missions, and on the measurement of their effectiveness, illustrates key difficulties which remain. The first is the dominance of the voices of the global North in the Olympic domain, and thus the contrast with what is often a lack of space for local actors and bodies to articulate local needs and priorities. The second is the weaknesses in terms of the technocratic construction of evaluation frameworks, which again favour actors/reviewers/evaluators from the global North but which do not necessarily solve problems of data deficiency, and where purported objectivity may be undermined by the need to place governmental or commercial sponsors in a positive light.

Notes

1   The EPAS Consultative Committee comprises 25 international NGOs and institutions in the sports field. As a partnership body, it provides advice for the 38 countries that are members of the Enlarged Partial Agreement on Sport under the Council of Europe.

2   Conceptually the way in which Net Impact is estimated is as follows: Net Impact = Gross Impact (1-leakage)(1-substitution)(1-displacement)(1+multiplier).

References

Al-Tauqi, M. (2003). Olympic Solidarity: Global Order and the Diffusion of Modern Sport between 1961 and 1980. PhD Thesis, School of Sport and Exercise Sciences, Loughborough University.

Canadian Encyclopedia. (2016). Entry on Right to Play. Available at: www.thecanadianencyclopedia.ca/en/article/right-to-play/ (accessed 23 November 2017).

Chatziefstathiou D., Henry I., Theodoraki E. and Al-Tauqi M. (2006). Cultural imperialism and the diffusion of Olympic sport in Africa: A comparison of pre-and post-second world war contexts. *8th International Symposium for Olympic Research*. Ontario, Canada: University of Western Ontario.

Chatziefstathiou, D. (2005). The Changing Nature of the Ideology of Olympism in the Modern Olympic Era. PhD Thesis, School of Sport and Exercise Sciences, Loughborough University.

Chatziefstathiou, D. (2009). Reading Baron Pierre de Coubertin: Issues of race and gender. *The Journal of Sport Literature: Aethlon, 25*(2).

Chatziefstathiou, D. (2012). Changes and continuities of the ideology of Olympism in the modern Olympic movement. In H. Dichter and B. Kidd *(eds), Olympic Reform Ten Years Later. Sport in the Global Society – Contemporary Perspectives*. London: Routledge.

Chatziefstathiou, D. and Henry, I. P. (2009) Technologies of power, governmentality and Olympic discourses: A Foucauldian analysis for understanding the discursive constructions of the Olympic ideology. *Esporte y sociedad, 4*(12). Available at: www.esportesociedade.com/.

Chatziefstathiou, D. and Henry, I. P. (2012). *Discourses of Olympism: From the Sorbonne 1894 to London 2012*. London: Palgrave.

Chatziefstathiou, D., Henry, I., Al Tauqi, M. and Theodoraki, E. (2008). Cultural imperialism and the diffusion of Olympic sport, in Africa: A comparison of pre and post Second World War contexts. In H. Ren, L. P. Dacosta, A. Miragaya and J. N. (eds), *Olympic Studies Reader. A Multidisciplinary and Multicultural Research Guide* (Vol. 1). Beijing: Beijing Sports University Press, pp. 111–121.

Chen, S., Henry, I, Ko, L-M (2014). Meta-evaluation, analytic logic models and the assessment of impacts of sports policies. In Henry and L.-M. Ko (eds), *Handbook of Sport Policy*. London: Routledge.

Connolly, C. A. (2012) The politics of the games of the new emerging forces (GANEFO) *The International Journal of the History of Sport, 29*(9), 1311–1324.

Coubertin, P. (1896) The Olympic Games of 1896. In N. Muller (ed.), *Pierre de Coubertin 1863–1937. Olympism, Selected Writings*. Lausanne: International Olympic Committee, p. 359.

Coubertin, P. (1908). Why I revived the Olympic games. In N. Muller and P. de Coubertin (eds), 1863–1937. *Olympism, Selected Writings*. Lausanne: International Olympic Committee, p. 545.

Coubertin, P. (1928) Educational use of athletic activity. In N. Muller (ed.), *Pierre de Coubertin 1863–1937. Olympism, Selected Writings*. Lausanne: International Olympic Committee, p. 188.

Coubertin, P (1931) Colonisation sportive. *Bulletin de Bureau International du Pedagogie Sportive, 5*, 12–14. In N. Muller (ed.), *Pierre de Coubertin 1863–1937. Olympism, Selected Writings*. Lausanne: International Olympic Committee.

Darnell, S. C. (2007). Playing with race: Right to play and the production of whiteness in development through sport. *Sport in Society, 10*(4), 560–579.

Davis, S. (2018). 'What abandoned Olympic venues from around the world look like today'. *Business Insider UK*. Available at: http://uk.businessinsider.com/abandoned-olympic-venues-around-the-world-photos-rio-2016-8 (accessed 24 February 2018).

Gordon, I, Lewis, J. and Young, K (1999). Perspectives in policy analysis. In T. Miyakawa, (ed.), *The Science of Public Policy: Policy Analysis*. New York: Routledge.

Guttmann, A. (1992). *The Olympics a history of the Modern Games*. Chicago: University of Illinois Press.

Henry, I. (2011). The Olympics: Why we should value them. In H. Lenskyj and S. Wagg (eds), *A Handbook of Olympic Studies*. Basingstoke: Palgrave.

Henry, I. (2015). *The Role of Sport in Fostering Open and Inclusive Societies*. Brussels: European Parliament: Culture and Education Committee.

Henry, I. and Al-Tauqi, M. (2008). The development of Olympic solidarity: West and non-west (core and periphery) relations in the Olympic world. *International Journal of the History of Sport, 25*(3), 355–373.

Henry, I., Amara, M., Aquilina, D., Argent, E., Betzer-Tayar, M., Coalter, F. and Taylor, J. (2005). *The Roles of Sport and Education in the Social Inclusion of Asylum Seekers and Refugees: An Evaluation of Policy and Practice in the UK.* European Year of the Education through Sport, Report to DG Education and Culture, European Commission Loughborough, Institute of Sport and Leisure Policy, Loughborough University.

Henry, I., Kay, T. and Coalter F. (2011). *Evaluation of Stage 1 of the International Inspiration Development through Sport Programme.* Loughborough: Centre for Olympic Studies and Research, Institute of Youth Sport, Loughborough University.

Henry, I. and Robinson, L. (2010). *Gender Equity and Leadership in Olympic Bodies: Women, Leadership and the Olympic Movement.* Lausanne: International Olympic Committee and Centre for Olympic Studies and Research, Loughborough University.

IOC. (n.d.). IOC Note relating to Sport and the UN's Agenda 2030 Sustainable Development Goals. Available at: https://stillmed.olympic.org/media/Document%20Library/OlympicOrg/News/2017/06/2017-Sustainable-development-en.pdf (accessed 12 January 2018).

IOC. (2009). Olympic Principles are United Nations Principles IOC Report of the speech by Ban Ki-Moon, September 2009. Available at: www.olympic.org/cooperation-with-the-un (accessed 3 November 2017).

IOC. (2014). Sport and Sustainable Development goals. Available at: www.un.org/sport/content/why-sport/sport-and-sustainable-development-goals (accessed 5 January 2018).

IOC. (2015). Olympic Truce Factsheet, Lausanne: IOC. Available at: https://stillmed.olympic.org/Documents/Reference_documents_Factsheets/Olympic_Truce.pdf (accessed 17 December 2017).

IOC (2017). Olympic Charter. International Olympic Committee: Lausanne Available at: www.olympic.org/olympic-studies-centre/collections/official-publications/olympic-charters (accessed 17 November 2017).

IOC. (2017). IOC Launches Olympic Refuge Foundation in its Commitment to Support Refugees. Available at: www.olympic.org/news/ioc-launches-olympic-refuge-foundation-in-its-commitment-to-support-refugees.

Lenskyj, H. (2000). *Inside the Olympic Industry: Power, Politics, and Activism.* Albany, NY: State University of New York Press.

Lenskyj, H. (2002). *The Best Olympics Ever?: Social Impacts of Sydney 2000.* Albany, NY: State University of New York Press.

Lenskyj, H. (2008). *Olympic Industry Resistance: Challenging Olympic Power and Propaganda.* Albany, NY: State University of New York Press.

Lewis, A. (2017). Migrant workers subjected to heat and humidity being put at risk, says Human Rights Watch, CNN Sport. Available at: https://edition.cnn.com/2017/09/27/football/qatar-2022-world-cup-workers-heat-humidity-human-rights-watch/index.html (accessed 12 December 2017).

Lutan, R. and Fan, H. (2005). The politicization of sport: GANEFO–A case study, *Sport in Society*, 8(3), 425–439.

MacEwan, C. (2009) *Postcolonialism and Development.* London: Routledge.

Muller, N. (ed.) (2000). *Pierre de Coubertin 1863–1937. Olympism, Selected Writings.* Lausanne: International Olympic Committee.

Parry, J. (1988). Olympism at the beginning and end of the twentieth century – immutable values and principles and outdated factors. *International Olympic Academy: 28th Young Participants Session.* Olympia: International Olympic Academy, pp. 81–94.

Parry, J. (1994). The moral and cultural dimensions of Olympism and their educational application. *34th Session of Young Participants*, Olympia, Greece: International Olympic Academy.

Parry, J. (2006). Sport and Olympism: Universals and multiculturalism. *Journal of the Philosophy of Sport, 33*(2), 188–204.

Pawson, R. and Tilley, N. (2004). *Realist Evaluation.* London: Cabinet Office, UK Government.

Play the Game. (2017) Resolution of the EPAS Consultative Committee on the closure of UNOSDP. Available at: www.playthegame.org/media/6300122/EPAS-CC-resolution-on-closure-of-UNSODP-English.pdf (accessed 20 November 2017).

Right to Play. (n.d.). What is Sport for Development and Peace? Right to Play: Toronto. Available at: http://toolkit.ineesite.org/toolkit/INEEcms/uploads/1088 (accessed 23 November 2017).

Right to Play. (n.d.). What we do. Available at: www.righttoplay.com/Learn/ourstory/Pages/What-we-do.aspx (accessed 23 November 2017).

Sartori, G. (1970). Concept misformation in comparative politics. *American Political Science Review, LXIV*(4), 1033–1053.

Sharp, J. and Briggs, J. (2006) Postcolonialism and development: New dialogues. *The Geographical Journal*, *172* (1), 6–9.

United Nations. (2014a). Secretary-General Appoints Jacques Rogge of Belgium Special Envoy for Youth Refugees and Sport. Available at: www.un.org/press/en/2014/sga1459.doc.htm (accessed 3 November 2017).

United Nations. (2014b). General Assembly 69th Session 16 October 2014 Agenda Item 11 Sport for Development and Peace. Available at: www.un.org/ga/search/view_doc.asp?symbol=A/69/L.5 (accessed 10 November 2017).

United Nations. (2017). UN Press Briefing 4 May 2017. Available at: www.un.org/press/en/2017/db170504.doc.htm (accessed 27 November 2017).

Zammit, M. and Henry, I. (2014). Evaluating Olympic solidarity 1982–2012. In I. Henry and L.-M. Ko (eds), *Handbook of Sport Policy*. London: Routledge.

9

SDP and corporate social responsibility

Roger Levermore

Introduction

In some ways when compared to say NGOs, governments and multilateral organizations, corporations (also known as firms, businesses, companies, the private sector etc.) are fairly minor players in the processes of international development. The Overseas Development Institute noted in 2012 that 'the private sector still remains tangential to mainstream development policy and practice' (Overseas Development Institute 2012: 1). This peripheral engagement in international development is often measured in terms of a lack of investment by companies to countries that constitute the so-called developing areas of the world. However, the positive and negative impacts by private or state-owned companies in both the formal and growing informal sectors extends to creating jobs, developing technology that can be transferred to other uses, lending expertise to develop small, local businesses, developing infrastructure, supporting specific corporate social responsibility (CSR) projects in areas of the world in which international development is focused on, and creating/addressing environmental issues such as pollution and the changing habitat of ecosystems (Edelman *et al.* n.d.).

Partly because of the negative impacts on society, one of the most visible ways in which corporations from the formal economy are seen to engage with international development is through this ubiquitous and much-derided term – CSR. Organizations such as the World Bank link CSR directly to international development, noting that: 'CSR is the commitment of business to sustainable economic development… to improve quality of life' (World Bank 2003). With this in mind, the main focus of this chapter is on how corporations interact with international development by using CSR associated with sport.

Before focusing on the way sport is used through CSR to advance development, it is important to chart critically the context of CSR. CSR starts with the long history of distrust of business in the way that companies impact on society especially in their neglect of social responsibilities. For example, the 'robber barons' of nineteenth/twentieth century US, were regularly criticized for the excessive wealth they generated while paying employees derisory salaries, their environmental destruction, and their failure to pay any respect to the local communities in which their operations were located. That these same business owners were also very generous supporters of philanthropy was not an irony lost on critics who argued that supporting charity was just a way of disguising their gross social irresponsibility (Frankental 2001). Business today faces the same accusations. For instance, the latest annual Edelman trust survey of institutions indicates that business faces a crisis of confidence among members of the general public: globally, only 52 per cent of respondents said that they trust business – this figures falls to 29 per cent for South Korea, 34 per cent for Hong Kong and 39 per cent for Russia (Edelman 2017). The situation is worse for the credibility of chief executives; only 37 per cent of respondents said that CEOs were credible (falling to 18 per cent for Japan and 23 per cent for France and Poland, 25 per cent for Canada and 26 per cent for Australia).

On top of this, CSR is still criticized for the way businesses have used their CSR outreach in a duplicitous manner; presenting a virtuous side when the reality is core business operations that cause damage to the human and natural environments, and/or where poor ethical and legal decision-making takes place (Banerjee 2008). More specifically, CSR is often seen as either:

- being used primarily in political lobbying to soften the image of corporations to appeal more to governments and consumers (Edward and Willmott 2008; Salamon and Siegfried 1977);
- an inadequate attempt to redress the much-publicized widespread abuse by corporations of a wide range of stakeholders (Gold 2003);
- having very little long-term substance especially in improving standards of living to poorer parts of society (Frankental 2001; Waddock 2008; Banerjee 2014);
- a deliberate attempt to 'greenwash' the negative public image of the company through highlighting its good deeds (especially prevalent in low and medium income areas of the world (Fig 2005; Kallio, 2007).

One of the staple but weakest aspects of CSR – philanthropy– is actually omitted from some definitions. For example, the International Organization for Standardization (ISO) 26000 defines CSR as 'taking responsibility for your impact on society and environment, rather than as charity. It emphasizes sustainable aims, engaging with stakeholders and respecting international norms' (ISO 2010).

Therefore it should come as little surprise that the term CSR is an increasingly devalued term that is used in a 'catch all' manner to include a multitude of terms that relate to, or are alternative names for, CSR. For instance, CSR is used to describe a range of activities including (but not limited to) employee rights, social development, bribery/corruption, impact on the natural environment (pollution, waste management), issues across the supply chain, core management practices (corporate governance), philanthropy, human rights or awareness campaigns. Dahlsrud (2008) has suggested 37 definitions exist.[1] CSR therefore can be regarded as a ubiquitous and meaningless term.

While CSR arguably fails to convince many that companies are taking their social responsibilities more seriously (especially the philanthropy dimension), there has been a growing trend in the last decade towards a more 'hard-edged' form of CSR that is targeted towards ensuring that companies engage more fully with a wider range of stakeholders and issues, even if the motive to do so is to reduce the record levels of financial penalties which businesses are receiving for their illegal or unethical decision-making. Some refer to this form of CSR as 'ESG'; this stands simply for the terms/words of 'environmental, social and governance'. Indeed, there is a growing level of contemporary research which shows that companies with 'good ESG' (opposed to 'bad ESG') increase their revenue and profit *because* of their record of good ESG (Eccles *et al.* 2011).

This chapter represents a departure from my previous work on this subject area, which has been highly critical of the relationship between sport, corporations and CSR (see for example, Levermore 2013). Instead, the main focus is to show how sport's use in sport for development and peace (SDP), particularly via CSR – which has undeniably focused almost exclusively on philanthropy and the weaker dimensions of CSR – might be recalibrated to focus more on ESG to the benefit of both longer-term societal requirements as well as the financial bottom line that is so important to the business community. The chapter progresses by charting the relationship between sport, corporations and CSR. It then focuses on the growing trend of 'ESG' and suggests ways in which sport CSR might be revised to pivot towards ESG, and in the process hopefully reduce some of the weaknesses associated with CSR/ESG.

CSR and SDP

Examples of sport used as part of CSR to advance development that I have catalogued previously and have been initiated since 2005 (some of these are no longer in existence) include:

- Ferrero Kinder and Sport global programme, which is directed at the development of children to have a healthy lifestyle in a range of developed and developing societies;
- Huawei, which uses philanthropic donations to support sports events across sub-Saharan Africa;
- Lenovo, Microsoft, eBay, Bloomberg (and many other) organizations that support the largest sports NGO – Right to Play – through philanthropic donations;
- Adidas, through donations to a variety of SDP projects;
- Bayer, whose 'Bayer Care' initiative in Brazil includes the creation of a football academy with the stated intention of encouraging disadvantaged children to attend school;
- BHP Billiton, which supports educational development through its 'Kicking Goals' education programme;
- CLSA Bank, whose Indochina Starfish programme runs in Cambodia; philanthropic support for a project using football to improve education;
- BP, sponsors of Football for Peace, a UNICEF-run football league that aims to generate peace and incorporate children affected or involved in the civil war back into society;
- Charlton Athletic Football Club (London, UK) partners with a range of organizations (British Airways and the police) to provide crime awareness/distraction programmes in London and Johannesburg;
- Deloitte (South Africa) run a range of employment skills classes linked to sports events;
- Diageo, whose employee volunteer scheme in Latin America centres on education programmes that use sport as a vehicle to encourage attendance and engagement;
- Catrol, whose Skillz holiday programme uses grassroots football to assemble young people in South Africa; part of the programme is used to help generate HIV/Aids awareness and testing;
- FC Barcelona, who have pledged to allocate at least 0.7 per cent of their turnover each year to international development programmes that include social integration and conflict alleviation (such as in the Israeli-Palestinian conflict);
- FIFA, whose 'Football for Hope' scheme works with NGOs on a range of educational, social integration and empowerment initiatives;
- Nike, whose various SDP initiatives include philanthropic support for 'Together for Girls' in refugee camps in east Africa, to help the empowerment of women through leadership training;
- UC Rusal, which helped build sports facilities for able/disabled young people in some developing regions of the world; some of these are linked to health programmes.[2]

This leads us to the term 'Sport CSR', which refers to two types of corporations using sport as a vehicle to assist a range of society initiatives; in this context, for development and peace. The first type is from companies outside of the sports industry (such as financial institutions) and the second is from within the sports industry. As the summary above highlights, both tend to provide largely philanthropic support (such as charitable donations and employee volunteerism) to support NGOs using sport to assist development.

Because of this connection with philanthropy, 'Sport CSR' in particular is associated with the criticisms sketched in the introduction from society perspectives. Chen *et al.* (2008) were one of the first to highlight this link between sport and weak CSR for four reasons. First, most philanthropy and awareness campaigns are a 'pet project' linked to those leading an organization and are inevitably short term (for example, the average length of tenure for CEOs of the largest 500 US companies was down to 4.6 years in 2013). Second, these are the areas most likely to be associated with greenwashing. In the sports industry, athletes and agents have realized that generates 'positive association' to help offset negative media attention (headlines that focus on drug-taking, greed, racism, sexism and violence etc.) (Babiak and Mills 2012). Third, the goals of both are often unrelated to the core strategies of a company and therefore rarely relate to the direction that the company and its employees are heading in (meaning the employees often resent having to volunteer to work on these programmes). Fourth, the most extreme criticism is the concern that philanthropy not only distorts decision-making to the advantage of the corporation which makes the donation but is also a conduit used to launder money (Wulfson 2001; Barnes 2005).

Replacing CSR with ESG?

These concerns raised by 'critical CSR' tend to be voiced by NGOs, the media and civil society groups. From within business, there are other approaches critical of CSR – especially those that view it as a drain on financial and employee resources (Karnani 2010). Ultimately, the criticisms of the effectiveness of CSR, as well as the meaningless and over-used term it has become, has led to much dissatisfaction in the corporate and academic worlds (Edward and Willmott 2008).

Combined, the criticism towards CSR and the way it has become a largely meaningless term has resulted in both a more concerted attempt to identify which aspects of CSR work for both society and business, and to disaggregate CSR into its 'compartments' (Osuji 2011: 31). Debate relates to the level of commitment that an organization shows in applying CSR. Is CSR integral to the 'layers of responsibility' that are expected within a corporation, the most important being economic, then legal responsibilities, then ethical decision-making with philanthropy the least important (Carroll 1991)? Or is CSR applied in a residual, 'distant' and disengaged manner (compared to proximate and engaged) (Ponte *et al.* 2009)? Carroll's 'pyramid of CSR' suggests that the social responsibilities of companies start with having a strong economic base (the largest responsibility that they have), with knowledge of, and adherence to legal obligations (second priority) followed by the need to make decisions that are ethical, taking into account a wide group of stakeholders when decisions are being made. It is only at the apex of the pyramid where philanthropy (the least important of the four) is located.

This drive has ushered in the relatively new term of ESG; 'E' stands for environmental issues; 'S' for social and 'G' for governance. The intention is for ESG to be less meaningless compared to CSR, reduce the weighting that CSR has placed on philanthropy and tie initiatives associated with ESG more closely to the central business operations of an organization. To show how effective ESG can be to these operations and the economic responsibilities aspect of the Carroll pyramid, there has been a significant growth in research, which suggests that companies with clearly targeted and long-term, strong ESG commitments are becoming more likely to see strong corporate financial returns as a result when compared to weaker forms of ESG. The seminal work of Eccles *et al.* (2011) focused on 180 US companies (of the same size and in comparable industry sectors), and those that voluntarily decided before 1993 to adopt policies consistent with 'high sustainability' outperformed the 'low sustainability' companies in financial terms. 'High sustainability' means companies that build long-term environmental and social policies into the core business model of the corporation and that the governance of the company is clearly concerned about its environmental and social impact – potentially at the cost of raising its profits. These companies are also likely to demonstrate visible signs of actively addressing and managing stakeholder concerns (with stakeholder feedback going directly to the senior management of the company) and have sophisticated measurement and reporting mechanisms. Another important trait of high sustainability companies is that senior directors are responsible for ESG issues rather than it being delegated to junior members in the public relations, marketing or human resources departments, and that a sustainability committee reports to the board. Some of the companies may well include ESG satisfaction metrics as part of the annual bonus received by the CEO of the company (Eccles *et al.* 2011: 3–4).

It should be noted here that more research is required to further substantiate these findings. Other studies (such as McKinsey 2009) suggest that this positive correlation usually occurs on the basis of three 'ifs': the company has (1) a long term commitment to CSR; (2) engages in 'good quality' CSR; and (3) is selective with focused CSR (so, environmental, social or governance or two of these but not all three). McKinsey (2009) even suggest that companies operating outside of the most developed economies are more likely to see better corporate financial performance (CFP) than companies operating in more mature CSR regions. At this juncture, it is important to note a difference between the theory of the term ESG and its use in practice. Many companies and practitioners who speak of 'ESG' are simply replacing the term of CSR without changing company practices that are at the heart of the criticism of CSR (in other words, philanthropy is still the main focus with fragments of environment, social or governance issues attached to it).

Applying 'good ESG' to CSR and SDP?

Having highlighted the criticisms associated with sport CSR – especially in its lack of meaningful long-term impact on development – this section suggests a tentative direction in which SDP might be viewed and engaged through this prism of ESG. The section sketches out a starting point for the kind of research that others in this field might want to take further. That starting point needs to take on board some of the salient points from the preceding section – namely, that the companies which are best focused on whether their ESG policies benefit both society and CFP need to:

- **Be proximate to SDP,** meaning that the *type of industry* that they are based in has strong resonance with sports as it means that ESG engagement is likely to be something of strong relevance to their business model. At the same time, the companies also need a *presence in parts of the world where SDP takes place* (such as lower income countries in sub-Saharan Africa or Asia).
- These companies need to have built **long-term environmental and social policies** into the core business model of the corporation, and the governance of the company should be clearly concerned about its environmental and social impact – potentially at the cost of raising its profits.
- These companies are also likely to demonstrate **visible signs of actively addressing and managing stakeholder concerns** (with stakeholder feedback going directly to the senior management of the company).

- Senior directors are responsible for ESG issues rather than it being delegated to junior members in the public relations, marketing or human relations departments and that a sustainability committee reports to the board.
- Have **sophisticated measurement** and reporting mechanisms.
- Some of the companies may well include an **ESG satisfaction metric** as part of the annual bonus received by the CEO of the company.

If these conditions are met, we would expect that the companies will have a good ESG reputation (as measured by a range of independent indicators) and that their CFP would also have increased in the past 10–20 years. For this chapter, I have selected four of the largest companies in the sports apparel industry – Nike, Adidas, VF Corporation and Under Armour. This is an industry expected to be worth US$184.6 billion by 2020 (Allied Market Research n.d.) and has a manufacturing footprint across many parts of the world in which SDP takes place, with signs of a slow shift from its Asia heartlands of China, Vietnam, Cambodia and Bangladesh to east Africa (because of rising labour costs) and arguably back towards its HQ base (partly due to political pressure in countries such as the USA). A summary of their business operations (history, size, where they operate) is included in Table 9.1 below. The table also provides a summary of their ESG processes and framework – as much as can be discerned from publicly available information.

So, all of these companies are in an industry that can be regarded as being proximate to SDP and have operations in countries where SDP takes place. The next step is to assess the extent to which their ESG engagement has been considered to be 'strong' or 'weak' versions. Researchers who assess this relationship in detail should cross-check the companies in depth against the categories noted above. This chapter turns to two ESG/CSR ratings agencies – Sustainalytics and CSR Hub[3] – who provide historical data to assess the extent to which ESG is rated against these four companies and, in so doing, touch upon these categories. A summary of their rankings is presented in Figures 9.1–9.5.

Based on the data derived from these two ratings agencies, the ranking order of the four companies would seem to indicate that Adidas be ranked first, Nike second, with VF lagging closer to industry average in third and Under Armour below industry average in fourth place. Sustainalytics has Adidas leading – or close to leading – in most ESG categories when compared with 52 other companies in this sector. It has a particularly strong record for environment and social, while performing strongly in governance. For environmental issues, Adidas receives credit for its clear, top-level management, policy, initiatives to reduce greenhouse gas emissions, commitment to renewable energy and reducing the use of carbon in the manufacturing process. Its only recorded weakness is in its failure to disclose water usage. Under social, Adidas is the only one of the companies focused on here which attempts at some level of transparency of its supply chain, openly listing its independent manufacturers on its website. It scores highly in discrimination and diversity policies but poorly in health and safety certifications. For governance, it (among many full grades) receives top grades for ESG governance and performance targets but is poorly graded for ESG reporting and independent verifications of ESG statements.

Nike has also some way above the average ESG ratings for the sector, although it has transformed from being close to a leader in 2013 to industry average in 2017. It has seen a decline in all three aspects of ESG, with governance being its weakest indicator. Under social issues, it performs well in reducing employee fatalities and for having diversity programmes but poorly in health and safety management and in addressing discrimination. For environmental aspects, Nike shows no evidence of a formal policy (it also insufficiently discloses water usage or carbon emissions) but does implement a strong environmental management system (it has a

Table 9.1 An overview of four sports apparel companies

Company name	Adidas	Nike	Under Armour	VF Corp
History/countries operated in	Founded in 1948. This is a German sports apparel manufacturer that sources its products to over 1,000 suppliers that span 61 countries (including Bangladesh, Cambodia, Nicaragua, Myanmar, South Africa and Pakistan). It has 57,620 employees	This sports apparel and sports equipment company was founded in 1964 (as Blue Ribbon Sports) in the US. It operates in over 120 countries with supplies from countries including Indonesia, China, Taiwan, India, Thailand, Vietnam, Pakistan, the Philippines and Malaysia. Employs more than 44,000 people	A sports apparel and footwear company, founded in 1996 in Baltimore, US. As recently as 2015 65% of its products were produced in 14 low costs countries (including China, Jordan, Vietnam and Indonesia). However, it has stated plans to manufacture more of its apparel in the US. 5,800 employees worldwide	A company founded in the US in 1899 that specialises in lifestyle apparel, footwear and equipment that includes sports apparel (mainly outdoor and action sports). It is the name behind powerful brands such as Timberland and North Face. Goods are sourced from China (16%), Americas (31%), Vietnam (15%), Bangladesh (15%), Cambodia (5%). Employs 54,000 people
Financial size	Second largest global sportswear manufacturer. It has a current market capitalisation of €31.26 billion	Market capitalization of US$93.01 makes Nike the largest company in this sector	Market cap of US$8.9 billion making it the third largest company in the sector. It is the second largest company in its sector in the US (after Nike)	Market cap of US$20.82 billion. In some aspects of the sports apparel industry (such as US sports footwear industry), this is the second largest company in its bracket

Sources: Company websites, industry reviews and the *Financial Times* company review pages

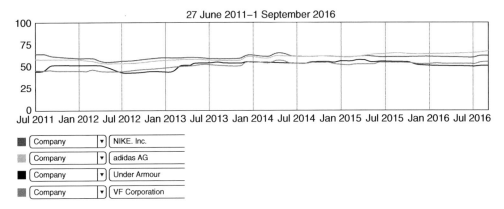

Figure 9.1 Comparing ESG ratings from Adidas, Nike, Under Armour and VF Corporation
Source: CSR Hub 2017

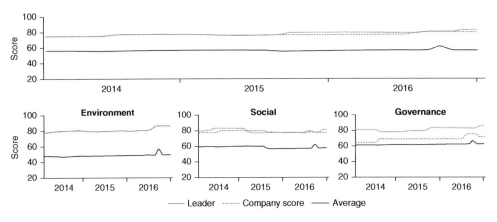

Figure 9.2 ESG analysis of Adidas
Source: Sustainalytics

board member responsible for environmental issues – as well as one overseeing ESG). Under governance, it scores highly for ESG reporting, an independent audit committee, gender diversity at board level but poorly for ESG performance targets, verification of its ESG reporting (not externally verified) and for engaging in political lobbying.

VF Corp is currently in a similar ESG situation to Nike, although historically it has a lower grading than its bigger competitor. Labour relations are its poorest ranking and it is mid-range for environmental policy/management, working conditions, discrimination and diversity policies, and employee fatalities, and very low for renewable energy, disclosing water and carbon usage, health and safety certifications, ESG performance targets and ESG reporting/verification of ESG engagement. Under Armour is very much the ESG laggard with an environmental performance much lower than industry average, social being slightly below average and governance slightly above average (due partly to a board member being responsible for governance only – there is no board member responsible for the E and S issues).

It needs to be stated here that these ESG ratings can be contested as the 'top level' (summary of) results because they tend to normalise grades for an industry by conveniently overlooking

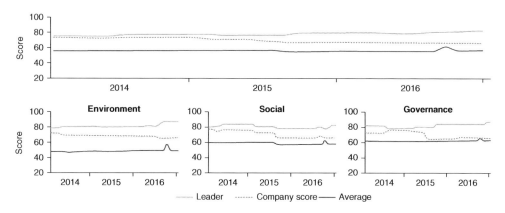

Figure 9.3 ESG analysis of Nike
Source: Sustainalytics

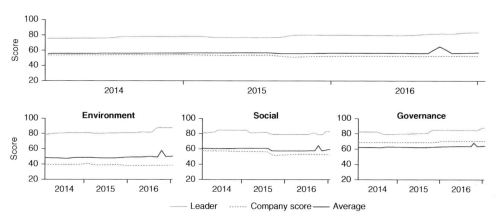

Figure 9.4 ESG analysis of Under Armour
Source: Sustainalytics

the fact that the textile and footwear industry is regarded as the second most polluting industry on the planet with very high water usage required to manufacture its products. It also has a poor record in governing its supply chain, with significant social issues including child labour, low pay, very poor working conditions and other exploitation of workers (the full reports on the companies actually show where the industry sits across the ESG sub-categories and gives a more complete picture).[4] Even the highest ranking of the companies faces accusations of labour rights issues (Adidas), human rights infringements (Adidas) and bribery/corruption (Nike). The ESG rankings I have shown here therefore do not convey the full context of the ESG issues facing these companies. That said, the indicators shown do usefully rank the organizations examined here and help paint a picture as to some of the strengths and weaknesses that the companies have – relative to each other.

Moving on, according to the argument presented throughout this chapter, companies with strong ESG should be rewarded with strong corporate financial performance. For the purposes of analysis, there are a great multitude of potential indicators to choose from to assess CFP and thorough research papers that might be conducted in the future that take on board a more diverse

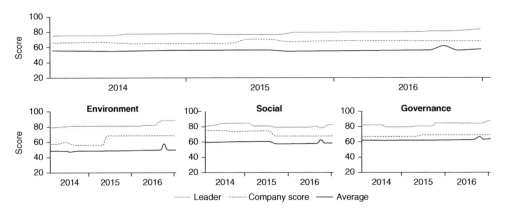

Figure 9.5 ESG analysis of VF Corp
Source: Sustainalytics

set of statistics than the one chosen for this chapter. The data chosen for this chapter relates to the profitability of each corporation, especially its net profit margin (the ratio of profits to total revenues) – companies can show profits of many millions or billions but if the net profit margin is a low percentage then marginal increases in operating costs, currency fluctuations, or an increase in the competitive advantage of competitors can prove perilous to that organization. Net profitability is one of the key indicators economists use to assess the financial health (and therefore CFP) of companies.

The 15-year financial performance of the four companies from publicly available financial data indicates that Nike has on average the highest net profit margins, rarely approaching as low as 5 per cent (in 2009) with most years performing in the 10–15 per cent range. Next comes VF Corp, with a greater level of volatility, dipping under 5 per cent at some intervals in the timespan focused on, but also occasionally rising above the 10 per cent net profit margin. Adidas has a fairly steady margin, largely averaging at the 5–6 per cent range but occasionally under 1 per cent (with a negative score at the start of 2013). Under Armour shows the greatest level of volatility; each year it has quarters showing a net profitability percentage between 0–2.5 per cent and other times of the year at 7.5–10 per cent. What to make of such CFP performance? Nike and VF Corp, ranked close together under ESG rankings, perform better on the indicator selected for the purposes of this chapter. Adidas – the best ESG performer – is marginally (and arguably) better in the past decade than Under Armour. This may well show that there is not a strong correlation between strong ESG and strong CFP – especially using the data selected here. Anecdotal evidence at the time of writing would suggest that Adidas (Fortune 2016a) has had the best financial performances of 2016, with Nike, VF Corp and (especially) Under Armour (Fortune 2016b) all in some financial turmoil. If this thread turns into a longer-term trend, then perhaps this linkage of net profit margin to CFP and ESG performance could be developed further. Likewise, more sophisticated analyses using stronger justifications for interpreting CFP (and ESG) offer one area of study that future researchers might like to pursue. I do need to reiterate at this stage that this is just a starting point of the research and that a more thorough investigation is required both of the strengths of ESG of the companies with a more nuanced unpacking of CFP, and then a better way of trying to assess whether a positive correlation exists between the two.

Conclusion

This chapter marks a slight departure from my prior work on how sport is used as a vehicle by companies towards achieving corporate social responsibility, and enhancing development and peace. In previous work, I have been very critical of the ability that sport CSR has in making positive, sustained contributions to society in countries and regions that fall under the definition of international development. I have suspended some of that scepticism for this chapter to follow an emerging line of thinking from management studies that echoes some views from development studies: that the impact of CSR both for the company (increased CFP) and society improves if there is a long-term commitment by the company to CSR (meaning strong ESG).

Therefore, the chapter has attempted to show that although business has some way to go to becoming a strong 'steward in society' (Blowfield and Murray 2008: 10), the recalibration of CSR around the concept of ESG might be a worthy pursuit for those hoping to balance the primary requirement of the private sector to focus on its economic responsibilities while also strengthening its legal, ethical, environmental, social and governance capabilities. The relationship between sport, the private sector and CSR in SDP shows that weak CSR pervades this connection and is in dire need of revising its approach; to wean itself off philanthropy (often excluded from definitions of CSR let alone strong ESG) and to ensure a closer connection between its core business model and the SDP with which it engages.

To help progress this relationship further, this chapter has reflected on recent literature that provides a glimpse of the linkage between CFP and strong ESG. I have taken four companies that are proximate to SDP and summarized how all four are regarded in relation to ESG engagement and also highlighted one aspect of CFP. The data points I have used have reflected the ESG rankings of each company and one basic economic variable. That a strong correlation does not exist might suggest that the tenuous nature of CSR is still inherent in ESG – and that changing the name has not resulted in a changing orientation or meaning. However, failing to find a positive correlation here might also be due to incorrect data points being sought, especially concerning CFP. I hope that future papers and research will take this argument further.

Notes

1   This includes corporate social performance, corporate social responsiveness, corporate sustainability (the environment features prominently in many CSR initiatives), corporate citizenship, corporate philanthropy, corporate social investment (CSI), creating shared value (CSV), economic/social/governance (ESG), corporate accountability, corporate moral agency, and social entrepreneurship.
2   Some of these have previously been referenced as Levermore (2010; 2013).
3   In terms of full disclosure, Sustainalytics provided this research data. Sustainalytics is a global for profit organization that has developed data on ESG for a range of clients for over 25 years. CSR Hub – a similar organization – also provided some additional information.
4   For instance, Sustainalytics reports that the sports apparel and footwear sector is in the lowest category (0 out of 5) for waste management, labour relations, human rights, occupational health and safety and environmental impact of products.

References

Allied Market Research. (n.d.). Sports Apparel Market by End User (Men, Women, Kids) and Mode of Sale (Retail stores, Supermarkets, Brand outlets, Discount stores, Online stores) – Global Opportunity

Analysis and Industry Forecast, 2014–2020. Available at: www.alliedmarketresearch.com/sports-apparel-market (accessed 1 February 2017).

Babiak, K. and Mills, B. (2012) An investigation into professional athlete philanthropy: Why charity is part of the game. *Journal of Sport Management, 26*(2), 150–176.

Banerjee, S. B. (2008) Corporate social responsibility: The good, the bad and the ugly. *Critical Sociology, 34*(1), 51–79.

Banerjee, S. B. (2014). A critical perspective on corporate social responsibility: Towards a global governance framework. *Critical Perspectives on International Business, 10*(1/2), 84–95.

Barnes, S. (2005). Global flows: Terror, oil and strategic philanthropy. *Review of African Political Economy, 32*(104/5), 232–252.

Blowfield, M. and Murray, A. (2008). *Corporate Responsibility*. Oxford & New York: Oxford University Press.

Carroll, A. (1991). The pyramid of corporate social responsibility: Toward the moral management of organizational stakeholders. *Business Horizons, 34*(4), 39–48.

Chen, J. C., Patten, D. M. and Roberts, R. W. (2008). Corporate charitable contributions: A corporate social performance or legitimacy strategy. *Journal of Business Ethics, 82*(1), 131–144.

Dahlsrud, A. (2008). How corporate social responsibility is defined: An analysis of 37 definitions. *Corporate Social Responsibility and Environmental Management, 15*(1), 1–13.

Eccles, E. G., Ioannou, I. and Serafim, G. (2011). The Impact of Corporate Sustainability on Organizational Process and Performance, Harvard Business Working Paper.

Edelman, Harvard University Kennedy School of Government and International Business Leaders Forum. (n.d.). Business and International Development: Opportunities, Responsibilities and Expectations. Available at: www.hks.harvard.edu/m-rcbg/CSRI/publications/report_5_edelman_survey.pdf (accessed 12 January 2017).

Edelman. (2017). 2017 Edelman Trust Barometer. Available at: www.edelman.com/trust2017/ (accessed 28 January 2017).

Edward, P. and H. Willmott. (2008) Dialogue: Corporate Citizenship: Rise or Demise of a Myth? *Academy of Management Review, 33* (3), 771–775.

Fig, D. (2005). Manufacturing amnesia: Corporate social responsibility in South Africa. *International Affairs, 81*(3), 599–617.

Fortune. (2016a). Why Adidas Is Outperforming Nike, Under Armour. Available at: http://fortune.com/2016/08/04/adidas-outperforming-nike-ua/ (accessed 10 February 2017).

Fortune. (2016b). Why Shares of Under Armour Are Tanking. Available at: http://fortune.com/2016/10/25/under-armour-shares-tumble/ (accessed 10 February 2017).

Frankental, P. (2001). Corporate social responsibility – a PR invention? *Corporate Communications: An International Journal, 6*(1), 8–23.

Gold, D. (2003). Thinkpiece – CSR is No More Than a Fig Leaf for Corporates. *Third Sector*. Available at: www.thirdsector.co.uk/opinion-thinkpiece-csr-no-fig-leaf-corporates/article/611190 (accessed 22 June 2018).

ISO (International Organization for Standardization). (2010). ISO 26000 – Social Responsibility. Available at: www.iso.org/iso/home/standards/iso26000.html (accessed 21 May 2018).

Kallio, T. J. (2007). Taboos in corporate social responsibility discourse. *Journal of Business Ethics, 74*(2), 165–175.

Karnani, A. (2010). The case against corporate social responsibility. *Wall Street Journal, 23*(14), 1–5.

Levermore, R. (2010) CSR for development through sport: Examining its potential and limitations. *Third World Quarterly, 31*(2), 223–241.

Levermore, R. (2013). CSR through sport from a critical perspective: Failing to address gross corporate misconduct? *The Routledge Handbook of Sport and Corporate Social Responsibility*. London: Routledge, pp. 52–61.

Levermore, R., and Moore, N. (2015). The need to apply new theories to 'Sport CSR. *Corporate Governance: The International Journal of Business in Society, 15*(2), 249–253.

McKinsey. (2009). Valuing Corporate Social Responsibility – McKinsey Global Survey Results. Available at: www.mckinsey.com/business-functions/strategy-and-corporate-finance/our-insights/valuing-corporate-social-responsibility-mckinsey-global-survey-results (accessed 10 October 2016).

Osuji, O. (2011). Fluidity of regulation-CSR nexus: The multinational corporate corruption example. *Journal of Business Ethics, 103*(1), 31–57.

Overseas Development Institute. (2012). Let's do Business Together – the role of the private sector in international development. Available at: www.odi.org/sites/odi.org.uk/files/odi-assets/publications-opinion-files/7734.pdf (accessed 12 December 2016).

Ponte, S., Richey, K. A. and Baab, M. (2009). Bono's product (RED) initiative: Corporate social responsibility that solves the problems of 'distant others'. *Third World Quarterly, 30*(2), 301–317.

Salamon, L. M. and Siegfried, J. J. (1977) Economic Power and Political Influence: the impact of industrial strategy on public policy. *The American Political Science Review, 71*(3), 1026–1043.

World Bank. (2003). Public Policy for Corporate Social responsibility. Available at: info.worldbank.org/etools/docs/library/../publicpolicy_econference.pdf, (accessed 30 April 2016).

Waddock, S. (2008). Corporate citizenship: The dark-side paradoxes of success. In G. Flynn (ed.), *Leadership and Business Ethics*. London: Routledge.

Wulfson, M. (2001). The ethics of corporate social responsibility and philanthropic ventures. *Journal of Business Ethics, 29*(1–2), 135–145.

10

SDP and the Sustainable Development Goals

Oliver Dudfield

Introduction

In September 2015 the United Nations General Assembly adopted the *2030 Agenda for Sustainable Development*. Central to this Agenda are 17 Sustainable Development Goals (SDGs) which 'set out the bold and transformative step urgently needed to shift the world onto a sustainable and resilient path' (UNGA 2015). The 2030 Agenda recognises that sport can be 'an important enabler of sustainable development' (ibid.: 37). This represents the first time that the intentional use of sport-based approaches to contribute to sustainable development, or Sport for Development and Peace (SDP), has been recognized in an overarching global development plan and policy agenda.

The SDGs extend on the reach of the preceding Millennium Development Goals (MDGs). While eradicating poverty remains a central issue, there is a greater emphasis in the SDGs on social and environmental development issues, many of which have been exacerbated through accelerated globalization. Critically, the SDGs are positioned as being relevant to each country and across contexts. At the same time, sections of academia and civil society have questioned whether the SDGs go far enough in setting out a plan to address growing global inequality and institute necessary reform of the global development architecture (Howard and Wheeler 2015; Sexsmith and McMichael 2015; Deacon 2016; van Bergeijk and van der Hoeven 2017). Amid these debates, the global community declared that the SDGs will define the 'agenda for global action for the next 15 years' (UNGA 2015: 51). Accordingly, they provide an important reference point for all government, private sector and civil society actors – including those within sport.

This chapter posits that reference to 'the growing contribution of sport to the realization of development and peace' (UNGA 2015: 37) in the 2030 Agenda, represents an important milestone in the recognition of the role of sport in development. But, as the single reference to sport in the 2030 Agenda, it is limited in scope, meaning there is need for further critical reflection on the role of sport-based interventions in efforts to achieve the SDGs.

To facilitate this reflection, this chapter identifies key tenets of the 2030 Agenda most relevant to the SDP field and, in doing so, proposes that a measured approach is most suitable in analysing the potential contribution of sport. The chapter starts by introducing the SDG agenda and the implications for the SDP field. It then proceeds to outline an approach to analyse the contribution of SDP to the SDGs, before concluding with a presentation of exemplar analysis of the contribution SDP-orientated policies and interventions could make to selected SDGs and associated targets.

SDP and global development goals

Acknowledgement in the 2030 Agenda that sport can be an important enabler of sustainable development builds on a range of previous international declarations and policy statements. Between 2003 and 2016 the United Nations General Assembly passed ten resolutions on sport as a means to promote education, health, development and peace.[1] The *Revised International Charter on Physical Education Physical Activity and Sport* (UNESCO 2015) alongside the *Kazan Action Plan* (UNESCO 2017b) *and Declaration of Berlin* (UNESCO 2013) – the key outcome documents of the last two International Conferences of Ministers and Senior Officials Responsible for Physical Education and Sport – also identify that sport-based approaches, when appropriately designed and delivered, can yield benefits to individuals, communities and society at large. Commonwealth governments have also been prominent in recognising and endorsing the potential contribution of sport to sustainable development (Commonwealth Secretariat 2014; 2016). These international policy declarations have coincided with a substantial growth in the number of projects and programmes employing sport in development and peacebuilding efforts, and a growth in academic work focused on SDP (Kidd 2008; Schulenkorf and Adair 2014).

The MDGs and the growth of the SDP field

The adoption of the first set of global development goals was an important catalyst for the growth and formalization of SDP. Deriving from the United Nations Millennium Declaration, these goals, known as the Millennium Development Goals (MDGs), have been applauded for galvanizing action, while at the same time critiqued for being too narrow in focus, for paying insufficient attention to structural issues affecting global development and for containing only limited mechanisms to measure progress (Sumner and Tiwari 2010; Fukuda-Parr 2012; 2014). When these goals expired in 2015, significant global progress had been made in a number of areas prioritized, but ultimately a number of the targets had not been achieved (United Nations 2016).

The galvanizing effect of the MDGs extended to the SDP field. They became an important reference point for advocates promoting the role of sport in development. These efforts culminated in a number of high profile international conferences, the establishment of the United Nations Office on Sport for Development and Peace and the publication of a range of policy documents promoting the role sport could play in delivering the MDGs (Lindsey *et al.* 2017). The Millennium Declaration itself called on member states to 'observe the Olympic truce and … support the International Olympic Committee's efforts to promote peace and human understanding' (UNGA 2000: 10).

Fifteen years on, reference to sport as an enabler of sustainable development in the 2030 Agenda was more substantial. Even so, it would be premature to conclude that the references in the SDGs framework, which are limited in scope, will lead to a significant increase in support and resourcing for SDP. The reference to sport in the preamble of the 2030 Agenda is its solitary mention across the SDG documentation. Physical activity, physical education and play also do not feature. Given the scant guidance provided to SDP field in the SDG documentation further analysis is required.

The transformative agenda of the SDGs and the implications for SDP

Examining the scope and central tenets of the SDGs provides an important starting point in assessing the implications for SDP. Three aspects are particularly noteworthy. First, the SDGs have been positioned as universal and relevant across developing and developed contexts alike. Second, there is recognition that the new agenda must 'leave no one behind'. And third, the 2030 Agenda gives emphasis to the interconnectivity of the economic, social and environmental dimensions of sustainable development.

A universal agenda

The SDGs are presented as involving the entire world, developed and developing countries alike' (UNGA 2015: 5). This focus represents important progress on the MDG agenda, which was perceived as being overly focused on actions in, and by, developing countries (Ojogwu 2009; Fukuda-Parr 2012). Associated criticism has been levelled at the SDGs, questioning whether they go far enough in calling for reform of the global development architecture or in instituting mechanisms to enforce implementation (Hajer *et al.* 2015; Sexsmith and McMichael 2015). There is also concern whether a trend towards prioritizing national interest over multi-lateral cooperation will limit the catalysing effect of the SDGs (Deacon 2016). While these debates are important to note, efforts to position the SDGs as relevant 'for all nations and people and for all segments of society' (UNGA 2015: 4) is a key theme and of particular relevance to SDP.

The value of sport as a 'universal language' is among the key assets promoted by SDP stakeholders. Many SDP actors advocate that sport can be used as a valuable tool in promoting tolerance, mutual understanding and forging cross-cultural linkages (SDPIWG 2008; UNOSDP 2011). They posit that the popularity and universality of sports is sufficient that its reach cuts across economic, social and cultural boundaries. However, positioning sport as universal and politically neutral should be approached with caution. The impact of sport on individuals and communities is malleable. While often positive, sport can also be a platform for racist, discriminatory and divisive attitudes (Collins and Kay 2014; Hylton *et al.* 2015; Kilvington and Price 2017).

The relationship between sport and globalization also warrants attention. Debate on the extent to which the SDGs address the impacts of globalization and growing inequality linked with aspects of neoliberal economic policies are likely to intensify (Ostry *et al.* 2016). It is probable that these debates will, in turn, be amplified within sport. Reflecting on the link between sport and globalization is also pertinent in specific analysis of SDP-orientated policy and practice. Much of the discourse in this field over the last two decades has been framed by 'the perception that the use of sport may assist the international development process' (Levermore and Beacom 2009: 9). This dynamic underscores the relevance of academic critiques arguing for more equitable relationships between actors from the global north and global south (Darnell 2012; Mwaanga and Mwansa 2013), the prioritization of locally led approaches (Lindsey *et al.* 2017) and enhanced consideration for South-South approaches in the SDP field (Huish 2011; Darnell and Huish 2015).

The disconnect between international and domestically focused SDP policy and practice has received less critical attention; despite domestic policy frameworks being underdeveloped in many contexts (Dudfield 2014; Keim and De Coning 2014; Lindsey 2016; Sanders *et al.* 2017). The need to strengthen SDP-orientated domestic policy frameworks has been explicitly recognized by Commonwealth (Commonwealth Secretariat 2014) and international meetings of ministers of sport (UNESCO 2017b). In adopting the 2030 Agenda, global leaders also emphasized the importance of 'respecting national policies and priorities … in particular for developing states' (UNGA 2015: 21). This emphasis provides an impetus to scale up domestic SDP policy, partnerships and programming. There are promising examples emerging in developed and developing contexts, with Mauritius (Republic of Mauritius 2017), Sierra Leone, Rwanda, Zambia, (Lindsey and Chapman 2017) Singapore (MCCY, n.d.) and the United Kingdom (DCMS 2015) among the growing number of countries who have bolstered SDP-orientated domestic policy in recent years.

Leave no one behind

A rallying call at the centre of the 2030 Agenda is to 'leave no one behind'. This principle is grounded in the universal declaration of human rights and recognition of growing inequality across and within contexts (UNGA 2015). In adopting the SDGs, global leaders resolved 'to combat inequalities within and among countries' (ibid.: 3), acknowledging that the SDGs will only be achieved 'if wealth is shared and income inequality is addressed' (ibid.: 27). While there are critiques of the level to which issues of inequality are addressed in the SDG framework (van Bergeijk and van der Hoeven 2017), in emphasizing 'leaving no one behind', the 2030 Agenda does provide an aspirational and ethical social policy norm that can be applied across sectors (Deacon 2016).

As the contribution of sport 'to combating discrimination and marginalization, (and) enabling the full and equal participation of all in societal life' is regularly promoted by SDP advocates (UNOSDP 2011: 9), the central tenant of 'leave no one behind' in the SDG framework is particularly relevant. The potential to employ sport-based interventions in support of youth development, gender empowerment, the inclusion of people with a disability and in engaging marginalized groups features prominently in SDP policy publications and among the outcomes reported by SDP NGOs (Kay and Dudfield 2013). However, aligning the championing of sport as tool to promote equality and the 'leave no one behind' agenda of the SDGs should be approached with a degree of nuance and must be more cognisant of structural inequalities in both sport and the SDP field.

The 2030 Agenda emphasizes that addressing institutional and, to some extent, structural issues will be important in tackling inequality. Targets on equitable representation in governance structures, enhancing social protection systems and access to justice are included in the SDG framework. In contrast, SDP interventions have predominantly been targeted towards individual 'empowerment' and on delivering programmatic-level outcomes (Sanders 2016). Less emphasis has been placed on broader governance, policy and structural issues (Lindsey 2016).

Addressing this incoherence therefore becomes an important consideration in analysing potential contributions of SDP to the leave-no-one-behind agenda central to the SDGs. Organizations promoting sport as a development tool will need to increasingly exemplify principles of equality and equity, not just in the rhetorical language used to describe their interventions, but also in structure. This applies equally to organizations with a primary focus on SDP and those in 'mainstream sport' promoting their activities as a vehicle to champion and advance equality. Consider, for example, that in 2016 less than 20 per cent of the members of the governing boards of international sport federations and national Olympic committees were women (Women on Boards 2016). There is limited disaggregated data on the governance and management of SDP organizations, but anecdotal evidence suggests similar inequalities exist.

A number of SDG targets and indicators provide a reference point for organizational reform programmes to address inequalities of this nature. These include SDG Target 5.5 on women's participation in leadership and decision making (UNGA 2015), SDG Target 10.3 on eliminating discriminatory laws, policies and practices and SDG indicator 16.7.1 related to the proportion of positions in public bodies disaggregated by sex, age, persons with disabilities and population groups (UN Statistics Commission 2016).

The response of SDP stakeholders, along with mainstream sport, to addressing inequalities within sport will be an important indicator of the level to which sport-based approaches can actually contribute to the leave no one behind agenda integral to the SDGs. Institutional reform to promote equality therefore becomes a critical area for increased attention and analysis for all actors.

The integrated dimensions of economic, social and environmental development

The 2030 Agenda emphasizes the integrated and indivisible nature of the economic, social and environmental dimensions of sustainable development. This focus underscores that an over-emphasis on economic development, at the expense social and environmental sustainability, can negatively impact on human well-being (Bhattacharya *et al.* 2015; Helliwell *et al.* 2015). Predominantly, SDP has been positioned to contribute to social development themes such as health, education, disability and social cohesion (Kay and Dudfield 2013; Schulenkorf *et al.* 2016). Economic development and environmental sustainability have not typically been a substantial part of SDP. The emphasis on the integrated nature of these three domains of sustainable development in the SDGs suggests there is value in the SDP field considering environmental sustainability and economic development issues in more depth.

A correlation can be drawn between the strong emphasis on social policy issues in SDP and the aforementioned focus on programmatic delivery and community level outcomes (Lindsey and Grattan 2012; Sanders 2016). Environmental sustainability and economic development issues have typically been the premise of actors with a substantive focus on macro and population-level outcomes. As such these have been areas that have had only limited attention in SDP discourse to date. To ensure greater relevance of SDP in relation to the interconnectivity agenda of the SDGs, there is a need to broaden perceptions of SDP to encompass the deliberate use of sport to contribute to population-level outcomes. This will require the engagement of a broader range of stakeholders, including those with macro and population-level foci (Dudfield and Dingwall-Smith 2015).

There are emerging examples of such a population-level and policy orientated SDP approaches and analysis. The *Designed to Move* report, which positions sport in a broader physical activity and active lifestyle agenda, argues that without targeted action, by 2030 the direct cost of physical inactivity will amount to US$7.5 billion in India, US$26.0 billion in the UK, US$67.5 billion in China and US$191.7 billion in the United States (Whitehead *et al.* n.d.). Research showing that participation in sport in the United Kingdom results in health costs savings of GBP £903.7 million per annum is another example (Fujiwara *et al.* 2015). Modifying tax, fiscal policy and accounting approaches to stimulate the sport economy (Lindsey and Chapman 2017); and instituting standards for the sustainable management of mega sport events (International Organization for Standardization 2012), are other pertinent examples of sport-based policy and strategy focused on macro outcomes and economic and environmental issues. In the context of the interconnections prioritized in the 2030 Agenda, further policy direction in the SDP field that is cognisant of the integrated nature of economic, environmental and social development outcomes will be required.

A more integrated approach to SDP policy and programme design could also provide important checks and balances. The development of the *International Safeguards for Children in Sport* (International Safeguarding Children in Sport Working Group 2016) and efforts to apply the UN Guiding Principles on Business and Human Rights in sport (Mega Sporting Events Platform on Human Rights 2017) are examples of human rights and social development issues being considered more extensively across sport, including by commercially orientated stakeholders. The prominent role of SDP stakeholders in developing these initiatives provides a model for future action. More nuanced engagement with economic development policy and financing arrangements would also benefit many SDP stakeholders. Public-private financing models, emphasized in the 2030 Agenda, and social impact investment are two areas that stand out for further attention.

There are risks that an enhanced focus on economic outcomes within SDP policy and practice may further promote neoliberal policy direction. However, private sector and commercial interests are already influential in the SDP field (Giulianotti 2011). More overtly considering the social, environmental and economic dimensions of SDP policy and practice, may in fact provide a framework for more transparency on the objectives and expectations of different actors and could actually work to position social justice issues more prominently (Forde and Kota 2016; Giulianotti 2015).

Often when sport and social justice issues are raised, SDP actors are quick to delineate elite and commercially orientated sport from community sport and SDP. However, actors and policy considerations in these domains are becoming increasingly intertwined (Giulianotti 2011; Bailey and Talbot 2015). It is therefore likely that the growing recognition of governance issues, corruption, doping and abuse in sport (Geeraert *et al.* 2014; Masters 2015; McPherson *et al.* 2015; Rhind *et al.* 2015), will impact more significantly on SDP policy and practice. Consequently, SDP stakeholders – who overtly leverage the 'positive' attributes of sport within their programme theories – must be prepared to respond. Commonwealth sports ministers emphasized as much at their biannual meeting in 2016, stating 'efforts to address sport integrity issues must be interconnected and embedded in advancing Sport for Development and Peace' (Commonwealth Secretariat 2016).

A model positing that the contribution of sport to sustainable development can occur both *through* sport (i.e. using sport as tool) and *within* sport (deliberate policy and strategy to address sport integrity issues) provides a conceptual framework that responds to this dynamic. In applying such a model to sport and the SDGs, the parameters of SDP policy and practice can be extended to encompass intentional action *within* sport to deliver against SDG targets, as well as the intentional use of sport as a tool to contribute broader sustainable development outcomes.

A targeted approach to analyse sport and the SDGs

In considering the specific contribution of sport to the SDGs it is important to first offer cautionary remarks. Warnings that too often the beneficial effects of sport are taken for granted, and that SDP actors ignore the complex dynamics of development, should be heeded (Coalter 2010; Langer 2015). While sport-based interventions may, in particular contexts, make a tangible contribution to development objectives, the positive contribution of sport to development should not be considered automatic. The type and scale of outcomes achieved will be influenced by individual, relational, structural and socio – cultural factors (Lindsey and Chapman 2017). Accordingly, guidance published by the Commonwealth Secretariat underscores the importance of basing SDP-orientated policy and strategy on robust programme theories and available research (Dudfield and Dingwall-Smith 2015), and that any use of sport in development should be underpinned by quality, inclusive sport programming that emphasizes the well-being and protection of all participants (Kay and Dudfield 2013). This guidance is echoed by a growing body of literature highlighting the design and application of sport-based approaches which are critical in determining the scope and type of outcomes delivered (Svensson *et al.* 2016). Applying these considerations to the analysis of sport and the SDGs suggests that a targeted approach is required. This means that rather than positioning sport as a generic and unproblematic catalyst for development, identifying specific 'development objectives to which sport can contribute' must be fundamental (Kay and Dudfield 2013: 65). Equally important is debunking notions that sport has the utility to contribute across all components of the SDG agenda.

SDG 8, which focused on economic growth and productive employment for all, offers a relevant example. Targets 8.3, 8.5 and 8.6, on reducing unemployment among young people and persons with disabilities, are specific SDG targets where sport-based approaches may make a measured contribution. These are particularly urgent priorities given that globally over 200 million people are unemployed, of which 73 million are young people (ILO 2013; United Nations 2015). Supporting vocational skill development, employability and the improved entrepreneurial capability of young people are typical policy interventions in response to youth underemployment and unemployment. The popularity of sport and its potential to be used as a 'hook' for young people, means that well-designed sport-based interventions, linked to broader employability strategies, can contribute to this policy direction. (OECD, 2009; ILO 2013; Ratten 2014). SDP interventions cannot, however, address market and structural issues that impact on employment levels (Coalter *et al.* 2016) and are the focus of other targets under this goal. Hence, a targeted approach, positioning specific types of well-planned sport-based approaches as best placed to contribute to the aforementioned targets is most appropriate.

Analysis at target level also supports more precise policy and programme design. Consider for example SDG Target 5.1, focused on ending all forms of discrimination against all women and girls, and SDG Target 5.5, which aims to ensure women's full and effective participation and equal opportunities for leadership at all levels. As highlighted by Lindsey and Chapman (2017), analysis of these targets dictates SDP stakeholders consider: establishing targets for girls' and women's involvement at all levels of programming and governance; developing appropriate strategies, provision and monitoring to advance the full participation of women and girls; using sport as a tool to engage men and boys with gender issues; and, engaging with other (non-sport) stakeholders working to advance gender equality.

The official list of SDGs indicators is also relevant in adopting a targeted approach. This indicator framework was developed based on recognition of the 'importance of adequate data for the follow-up and review of progress made in implementing the Goals and targets of the 2030 Agenda' (UN Statistics Commission 2016: 5). The indicators for SDG Target 3.4, focused on reducing mortality from non-communicable disease and improving mental health and well-being, provides a relevant example. Indicators 3.4.1 and 3.4.2 measure mortality attributed to non-communicable disease and suicide. The design of these indicators highlight the importance of explicitly addressing risk factors for non-communicable disease in the design of 'sport for health' policy and programming. Encouraging regular physical activity participation at the prescribed rate to achieve health benefits is the most obvious example (WHO 2010).

A targeted approach was employed by the Commonwealth Secretariat and mirrored by other government, sport and academic stakeholders in analysing the potential contribution of sport to the SDGs (Dudfield and Dingwall-Smith 2015; IOC 2015; Bailey *et al.*, 2016; UNESCO, 2017a). This analysis informed decisions by the 8th Commonwealth Sports Ministers Meeting (Commonwealth Secretariat 2016) and Sixth International Conference of Ministers and Senior Officials Responsible for Physical Education and Sport (MINEPS VI) to design future sport policy to contribute to prioritized SDGs (UNESCO 2017b). MINEPS VI identified nine prioritized SDGs and 36 SDG targets where sport-based approaches can make effective and cost-efficient contributions (UNESCO 2017b). These SDG goals and targets cover diverse policy areas, ranging from individual-level health, education and employability outcomes, to environmental sustainability, reducing societal violence and issues of institutional governance.

Measuring the contribution of sport to the SDGs

The challenge of measuring and evaluating the impact of SDP is well recognized (Levermore 2011). There is acknowledgement that providing 'proof' of the direct impact of sport-based approaches on non-sport development outcomes is extremely challenging if not impossible (Lindsey and Chapman 2017), and that the scale and quality of evidence for SDP approaches is varied across contexts and policy domains (Schulenkorf *et al.* 2016; Lindsey *et al.* 2016). Opinion on how to strengthen the measurement and evaluation of SDP is varied. On one hand, researchers have argued the need for increased independent evaluation based on clearly defined theoretical frameworks (Coalter 2013), while other researchers have championed more participatory approaches (Darnell and Hayhurst 2011). The latter responds to criticism that many approaches to SDP measurement and evaluation are 'top-down' and geared towards the priorities of donor agencies (Kay 2012).

It is beyond the scope of this chapter to consider measuring and evaluating the contribution of sport to the SDGs in detail. Nevertheless, it is clear that careful consideration of this issue is required in the context of the 2030 Agenda. While the Official SDG Indicators List provides an important reference point (UN Statistics Commission 2016), the scope of these indicators extends far beyond the contributions of sport-based initiatives. It is on this basis that one of five priority actions adopted by MINEPS VI was to 'develop common indicators for measuring the contribution of physical education, physical activity and sport to prioritized SDGs and targets' (UNESCO 2017b: 19). In considering how to advance this complex and challenging undertaking it is useful to reference Lindsey and Chapman's (2017) guidance on the importance of assessing and triangulating contributory evidence from various sources to make reasoned judgements as to the contribution of sport-based interventions to the SDGs. These include national and international-level data sets, regional and local-level data, evidence drawn from monitoring and evaluation of discrete initiatives, and evidence from academic research where available.

Concluding comments on the implications for SDP

The implications of the adoption of the SDGs for SDP may be best considered from two angles. First, the impact the transformative shifts represented by the 2030 Agenda will have on future policy development and programme design in the field; and second, the most appropriate approach to analyse and articulate the potential contributions of sport to the 2030 Agenda. As a framework for future action, the cross-contextual relevance of the SDGs, emphasis on the interconnectivity of the social, environmental and economic dimensions of development, and need to address growing inequality stand out. In response, the following questions for the SDP field are pertinent.

- Would framing SDP as a domestic policy issue, as opposed to being primarily located within international development, better address local need and scale impact?
- Can SDP actors do more to address issues of systemic and structural inequality?

- Is an SDP model emphasizing action *within* sport, as well as *through sport*, most effective in working to enhance the positive contributions of sport towards achievement of the SDGs?

These questions, coupled with the scope and scale of the challenges addressed by the 2030 Agenda, calls for well-considered and robust analysis ahead of rhetorical advocacy for SDP. Undertaking this analysis at SDG target level, drawing on available research and well-developed programme theories has proven most instructive to date. This work posits that sport-based approaches may offer a valuable tool to support the achievement of specific SDP targets in specific contexts. However, it also underscores that the use of sport should be integrated and complimentary to the suite of policy and programmatic responses required to deliver sustainable social, economic and environmental development and that action to protect the integrity of sport and human rights in sporting contexts must be integral to future SDP-orientated policy and practice.

Overall, recognition of sport as an enabler of sustainable development in the 2030 Agenda is a significant milestone for SDP. Ideally, this will be a catalyst for further critical reflection and measured responses that result in enhanced policy, practice and research that maximise the positive contribution of sport to achieving the SDGs, and limit potential negative outcomes of this approach.

Note

1 See www.un.org/sport/resources/documents/general-assembly-resolutions.

References

Bailey, R., Glibo, I., Martirosyan, A., Concalves, S. and Flachsbart, G. (2016). *The International Conference of Ministers and Senior Officials Responsible for Physical Education and Sport – MINEPS VI, Literature Review*. Berlin: International Council of Sport Science and Physical Education. Available at: www.icsspe.org/system/files/MINEPS%20VI%20Literature%20review_0.pdf (accessed 19 January 2017).

Bailey, R. and Talbot, M. (eds) (2015). *Elite Sport and Sport-for-all: Bridging the Two Cultures?* London: Routledge.

Bhattacharya, A., Oppenheim, J. and Stern, N. (2015). Driving Sustainable Development Through Better Infrastructure: Key Elements of a Transformation Program. Brookings Global Working Paper Series.

Coalter, F, Wilson, J, Griffiths, K. and Nichols, G. (2016). *Sport and Employability – A Report of the Sport Industry Research Centre at Sheffield Hallam University for Comic Relief UK*. London: Comic Relief. Available at: www.uploadlibrary.com/LaureusWorldSportsAwards/2015_Sport_and_Employablity_Report_by_Comic_Relief.pdf (accessed 22 February 2018).

Coalter, F. (2010). The politics of sport-for-development: Limited focus programmes and broad gauge problems? *International Review for the Sociology of Sport*, September 2010, *45*(3), 295–314.

Coalter, F. (2013). *Sport-for-Development: What Game Are We Playing?* London: Routledge.

Collins, M. and Kay, T. (2014). *Sport and Social Exclusion*. New York: Routledge.

Commonwealth Secretariat. (2016). *8th Commonwealth Sports Ministers Meeting Communique*. Rio de Janeiro, Brazil. Available at: http://thecommonwealth.org/sites/default/files/inline/8CSMM%20Communiqu%C3%A9%20-%20FINAL%20-%2004.08.16.pdf (accessed 25 February 2018).

Commonwealth Secretariat. (2014). *7th Commonwealth Sports Ministers Meeting Communique*. Glasgow, UK. Available at: http://thecommonwealth.org/sites/default/files/news-items/documents/7CSMM%20Final%20Communique.pdf (accessed 22 February 2018).

Darnell, S. (2012). *Sport for Development and Peace: A Critical Sociology*. London: Bloomsbury.

Darnell, S. and Hayhurst, L. (2011). Sport for decolonization: Exploring a new praxis of sport for development. *Progress in Development Studies*, *11*(3), 183–196.

Darnell, S. C. and Huish, R. (2015). Cuban sport and the challenges of South-South solidarity. *Beyond Sport For Development And Peace: Transnational Perspectives On Theory, Policy And Practice*, pp.35–46.

Deacon, B. (2016). Assessing the SDGs from the point of view of global social governance. *Journal of International and Comparative Social Policy*, *32*(2), 116–130.

De Coning, C. and Keim, M. (2014). Sport and development policies in selected African countries: Sport administration. *African Journal for Physical Health Education, Recreation and Dance*, *20*(Supplement 2), 296–315.

Department for Culture, Media and Sport, United Kingdom Government (DCMS). (2015). *Sporting Future: A New Strategy for an Active Nation*. London: Cabinet Office.

Dudfield, O. (2014). Sport for development and peace: Opportunities, challenges and the Commonwealth's response. In O. Dudfield (ed.), *Strengthening Sport for Development and Peace: National Policies and Strategies*. London: Commonwealth Secretariat, pp. 1–12.

Dudfield, O. and Dingwall-Smith, M. (2015). *Sport for Development and Peace and the 2030 Agenda for Sustainable Development: Commonwealth Analysis Report*. London: Commonwealth Secretariat.

Dudfield, O. and Kidd, B. (2012). Everything to play for. Global – The International Briefing. Available at: www.global-briefing.org/2012/07/everything-to-play-for/.

Forde, S. D. and Kota, A. (2016). Football as a terrain of hope and struggle: Beginning a dialogue on social change, hope and building a better world through sport. *Qualitative Research in Sport, Exercise and Health*, *8*(5), 444–455.

Fujiwara, D., Kudrna, L., Cornwall, T., Laffan, K. and Dolan, P. (2015). *Further Analysis to Value the Health and Educational Benefits of Sport and Culture*. London: Department for Culture, Media and Sport, United Kingdom Government. Available at: www.gov.uk/government/uploads/system/uploads/attachment_data/file/446273/Health_and_educational_benefits_of_sport_and_culture.pdf (accessed 19 January 2017).

Fukuda-Parr, S. (2012). Should Global Goal Setting Continue, and How, in the Post-2015 era? DESA Working Paper No 117 ST/ESA/2012/DWP/117, United Nations Department of Economic and Social Affairs. Available at: www.un.org/esa/desa/papers/2012/wp117_2012.pdf (accessed 19 January 2017).

Fukuda-Parr, S. (2014). Global goals as a policy tool: Intended and unintended consequences. *Journal of Human Development and Capabilities*, *15*(2–3), 118–131.

Geeraert, A., Alm, J. and Groll, M. (2014). Good governance in international sport organizations: An analysis of the 35 Olympic sport governing bodies. *International Journal of Sport Policy and Politics*, *6*(3), 281–306.

Giulianotti, R. (2015). Corporate social responsibility in sport: Critical issues and future possibilities. *Corporate Governance*, *15*(2), 243–248.

Giulianotti, R. (2011). The sport, development and peace sector: A model of four social policy domains. *Journal of Social Policy*, *40*(04), 757–776.

Hajer, M., Nilsson, M., Raworth, K., Bakker, P., Berkhout, F., de Boer, Y., Rockström, J., Ludwig, K. and Kok, M. (2015). Beyond cockpit-ism: Four insights to enhance the transformative potential of the sustainable development goals. *Sustainability*, *7*(2), 1651–1660.

Helliwell, J. F., Layard, R. and Sachs, J. (eds) (2015). *World Happiness Report 2015*. New York: Sustainable Development Solutions Network.

Herrick, C. (2014). (Global) health geography and the post-2015 development agenda. *The Geographical Journal*, *180*(2), 185–190.

Howard, J. and Wheeler, J. (2015). What community development and citizen participation should contribute to the new global framework for sustainable development. *Community Development Journal*, *50*(4), 552–570.

Huish, R. (2011). Punching above its weight: Cuba's use of sport for South–South co-operation. *Third World Quarterly*, *32*(3), 417–433.

Hylton, K., Long, J., Parnell, D. and Rankin-Wright, A. (2015). 'Race', racism and participation in sport. *Better Health Briefing*, *40*. Race Equality Foundation. Available at: http://eprints.leedsbeckett.ac.uk/2049/1/Hylton%20et%20al%20Race%20Equality%20Foundation%20Health%20Briefing%2040%20Final.pdf (accessed 23 February 2018).

International Labour Organisation. (2013). Global Employment Trends for Youth 2013: A Generation at Risk. Available at: www.ilo.org/global/research/global-reports/youth/2013/WCMS_212423/lang--en/index.htm (accessed 19 January 2017).

International Olympic Committee. (2015). The Contribution of Sport to the Sustainable Development Goals and the post-2015 Development Agenda, the Position of the International Olympic Committee, on behalf of the Olympic and Sport Movement. Available at: www.sportanddev.org/sites/default/files/downloads/sport_contribution_to_post_2015_agenda_eng_feb.pdf (accessed 19 January 2017).

International Organization for Standardization. (2012). Sustainable Events with ISO 20121. Available at: www.iso.org/iso/sustainable_events_iso_2012.pdf. (accessed 19 January 2017).

International Safeguarding Children in Sport Working Group. (2016). International Safeguards for Children in Sport. Available at: www.brunel.ac.uk/__data/assets/pdf_file/0009/484587/International-Safeguards-for-Children-in-Sport-version-to-view-online.pdf (accessed 19 January 2017).

Jarvie, G. (ed.) (2003). *Sport, Racism and Ethnicity*. London: Routledge.

Kay, T., and Dudfield, O. (2013). *The Commonwealth Guide to Advancing Development through Sport*. London: Commonwealth Secretariat.

Kay, T. (2012). Accounting for legacy: Monitoring and evaluation in sport in development relationships, *Sport in Society, 15*(6), 888–904.

Keim, M. and De Coning, C. (eds) (2014). *Sport and Development Policy in Africa: Results of a Collaborative Study of Selected Country Cases*. African Sun Media.

Kidd, B. (2008). A new social movement: Sport for development and peace. *Sport in Society, 11*(4), 370–380.

Kilvington, D. and Price, J. (eds) (2017). *Sport and Discrimination* (Vol. 72). London: Taylor & Francis.

Langer, L. (2015). Sport for development–a systematic map of evidence from Africa. *South African Review of Sociology, 46*(1), 66–86.

Levermore, R. (2011). Evaluating sport-for-development: Approaches and critical issues. *Progress in Development Studies, 11*: 339–353.

Levermore, R. and Beacom, A. (2009). Sport and development: Mapping the field. *Sport and International Development*. Basingstoke: Palgrave Macmillan.

Lindsey, I. (2016). Governance in sport-for-development: Problems and possibilities of (not) learning from international development. *International Review for the Sociology of Sport*, p.1012690215623460.

Lindsey, I. and Chapman, T. (2017). *Enhancing the Contribution of Sport to the SDGs*, London: Commonwealth Secretariat.

Lindsey, I. and Grattan, A. (2012). An 'international movement'? Decentring sport-for-development within Zambian communities. *International Journal of Sport Policy and Politics, 4*(1), 91–110.

Lindsey, I., Kay, T., Jeanes, R. and Banda, D. (2017). *Localizing Global Sport for Development*. Manchester: Manchester University Press.

Masters, A. (2015). Corruption in sport: From the playing field to the field of policy. *Policy and Society, 34*(2), 111–123.

McPherson, L., Atkins, P., Cameron, N., Long, M., Nicholson, M. and Morris, M. E. (2015). Children's experience of sport: What do we really know? *Australian Social Work*, pp.1–12.

Mega-Sporting Events Platform for Human Rights. (2017). Evaluating Human Rights Risks in a Sporting Context, Sporting Chance White Paper 1.1 Version 1, January 2017. Institute of Human Rights and Business. Available at: www.ihrb.org/megasportingevents/resource-view/white-paper-1.1-evaluating-human-rights-risks (accessed 23 February 2018).

Ministry of Culture, Community and Youth, Government of Singapore (MCCY). (n.d.). Vision 2030. Available at: www.mccy.gov.sg/en/Topics/Sports/Articles/Vision_2030.aspx (accessed 19 January 2017).

Mwaanga, O. and Mwansa, K. (2013). Indigenous discourses in sport for development: A case study of the ubuntu cultural philosophy in Edusport foundation, Zambia. In N. Schulenkorf and D. Adair (eds), *Global Sport-for-Development: Critical Perspectives*. Basingstoke: Palgrave Macmillan, pp. 115–133.

Ojogwu, C. N. (2009). The challenges of attaining Millennium Development Goals in education in Africa by 2015. *College Student Journal, 43*(2), 375–384.

Organisation for Economic Cooperation and Development. OECD. (2009). Promoting Pro-Poor Growth: Employment. Available at: www.oecd.org/dac/povertyreduction/43514554.pdf (accessed 19 January 2017).

Ostry, J. L. and Loungani, P. P. and Furceri, D. (2016). Neoliberalism: oversold? *Finance and Development, 53*(2), 38–41.

Ratten, V. (2014). Collaborative entrepreneurship and the fostering of entrepreneurialism in developing countries. *International Journal of Social Entrepreneurship and Innovation, 3*(2), 137–149.

Republic of Mauritius. (2017). Budget Speech 2017/17: Rising to the Challenge of Our Ambitions. pp. 32. Available at: http://budget.mof.govmu.org/budget2017-18/2017_18budgetspeech.pdf (accessed 23 February 2018).

Rhind, D., McDermott, J., Lambert, E. and Koleva, I. (2015). A review of safeguarding cases in sport. *Child Abuse Review, 24*(6), 418–426.

Sanders, B. (2016). An own goal in sport for development: Time to change the playing field. *Journal of Sport for Development, 4*(6), 1–5.

Sanders, B., De Coning, C. and Keim, M. (2017). Going to Scale? A critique of the role of the public sector in sport for development and peace in South Africa. *African Journal for Physical Activity and Health Sciences (AJPHES)*, *23*(4), 514–532.

Schulenkorf, N. and Adair, D. (eds) (2014). *Global Sport-for-Development: Critical Perspectives.* London: Palgrave Macmillan.

Schulenkorf, N., Sherry, E. and Rowe, K. (2016). Sport for development: An integrated literature review. *Journal of Sport Management*, *30*(1).

Sexsmith, K. and McMichael, P. (2015). Formulating the SDGs: Reproducing or reimagining state-centered development? *Globalizations*, *12*(4), 581–596.

Sport for Development and Peace International Working Group (SDPIWG). (2008). *Harnessing the Power of Sport for Development and Peace.* Toronto: Right to Play.

Sumner, A. and Tiwari, M. (2010). Global poverty reduction to 2015 and beyond: What has been the impact of the MDGs and what are the options for a post-2015 global framework?. *IDS Working Papers*, *348*(2010), 1–31.

Svensson, P., Hancock, M. and Hums, M. (2016). Examining the educative aims and practices of decision-makers in sport for development and peace organizations. *Sport, Education and Society*, *21*(4), 495–512.

United Nations. (2016). The Sustainable Development Goals Report 2016. New York: United Nations. Available at: https://unstats.un.org/sdgs/report/2016/ (accessed 19 January 2017).

United Nations Educational, Scientific, and Cultural Organization (UNESCO). (2013). *Declaration of Berlin, Outcome document of the Fifth International Conference of Ministers and Senior Officials Responsible for Physical Education and Sport (MINEPS V)*. Berlin, Germany: Author.

United Nations Educational, Scientific and Cultural Organisation (UNESCO). (2015). International Charter of Physical Education, Physical Activity and Sport. Paris, France: 38th Session of the General Conference of the United Nations Educational, Scientific and Cultural Organisation, November 2015.

United Nations Educational, Scientific, and Cultural Organization (UNESCO) (2017a). Sixth International Conference of Ministers and Senior Officials Responsible for Physical Education and Sport (MINEPS VI) Working Document, SHS/2017/4, 8 June 2017. Available at: http://unesdoc.unesco.org/images/0025/002510/251081E.pdf.

United Nations Educational, Scientific, and Cultural Organization (UNESCO). (2017b). Kazan Action Plan, Outcome Document of the Sixth International Conference of Ministers and Senior Officials Responsible for Physical Education and Sport (MINEPS VI). Kazan, Russia: Author.

United Nations General Assembly (UNGA). (2000). United Nations Millennium Declaration, United Nations General Assembly Resolution 55/2. Available at: www.un.org/millennium/declaration/ares552e.htm (accessed 19 January 2017).

United Nations General Assembly (UNGA). (2015). Transforming our World: The 2030 Agenda for Sustainable Development. United Nations General Assembly Resolution 70/1. Available at: https://sustainabledevelopment.un.org/post2015/transformingourworld/publication (accessed 19 January 2017).

United Nations Office on Sport for Development and Peace (UNOSDP). (2011). *Achieving the Objectives of the United Nations through Sport*, Geneva: United Nations.

United Nations Statistical Commission. (2016). Report of the Inter-Agency and Expert Group on Sustainable Development Goal Indicators. Available at: http://unstats.un.org/unsd/statcom/47th-session/documents/2016-2-IAEG-SDGs-Rev1-E.pdf. (accessed 19 January 2017).

van Bergeijk, P. A. and van der Hoeven, R. (2017). *Sustainable Development Goals and Income Inequality*. Abingdon: Edward Elgar.

Whitehead, J., MaCallum, L. and Talbot, M., (n.d.). *Designed to Move: A Physical Activity Action Agenda*, American College of Sports Medicine (ACSM), International Council of Sport Science and Physical Education (ICSSPE) and Nike. Available at: www.wfsgi.org/images/downloads/physical_activity/Designed_To_Move_Full_Report.pdf (accessed 19 January 2017).

Women on Boards. (2016). *Gender Balance in Global Sport Report*. Available at: www.womenonboards.org.au/pubs/reports.

World Health Organization. (2010). *Global Recommendations on Physical Activity for Health*. Geneva: World Health Organization. Available at: http://whqlibdoc.who.int/publications/2010/9789241599979_eng.pdf (accessed 19 January 2017).

World Health Organization. (n.d.).. Physical Inactivity: A Global Health Problem. Geneva: World Health Organization. Available at: www.who.int/dietphysicalactivity/factsheet_inactivity/en/ (accessed 19 January 2017).

11

SDP and monitoring and evaluation

Jutta Engelhardt

Introduction

This is a very prescriptive and detailed chapter which argues that development work can no longer do without quality control and evidence-based improvements. This article pledges for sophisticated data collection, meaningful donor-driven monitoring requirements and increased efforts in communicating and embracing learning from the field in development practice. By virtue of 20-years' experience of working within the development sector, coordinating and managing sport and play-based activities, the author of this article is well placed to highlight the lack of effective monitoring and evaluation (M&E) practices being applied and disseminated by SDP organizations. Personal interest and years of commitment to the exchange of knowledge between social sciences and programme rollout in practice, has directed the pursuit of improving evaluation, analysis and translating theory into practice and vice versa. This chapter will support practitioners, academics and grant-makers alike in anticipating, financing and processing learning from programme implementation by outlining the complexities of monitoring and evaluating in detail.

A call for more evidence to prove the effectiveness of sport for development has become a mantra at every conference and SFD meeting. In principle, a call for more scientific knowledge is a good thing. It helps us to know whether or not the form of intervention chosen is actually generating the desired results and addressing the social malaise we are trying to eliminate. It is good to know whether the children and youth participating for years in sport and education programmes actually read and write better and have the brighter future promised in the project proposal. It is also advantageous to verify whether the swimming lessons provided to local populations safeguard from drowning during annual floods or whether the number of drowned persons stays the same as we have only taught the children to swim, whereas the mothers are the primary group to drown. Identifying closely which group is affected most by flood-inflected mortality will have consequences on our project implementation and ultimately help to reach the self-defined project goals. It is thus good to realize that so-called unexpected results can counteract the desired results and that not all well-intended objectives actually lead to positive effects. To learn about the benefits and drawbacks of projects, we have to be willing to closely look at and understand the interventions' effects: we have to monitor and evaluate.

Long-term monitoring and scientifically sound evaluation reveals *good practice* in programme management; however, it also sheds light on the ambiguity of development aims, the relative arbitrariness of objectives and indicators, and the unexpected results of interventions. Processing such ambiguous information causes most readers to reflect on what they are doing, and to engage in critical dialogue about relevance, effectiveness and impact. Getting more people in development to talk about effectiveness is a first step. Being engaged and recognizing the complexity of development will make it harder to chant along with the lamenting crowd or to claim that SFD interventions can eliminate any social ill.

A dialogue about effectiveness and sustainability alone, however, will not resolve the social problems development work is trying to resolve. It is only the first step in the direction of adapting project management processes for the better, of setting realistic aims and of staying open to new types of interventions. If we do not participate in this evidence-informed dialogue, development work in general and SFD in particular will keep on turning in the same, almost seven decades' old circle of 'big development claim – little long-term results'. Monitoring and evaluation is not an end in itself, but the first step towards basing our work on evidence and improving implementation as we go. Meanwhile, learning how to rely on existing tools and methods to collect and interpret data, and to appreciate the complexity of data interpretation, is the first step towards embracing new knowledge; learning to read and understand existing evaluations and scientific conclusions while refraining from wanting to experience all possible pitfalls and mistakes ourselves is the second. Ultimately, our aim is to prove those wrong who cannot stop lamenting about the lack of data on the effectiveness of SFD interventions and to base programming, as well as political decision-making, on scientifically generated evidence.

What is monitoring?

The need for monitoring – and the process of doing it – is best explained by a technical analogy. When an airplane takes off, the pilot relies on the information provided to her by equipment measuring parameters such as outside temperature, wind speed, distance to destination and air traffic. No pilot will take off without the full functionality of this cockpit technology. Ignored danger warnings threatening the well-being of the passengers would result in the pilot being fired.

In development work, there is a need to keep to comparable standards for reasons of accountability, programme improvement and long-term learning of what works and what does not. Assuming that all interventions cause change, we have a duty – as much as the pilot – to protect programme participants from threats to their well-being. Making sure that those who operate in the SFD sector live up to the international standard of 'Do no harm', we need to observe the changes caused by the intervention and evaluate their effects on all stakeholders. It should therefore be obvious that programmes cannot take off without a solid monitoring system. This must allow for learning along the way and enable project managers to receive warnings of failed implementation or predefined objectives being out of sync with realistically achievable results. Monitoring needs to be considered an imperative, sustained, long-term and fluid process.

Planning, monitoring and evaluation

The ability to evaluate the effects of programmes relies on the monitoring data that the programme implementers or M&E officers can collect before and during the programme activities. To guarantee a good data set that truly represents the relationship between programme inputs, outputs, outcomes and impacts, a solid monitoring and evaluation framework is necessary. The planning process is an essential part of this framework development and entails the following steps.

Rephrasing programme objectives as questions

As a first step, it is necessary to clearly outline the key objective of an intervention and rephrase the short, medium and long-term objectives as questions. A project proposal might provide the key objective as a statement such as: 'Increase rural communities' access and quality of education in Afghanistan'. The short and medium-term objectives might read as 'train teachers in sport and education methods' or 'inform parents about the benefits of formally educated daughters'.

In the first step of planning for collecting data and evaluating success, these statements need to be rephrased into questions, reflecting the desire to learn how the intervention has contributed to reaching these objectives. The key objective would then read, 'Has the intervention contributed to increased access to education and higher quality teaching for rural communities in Afghanistan?' The question for medium-term objectives might read 'How effectively have teachers been trained in sport and education methods?' or 'Are parents aware of the benefits of their daughters being formally schooled?' These questions are the departure point for any investigation into how successful the intervention has been.

Developing a theory of change

Once the statements have been rephrased to questions, a theory of change needs to be developed. A 'theory of change is essentially a comprehensive description and illustration of how and why a desired change is expected to happen in a particular context' (Centre for Theory of Change) Based on this explanation, an intervention is developed to change the course of action channelling them into the direction of the desired outcome.

It is simplistic, but sadly very common, to believe that change happens by way of causal relationships arguing along the lines of common sense thinking. Many theories of change simply assume that the addressed situation (e.g. lack of quality education in rural Afghan communities) can be changed by simply providing *additional information to parents* or *training to teachers*, accelerating and diverting development into the desired direction. For the example of Afghanistan, programme initiators intervene based on the belief that the activities will build towards the greater development of the region and will support the local communities in being better equipped to face challenges. When developing a theory of change, however, it is important to keep in mind that human interaction is not necessarily based on causal coherence or 'logical connections'. Human interaction is instead shaped by norms and expectations, traditions and myths: behavioural change is hard to generate through only the provision of additional information. A theory of change must keep this 'human factor' in mind. It should be based in solid scientific findings about the human psyche and principles of social interaction while being culturally adapted based on knowledge of local traditions and norms.

Defining the scope of M&E efforts

When the theory of change is in place, the third step is to define the scope of the programme's monitoring and evaluation. This depends on factors such as:

1. The budget available.
2. The M&E expertise available in the programme team.
3. Expectations regarding the M&E results – to learn for future improved implementation or to seek minimum investigative effort to satisfy donors?
4. The audience of the evaluation report: the content and style of the M&E report will differ depending on whether parents want or are able to see the benefits of programme participation on their children or if the organization is planning to run a policy campaign proving the added value of the intervention.

The list of options for using the evaluation's findings go on and the way the data is collected should be spelled out prior to the project's outset. This will define the scope and methods of the M&E process and outcome. Depending on the needs of the organization or stakeholders, evaluation designs range from a rigorous impact assessment with a control group design to a simple descriptive analysis of final results. Any design and scope, chosen and carefully planned prior to implementation, is valuable as long as the design fits the needs and the argument defending it does not run solely along the lines of lack of funding. Unfortunately, very few programme managers take the time to fully conceptualize the scope of their M&E efforts, never properly investigating their needs and the resources available.

Timing of data collection

When the decision on the scope of the M&E has successfully been taken, it is necessary to define when exactly the monitoring data will be collected. This fourth step in M&E planning ensures that opportunities to monitor the effects of the intervention will not be missed. Important times for data collection are prior to programme implementation, mid-programming and at the end of a programme. However, specific moments within the programme implementation might also lend themselves to process monitoring and to verify specified assumptions.

Deciding for tools to collect data

The tools used to collect data need to be clearly specified. An understanding of the nature of what is being evaluated and who the target group is should drive choices regarding monitoring tools. A mixed-methods approach, consisting of qualitative and quantitative methods, allows for the most comprehensive picture of a programme's effects. This has become a minimum standard in monitoring and evaluation of social interventions today. A mixture of tools helps to capture information on a variety of aspects of the programme while including a range of stakeholders.

Choosing a questionnaire to collect data is helpful in a setting where reading and writing is the most common way to transfer information. Respondents will be used to expressing their thoughts in writing, be familiar with the format and will recognize the question types they are expected to answer (yes/no questions, multiple choice questions, finish the sentence questions, etc.). In settings in which oral forms of communication are highly valued, it is advisable to focus instead on other tools and to run interviews, group discussions or story-telling sessions to elicit the information desired. Programme implementers need to be flexible enough to move away from extensive interviewing or focus group discussions and dare to use more experimental tools such as videos, community mapping, story-telling and drawing.

Deciding on appropriate tools that are both culturally and age appropriate is important to avoid collecting data that is not representative or results in a mismatch between questions asked and answers provided. An example of such a mismatch is a choice of questionnaire meant to investigate children's opinions of the new teaching methods. Although the questions might be child appropriate in complexity, the format of a questionnaire will probably create difficulties. Children that do not yet read well (in English) will need support. Most programme managers will be tempted to ask the available teacher to read to the children and help them understand the questions. Children will, as a result, no longer be free to provide socially desired answers. They might feel unable to freely express their like or dislike of the new sport-based teaching methodology in front of the daily implementer of the activities. Choosing the right monitoring tools thus helps avoid tainted monitoring data and allows for solid conclusions. The use of age appropriate and more playful tools also supports grasping the unintended, and moving beyond the bias of the one collecting data. Collecting data with a mixture of tools helps to 'apprehend those invisible elements that constitute so much of what development is about' (Dlamini 2007: 4).

Breaking down the big questions

Asking ourselves which questions we would like most to be answered by programme participants, staff and important stakeholders to illustrate the process of change is the next relevant step. Reflecting on these, we are splitting big questions, for example, 'How can we prevent a lack of academic education for the next generation of Afghans?' into more specific questions, such as 'What increases the likelihood of girls going to school?' or 'Why do girls leave school after primary education?'

The ambition is to split the broad into the specific. Asking these more detailed questions allows those collecting data to receive answers to aspects of programme activities, which we assume, in our causal approach to theory of change, are building towards the biggest question of all: '*Has the intervention contributed to increased access to education and higher quality teaching for rural communities in Afghanistan?*' The specific answers will shed light on whether the measures taken in the programme implementation (inputs) achieve the desired results (outputs and outcomes).

Distinguish between inputs, outputs, outcomes and impact

All activities (project cycle management (PCM) training, SFD trainings, etc.) and goods (e.g. salaries paid and ICT devices distributed) can be considered project inputs. It does not matter whether they are planned or spontaneously added to the implementation as a consequence of monitoring that tells project staff that additional measures are needed.

Activities, which are measurable and countable as a direct consequence of the inputs provided, are called outputs. Examples include the number of trainings performed, the number of parents informed, and the number of sport and education units taught by the newly trained teachers or volunteers.

Outcomes, by contrast, are larger in scope and add to impact of the intervention. An example in the given project in Afghanistan would be the readiness of girls and young women to start their own business due to sufficient formal education and improvements to self-esteem triggered by the project.

To decide whether the results have been achieved, there is a need to measure the collected data against set quantifiable/qualifiable thresholds, the so-called indicators. These need to be set at the outset of a programme in the planning phase of M&E. All monitoring data is measured against the stated indicators. Participants' answers that play into expectations and confirm any assumptions help to verify whether the activities move towards the intervention's desired results.

Unexpected answers show where the model of implementation went wrong in its assumptions and allow the organization, in the course of the programme's duration, to change the implementation to reach set objectives.

Reciprocity of project-internal and project-external factors

The impact of a project is bigger than the sum of the project's activities, outputs and outcomes. For our sample community in rural Afghanistan the impact is more than the reduced mortality, the additionally acquired skill-set of swimming or the new knowledge about disaster preparedness. An important characteristic of 'impact' is the fact that many factors – including those external to the direct project outputs and outcomes – play into changing the situation and improving the overall well-being of the rural (female) population. By investigating the relationship between project-internal and project-external agents of change, we can outline the reciprocity of project results with project-external developments that support the cause defined as the key objective of the project. Impact is therefore always a combination of processes triggered by the project implementation and external factors that support or inhibit social change in moving in the desired direction.

Careful M&E planning thus has the following functions and builds towards a **monitoring and evaluation framework**:

1. To articulate programme goals and **measurable short, medium and long-term objectives**
2. To develop a stringent **theory of change**
3. To define **the scope of the M&E efforts,** ranging from randomized control trials to simple descriptive evaluation at the end of a project
4. To develop sound **monitoring and evaluation plans**, carefully coordinating the timing of the implementation of activities with monitoring and evaluation efforts
5. To choose the **correct monitoring tools** to collect data
6. To **break down the big questions** into smaller ones
7. To describe **relationships between inputs, outputs, outcomes and impacts**
8. To clarify the **reciprocity between programme activities and external factors**[1]

Evaluating monitoring data

Once data is collected and stored appropriately, it can be analysed by those who are trained to do so. A majority of development programmes are evaluated using the logical framework approach and a smaller number experiment with a newer approach called outcome mapping.

The logical framework approach (LFA), which was originally developed and applied to the military and commercial sector, was adapted for use in the development world in the 1960s. It is a linear model that relies on result chains and is based on the assumption of objective causal relationships between inputs, outputs, outcomes and impact. Connecting the programmes' components, users of the LFA attempt to illustrate how the binding element for these components is causality. The four by four matrix of the LFA contains a hierarchy of objectives, indicators that will show whether the objectives have been achieved, the sources of information for each indicator, and a set of assumptions concerning the necessary preconditions needed for a programme to succeed.

LFA is used for planning, monitoring and evaluating a programme and collecting and registering programme data. In 2005, the majority of respondents interviewed by the

Swedish International Development Agency told researchers that LFA was widely used, but far from widely liked (Bakewell and Garbutt 2005: 1). Programme implementers saw it as a requirement from donors, but doubted that the matrix, in its mathematical rigidity, is able to reflect the complex reality of development programmes implemented in multifaceted, and often unpredictable and culturally diverse, environments. Additionally, it became clear that programme implementers struggled with the fact that the standard matrix can only reflect planned outputs and outcomes whereas unplanned and unexpected outcomes, which occur in most programmes, cannot be accounted for. Whereas the LFA was liked by those planning an intervention, those that were monitoring had difficulties 'squeezing' the information into the matrix, losing mainly qualitative details on the way. The matrix therefore received the nickname 'lack-frame' and programme adaptation as well as learning from monitoring data collected is obviously not optimal.

To respond to the shortcomings of the LFA, the International Development Research Centre Canada (IDRC) developed an evaluation approach called 'Outcome Mapping' (OM) in 2001. The underlying assumption of OM is that changes are not one-dimensional, but that development occurs through changes in the behaviour of people. These changes do not necessarily occur as anticipated or planned. OM thus puts people and their behavioural learning processes first and accounts for unexpected outcomes that are seen as sources of innovation. The assets of OM lie in moving away from assessing the products of programmes and looking instead at changes in behaviour, relationships, actions and activities of people and organizations. In the programme planning process, OM is helpful in clearly defining the roles and responsibilities of the organizations involved and in defining milestones that reflect processes rather than results, while focusing attention on learning and accountability.

Despite the sophisticated and stringent alternative offered by OM, most organizations still use LFA for monitoring and evaluation. At first sight, OM does not differ much in terms of scope of data collected. The approach of being more people-centred allows for an analysis of data that accounts for deviation for the causality principle underscoring the LFA. The fact that OM is used less often might not only be due to the more social science-based approach of putting people and their learning first, but also be due to programme management and donors feeling more comfortable with LFA despite its shortcomings. After all, LFA has been used as a planning and evaluation approach for the last 50 years in development work.

The complexity of monitoring and evaluating sport and development interventions

When talking about an evaluation framework for SFD programmes, it is important to realize that all programmes embracing sport as a tool for development aim to trigger improvements in areas outside of the immediate sphere and influence of sport. Areas in which international players such as the Commonwealth Secretariat recommend using sport as a tool are:

- Youth development
- Health
- Access to and quality of education
- Gender equality
- Social inclusion and increased diversity
- Peace and stability

Kay and Dudfield (2013: 101) claim that,

the development areas to which sport is best placed to contribute are complex domains that usually encompass multi-sector approaches. Sport will often be one of multiple interventions employed, making it difficult to establish causal links between a sport-based intervention and stated development objectives.

When monitoring and evaluating SFD programmes, there is a need to recognize numerous complexities and keep the multi-sector approach in mind, which means that in M&E efforts we need to tackle at least two levels of investigation:

1. Proper monitoring and evaluation of the programme's effects and impact to improve the situation in the thematic area it addresses (increased health, gender equality, social inclusion, etc.).
2. Monitoring of sport's effect on social improvements and whether sport actually is the catalyst triggering such social change.

How (1) – the procedural programme monitoring – is done properly has been explained in detail in the above sections. It is important to measure the relationship between inputs and outputs, and to verify the outcomes. Overall impact is, as mentioned, intertwined with external factors and it is the evaluator's task to demonstrate how the performed activities contribute to triggering social change. It is obvious that a control group design, in which the absence of the intervention for a monitored cohort allows learning on what the programme actually accomplished, is not always possible, due to resource restraints, lack of capacity, or proportionality to programme size and relevance. There are also ethical implications that must be considered before using a control group design, which makes the approval of an ethics commission necessary.

Simpler research methods to monitor change can, however, also be explanatory enough to understand how youth can be supported, women and girls empowered, health issues addressed and social change initiated. But effect and impact measurements need to be performed with scientific ambition and technical solidity, to demonstrate the benefits and challenges of sport being used in reaching the set development objectives in the respective thematic area.

To shed light on (2) – sport's role as a catalyst – it is necessary to monitor the advantages and disadvantages sport can bring to reaching the intervention's objectives. Investigating the question of whether sport really makes a difference in the success of the intervention, it is necessary to consciously transcend the level of only measuring participation and to focus on concepts such as increased motivation, increased well-being and physical/mental self-perception through sport. For example, in sport and gender equity programmes, sport supposedly achieves all this and thus improves access to resources previously inaccessible for women and girls due to social barriers. The task is therefore to develop a monitoring and evaluation framework demonstrating that sport used as an intervention tool transcends these challenges and embraces the opportunities for target groups to genuinely benefit from catalytic effects of SFD. The ambition is to measure how sport can be used to reach the predefined development objectives. When using sport and play, expectations of improved programme success will be high, partly because SFD stakeholders claim the tool's effectiveness and partly because it seems so straightforward that sport can generate individual benefit and ultimately social change.

To verify this, a comparative effort is needed. Programmes in thematic fields in which SFD has been suggested as a useful form of intervention have often already been run without the use of SFD tools. These previous experiences provide knowledge on effectiveness, efficiency and sustainability. The analysis of benefits and shortcomings of other tools being used for such an intervention (e.g. media campaigns intended to change behaviour) can enable the validation of sport as a tool. It is obviously a challenge to separate the contributions made by sport-based approaches from all other non-sport and play-based approaches. This, however, should not lead to avoidance of the challenge. Assumptions, from the positive effects generated by sport-based approaches to the general acceptance and attractiveness of sport, need to be shown through solid M&E to withstand legitimate criticism. Just because youth are more likely to participate in, for example, gender equity training if programme methods are perceived as attractive does not mean that development objectives are reached more efficiently or maintained more effectively. All stakeholders need to be clear that measuring catalytic effects requires a comparative approach. Comparison is only possible if the evidence generated through monitoring and evaluation is compared to the results of projects implemented previously without sport or if the programme design incorporates a control group that is offered a similar intervention without sport and play.

Challenges of evaluation

Unfortunately not all programmes that achieve their goals and aims defined as indicators also deliver on their overall programme objective. Reasons for such failures are multiple. Only some can be mentioned here:

1. **Tools used for collecting data are not adequate** and thus do not enable the data collection process to generate representative results.
2. **The underlying theory of change is too simple**, ignoring that human interaction cannot be reduced to a chain of causally connected actions that lead to a predictable result: many programme implementers do not take into consideration that their programmes aim to change human behaviour and patterns of social interaction. Being used to thinking in causal chains, practitioners are often surprised that despite achieving the logically connected indicators (e.g. more boys and men learn about girls' and women's rights), the result is not reached (e.g. girls and women are not allowed equal access to education).
3. **The intricate process of evaluating monitoring data is done incorrectly** due to a lack of knowledge, a lack of resources, time restraints, a low prioritization of M&E and a lack of interest in lessons learnt.
4. **The conclusions drawn are biased** due to a lack of technical knowledge or cultural awareness. Using the standardized evaluation approaches – the Logical Framework Approach or Outcome Mapping – does not always enable a holistic understanding of the situation, the inclusion of unexpected results and a full understanding of how the programme objective relates to environmental factors relevant to impact claims.
5. **The multi-sector nature of the SFD intervention is too complex to trace the origin of success or failure** back to, for example, project implementation mistakes, lack of stakeholder management, mismatch of implementation tool (sport) and the overall objective (girls' education) and other factors.

Keeping these and further potential pitfalls in mind, evaluators have a great responsibility to process the data collected. This is especially the case if the data collection process has been carefully planned and many project stakeholders have contributed to the data set. The expectation towards evaluators is that data is processed by a sophisticated use of computer-based data interpretation programmes, that processes of change are highlighted and that results are presented in easily accessible graphs, pictures or text. Evaluators therefore need to have a solid level of technical expertise and should be well aware of the scientific discourse on project management, the thematic area of the intervention (e.g. access to quality education) and the implementation tool used (e.g. sport).

Reporting M&E findings

Structuring a report

Interpreting and reporting on project results, the DAC OECD[2] criteria provide a reference framework. The five criteria along which interpretation of data is meaningful and expected to run, are:

Relevance:
- To what extent are the objectives of the programme still valid?
- Are the activities and outputs of the programme consistent with the overall goal and the attainment of its objectives?
- Are the activities and outputs of the programme consistent with the intended impacts and effects?

Effectiveness:
- To what extent were the objectives achieved/are they likely to be achieved?
- What were the major factors influencing the achievement or non-achievement of the objectives?

Efficiency:
- Were activities cost-efficient?
- Were objectives achieved on time?
- Was the programme or project implemented in the most efficient way compared to alternatives?

Impact:
- What has happened as a result of the programme or project? Did the results yield direct or indirect effects and were they intended or unintended?
- What real difference has the activity made to the beneficiaries?
- How many people have been affected?

Sustainability:
- To what extent did the benefits of a programme or project continue after donor funding ceased?
- What were the major factors that influenced the achievement or non-achievement of the sustainability of the programme or project?

These criteria should guide the programme evaluation process. Structuring an evaluation report according to these key categories enables a solid representation of the data collected.[3]

Dissemination of findings

To counteract the complaints that too little data exists about the effectiveness and impact of SFD interventions, it is important that existing evaluation reports are meaningfully disseminated and findings are publicly discussed. It is therefore the programme owner's responsibility to clearly instruct an evaluator about the envisaged audience of the evaluation report. While planning M&E, collecting data and writing a report, the evaluator should have a clear audience in mind. She/he needs to make sure that the data collected, the results elaborated on and the style of reporting suits the needs of these addressees. Different needs of different audiences can be illustrated by simple examples:

1. A programme owner commissions an evaluation to enable internal learning of programme management staff. The project management personnel will probably be interested in whether the implementation can be rated as decently effective, well-managed and sustainable.
2. A programme owner has ambitions to convince the national government that new policies need to be developed based on using SFD as tool for improved education and health services for the local population. For governmental staff, it might be most intriguing to learn about the surplus value of using sport as an inexpensive and popular intervention tool for improved education and health services, caring significantly less about the concrete managerial aspects of the programme discussed.
3. A programme owner seeks support in demonstrating the long-term sustainability of the organization's activities in a certain region, to highlight its contribution to the SDGs in the mainstream media. For the media, it might be most important to access information of project relevance and impact, focusing less on a detailed description of how programme implementation has been conducted.

All three audiences are interested in different details and most likely require a different presentation format. For the first of the three – the project staff – the report needs to clearly reference project implementation phases, reflect the timing and incorporate budgetary reflections; for the second audience – the governmental decision-makers – the global relevance and feasibility of sport being used to fulfil international commitments is of more interest. When seeking to advise governments on incorporating sport as a tool to address the SDGs, it becomes necessary to report on the additional value that sport can bring in improving health, guaranteeing quality of education, promoting gender equality, facilitating economic growth, supporting good habitats and promoting peaceful societies. The third group – the media – is more interested in video and photographic material and favours eye witness reports over intricate graphs and pie charts.

Ultimately, it is the evaluator's responsibility to include the most relevant information for each of the audiences and to discuss upfront which format of presentation is most feasible. It is clear that information placement, digestibility and accessibility make all the difference in whether evidence will be consumed and reflected critically. It is the responsibility of those who generate new evidence to make the knowledge accessible and engage in discussions about programme effectiveness and sustainability. Only if active knowledge sharing will be made a part of the monitoring and evaluation efforts, can the lamenting be counteracted, which partly derives from being too lazy to read the existing – and, sadly, often boring – reports and partly from the unwillingness to deal with the ambiguity of lacking effectiveness which good evaluations might reveal.

Conclusion

If SFD is to establish itself on a broader scale in international development and claim more than the niche it currently holds it is necessary to prove effectiveness, efficiency and impact of the SFD interventions and present the results in a format that will be read by those that take decisions on implementing sport-based interventions. Arguments on triggering positive social development through sport can best be supported by solid and scientifically generated evaluations of sport-based interventions. The set of arguments for using sport should be readily available and easily understandable. The same holds true for the arguments that would rather pledge for choosing an alternative intervention tool, as a realistic judgement on what sport can accomplish is part of the equation.

Monitoring and evaluating programme results requires technical skills. Organizations should act on the bases of solid theories of change and programme staff needs to be trained to plan, perform or commission the data collection process and to seek answers for the proper predefined questions through monitoring the change that occurs during a sport-based intervention. Monitoring tools adequate for cultural settings, age groups and nature of information sought allow for feeding data collection matrixes like those of the well-known logical framework or the less used outcome mapping. While recording, it is important that data collectors and evaluators stay open for unexpected results and listen carefully to respondents.

Evaluating data also requires technical skills. Various computer-based support programmes can help to sort and store quantitative and qualitative data. Ultimately, however, data interpretation is the task of evaluators. Judgement of programme success will be measured against predefined objectives and is shaped by ideas of how social change happens. Evaluation is thus not solely a simple interpretation of data sets, but relies on social science findings that explain how human beings process information, change their behaviour or why they resist against consolidated knowledge. The evaluators' responsibility thus includes the linkage to latest social science findings, referencing relevant philosophical concepts and drawing conclusions for the practical programme implementation.

A final, and not to be neglected, step is the focused presentation of evaluation results. Format, style and the careful selection of information provided is important when addressing different audiences because not all evaluation results are relevant for the different addressees. Political decision-makers want comparative efficiency studies whereas programme managers are in need of programme process analysis. Keeping this in mind will help to drive the message home and can help to counteract the lamenting that too little adequate data exists in the field of SFD.

Notes

1   www.who.int/immunization/hpv/deliver/monitoring_and_evaluation_framework_path_2012.pdf.
2   Development Assistance Committee (DAC) of the Organisation for Economic Co-operation and Development (OECD).
3   www.oecd.org/dac/evaluation/daccriteriaforevaluatingdevelopmentassistance.htm.

Bibliography

Akindes, G. and Kirwin, M. (2009). Sport as international aid: Assisting development or promoting under-development in sub-Saharan Africa? In R. Levermore and A. Beacom, (eds), *Sport and International Development*. Basingstoke: Palgrave MacMillan, pp. 219–245.

Bakewell, O. and Garbutt, A. (2005). The use and abuse of the logical framework approach. *SEKA: Resulta tredovisiningsprojekt*. SIDA.

Center for Disease Control and Prevention (CDC). (n.d.) Brief 1: Overview of Policy Evaluation. Available at: www.cdc.gov/injury/pdfs/policy/Brief%201-a.pdf.

Center for Theory of Change. (n.d.). What is Theory of Change? Available at: www.theoryofchange.org/what-is-theory-of-change/.

Coalter, F. (2013). *Sport for Development: What Game are we Playing?* London & New York: Routledge.

Commonwealth. (2013). *Commonwealth Secretariat Strategic Plan 2013/14–2016/17*. London: Commonwealth Secretariat, 23 May.

Commonwealth Youth Sport for Development and Peace Working Group (CYSDP). (2015). *Sport for Development and Peace Youth Advocacy Toolkit*. London: Commonwealth Secretariat.

Darnell, S. (2014). Critical considerations for sport for development and peace policy development. In O. Dudfield (ed.), *Strengthening Sport for Development and Peace: National Policies and Strategies*. London: Commonwealth Secretariat, pp. 25–29.

Dlamini, N. (2007). Stories and M&E. Rethinking monitoring and evaluation. *ONTRAC*, *37*, September. Available at: https://evaluationinpractice.files.wordpress.com/2007/11/intrac-37.pdf.

Dudfield, O. and Dingwall-Smith, M. (2015). *Sport for Development and Peace and the 2030 Agenda for Sustainable Development*. London: Commonwealth Secretariat.

Earl, S., Carden, F. and Smutylo, T. (2001). *Outcome Mapping: Building Learning and Reflection into Development Planning*. Ottawa: International Development Research Centre (IDRC).

Gasper, D. (1999). Evaluating the 'Logical Framework Approach' – Towards Learning-Oriented Development Evaluation. The Hague: ISS Working Paper, Genera Series No. 303. Available at: http://pdf2.hegoa.efaber.net/entry/content/903/evaluating_the_LFA_Des_Gasper.pdf.

Giulianotti, R. (2014). Sport for development and peace policy options in the Commonwealth. In O. Dudfield (ed.), *Strengthening Sport for Development and Peace: National Policies and Strategies*. London: Commonwealth Secretariat, pp.13–24.

Hylton, K., Bramham, Peter, J., Dave and Nesti, M. (eds) (2001). *Sports Development: Policy, Process and Practice*. London & New York: Routledge.

Kay, T. and Dudfield, O. (2013). *The Commonwealth Guide to Advancing Development through Sport*. London: Commonwealth Secretariat.

Levermore, R. and Beacom, A. (2009). Opportunities, limitations, questions. In R. Levermore and A. Beacom (eds), *Sport and International Development*. Basingstoke: Palgrave MacMillan, pp. 246–268.

Organisation for Economic Co-operation and Development (OECD). (2008). *The Paris Declaration on Aid Effectiveness and the Accra Agenda for Action*. OECD Publishing. Available at: www.oecd.org/dac/effectiveness/34428351.pdf.

Organisation for Economic Co-operation and Development (OECD). (2012). *Measuring Regulatory: a Practitioners' Guide to Perception Survey*. OECD Publishing. Available at: http://dx.doi.org/10.1787/9789264167179-en; www.oecd.org/gov/regulatory-policy/48933826.pdf.

Path: A Catalyst for Global Health. (2012). Monitoring and Evaluation Framework. Available at: www.who.int/immunization/hpv/deliver/monitoring_and_evaluation_framework_path_2012.pdf.

Roduner, D., Schläppi, W. and Egli, W. (2008). Logical Framework Approach and Outcome Mapping: A Constructive Attempt of Synthesis. Zürich: Discussion Paper Agridea and NADEL ETH.

Simons, A. (2014). Evaluating the contribution sport makes to development objectives in the Pacific. In O. Dudfield (ed.), *Strengthening Sport for Development and Peace: National Policies and Strategies*. London: Commonwealth Secretariat, pp. 76–83.

Sustainable Development Solutions Network. (2015). Indicators and a Monitoring Framework for the Sustainable Development Goals: A Report by the Leadership Council of the Sustainable Development Solutions Network, Version 7, 20 March.

Synthesis Report of the Secretary-General on the Post-2015 Agenda. (2014). The Road to Dignity by 2030: Ending Poverty, Transforming All Lives and Protecting the Planet. New York: United Nations, 4 December.

UN General Assembly. (2006). Report of the Secretary-General A/61/373. New York: United Nations.

UN General Assembly 70/1. (2015). *Transforming our World: The 2030 Agenda for Sustainable Development*. Adopted by the General Assembly on 25 September 2015. New York: United Nations.

UN General Assembly Resolution 58/5. (2003). *Sport as a Means to Promote Health, Education, Development and Peace*. New York: United Nations.

Waddington, H., White, H., Snilsveit, B., Hombrados, J.G., Vojtkova, M., Davies, P., … and Tugwell P. (2012). *How to do a good systematic review of effects in international development: A toolkit, Journal of Development Effectiveness*, *4*(3), 359–387, DO I:10.1080/19439342.2012.711765.

www.oecd.org/gov/regulatory-policy/measuring-regulatory-performance.htm.

www.un.org/wcm/content/site/sport/home/sport.

www.sportanddev.org.

12
SDP and human rights

Peter Donnelly

Introduction

The year 2018 marked the 70th anniversary of the United Nations' endorsement of the Universal Declaration of Human Rights (UDHR) in 1948. And while none of the 30 articles in the UDHR refers specifically to sport, there are at least three articles that concern fundamental conditions for the practice of sport and recreational, physical activity (Veal 2015):

- Article 13 identifies the freedom of movement/travel, domestically and internationally, as a human right;
- Article 24 identifies rest and leisure (including reasonable limitation of working hours and periodic holidays with pay) as a human right; and
- Article 27 identifies the right freely to participate in the cultural life of the community.

In 1998, to mark the 50th anniversary of the UDHR, Bruce Kidd and I wrote the first comprehensive overview of the relationships between sports and human rights (Kidd and Donnelly 2000). That paper did not mention SDP, a movement that has emerged as a recognized aspect of international and social development, and grown exponentially in the 20 years since. Thus, it is fitting to revisit sport and human rights in the context of SDP. This is particularly important since SDP, and international and social development movements in general, are perhaps inevitable manifestations of 'the age of rights' (Bobbio 1982). United Nations' endorsement of SDP in the early 2000s (e.g. United Nations 2003) appeared to cement the relationship between SDP and human rights in terms of both the right to participate in sport and recreational physical activity and the rights that may be realized as a result of participation in sport. In fact, the most prominent and perhaps still best known SDP non-governmental organization (NGO), Right to Play, even appropriated a human right as the name/brand of the organization.

However, despite the foundational status of human rights, current discussions and analyses of SDP rarely refer to human rights. In the most recent comprehensive review of research in the field (Schulenkorf *et al.* 2016: 33), the word *rights* is mentioned only once: 'the advancement of access and rights for girls and women'. Governments that fund NGOs in the SDP movement may mention human rights, especially girls' and women's rights, but their agendas appear to range from diplomatic relations to the development of trade and economic opportunities. Corporations that fund NGOs in the SDP movement may mention equality, especially girls' and women's equality, but their agendas appear to range from corporate social responsibility concerns to low-cost labour and marketing opportunities. Hence, the importance of re-centring rights in discussions of SDP.

Recognizing this, the chapter begins with a consideration of human rights in 'the age of rights', and a reflection on the paradoxical and asymmetric use of human rights. It then addresses the growing attention paid to human rights in studies of sport, followed by critical analyses of the relationships between human rights and SDP, and concludes with some suggestions for strengthening those relationships.

The age of rights

Human rights are moral principles and norms of social behaviour that are now widely considered to be the *natural* entitlement of all humans. Their Western origins are often attributed to the English *Magna Carta* (1215), but the first major wave of debate and action to enshrine human rights occurred in Europe and the United States in the latter part of the eighteenth century. The French *Déclaration des droits de l'homme et du citoyen* (1789), and the United States *Bill of Rights* (1791) were declarations of the rights that humans could now expect in their respective post-revolutionary societies. These constitutional shifts to rights-based societies provoked a great deal of criticism, and Thomas Paine's *Rights of Man* (1791) was written by an American revolutionary in defence of the French Revolution against Edmund Burke's critique (*Reflections on the Revolution in France*, 1790).

It was quickly recognized that such rights were not universal. They did not apply to non-citizens, to slaves, or to women (see Mary Wollstonecraft's *A Vindication of the Rights of Woman*, 1792), and a *Universal Declaration of Human Rights* (UDHR) did not appear until 1948, after the horrors of two World Wars. The rights outlined in the UDHR are considered to be universal and inalienable – fundamental rights 'to which a person is inherently entitled simply because she or he is a human being' (Sepulveda *et al.* 2004), 'whatever our nationality, place of residence, sex, national or ethnic origin, colour, religion, language, or any other status' (UNOHCHR, n.d.). Bobbio (1982) refers to the period between the French and American Revolutions and the present day as The Age of Rights.

The UDHR, together with its two main implementing Covenants (International Covenant on Economic, Social and Cultural Rights; International Covenant on Civil and Political Rights – both adopted in 1966, coming into force with the status of treaties in 1976) came to be known as the International Bill of Rights. These were followed by a series of United Nations Conventions and Declarations outlining specific rights for various population segments, including:

- 1969 – International Convention of the Elimination of All Forms of Racial Discrimination (CERD)
- 1979 – International Convention on the Elimination of All Forms of Discrimination Against Women (CEDAW)
- 1989 – International Convention on the Rights of the Child (CRC)
- 1992 – International Declaration on the Rights of Persons Belonging to National or Ethnic, Religious or Linguistic Minorities
- 2006 – International Convention on the Rights of Persons with Disabilities (CRPD)
- 2007 – International Declaration on the Rights of Indigenous Peoples

With the fundamental conditions for the practice of sport and recreational physical activity outlined in the UDHR, the idea that there was a human right to participate in sport and recreational physical activity began to emerge in rights documents in the 1970s. The European Sport for All Charter (1976; revised in 1992 and 2001) was quickly followed by the UNESCO International Charter on Physical Education, Physical Activity and Sport (1978, revised in 2015), and by articles declaring the right to participate for girls and women (CEDAW 1979), children (CRC 1989), persons with a disability (CRPD 2006) and Indigenous peoples (2007). The International Olympic Committee finally included the right to participate in sport in the Olympic Charter in 1996.

Although there were earlier manifestations of SDP, often associated with missionary and colonial development, the initiatives that we currently recognize as SDP (along with most of the human development initiatives that started in the second half of the twentieth century) occurred in the wake of the UDHR. Many of these initiatives followed independence struggles, and were introduced in support of the newly independent former colonies of Belgium, Britain, France, the Netherlands, Portugal and Spain. The initiatives were established in the cause of human rights, and the link between human rights and SDP was clearly recognized in the early academic reviews of what was by then being referred to as the SDP 'movement' (Giulianotti 2004; Kidd 2008).

Paradoxes of human rights

Giulianotti (1999: 2), citing Frankovits (1998) notes that 'development is a subset of human rights'. This is evident in the *raison d'être* of the United Nations – peace and security, development and human rights – which encompass the topic of this chapter. When the UDHR was drafted and accepted by the members of the newly formed United Nations in 1948, it was timely in a number of ways. The recent World Wars, genocides and rampant violations of what were now to be considered as universal rights motivated their development and acceptance, but they were also connected to a widespread popular determination in the former warring nations not to return to the social inequalities that existed before the war.

That determination, in many of the democratic countries, resulted in the emergence of welfare states with the realization of a number of human rights through state-supported health care, retirement pensions, higher education and unemployment insurance. The framework of human rights also gave impetus to anti-colonial independence movements, and to equal rights movements (e.g. anti-racist movements such as the anti-apartheid and civil rights movements; gender equality movements; Indigenous rights movements; gay rights movements; and disability rights movements). And while these movements are engaged in ongoing struggles and have yet to fully realize equal rights, it is difficult to imagine how whatever progress has been made could have been achieved without the UDHR.

However, it is also important to recognize that human rights are contingent and political (Kidd and Donnelly 2000). When most countries endorsed 'universal' human rights in 1948, and every country endorsed them in 1993 (Vienna World Conference on Human Rights) and again in 2005 (UN World Summit, New York), the notion of 'universal' was aspirational. As Bobbio notes, 'human rights however fundamental are historical rights and therefore arise from specific conditions characterized by the embattled defence of new freedoms against old powers … [human rights] only come into existence when their existence is either essential or possible' (Bobbio 1982: xi). Tagliarina (2015) considers the 'vernacular' of human rights, where rights are negotiated and translated differently in different contexts and by different populations segments. Thus, 'rights are prime battle grounds for fights for social power, as the relatively disadvantaged can use rights to advance their claims, but so too can the powerful deploy rights talk to counteract efforts for social change' (Tagliarina 2015: 1202).

In practice, the way that human rights are structured and enforced creates a number of paradoxes. As Nash (2011: 1) points out: 'On the one hand state actors are held to be accountable as the violators of human rights. On the other hand, states are addressed in international terms as the guarantors of human rights'. The connection of rights to states compounds the paradox. Arendt (1973), writing with reference to 'the right to have rights', pointed out that since rights attach to states, there were no guarantors of the rights of refugees and other stateless persons. In other words, individuals who most need the protection of human rights are least likely to have them (see also Prellwitz 2016).

Douzinas (2013) takes the paradox further, pointing out that since 1948 there have continued to be massacres, genocides and ethnic cleansing. Thus, as human rights historian Lynn Hunt pointed out, 'human rights are still easier to endorse than to enforce' (Hunt 2007: 211). However, she goes on to argue that the success of human rights lies in the fact that it is no longer possible to pretend that some humans are less human than others; 'you know the meaning of human rights because you feel distressed when they are violated. The truths of human rights might be paradoxical in this sense, but they are nonetheless self evident' (Hunt 2007: 214). It is difficult to imagine the existence of human and social development programmes, including SDP, without the existence of a framework of human rights.

Sport and human rights

As Kidd and Donnelly (2000) pointed out, there were few acknowledgements of any connections between sport and human rights in the international sport community, or the academic community, by the 50th anniversary of UDHR. However, by 2006, in the lead up to the 2008 Beijing Olympics, the sport and academic communities were beginning to acknowledge the connections – including in relation to SDP. Donnelly outlined three ways that sport and human rights are related: (1) the right to participate in sports and recreational physical activity; (2) the possibility that sport may assist in the achievement of human rights; and (3) the use of sports to achieve rights for specific classes of persons, which combines aspects of the right to participate in sport and recreational physical activity with the more general use of sports to achieve human rights (Donnelly 2008: 384).

The right to participate in sports and recreational physical activity has been well established and endorsed over a number of charters and conventions. However, there is only one major example of sport assisting in the achievement of human rights – namely, the ways that sport was involved in the overthrow of apartheid in South Africa. This mainly occurred through non-participation in terms of international boycotts of white South African teams and athletes. Imprisoned leaders of the African National Congress also used sport by starting a soccer league on Robben Island; governance of the league – employing principles of fairness, equity and social justice – came to serve as a 'rehearsal' for the subsequent governance of South Africa (Korr and Close 2010).

In 2006, a hunger strike by Tibetan activists at the Turin Olympics started a long campaign of protests against human rights violations by China, and many (unsuccessful) calls to boycott the Games and/or to extract promises from the IOC and the Chinese government regarding the implementation of human rights. In 2007, a group of women ski jumpers brought an (unsuccessful) lawsuit, based on the Canadian Charter of Rights and Freedoms, against the organizers of the 2010 Vancouver Olympics for violating Canada's gender equity rights by not having a women's ski jumping event. The main focus of human rights activism in sports continued to be on major Games and other major sports events, including labour rights, athletes' rights, gender equality, environmental rights, housing rights, children's rights, and so on.

Amnesty UK typifies the growing calls for human rights in sports:

> Human rights have a vital role to play in sport that is often overlooked. From fighting racism, sexism and homophobia to standing up for the rights of the workers building stadiums, sport and human rights are intrinsically linked.
>
> *Amnesty n.d.*

Recent examples include: the United Nations and the IOC cementing their relationship through the United Nations Human Rights Council with a report on using sport to promote human rights (UNHCR 2015); FIFA revising its Human Rights Policy (2017) in time for the 2018 Russia World Cup; the World Players Association (the largest international athlete's union, and a branch of UNI Global Union) releasing its Universal Declaration of Player Rights (14 December 2017); and the Commonwealth Games Federation (CGF), building on its planned 'new standards for inclusivity and gender-equality' at the 2018 Gold Coast (Australia) Commonwealth Games by announcing a CGF Policy Statement on Human Rights (CGF 2017).

Human rights and SDP

Over the same period of time that mainstream sport has discovered its connections with human rights, SDP, grounded in human rights, seems to be losing its direct connection. As noted, Giulianotti (2004) and Kidd (2008) clearly identified the SDP – human rights connection, a connection that was always evident in the significant role played by the United Nations in supporting and promoting SDP. In 2001, Secretary-General Kofi Annan appointed Adolf Ogi as a special advisor on sport, precisely at the time that Olympic Aid was morphing into Right to Play. In 2002, Kofi Annan was invited to speak at the Olympic Aid Roundtable Forum held in association with the Salt Lake City Olympics, where he made the case for the use of sport for development:

> Sport can play a role in improving the lives of individuals, not only as individuals, I might add, but whole communities. I am convinced that the time is right to build on that understanding, to encourage governments, development agencies and communities to think how sport can be included more systematically in the plans to help children, particularly those living in the midst of poverty, disease and conflict,
>
> *Annan 2002, cited by Coalter 2010*

It was only a matter of time before Johann Koss (CEO of Olympic Aid/Right to Play) and others persuaded Annan to link sport to the achievement of the Millennium Development Goals (Kidd 2008) – the United Nations' human rights agenda for the new century – with a report that gave major impetus to the SDP movement (United Nations 2003).

Also in 2003, the first International Conference on Sport and Development, held in Magglingen, Switzerland, produced the 'Magglingen Declaration and Recommendations', again affirming the SDP – human rights connection (Giulianotti 2004). And in 2004, during the lead up to the United Nations declaring 2005 as the International Year of Sport and Physical Education, the Sport for Development and Peace International Working Group was established (IWG-SDP), and the post of Special Advisor to the Secretary-General on Sport for Development and Peace (UNOSDP) was established with an office in Geneva. The UNOSDP and the IWG, especially the IWG web site – sportanddev.org – have been an important backbone for the SDP movement, in many ways sustaining the connection to human rights through the UN connection.

The connection between human rights and SDP clearly fits into the third way that sport and human rights are related: 'the use of sports to achieve rights for specific classes of persons, which combines aspects of the right to participate in sport and recreational physical activity with the more general use of sports to achieve human rights' (Donnelly 2008: 384). This category was originally intended to characterize grassroots movements of 'marginalized groups and populations who have begun to announce their presence and claim their right to human rights with the use of sport' (Donnelly 2008: 387). Examples given at that time included the Homeless World Cup, the Railroad All Stars (a soccer team comprised of female sex workers in Guatemala), the Millennium Stars (a soccer team comprised of former child soldiers in Liberia) and, in West Africa, amputees' soccer teams comprised of victims of land mines and reprisal amputations. However, although not mentioned in the 2008 paper, it is clear that SDP fits well into this category, and that even some of the examples noted here (e.g. Homeless World Cup) have benefited from the involvement of NGOs recognized as part of the SDP movement.

So how has the SDP movement shifted from this fundamental connection to human rights to a situation where, as noted, Schulenkorf et al. (2016) only mention the word 'rights' once in their recent review of the field; where a review of recent SDP research by Darnell et al. (2016) only mentions rights once, in terms of the Convention on the Rights of the Child?; and where scant mention is given to rights in a Dutch review of academic research on SDP between 1998 and 2013? (Van Eekeren et al. 2013).

Perhaps the relationship with human rights has become normalized; it is assumed and accepted to the point where it does not need to be mentioned. Or perhaps, as Coalter (2010: 301) argues, to the increasingly neoliberal governments and corporations who fund SDP programmes, 'rights' has become a dirty word. For capitalist states, the Covenant on Economic, Social and Cultural Rights was far more problematic than the Covenant on Civil and Political Rights, even in 1948. Health care, higher education, food, clothing, housing, jobs and even sport have been referred to as 'new' rights by right wing critics: 'Food, jobs and housing are certainly necessities. But no useful purpose is served by calling them "rights"' (Munoz 2007). While it has become de rigueur to support identity rights, especially gender equality, actual support to improve the material, social and cultural conditions of life is more difficult to obtain for SDP programmes. And it is under the continual scramble for funding that, as Coalter notes, 'projects [are] being developed to fit the funding criteria' (Coalter 2010: 307), 'NGOs make inflated promises in order to obtain funding' (ibid.: 308), and there is a tendency to exaggerate achievements in order to sustain funding.

SDP, neocolonialism and human rights

If SDP is to be grounded in human rights, which specific rights are in its purview? SDP may contribute in a small way to the realization of gender equality rights, to disability inclusion rights, to the rights of children, to the right to education and the right to health (e.g. AIDS prevention programmes, vaccination programmes). Such contributions are, in part, contingent on the sustainability of a programme (dependent on funding) or the ability of an NGO to ensure that local capacity and infrastructure are in place to sustain the programme when NGO funding runs out. SDP may even contribute in a small way to attaining the right to peace and security: 'Sport may not change the world, but children playing with their enemies might' (Sugden and Tomlinson 2018: 131).

However, SDP does *not* ensure the 'right to play' for children living in poverty. Despite its advertising, it would be a mistake to think that no play occurred until Right to Play (or other SDP NGOs) arrived at a refugee camp, Indigenous reserve, or low-income village. Unless incapacitated by sickness, injury or starvation, or otherwise prevented, children (will) always play. Recent images of children playing in the bombed out streets of Syrian cities are a reminder of this, and Eisen's research (1985; 1990) even provided evidence of children's play in the concentration camps before and during World War II. So, rather than ensuring the 'right to play', it is more accurate to say that SDP NGOs organize and direct particular ways of playing.

As Bruce Kidd noted in 2008, SDP was 'still in its infancy, woefully underfunded, completely unregulated, poorly planned and co-ordinated and largely isolated from mainstream development efforts' (Kidd 2008: 376). Recent critiques suggest that little has changed, and that there are ongoing concerns with regard to sustainability (cf. Donnelly *et al.* 2011), claimed achievements and evidence (cf. Coalter 2013), and the paternalism and neocolonialism associated with SDP programmes (cf. Darnell and Hayhurst 2012). Here, I focus on this latter critique because, while overlapping in various ways with the sustainability and evidence critiques, it is the issue that is most directly related to human rights.

The neocolonialist critique of SDP programmes has been used in a rather cavalier way since the mid-2000s. The criticism refers to factors ranging from the 'white savior syndrome' of some volunteers and NGO leaders to the implicit assumption, motivating many SDP programmes, that showing how things are done in the global North is the path to development. Because most of the places in receipt of development initiatives are former colonies of European countries or, in the case of the white settler nations of Abya Yala, Aotearoa and 'Australia',[1] still colonizers of indigenous peoples; are former sites of Cold War struggles between the USA and the Soviet Union; and/or economic colonies of East Asia, Europe and North 'America', neocolonial seems an apt term to describe the actions of many of the SDP NGOs that have been studied.

More recently there have been some more nuanced attempts to outline the paternalistic nature of SDP and the relationships between development and dependency. For example, Darnell (2012) outlined how Edward Said's critique of imperialism provided important insights into the ways that SDP is viewed in the global North. Mwaanga (2013) employs a postcolonial perspective to point out that the global North uses 'modernization' as the primary theory of development. And Mwaanga and Adeosun (2017) have been able to show that the use of a critical participatory paradigm in research may add some praxis to the principles of decolonization in an SDP programme.

It is disturbing to think about the number of ways that neocolonization may occur in SDP programmes – not just in the specific programme agendas that are more often determined by global North funders than by the fieldworkers and recipients, but also in the mindset which assumes that knowledge and practices from the global North are always superior to local knowledge and practices. In addition, the sports and activities employed in SDP programmes are frequently the colonizers' sports and activities (e.g. soccer, basketball, ice hockey, rugby and so on). And while it is appropriate to argue that soccer is incredibly popular in, for example, the countries of sub-Saharan Africa – and thus makes an important and immediate connection between development workers and recipients – it is also appropriate to acknowledge that the popularity of soccer (and the virtual eradication of many local physical cultures) is an artefact of the overwhelming hegemonic impact of colonization. Revival of traditional games, dances and sports is an important step toward decolonization, although, as Mrozek cautions: 'the consciousness of having to preserve the culture fundamentally alters what is preserved – [potentially] turning it into a museum piece' (Mrozek 1987: 38).

The crucial right that is being violated here is the right to self-determination. This right is enshrined in a number of major Charters, Conventions and Declarations of human rights, most recently in the United Nations Declaration on the Rights of Indigenous Peoples, where Article 3 states: 'Indigenous peoples have the right to self-determination. By virtue of that right they freely determine their political status and freely pursue their economic, social and cultural development'.

This right was recognized even when the mandate of the Special Advisor on SDP was being established in 2004, where one of the six key elements stated: '*Ensure due attention is accorded to cultural and traditional dimensions*, respect upheld for principles of human rights – especially youth and child rights – human diversity, gender equality, social insertion and environmental sustainability' (cited by Beutler 2008: 364, emphasis added). And it was further acknowledged in the 2007 *Literature Reviews on Sport for Development and Peace*:

> It is important to note that … no country ever achieves a final state of being 'developed' – as the UN Declaration notes, development is a process of 'constant improvement'. However, key questions remain: 'who determines the form of development in a country?' and 'what are the appropriate roles for foreigners in the development of another country'.
>
> *Donnelly et al. 2007: 11*

Of course, the right to self-determination is also recognized by, and part of the agency of the recipients of development programmes. The principle of 'Nothing about us without us' is often associated with the disability community, although it is a much older political principle. Australian Indigenous activist, Lilla Watson gave the following version: 'If you have come here to help me, you are wasting your time. But if you have come because your liberation is bound up with mine then let us work together'. Donnelly, *et al.* (2011: 597) outlined a scenario where a supposed consultation was taking place between NGO representatives and local community representatives regarding a SDP programme to be implemented. The scenario imagines how the two sides might talk past one another, with the NGO representatives believing that they have consulted with local people, and local people not feeling empowered to negotiate in case their concerns would jeopardize the provision of equipment and expertise by the NGO. A more complete acknowledgement and implementation of the right to self-determination is crucial if SDP is to shed its neocolonial tendencies.

Conclusion

The 'problematic ambitions' and 'noble intentions' of SDP (Guest 2009: 1338) become most evident in the cultural struggles between the *right to play* (sport as an end in itself) and the *right to play in the neocolonizer's way* (sport as a means to an end). After outlining the anecdotal evidence, and evidence based on qualified research support for the right to play, Qualter Berna argues that:

> this might be enough. Practicing sport for sport's sake is imperative. It is worth every penny to build sports infrastructure, promote sports programming and develop sports champions and teams. Sport is the right of every individual and it is beneficial for communities in countless ways … Perhaps it is sufficient to ensure this basic child right and happiness alone is a strong enough measure.
>
> *Berna 2006: 36, 37*

With this in mind, there is something of an inevitability that sport (and SDP) would be loaded with functionalist baggage and become a means to an end. This has not been helped since the

1980s by the continuing, self-justifying, and often unsubstantiated claims of physical educators, recreation programmers and exercise scientists in the global North that sport and physical activity can cure many social, physical and mental ills (see Coalter 2007 for evidence of the lack of evidence). This mantra was adopted by many well-meaning people who felt that their own lives had been enriched by their participation in sport and who wanted to 'give something back' by starting or becoming involved in a SDP NGO. They often saw themselves as using the benefits of sport to bring human rights to those without rights, but ran into the same problems of evidence and causality that had become apparent to critics of development programmes using sport and recreation in the cities of the global North:

> With regard to the [psychological, social and community] benefits of sport participation identified in the research literature … *the evident benefits appear to be an indirect outcome of the context and social interaction that is possible in sport* rather than a direct outcome of participating in sport. Critical analysis of a broad range of research findings provides overwhelming support for this conclusion.
>
> *Kidd and Donnelly, 2007: 4, emphasis added*

Although SDP programmes are essentially concerned with social transformation, it has been pointed out (e.g. Hartmann and Kwauk 2011) that the often externally determined functionalist elements of the programmes may in fact serve to maintain and reproduce the status quo in terms of established class and material power relations. Where social transformations may occur, they are more likely to be in the area of identity rights (gender equality, disability inclusion and so on) rather than disrupting structural inequalities. This critique has, to some extent, been taken up by some in the SDP NGO community. While still attempting to serve the demands of their funding 'masters' who are concerned primarily with programme outcomes, some have begun to draw on philosophy and economics to implement a 'capability' approach (cf. Svensson and Levine 2017) in an attempt to support programme participants in the realization of their human rights. Others are advocating an Ubuntu approach whereby the right to self-determination is realized through a community-based democratic approach (Mwaanga and Banda 2014). And anticolonial researchers are pointing out the need to consider the different approaches to teaching between, for example, European and indigenous communities, which may have a significant effect on SDP programme delivery (e.g. Battiste 2002).

In conclusion, I argue that the 'development of sport-for-development' (Coalter 2011: 311) would benefit in significant ways from a re-focus on human rights. For example, any SDP programme concerned with children and youth (as most of the programmes are) should use the UN Convention on the Rights of the Child as a starting point. More than half of the 42 Articles have direct and important relevance for SDP programmes, and form a template for a human rights based programme – ranging from Article 3 (best interests of the child) to Article 12 (respect for the views of the child) to Article 15 (freedom of association) to Article 17 (access to information) to Article 19 (protection from all forms of violence) to Article 27 (adequate standard of living) to Articles 28 and 29 (education) and, of course, to Article 31 (leisure, play and culture). In the final analysis though, discovering ways to enshrine the right to self-determination in SDP programmes may be the most difficult challenge, and the most important goal.

Note

1   Given this critique of colonialism and neocolonialism it is appropriate, where possible, to use a more postcolonial/anticolonial terminology. Aotearoa is the Maori name for New Zealand, and Abya

Yala (Kuna) is increasingly being used to refer to the 'Americas'. Its use is attributed to ('Bolivian') Aymara leader, Takir Mamani: 'To name our cities, towns and continents with a foreign name is equivalent to submitting our wills to the identity of our invaders and their heirs' (cited by Albo 1995: 33).

References

Albo, X. (1995). Our identity starting from pluralism in this base. In J. Beverley, J. Oviedo and M. Aronna (eds), *The Postmodern Debate in Latin America* Durham, NC: Duke University Press, pp. 18–33).

Amnesty. (n.d.) Available at: www.amnesty.org.uk/issues/Sport-and-human-rights.

Arendt, H. (1973). *The Origins of Totalitarianism*. New York: Houghton Mifflin Harcourt.

Battiste, M. (2002). *Indigenous Knowledge and Pedagogy in First Nations Education: A Literature Review*. Ottawa: National Working Group on Education. Available at : www.afn.ca/uploads/files/education/24._2002_oct_marie_battiste_indigenousknowledgeandpedagogy_lit_review_for_min_working_group.pdf.

Berna, A. Q. (2006). Sport as a human right and as a means for development. *Sport and Development*. Ch.2. Leuven: Uitgeverij Lannoo Campus, pp. 35–42.

Beutler, I. (2008). Sport serving development and peace: Achieving the goals of the United Nations through sport. *Sport in Society*, 11(4), 359–369.

Bobbio, N. (1982). *The Age of Rights*. Cambridge: Polity.

CGF. (2017). Press release: Gold Coast Ceremonies Concept, CGF Human Rights Statement and 2022 Candidate City Process Extension approved in Colombo. 6 October 2017: http://mailchi.mp/bc87b1158f2e/gold-coast-ceremonies-concept-cgf-human-rights-statement-and-2022-candidate-city-process-extension-approved-in-colombo.

Coalter, F. (2007). *A Wider Social Role for Sport: Who's Keeping the Score?* London: Taylor & Francis.

Coalter, F. (2010). The politics of sport-for-development: Limited focus programmes and broad gauge problems? *International Review for the Sociology of Sport*, 45(3), 295–314.

Coalter, F. (2013). *Sport for Development: What Game Are We Playing?* London: Routledge.

Darnell, S. (2012). *Sport for Development and Peace: A Critical Sociology*. London: Bloomsbury.

Darnell, S., Chawansky, M., Marchesseault, D., Holmes, M. and Hayhurst, L. (2016). The state of play: Critical sociological insights into recent 'sport for development and peace' research. *International Review for the Sociology of Sport*, doi:10.1177/1012690216646762.

Darnell, S. and Hayhurst, L. (2012). Hegemony, postcolonialism and sport for development: A response to Lindsey and Grattan. *International Journal of Sport Policy and Politics*, 4(1), 111–124.

Donnelly, P. (2008). Sport and human rights. *Sport in Society*, 11(4), 381–394.

Donnelly, P., Atkinson, M., Boyle S. and Szto, C. (2011). Sport for development and peace: A public sociology perspective. *Third World Quarterly*, 32(3), 581–593.

Donnelly, P., Darnell, S., Wells, C. and Coakley, J. (2007). The use of sport to foster child and youth development and education. In B. Kidd and P. Donnelly (eds), *The Benefits of Sport in International Development: Five Literature Reviews*. Geneva: Switzerland: International Working Group for Sport, Development and Peace, pp. 7–47.

Douzinas, C. (2013). The paradoxes of human rights. *Constellations*, 20(1), 51–67.

Eisen, G. (1985). Coping in adversity: Children's play in the Holocaust. In G. A. Fine (ed.), *Meaningful Play, Playful Meaning*. Champaign, IL: Human Kinetics, pp. 129–141.

Eisen, G. (1990). *Children and Play in the Holocaust: Games Among the Shadows*. Amherst, MA: University of Massachusetts Press.

Giulianotti, R. (1999). Sport and social development in Africa: Some major human rights issues. Proceedings of the First International Conference on Sports and Human Rights, 1–3 September. Available at: www.ausport.gov.au/fulltext/1999/nsw/p18-25.pdf.

Giulianotti, R. (2004). Human rights, globalization and sentimental education: The case of sport. *Sport in Society*, 7(3), 355–369.

Guest, A. (2009). The diffusion of development-through-sport: Analyzing the history and practice of the Olympic Movement's grassroots outreach to Africa. *Sport in Society*, 12(10), 1336–1352.

Hartmann, D. and Kwauk, C. (2011). Sport and development: An overview, critique, and reconstruction. *Journal of Sport and Social Issues*, 35(3), 284–305.

Hunt, L. (2007). *Inventing Human Rights: A History*. New York: W. W. Norton.

Kidd, B. (2008). A new social movement: Sport for development and peace. *Sport in Society*, *11*(4), 370–380.

Kidd, B. and Donnelly, P. (2000). Human rights in sport. *International Review for the Sociology of Sport*, *35*(2), 131–148.

Kidd, B. and Donnelly, P. (eds) (2007). *The Benefits of Sport in International Development: Five Literature Reviews*. Geneva: Switzerland: International Working Group for Sport, Development and Peace.

Korr, C. and Close, M. (2010). *More Than Just a Game – Soccer vs. Apartheid: The Most Important Soccer Story Ever Told*. New York: St. Martin's/Dunne.

Munoz, C. (2007). Human rights. Dangerously blurred. *The Economist*, 22 May Available at: www.economist.com/opinion/displaystory.cfm?story_id=8888856.

Mwaanga, O. (2013). International sport and development. In K. Hylton (ed.), *Sport Development: Policy, Process and Practice*. New York: Routledge.

Mwaanga, O. and Adeosun, K. (2017). Decolonisation in practice: A case study of the kicking AIDS out programme in Jamaica. *Journal of Sport for Development*, *5*(9), 58–69.

Mwaanga, O. and Banda, D. (2014). A postcolonial approach to understanding sport-based empowerment of people living with HIV/AIDS (PLWHA) in Zambia: The case of the cultural philosophy of Ubuntu. *Journal of Disability and Religion*, *18*(2), 173–191.

Nash, K. (2011). States of human rights, *Sociologica*, 1. Available at: www.rivisteweb.it/doi/10.2383/34620.

Prellwitz, M. (2016). Protecting the Rightless – Are Refugee Rights still the Paradox of Human Rights?: A case study of refugee children's access to education in Lebabon. Master's thesis, University of Uppsala, SWEDEN. Available at: www.diva-portal.org/smash/record.jsf?pid=diva2%3A931973anddswid=7496#sthash.vhkYJGUH.dpbs.

Schulenkorf, N., Sherry, E. and Rowe, K. (2016). Sport for development: An integrated literature review. *Journal of Sport Management*, *30*(1), 22–39.

Sepúlveda, M., van Banning, T., Gudmundsdóttir, G., Chamoun, C. and van Genugten, W. (2004). *Human Rights Reference Handbook* (3rd edn rev.). Ciudad Colon, Costa Rica: University of Peace.

Sugden, J. and Tomlinson, A. (2018). *Sport and Peace-Building in Divided Societies: Playing with Enemies*. London: Routledge.

Svensson, P. and Levine, J. (2017). Rethinking sport for development and peace: The capability approach. *Sport in Society*, *20*(7), 905–923.

Tagliarina, D. (2015). Power, privilege and rights: How the powerful and powerless create a vernacular of rights. *Third World Quarterly*, *36*(6), 1191–1206.

UNHRC. (2015). Final Report of the Human Rights Council Advisory Committee on the possibilities of using sport and the Olympic ideal to promote human rights for all and to strengthen universal respect for them. New York: UN General Assembly, 17 August.

UNOHCHR. (n.d.). The United Nations, Office of the High Commissioner of Human Rights, What are human rights? Available at: www.ohchr.org/en/issues/pages/whatarehumanrights.aspx (accessed 15 January 2017).

United Nations. (2003). Sport for Development and Peace: Towards Achieving the Millennium Development Goals. Report from the United Nations Inter-Agency Task Force on Sport for Development and Peace. Geneva: United Nations.

Van Eekeren, F., ter Horst , K. and Fictorie, D. (2013). *Sport for Development: The Potential Value and Next Steps – Reviews of Policy, Programs and Academic Research, 1998–2013*. 's-Hertogenbosch, Netherlands: International Sport Alliance, KNVB, Right to Play Netherlands.

Veal, A. (2015). Human rights, leisure and leisure studies. *World Leisure Journal*, *57*(4), 249–272.

13

SDP and social exclusion

Ruth Jeanes, Ramon Spaaij, Jonathan Magee and Tess Kay

Introduction

The previous two decades have witnessed an increasing abundance of Sport for Development and Peace (SDP) initiatives within the global North and South that seek to use sport to counter social exclusion. Global North SDP programs tend to target specific populations categorised as 'at risk'. This can be related to numerous factors including low educational attainment, unemployment, homelessness and involvement in crime (for project examples see Positive Futures, Street Chance www.chancetoshine.org/street/chance-to-shine-street and Street Soccer www.thebigissue.org. au/community-street-soccer/about/ initiatives). There is an extensive literature examining the value of sport in addressing social exclusion across these contexts (Crabbe 2000; Nichols 2010; Collins 2014). Although it is difficult to generalise findings, these studies typically suggest that depending on how sport is used and managed it can contribute to a range of health, social and economic outcomes (Bailey 2005). Global South initiatives have similarly focused on young people. Due to higher rates of poverty within global South countries, SDP programs frequently work with whole communities rather than adopting the global North approach of targeting a small number of 'at-risk' individuals. SDP initiatives within global South contexts often provide support for young people to access education and develop life skills, and for addressing social exclusion within impoverished communities.

Despite the obvious connection between SDP and social exclusion, the term itself is not commonplace within SDP policy and practice. Other related concepts are more familiar including social development (Marshall and Barry 2015), social mobility (Spaaij 2013) and social capital (Coalter 2007). Yet, we argue that SDP is underpinned by a desire to reduce social exclusion and seeks to tackle some of the core mechanisms that render individuals and communities excluded or marginalised. In this chapter, we firstly outline how social exclusion has been conceptualised in mainly global North literature and consider how applicable these frameworks are within the global South. The second part of the chapter discusses a case study of an SDP program that aims to address social exclusion among young women by providing access to sports participation, education and life skills development. The initiative has been organised by a nongovernmental organisation (NGO) in Lusaka, Zambia. Through this case study, we highlight ways in which SDP can contribute to addressing aspects of social exclusion in the global South, but also consider some of the constraints that projects encounter. The chapter draws on insights and observations gathered from several years of primary research in Lusaka, where longitudinal data was collected via interviews and focus groups with participants, NGO staff, peer leaders and community members.

Understanding social exclusion

The concept of social exclusion originated in France in the 1970s and has subsequently become part of policy discourse in several other countries. Despite its widespread use, the concept remains vague and difficult to define. To be socially excluded is essentially to be shut out of mainstream society. In this sense, the term relates to marginalisation, poverty, disadvantage and social closure. However, social exclusion does not occur statically or in binary form (Spaaij *et al.* 2014). It is not the case that individuals and communities are either excluded or included or that they will always be one or the other. Instead, it is valuable to consider social exclusion as a dynamic process that is driven by power relations connected to social, political and cultural norms. Individuals and communities can be excluded by multiple dimensions; they may feel included in certain aspects of their lives but excluded in others (Spaaij *et al.* 2014). For example, individuals may consider sport, or certain sport-related activities, as exclusionary but feel included within other cultural and social arenas.

Social exclusion, therefore, tends to occur in degrees. Very few individuals are absolutely excluded, but many may experience multiple dimensions of exclusion that lead them to be highly vulnerable and experience 'deep social exclusion' (Levitas *et al.* 2007). Various scholars, predominantly from the global North, have developed conceptual frameworks that seek to capture the multidimensional nature of social exclusion (e.g. Hills *et al.* 2002; Bhalla and Lapeyre 2004). Most of these frameworks highlight that social exclusion is a consequence of exclusion from the economic, social, cultural and political domains, leading to lesser quality of life, well-being and poorer living conditions. For example, Levitas *et al.* (2007: 25) define social exclusion as follows:

> A complex multi-dimensional process. It involves the lack, or denial, of resources, rights, goods and services, and the inability to participate in the normal relationships and activities available to the majority of people in a society, whether in economic, social, cultural or political arenas. It affects both the quality of life of individuals and the equity of society as a whole.

There are several aspects we can take from this definition to assist in understanding what social exclusion is and how it is experienced. While poverty is a key contributor to social exclusion, Levitas and others highlight that this is one of a host of factors. Social exclusion can be experienced at the micro level, by individuals, but also at a meso and macro level across families, communities and societies (Spaaij *et al.* 2014). As Levitas *et al.* (2007) concludes, social exclusion is generally associated with negative consequences for both individuals and societies. Research consistently suggests that the effects of social exclusion are negative for individual's psychological and material well-being as well as creating communities that are more susceptible to conflict, inequality and mistrust (Abrams *et al.* 2005).

Social exclusion and the global South

Social exclusion is a predominantly global North discourse. It has relevance within the global South (Gore and Figueiredo 1997), but cannot be adopted uncritically. In the global North, social exclusion is usually associated with a marginalised minority who are unable to fully and equitably participate in 'normal' activities (Levitas *et al.* 2007) or experience a sufficient standard of living. In contrast, within the global South the majority of populations may live in poverty, be excluded from formal labour markets and receive little protection by the state (Spaaij *et al.* 2014). What conditions are considered exclusionary within the global North may, therefore, be a regular part of life in the global South. Much of the focus on social exclusion by European scholars is on non-participation in paid employment and economic activity. However, a rights-based understanding of social exclusion can be more relevant within the global South (Mathieson *et al.* 2009), where denial of political, civil or social rights is a defining feature of marginalisation. Rights-based approaches suggest that social exclusion negatively impacts on human dignity and recognition, issues that are rarely considered within Northern theories (Spaaij *et al.* 2014). Northern theories have also tended to underplay the role of violence and lack of personal safety as a key mechanism of social exclusion. Violence, such as domestic violence against women and children, contributes to exclusionary processes, impacts on dignity and well-being, and restricts the ability of individuals to occupy particular spaces.

To understand how SDP seeks to address social exclusion within global South contexts, we advocate for a broader understanding of social exclusion than what is commonly presented by Northern scholars. In this chapter, we draw on the definition and understanding of social exclusion we have developed elsewhere as 'a (set of) process(es) that negatively affects the rights, recognition and or/resources' of individuals and communities 'and/or their opportunity to participate in key activities in different societal domains' (Spaaij *et al.* 2014: 33). Social exclusion is understood as a process that marginalises individuals, families and communities and prevents them accessing a fair share of social, economic, cultural and political resources and social recognition. Understanding social exclusion as a process influenced by numerous factors is also important for shifting away from a deficit model that attributes the cause of social exclusion to individuals' 'deficits', such as low employability or lack of character.

Social exclusion in SDP contexts

SDP projects frequently seek to address aspects of social exclusion in their work. SDP has been utilised as a tool to address gender inequity and support female empowerment (Kay 2009; Saavedra 2009; Chawansky 2011), promote intercultural contact and social cohesion (Schulenkorf 2010), reduce HIV/AIDS infection and other communicable diseases and support entry into education (Mwaanga and Banda 2014). In doing so, SDP projects often ambitiously seek to increase the access individuals living in impoverished communities have to the systems and structures influencing inclusion, such as health care, education and employment. Sport can have multiple purposes within this process. It attracts vulnerable participants to settings where they can subsequently access other resources, support and education to address broader challenges (Coalter 2010). Participation in sport can also, in its own right, begin to address exclusion by providing a space to connect vulnerable people, providing physical and mental health benefits, and enabling participants to develop certain skills such as leadership, team building and negotiation (Lindsey *et al.* 2017). Although such outcomes will not necessarily address social exclusion on their own, they can provide a foundation for doing so by equipping young people with various 'life skills' that may assist them in navigating broader challenges. It is this process that we will explore in the remainder of the chapter through a case study of a sport-based female empowerment program managed by an Indigenous NGO in Lusaka, Zambia.

SDP, social exclusion and young women in Zambia

The SDP program analysed here has been running for almost two decades and during this time has received funding support from various international donors. The program works with young women living in impoverished 'compound' communities, high-density shantytowns located on the outskirts of Lusaka. Female participants are socially excluded by a vast array of social, cultural, economic and political factors.

Traditional gender hierarchies which position women as subordinate to men are deeply entrenched within Zambian society and play an overarching role in young women's exclusion (Evans 2014). Mwaanga and Prince (2016: 593) suggest that Zambian women with low educational attainment in particular 'are expected to fulfil "birth jobs": preparing food, washing clothes, collecting firewood'. Females within compound communities are often excluded from public space, have little opportunity to contribute to or influence political matters and have little social standing within their communities (Schlyter 1999). Mwaanga and Prince (2016: 593) suggest that often 'women and girls have little or no access to basic amenities including food, education, healthcare or shelter'.

Families within compound communities tend to prioritise the education of male children, which perpetuates the cycle of inequality experienced by young women (Schlyter 1999). With limited resources and capacity to enter the labour market, young women are rendered dependent on their families and ultimately their husbands for security. This dependency leaves young women highly vulnerable to abuse and domestic violence. The HIV/AIDS pandemic that ravaged Zambia in the 1980s and 1990s disproportionately affected women, with females five times more likely to be infected than males. This is a further consequence of the disempowerment impoverished women experience in Zambian society (Gari et al. 2013). For young women, negotiating safe sexual behaviour while having limited authority within their relationships is also difficult (Jewkes et al. 2010). Here, gender-based norms intersect with poverty to create conditions that limit women's rights, their ability to participate in social life and their capacity to change their day-to-day lives.

Using sport to address social exclusion

The SDP initiative in Lusaka sought to address these aspects of exclusion in multiple ways. The program was delivered using a peer leader model, whereby NGO staff provided training and support for young women within local communities to lead and organise sport sessions. Peer leaders were responsible for recruiting and supporting the participation of other young women. Part of this role included liaising with families to negotiate access for young women. The project sought to address exclusion through multi-layered approaches. At a fundamental level, providing the opportunity for young women to engage in sport in public spaces challenged repressive gender stereotypes. A key aspect of the program was providing a 'safe space' (Spaaij and Schulenkorf 2014), where young women could come together and form networks and social relationships free from violence or abuse. Additional aspects of the program that moved beyond participation in sport included the provision of scholarships to support young women to attend local schools and the opportunity for females to undertake 'internships' within the NGO. Internships opportunities were facilitated by the NGO to provide opportunities for work experience that would support young women in gaining employment. Peer leaders were also encouraged to facilitate education sessions with participants, underpinned by critical pedagogy that encouraged young women to discuss key issues within their lives. Such discussions often related to health issues, particularly HIV/AIDS, with participants discussing their potential risk of infection and sharing ways that they could mitigate or minimise such risks. Additional areas of focus included women's rights, domestic violence and strategies to manage this. From this brief overview, it is possible to see the ways in which the NGO used sport to address exclusion across social, cultural and economic domains. The project sought to make young women visible within their communities, challenge limiting gender stereotypes and extend participants' capabilities through enabling access to education and workforce opportunities.

How does SDP address social exclusion?

Young women in the Zambian SDP program described a range of benefits from their participation. Many talked about the project providing them with a focus, and peer leaders in particular talked about the pride they gained from establishing opportunities and bringing young women together. Participation also provided young women with a sense of hope, allowing them to reconceive their lives and the potential of new possibilities. The importance of hope has been discussed extensively in literature examining HIV/AIDS protection (Yadav 2010), making this a valuable benefit of engagement in SDP. This was also valuable considering that opportunities for meaningful social connection, the facilitation of hope and the space to consider alternative life courses were rare in other aspects of the young women's lives.

The friendship networks established through SDP were fundamental to creating a safe space for young women. As Spaaij and Schulenkorf (2014: 635) document, 'safe space is critical both to the provision of inclusive and equitable sport opportunities and to leveraging the positive social impact that can flow from those opportunities'. They suggest the creation of safe space does not simply happen but takes careful planning. Several young women talked about sessions as providing a physical safe space, a place where they could interact meaningfully with peers and somewhere where they felt respected and trusted. These aspects reflect the multidimensional nature of safe space highlighted in Spaaij and Schulenkorf's analysis.

The value of the SDP project for facilitating trusting relationships and developing a collective identity was also repeatedly highlighted in the women's accounts. They described the support networks as becoming a central part of their lives. Many likened these connections as similar to family bonds, resulting in young women feeling they were part of a collective that shared challenges together. Coalter (2012) similarly illustrates the importance of relationships within SDP processes while Lindsey *et al.* (2017) outline the notion of a 'sport for development family' that provides young people with critical resources and support. A crucial way therefore that this particular SDP program began to challenge social exclusion was by allowing young women to share experiences, gain support and reduce their isolation. Many talked about not 'feeling alone' since they connected with others in and through the SDP initiative. While they remained excluded in other aspects of their lives, particularly economically and politically, they felt included, valued and respected among their peers within the SDP setting.

A further outcome was that young women countered and contested gender stereotypes that confined their movement around their local community. By participating in sport, they became highly visible within their communities. This process is not without risk; for some women, such a visible presence can render them highly vulnerable to community disapproval, stigmatisation and abuse (Meier and Saavedra 2009). However, the young women in this case study stated that participation in sport allowed them to challenge the gender stereotypes which positioned them as weak and vulnerable. Indeed, for several participants, the SDP program offered the only opportunity they had to move beyond the immediate vicinity of their homes.

Outlining some of the benefits experienced by program participants assists with identifying how SDP may contribute to reducing social exclusion among marginalised individuals. The discussion above illustrates the importance of understanding social exclusion as a process in order to enable an in-depth analysis of the ways in which exclusion occurs and the subtle ways SDP can begin to counter these mechanisms.

Addressing social exclusion through SDP: tensions and challenges

The previous section points to some of the ways SDP can counter aspects of social exclusion. Yet, the constraints in this process also need to be recognised. A fundamental consideration is whether SDP initiatives are able to reach highly vulnerable and deeply socially excluded individuals within communities. Here it is relevant to return to our initial conceptualisation of social exclusion which acknowledges how individuals usually experience degrees of exclusion and can simultaneously be included in certain contexts and excluded in others. This is fruitful for understanding some of the benefits young women gained from feeling included within the space of the SDP program, while still remaining excluded in other aspects of their lives. The notion of degrees of exclusion is also useful when considering the peer leaders and participants. There were several examples of young women in the local area who experienced more extreme exclusion than those who were engaged in the program as peer leaders or participants. For example, very few participants were homeless; they all lived in basic homes with limited facilities.

Similar to recent studies that foreground the importance of family in supporting young women's participation in SDP (Kay and Spaaij 2012; Chawansky and Mitra 2015;), many of the young women in the program received considerable family support, particularly from elder female relatives. Frequently it was this family support that had prompted them to participate in the program. When their families attempted to restrict their participation the young women successfully negotiated access. For example, several of the young women discussed family members suggesting they could not participate because it was not appropriate for females to participate in sport in public settings. So the young women successfully contested this notion and were able to participate. Crucially, they had the resources and agency to hold these negotiations with (often) senior male members of their families. Many therefore did not experience the severe types of domestic constraints outlined earlier in this chapter. To return to Levitas *et al.* (2007), many of the participants did not experience 'deep social exclusion' that rendered them almost completely excluded from all facets of society. Participants and particularly peer leaders had certain resources and support available to them that supported their engagement in SDP initiatives. By contrast, it is reasonable to speculate that young women experiencing more acute marginalisation would have difficulty negotiating access to SDP programs such as this. Indeed, several of the peer leaders mentioned that they knew of girls who would like to attend but were unable because of family or partner regulation.

Research emanating from the global North has raised similar concerns regarding the capacity of sports programs to reach those who experience deep social exclusion. For example, project workers in Spaaij, Magee and Jeanes' (2012) analysis of sport-based youth employment initiatives reported that they chose not to work with highly marginalised individuals because the issues these individuals faced were too complex to be addressed through SDP. Staff argued that their limited resources were better invested in individuals experiencing less complex forms of social exclusion and upon whom they were more likely to have some positive impact. In the present case study, there was no deliberate intent to avoid supporting highly marginalised young women, but the project relied heavily on women who had some autonomy to negotiate their initial access. NGO staff and peer leaders did a vast amount of work within local communities to raise the profile of the project and encourage families to allow young women to attend, but partici-pation remained difficult for many highly vulnerable young women.

More broadly, therefore, part of the challenge for SDP when seeking to address social exclu-sion is to recognise that project participants are not homogenous (Mwaanga and Prince 2016). Samie *et al.* (2015: 934) discuss the 'crude totalitarian re/presentations' of young women in the Global South that position them all as 'other' and powerless. In turn, SDP has been critiqued for perpetuating the neo-colonial assumption that all young people from the global South require saving (Mwaanga and Prince 2016). This problematic discourse has led to some SDP programs failing to differentiate their approach to support the complex array of mechanisms and the varying ways that exclude certain individuals more than others

A further point of debate is the capacity of SDP to address or reconfigure structural mechanisms of social exclusion. Giulianotti (2004) suggests that SDP programs need to move beyond individual-focused or surface-level change and instead consider how they might influ-ence the problems that underpin inequalities. The overview of benefits above suggest that young women, once they have gained entry to SDP, can address some of the more fundamental barriers to social inclusion, such as their lack of education and economic dependency. However, even though initiatives can support some young women to gain some degree of autonomy and agency, they do not fundamentally address the causes of exclusion through structural change or the redis-tribution of power towards excluded groups (Hayhurst 2014; Spaaij, Magee and Jeanes 2014).

These critiques are both valid and relevant within the case study context, where young women were supported to gain skills that could help them enter the labour force. At a very practical level, the value of developing young women's skills was diminished because of the small number of employment opportunities. The development of employment skills only led to what Lawson (2005) describes as 'narrow empowerment', where short-term impacts are facilitated. Unemployment was high within compound communities among both men and women, and the limited work available was usually short-term, casual and ad hoc. Consequently, employers were unlikely to consider young women for the limited opportunities that did arise. The case study illustrates one of the fundamental critiques of SDP: it struggles to substantially alter mechanisms of social exclusion (Black 2010; Darnell and Hayhurst 2011; Hartmann and Kwauk 2011). Within the case study, there were examples of young women who successfully negotiated various constraints and were able to secure at least some form of casual employment such as cleaning or working at market stalls. These were important yet atypical examples. Despite engagement in the project for many years, during which young women developed a range of skills and accessed various work experience opportunities, many were unable to secure any form of stable employ-ment, continuing to render them economically dependent on families and partners.

Similarly, while the SDP initiative provided vital support that enabled many of the young women to attend school, this did not necessarily result in greater social inclusion. Several of the young women who gained scholarships discussed how they found school challenging because they had not been afforded the opportunity to attend from a young age. This was particularly noticeable among young women who received scholarships to attend government high schools. It was only at these schools that young women could take their grade 10 and grade 12 examinations which would provide them with recognisable certification and allow access to better employ-ment opportunities or further education. Many of the young women also discussed significant challenges when moving from a volunteer-run community school located within their com-pound to one of the city's government high schools. They had not had the opportunity to gain either the skills or the knowledge in their foundational education years to equip them with the demands of undertaking exams. Consequently, several young women were unable to successfully complete their examinations. This example usefully highlights that gaining access to resources and opportunities is only a starting point in addressing social exclusion. It is not enough to place an individual in an environment or context that they were previously excluded from, without also recognising that they will likely have been excluded from the skills, resources and knowledge that will enable them to survive and thrive within that context. Whether it is within the realm or capacity of SDP programs to provide such resources is open to debate, but it is important to acknowledge that while SDP can provide support to begin to address social exclusion, this alone may not significantly impact on the root causes of social exclusion (Spaaij 2013).

Conclusion

Social exclusion is a complex and multifaceted process that prevents individuals, families and communities from engaging fully in many aspects of society. SDP has at its core a strong commitment to use sport to reduce social exclusion across multiple domains. We nevertheless need to be cautious regarding the extent to, and ways in which, SDP can counteract the structural mechanisms that shape social exclusion. Participation can have a significant impact on the lives of young people facing social exclusion, particularly through its capacity to offer a space to escape, a place to connect and a setting where they can feel included, valued and empowered for at least the time they occupy it. As Spaaij and Schulenkorf (2014) highlight, cultivating a setting where participants feel supported, respected and valued requires ongoing effort from those organising, managing and participating in SDP. When a safe space is being cultivated, SDP can provide a platform to begin to leverage other outcomes (Hershow *et al.* 2015). However, to seriously address social exclusion as it is experienced in highly marginalised communities, SDP needs to be only one piece of a larger approach seeking to transform exclusionary structures and reconfigure power relations.

Research suggests that for SDP to effectively provide a starting point to address social exclusion, it needs to be delivered and managed in particular ways. Traditional Northern driven approaches to SDP have typically given relatively little consideration to local context and sought to develop outcomes that may be meaningless and irrelevant to individuals and communities within the global South, as well as short-term in nature (Black 2010; Darnell and Hayhurst 2011; Mwaanga and Prince 2016). Recent research offers insight into alternative approaches that counter the Northern dominance of SDP and have the potential to influence more significant change within local communities (Giulianotti 2011; Hartmann and Kwauk 2011; Spaaij and Jeanes 2013). Scholars and practitioners are increasingly advocating for community-driven approaches to SDP that are culturally and locally relevant and underpinned by critical pedagogy and participatory action research approaches (Hayhurst *et al.* 2015; Mwaanga and Prince 2016). Such approaches place local knowledge and needs at the heart of their programming. SDP programs that utilise critical pedagogy seek to raise participants' critical awareness of the ways in which they are socially excluded (Spaaij *et al.* 2016). An SDP approach underpinned by critical pedagogy would, therefore, seek to support groups facing social exclusion to develop strategies and facilitate action based upon their critical awareness (Mwaanga and Prince 2016). As illustrated in the case study, and elsewhere (Jeanes and Spaaij 2015), a community-led, critical approach to SDP will not instantly transform social relations but it can challenge hegemonic discourses and, over time, offer a public space where alternative discourses are presented and experienced.

References

Abrams, D., Hogg, M. A. and Marques, J. M. (2005). A social psychological framework for understanding social inclusion and exclusion. In D. Abrams, M. A. Hogg and J. M. Marques, (eds), *The Social Psychology of Inclusion and Exclusion*, New York: Psychology Press.

Bailey, R. (2005). Evaluating the relationship between physical education, sport and social inclusion. *Educational Review*, *57*(1), 71–90.

Bhalla, A. and Lapeyre, F. (2004). *Poverty and Exclusion in a Global World*, Basingstoke: Palgrave Macmillan.

Black, D. R. (2010). The ambiguities of development: implications for 'development through sport'. *Sport in Society*, *13*(1), 121–129.

Chawansky, M. (2011). New social movements, old gender games? Locating girls in the sport for development and peace movement. *Research in Social Movements, Conflicts and Change*, *32*: 121–134.

Chawansky, M. and Mitra, P. (2015). Family matters: Studying the role of the family through the eyes of girls in an SfD programme in Delhi. *Sport in Society*, *18*(8), 983–994.

Coalter, F. (2007). *A Wider Social Role for Sport: Who's Keeping the Score?* London: Routledge.

Coalter, F. (2010). The politics of sport-for-development: Limited focus programmes and broad gauge problems? *International Review for the Sociology of Sport*, *45*(3), 295–314.

Coalter, F. (2012). 'There is loads of relationships here': Developing a programme theory for sport-for-change programmes. *International Review for the Sociology of Sport*, *48*(5), 594–612.

Collins, M. (2014). *Sport and Social Exclusion.* London: Routledge.

Crabbe, T. (2000). A sporting chance? Using sport to tackle drug use and crime. *Drugs: Education, Prevention and Policy*, *7*(4), 381–391.

Darnell, S. C. and Hayhurst, L. M. (2011). Sport for decolonization: Exploring a new praxis of sport for development. *Progress in Development Studies*, *11*(3), 183–196.

Evans, A. (2014). 'Women can do what men can do?': The causes and consequences of growing flexibility in gender divisions of labour in Kitwe, Zambia. *Journal of Southern African Studies*, *40*(5), 981–998.

Gari, S., Doig-Acuña, C., Smail, T., Malungo, J. R., Martin-Hilber, A. and Merten, S. (2013). Access to HIV/AIDS care: A systematic review of socio-cultural determinants in low and high-income countries. *BMC Health Services Research*, *13*: 198.

Giulianotti, R. (2004). Human rights, globalisation and sentimental education: The case of sport. *Sport in Society*, *7*(3), 355–369.

Giulianotti, R. (2011). The sport, development and peace sector: A model of four social policy domains. *Journal of Social Policy*, *40*(04), 757–776.

Gore, C. and Figueiredo, J. B. (eds) (1997). *Social Exclusion and Anti-Poverty Policy: A Debate.* Geneva: International Institute for Labour Studies.

Hartmann, D. and Kwauk, C. (2011). Sport and development: An overview, critique, and reconstruction. *Journal of Sport and Social Issues*, *35*(3), 284–305.

Hayhurst, L. M. (2014). The 'Girl Effect' and martial arts: Social entrepreneurship and sport, gender and development in Uganda. *Gender, Place and Culture*, *21*(3), 297–315.

Hayhurst, L. M., Giles, A. R. and Radforth, W. M. (2015). 'I want to come here to prove them wrong': Using a post-colonial feminist participatory action research (PFPAR) approach to studying sport, gender and development programmes for urban Indigenous young women. *Sport in Society*, *18*(8), 952–967.

Hershow, R. B., Gannett, K., Merrill, J., Kaufman, E. B., Barkley, C., DeCelles, J. and Harrison, A. (2015). Using soccer to build confidence and increase HCT uptake among adolescent girls: A mixed-methods study of an HIV prevention programme in South Africa. *Sport in Society*, *18*(8), 1009–1022.

Hills, J., Le Grand. J. and Piachaud, D. (eds) (2002). *Understanding Social Exclusion.* Oxford: Oxford University Press.

Jeanes, R. and Spaaij, R. (2015). Examining the educator. In L. M. Hayhurst, T. Kay and M. Chawansky (eds), *Beyond Sport for Development and Peace: Transnational Perspectives on Theory, Policy and Practice*, London: Routledge, pp. 155–168.

Jewkes, R. K., Dunkle, K., Nduna, M. and Shai, N. (2010). Intimate partner violence, relationship power inequity, and incidence of HIV infection in young women in South Africa: A cohort study. *The Lancet*, *376*(9734), 41–48.

Kay, T. (2009). Developing through sport: Evidencing sport impacts on young people. *Sport in Society*, *12*(9), 1177–1191.

Kay, T. and Spaaij, R. (2012). The mediating effects of family on sport in international development contexts. *International Review for the Sociology of Sport*, *47*(1), 77–94.

Lawson, H. A. (2005). Empowering people, facilitating community development, and contributing to sustainable development: The social work of sport, exercise, and physical education programs. *Sport, Education and Society*, *10*(1), 135–160.

Levitas, R., Pantazis, C., Fahmy, E., Gordon, D., Lloyd, E. and Patsios, D. (2007). *The Multi-Dimensional Analysis of Social Exclusion.* Bristol: University of Bristol.

Marshall, S. K. and Barry, P. (2015). Community sport for development: Perceptions from practice in Southern Africa. *Journal of Sport Management*, *29*(1), 109–121.

Mathieson, J., Popay, J., Enoch, E., Escorel, S., Hernandez, M., Johnston, H. and Rispel, L. (2009). *Social Exclusion: Meaning, Measurement and Experience and Links to Health Inequalities: A Review of Literature*. Geneva: WHO Social Exclusion Knowledge Network.

Meier, M. and Saavedra, M. (2009). Esther Phiri and the Moutawakel effect in Zambia: An analysis of the use of female role models in sport-for-development. *Sport in Society*, *12*(9), 1158–1176.

Mwaanga, O. and Banda, D. (2014). A postcolonial approach to understanding sport-based empowerment of people living with HIV/AIDS (PLWHA) in Zambia: The case of the cultural philosophy of Ubuntu. *Journal of Disability and Religion*, *18*(2), 173–191.

Mwaanga, O. and Prince, S. (2016). Negotiating a liberative pedagogy in sport development and peace: understanding consciousness raising through the Go Sisters programme in Zambia. *Sport, Education and Society*, *21*(4), 588–604.

Nichols, G. (2010). *Sport and Crime Reduction: The Role of Sports in Tackling Youth Crime*. London: Routledge.

Saavedra, M. (2009). Dilemmas and opportunities in gender and sport-in-development. In R. Levermore and. A. Beacom (eds), *Sport and International Development*. Basingstoke; Palgrave Macmillan, pp. 124–155.

Samie, S. F., Johnson, A. J., Huffman, A. M. and Hillyer, S. J. (2015). Voices of empowerment: women from the global south re/negotiating empowerment and the global sports mentoring programme. *Sport in Society*, *18*(8), 923–937.

Schlyter, A. (1999). *Recycled Inequalities: Youth and Gender in George Compound, Zambia* (Vol. 114). Uppsala: Nordic Africa Institute.

Schulenkorf, N. (2010). Sport events and ethnic reconciliation: Attempting to create social change between Sinhalese, Tamil and Muslim sportspeople in war-torn Sri Lanka. *International Review for the Sociology of Sport*, *45*(3), 273–294.

Spaaij, R. (2013). Changing people's lives for the better? Social mobility through sport-based intervention programmes: Opportunities and constraints. *European Journal for Sport and Society*, *10*(1), 53–73.

Spaaij, R. and Jeanes, R. (2013). Education for social change? A Freirean critique of sport for development and peace. *Physical Education and Sport Pedagogy*, *18*(4), 442–457.

Spaaij, R., Magee, J. and Jeanes, R. (2012). Urban youth, worklessness and sport: A comparison of sports-based employability programmes in Rotterdam and Stoke-on-Trent. *Urban Studies*, *50*(8), 1608–24.

Spaaij, R., Magee, J. and Jeanes, R., (2014). *Sport and Social Exclusion in Global Society*. Abingdon, Oxon: Routledge.

Spaaij, R., Oxford, S. and Jeanes, R. (2016). Transforming communities through sport? Critical pedagogy and sport for development. *Sport, Education and Society*, *21*(4), 570–587.

Spaaij, R. and Schulenkorf, N. (2014) Cultivating safe space: Lessons for sport-for-development projects and events. *Journal of Sport Management*, *28*(6), 633–645.

Yadav, S. (2010). Perceived social support, hope, and quality of life of persons living with HIV/AIDS: A case study from Nepal. *Quality of Life Research*, *19*(2), 157–166.

Part II
The social study of SDP

14

SDP and social theory[1]

Laura Zanotti and Max Stephenson Jr

Introduction

International interest in sport as a mechanism for advancing peace and international development first emerged formally in 2001. In that year, the United Nations (UN) officially recognized sport as a strategy to achieve development goals as well as to encourage peace. The UN institutionalized sport's newfound status as an international intervention in that same year when it established the position of Special Advisor on Sport for Development and Peace (SDP) to the United Nations Secretary-General. In the period since, the United Nations formed an Inter-Agency Task Force on Sport for Development and Peace in 2002, established the Sport for Development and Peace International Working Group in 2004 and designated 2005 as the International Year for Sport and Physical Education (Beutler 2008). All of these steps represented evidence of growing interest in the use of sport for peacebuilding and development. That interest has only deepened in the ensuing period.

While the UN has clearly been a key player in this domain, other actors have also taken up the charge. International non-governmental organizations (INGOs), such as Right to Play and the Fédération Internationale de Football Association (FIFA) particularly, national governments and corporations have joined the cause. Additionally, sportanddev.org the International Platform on Sport and Development, connects various interested actors across the world by offering space for information sharing and analysis of their common challenges. These and similar groups have increased support for the growth of sport programs linked to such goals as health, disease prevention, education and gender equality within the United Nations and among governments and other NGOs alike.

The UN Inter-Agency Task Force on Sport for Development and Peace released a report in 2003 that outlined the potential benefits of sport as a development and peace intervention. The effort characterized such initiatives as 'cost-effective' and suggested that as a group they promote beneficial values and goals, including exercise for improved health; greater awareness of the value of education; sustainable development; peace; improved interpersonal communication skills; partnerships between UN, state, INGOs and community entities; and increased awareness of HIV/AIDS (United Nations 2003: V).

The Task Force also argued that sport could play roles in reducing crime and anti-social behaviour, in workforce development by imbuing participants with employment-relevant capacities, in empowering women and girls, in building social capital, in preventing social conflict, in rehabilitation and reintegration of wounded or injured citizens, in improving social communication capacities and in securing human rights (Beutler 2008).

Few would question the concept of sport as a potentially positive social intervention, as the Task Force suggested. Nonetheless, the prosocial nature of sport may prevent a critical, substantive examination of its strengths and weaknesses in the various domains in which it is employed. Indeed, some critical and post-colonial theorists have raised substantial and warranted concerns about dominant conceptions of development as imposing a neoliberal frame on nations that do not fit the definition of 'developed'. In the specific context of sport, several authors have suggested that SDP is part of a 'hegemonic discourse' (Darnell 2012; 2014) that relies on a positivist understanding of 'evidence' that dismisses forms of knowledge possessed by residents and practitioners from the global South (Nicholls *et al.* 2010: 250). Others have suggested a problematic 'neoliberal discourse' has pervaded both UN claims about sport and global funding choices (Hayhurst 2009; 2014). We share these concerns.

This chapter provides an overview of salient characteristics of the sport for development and peacebuilding theoretical challenge and the diverse ways that scholars have treated those concerns at different analytical scales. We also survey various investigators' attempts to describe the phenomenon adequately and to track its dynamics and implications in light of multiple evaluative criteria. We contend, along with other scholars in this field, that sport-based interventions are multi-scalar, depend on complex social diffusion processes for their efficacy, must always be contextualized by their purveyors, and inevitably demand broadly focused social theorizations to capture their nuanced effects on the populations they both reflect and whose norms and behaviours they seek to shape.

Theoretical resources for analysing sports, development and peacebuilding

Substantial bodies of theory are available to describe and support research on sport and development at the individual, organizational and national/transnational scales. At the individual level, educational development theories (Piaget 1948; Kohlberg 1981) that assay changes in the complexity of thought, skills and aptitude development of participants allow investigation of the links among personal development, sport and the adoption of key social norms. While we believe these sorts of studies are important, we are more interested in the larger claims of 'development' and 'peace' as phenomena that must be addressed at the subnational, national and international levels. We therefore focus on theories that address those realms.

One instructive starting point for situating sport as a strategy in development and peacebuilding is to consider the contexts in which such efforts are pressed. One thoughtful observer of these situations is John Paul Lederach, a practitioner and scholar, who has been active in the peacebuilding field for several decades. Lederach has suggested that conflict in 'deeply divided societies' is most often intra-national, occurring predominantly in the developing world (Lederach 1997: 11–12). In consequence, such strife is typically best characterized as communal or inter-communal (Lederach 1997:12). Likewise, fragile state politics and legitimacy may exacerbate community-level conflict.

Theories of national governance suggest that the role of the state is pivotal in post-conflict situations. Specifically, weak national governments may often actually encourage violence while strong ones may help to ameliorate it by obtaining or regaining the confidence of the people. For example, Gaventa (2006: 264) has distinguished among four types of democracy, each progressively deeper in its participatory practices: building civil society; participation and participatory governance; deliberative democracy; and empowered participatory governance.

These categories suggest the politics of reconciliation must address these complex phenomena together if genuine change is to occur and conflict to be overcome successfully. Outcomes of sport-related interventions in such circumstances are not easily measurable or readily discerned, but occur in the shifting contours of relationships at the local, regional and state levels. They must occur too in the face of ingrained social norms; whose change by definition requires sustained effort and a clear vision of new possibilities and their implications for the principal stakeholders affected.

Theories of organizational and network learning may be used profitably to examine the roles of sport in development and peacebuilding, because they can address intra-communal relationships and tensions. The creation of new networks among formerly conflicting parties can serve as a fresh basis for interaction. Podolny and Page have underscored the knowledge-sharing and inculcating benefits of networks: 'Network forms of organization foster learning because they preserve greater diversity of search routines than hierarchies and they convey richer, more complex information than the market' (Podolny and Page 1998: 62). These authors argued that networks can serve as vehicles for the transmission of learning because of their internal complexity and connectivity. Intriguingly, Phan and Peridis have suggested conflict may also heighten the potential for learning precisely because it is often 'associated with the tension between alliance partners of different cultural origins' (Phan and Peridis 2000: 201). Thus, while these stresses are doubtless present in post-conflict societies, building mechanisms for ready and persistent interaction among participants that seek to address them more or less systematically and self-consciously could channel conflict in constructive directions.

Several authors have argued that bonding social capital occurs within networks of association comprised of participants from a variety of backgrounds (Gittell and Vidal 1998; Taylor 1996; Pautz and Schnitzer 2008).[2] Szreter has described this form of social capital as

> networks formed from perceived, shared identity relations. The reason for assenting to membership is that others are considered to be 'like' one's self and so no further justification is required for a default assumption that cooperation and trust are appropriate … The possible networks of bonding social capital in any given society are, of course multiple and diverse, influenced by the whole range of complex, politically-negotiated ideas about social identities and by individuals' own interpretations of their paths within this forest of meanings.
>
> *Szreter 2002: 576*

Studies of group/organizational change also lend themselves to the exploration of contexts through network analyses. Walseth (2008), for example, has documented the development of bridging and bonding social capital among immigrant children participating in sports clubs. Bridging social capital is particularly important for loosely organized publics, enabling individuals to make connections. Gittell and Vidal have described bridging social capital as occurring within 'networks of association' comprised of participants from a wide variety of backgrounds (cited in Szreter 2002: 576).

Woolcock (1998) has developed the concept of linking social capital specifically to address exchanges between groups of unequal powers. This construct describes how organizational actors build connections and ties across boundaries. These sorts of links can also encourage new and alternative associations among sporting participants. Brady has credited sport with building social networks for adolescent girls, 'a close-knit social network of peers, which is clearly offered by sport, can give girls an identity outside of those conventionally assigned to them (e.g. daughter, sister, future wife, mother)' (Brady 2005: 45).

Szreter (2002: 574) has argued that social capital analyses have insufficiently accounted for issues of power. Nonetheless, such efforts may be useful in characterizing how relationships and trust-building are formed through sporting activities as well as how individual and shared identities may evolve through these sorts of complex associations.

Several organizational learning theories allow scholars to traverse levels of analysis. Crossan *et al.* (1999), for example, have provided an institutional analysis and framework in which they argue that learning travels from individuals to groups and finally to the organizational level and beyond. Crossan's framework suggests one means by which individual learning may be transferred within SDP programs and may thereafter potentially begin to (re)shape prevailing social norms. Notably, however, this research did not specifically treat trauma and violence or situations of uneven distribution of social and economic power among the groups involved.

Among social theorists, Pierre Bourdieu *et al.* (1998) specifically addressed the challenge of unequal power among individuals in groups as well as in networks in his analysis of sport. Bourdieu's field theory incorporated the array of stakeholders outlined above, constituting the field of sport. His approach was noteworthy because it placed local athletics within a broader social, cultural and political context. Bourdieu viewed fields as sites of struggle in which actors are arrayed on the basis of power relationships in which everything is contested, including their boundaries (Wacquant 1989: 6).

Bourdieu's vision of contested fields could usefully be applied more broadly to sport as a venue in which conflicting groups engage across power differentials. Indeed, this seems a particularly fruitful area of inquiry, but one in which theory building depends on self-conscious awareness that such, in fact is occurring as studies are undertaken. That is, as Bourdieu (1998) argued, researchers cannot simply accept sport as a benign intervention. Fields exhibit uneven distributions of various forms of capital: social, economic and cultural. Transcending those inequalities requires consistent attention to relational change. Nicholls, *et al.* (2010) have explored the question of whether sport is used as a top-down initiative to impart development goals or whether it can serve as a medium for understanding local knowledge and thereby as a key basis for social change.

In short, there is ample theoretic reason to explore the outcomes of sport for development and peacebuilding initiatives in the specific socio-political and economic contexts of their deployment. The most robust analytic frameworks to date in the field have pointed up this characteristic and have argued that SPD must be considered in multi-scalar terms, must consider power differentials among its participants and must find ways and means to characterize and capture its dynamics in the social contexts in which they unfold. This is not only true descriptively, but also essential if ways and means are to be found to model successfully the potential social-behavioural changes latent in sport. We treat these concerns in the remainder of this analysis. As such, it is important to recall that while sport is perhaps most often viewed as a tool for use at the local level, its reach can extend to the national scale through leagues, as well as to transnational events; such as the World Cup, Pan American Games, the Olympics and Paralympics. UN Goodwill ambassadors extend sport's reach as well. In this regard, Nancy Fraser's (2005) exploration of the notion of the public sphere at both national and transnational levels may offer a theoretical frame to trace the links between the local and transnational realms, in which civil society actors can be joined across space to form global action networks.

Theory for sport, development and peacebuilding: exploring some intersections

The importance of theory for understanding sport has been the subject of recent debates and explorations (Lyras and Peachey 2011; Edwards 2015). We have argued that existing analyses are diverse and inspired by different streams of research in the social sciences. These differing perspectives reveal the complex nature of sport, in terms of potential foci of study (individual development projects, implications for social organization and order, relations with broader strategies of development, North–South relations, etc.) We turn next to a review of a share of this research.

Embracing an optimistic vision of the role of sport for providing a number of social goods expressed in the 2006 Report of the UN Secretary-General on Sport for Development and Peace (United Nations 2006), a number of authors have highlighted the benefits of athletics for individual health and well-being. Fountain (1999), for example, has discussed the positive impacts of sport for the behavioural and social development of children, as evidenced by programs in Rwanda, Burundi and Sudan. Walseth (2008) also embraced this view in her study of young immigrant girls in several geographic locations, including Norway. Other authors have emphasized the role sport can play in disseminating information. Koss and Alexandrova (2005), for example, have suggested athletic engagement can support HIV/AIDS education and prevention. Participants in several 'e-debates' on sport and development noted the potential positive impacts of sport on education and health, when done 'right' (Van Kempen 2009a: 6). Other analysts have sought to bridge the individual level at which sport always operates with broader social development analyses by employing Sen's Capability Approach (Svensson and Levine 2017).

As mentioned above, while not disputing the individual level impacts that accrue to participants in sport, we believe the phenomena of development, and still more so peace, are appropriately studied as subjects involving collectivities: non-governmental organizations, communities and governments. For this reason, social theories, especially those that emphasize the relational nature of interventions aimed at bringing about development and peace, are key to illuminating SDP. We next provide an overview of some perspectives that emphasize the deeply social and cultural character of sport and the need to design and assess sport and peace and development interventions with strong attention to context.

Notwithstanding the many aspirational declarations of the United Nations on the topic to date, Gasser and Levinsen (2004: 457) have suggested the use of sport to influence behaviour can be a double-edged sword: 'A complicated picture emerges: in some situations, sport contributes to social harmony, and in others it feeds conflict'. They explored the work of the Open Fun Football Schools (OFFS), which had been founded by Levinsen, in helping to reintegrate young people from divided areas following conflict. In the case of Bosnia-Herzegovina, they observed:

> OFFS is based on the concept of 'fun football,' as developed by the Danish Football Association. Their philosophy is derived from the Danish public sport culture that is characterized by a strong local focus, democratic principles, volunteerism, parent support, and the basic principle of 'sports for all'.
>
> *Gasser and Levinsen 2004: 462*

In a similar vein, Spaaij and Jeanes (2012) and Spaaij et al. (2016) have employed a Freirean lens to criticize the standardized approach to education privileged by SDP initiatives and advocated a more critical, flexible and contextualized curriculum aimed at developing transformative education processes through sport.

Other authors have considered the potentially productive role of partnerships for improving the efficacy of sport as a peacebuilding strategy (Koss and Alexandrova 2005; United Nations 2006; Kidd 2008). Kidd has highlighted the potential for collaboration among, 'national and international sports organizations, governments and non-governmental organizations (NGOs), universities and schools' (Kidd 2008: 370). However, he has also argued that the prevalence of, and competition among, NGOs may impair the development of a host developing state's potential infrastructure for sport (Kidd 2008). As he has explained: 'In fact, in the competition for donors, photo ops, and placements for volunteers, NGOs not only compete against each other, but also against state schools' (Kidd 2008: 376).

This contention raises the issue of NGO accountability to states and to those served, in addition to donors. Other critics have expressed concerns about the sustainability of donor-dependent NGO-led sport for development and peace programs (Van Kempen 2009b:10). The role of the news media can also be problematic. For example, while largely praising television and print journalists for raising awareness and highlighting the success of sport initiatives, Adam and Holguin (2003: 4) have also lamented their tendency to sensationalize individual scale conflicts in war-torn countries.

Critiques of whether sport may be taken to be a universal good fall along three major lines: its potential to rouse or even to kindle violent nationalisms; and, the tendency for outside funding and INGO or NGO intervention to eclipse its otherwise local character and the attendant issue of its possible commercialization.[3] The level of analysis for these criticisms tends to be national rather than local. Nevertheless, these critiques point to a grey area in which sport evolves from informal, local initiatives to more formal (and possibly thoroughly nationalized) leagues.

Scholars have examined this dual character of sport. A special issue of *The International Journal of Sport Policy* (2009), for example, pointed to this characteristic in an analysis of the European Commission's White Paper on Sport (2007). Specifically, Coenen (2009) studied the issue of public disorder during athletic events, while Mutz (2009) probed sports club membership and adolescent violence. Indeed, public disorder can be casually observed in professional European football. Mutz, however, raised concerns about the frequency of sport and violence in less formal settings as well. Competitive sport also has a violent history in the Southern Hemisphere. Finally, and more broadly, Finn and Giulianotti (1999) is one of several scholars who have traced the legacy of sport as a mechanism of European colonization.

Toohey has extended this argument to terrorism, citing '168 sport-related terrorist attacks occurred between 1972 and 2004' (2008: 429). While not per se a critique of SDP, Jarvie and Reid have analysed the strong ties among sport, culture and nationalism, using Scotland as their case. They highlighted the innately political nature of sport:

> Studies of sport and domestic government policies, sport and International relations and sport and political ideologies are now quite common and have contributed to our understanding of the close relationship between sport, culture and society.
>
> *Jarvie and Reid 1999: 24*

Meanwhile, Platts and Smith (2009: 323) and Mutz and Baur (2009) have suggested a 'sub-culture of sport' that encourages nationalism and violent confrontation is developing. Intentionally or not, the Olympics and the World Cup have each demonstrated capacity to promote nationalism through displays and symbols and have thereby often acted as a divisive force. Under politically volatile conditions, the association between sport and nationalism may degenerate into violence, as occurred in the former Yugoslavia (Gasser and Levinsen 2004). Indeed, sport is likely to be mediated or characterized by existing conflicts arising from racial, ethnic, religious or tribal differences. Sport sits uneasily on a razor's edge between potentially encouraging interaction and building empathy and shared ties among factions and exacerbating existing divisive conflicts among groups.

SDP scholars have thus far been reluctant to generalize concerning the possible impacts of sport, and instead have emphasized that its benefits are contingent on local circumstances (Van Kempen 2009a). Gasser and Levinsen (2004: 467), for example, have stressed that those employing sport as a development or peace strategy must possess 'intimate knowledge of their own terrain and its particular risks and advantages'.

Other authors have also observed a need for contextual knowledge to position SDP efforts for success. Finn and Giulianotti (1999), for example, have argued that sport's use for development or peacebuilding is highly situational. Their review of football practices raised important issues concerning the role of difference and identity in sport. Citing Rorty's use of the term 'sentimental education' as essential in creating a universal culture of human rights predicated on empathy, Giulianotti (2004: 366) has argued sport can play a positive role in 'conflict zones, to promote rehabilitation and reconciliation'. He has also suggested 'Sport arguably provides for cross-cultural encounters with the other, forcing us into bodily and normative dialogue with those that we might find "irrational" or culturally abominable' (Rorty 1993; Giulianotti 2004: 366).

In an analysis of UN Sport for Development and Peace initiatives Kidd characterized 'SDP (as a) timely, progressive impulse, one of the most encouraging initiatives in sport in the last few years' (Kidd 2008: 376). Yet he also stressed the importance of scale, coordination, training and qualifications of personnel as well as the need to tailor intervention forms to regional needs. Where NGOs have played generative roles in advancing sport interventions, Kidd recommended that governments assume leadership in the future, in order to ensure sustainability and positive long-term consequences in addressing or preventing conflict.

On our part, and using Foucauldian theoretical tools, we have argued that the role of sport as a peacebuilding strategy through 'bottom-up' transformation of conflict societies must be understood in the context of a broader intensification of the biopolitical and disciplinary trajectories of the liberal peace (Zanotti et al. 2015). As Zanotti (2006; 2011) earlier argued, the United Nations' decision to redefine its role in collective security as protecting the well-being of populations, instead of preserving the existing international order, suggested the post-Cold War international security regime was becoming increasingly biopolitical in character.

For Foucault, biopolitics described the managerial inclination of governments to regulate the behaviours of populations directly with an eye to attaining an equilibrium of social order and security. The UN and other international entities' adoption and development of an array of regulatory mechanisms after 2000 that targeted people's everyday lives constituted a similar trajectory in international security. With this turn, international organization discourses now reflected increasing concern with identifying, managing and protecting the health and wealth of populations under what came to be called the 'Responsibility to Protect' umbrella. In this framework, the use of sport in peacebuilding is biopolitical because as a technique it aims to govern societies by targeting and changing people's ways of living together in order to achieve social order and stability. They are disciplinary because such efforts, via sport in the present instance, view social change as resulting from crafted interventions that reform 'the souls' of disorderly individuals by training their bodies and enhancing their overall ability to coordinate with others to produce desired results. In this sense, sport can be regarded as a tool to foster and maintain an international order that encompasses social engineering processes that are capillary, decentralized and increasingly focused on shaping individuals and societies. As such, we agree with other SDP scholars that the effects of such initiatives for peace and development must be assessed in the specific contexts in which they are employed.

Conclusion

This selective review of literature concerning theory building aimed at describing the roles of sport for peace and development has highlighted the fact that the relevant scholarly literature is still nascent. The many case studies of sport as a strategy for peacebuilding or development offer a potentially strong base for inductive research and theory building. However, there is also a need for more research grounded in theory that can improve description and evaluation of these initiatives. However consequential sport may be as a development, conflict management or peacebuilding strategy, its success and the effects it may have on individuals and communities can never be assumed in the abstract. We embrace Coalter's scepticism concerning the claims of what he has called 'sports for development evangelists and conceptual entrepreneurs' (2010: 311) while sympathizing with his admiration for the 'optimism of the will' of many SDP practitioners. Our exploration of SDP has suggested such efforts are highly contextually dependent. Thus, analyses of the dynamics of individual programs continue to be appropriate.

The field continues to suffer from a relative lack of theory-driven long-term studies of specific initiatives at all analytical scales. Indeed, in certain locations, there may already be some basis for longer-term project and program analyses and evaluations.

Sport for development and peace has demonstrated potential for interdisciplinary research across several levels of analysis. This chapter has highlighted individual, group, national and transnational investigations of SDP initiatives. We have suggested throughout that sport is certainly not a panacea for all social ills or even for most social conflict. It is also clear that sport for development and peace interventions are contingent on specific conditions of conflict, poverty and other socially conditioned factors. For this reason, field and network theories may be needed to determine how sports initiatives ought to be assessed in each setting, while social theories may connect such analyses to broader socio-political and economic concerns.

Sociologists and psychologists may help to provide the network analyses that can chart the individual and group attributes and behaviours that accompany and determine the effects of SDP interventions. Political scientists, anthropologists, geographers and sociologists can highlight the role of governance and of power in these efforts. In particular, theoretical perspectives drawn from network theories and Foucauldian positions may help chart and describe these dynamics by placing SDP in the context of broader analyses of the places and spaces within which they are undertaken. We contend that sport must be addressed as a tool; the adequacy of which should be assessed in light of the specific contexts in which it is employed. There is much work to be done.

Notes

1   Our earlier work with our colleagues Marcy Schnitzer and Yannis Stivachtis has helped to shape this chapter. We thank them.
2   We use the term 'social capital' advisedly, recognizing the 'dark side' of the term highlighted by Bourdieu (1985). That is, social capital also represents distinctions based upon various forms of exclusionary attainment. Here, we employ the term to describe the interactional impacts that can accrue through mutual engagement in sporting events.
3   An extensive body of literature exists concerning cricket in this regard. For examples see Appadurai (1996), Majumdar and Brown (2007), and Mannathukkaren (2001).

References

Adam, G. and Holguin, L. (2003). The Media's Role in Peace-Building: Asset or Liability? Our Media 3 Conference, Barranquilla, Colombia, 19–21 May 2003.

Argyris, C. and Schon, D. (1996). *Organizational Learning II: Theory, Method, and Practice.* Reading, MA: Addison-Wesley.

Appadurai, A. (1996). *Modernity at Large: Cultural Dimensions of Globalization.* Minneapolis, MN: University of Minnesota Press.

Benson, R. (2006). News media as a 'journalistic field': What Bourdieu adds to new institutionalism, and vice versa. *Political Communication, 23*(2), 187–202.

Beutler, I. (2008). Sport serving development and peace: Achieving the goals of the united nations through sport. *Sport in Society, 11*(4), 359–369.

Bourdieu, P. (1985). The social space and the genesis of groups. *Social Science Information, 24*(2), 195–220.

Bourdieu, P. (1986). The forms of capital. In J. Richardson (ed.), *Handbook of Theory and Research for Sociology of Education.* New York: Greenwood Press, pp. 241–258.

Bourdieu, P., Dauncey, H. and Hare, G. (1998). The state, economics and sport. *Sport in Society. 1*(2), 15–21.

Brady, M. (2005). Creating safe spaces and building social assets for young women in the developing world: A new role for sports. *Women's Studies Quarterly, 33*(1&2), 44–45.

Chisholm, R. F. (1998). *Developing Network Organizations.* Reading, MA: Addison-Wesley.

Coalter, F. (2010). The politics of sport-for-development: Limited focus programmes and broad gauge problems? *International Review for the Sociology of Sport, 45*(3), 295–314.

Coenen, P. (2009). The proposed Dutch football law and lessons learned from the English approach to spectator violence associated with football. *International Journal of Sport Policy, 1*(3), 285–303.

Crossan, M., Lane, H. and White, R. (1999). An Organizational Learning Framework: from Intuition to Institution. *Academy of Management Review, 24*(3), 522–537.

Darnell, S. C. (2012). *Sport for Development and Peace: A Critical Sociology.* London: Bloomsbury Academic.

Darnell S. C. (2014). Orientalism through sport: Towards a Said-ian analysis of imperialism and 'sport for development and peace'. *Sport in Society, 17*(8), 1000–1014.

Edwards, M. (2015). The role of sport in community capacity building: An examination of sport, for development research and practice. *Sport Management Review, 18:* 6–19.

Finn, G. and Giulianotti, R. (1999). Local contests and global visions: Sporting difference and international change. *Sport in Society, 2* (3), 1–9.

Fountain, S. (1999). Peace Education in UNICEF. Working Paper. Education Section. Programme Division. New York: UNICEF.

Fraser, N. (2007). Special section: Transnational public sphere: transnationalizing the public sphere: On the legitimacy and efficacy of public opinion in a post-Westphalian world. *Theory, Culture and Society, 24*(4), 7–30.

Gaventa, J. (2006). *Triumph, Deficit or Contestation? Deepening the 'Deepening Democracy' Debate.* Oxford: Institute for Development Studies.

Gittell, R. and Vidal, A. (1998). *Community Organizing: Building Social Capital as a Development Strategy.* Newbury Park, CA: SAGE.

Giulianotti, R. (2004). Human rights, globalization and sentimental education: The case of sport. *Sport in Society, 7*(3), 355–339.

Hayhurst, L. M. (2009). The Power to Shape Policy. *International Journal of Sport Policy, 1*(2), 203–227.

Hayhurst, L. M. (2014). 'The girl effect' and martial arts: Social entrepreneurship and sport, gender and development in Uganda. *Gender, Place and Culture, 21*(3), 297–315.

Jarvie, G. and Reid, I. (1999). Scottish sport, nationalist politics and culture. *Sport in Society, 2*(2), 22–43.

Kidd, B. (2008). A new social movement: sport for development and peace. *Sport in Society, 11*(4), 370–380.

Kohlberg, L. (1981). *The Philosophy of Moral Development: Moral Stages and the Idea of Justice,* New York, NY: HarperCollins.

Koss, J. and Alexandrova, A. (2005). HIV/AIDS prevention and peace through sport. *Lancet, 366,* 53–54.

Lederach, J. P. (1997). *Building Peace: Sustainable Reconciliation in Divided Societies.* Washington, DC: United States Institute of Peace.

Lindsey, I., Kay, T., Jeanes, R. and Banda, D. (2017). *Localizing Global Sport for Development.* Manchester: Manchester University Press.

Lyras, A. and Peachey, W. (2011). Integrating sport-for-development theory and praxis. *Sport Management Review, 14:* 311–326.

Majumdar, B. and Brown, S. (2007). Why Baseball, Why Cricket? Differing Nationalisms, Differing Challenges. *International Journal of the History of Sport*, 24(2), 139–156.

Mannathukkaren, N. (2001). Subalterns, cricket and the 'Nation': The silences of 'Lagaan'. *Economic and Political Weekly*, 36(49), 4580–4588.

Mutz, M. and Baur, J. (2009). The role of sports for violence prevention: Sport club participation and violent behaviour among adolescents. *International Journal of Sport Policy*, 1(3), 305–321.

Nicholls, S., Giles, A. R. and Sethna, C. (2010). Perpetuating the 'lack of evidence'. Discourse in sport in development: Privileged voices, unheard stories and subjugated knowledge. *International Review for the Sociology of Sport*, 46(3), 249–264.

Pautz, M. and Schnitzer, M. (2008). Policymaking from below: The role of environmental inspectors and publics. *Administrative Theory and Praxis*, 30(4), 450–475.

Phan, H. and Peridis, T. (2000). Knowledge creation in strategic alliances: Another look at organizational learning. *Asia Pacific Journal of Management*, 17(2), 201–222.

Piaget, J. (1948). *The Moral Judgment of the Child*, Glencoe, Ill: Free Press.

Platts, C. and Smith, A. (2009). The education, rights and welfare of young people in professional football in England: Some implications of the white paper on sport. *International Journal of Sport Policy*, 1(3), 323–339.

Podolny, J. M. and Page, K. L. (1998). Network forms of organization. *Annual Review of Sociology*, 24(S), 57–76.

Rorty, R. (1993). Human rights, rationality, and sentimentality. In S. S. Hurley (ed.), *On Human Rights: The Oxford Amnesty Lectures*. London: Basic Books.

Sen, A. (2001). *Development as Freedom*. Oxford: Oxford University Press.

Spaaij, R. and Jeanes, R. (2012). Education for social change? A Freirean critique of sport for development and peace. *Physical Education and Sport Pedagogy*, 18(4), 1–16.

Spaaij, R., Oxford, S. and Jeanes, R. (2016). Transforming communities through sport? Critical pedagogy and sport for development. *Sport, Education and Society*, 21(4), 570–587.

Svensson P. G. and Levine, J. (2017). Rethinking sport for development and peace: The capability approach. *Sport in Society*. Available at: http://dx.doi.org/10.1080/17430437.2016.1269083.

Szreter, S. (2002). The state of social capital: Bringing power, politics, and history back in. *Theory and Society*, 31(5), 573–621.

Taylor, M. (1996) Good Government: On Hierarchy, Social Capital and the limitations of Rational Choice Theory. *Journal of Political Philosophy* 4 (1), 1–28.

Toohey, K. (2008). Terrorism, sport and public policy in the risk society. *Sport in Society*, 11(4), 429–442.

United Nations. (2003). *Sport as a Tool for Development and Peace: Towards Achieving the United Nations Millennium Development Goals*. Geneva: UN Inter-agency Task Force on Sport for Development and Peace.

United Nations. (2006). Sport for Development and Peace: The Way Forward. Report of the Secretary-General report A/61/373, 22. New York, NY: United Nations. Available at: www.un.org/sport2005/resources/statements/N0653114.pdf.

Van Kempen, P. (2009a). In Search for the Optimal Balance Between Sport and Education in Health Awareness Programmes. Draft results of round 1 of the Sport and Development eDebate. International Platform on Sport and Development. Available at: www.sportanddev.org/newsnviews/sport___development_e_debate/.

Van Kempen, P. (2009b). Aims and challenges for Sport and Development Interventions. Draft results of Round 2 of the Sport and Development eDebate. International Platform on Sport and Development. Available at: www.sportanddev.org/sites/default/files/downloads/draft_summary_round_2.pdf.

Wacquant, L. (1989). An interview with Pierre Bourdieu: For a socio-analysis of intellectuals: On homo academicus. *Berkeley Journal of Sociology*, 34(1), 1–29.

Walseth, K. (2008). Bridging and bonding social capital in sport: Experiences of young women with an immigrant background. *Sport, Education and Society*, 13(1), 1–17.

Zanotti, L. (2006). Taming chaos: A Foucauldian view on UN peacekeeping, democracy and normalization. *International Peacekeeping*, 13 (2), 150–167.

Zanotti, L. (2011). *Governing Disorder. UN Peace Operations, International Security, and Democratization in the Post–Cold War Era*. University Park, PA: Penn State University Press.

Zanotti, L., Stephenson, M. and Schnitzer, M. (2015). Biopolitical and disciplinary peacebuilding: Sport, reforming bodies, and rebuilding societies. *International Peacekeeping*, 22(2), 1–16.

15

SDP and research methods

William V. Massey and Meredith A. Whitley

Introduction

Discussing the critical issues related to current (and future) research in the area of Sport for Development and Peace (SDP) presents several unique challenges. Chief among these is the question: What exactly is SDP? Moreover, one could ask: What is Sport-Based Youth Development? How does this differ from SDP? What is simply Sport for Development? And why differentiate between Sport for Development and Sport for Development and Peace? To complicate matters, 'development' and 'peace' are often vaguely defined terms (Levermore and Beacom 2014; Sugden 2010) that can refer to, among other things, the absence of conflict, poverty reduction, education, economic growth, health, and gender equity. While the purpose of this chapter is not to argue the merit or utility of various terms, it is worth pointing out that the lack of clarity around the SDP field, and what defines SDP, can provide confusion as to what constitutes SDP research, and how SDP research should move forward in a coherent form.

For the purposes of this text, SDP is understood to occur when sport, play, or physical activity (PA) are used in the service of social development, health promotion, gender empowerment, and social inclusion, as well as conflict resolution and community building in post-conflict contexts. Previously, we have argued (Massey *et al.* 2015) that what is considered 'sport', 'development', and/or 'peace' is less important than working towards 'a state of human existence characterised by sustainable levels of human development and healthy processes of societal change' (Ricigliano 2012: 15). Thus, this chapter broadly focuses on research that aims to use sport, play, and/or PA to increase human development in its many forms and improve healthy processes of change. In our discussion below, we outline trends in SDP research, with a focus on theoretical, philosophical, methodological, and rigour concerns. From there, we highlight some key disciplinary differences and argue for the need to embrace a transdisciplinary field of SDP. Finally, we propose a path forward in SDP research, providing recommendations to scholars for planning and implementing research within the SDP field.

Current trends and challenges in SDP research

Contributing to the questions raised above is fact that SDP is composed of researchers from different academic disciplines (e.g. sport psychology, sport sociology, sport management, pedagogy). While coming to a common ground regarding best research practices can be difficult within a single academic discipline (e.g. Darnell 2012; Coalter 2013), doing so across multiple academic disciplines and training paradigms presents an even greater challenge. Disciplinary and paradigmatic trends connected to theory, philosophy, and methodology have emerged – often isolated within singular fields of study – with direct implications on the quality of research within SDP. Moreover, there are vested interest groups (e.g. practitioners, academics, funders, policy-makers, governmental bodies, multilateral institutions, corporations, international non-governmental organizations) from both sport and non-sport sectors (e.g. non-profit management, international development, peacebuilding efforts, corporate social responsibility) that shape research within SDP, including but not limited to theory, philosophy, methodology, and rigour. Given this, and based on recent evidence and reviews of literature in SDP (Langer 2015; Massey *et al.* 2015; Darnell *et al.* 2016a; Schulenkorf *et al.* 2016; Holt *et al.* 2017; Whitley *et al.* 2018; Whitley *et al.* 2017), we have identified three inter-related areas warranting further discussion: (a) theoretical and philosophical underpinnings to SDP research; (b) methodologies and methodological rigour in SDP research; and (c) disciplinary trends in SDP research.

Theoretical and philosophical underpinnings to SDP research

A common critique levied against SDP research has been its atheoretical and aphilosophical nature (Coalter 2010; Massey *et al.* 2015). Despite these critiques, substantial progress has been made with the theoretical and philosophical underpinnings of SDP research in the last eight years. Perhaps the most substantial advances in theoretical and philosophical thought have come from scholars within sociology, with theorists arguing that SDP research cannot be detached from the social and political conditions in the local context. Given the complexity of social systems and structures that exist, broad or context-devoid theories are likely to render themselves ineffective and irrelevant. For example, Darnell (2012) has argued for the use of Gramscian, Foucauldian, and postcolonial theories, as well as theoretical approaches that politicize research and practice within SDP (i.e. political economy, governmentality, feminist theories; Darnell *et al.* 2016a). Moreover, Spaaij and Jeanes have explored the potential for Freire's critical pedagogy as a theoretical framework to study SDP, particularly in the global South (Spaaij and Jeanes 2013; Jeanes and Spaaij 2016). This theorizing has led to more contemporary SDP research firmly grounded in sociological theory that considers both the politics and ethics of conducting this work (e.g. Hayhurst *et al.* 2015; Burnett 2016; Shehu, 2016; Spaaij *et al.* 2016; Gardam *et al.* 2017). In addition to this research, Sugden (2010) developed the 'ripple effect' model to illustrate ways in which social impacts experienced through interventions at the individual and group levels can lead to change in the broader community and society, resulting in research grounded in critical left-realism (e.g. Sherry *et al.* 2017).

Aside from those in sport sociology, sport management scholars have used social capital theory (e.g. Intergroup Contact Theory; Allport 1954) to measure individual and collective development among participants, stakeholders, and communities (e.g. Magee and Jeanes 2013; Welty Peachey *et al.* 2015a; Welty Peachey *et al.* 2015b), with this guiding the development of the sport-for-development theory (Lyras and Welty Peachey 2011). This theory is grounded in the need for proximity and intergroup contact in an effort to facilitate change, with sport management scholars examining SDP research through this theoretical lens (e.g. Marshall and Barry 2015; Welty Peachey *et al.* 2013). Moreover, those studying SDP within the pedagogical and psychological sciences have utilized a range of theories (e.g. bioecological systems theory, self-determination theory) and frameworks (e.g. positive youth development, teaching personal and social responsibility) to contextualize their research.

Yet, what remains largely problematic for theory development within SDP research is that various theories remain isolated to specific disciplines of study. That is, sociologists tend to draw from sociological theory, psychologists from developmental and behavioural psychology theories, with other disciplines acting accordingly. A needed area of growth, and perhaps an emerging trend within SDP research, is integration across various academic disciplines, particularly as it relates to the philosophy of knowledge production and consideration of theoretical lenses through which to examine data. For example, Massey and colleagues (2015) have argued for the need to examine SDP through a systems theory lens, which is consistent with more recent writing from those in a range of academic disciplines (e.g. Whitley *et al.* 2016; Schulenkorf 2017; Sugden 2010). Thus, and as elaborated on further below, studying SDP through systems science may allow for SDP to become a transdisciplinary field of study that unites, rather than silos, those from divergent research traditions.

Research methodologies and methodological rigour in SDP research

Often tied to such debates regarding theoretical frameworks, philosophy of knowledge production, and diverging research traditions are issues related to methodological practices in SDP research. Many SDP scholars have argued that top-down, traditional monitoring and evaluation approaches are inappropriate for SDP programme design and evaluation (e.g. Black 2010; Darnell and Hayhurst 2011; Levermore and Beacom 2014; Schulenkorf and Adair 2014). Darnell and Hayhurst (2011: 188) suggested, 'sport does not, and most likely cannot, usurp the social-political relations and challenges of international development organization, policy, and implementation'. In this way, scholars have questioned the reliability of instrumental (often positivist) research, as it is thought to reinforce systems of hegemony and oppression of marginalized groups (Nicholls *et al.* 2010; Darnell and Hayhurst 2012; Lindsey and Grattan 2012). Still others maintain the need for evidence based on a scientific definition of 'truth' (Raphael 2000). Yet dismissing certain types of research based on underlying epistemology inherently presents issues of power, regardless of the directionality of the argument. Thus, rather than lay blanket critiques across different research paradigms and epistemologies, there is a need to discuss higher levels of sophistication in both instrumental/positivist (i.e. quantitative) and descriptive/critical (i.e. qualitative) SDP research (Darnell *et al.* 2016a; Holt *et al.* 2016).

In their comprehensive review of the state of research in SDP, Schulenkorf *et al.* (2016) noted that positive youth development and social capital theory were the frameworks most frequently cited in SDP research. As highlighted by Darnell and colleagues (2016a), these approaches likely indicate an instrumental view of research, grounded within positivist assumptions. Within these positivist (and post-positivist) assumptions, research is primarily focused on solutions, or questions of what works and under what conditions. From a methodology and methodological rigour standpoint, the positionality of this research assumes a need to reduce bias in an effort to isolate the causes of any positive (or negative) effects stemming from the intervention (Coalter 2013). Yet, the methodological rigour seen within positivist studies in SDP to date often falls short of being able to make definitive claims regarding the effectiveness of SDP programmes (Langer 2015; Whitley *et al.* 2018; 2017). Notably, a profusion of studies in SDP rely on single time point, single programme, and/or single group studies. This becomes problematic when considering application of research to practice in SDP because it assumes the effects reported in the literature take place in a vacuum, without critical analysis of contextual factors in various environments, as well as changes over time.

As one example of the comments illustrated above, multiple single group pre-post studies examining the effects of the Girls on the Run programme (e.g. Waldron 2007; DeBate *et al.*

2009; Rauscher *et al.* 2013) show consistent positive improvements over time. However, when adding a comparison group to the study design, Gabriel *et al.* (2011) show no differences in results between those who were exposed to the programme, and those with no programme exposure. Thus, aside from the intervention, the results could also be explained by natural changes over time (maturation bias), selecting participants more likely to respond positively to the programme (selection bias), participants reporting more positive scores so as not to disappoint the programme leaders (reporting bias), or factors related to programme context and implementation. Also present in the SDP literature are issues of: (a) methodological rigour related to the use of valid, reliable, culturally relevant, and behaviourally based measures; (b) reporting fidelity to intervention/programme protocols; (c) accounting for likely covariates that may influence results; and (d) the appropriateness of statistical analyses and reporting. As revealed by Langer (2015: 78), evidence of SDP programmes in Africa have 'failed to adequately measure final and impact outcomes'. This can be seen in both the lack of follow-up on outcome measurement in SDP research, along with a tendency to focus on knowledge and attitudes, as opposed to actual behaviour change or public health impacts (Langer 2015; Whitley *et al.* 2018).

Our intent here is not to overly criticise the important work that colleagues have conducted within SDP, as we certainly recognize (and have experienced) the challenges inherent in conducting research in the SDP field (e.g. Whitley *et al.* 2014; Whitley and Johnson 2015). Rather, our intent is to call attention to methodological issues that will strengthen the SDP evidence base moving forward. In providing a sociological critique to SDP research, Darnell *et al.* (2016a) argued for the need to offer a more critical perspective, as opposed to the often apolitical perspectives taken by those conducting positivist research. Specifically, Darnell and colleagues (2016a: 13) commented that, 'more research does not necessarily yield better insights'. While we concur with this sentiment, we would also suggest (a) the continued need for instrumental, outcomes-based research; and (b) higher quality of instrumental, outcomes-based research. To date, very few studies have utilized multiple group and/or experimental designs within SDP research, with those adhering to more rigorous standards showing both mixed (e.g. Fuller *et al.* 2013; Snelling 2015; Butzer *et al.* 2017) and negative impacts (e.g. Richards *et al.* 2014). These mixed findings could suggest cherry picking of evidence to support the notion that sport can be a simplistic solution to complex problems (Coalter 2010; Langer 2015). Moreover, the relative dearth of longitudinal studies (e.g. Weiss *et al.* 2016) leaves questions as to whether any benefits reported in an evaluation study are maintained. This overwhelming focus on immediate, positive outcomes is likely a response to external pressures from various stakeholders (e.g. funders, policy-makers, governmental bodies, corporations) to explain and justify SDP programmes and processes (Burnett 2011; Schulenkorf and Adair 2014). In spite of this climate, there is the need for research that is multi-site and multi-group, along with research which considers the contextual environment and includes a longitudinal analysis of outcomes over time. This will result in higher quality instrumental research that will advance the SDP field.

While instrumental (and often positivist) research has been critiqued as being devoid of context (Lindsey and Grattan 2012), descriptive and/or qualitative work can fall into similar trappings. For example, there has been an increased focus on 'giving voice' to participants within SDP research paradigms. Yet intakes of participants' views, and perceptions of an SDP programme without consideration of the structural, social, political, and economic forces that create disparities in the first place, are also at risk of being devoid of context. The field of SDP operates within messy, complex, and dynamic social systems, with long histories and structures of inequity. Thus, it would behove researchers to strongly consider the philosophical, theoretical, methodological, and analytical underpinnings of their research. When researchers explicitly address how their ontology and epistemology shape decisions related to theory, methodology, and methods, other stakeholders can assess if the tools and approaches used to collect, analyse, and interpret the data were coherent. Similarly, detailed descriptions of the methodology and methodological procedures (i.e. how data were collected, how data were analysed, how decisions were made) allow for a nuanced understanding and assessment of the research methods. Yet to date, these underpinnings and decision making processes are inconsistently reported (e.g. Holt *et al.* 2017), with recent systematic reviews from Whitley *et al.* (2018; 2017) indicating that integration across philosophical, theoretical, methodological, and analytical perspectives rarely occurs in qualitative SDP research.

This presents a need for philosophical, theoretical, methodological, and analytical creativity and diversity to 'build theory, research, and praxis that is relevant, contextual, decolonizing, and postcolonial' (Darnell *et al.* 2016b: 574) within SDP. This may include, but is not limited to, research that engages with, rather than makes claims about, people on the ground (Lindsey *et al.* 2017), with the researcher stepping out from their impartial and disconnected lens, and considering their role as facilitators, collaborators, and advocates. In doing so, the questions asked in SDP research should be driven by exploration and curiosity, and contextualized within the social, cultural, and political history and climate (Whitley *et al.* 2018; 2017), rather than being reduced to box ticking exercises (Levermore 2011). Moreover, similar to critiques levied at instrumental/positivist research, there continues to be a need for critical and descriptive research that is multi-site, considers the contextual environment, and includes a longitudinal analysis of outcomes over time.

Disciplinary perspectives in SDP research

In reviewing the literature presented above, disciplinary trends related to the process of conducting SDP research emerged as worthy of discussion, despite the limitations associated with abridged summaries (e.g. exceptions to trends, exclusion of trends). Our purpose in highlighting these differences is not to splinter or drive apart disciplines, but rather highlight areas in which scholars may consider collaboration across disciplines. Moreover, while we recognize that SDP research and practice takes place both within and outside sport-specific academic domains, we have limited this discussion to those doing work in sport management, sport psychology, sport sociology, and sport pedagogy.

Sport management scholars tend to focus on the management and organizational aspects of SDP initiatives, from events with short-term, intensive activities to programmes with scheduled activities over longer periods of time. In his review of SDP research in the sport management field, Schulenkorf conceptualized this managerial and organizational focus as critical to the growing body of SDP research, explaining how it 'shifts the emphasis from merely investigating specific programme contexts or impacts to strategically designing, managing, and leveraging SFD initiatives for (wider) community benefit' (Schulenkorf 2017: 245) Often, this research is informed by social capital theory (e.g. Intergroup Contact Theory; Allport, 1954), with sport management researchers examining ways in which SDP events and programmes can be managed, organized, and leveraged to maximise social capital outcomes within and beyond the initiatives (e.g. Schulenkorf and Edwards 2012; Welty Peachey *et al.* 2015b).

Sport psychology trained researchers conducting SDP work are generally influenced by the larger positive youth development (PYD) movement within psychology (Pittman and Irby 1998), with PYD identified as one of the most popular and recurring approaches to studying SDP (Schulenkorf *et al.* 2016). From a historical perspective, PYD emerged as a counter to prevention science, yet was grounded in empirical positivism. This has led to a focus more on individualistic outcomes, particularly those related to mental health and well-being. The PYD movement was originally grounded in bioecological systems theory (Bronfenbrenner 1995), which should necessitate the examination of outcomes on multiple levels (i.e. individual, community, societal). However, to date little SDP work in sport psychology has explicitly utilized a bioecological lens (e.g. Holt *et al.* 2008; Holt *et al.* 2011; Massey and Whitley 2016; Whitley *et al.* 2016), perhaps signifying a need to collaborate with their sociological counterparts in an effort to better examine how upstream factors might influence individual behaviour.

While the dominant theoretical paradigms in sport psychology (i.e. PYD) and sport management (i.e. social capital) suggest 'solutions to development inequalities through sport', sport sociologists more frequently ask 'how sport aligns with or diverges from (or even resists) the histories and structures of inequality' (Darnell *et al.* 2016a: 6). This results in a more instrumental (and often positivist) approach to SDP research in sport management and sport psychology, compared with a more descriptive, critical, and politicized study of SDP in sport sociology. Thus, sport sociologists tend to focus on broader social, political, and structural issues related to SDP (e.g. societal constraints, structural change; Sherry *et al.* 2017). Further, when compared to those in other SDP sub-disciplines, sociologists engaged in SDP research tend to conduct their work in communities not native to their university or living quarters. This immediately raises different moral and ethical issues around knowledge production and neocolonialism through sport (Collison *et al.* 2016), and ultimately shapes theoretical and philosophical underpinnings of the research. Collison *et al.* (2016) discussed the tensions inherent in conducting field-based anthropological research in SDP, noting both the need for non-instrumental research and the ongoing push for studies that are 'practical and useful' for local populations. Thus, as scholarship in SDP continues to grow, an ongoing presence from anthropology researchers can shed important theoretical and critical insight into how sport may operate within local communities.

Another area of growth within SDP research comes from those studying sport pedagogy. Perhaps the largest contribution came from Don Hellison and the development and use of the Teaching Personal and Social Responsibility (TPSR) model (Hellison 2011). Scholars within this field have often taken a pragmatic approach to programme evaluation to examine whether SDP programmes have met the intended goals of the TPSR model. While the methodological rigour of this work is not without critique (Whitley *et al.* 2017), pedagogical scholars utilizing the TPSR model have shed important light on best practices in programme implementation (e.g. Schilling *et al.* 2007; Wright and Burton 2008), which is imperative for scholars seeking to understand how programme fidelity might impact SDP outcomes. As these components are likely to shift across contexts, collaborations between those in pedagogy and other academic disciplines engaged in SDP research are likely to improve the quality of SDP design and evaluation.

Futures directions in SDP research

What then can be said about the future of research in SDP? There is pressure in many fields of study to conform to the paradigm of evidence-based practice, so as not to be stigmatized as an evidence-less field of inquiry. Yet, evidence-based practice promotes hierarchies that privilege carefully controlled and manipulated experiments, which are often ineffectual in the real world of messy, complex, and dynamic social ecological systems. While we argued above that there is a need to improve instrumental/positivist research, we maintain that simply using 'better' forms of reductionist research is still likely to widen the gap between researchers and practitioners in SDP. Moreover, while we highlighted a need for more critical forms of research (e.g. Darnell *et al.* 2016a), we also maintain that critical discourse without action is equally problematic. To this end, we suggest that a systems theory approach offers great potential for SDP researchers. Rather than attempt to accumulate knowledge through inductive or deductive principles, a systems theory approach allows for knowledge through simulation and the promotion of planning, action, and learning cycles, resulting in a field grounded in practice-based evidence (Green 2006). It seems as though Green's call to improve research in public health is also applicable to SDP, which will 'help us get a handle on the multiplicity of influences at work in the real world of practice, so that the evidence from our study of interventions and programmes can reflect that complex reality rather than mask it' (Green 2006: 406).

There are several advantages when considering a systems theory approach to SDP scholarship. First, systems theories require a holistic focus, which often includes structural, attitudinal, and transactional facets of a system (Ricigliano 2012). Inherently, this necessitates knowledge and input from a broad and diverse coalition of 'participants', addressing various concerns around what is considered evidence (Harris and Adams 2016) and the need for input from a range of stakeholders (Darnell *et al.* 2016b). This also aligns with calls for more participatory research paradigms within SDP (e.g. Hayhurst *et al.* 2015; Collison and Marchesseault 2016) that can work towards flattening traditional power differentials between researchers and the researched (Hayhurst 2016). Moreover, we posit that a systems theory approach demands the use of transdisciplinary research teams, addressing the need for 'an increasingly holistic approach to SDP research, rather than an exclusive or bordered one' (Darnell *et al.* 2016a: 15). This team approach will enable scholars from various disciplines to bring their diverse theories and methodological tools to the table, resulting in a more rigorous, theoretically diverse, and methodologically encompassing approach. This will allow for more complex and meaningful research questions to be explored.

A systems theory approach to SDP research can lead to the study of multiple systems levels (e.g. microsystem, mesosystem, exosystem, macrosystem), across various levels of influence (e.g. individual, school, community, policy) and influencers (e.g. parents, peers, youth workers, funders, governments, corporations), and the interaction of these factors over time and within an historical context. For example, sociologists can examine structural systems factors by engaging in macro-level analyses that focus on, 'the physical environment and issues of ecology and sustainability; the geo-politics of underdevelopment; and sport and SDP policy (at both international and national levels) as well as the historical underpinnings of SDP' (Darnell *et al.* 2016a: 8). Concurrently, sport managers can explore attitudinal level factors by studying various exosystem and mesosystem level influencers and how interactions between various groups and events influence behaviour and development at individual and collective levels. Further, collaborating scientists within sport psychology can examine behaviour change at an individual level, giving insight into questions of what works and under what conditions, while those in pedagogy can ensure learning and action cycles take place and knowledge is transferred across domains. These collaborations across levels enable the examination of both upstream and downstream influences, allowing for a more dynamic understanding of causality that takes into account historical, structural, community, and individual level influences in SDP. Additionally, transdisciplinary teams taking a systems theory approach are better equipped to explore emerging questions about collective impact (e.g. Kania and Kramer 2011) and transnational/global impact (e.g. Darnell *et al.* 2016a). While this will certainly not be an easy path forward in SDP research, and might require more creativity in research funding and research design, prominent scholars across multiple disciplines have begun to express similar views (e.g. Darnell *et al.* 2016a; Holt *et al.* 2016; Schulenkorf *et al.* 2017). The key, we believe, is to move forward in collaborative ways that cross traditional disciplinary and epistemological boundaries to examine and ultimately advance the current evidence base in SDP.

References

Allport, G. W. (1954). *The Nature of Prejudice*. Cambridge, MA: Addison-Wesley.

Black, D. R. (2010). The ambiguities of development: Implications for 'development through sport'. *Sport in Society, 13*, 121–129.

Bronfenbrenner, U. (1995). Developmental ecology through space and time: A future perspective. In P. Moen, G. H. Elder and K. Lüscher (eds), *Examining Lives in Context: Perspectives on the Ecology of Human Development*. Washington, DC: APA, pp. 619–647.

Burnett, C. (2011). Local agency as a strategic imperative in sport for development. *African Journal for Physical, Health Education, Recreation and Dance, 17*, 916–935.

Burnett, C. (2016). Relevance of Olympism education and sport-for-development programmes in South African schools. *South African Journal for Research in Sport, Physical Education and Recreation, 38*(3), 15–26.

Butzer, B., LoRusso, A., Shin, S. H. and Khalsa, S. B. S. (2017). Evaluation of yoga for preventing adolescent substance use risk factors in a middle school setting: A preliminary group- randomized controlled trial. *Journal of Youth and Adolescence, 46*(3), 603–632.

Coalter, F. (2010). The politics of sport-for-development: Limited focus programmes and broad gauge problems? *International Review for the Sociology of Sport, 45*(3), 295–314.

Coalter, F. (2013). *Sport for Development: What Game are We Playing?* Abingdon: Routledge.

Collison, H., Giulianotti, R., Howe, P. D. and Darnell, S. (2016). The methodological dance: Critical reflections on conducting a cross-cultural comparative research project on 'Sport for Development and Peace'. *Qualitative Research in Sport, Exercise, and Health, 8*, 413–423, doi:10.1080/2159676X.2016.1206610.

Collison, H. and Marchesseault, D. (2016). Finding the missing voices of sport for development and peace (SDP): Using a 'participatory social interaction research' methodology and anthropological perspectives within African developing countries. *Sport in Society*, doi:10.1080/17430437.2016.1179732.

Darnell, S. C. (2012). *Sport for Development and Peace: A critical sociology*. London: Bloomsbury Academic.

Darnell, S. C., Chawansky, M., Marchesseault, D., Holmes, M. and Hayhurst, L. M. C. (2016a). The state of play: Critical sociological insights into recent 'sport for development and peace' research. *International Review for the Sociology of Sport*, 1–19, doi:10.1177/1012690216646762.

Darnell, S. C. and Hayhurst, L. M. C. (2011). Sport for decolonization: Exploring a new praxis of sport for development. *Progress in Development Studies, 11*(3), 183–196.

Darnell, S. C. and Hayhurst, L. M. C. (2012). Hegemony, postcolonialism and sport-for-development: A response to Lindsey and Grattan. *International Journal of Sport Policy and Politics, 4*(1), 111–124.

Darnell, S. C., Whitley, M. A. and Massey, W. V. (2016b). Changing methods and methods of change: Reflections on qualitative research in sport for development and peace. *Qualitative Research in Sport, Exercise, and Health, 8*(5), 571–577, doi:10.1080/2159676X.2016.1214618.

DeBate, R. D., Gabriel, K. P., Zwald, M., Huberty, J. and Zhang, Y. (2009). Changes in psychosocial factors and physical activity frequency among third-to eighth-grade girls who participated in a developmentally focused youth sport program: A preliminary study. *Journal of School Health, 79*(10), 474–484.

Fuller, R. D., Percy, V. E., Bruening, J. E. and Cotrufo, R. J. (2013). Positive youth development: Minority male participation in a sport-based afterschool program in an urban environment. *Research Quarterly for Exercise and Sport, 84*(4), 469–482.

Gabriel, K. K. P., DeBate, R. D., High, R. R. and Racine, E. F. (2011). Girls on the run: A quasi- experimental evaluation of a developmentally focused youth sport program. *Journal of Physical Activity and Health, 8*(S2), S285–S294.

Gardam, K., Giles, A. R. and Hayhurst, L. M. C. (2017). Understanding the privatisation of funding for sport for development in the Northwest Territories: A Foucauldian analysis. *International Journal of Sport Policy and Politics, 9*(3), 541–555.

Green, L. W. (2006). Public health asks of systems science: To advance our evidence-based practice, can you help us get more practice-based evidence? *American Journal of Public Health, 96*(3), 406–414.

Harris, K. and Adams, A. (2016). Power and discourse in the politics of evidence in sport for development. *Sport Management Review, 19*(2), 97–106.

Hayhurst, L. M. C. (2016). Sport for development and peace: A call for transnational, multi-sited, post-colonial feminist research. *Qualitative Research in Sport, Exercise, and Health, 8*(5), 424–443.

Hayhurst, L. M. C., Giles, A. R. and Radforth, W. M. (2015). 'I want to come here to prove them wrong': Using a post-colonial feminist participatory action research (PFPAR) approach to studying sport, gender and development programmes for urban indigenous young women. *Sport in Society, 18*(8), 952–967.

Hellison, D. (2011). *Teaching Personal and Social Responsibility Through Physical Activity*. Champaign, IL: Human Kinetics.

Holt, N. K., Deal, C. J. and Smyth, C. L. (2016). Future directions for positive youth development through sport. In N. K. Holt (ed.), *Positive Youth Development Through Sport*. Milton Park: Routledge, pp. 231–240.

Holt, N. L., Kingsley, B. C., Tink, L. N. and Scherer, J. (2011). Benefits and challenges associated with sport participation by children and parents from low-income families. *Psychology of Sport and Exercise*, *12*(5), 490–499, doi:10.1016/j.psychsport.2011.05.007.

Holt, N. L., Tink, L. N., Mandigo, B. and Fox, K. R. (2008). Do youth learn life skills through their involvement in high school sport? A case study. *Canadian Journal of Education*, *31*(2), 281–304.

Holt, N. L., Neely, K. C., Slater, L. G., Camiré, M., Côté, J., Fraser-Thomas, J., … Tamminen, K. A. (2017). A grounded theory of positive youth development through sport based on results from a qualitative meta-study. *International Review of Sport and Exercise Psychology*, *10*(1), 1–49, doi:10.1080/1750984X.2016.1180704.

Jeanes, R. and Spaaij, R. (2016). Examining the educator: Towards a critical pedagogy of sport development and peace. In L. Hayhurst, T. Kay and M. Chawansky (eds), *Beyond Sport for Development and Peace: Transnational Perspectives on Theory, Policy and Practice*. London: Routledge, pp. 155–168).

Kania, J. and Kramer, M. (2011). Collective impact: Large-scale social change requires broad cross-sector coordination, yet the social sector remains focused on the isolated intervention of individual organizations. *Stanford Social Innovation Review*, *9*(1), 36–41.

Langer, L. (2015). Sport for development: A systematic map of evidence from Africa. *South African Review of Sociology*, *46*(1), 66–86.

Levermore, R. (2011). Evaluating sport-for-development: Approaches and critical issues. *Progress in Development Studies*, *11*(4), 339–353.

Levermore, R. and Beacom, A. (2014). Reassessing sport-for-development: Moving beyond 'mapping the territory'. *International Journal of Sport Policy and Politics*, *4*(1), 125–137, doi:10.1080/19406940.2011.627362.

Lindsey, I. and Grattan, A. (2012). An 'international movement'? Decentring sport-for-development within Zambian communities. *International Journal of Sport Policy and Politics*, *4*(1), 91–110.

Lindsey, I., Kay, T., Jeanes, R. and Banda, D. (2017). *Localizing Global Sport for Development*. Manchester: Palgrave Macmillan.

Lyras, A. and Welty Peachey, J. (2011). Integrating sport-for-development theory and praxis. *Sport Management Review*, *14*(4), 311–326, doi:10.1016/j.smr.2011.05.006.

Magee, J. and Jeanes, R. (2013). Football's coming home: A critical evaluation of the Homeless World Cup as an intervention to combat social exclusion. *International Review for the Sociology of Sport*, *48*,(1), 3–19, doi:10.1177/1012690211428391.

Marshall, S. K. and Barry, P. (2015). Community sport for development: Perceptions from practice in Southern Africa. *Journal of Sport Management*, *29*(1), 109–121.

Massey, W. V. and Whitley, M. A. (2016). The role of sport for youth amidst trauma and chaos. *Qualitative Research in Sport, Exercise, and Health*, *8*, 487–504, doi:10.1080/2159676X.2016.1204351.

Massey, W. V., Whitley, M. A., Blom, L. C. and Gerstein, L. H. (2015). Sport for development and peace: A systems theory perspective on promoting sustainable change. *International Journal of Sport Management and Marketing*, *16*, 18–35, doi:10.1504/IJSMM.2015.074921.

Nicholls, S., Giles, A. R. and Sethna, C. (2010). Perpetuating the 'lack of evidence' discourse in sport for development: Privileged voices, unheard stories and subjugated knowledge. *International Review for the Sociology of Sport*, *46*(3), 249–264.

Pittman, K. and Irby, M. (1998*). Reflections on a Decade of Promoting Youth Development*. Washington, DC: American Youth Policy Forum.

Raphael, D. (2000). The question of evidence in health promotion. *Health Promotion International*, *15*(4), 355–367.

Rauscher, L., Kauer, K. and Wilson, B. D. M. (2013). Organizational and interactional influences on pre-adolescent girls' body image in Los Angeles. *Gender and Society*, *27*(2), 208–230.

Richards, J., Foster, C., Townsend, N. and Bauman, A. (2014). Physical fitness and mental health impact of a sport-for-development intervention in a post-conflict setting: Randomised controlled trial nested within an observational study of adolescents in Gulu, Uganda. *BMC Public Health*, *14*(1), 619.

Ricigliano, R. (2012). *Making Peace Last: A Toolbox for Sustainable Peacebuilding*. Boulder, CO: Paradigm.

Schilling, T., Martinek, T. and Carson, S. (2007). Youth leaders' perceptions of commitment to a responsibility-based physical activity program. *Research Quarterly for Exercise and Sport*, *78*(2), 48–60.

Schulenkorf, N. (2017). Managing sport-for-development: Reflections and outlook. *Sport Management Review*, *20*(3), 243–251.

Schulenkorf, N. and Adair, D. (2014). *Global Sport-for-Development: Critical Perspectives*. Palgrave Macmillan: London.

Schulenkorf, N. and Edwards, D. (2012). Maximizing positive social impacts: Strategies for sustaining and leveraging the benefits of intercommunity sport events in divided societies. *Journal of Sport Management*, *26*(5), 379–390.

Schulenkorf, N., Sherry, E. and Rowe, K. (2016). Sport for development: An integrated literature review. *Journal of Sport Management*, *30*(1), 22–39.

Shehu, J. (2016). Theorizing sport for development: Intersections among sport, gender and development. In L. Hayhurst, T. Kay and M. Chawansky (eds), *Beyond Sport for Development and Peace: Transnational Perspectives on Theory, Policy and Practice*. London: Routledge, pp. 12–28.

Sherry, E., Schulenkorf, N., Seal, E., Nicholson, M. and Hoye, R. (2017). Sport-for-development in the South Pacific region: Macro-, meso- and micro-perspectives. *Sociology of Sport Journal*, *34*(4), 303–316.

Snelling, M. (2015). Breaking Cycles of Violence, One Wave at a Time: A Formative Evaluation of the Waves for Change Surf Therapy Programme. Unpublished Master's thesis. University of Cape Town, South Africa.

Spaaij, R. and Jeanes, R. (2013). Education for social change? A Freirean critique of sport for development and peace. *Physical Education and Sport Pedagogy*, *18*(4), 442–457.

Spaaij, R., Oxford, S. and Jeanes, R. (2016). Transforming communities through sport? Critical pedagogy and sport for development. *Sport, Education and Society*, *21*(4), 570–587.

Sugden, J. (2010). Critical left-realism and sport interventions in divided societies. *International Review for the Sociology of Sport*, *45*(3), 258–272.

Waldron, J. J. (2007). Influence of involvement in the Girls on Track program on early adolescent girls' self-perceptions. *Research Quarterly for Exercise and Sport*, *78*(5), 520–530.

Weiss, M. R., Bolter, N. D. and Kipp, L. E. (2016). Evaluation of The First Tee in promoting positive youth development: Group comparisons and longitudinal trends. *Research Quarterly for Exercise and Sport*, *87*(3), 271–283.

Welty Peachey, J., Bruening, J., Lyras, A., Cohen, A. and Cunningham, G. B. (2015a). Examining social capital development among volunteers of a multinational sport-for-development event. *Journal of Sport Management*, *29*(1), 27–41.

Welty Peachey, J., Lyras, A., Borland, J. and Cohen, A. (2013). Street soccer USA cup: Preliminary findings of a sport-for-homeless intervention. *ICHPER-SD Journal of Research*, *8*(1), 3–11.

Welty Peachey, J., Lyras, A., Cunningham, G. B., Cohen, A. and Bruening, J. (2015b). The influence of a sport-for-peace event on prejudice and change agent self-efficacy. *Journal of Sport Management*, *29*(3), 229–244.

Whitley, M. A., Forneris, T. and Barker, B. (2014). The reality of evaluating community-based sport and physical activity programs to enhance the development of underserved youth: Challenges and potential strategies. *Quest*, *66*(2), 218–232.

Whitley, M. A. and Johnson, A. (2015). Using a community-based participatory approach to research and programming in northern Uganda: Two researchers' confessional tales. *Qualitative Research in Sport, Exercise and Health*, *7*(5), 620–641.

Whitley, M. A., Massey, W. V. and Leonetti, N. (2016). Greatness (un)channelled: The role of sport in the life of an elite athlete who overcame multiple developmental risk factors. *Qualitative Research in Sport, Exercise, and Health*, *8*(5), 194–212, doi:10.1080/2159676X.2015.1121913.

Whitley, M. A., Massey, W. V., Blom, L., Camiré, M., Hayden, L. and Darnell, S. C. (December, 2017). Sport for Development in the United States: A Systematic Review and Comparative Analysis. Report submitted to the Laureus Sport for Good Foundation USA.

Whitley, M. A., Massey, W. V., Camiré, M., Blom, L. C., Chawansky, M., Forde, S., … Darnell, S. C. (2018). A systematic review of sport for youth development interventions across six global cities. *Sport Management Review*. https://doi.org/10.1016/j.smr.2018.06.013.

Wright, P. M. and Burton, S. (2008). Implementation and outcomes of a responsibility-based physical activity program integrated into an intact high school physical education class. *Journal of Teaching in Physical Education*, *27*(2), 138–154.

16

SDP and research ethics

Andrew Bloodworth, Mike McNamee and Steve Olivier

The process of undertaking worthwhile research in sport for development and peace (SDP) generates significant ethical challenges, only a few of which we can address here. We discuss first some general ethical considerations concerning what is taken to do good research in SDP, and in particular whether good research must *ipso facto* be ethically conceived and conducted. We argue that in successful SDP research, the benefits ought to be both to the host community and the broader academic community in terms of knowledge production. Next, we discuss the issue of consent since it is often taken as the key concept of ethical research and because the challenges here are considerable for SDP research in particular. We show that while the dominant norm is for first person written consent to participate in research on the basis of a voluntary and informed choice, competing models of consent have arisen that are worthy of consideration for SDP researchers. Finally, we situate these understandings in the contexts of transcultural research.

Ethical concerns for SDP research

Any new or developing field of investigation generates methodological and ethical questions. Where research directly affects peoples' lives, both in the long and short term, an array of ethical considerations present themselves in terms of the execution of research processes from conceptualization to data collection and reporting. This is undeniably the case for the emerging field of SDP. While researchers, largely social scientists, can of course draw on a rich tradition of applied ethics and methodology from fields as diverse as anthropology and ethnography, the SDP research community must itself consider the form that ethical challenges take.

Part of the challenge will concern the very *raison d'être* of the field and the aims it pursues. Not least among these is the nature of sport itself, and whether it is the often unchallenged 'good' that it is presumed to be, in the contexts under consideration. For what unites people may also force them apart: sport interventions can exacerbate or initiate conflict rather than generate intended peaceful outcomes. In this short offering we consider that those are primarily questions for practitioners and experts in the SDP field, such as we are not. Nevertheless, our concern is rather with some key procedural issues, and this means that ethical challenges should be seen alongside methodological ones. Though it may be surprising to the neophyte researcher, less callow souls who have the scars of fieldwork in challenging settings know only too well that methodological and ethical issues often present themselves in an uncomfortable combination (Collison *et al.* 2016). What makes this even more problematic is that ethical theory and practice is itself highly contested. And if that were not enough, greater complications confront researchers in SDP where cultural differences are part of the very foundation of the research itself. Where the norm for much social science in sport is monocultural, by contrast, the majority of research in SDP is likely to be transcultural in nature. This raises serious questions about respect and comprehension, patriarchy, models of decision-making, trust, oral versus written forms of agreement or permission, access to participants in projects, and so on. One cannot entertain these problems in a vacuum. These are not simply theoretical matters to be saved for rainy days. Rather, the existence of regulatory frameworks, in the shape of Review Boards or Research Ethics Committees, mean that it is essential that researchers consider these issues prior to engagement in the research.

Methodology and ethics

A very general question concerning SDP, both to ethics review boards, committees, and to researchers, is whether bad science is *ipso facto* unethical? On the face of it, we ought answer 'yes' to this question since to waste time and other resources on research that does not deliver products properly thought of as knowledge is itself ethically problematic. Of course, *ceteris paribus*, a research study that actually results in harm to its participants, whether physical or psychological is unconscionable. Many guidelines also explicitly hold that scientifically invalid research is unethical. The Council for International Organizations of Medical Sciences (CIOMS) states that 'researchers, sponsors, research ethics committees, and health authorities, must ensure that proposed studies are scientifically sound, build on an adequate prior knowledge base, and are likely to generate valuable information'(CIOMS 2016). The notion of valuable information, and its likely production being a requirement for ethically sound research, may need further explanation and deliberation in some contexts. It has been argued elsewhere (McNamee *et al.* 2006) that the situation is less straightforward. It may not be the case, for example, that undergraduate student projects have likely benefits beyond those that accrue to the researcher her or himself.

For present purposes, we shall assume that for the vast majority of SDP work, where humans are active participants in the research – as opposed to mere subjects – and where benefit to individuals and societies is at least implicit in the mission of the discipline, bad research practice should in itself be considered unethical. Moreover, in designing research projects we need to consider the potential effect of quasi-methodological issues such as raising expectations (e.g. so-called legacy effects), damage caused by dissemination or publication of invalid results, and friction in communities (Liamputtong 2008).

The challenge for SDP researchers is to convince ethics review boards that the work they do satisfies the following criteria:

1. Research involving human participants is ethically justifiable only if it holds out some realistic prospect of longer-term benefit to individuals, groups, or societies;
2. Participation may involve some risk or costs to the participants;
3. Such risks or costs (e.g. injury while participating in a sports programme) are ethically justifiable if they are non (reasonably) foreseeable, and proportionate to the importance or benefit of the research;
4. Benefits of research might include the production of new knowledge, and/or tangible individual or societal benefits arising from participation and the incorporation of legacy effects; and

5. Projects where the generation of new knowledge is not guaranteed or anticipated can be ethically justified when the risks and costs are proportionate to other benefits produced.[1]

While research design and ethical review in SDP research are perhaps not as closely aligned as is the case in good biomedical research, it is still important to construct a project according to sound principles, even when potential outcomes might not be wholly clear. For SDP research, primacy should, in our opinion, be given to benefits to participants, with the generation of new knowledge occupying a highly important but secondary role.

Sport as a force for good

Sport itself can be harmful, and some sports (e.g. boxing, mixed martial arts) are explicitly designed to be so. In others, injury is an obvious possibility (e.g. rugby, skiing), or the possibility of fatality is even seen as an inherent part of the nature of the activity (e.g. climbing, big-wave surfing, freediving) (Olivier 2006). Certainly the last few years have seen a plethora of research that challenges the prevalence and severity of head injuries in sports (Hecht 2002; McNamee and Partridge 2013; McNamee *et al.* 2015).

Some of these activities, such as football or rugby, are commonly incorporated into SDP interventions with the aim of inculcating positive values such as teamwork, reconciliation, improved health, gender awareness, bridging cultural divides, and various other social and educational initiatives. Moreover, specifically in a SDP context, it has been pointed out (Giulianotti and Darnell 2011), that sport interventions or programmes 'may be associated with disorderly, disruptive, or harmful incidents such as violence involving rival players or spectators. The potential for these unintended consequences is heightened when cultural, political, or historical tensions are at play. Attitudes are long-term, relatively stable evaluative predispositions to respond to given situations. Particularly when formed early they can be resistant to change, so it might be unrealistic or naïve to expect a short-term SDP intervention to effect meaningful change.

George Orwell's (1945) famously negative view of organized sport, expressed in an essay titled 'The Sporting Spirit', was an expression of his negative views on nationalism and its various manifestations. He wrote that 'Serious sport has nothing to do with fair play. It is bound up with hatred, jealousy, boastfulness, disregard of all rules and sadistic pleasure in witnessing violence. In other words, it is war minus the shooting' (ibid.). It could, of course, be plausibly argued that after his experiences in the Spanish Civil War, Orwell knew a great deal about military conflict but perhaps less about sport. Orwell's rather extreme view ignores any positive effects, such as those expressed by Nelson Mandela (2000) who famously remarked that

> Sport has the power to change the world. It has the power to inspire. It has the power to unite people in a way that little else does. It speaks to youth in a language they understand. Sport can create hope where once there was only despair. It is more powerful than government in breaking down racial barriers.
>
> *Mandela 2000*

The idea of harnessing 'Sport for good' has its antecedents in the promotion of 'Muscular Christianity', a movement that gained popularity in the Victorian era, espousing 'virtues' such as masculinity, productivity, self-improvement, character development, and so on (Mangan and Walvin 1991; MacAloon 2013). Many SDP programmes still embody some of these and other ends, often justifiably so. Nevertheless, it is well to recognize, in design, implementation and legacy phases, the potential that programmes have for ideological conformity, social control, imperialism, nationalism, militarism, and commercialism (Donnelly 2011).

We authors are sportspersons. We ascribe positive values and outcomes to sport participation. Yet we recognize too that contradictions abound in sport: health promotion clashes with intentional harming of opponents; sporting superiority may be seen as a surrogate for ideological superiority; exclusion in selection clashes with egalitarianism. Sport is valuable, but not a universal panacea (Carr 1998) wherein the United Nations Millennium Development Goals (United Nations 2016) will somehow magically be achieved. SDP practitioners must realize that good intentions are not sufficient. An understanding of regional history and culture, proper training of those involved, and serious consideration of consequences need to be factored into ethical consideration from the beginning.

We have seen then that the guiding ethical principle of SDP research is predicated on benefits to the participants; it is research for and with the relevant community, not *on* them. This demands that researchers critically explore the selection of sports, the mode of their engagement, and the structuring of suitably pedagogical forms of sporting contests. We turn now to the engagement of those individual participants and communities and we highlight in particular the notion of informed consent, which is widely regarded as the most important ethical concept for researchers to respect.

The vagaries of informed consent[2]

Informed consent ties together several ethical concepts and concerns which will be key to researchers and participants in SDP studies and practices. We cannot present here a detailed exploration of the many and varied functions of informed consent such as protecting the anonymity and confidentiality of participants and their data given the scope of this essay. Yet its history, emerging from the Nuremberg Code and Trials (Annas and Grodin 1992) which adjudicated on unethical research with captive populations such as prisoners of war and Jewish detainees must be acknowledged. The World Medical Association (2013) updates the subsequent Declaration of Helsinki that emerged from this the Code with the aim of protecting participants of research. Two fundamental conceptual pillars of the traditional model of consent are voluntariness and informedness. Voluntariness refers to the requirement that decisions be made by participants in a manner free from coercive pressure or improper influence. Informedness refers to the degree to which the participant has a reasonable grasp of the salient information in order to consent or withhold consent based on that information. While readily comprehensible in theory, the application of this principle can be challenging. What kind of, and how much, persuasion is allowed before one's behaviour counts as duress? and, how much, and what quality, of information is required for informedness? Navigating these challenges in the light of the complexities of the research, and the competence of the participant, is a tricky affair. This difficulty is amplified when one considers the variety of forms of political and cultural association that do not conform to Western liberal values, where respect for individual autonomy is prized, perhaps paramount, in research ethics thinking.

Autonomy is understood as self-governance. It is often transposed under the legal term of 'competence' but refers essentially to the capacity of acting in an informed and self-directed manner consistent with researchers' goals and aims (Christman 2015). The dominant norm for consent is that it takes a written form, where suitable surrogates are permissible for those without competence. Typically researchers consider whether the participant is lawfully and ethically capable of authorizing their participation. The list of incompetent persons and populations are children and youth (in certain circumstances) and those persons by context (perhaps age, limited cognitive ability, captive populations, etc.) that are deemed vulnerable in some way and thereby owed greater protections.

The grammatically incorrect verb 'consenting' is ubiquitous in clinical medical language and has creeped into research contexts. It is improper in the sense that it assumes one person (e.g. a researcher or clinician) may consent another, whereas the very point and purpose of informed consent is that the participant authorizes the researcher to engage with them, not the other way around. This ethically unacceptable practice is a form of disrespect to the participant, host community or group predicated on the assumption that the purposes of the research, and the researchers' motivations trump any respect for the consent process proper. It is often compounded by researchers' attitudes to consent as a tick-box exercise. We are all familiar with this process in terms of agreeing to (e.g.) conditions of use for an IT application or for a website before ticking the 'I have read and accept these terms' box (without ploughing through reams of particular specifications). This excessively casual use of consent processes leads to 'ritualization' (Manson and O'Neill 2007) and a diminishment of respect for the participant and the research. In contrast, consent properly understood, should be a process rather than a single event where the researcher merely secures the signature and date of agreement. This concept is especially applicable in longitudinal research. Where research participants engage in a one-off event of limited duration there is less pressure on the process conception, but in SDP work there is likely to be sustained community engagement. Ensuring that all partners or participants still concur with the stated aims and methods of data capture, sharing, storage, and analysis is a matter of principle. And that principle is the well-known Kantian one of mutual respect among persons.

Challenges to informed consent in SDP research

First person, written, informed consent is seen as the 'gold standard' and has been a cornerstone of biomedical research since the Nuremburg Code. We shall refer to it as the 'traditional model'. This model is widely perceived to offer the best protection for autonomy and has been imported from clinical to data-based research in most spheres.

Even in the traditional model, however, concerns remain as to whether participants sufficiently comprehend the foreseeable implications of engaging with research projects. Information may be given but not read, or read but not understood; care may or may not be taken to check comprehension of what is being authorized. But what ought we to think in cases where this formalized process – normally thought of as respectful – is itself ethically problematic?

Despite the traditional requirement for first person written consent as an ethical and legal standard there are parts of the globe where the dominant culture is an oral one. Alternatively, there may be contexts where, for example, participants do not write for some other reason. Here the demand for first person written consent may be considered distrustful; that the researcher is trying to force the participant(s) into a procedure they may not wish to engage with. Review boards or research ethics committee, may not accept a statement to the effect that a verbal assurance is satisfactory. Typically it will want to see evidence and typically that will be written. Mobile phones or tablets may be a reasonably inexpensive way to facilitate verbal consent in ways that do not undermine respect.

Blanket consent

Another form of consent that has arisen in biomedical research is called 'blanket consent' (Caulfield 2007). As opposed to precisely specifiable aims and methods, this technique is used when consent is sought and given for investigations, or data uses, where the research is open ended. So, for example, I may wish to take a sample from a participant in relation to the genetic basis of X condition, but want to store and re-analyse in terms of conditions Y and Z as they arise. And under blanket consent no further permissions are sought by the researcher. Safeguards are usually put in place to 'wash' the data of all identifying characteristics. This gives considerable power to the researcher(s) but approaches consent as a tick box event. It is highly efficacious in terms of accessing a larger population. And there may be some justification for hard to reach, underrepresented sample populations, and of course for cost reasons too. Though it makes life considerably easier for the researcher it is hard to imagine the ethical justification for this in SDP research where one works with the host population. Here viewing consent as a process, and being specific about the purposes of the engagement, are critical in terms of generating trust and therefore trustworthy data. Thus, while blanket consent may be justifiable where the risk is minimal, all forms of consent and governance should reflect societal values, and people express preferences over the types of research they wish to be a part of. Blanket consent expressly denies this opportunity and should not be adopted in SDP research.

Broad consent

An alternative to blanket consent, but similar in leaving open the specific aims and uses of the data is the notion of 'broad consent', which provides some greater control for the participant. Here the researcher would specify *some* general parameters for the work being undertaken. While this model is also used in many biobanks (Holland 2007; Benatar and Singer 2010), it can be argued that this is not a valid form of consent because of the failure to meet the requirements of the informedness of consent proper. Nevertheless, one can see how it has an attraction for SDP researchers where fluidity of interactions are commonplace. One may engage with a particular cultural group or groups with a stated aim only to realize – in the thick of things – that the stated goals are inoperable, undesirable, or misconceived. Broad consent gives one the opportunity to shift the goals to a reasonable degree as the cultural context itself shifts or becomes better known to the researcher(s).

This open textured consent seems to present a model of efficiency for the researcher. Moreover, there is precedent for it. But to what extent, as with blanket consent above, does biobanking research really provide a good analogy for SDP research? One crucial difference can be seen in what the host participants or community are agreeing to. In biobanking research there is a regulatory framework and lead body to oversee research (Benatar and Brock 2011). In broad consent it seems that the participant is accepting engagement and transferring authority to the regulatory body – in trust – so to speak. This assumes a fairly high degree of comprehension by the participant. SDP by contrast is a much more personalized engagement with a host community and because of the transcultural and multi-linguistic nature of the researcher: researched interaction, such an assumption is unlikely to be warranted. The quality of social interaction between both parties is critical to the success of the endeavour in terms of economic, social, or epistemic gains. Such a consideration would look more like 'blind trust' or a leap of faith the like of which will not be a product of some initial meeting but gained only over considerable time and tested in the quality of ongoing interaction.

Dynamic consent

A further model, again to be distinguished from traditional first order specified consent is called 'dynamic consent'. While not open ended like broad or blanket consent, it does recognize powerfully a 'consent as process' approach. The approach emanates from legal requirements for researchers to confirm consent as new uses for the data emerge. Although this may reflect a 'gold standard' of informed consent in biomedical research, it is not without problems on its own terms let alone in application to social scientific research that is largely conducted *in situ*, as is the case with SDP. By contrast the background assumption seems to be a clear separation between researcher and researched such that one has to 'go back' to assure ongoing consent. A phenomenon that might be labelled 'consent fatigue' is likely to arise due to repeated re-contacting of the consenting participants. Moreover, if consent becomes routinized, this may undermine the very quality that first assured its validity. Other questions include considering how distinct the new use has to be from those consented in order to need re-consent and who decides the boundaries for this. The thrust of dynamic consent is a good one: continue to respect the participant or host community. Nevertheless, one would hope that trust between the parties will be fostered in other ways. Moreover, where aims and methods significantly vary over time one would properly seek revalidation of the approval for the research granted by the relevant review board or ethics committee.

Particular challenges in transcultural research

We have charted the contested territory of informed consent and noted how recent innovations from biomedical science might grant greater latitude than traditional consent, but noted how each of them are left wanting in relation to SDP research where immersion in a host community is extended in time. Our earlier point about benefits being accorded primacy over knowledge generation endorses Liamputtong's (2008) view that in socially responsible projects, cultural norms should be taken into account so that the research benefits local people. Nevertheless, as we shall argue below, this neither entails accepting host norms uncritically nor embracing relativistic notions of research ethics.

Transcultural research – research across cultures – poses many methodological and ethical challenges. It may be the case, however, that a number of these challenges are encountered elsewhere in social science research. The aim of many forms of social science research is an understanding of the point of view of the participant(s). The extent to which we are able to understand the experiences of others, in light of our own personal history, has been the subject of interest in the philosophy of social sciences (e.g. Fay 1996). Some philosophers have suggested the requirement for some sort of shared sentiment, in order to properly conduct social scientific research. Winch for example states that 'a historian or sociologist of religion must himself have some religious feeling if he is to make sense of the religious movement he is studying and understand the considerations which govern the lives of its participants' (Winch 1958: 89). The central claim here is the need to understand the rules and norms that govern the lives of the research participants. Without such an understanding there is no anchor from which to begin to contemplate the lives of the research participants. This view generates complex epistemological debates, the subtleties of which we cannot address here. They do, however, raise central concerns for social scientific research, which relies upon an understanding of others, where one must grapple with the challenges of such an understanding. Indeed the aim of many researchers may not be to convey the experiences of research participants. Researchers must be aware of the tensions this gives rise to. For example, evaluating the sometimes sensitive or private experiences and lives of others, in terms that they may neither use nor share, raises ethically challenging questions, particularly when the purpose of research is to portray the viewpoint of its participants. A reasonable start point from a researcher's point of view is to note potential limitations in understanding, and indeed their own assumptions or preconceptions as they enter into the research field.

Widespread as it is, the commonly accepted concept of informed consent is still something of a Western construct, deeply rooted in the notion of individual autonomy. Attempting to employ the principle in practice without thought to local norms in non-Western setting may be to display a certain cultural insensitivity. This can prevent participation in an SDP project, or adversely affect the quality of that participation.

An obvious starting place is to consider language, literacy, and comprehension. Although the traditional model of consent requires written first person consent, much valuable research takes place in non-literate populations or societies where norms differ significantly from the Western world. If researchers cannot converse in a local language, it may be necessary to employ a translator or interpreter, or a bilingual research assistant. In either case, it should not be assumed that the translator's language proficiency is taken to imply that he or she can represent a given host community, or knows it sufficiently well to navigate the minefield of cultural sensitivities or taboos. Therefore, 'back translation' (returning to the participants to verify their intentions and meanings) and early pilot testing of the consent process is strongly advisable in order to detect errors of interpretation.

Ideally, the person involved in translation should be immersed in the research, having undertaken a thorough course of training and induction. Furthermore, significant emphasis should be placed on the building of trust, gaining the confidence of participants, and the provision of *relevant* information to the hosts prior to their acceptance of the researchers' intrusion into their life world. Obtaining consent in transcultural situations should never be treated as a mechanistic, or tick-box, process. SDP projects or research often involve marginalized or vulnerable groups, and such marginalization might be consistent with a lack of literacy. This does not mean that they are not competent to make their own decisions: serious inequities can be introduced if people are excluded from potentially beneficial participation simply because of rigid consent procedures.

Also, the value of written forms varies from society to society. In the West, appending a signature to documents is commonplace, whether signing for a parcel delivery or on an informed consent form. In other societies signatures are reserved for important life events; for example, in Egyptian society, this could be for marriage, property, or legal matters (McNamee *et al.* 2006).

In cultures with an oral tradition, a perceived overload of written information may predispose against participation, or affect validity of it. It can also lead to distrust, particularly where there is a surfeit of exculpatory language designed to diminish or prevent researchers' accountability. This might be particularly true in areas where a history of colonialism, giving rise to negative effects on participation rates or the meaningfulness of that participation. When signatures are required, anonymity, at least on the face of it, may be compromised, and promises of confidentiality too.

In the case of non-literate populations a written form on its own is inappropriate, as relying just on that clearly negates the comprehension element of informed consent. In such cases oral, perhaps recorded, consent can be obtained. The same procedures could be followed in societies that follow oral traditions, as in the case of some Aboriginal groups in Australia. Whether orally or in writing, it is recommended that consent be obtained in the language of the participants, and that translation includes back-referencing, that is, a form is translated from English to another language, and then independently back into English, to improve accuracy.

The need to be aware of cultural sensitivities extends to situations where societies have a tradition of communitarian decision-making, or where patriarchy is the norm. Culture is a constantly developing and dynamic process, stemming from adaptations to different environmental and social factors (McNamee *et al.* 2006). Individuals in different cultures, and perhaps groups in a collective sense, view the world through different lenses (Benatar 2002) and applying rigid Western guidelines could even do harm in a particular society by undermining the traditional notion of community and shared decision-making. This does not mean that those who engage with the research are not to be respected simply because of a patriarchal gatekeeper who grants access to the research domain. Rather, it means that they must be approached to secure such access *and* that when engaging with the participants one should make sure that their participation has not been the product of non-voluntariness or even coercion.

In the liberal West, a somewhat atomized notion of individualism, self-sufficiency, autonomy, technology, materialism, and the power of science to solve problems has been privileged for at least two centuries. This contrasts with some African, central American, and Asian cultures, where notions of community, group involvement, the consequences for the collective, deference to elders, and a reliance on religious beliefs predominate (McNamee *et al.* 2006). Viewing people as ends in themselves is an essentially deontological Western concept, which is at variance with a notion of the embeddedness of people in society, with an emphasis on relational definitions of personhood (Christakis 1992). As Honan *et al.* (2013) note, the communal orientation of some societies has resisted the march of liberal individualism.

These differences have practical implications in research ethics contexts. For example, researchers should consider whether they ought to consult elders or designated authorities before approaching individuals. While this might be thought to offend Western sensibilities of 'freedom', it is worth bearing in mind that individuals might value their so-called bondage. In Japan, many parts of Africa, and in some Maori groups, great store is set by decision-making by an extended family or collectively by a community, illustrating that an autonomy-driven model of ethics might not be universally applicable or effective (Hipshman 1999; Liamputtong 2008). Nevertheless, a note of caution should be sounded in cases where authorities are distrusted by the communities who engage with the researcher; it would be unjustifiable merely to obtain consent from such authorities.

Some cultures practice patriarchal decision-making, where the husband (or in his absence perhaps the elder son) makes important decisions on behalf of others (notably female or younger members) in the family or group. In these instances researchers might find women reluctant to make individual decisions. Outright rejection of such decision-making systems can rule out participation, with the attendant loss of benefits. Of course, researchers should also be aware that power differentials in a society, where, for example, women are seriously marginalized, may predispose *towards* participation. In such cases the potential participants might feel unable to resist the entreaties to participate from supposedly powerful authority figures (in the form of researchers from the outside). Researchers must be especially careful in these circumstances to ensure that the individual's participation is free from coercion.

Having advocated the need for researchers to display cultural sensitivity, we have not suggested the adoption of a relativistic stance. There is still an element of universality here. Research participants must be respected. This entails that our principles, processes, and practices are fundamental and ought to be applied transculturally but with sensitivity to the forms that respect can take. With the Western-inspired notion of research ethics being based on the principles of beneficence, justice, and non-maleficence, universality is an attractive proposition. On the other hand, a relativistic stance may seem more reasonable in the face of cultural diversity. Nevertheless, relativism must be rejected – not on the grounds that one must treat everyone the same, but rather because we reject the notion that every way of life is equally valuable. That is, after all, why notions such as international human rights exist. Such a permissive position, would allow that racist, or patriarchal, or any other discriminatory culture was equally valuable with ones characterized by such norms as equality and justice. As Bernard Williams (1972) once remarked, 'when in Rome do as the Romans do' may be helpful advice, but it is not a *moral* principle. We therefore embrace certain moral imperatives such as beneficence, justice, and respect for persons, with the latter taking into account the complex interplay between individual rights and the cultures/societies that they inhabit. Informed consent is a process based on the principle of respect for persons, but does not demand an inflexible process that disaffects individuals or groups. Researchers in SDP contexts may find themselves submitting proposals to ethical review boards that are not well-versed in matters where transcultural contexts affect the relationships between participants and those doing the research. In short, in biomedical and behavioural research in particular, well-documented abuses have led to legislative and regulatory responses and the widespread formation of Institutional Review Boards (IRBs) or Research Ethics Committees (McNamee *et al.* 2006), with funding dependent on clearance. The structure, function and expertise of these committees varies and we would contend that despite significant improvements, members' expertise in methods generally employed in SDP research lags behind those used in biomedical or conventional scientific projects. Along with the perceived bureaucratization of the ethics approval process, this means that SDP researchers may have some difficult hurdles to clear, or to quote Mosher (1988: 379) 'The institutionalisation of IRBs creates a growing bureaucracy that chills science by reducing creative nonconformity'.

Formal and informal regulation of SDP

Even though the bureaucracy of ethics scrutiny can weigh heavily, it exists to promote ethically justifiable research and in so doing to protect participants, to evaluate whether there is value in the knowledge being sought, and to provide some comment on the validity of the methods to be employed. Whether they seek an educative role or not, it may be necessary for researchers to inform Review Boards or Research Ethics Committees of the peculiarities, benefits, and methods of SDP research. Fleming (2013), using the example he calls 'Mcfee's friends' (effectively an argument from non-maleficence) makes a case for how proceeding with research without informed consent might be advanced successfully. He holds that when arguments are grounded in concerns for ecological validity, practical difficulties, forestalling alarm, the value of the research, coupled with acting in the best interests of participants, may generate a legitimate case for dispensing with formal informed consent processes.

Fleming's arguments are persuasive, but we contend that they are unlikely to be wholeheartedly embraced by RECs – most of which are risk-averse on a large scale – in the very near future. The 'deparochialisation of the research imagination' (Appadurai 2001 in Honan *et al.* 2013) will not occur overnight. Guidance to researchers submitting proposals would be to focus on the base principles of research ethics (see earlier). To this should be added considerations of cultural sensitivity and context, with an explicit exposition of reflexive consideration of how the base principles relate to a specific setting, e.g. how does one show respect in a different cultural context? (Honan *et al.* 2013). In ethics submissions, SDP researchers – like others – must be prepared to not just consider such issues, but explain *how* they have done so.

So how do SDP researchers make decisions on the ethics elements of their projects, in so doing assisting the passage of the proposal through ethical review? Most committees will adopt a casuistic approach,[3] incorporating and combining utilitarian (consequence-based) and deontological (rights-based) approaches, with considerations of virtue theory (how we should be rather than just how we should act – character rather than conduct) thrown into the mix. Researchers should thus anticipate questions regarding: the importance of anticipated results (utilitarian); the risk/benefit ratio (utilitarian); voluntary informed consent (deontological); whether considerations such as privacy, cultural factors; language; mode of decision-making; and so on, set limits on the conduct of the research. The considerations dealing with utility could be viewed as necessary but not sufficient conditions for research to proceed, while the unjustified absence of the deontological ones may invalidate the proposal. It is thus evident that we hold the position that while serious consideration needs to be given to matters of cultural sensitivity, primacy is accorded to principles based on duty, rights and obligations underpinning cost-benefit evaluations.

Concluding remarks

We have examined research ethics issues that arise in the process of conducting research in sport for peace and development in a manner consistent with the established social scientific literature on research ethics. In doing so we articulated an ethical rationale for such research, on the basis of potential benefits to participants, stemming from projects working with participants *in situ*. We dealt in some detail with the notion of informed consent and analysed the general notion, alongside many of the progeny the concept has spawned since the Nuremburg Trials. This facilitated some of the key challenges faced in transcultural research which is typically the form that SDP research takes. We attempted to account for ways in which to ensure (a) meaningful consent; (b) that potential participants are not excluded from the benefits of research; and (c) that such research is conducted respectfully in a way that eschews ethical relativism. We have nonetheless appealed to ethical principles as a way in which to resist and challenge ethically problematic norms in host cultures, rather than accept them uncritically.

Notes

1   Adapted from McNamee *et al.* (2006).
2   The following discussion of consent is an abbreviated and modified version of a part of Thompson and McNamee (2017).
3   Taken here to mean simply the making ethical decisions through the particularized application of theoretical rules, where each instance is taken with a high degrees of sensitivity to individual circumstances.

References

Annas, G. and Grodin, M. A. (eds) (1992). *The Nazi Doctors and the Nuremberg Code.* Oxford: Oxford University Press.

Benatar, S. R. (2002). Reflections and recommendations on research ethics in developing countries. *Social Science and Medicine, 54*(7), 1131–1141.

Benatar, S. and Singer, P. A. (2010). Responsibilities in international research: A new look revisited. *Journal of Medical Ethics, 36*(4), 194–197.

Benatar, S. and Brock, G. (2011), *Global Health and Global Health Ethics.* Cambridge: Cambridge University Press.

Caulfield, T. (2007). Biobanks and blanket consent: The proper place of the public good and public perception rationales. *King's Law Journal, 18*(2), 209–226.

Carr, D. (1998). What moral educational significance has physical education? A question in need of disambiguation. In McNamee, M. J. and Parry, S. J. (eds), *Ethics and Sport.* Abingdon: Routledge, pp. 119–133.

Christakis, N. A. (1992). Ethics are local: Engaging cross-cultural variation in the ethics for clinical research. *Social Science and Medicine, 35*(9), 1079–1091.

Collison, H., Giulianotti, R., Howe, P. D. and Darnell, S. (2016). The methodological dance: Critical reflections on conducting a cross-cultural comparative research project on 'sport for development and peace'. *Qualitative Research in Sport, Exercise and Health, 8*(5), 413–423.

Council for International Organizations of Medical Sciences (CIOMS). (2016). International Ethical Guidelines for Health-related Research Involving Humans. Available at: http://cioms.ch/shop/wp-content/uploads/2017/01/WEB-CIOMS-EthicalGuidelines.pdf (accessed 30 May 2017).

Christman, J. (2015). Autonomy in moral and political philosophy. In E. N. Zalta (ed.), *The Stanford Encyclopedia of Philosophy* (Spring 2015 edn). Available at: https://plato.stanford.edu/archives/spr2015/entries/autonomy-moral/ (accessed 30 May 2017).

Donnelly, P. (2011). From war without weapons to sport for development and peace: The Janus-face of sport. *SAIS Review of International Affairs*, *31*(1), 65–76.

Fay, B. (1996) *Contemporary Philosophy of Social Science*. Cambridge MA: Blackwell.

Fleming, S. (2013). Social research in sport (and beyond): Notes on exceptions to informed consent. *Research Ethics*, *9*(1), 32–43.

Giulianotti, R. (2011). Sport, peacemaking and conflict resolution: A contextual analysis and modelling of the sport, development and peace sector. *Ethnic and racial studies*, *34*(2), 207–228.

Hecht, A. N. (2002). Legal and ethical aspects of sports-related concussions: The Merril Hoge story. *Seton Hall Journal of Sports Law*, *12*(17), 43–44.

Hipshman, L. (1999). Attitudes towards informed consent, confidentiality, and substitute treatment decisions in southern African medical students: A case study from Zimbabwe. *Social Science and Medicine*, *49*(3), 313–328.

Holland S. (2007). *Public Health Ethics*. Cambridge: Polity.

Honan, E., Hamid, M. O., Alhamdan, B., Phommalangsy, P. and Lingard, B. (2013). Ethical issues in cross-cultural research. *International Journal of Research and Method in Education*, *36*(4), 386–399.

Liamputtong, P. (2008). Doing research in a cross-cultural context: Methodological and ethical challenges. In P. Liamputtong (ed.), *Doing Cross-Cultural Research: Ethical and Methodological Perspectives*. Dordrecht, The Netherlands: Springer, pp. 3–20.

MacAloon, J. J. (2013). *Muscular Christianity and the Colonial and Post-Colonial World*. Abingdon: Routledge.

Mangan, J. A. and Walvin, J. (eds) (1991). *Manliness and Morality: Middle-class Masculinity in Britain and America, 1800–1940*. Manchester: Manchester University Press.

Manson, N. C. and O'Neill, O. (2007). *Rethinking Informed Consent in Bioethics*. Cambridge: Cambridge University Press.

McNamee, M. J., Olivier, S. and Wainwright, P. (2006). *Research Ethics in Exercise, Health and Sports Sciences*. Abingdon: Routledge.

McNamee, M. J., Partridge, B. and Anderson, L. (2015). Concussion in sport: Conceptual and ethical issues. *Kinesiology Review*, 4(2), 190–202.

McNamee, M. J. and Partridge, B. (2013). Concussion in sports medicine ethics: Policy, epistemic and ethical problems. *The American Journal of Bioethics*, *13*(10), 15–17.

Mandela, N. (2000) Speech by Nelson Mandela at the Inaugural Laureus Lifetime Achievement Award, Monaco 2000. Available at: http://db.nelsonMandela.org/speeches/pub_view.asp?pg=itemandItemID= NMS1148 (accessed 30 May 2017).

Mosher, D. L. (1988). Balancing the rights of subjects, scientists, and society: 10 principles for human subject committees. *The Journal of Sex Research*, *24*: 378–385.

Olivier, S. (2006). Moral dilemmas of participation in dangerous leisure activities. *Leisure Studies*, *25*(1), 95–109.

Thompson, R. and McNamee, M. J. (2017). Consent, ethics and genetic biobanks: The case of the Athlome project, *Biomed Central Genetics*, *18*(S8), 830.

United Nations. (2016). Millennium Development Goals and Beyond. Available at: www.un.org/millenniumgoals/ (accessed 30 May 2017).

Winch, P. (1958). *The Idea of a Social Science and its Relation to Philosophy*. London: Routledge.

WMA, World Medical Association (2013). Declaration of Helsinki: Ethical principles for medical research involving human subjects. *Journal of the American Medical Association*, *227*(11), 925–926.

17

SDP and feminist theory

Mary G. McDonald

Discerning the relationship between feminist theory and development – including Sport for Development and Peace (SDP) initiatives – is a difficult task. Just as there is a diversity of development projects so too is there a diversity of feminist-inspired theoretical positions and projects. Several scholars have noted the diverse ways that feminism has been imagined within sport and Sport Studies scholarship. For example, Birrell (2000: 61) suggests that 'feminist theory is a dynamic, continually evolving complex of theories or theoretical trajectories that take as their point of departure the analysis of gender as a category of experience in society'. Rather than offering a singular definition, this fluidity means that it may be more 'useful to conceive of feminist theories in the plural, as a series of theoretical approaches marked by rapid development and comprised of an intermix of voices and responses to earlier theoretical traditions' (Birrell 2000: 61).

Recognition of the diversity of theoretical voices within feminism has helped to disrupt uncritical appeals, typically generated in the global North, to a unified 'global sisterhood'. That is, pleas for sisterhood presume commonalities in experiences and gender oppression regardless of culture and nation. This position ignores local histories, politics, and distinctive feminist actions to instead falsely universalize a vision of women as always and everywhere (equally) constrained within patriarchal gender relations (Mohanty 2003). Instead critical feminist analyses suggest that such a framing ignores the ways in which men and women are differently positioned within local communities across the globe as well as the ways in which other social forces such as economic inequality, imperialism, nationalism, and racism continue to shape opportunities in and out of local sport settings.

Equally problematic, according to critics, are those SDP initiatives grounded in the belief in sports' universal emancipatory potential. Such an optimistic perspective seems to be enshrined in the United Nation's sponsored Sustainable Development Goals, the initiative that builds upon the Millennium Development Goals (MDG). Both projects are designed to reduce poverty and inequality. The Declaration of the 2030 Agenda for Sustainable Development lauds the apparently worldwide applicability of sport within development contexts regardless of local histories observing:

> Sport is also an important enabler of sustainable development. We recognize the growing
> contribution of sport to the realization of development and peace in its promotion of

tolerance and respect and the contributions it makes to the empowerment of women and of young people, individuals and communities as well as to health, education and social inclusion objectives.

United Nations 2015: 37

Such grand claims about universal empowerment – a type of 'global sport sisterhood' – ignore the vastly different ways in which sport is organized, experienced, represented, and understood across the globe. Against critical feminist sensibilities, which embrace multiplicity, grand claims about a worldwide sport sisterhood also ignore the ways in which contextually specific inequitable power relations continue to impact local communities differently. Rather than embrace romantic characterizations of sport's transcendent qualities, it is far more useful to consider the words of Martha Saavedra (2009: 124) who instead argues that gender-related sport development projects encompass both 'dilemmas and opportunities'.

This later view recognizes that – much as with feminism, and in the midst of highly visible hegemonic forms – sport is replete with multiple meanings and different aims. And if we also take Birrell's comments to heart and start with gender as a point of departure, it is clear that particular articulations of sport offer the potential for disrupting local gender norms, many of which too frequently ideologically suggest that sporting participation is the domain of men.

Despite notable challenges and competing formations, in many places across the globe, many sports are still hegemonically aligned with norms of masculinity – as sites where such qualities as aggressiveness, assertiveness, and forcefulness are culturally celebrated. These sensibilities are not simple preferences but are culturally created and performed constructions that exist within spatially specific unequal relations of power. For example, Shehu (2010) argues that in several African countries the very presence of girls and women in sport is seen as an intrusion into men's 'natural' territory and as a threat to the existing gender order. As such women and girls who transgress these masculinist norms and spaces too frequently 'become targets of toxic myths, stigmas and harassment in sport spaces to perpetuate the domination of those spaces by heterosexual, masculine males' (Shehu 2010: X).

Saavedra (2009) further suggests that objections to women's general involvement in sport (which varies according to the type of sport and location) often rest on the ways in which 'gender norms … are challenged by external forces, which can range from NGOs to the state and to international cultural flows' (Saavedra 2009: 124). Paradoxically, the ability of young girls and women to challenge local gender relations through sport speaks to the powerful role played by dominant sporting forms historically in seeking to naturalize the relationship between sport, masculinity, and maleness. And despite the aforementioned 'variation across settings' there still 'remains a strong link between sport, body practices, gender and sexuality' (Saavedra 2009: 124).

In this chapter, I briefly outline some related dilemmas and opportunities in regard to local and global gender relations documented within feminist SDP scholarship. Organizationally I accomplish this goal by first building upon the work of feminist development and SDP scholars to highlight the complicated state of feminist and women-center approaches within post-World War II development agendas. As will be demonstrated more fully via this historical tracing, competing visions of how best to conceive of gender – and associated inequalities – have long fueled debates about the best ways to enact international development aims. Postcolonial feminist perspectives are particularly salient to this discussion in linking development aims to histories of colonial occupation.

This perspective is additionally important as it challenges the centrality of Western knowledge production including the neocolonial gaze of dominant strands of Western liberal feminist thought. Too frequently this liberal gaze ignores context and diversity to instead create a highly problematic vision of a normalized 'Third World woman' in need of rescuing (Mohanty 2003). There are a small number of scholars who analyze SDP agendas using a postcolonial feminist lens, and Lyndsay Hayhurst's work is particularly exemplary in applying concepts developed within postcolonial feminist theorizing to more fully illuminate and critique SDP endeavors (Hayhurst 2011; 2013; 2014; Hayhurst *et al.* 2014; Hayhurst *et al.* 2015; Hayhurst *et al.* 2016) With Simon Darnell, Hayhurst suggests the postcolonial feminist perspectives and methods offer participants, practitioners, and scholars important insights. These insights are useful for the analysis of material relations, and the decolonization of representations and knowledge while helping to facilitate ethical encounters (Darnell and Hayhurst 2014).

Feminist postcolonial perspectives challenge the masculinist bent of much postcolonial musing on power while seeking to expose and disrupt the unequal power relationships that exist between and within the global North and South. This later focus is particularly relevant given that the majority of sport development projects studied are those initiated and financially supported by Northern states, donors, corporations, and NGOs – and are disproportionately located in the global South. An additional emerging trend is the increased development attention given to marginalized communities in the North, particularly via the 'targeting of Indigenous young women' (Hayhurst *et al.* 2016). Postcolonial feminism also provides useful insights to help analyse this state of affairs.

After providing this brief historical tracing, I then offer a highly selective reading of English-language feminist scholarship, which analyzes feminism and women–centered initiatives in contemporary SDP settings. As will become more apparent in what follows, this scholarship reveals a highly contested terrain as not everyone equally embraces SDP initiatives. Indeed many feminists, especially those using postcolonial feminist theories as well as local community members, may acknowledge possibilities – but still remain 'highly critical of "development," itself, both as a concept and as a set of practices' and instead locate development 'within analyses of imperialism and neoliberalism' (Wilson 2013: 84).

Far from an exhaustive account, I have chosen to highlight three examples of research that critically examines notions of 'empowerment' differently mobilized in SDP settings, cases that clearly show limitations of the Northern/Western development representations and programming agendas. These SDP accounts – scholarly narratives about an Ugandan martial arts program, NGO Right to Play's HIV/AIDS education strategies, and Nike's Girl Effect – are situated knowledges, mainly written by scholars in the global North. As such these examples do not say all that can be said regarding postcolonial feminism contributions, nor is postcolonial feminism the only suitable lens that may be used to interrogate development practices. Rather this dialogue seeks to promote the decolonization of SDP knowledge and practices, and encourages further analyses, critique, and revision.

The chapter concludes by engaging scholarship that further discusses an important tenet of feminisms, the need for self and community reflections within development agendas as well as the continuing need for critical feminist research, engagements, and activism. Such projects and scholarship are important in revealing and resisting the multiple ways in which power is embodied and challenged in development projects. This sensibility also points toward the need for additional research agendas as well as praxis in working across differences to challenge inequalities.

Contesting gender relations and feminisms within development

Contemporary SDP curriculums and representations take place with in a variety of contexts including a history of broader development ventures in regard to women and gender. These efforts are interventions into what Parpart and Marchand (2001) term the 'development enterprise'. This enterprise is largely rooted in the liberal approach to development that emerged after World War II, a time period when Western economists argued that development could be achieved across the globe via a simple adoption of Western political and economic systems. At the time, even those Marxist critical of international capital and development frequently reified problematic Western assumptions in not questioning development framing as a common-sense linear journey on the path to progress. That is, post-War development frameworks typically assumed that people or nations moved from underdeveloped (read connected with traditional institutions and values) to full development as embodied by 'modern/rational/industrialized societies based on the Northern model' (Parpart and Marchand 2001: 522; also see McDonald 2015).

Still, Jacqui Alexander and Chandra Mohanty (1997: XV) argue that one effect of heightened globalization over the last several decades is a 'new visibility of women's issues on the world stage' including 'the large number of international conferences on the topics like violence against women, women's health, reproductive politics and "population control"'. Furthermore, globalization has helped to proliferate several distinctive development approaches (Momsen 2010) and while some attention focuses on men and masculinity, most of focus within these paradigms is on women and girls.

Among these tactics is the Women in Development (WID) approach, which gained visibility via the 1975 UN International Year for Women and International Women's Decade (1976–1985). A key initial aim of 'WID was to integrate women into economic development by focusing on income generation projects for women' (Momsen 2010: 12). While challenging male bias in seeking to eradicate poverty by emphasizing 'the unique problems facing women especially in the South' WID was additionally characterized by debate and disagreement. The WID framework was criticized by self-described 'Third World' feminists for promoting access as a panacea while treating 'women as a homogenized group' and for failing to fully integrate challenges to long-standing inequalities related to class, race, gender, and dependency (Parpart and Marchand 2001: 525; Momsen 2010: 13). For instance, 'while early WID interventions encouraged a shift of emphasis from reproductive to productive activities' critics point out how this shift 'failed to challenge the racialised population control policies, which drew on the pathologisation of the sexuality of women in the global South' (Shain 2013: 6).

The Women and Development agenda offered more radical approaches, for example, suggesting women-only solutions. However, this framing also failed to account for differences among women across the globe (Saavedra 2009). The Gender and Development (GAD) paradigm emerged in an era of structural readjustment programs to critically assess inequalities as well as resistance performed by those marginalized by gender, race, class, and national identities. A highly diverse paradigm, since the 1980s this alternative framework has also included post-colonial and transnational perspectives to recognize that 'the construction of gender relations interacts with all forms of imperialism to shape the dominant ideologies of development' (Shain 2013: 7). While critics argue that the radical edge of this approach is lost as ideas are translated into policy, some strands of GAD also provide for the interrogation of 'power and difference with close attention to the power of language and discourse that are refracted through global disparities' (Saavedra 2009: 133).

This very brief review makes clear that development and poverty eradication have a complicated history with competing gender-related paradigms operating within many national, NGO, corporate, and United Nations initiatives. Advocacy for sport and physical activity has also appeared within these and related enterprises. For example, 280 delegates from 82 countries representing governmental and non-governmental organizations helped to craft the Brighton Declaration on

Women and Sports in 1994 (Brady 1998). The manifesto offered guiding principles 'to increase the involvement of women in sports at all levels, and in all functions and roles' (Brady 1998: 81). The UN's Platform for Action form the Fourth World Conference on Women: Action for Equality, Development and Peace held in 1995 in Beijing included references to the importance of physical activity and sports for women and girls (Brady 1998: 81).

The advent of the United Nations' Millennium Development Goals (MDG) in 2000 marked a concerted attempt to use sport as a tool of development while also addressing gender-specific aims. The broader MDG project was designed to 'eradicate poverty, hunger, and disease as well as to promote gender equality, health, education and environmental sustainability on a global scale' (Hancock *et al.* 2013). Both the MDG and the related Sport Millennium Development Goals suggest that sport plays an important role in realizing development aims. For example, Sport Millennial Goal 3 specifically suggests that sport can 'promote gender equality and empower women' by building 'confidence' and providing 'integration' which can 'help overcome prejudice that often contributes to social vulnerability of women and girls in a given society'. Very similar optimistic views about sport have been integrated into the project that replaced the MDG; the previously mentioned Sustainable Development Goals.

There are a variety of State actors including, but not limited to the UK, Australia, and Sweden; non-State actors including NGOs and sporting organizations such as Women Win, Right to Play and the International Olympic Committee (IOC); and transnational corporations such as Nike (to mention but a few) who use sport as a tool for development. The visibility of these actors clearly reveals that the UN's encouragement of sports-related proposals has helped facilitate a proliferation of SDP agendas, although it is still difficult to ascertain the exact number of programs currently in operation globally. Hancock *et al.* (2013) offered one estimate based upon their 2010 review of Internet sites suggesting the existence of over 1,000 SDP sites with '440 programmes, or 42.5 per cent of all programmes, specifically targeting girls and women' (Hancock *et al.* 2013).

In addition to offering these estimates, the authors analyzed and then categorized 'gender and development agendas (SGD)' (Hayhurst 2014) as articulated through programming content foci as stated on organizations' websites. Most prevalent was content that conceived of sport as a tool for social inclusion, a goal consistent with UN aims and designed to ensure that girls and women have access to sport. This position is 'particularly important in communities with strict cultural or religious practices'. As such, SGD 'social inclusion programmes were prevalent in Asian, African and eastern European counties' (Hancock *et al.* 2013). An additional strategy was the use of sport as a 'hook' to attract participants for 'educational programming (e.g. HIV/AIDS, reproductive practices, mental health, self-efficacy, skill development)' (Hancock *et al.* 2013). This strategy, again consistent with UN aims, is found in places across the globe where girls and women have some measure of access to sporting opportunities. On the whole, these

> projects promise positive change through sport trainings and varied life skills curricula that endeavour to educate girls on topics such as reproductive health, hygiene, effective communication and financial literacy, but the evidence and research on these types of programmes is limited at best.
>
> *Chawansky and Hayhurst 2015: 878*

These programs no doubt provide unique even pleasurable experiences for participants. However, in further thinking about the efficacy of these programs, it is useful to return to the competing paradigms of development especially the WID and GAD frameworks. In privileging access and the removal of barriers as important strategies of getting women and girls 'into the game,' many of the programs discussed by Hancock *et al.* (2013) are strategically aligned with the sensibilities and limitations of Western liberal feminist approaches articulated through WID agendas.

In contrast to liberal WID approaches the GAD framework, especially its postcolonial iterations, offers criticism of structural, imperialistic, and capitalist-inspired inequalities. This approach interrogates power imbalances while inspiring alternative methods and tactics in the movement toward broader social change. Samie and colleagues conceptualize the synergies between critically oriented SDP efforts and GAD as they work to

> (1) question and challenge, for instance, an existing gender order and various forms of unequal hierarchies that sustain poverty, oppression and inequity against both males and females (i.e. the GAD approach) and (2) mobilize sport for the purposes of nurturing broader forms of economic, social, cultural and political change in typically disadvantaged communities and/or post-conflict regions around the world (i.e. the SDP approach).
>
> *Samie et al. 2015: 924*

While there is overlap between WID and GAD approaches in practice, distinctions in philosophy are quite evident. Sports programs aligned with WID sentiments optimistically promise to 'empower' women and girls in advancing access, education, 'health, gender equity and social integration' through sport participation (Hancock *et al.* 2013). This WID perspective frequently encompasses neoliberal market-driven approaches to development. GAD frameworks critique broader relations of power including normative Western feminist ideals, and structural inequalities.

Postcolonial feminist perspectives additionally explore the representational politics whereby the North defines itself through highly problematic images of the South as other. 'For instance, females from the GS [global South] have been particularly subject to crude processes of categorization that confines "Them" as a "homogeneous", "powerless" group victimized by their own men, and their cultural and socio-economic systems and political basis' (Samie *et al.* 2015: 926). This orientalist framing in turn problematically positions Western/Northern women as the normative referent as 'educated, as modern, as having control over their own bodies and sexualities and the freedom to make their own decisions' (Mohanty 2004: 22). The next section highlights three cases of critical feminist scholarship, which further contextualize and ethically explicates SGD paradigms and the politics of representation, particularly in relationship to competing notions of empowerment.

Challenging discourses of sport and empowerment through feminist research

A reoccurring focus within feminist scholarship on SGD is the interrogation of notions of 'empowerment' (Chawansky 2011; Hayhurst 2014; Samie *et al.* 2015). This is understandable given the widespread popular promotion of the apparent need to empower women in both development and sport development spaces. The recently implemented Sustainable Development Goals (SDG) at times use language also found in the Millennium Development Goals including SDG Goal 5, which is to 'achieve gender equity and empower all women and girls'. As stated on the UN's website, the related Sport and Sustainable Development Goals suggest that sport 'can contribute to the elimination of discrimination against women and girls by empowering individuals, particularly women, and equipping them with knowledge and skills needed to progress in society'.

It is important to note that the dominant meanings of 'empowerment' have transformed over time within development agendas. At the time of the Fourth World Conference on Women, empowerment was most commonly understood as encompassing the 'transformation of gender relations ... and other power relations ... between individuals and social groups' (Drydyk 2013: 250). More recently within market-driven development agendas the term has come to signify one's ability to make informed choices and realize one's greatest potential (Drydyk 2013). As Drydyk suggests this later notion of 'empowerment as choice-expansion is neither relational nor transformative; it has no connotations referring to gender relations or other power relations; nor does it imply any transformation of social relations' (Drydyk 2014: 250).

The competing definitions between the activist-oriented understanding about the need to transform unequal power relations versus neoliberal and individualistic notions about the need to transform women is also readily apparent in feminist-inspired SGD literature. For example, Hayhurst and colleagues (2014) examine a martial arts self-defense program facilitated by a NGO in rural Uganda. In doing so they reveal the limits of uncritical deployments of empowerment. This particular Ugandan program promised to teach female participants leadership skills and enhance their self-defense capabilities in light of the community's considerable problems with domestic and gender-based violence. Seeming these young women were the beneficiaries of leadership skills and martial arts practices as 'lessons of empowerment' (Hayhurst *et al.* 2014: 158).

Yet the authors argue that these lessons actually serve as governing strategies where the young

> women were positioned as having gendered identities that needed to be reframed, augmented or changed. Thus, the onus seemed to be on these young women to change *their* behaviours, actions and attitudes in order to achieve gender equality, while seeming to ignore the need to enlist men, boys and adult women in the community in accomplishing this deed.
>
> *Hayhurst et al. 2014: 161*

That is, the aim of the martial arts venture was to instill the discipline and confidence necessary for individual women to overcome gender norms on the pathway toward defending themselves. While some young women embraced this vision, all did not necessarily incorporate these messages into their lives in the same way. Nor did community members including boys and young men all support the young women's foray into the martial arts.

Furthermore, the program's exclusive emphasis on girls and women reinforced heteronormative framings – a common occurrence in SDP programming and scholarship (see Carney and Chawansky 2016) – and sidestepped important issues related to gender and sexual-based violence against gays in Uganda. Given these framings and absences, the program serves to reinforce a problematic binary of men as perpetrators and women as victims in regard to gender and sexual-based violence. What is additionally relevant to this discussion is that the program's emphasis on individualized behavioral transformation without wider community commitments to social change, 'potentially do little to actively alter the patriarchal ideologies, social institutions, social relations, and structures that promote and encourage gender-based and sexual violence against (young) women and girls in the first place' (Hayhurst 2011; Hayhurst *et al.* 2014: 159).

The Ugandan case is not unique. Critical analysis of the Right to Play, a large NGO which uses sport 'as a hook' to deliver programming including HIV education and prevention materials reveals a similar logic. In many spaces across the globe women are worse off than men in terms of 'prevalence, new infection rates, and knowledge' about HIV/AIDS (Forde and Frisby 2015: 884). Right to Play educational text, *Live Safe Play Safe* acknowledges these conditions while also recognizing that sexual violence puts girls at greater risk of acquiring HIV/AIDS.

Still, girls and young women are framed within the *Live Safe Play Safe* manual as vulnerable, yet paradoxically, with the ability to become empowered. The manual teaches life skills as a strategy to educate and prevent HIV/AIDS. According to Forde and Frisby (2015: 882) the manual's texts further assumes heteronormativity and constructs 'girls as deficient because of their minds and bodies'. This particular framing also makes boys and men invisible while positioning girls 'as being responsible for preventing HIV/AIDS by becoming more self-interested and assertive' (Forde and Frisby 2015: 882). This analysis and that of the Ugandan martial arts program both reveal the importance of not simply changing girls and women, but instead recognizing the relational ways through which power operates.

Several scholars have excavated the cultural, social, political, and economic contexts which have helped to elevate particular notions of empowerment. The increasing presence of NGOs and transnational corporations in the SGD landscape too frequently means that even the 'most powerful feminist-oriented NGOs end up compromising "radical politics" by prioritizing interventions that serve the interests of global capital' (Hayhurst 2014: 301). Nowhere is this phenomenon more evident than in discussions about the 'the Girl Effect'. In 2005 the Nike Foundation partnered with the NoVo Foundation to initiate a social responsible crusade 'the global Girl Effect "movement"' that 'consists of hundreds of projects and campaigns targeting adolescent girls across the poorest countries in the areas of education, sport and health' (Shain 2013: 10). The Girl Effect website is a testimony to Nike's considerable branding power, using emotional appeals to urge potential donors to see girls as just as capable as, or more capable than, boys in the global South.

This campaign is one mainstream response to the UN's goals of promoting gender equity and eliminating poverty by asserting 'the unique potential of 600 million adolescent girls to end poverty for themselves and the world' (The Girl Effect website as cited in Hayhurst 2014: 297). The Girl Effect is based upon the claim promoted by agencies such as the World Bank 'that when given the opportunity, women and girls are more effective at lifting themselves and their families out of poverty, thereby having a multiplier effect within their villages, cities, and nations' (Shain 2013: 3). This strategy encourages citizens and transnational organizations in the North to see the potential of girls in the South and to invest in that potential.

At first glance this campaign appears to offer a compelling intervention; however, this framework's logic is limited. It assumes that by assisting girls achieve an education – and thus presumably delaying marriage and childbirth, girls can overthrow patriarchal barriers – often represented as local 'backward customs' – thus fueling economic growth for local communities (Shain 2013). Koffman and Gill (2013) highlight the cultural assumptions embedded in such notions of empowerment as ignoring 'immense variation in education, marriage and fertility patterns across different developing countries'. Related promotional web content further disseminate a racialized and overly simplistic image of 'life in the Global South as plagued by "child marriage", teenage motherhood and HIV/AIDS' (Koffman and Gill 2013). Poverty is not seen as a structural issue in this campaign, but rather 'emphasis is placed on women's domestic role and their high fertility … the possibility that some women may value early motherhood, or indeed a large family, remains unthinkable' (Koffman and Gill 2013).

These Girl Effect narratives additionally reproduce the standardized referent of the Northern woman/girl as educated, liberated, and in control of her reproductive capabilities – even though vast inequalities also exist within the North. The narratives also add a new twist on the homogenized version of the 'Third World' woman – now younger and contradictorily represented. Girl Effect narratives represent girls in the South 'as capable and hardworking but culturally constrained; as agentic but still dependent and in need of assistance from donors and investors' (Shain 2013: 4). Here the solution to gender inequality and poverty relies upon an uncritical embrace of neoliberal capitalist goals of efficacy and personal perseverance all under the guise of 'smart economics' (Shain 2013). In this way, the Girl Effect campaigns serve as a type of neoliberal feminism devoid of radical critique and problematically committed to 'creating self-reliant girls as disseminators of social change' (Hayhurst 2014: 309).

Conclusion: final thoughts, future research, and action

One axiom of critical feminist-inspired development strategies is to offer alternative ways of thinking and being beyond dominant normative values and practices. As established in the opening words of this chapter, feminist theory represents a process of engagement with competing traditions and one such engagement is articulated via the aforementioned GAD agendas. In particular, postcolonial feminist understandings of GAD continue to disrupt and replace standard models that reaffirmed narrow notions of feminism emanating from the North/West.

While purporting to usher in change, Eurocentric development frameworks reinforce dominant interests by eliding 'the diversity of women's agency in favor of a universalized Western model of women's liberation that celebrates individuality and modernity' (Grewal and Kaplan 2002). The possibility that 'modernization' and 'progress' may be both unobtainable and/or undesirable goals within international contexts historically has been rarely interrogated within normative development perspectives (Parpart and Marchand 2001: 518). Too frequently strands of Western feminist thought suggests the enhancement of women's rights demands a particular form of democratization and economic liberalization throughout the world. These powerful ideological beliefs reflect well-financed neoliberal economic interests and problematically reify Western notions of freedom and governance (Parpart and Marchand 2001).

Advocates for critical and feminist agendas challenge these models ethically recognizing the centrality of the voices, life experiences, competing worldviews, and political contexts of marginalized groups. This recognition is important given the ways in which power imbalances frequently operate to silence the multiple standpoints of those girls and women directly targeted for Western development assistance. As Samie and colleagues' interviews with participants in a global sports mentoring project reveal, attempts at 'development should be "by the people", as opposed to being designed for them' (Samie 2015: 933). The women interviewed further offered competing notions of empowerment, and many saw 'empowerment as not only a broad process that 'encompasses progress in social and political participation, cultural expression, and access to equitable legal rights' (Swai 2010: 170) but also a transformation in gender relations' (Samie *et al.* 2015: 935).

The sensibility articulated in these interviews is aligned with those suggesting that current and future development practices are best served by addressing 'local needs in a bottom-up approach of a programme that is community-driven as opposed to being merely community-based' (Burnett 2009: 1195). Hayhurst and colleagues (2015) also point out the need for centering local ways of knowing to 'decolonize' dominant knowledge formations within SGD research and practices. That is, 'research that is truly decolonized recognizes and works within the understanding that non-Western knowledge forms are silenced from and/or marginalized within most research paradigms and development work' (Hayhurst *et al.* 2015: 4). This standpoint not only suggests the need for more research from global South scholars including those located in understudied regions, but also that scholars and practitioners in the global North reflectively recognize the political salience of such knowledge formations. Future critical and feminist scholarship additionally must recognize the 'need to identify and better understand how SDP is being taken up in new and/or previously overlooked contexts' including within South to South interactions as well as within marginalized Northern communities (Hayhurst *et al.* 2016: 9).

Yet questions and problems still remain including those related to how best to use the knowledge gleaned through researcher, practitioner, and activist discussions as praxis. Hayhurst and colleagues (2015) advocate connecting SDP initiatives to local social movements such as connecting the Idol No More social movement with 'targeted' Indigenous communities within Canada. Still others recognize one downside to such connections fearing that this strategy might elide local concerns (Lahey 2016). Strategies for moving forward must further recognize the tensions between the ability of donors to provide resources through policy and practices, and working against the larger social and economic structures including gendered and racialized colonial legacies that produce those inequalities in the first place. This chapter has offered postcolonial feminist sensibilities as a means to think through these and additional dilemmas and opportunities.

References

Alexander, J. and Mohanty, C. (1997). Introduction: Genealogies, legacies, movements. In J. Alexander and C. Mohanty (eds), *Feminist Genealogies, Colonial Legacies, Democratic Futures*. New York: Routledge.

Birrell, S. (2000). Feminist theories for sport. In J. Coakley and E. Dunning (eds). *Handbook of Sports Studies,* New York: SAGE.

Brady, M. (1998). Laying the foundation for girls' healthy futures: Can sports play a role? *Studies in Family Planning, 29*(1), 79–82.

Burnett, C. (2009). Engaging sport-for-development for social impact in the South African Context. *Sport in Society, 12*(9), 1192–1205.

Carney, A. and Chawansky, M. (2016). Taking sex off the sidelines: Challenging heteronormativity within sport in development. *International Review for the Sociology of Sport, 51*(3), 284–298.

Chawansky, M. (2011). New social movements, old gender games? Locating girls in the sport for development and peace movement. In A. C. Snyder and S. P. Stobbe (eds), *Critical Aspects of Gender in Conflict Resolution, Peacebuilding, and Social Movements*. Bingley, UK: Emerald Group.

Chawansky, M. and Hayhurst, L. (2015). Girls, international development and the politics of sport: introduction. *Sport in Society: Cultures, Commerce, Media, Politics, 18*(8), 877–881.

Darnell, S. C. and Hayhurst, L. M. C. (2014). Decolonizing the politics and practice of sport-for-development: Critical insights from post-colonial feminist theory and methods. In N. Schulenkorf and D. Adair (eds), *Global Sport-for-Development: Critical Perspectives*. New York: Palgrave McMillan.

Drydyk, J. (2013). Empowerment, agency, and power. *Journal of Global Ethics, 9*(3), 249–262.

Forde, S. D. and Frisby, W. (2015). Just be empowered: How girls are represented in a sport for development and peace HIV/AIDS prevention manual. *Sport in Society, 18*(8), 882–894.

Grewal, I. and Kaplan, C. (2002). Transnational feminist practices and the question of post modernity. In I. Grewal and C. Kaplan (eds), *Scattered Hegemonies: Post Modernity and Transnational Feminist Practices*. Minneapolis: University of Minnesota.

Hancock, M., Lyras, A. and Ha, J. P. (2013). Sport for development programmes for girls and women: A global assessment. *Journal of Sport for Development, 1*(1), 15–24.

Hayhurst, L. M. C. (2011) Corporatising sport, gender and development: Postcolonial feminisms, transnational private governance and global corporate social engagement. *The Third World Quarterly, 32*(3), 531–549.

Hayhurst, L. M. C. (2013) Girls as the 'new' agents of social change? Exploring the 'Girl Effect' through sport, gender and development programs in Uganda. *Sociological Research Online, 18*(2), 8.

Hayhurst, L. M. C. (2014). The girl effect' and martial arts: Social entrepreneurship and sport, gender and development in Uganda. *Gender, Place, and Culture, 21*(3), 297–315.

Hayhurst, L. M. C., Giles, A. R., Radford, W. and the Aboriginal Friendship Centre Society. (2015). 'I Want to come here to prove them wrong': Using a post-colonial feminist participatory action research (PFPAR) approach to studying sport, gender and development programmes for urban indigenous young women. *Sport in Society*. Available at: http://dx.doi.org/10.1080/17430437.2014.997585.

Hayhurst, L. M. C., Kaye, T. and Chawansky, M. (eds) (2016). *Beyond Sport for Development and Peace: Transnational Perspectives on Theory*. London: Routledge.

Hayhurst, L. M. C., MacNeill, M., Kidd, B. and Knoppers, A. (2014). Gender relations, gender-based violence and sport for development and peace: Questions, cautions and concerns emerging from Uganda. *Women's Studies International Forum, 47*(1), 157–167.

Koffman, O. and Gill, R. (2011). The revolution will be led by a 1-year-old girl: Girl power and global biopolitics. *Feminist Review, 105*(1), 83–102.

Lahey, W. (2016). Reflection on the benefits and challenges of girl-focuses indigenous SDP programs in Australia and Canada: A practitioner's critique of Hayhurst, Giles and Wright (2015) using experiences from two case studies in the NWT. In L. Hayhurst, T. Kaye, T. and M. Chawansky (eds), *Beyond Sport for Development and Peace: Transnational Perspectives on Theory*, London: Routledge.

McDonald, M. G. (2015) Imagining neoliberal feminism: Thinking critically about the US diplomacy campaign, 'empowering women and girls through sports'. *Sport in Society: Cultures, Commerce, Media, Politics, 18*(8), 909–922.

Mohanty, C. (2003). 'Under western eyes' revisited: Feminist solidarity through anti-capitalist struggles, *Signs 28*(2), 499–535.

Mohanty, C. (2004). *Feminism Without Borders: Decolonizing Theory, Practicing Solidarity*. Durham, NC: Duke University.

Momsen, J. (2010). *Gender and Development*. New York: Routledge.

Parpart, J. and Marchand, M. (2001). Exploring the cannon. In K. Bhavnani (ed.), *Feminism and 'Race'*. Oxford: Oxford University.

Saavedra, M. (2009). Dilemmas and opportunities in gender and sport-in-development. In R. Levermore and A. Beacom (eds), *Sport and International Development*. New York: Palgrave Macmillan.

Samie, S. F, Johnson, A. J., Huffman, A. M. and Hillyer, S. (2015). Voices of empowerment: Women from the global south re/negotiating empowerment and the global sports mentoring programme. *Sport in Society: Cultures, Commerce, Media, Politics, 18*(8), 923–937.

Shain, F. (2013). 'The Girl Effect': Exploring narratives of gendered impacts and opportunities in neoliberal development. *Sociological Research Online, 18*(2), 9.

Shehu, J. (ed.) (2010). *Gender, Sport and Development in Africa: Cross-Cultural Perspectives on Patterns of Representations and Marginalization*. Dakar: Council for Development of Social Science Research in Africa.

Swai, E.V. (2010). *Beyond Women's Empowerment in Africa: Exploring Dislocation and Agency*. New York: Palgrave Macmillan.

United Nations (UN). (2015). Transforming our World: The 2030 Agenda for Sustainable Development. Available at: https://sustainabledevelopment.un.org/post2015/transformingourworld.

Wilson, K. (2013). Agency as 'smart economics': Neoliberalism, gender and development. In S. Madhok, A. Phillips and K. Wilson (eds), *Gender, Agency and Coercion*. New York: Palgrave MacMillan.

18

SDP and postcolonial theory

Martha Saavedra

What is 'postcolonial theory' and what does it contribute to knowledge and practice in the realm of 'sport for development and peace'? This chapter provides an introduction to postcolonial theory, examines how 'it' has and could be used in sport for development and peace theory, research and practice, and offers a few sign-posts for future work. Particularly useful insights from postcolonial theory include a specific historical understanding of how colonialism and its legacies have shaped modern sport, and how modern sport intersects with notions and practices of 'Development' that are hallmarks of the postcolonial condition.

Introduction: a history of the present

Postcolonial theory came into use in the late 1970s among Anglophone academics as a means to assess and highlight the impact of colonialism on a broad array of contemporary practices, relationships, as well as ways of thinking and speaking. As such, postcolonial theory asserts that the historical experience of colonialism deeply structures the present, impacting institutions, opportunities, and choices of everyone, whether located in a high, low or middle-income country. At the same time, proponents and critics have strongly contested what postcolonial theory is, what methods are appropriate within it, and what actionable conclusions emerge from applying it. Those new to postcolonial theory may well find it both compelling and frustrating.

As a means of organizing knowledge and hypotheses about social interactions between countries, regions and peoples, postcolonial theory serves as a paradigm for mapping and appreciating the overall dynamics of social and historical global processes underway. Postcolonial theorists historicize contemporary configurations of power, privilege and resource distribution, scrutinize the impact of discourse, tease out legacies of Eurocentric imperialism and colonialism, and, most especially, amplify and even insist on the primacy of voices and experiences of 'subalterns' – i.e. the most marginalized (see p. 210). The significance of historical-spatial specificity is central. Postcolonial theory is fastened explicitly to a historical arc that has its fulcrum in colonial interactions between Europe and the rest of the world. Colonialism, hegemony, subjugation, resistance, cooptation, mimicry, collaboration, coping, hybridity and anti-colonialism are the substance of these relations, with the present moment experienced as a historical outcome of these relations.

In this way, postcolonial theory directly engages with both the results and the practice of what it called 'development'. It provides a critical analysis of what Hart refers to as little 'd' *development*, i.e. changes and reconfigurations in social, political, economic and technological realms, which affect the well-being and life trajectories of individuals, communities and other levels of socio-political groupings (Hart 2010). Postcolonial theory also provides a lens on big 'D' *Development*, i.e. the intentional interventions by governments and institutions to 'modernize' economies and improve well-being with a focus on economic growth. This practice of *Development* emerged in the post-World War II era of decolonization and the cold war and has become an industry in and of itself (Hart 2001: 650; 2010). Postcolonial theory encourages the interrogation of motivations, methods and outcomes of specific interventions and major enterprises. It is less a set of specific tools guiding implementation of *Development* interventions, and more a paradigmatic frame. Indeed, a perspective informed by postcolonial theory can lead to such deep skepticism of the aims, methods and structures of standard development projects that active participation in *Development* at all may be obviated on moral, ethical and empirical grounds. Intense self-reflexivity often marks the work of practitioners and researchers who adopt a postcolonial paradigm and who stay engaged with development, whether little 'd' or big 'D'. The paradigm highlights normative dilemmas and provokes questions around accountability and ethics for researchers, including those studying sport, development and peace, who must wrestle with the methodological and ethical implications of operating in a postcolonial environment.

There are ironies within postcolonial theory. For example, one trajectory of postcolonial studies seeks to de-center and provincialize the West and challenge the importance of Western frames in defining particular subjectivities. Recognizing the historicity and idiosyncrasy of European colonialism, one can see the resulting hegemony of Euro-American-'Western' power as precarious and mutable – especially given the contemporary manifestation of Chinese global power. Yet, within most studies adopting a postcolonial frame, the 'West' remains the central referent. Indeed, postcolonial theory insists that in the here-and-now, the half-life of European colonialism is substantive, persistent and relevant. As Spivak has suggested in questioning whether the subaltern can ever speak (Spivak 1988), it is nearly impossible to move beyond the imprint of Western concepts and languages given their invasive dominance. One outcome of this is that postcolonial perspectives may be more radical, explanatory and relevant in their application to the lasting impact of colonialism within the postcolonial West itself rather than in the reality of lives outside of the West. Mbembe's (2011) analysis of contemporary French intellectual and political life is an example of this.

Postcolonial theory: key concepts

With the broad scope of its subject and the range of interventions, postcolonial theory offers a plethora of concepts and mechanisms that seek to interpret the social and political world (see Ashcroft *et al.* 2013). The following section highlights a few concepts of particular importance in the field of sport and development: discourse, hegemony, hybridity, agency and the subaltern.

A central concern of postcolonial theory has been how **discourse** constructs subjectivities, shapes knowledge, justifies practice and normalizes particular distributions of power. In *Orientalism* (1978), for instance, Edward Said argues that a post-Enlightenment European intellectual tradition, a 'systematic discipline of *accumulation*' about the 'Orient' (Said 1979: 123), employed stereotypes and assumptions to create an 'Other' that was not only different, but ultimately unequal to and less than the European or 'Occidentals'. This and similar Eurocentric intellectual traditions contributed to normalizing imperial and colonial authority over an 'Other', who was rendered primitive, backward or childish relative to the modern and superior European.

These discourses also contributed to emerging notions of race and racial hierarchies that further legitimized colonial domination. Postcolonial theorists commonly locate, interrogate and deconstruct these discourses of power and representations of the 'Other'. They also examine the persistence and evolution of these discourses, even as they become more diffuse over time, especially in the practice of 'Development'.

How discourse functions to bolster hegemony also gives insight into how power and domination within postcolonial theory are understood. Discourses that construct the 'Other' and sociopolitical and racial hierarchies are not just used by those wielding the most blatant power, but they become accepted among those dominated through practices of governance, via law, education, commercial regulation, the media and, of course, sport. Here is where the concept of **hegemony**, most closely identified with the Italian theorist Antonio Gramsci, is useful (see Gramsci 2011). In hegemony, domination is not imposed by raw force, but through consent and complicity, and with ongoing negotiation and compromise. It is a work in progress, with resistance possible, but ultimately ceding to Eurocentric modes of valuation (Rowe 2004: 102–103; Ashcroft *et al.* 2013: 106–107). An example of this is that while football is practiced globally, the European leagues garner the most attention and money.

The ongoing negotiation of hegemony initially within the colonial and then the postcolonial experience impacts all parties and leads to a condition of **hybridity**, a term particularly associated with the literary theorist, Homi Bhabha, but also with Frantz Fanon. Hybridity may be most obvious in the political, social, material and physical cultures of those who have been colonized. Mimicry occurs – the colonized adopts aspects of the colonizer's culture, but what is copied is blurred and the results may be a creolization of languages, music, food, architecture, religion, government institutions, *and* sport. (Prabhu 2007; Fanon 2008; Bhabha 2012; Ashcroft *et al.* 2013: 108–111). The colonizer also is changed, given the mutually constitutive *relationship* of hegemonic domination. Mbembe (2011) among others suggests that this change may be quite profound and unsettling over time (e.g. Rigney 2003 and the rhetoric of the 2017 French presidential elections).

While the hegemonic power of Eurocentric discourse is considerable, hybridity suggests that those dominated have options to adopt, resist or exit aspects of colonialism, imperialism and their legacies. Hence, the notion of **agency**, or the capacity to act and the choice to act, is important in postcolonial theory. Acknowledging that those dominated have agency emphasizes their consent and complicity within imperialism. This can also highlight mechanisms for coping and survival (Green 1999). Claiming agency is also a means to assert the possibilities of conscious resistance and transformative change, 'to "exit" from habitually imperial assumptions and practices of relation, and take the opportunity to reconstruct modes of social existence upon an alternative, non-imperial political and ethical basis' (Bignall 2010: 3–4). While much of postcolonial theory is an effort to describe the ongoing legacy of colonialism and explain the mechanisms of power, there is also an impulse to seek social justice and create a *future* that is actually *post*-colonial, albeit how power would be structured, performed and distributed in such a future is still to be determined.

The **subaltern** is another key concept in postcolonial theory. Introduced by Gramsci, it was taken up by South Asian scholars such as Ranajit Guha and Gayatri Spivak in the Subaltern Studies Group to counter historiographies that privileged elites who both opposed and colluded with the colonialists. A subaltern emphasis centers on the masses and most marginalized, the 'laboring population and intermediate strata in town and country', as the principal actors (Guha 1982: 4). The subaltern can be a mover of history, but also may bear the brunt of injustice and epistemic violence. Furthermore, not all subjected to domination are necessarily subaltern. Postcolonial theorists often focus on the lives, histories, actions and experiences of the subaltern. Critical consideration of the subaltern also circles back to issues of representation and positionality, and ultimately leads to questions of voice, authenticity and agency, especially within the practice of research itself (Jazeel and McFarlane 2010). As Spivak notes in her classic essay, 'Can the Subaltern Speak' there is a contradiction in valorizing 'the concrete experience of the oppressed, while being so critical about the historical role of the intellectual' (Spivak 1988: 275).

Sport, development and postcolonial theory

Sport as experienced in the contemporary world is comprised of institutions, practices and phenomena that can be interrogated with a postcolonial lens. Modern sport's historical roots are entangled with those of the global postcolonial present. Colonial powers employed sport to serve the nation, recruit imperial officers, train soldiers, and discipline and distract colonial subjects. Those colonized engaged with and adapted sport to collaborate and cope with imperialism as well as to resist it. Moreover, one can argue that imperial powers did not simply disseminate the institutions of modern sport. It is true that discursive frameworks around sport normalize a hierarchy that gives primacy to European and 'Western' sporting practice and power. Yet, modern sport was born in the crucible of imperialism, and is suffused with both hegemony and hybridity. Colonized subjects and subaltern actors may have been 'obscured' but nonetheless shaped the contours of sport. A postcolonial view highlights these histories, discourses and relationships and delves into the uncomfortable contradictions and ambiguities that arise (e.g. Stoddart 1988; Searle 1990; Darby 2002; Dine 2002).

Though written long before postcolonial theory emerged as a paradigm, C.L.R. James' 1963 memoir and social history of cricket, *Beyond a Boundary* (2013) provides an example of a postcolonial analysis of sport. Written from the perspective of cricket in the West Indies, his work delves into issues of race, class, color, religion, occupation and power within the wider cricketing world and how this reflected a history of slavery and colonialism. Thoroughly embracing and mastering the 'colonial' game, he also exemplifies the consent, complicity, internalization and resistance of the colonized. The struggle for recognition and justice within West Indian cricket which James critically chronicles can also guide sport and development scholars and practitioners (Needham 1993; Stoddart 2004; James 2013; Darnell and Kaur 2015).

In the early twenty-first century, cricket again showed how sport can engender rich scholarly discussion about the nature of colonialism and its relationship to the present via analyses of the 2001 Bollywood film, *Lagaan*. The film depicts a fictional story of a diverse group of Indian villagers fighting injustice through a cricket match against British colonial officers. With the full dimensions well beyond the confines of this chapter, the scholarly debate highlights the contributions and limitations of a postcolonial approach. Majumdar (2002) emphasized how the fictional story mapped onto cultural resistance and popular nationalism found in the history of South Asia cricket, Mannathukkaren (2001) responded with a critique of how that nationalism glossed over the material realities of subalterns and disguised hegemonic elite and class consolidation within South Asia. Chakraborty (2003; 2004) argued that popular culture can contribute to decolonizing subaltern consciousness. Brown and Farred in various ways showed how the postcolonial political present intervenes in representations of the past (Brown 2004; Farred 2004).

While there already was a growing literature on colonialism and its legacies in sport (e.g. Baker and Mangan 1987; Martin 1995; Bale and Sang 1996; Deville-Danthu 1997; Black and Nauright 1998; Booth 1998), Bale, Cronin and the contributors to *Sport and Postcolonialism* (2003) were among the first to move beyond cricket and explicitly invoke postcolonial theory to analyze sport more broadly. Bale and Cronin (2003: 2) emphasized that sport and postcolonial theory had common themes of the body and bodily practices. They sketched out an agenda for using postcolonial theory to study sport that included exploring how sport contributed to colonial domination and resistance against it, examining the representation of sport within colonial discourse, delinking sport from metropolitan theory, and recovering the hidden spaces and meanings of colonial and postcolonial body practices (Bale and Cronin 2003: 8). The contributors explored the continuity, disjuncture, transgression, resistance, hegemony and ambiguity found in sporting experiences in the past and present in multiple postcolonial places, sports and institutions.

Since then postcolonial theory has continued to influence the study of sport (e.g. Mills 2005; Creak 2010; Riot 2010; Rollason 2010; Aung-Thwin 2012; Bancel 2015). However, it is scholars analyzing the contemporary field of Sport, Development and Peace – with emphasis on big 'D' Development – who have found it particularly relevant. The basic argument is as follows: legacies of colonialism entangle both modern sport and development. Hence, when sport is used explicitly as a tool to achieve development outcomes, there is a high likelihood that the effort will do more to reinforce the hegemony of the global North than contribute to greater well-being, equality and justice. Furthermore, the representation of poverty and marginality in SDP often undermines the agency of those portrayed for the purposes of fundraising. (Darnell 2012)

Scholars employing postcolonial theory and methods offer cautionary critiques of the discourse, structures and practices within the SDP movement that perpetuate inequalities in power, resources and influence. They also explore mindsets and methods that might contribute to decolonizing both research and practice and more directly tackle inequality, racism and injustice. Some focus explicitly on subaltern experiences and agency, recovering 'hidden spaces'.

One focus of research has been to interrogate SDP discourse. For instance, Lyndsay Hayhurst (2009) analyzed six key policy documents produced from 2003 to 2008 representing prominent institutions and voices within the movement, i.e. the United Nations and the Sport for Development and Peace International Working Group (SDP IWG). She did find some encouraging elements, e.g. increased emphasis on participatory approaches and attention to discrimination and difference, albeit not to racial differences (Hayhurst 2009: 223). It was also clear that choices were made to graft SDP policy onto the Millennium Development Goals, especially goal 8 emphasizing partnerships (ibid.: 216). Sport was to be part of the technical toolbox through which knowledge would be delivered to recipients of SDP programs. Amid ambiguity on policy specifics, the documents also stressed the important role of non-governmental organizations (NGOs) and the private sector (ibid: 220). Hayhurst concludes the SDP 'policy models are wedded to the neoliberal discourses of international development interventions' (ibid.: 222).

In another example, Simon Darnell employs Said's methods in *Orientalism* to investigate the construction of cultural knowledge of SDP with a discursive analysis of a 2011 *Sports Illustrated* article, 'Sports Saves the World'. The narrative creates a body of knowledge 'that secures hierarchies of dominance and inequality' and appeals specifically to Western audiences (Darnell 2014: 1007). This is accomplished through tropes of 'uncovering truths' (AIDS is about taboos and soccer can overcome them), 'Othering' (boxing can transform the bloodlust of a young man in the *favelas*), and the availability of 'benign' platforms for benevolent encounters (SDP can address these ills). The narrative of the article glosses over specific socio-economic complexities, political conflicts and entrenched inequalities, i.e. the political economy of underdevelopment, that structures the lives of those profiled. Instead, redemption is about individual choices, lifestyles and behavior. Darnell argues that '[t]here remains a need for continued historical, critical and *contrapuntal* readings of SDP and its social and political implications' that challenge imperialism and 'upset the normativity and presumed universality of SDP' (Darnell 2014: 1011–1012).

Nicholls, Giles and Sethna invoked Foucault and feminist, poststructural and postcolonial theory to examine subjugated knowledge and offered an alternative – feminist participatory action research (F-PAR) (Nicholls 2009; Nicholls *et al.* 2010). Nicholls critiqued the 'vertical hierarchy' she had observed in the SDP movement that places youth at the bottom delivering programming, but not involved in *developing* policy or programs (Nicholls 2009: 158). At the same time, global SDP policy leaders lamented the lack of empirical evidence on the impact of sport (Nicholls *et al.* 2010: 251). The expertise of peer educators, however, was overlooked. To challenge the dominant knowledge paradigm, Nicholls, Giles and Sethna (2010: 254) used F-PAR in 'a conscious effort to surface participants' subjugated knowledges and to recognize them as distinct and valid in an effort to inspire critical reflections on the power relationships that pervade research'. Peer educators collaborated in the design of a study of Kicking AIDS Out network, and interviewees co-produced the report. The authors document the barriers to co-creation of knowledge, the politics of partnership, donor-driven priorities and top-down approaches. To better negotiate 'the power/knowledge nexus', they recommend recognizing local knowledge as valid and nurturing the links between donors, academics and practitioners. (2010: 261). Sherry *et al.* echo these methods (2017)

Mwaanga and Banda (2014) explicitly adopt a postcolonial approach to praxis and research in their study of how the *Ubuntu* cultural ethos shapes the Positive and Kicking SDP program in Zambia. They intend 'to destabilize the dominant, ethnocentric discourses of the Global North worldview' by including 'more local, Indigenous understandings/inputs' and creating 'spaces for marginalized groups to speak out against dominant discourses'. They also seek to recover lost voices, agency and resistance 'through a radical reconstruction of knowledge production' (Mwaanga and Banda 2014: 177–178). A contested concept, Ubuntu is a southern African philosophy that asserts the individual is only complete within a community (ibid.: 175). They find that people living with HIV/AIDs use aspects of their local Ubuntu culture, such as mutual support, promoting senses of community, sharing, and social relationships encouraged through team sports, to 'achieve collective empowerment' (ibid.: 186). This contrasts with SDP programs that rely on medicoscientific discourses that emphasize the sharing of health-related knowledge as a universal solution to HIV/AIDS. They conclude that local culture and the agency of participants should be central platforms in SDP research and practice (ibid.: 187).

Tarminder Kaur builds on these ideas further in her ethnography of the sporting lives of the subaltern – workers on commercial grape and wine farms in the Western Cape, South Africa. (Kaur 2016). Her work is grounded in the lived experience of the farm workers and contextualized within the concatenated local/global political economy. Two key points from her deeply rich study follow. First, as an ethnographer, she adopted a critical self-reflective approach, aware of her own shifting positionality and privilege (Chapter 2). She notes that 'every relationship and every interaction had its unique dynamics', (Kaur 2016: 57) and acknowledges her own 'complicity in the politics of the social world one enters to study' (ibid.: 61). Second, while more formal SDP efforts 'targeted' the farm workers, the workers' sporting lives were community based and self-organized. In those spaces, participants gained experiences and benefits, including organizational skill building, leadership training, community empowerment, etc. that many would ascribe to more intentional or 'official' SDP programs. Yet, they were also part of political and economic struggles for equity and justice and subject to the vagaries of intensely unequal racial and class systems.

Critiques and next steps

Postcolonial theory certainly has impacted the field of SDP research. However, it has not engendered a significant body of criticism as has the general field of postcolonial theory. One direct critique has come from Fred Coalter (2013), who has specifically addressed it in terms of monitoring and evaluation and evidence and knowledge building. Coalter identifies the postcolonial approach as 'liberation' theory, and is troubled by what he sees as its dismissal of quantitative research in favor of qualitative research. In his view, postcolonial theory labels any quantitative, positivist work as oppressive and a product of neocolonialism. Yet, it does not clearly define 'positivism' and overlooks long-standing sophisticated debates on social science methods. Arguments are framed in terms of homogenized polarities that lack specificity. Ultimately, he sees it as a displacement of scope and ideological overreach (Coalter 2013: 45–49). Yet, Coalter's later argument for nuanced understanding of context, is very similar to the arguments of many in postcolonial theory to pay attention to the circumstances and complexities of people, places and institutions involved.

Coalter does raise questions that many postcolonial theorists considering SDP confront. What are the appropriate ethics and methods for research and how does one define success? One discipline that has not delved into postcolonial theory per se is economics. Often at the forefront of development interventions, the World Bank and development economists have of late been focused on rigorous impact evaluation that employs randomized controlled trials (e.g. see the work of the Center for Effective Global Action at UC Berkeley and the Poverty Action Lab at MIT). Could postcolonial theory frames be used to create a quantitative evaluation? There are studies such as those investigating the impact of stereotype threat that do test for the impact of biases (Steele and Aronson 1995; Steele 2011) or the likelihood of radicalization (Lyons-Padilla *et al.* 2015). Yet, coming up with appropriate indicators and tests to measure impact is difficult. Indicators 'can present "oversimplifications of complex social phenomena," which can, in turn, mask important issues of power that affect networks beyond decision-making processes' (Henne 2017: 4). Still it may be worth trying.

An obvious next step arises from a concern raised by the postcolonial critique itself, i.e. representation. Who does research on what and where and how is it disseminated? It is obvious that authors from and located in low and middle-income countries – a proxy for, though not equivalent to, the 'global South' – are not well represented in published scholarship on SDP. Schulenkorf, Sherry and Rowe report that 92 percent of researchers in their integrated literature review were from North America, Europe and Australia (NA/E/A), with only 5 percent of authors from African countries, and few from Asia, Latin America and the Pacific Islanders although 20 percent of the studies were located in those regions. Yet, based on *registered* projects on the SAD's Platform for Sport and Development over half of all SDP projects are in Africa, Asia and Latin America (Schulenkorf *et al.* 2016: 34). My own observations via research and coaching over the last 20 years as well as Kaur's study of farmworker sporting lives (2016) suggest that there are many more instances of what might be classified as SDP 'projects' that do not make it onto the Platform or other signifying registries. Schulenkorf, Sherry and Rowe's review also found that only 50 percent of the projects *studied* used local staff as opposed to 'international experts'. Whether this results from a selection bias in the kind of SDP projects that NA/E/A researchers choose to study is unknown, though Lindsey and Grattan's (2012) research on locally driven projects in Lusaka suggests this may be the case. Postcolonial and subaltern theory would also caution one to not conclude that the geographic origin of an author alone determines the positionality and power of a researcher and how that impacts research undertaken. Class, caste, lineage, neighborhood, religion, ethnicity, race, gender, sexuality, occupation, income, education, language abilities, age, birth-order, able-bodiedness, life-histories and dumb luck all impact the circumstance shaping any particular researcher's engagement with a particular research project. Autochthony and authenticity are valuable perspectives, but never absolute, especially in dynamic and ever-shifting contemporary environments. However, one cannot escape that the existing SDP published scholarly literature in many ways is unrepresentative of the world as it exists. On one hand, this could be ascribed to the process of discovery. There is much more out there empirically to find, and SDP as a 'discipline' has just begun. The relative lack of circulating research by scholars from the global South though is of concern to the field of SDP and most other areas of scholarly inquiry.

Academics with privilege who take to heart a postcolonial perspective can address this. They can make their own work accessible both digitally and in hard-copy, especially in communities and groups involved in the research. They can more diligently seek out, read and cite existing research by scholars in the 'global South', much of which is not digitized or catalogued, by visiting research institutions, libraries and archives. The Institut National Supérieur de l'Education Populaire et du Sport in Dakar Senegal, for instance, has over 546 theses, only some of which are available online.[1] As ever more institutions globally provide digital access to theses and research papers, this becomes easier. A more direct step is to collaborate with local students and scholars on projects from conception through fieldwork to presentation and publication. Citation, engagement and collaboration though do not necessarily address imbalances of power, resources and opportunities. Intellectual property rights and appropriation of knowledge for whose benefit can become issues. There are also the particular discursive realms of both the 'Academy' and 'Development' that sanction and legitimate particular kinds of questions, methods, theories and dissemination. One returns to the questions of hegemony, voice and agency in the production of knowledge.

It may be worthwhile for scholars inclined towards postcolonial theory to also engage with and seek inspiration in other forms of knowledge production, particularly within popular culture, where sport also exists. Afrofuturism is an example in which imagination, hope and an orientation towards the future incorporates the past, sometimes in a painful confrontation, by seeking to correct inequities and transcend legacies (e.g. Yaszek 2006; Anderson 2015). Yuval-Davis argues that imagining is an important creative process to move between knowledge and practice 'from positionings to practices, practices to standpoints, knowledge, meaning, values, and goals' (Yuval-Davis 2012). Within athletic training, visualization and thinking about specific muscles movements and positionality in a future place and state of being is a trusted technique to improving performance. Within SDP this can also be applied with knowledge of the past foregrounded. Hence, perhaps through systematic and reflexive processes, SDP scholars and practitioners can imagine new futures for inquiry, knowledge production and practice that build on, but, ultimately, transcend postcolonial frames.

Note

1 See www.beep.ird.fr/cgi-bin/library.cgi?site=localhostanda=pandp=aboutandc=insepsandl=frandw=utf-8.

References

Anderson, R. (2015). Critical afrofuturism: A case study in visual, rhetoric, sequential art and postapocalyptic black identity. *The Blacker the Ink: Constructions of Black Identity in Comics and Sequential Art.* New Brunswick, NJ: Rutgers University Press, pp. 171–192.
Ashcroft, B., Griffiths, G. and Tiffin, H. (2013). *Post-Colonial Studies: The Key Concepts.* London: Routledge.

Aung-Thwin, M. (2012). Towards a national culture: Chinlone and the construction of sport in post-colonial Myanmar. *Sport in Society, 15*(10), 1341–1352.

Baker, W. J. and Mangan, J. A. (1987). *Sport in Africa: Essays in Social History*. New York & London: Holmes & Meier.

Bale, J. and Cronin, M. (2003). *Sport and Postcolonialism*. Oxford & New York: Berg.

Bale, J. and Sang, J. (1996). *Kenyan Running: Movement Culture, Geography, and Global Change*. London: Routledge.

Bancel, N. (2015). Physical activities through postcolonial eyes: A place of epistemologic and historiographical experimentation. *The International Journal of the History of Sport, 32* (7), 862–875.

Bhabha, H. K. (2012). *The Location of Culture*. Florence, KY: Routledge.

Bignall, S. (2010). *Postcolonial Agency: Critique and Constructivism*. Plateaus – New Directions in Deleuze Studies : Edinburgh: EUP.

Black, D. R. and Nauright, J. (1998). *Rugby and the South African Nation: Sport, Cultures, Politics, and Power in the Old and New South Africas*. International Studies in the History of Sport. Manchester & New York: Manchester University Press; Distributed exclusively in the USA by St. Martin's Press.

Booth, D. (1998). *The Race Game: Sport and Politics in South Africa*. Abingdon: Frank Cass.

Brown, R. M. (2004). Lagaan: Once upon a time in India. *Film and History: An Interdisciplinary Journal of Film and Television Studies, 34*(1), 78–80.

Chakraborty, C. (2003). Subaltern studies, Bollywood and 'Lagaan'. *Economic and Political Weekly, 38*(19), 1879–84.

Chakraborty, C. (2004). Bollywood motifs: Cricket fiction and fictional cricket. *The International Journal of the History of Sport, 21*(3–4), 549–572.

Coalter, F. (2013). *Sport for Development: What Game Are We Playing?* London: Routledge.

Creak, S. R. (2010). *'Body Work': A History of Sport and Physical Culture in Colonial and Postcolonial Laos*. Canberra: Australian National University.

Darby, P. (2002). *Africa, Football and FIFA: Politics, Colonialism and Resistance*. Sport in the Global Society. London & Portland, OR: Routledge.

Darnell, S. C. (2012). *Sport for Development and Peace : A Critical Sociology*. London & New York: Bloomsbury Academic.

Darnell, S. C. (2014). Orientalism through sport: Towards a Said-ian analysis of imperialism and 'sport for development and peace'. *Sport in Society, 17* (8), 1000–1014.

Darnell, S. C. and Kaur. T. (2015). C.L.R. James and a place for history in theorising 'sport for development and peace'. *International Journal of Sport Management and Marketing, 16* (1–2), 5–17.

Deville-Danthu, B. (1997). *Le Sport En Noir et Blanc: Du Sport Colonial Au Sport Africain Dans Les Anciens Territoires Français d'Afrique Occidentale (1920–1965)*. Collection 'Espaces et Temps Du Sport'. Paris: L'Harmattan.

Dine, P. (2002). France, Algeria and isport: From colonialism to globalisation. *Modern and Contemporary France, 10*(4), 495–505.

Fanon, F. (2008). *Black Skin, White Masks*. Translated by Richard Philcox. New York: Grove.

Farred, G. (2004). The double temporality of Lagaan: Cultural struggle and postcolonialism. *Journal of Sport and Social Issues, 28*(2), 93–114.

Gramsci, A. (2011). *Prison Notebooks (Vols 1, 2 and 3)*. Edited and translated by Joseph A. Buttigieg and Antonio Callari. New York: Columbia University Press.

Green, D. (1999). Gender violence and the politics of disengagement. *Gender Violence in Africa : African Women's Responses*, New York: St. Martin's, pp. 151–197.

Guha, R. (1982). On Some Aspects of the Historiography of Colonial India. In P. Chatterjee and G. Pandey (eds), *Subaltern Studies: Writings on South Asian History and Society* (Vol. 1). Delhi: Oxford University Press.

Hart, G. (2001). Development critiques in the 1990s: Culs de sac and promising paths. *Progress in Human Geography, 25*(4), 649–658.

Hart, G. (2010). D/Developments after the meltdown. *Antipode, 41*(S1), 117–141.

Hayhurst, L. M. C. (2009). The power to shape policy: Charting sport for development and peace policy discourses. *International Journal of Sport Policy and Politics, 1*(2), 203–227.

Henne, K. (2017). Indicator culture in sport for development and peace: A transnational analysis of governance networks. *Third World Thematics: A TWQ Journal, 2*(1), 1–18.

James, C. L. R. (2013). *Beyond a Boundary: 50th Anniversary Edition*. Durham, NC: Duke University Press.

Jazeel, T. and McFarlane, C. (2010). The limits of responsibility: A postcolonial politics of academic knowledge production. *Transactions of the Institute of British Geographers, 35*(1), 109–124.

Kaur, T. (2016). Sporting Lives and Development Agendas: A Critical Analysis of Sport and Development Nexus in the Context of Farm Workers of the Western Cape. School of Government, Faculty of Economics and Management Sciences, University of the Western Cape.

Lindsey, I. and Grattan, A. (2012). An 'international movement'? Decentring sport-for-development within Zambian communities. *International Journal of Sport Policy and Politics, 4*(1), 91–110.

Lyons-Padilla, S., Gelfand, M. J., Mirahmadi, H., Farooq, M. and van Egmond, M. (2015). Belonging nowhere: Marginalization and radicalization risk among Muslim immigrants. *Behavioral Science and Policy, 1*(2), 1–12.

Majumdar, B. (2002). Cultural resistance and sport: Politics, leisure and colonialism-lagaan-invoking lost history. *Sport in Society, 5*(2), 29–44.

Mannathukkaren, N. (2001). Subalterns, cricket and the 'nation': The silences of 'Lagaan'. *Economic and Political Weekly, 36*(49), 4580–4588.

Martin, P. (1995). *Leisure and Society in Colonial Brazzaville.* African Studies Series 87. Cambridge: Cambridge University Press.

Mbembe, A. (2011). Provincializing France? *Public Culture, 23*(1), 85–119.

Mills, J. H. (2005). *Subaltern Sports: Politics and Sport in South Asia.* London: Anthem.

Mwaanga, O. and Banda, D. (2014). A postcolonial approach to understanding sport-based empowerment of people living with HIV/AIDS (PLWHA) in Zambia: The case of the cultural philosophy of Ubuntu. *Journal of Disability and Religion, 18*(2), 173–191.

Needham, A. D. (1993). Inhabiting the metropole: C.L.R. James and the postcolonial intellectual of the African diaspora. *Diaspora: A Journal of Transnational Studies, 2*(3), 281–303.

Nicholls, S. (2009). On the backs of peer educators: Using theory to interrogate the role of young people in the field of sport-in-development. *Sport and International Development*, 156–175. Springer.

Nicholls, S., Giles, A. R. and Sethna, C. (2010). Perpetuating the 'lack of evidence' discourse in sport for development: Privileged voices, unheard stories and subjugated knowledge. *International Review for the Sociology of Sport, 46*(3), 249–264.

Prabhu, A. (2007). *Hybridity: Limits, Transformations, Prospects.* Albany, NY: State University of New York Press.

Rigney, D. M. (2003). *Sport, Indigenous Australians and Invader Dreaming: A Critique.* New York: Berg.

Riot, T. (2010). Le football Rwanda: Un simulacre guerrier dans la creolisation d'une société (1900–50). *Canadian Journal of African Studies/La Revue Canadienne Des Études Africaines, 44*(1), 75–109.

Rollason, W. (2011). *We Are Playing Football: Sport and Postcolonial Subjectivity, Panapompom, Papua New Guinea.* Cambridge Scholars Publishing.

Rowe, D. (2004). Antonio Gramsci: Sport, hegemony and the national-popular. In R. Giulianotti (ed.), *Sport and Modern Social Theorists.* Basingstoke & New York: Palgrave MacMillan, pp. 97–110.

Said, E. (1979). *Orientalism.* New York: Vintage.

Schulenkorf, N., Sherry, E. and Rowe, K. (2016). Sport for development: An integrated literature review. *Journal of Sport Management, 30*(1), 22–39.

Searle, C. (1990). Race before wicket: Cricket, empire and the white rose: For C.L.R. James (1901–1989). *Race and Class, 31*(3), 31–48.

Sherry, E., Schulenkorf, N., Seal, E., Nicholson, M. and Hoye, R. (2017). Sport-for-development: Inclusive, reflexive, and meaningful research in low- and middle-income settings. *Sport Management Review, 20*(1), 69–80.

Spivak, G. C. (1988). Can the subaltern speak? In C. Nelson and L. Grossberg (eds), *Marxism and the Interpretation of Culture*, Urbana and Chicago: University of Illinois Press, pp. 21–78.

Steele, C. M. (2011). *Whistling Vivaldi: And Other Clues to How Stereotypes Affect Us (Issues of Our Time).* New York: WW Norton.

Steele, C. M. and Aronson, J. (1995) Stereotype threat and the intellectual test performance of African Americans. *Journal of Personality and Social Psychology, 69*(5), 797.

Stoddart, B. (1988). Sport, cultural imperialism, and colonial response in the British Empire. *Comparative Studies in Society and History, 30*(4), 649–673.

Stoddart, B. (2004). Sport, colonialism and struggle: C.L.R. James and cricket. In R. Giulianotti, *Sport and Modern Social Theorists*, UK: Palgrave Macmillan, pp. 111–128.

Yaszek, L. (2006). Afrofuturism, science fiction, and the history of the future. *Socialism and Democracy, 20*(3), 41–60.

Yuval-Davis, N. (2012). Dialogical epistemology: An intersectional resistance to the 'oppression Olympics'. *Gender and Society, 26*(1), 46–54.

19

SDP and social anthropology

Holly Collison

Introduction

Academic inquiry within sport for development and peace (SDP) has produced a rich body of literature, knowledge production, critical perspectives, advocation and directions for the future. This handbook highlights the numerous methodological challenges, opportunities and approaches within the research of the SDP sector. Yet there are limited anthropological examinations within the context of sport and more specifically SDP. Leading academics in the sector have called for more anthropological approaches to SDP research. For example, in 2009 Hayhurst proposed that future research should advocate for increased 'anthropological perspectives to uncover how those on the "receiving end" of SDP policies are influenced and challenged by taking up the solutions and techniques prescribed for them' (Hayhurst 2009: 203). The suggestion made here is valid and shared by others in the SDP space, it is the contextualisation and deeper understandings of culture, the 'local' and the 'locals' that are too often missing in both the process and product of SDP research.

This chapter has three main aims. First it attempts to examine existing anthropological literature within both sport and development contexts; second it highlights the opportunities that anthropology can bring to the SDP field with regard to social process, cultural understandings and challenging assumptions of the local; and third, the chapter aims to demonstrate the ethical advantages of researching with local populations, organisations and recipient populations as opposed to 'on' them, giving prevalence to cultural specificity and local voices.

Social anthropology

Before I turn to the anthropology of sport and development landscape I think it is important first to define, albeit broadly, social anthropology as an academic discipline. Put simply, 'Anthropology is the study of people; social anthropology is the study of human society ... Social anthropology can also be characterised as the translation of culture' (Layton 1997: 1). Thomas Hylland Eriksen's account of anthropology takes into consideration the ways in which the discipline may be useful when making sense of the contemporary world, he sums this up well by claiming, there is a need for a perspective on humanity which does not take preconceived assumptions about human societies from granted, which is sensitive to both similarities and differences, and which simultaneously approaches the human world from a global and local angle. The only academic subject which fulfils these criteria is anthropology, which studies humans in societies under the most varying circumstances imaginable, searches for patterns and similarities, but is fundamentally critical of quick solutions and simple answers to complex questions. There is also an explicit ambition among anthropologists not to see the world from a European or North American vantage-point, but to establish a truly global, comparative perspective where as many voices and life-worlds as possible are taken seriously.

Eriksen 2017: 6–7

Some may still need convincing regarding, (a) the boundaries between sociological and anthropological methodological approaches and perspectives towards sport and development, and (b), the distinct advantages the discipline can bring to the subject area. I will address the first tension now and return to the second in the latter part of this chapter.

The distinctiveness or differences between sociology and anthropology is often centred around the pursuit of ethnographic fieldwork, as Akhil Gupta and James Ferguson claim, 'The single most significant factor determining whether a piece of research will be accepted as (that magical word) "anthropological" is the extent to which it depends on experience in the field' (Gupta and Feguson1997: 1). This claim is supported by Eriksen who advocates for fieldwork as the distinguishing factor for anthropology and the most important source of new knowledge about society and culture (Eriksen 2001: 24). John Van Maanen's *Tales of the Field: On Writing Ethnography* is an important resource for anthropologists and anthropologists in training to discover and explore the connections, challenges and credentials of 'doing fieldwork' and 'being in the field' (Maanen 1988). This guide introduces the key principles of ethnographic fieldwork which suggests 'fieldwork demands the full-time involvement of a researcher over a lengthy period of time (typically unspecified) and consists mostly of ongoing interaction with the human targets of study on their home ground' (Maanen 1988: 2). This initial description maybe considered overly simplistic, however, the description develops to include pursuits such as the first hand sharing and experiencing of environment, problems, background, language, rituals, belief systems and the social relations of a specified group of people. Fieldwork as positioned as the means to an end that allows for a 'rich, concrete, complex and truthful account of the social world being studied' (ibid.). It is the idea of 'fieldwork as a means to an end' to which I now turn.

If fieldwork is positioned as the necessity for anthropological investigation, what is the end goal? Often this is summarised through the expression and portrayal of culture. Ethnographies connect culture and fieldwork, it is the written representation of culture and cultural groups and importantly represents two worlds of meaning, that of the ethnographer and that of the individuals and cultural groups under examination. It is the position, interpretation and reflection of the ethnography that is another stand out principle of anthropology. In line with Clifford Geertz use of 'thick description', interpretative anthropology saw a shift in epistemological standpoints, personalised accounts and the use of 'I' in cultural examinations which allowed for personal authority within research (Geertz 1973). Michael Schnegg (2014:34) highlights this ethnographic approach by using the example of Geertz analysis of the Balinese cockfight, in which Geertz describes being caught by the police as part of larger group watching an illegal cockfight and how this transformed their relationship with the community. After the incident the village 'opened up to them' and they were 'in' (Geertz 1973: 416).

To some the use of personal reflection and personalising research accounts feels unnatural and potentially uncomfortable. In my own ethnography examining 'youth' and the use of football as a development tool in post-conflict Liberia, it was often fieldwork 'incidents', my own personal methodological challenges and unpredictable events that I found myself in which constructed and evolved 'My Journey' (Collison 2016). In this case, adopting 'my' and 'I' in written accounts in conjunction with the narratives and reflections of those being researched allowed for a 'local' perspective to be intersected to empower both myself as an anthropologist and those I lived with, interacted with and observed.

Without wishing to abruptly leave this important epistemological principle found within ethnography, I now turn to an important source of its application within SDP. Megan Chawansky's (2015) *You're Juicy: Autoethnography as Evidence in Sport for Development and Peace (SDP) Research* demonstrates the benefits of writing from the perspective of her embodied self. By doing so she proposes that through her own research experiences 'in the SDP realm and in foregrounding the body as something that one can know with, about, and through, she highlights the complexities of SDP subjectivities' (Chawansky 2015: 1). Chawansky's personal accounts highlight the value of constructing evidence through experience to produce new knowledge and understandings of SDP spaces (ibid.: 10). By doing so, and by advocating for autoethnographic narratives she claims that 'the myth' of objective social research can be diminished.

Despite the romanticism associated with cultural exploration and conducting fieldwork in foreign lands, the challenges and limits of fieldwork and ethnography are notable. First, the idea of structure, rules or a methodological formula is rejected or questioned by many anthropologists, 'ethnographic research cannot be programmed … it is not a matter of following methodological rules, nor can all the problems be anticipated, or for that matter resolved' (Hammersley and Atkinson 2007: 20). Eriksen (2001: 26) captures this challenge well by claiming, 'There is – alas – no simple recipe for fieldwork'. Aside from the unpredictability of ethnographic fieldwork, much of what is later positioned in terms of 'success' or 'failure' in the field is evaluated via the ability of the researcher to manage, mediate, negotiate, engage, gain access and embed him/herself in a variety of environments or specific events or spaces. The personality characteristics, bias, skills, gender, age, ethnicity or willingness to adapt and evolve according to others and the cultural climate may be a source of limitation. An all too familiar challenge is the limitations placed on the researcher by virtue of funding and time allocated to pursue fieldwork either directly connected to research budgets or institutional permissions and approval. The difficulty associated with translation is also a concern and point of contestation within the social sciences.

Questions pertaining to misinterpretation, distortion and the critical process of connecting analytical concepts to alien social and cultural worlds are ever present. Many of these challenges expose the 'my' and 'I' within anthropological research projects and questions the abilities of the researcher to adapt and ultimately find a way 'in' and sustain this in a meaningful way. Post-fieldwork the researcher will remain challenged in her/his ability, style and skill to translate, describe, analyse and reflect cultural norms and practices from within and outside of alien social worlds.

Traditionally it is the methodological commitment to intensive participant observation (Clifford 1992), the principle that fieldwork should be experienced as performed (as opposed to communicated in dialogue) (Hastrup and Hervik 1994: 3) and long-term fieldwork and immersion that distinguishes anthropological examinations (Okely 1992). Vered Amit's (2003) edited collection of ethnographic fieldwork acknowledges such traditions but importantly paves the way to reconsider some of these, until recently unchallenged, principles of ethnographic fieldwork. This is a positive step forward. Away from the rigid confines of *total* immersion or exotic exploration, those drawn to contextual and deeper understandings of SDP may now be able to pursue credible anthropological examinations of organisational cultures, recipient experiences, local narratives and culture in a more fluid methodological framework that aligns with an anthropological perspective. Social anthropology can be more viable and accessible than once thought due to contemporary fieldwork pursuits which demonstrate and advocate for a shift in our understandings of ethnographic fieldwork in a rapidly changing world.

The anthropology of sport

Anthropology has a long tradition of exploration and the considered study of religion, kinship, political economy, identity and social behaviour and organisation. The examination of sport, play and games has and continues to sit on the peripheral of serious study, as Sands argues, 'Primitive play and games were rarely considered by anthropologists, it is only in the last 50 years that the study of sport and culture has emerged and this has been accomplished in academic fields other than anthropology' (Sands 2002: 1). Despite the observations made by Sir Edward Burnett Tylor, in *The History of Games* (1879) in which he explored sport as a vehicle for the analysis of broader cultural processes and historical connections, the uptake of sport and games as a legitimate site of anthropological enquiry did not catch on. There were some exceptions of course, most notably, James Mooney the *Cherokee Ball Game* (1890), Stewart Culin *American Indian Games* (1903), Raymond Firth *A Dart Match in Tikopia* ([1931], 1990), Alexander Lesser *The Pawnee Ghost Dance Hand Game* (1933) and John Roberts, Malcolm Arth and Robert Bush *Games in Culture* (1959). Yet the anthropology of sport still lacked legitimacy and remained superfluous to more traditional research topics.

It was not until the 1970s through the advocation of scholars such as Edward Norbeck and the formation of The Anthropological Association for the Study of Play (TAASP) that play and games were, to a limited extent, introduced as an important research area that paved the way for the emergence of sport as a central research theme. Blanchard (1985: 293) claimed, 'No longer is sport simply a topic of idle conversation and pastime activity amongst anthropologists; it has become a legitimate subject of serious study', again, I might argue that this claim was a little premature within anthropological contexts. Anthropologist Noel Dyck (2000) has for some time has questioned the lack of anthropological enquiry within emerging sports contexts and maintains the stance that sport is considered as non-serious and at times inconsequential. Advocation has followed as the social relationships, organisation, power and cultural aspects embedded in sports, and has been critiqued through an anthropological lens (see, for example, Carter 2002). A shift in recognition and legitimacy of the anthropology of sport and its application within the development sector and in diverse national contexts is emerging.

Anthropology and SDP

The rapid acceleration of the SDP movement (Kidd 2008) has given anthropological enquiry an opportunity. In 2009, Tess Kay called for an increase in 'reflexive forms of research (that) provide a mechanism for the expression of local understandings and knowledge that are crucial to the assessment of the "social impact" of sport for development contexts' (Kay 2009: 1190). This statement provides the rationale for an increase in social anthropology research within SDP, especially in relation to participant engagement, transferability and impact. One example of ethnographic inquiry is provided by Ramon Spaaij, by his account of the lived experience of Somali people from refugee backgrounds in Australia to examine the role of sport as an indicator or means of social integration. His three-year ethnography explores in a meaningful way the everyday realities and experiences of Somali Australians' and the use of sport as a means for bonding and its links to social capital (Spaaij 2012). This in-depth approach and commitment to long-term engagement, first demonstrates credible and thoughtful discussion and analysis but second, positions Somali Australians' at the centre of the research through their lived experiences. It might also be worth noting the contemporary approach to conducting ethnographic research 'at home' in contrast with the traditional expectation of exotic exploration (see Dyck 2003: 40–61). Further examples of anthropological enquiries into SDP are provided later in this chapter.

Although sport is seemingly the central theme to many inquiries of SDP, the formula of international locales, diverse contexts, globalisation, the notion of development, ethnicity, religious division, varying political economies, cultural distinctiveness, performance, and social organisation and structures satisfies many traditional and emerging anthropological interests. This section will now draw upon some methodological opportunities already employed and advocated by academics in SDP which have the potential to compliment an anthropological lens. While I argue that SDP provides a rich space for anthropological investigation, I also note the lessons researchers in SDP can learn from anthropologists examining several top-down bottom-up perspectives in wider development studies. In order to construct a picture of the opportunities and potential of anthropology in SDP research I will attempt to introduce and intersect two schools of thought – and a significant source of tension – for both anthropology, SDP and development studies. This tension can, for now, be summarised through the pursuit of application, impact and action versus theoretical, conceptual and explorative purity.

Applied anthropology

The question of how anthropologists define themselves has long been contested. In Sarah Pink's edited collection of essays focused on the *Applications of Anthropology: Professional Anthropology in the Twenty-first Century* (2006), this tension is identified, discussed and justified throughout. This is appropriately identified as 'pure' (academic) or 'impure' (applied). The resistance is particularly present in the field of international development, with a natural tendency to question the very notion of 'development', directed change and defining change within the parameters of policy as is the norm for international development agencies (Escobar 1991; Sahlins 1999). Despite the scepticism and ethical standpoints, applied anthropology in the field of development significantly expanded in the 1980s and 1990s with a renewed consideration of poverty, social exclusion and marginality. Anthropologist Maia Green used the term '*cultural brokerage*' to describe the project of international assistance in the form of understanding the poor and cultural dispositions which seemed to work against the goals of modernisation (Green 2006: 118).

The *belief* in applied anthropology is assumed to be a shift related to modernity or the rapid growth of recent social and developments movements. However, Malinowski believed that a need to distinguish between applied and pure research was unhelpful. He suggested

> research in order to be of use must be inspired by courage and purpose … it must be briefed by the constructive statesmanship and use foresight which establish the relevant issues and have the courage to apply the necessary remedies.
>
> *Malinowski 1945: 4*

Colonial politics aside, Malinowski understood the blurred lines between application and academic opportunities and indeed obligations. Raymond Firth recalled Malinowski's belief that an anthropologists duty is to 'present facts, develop concepts, destroy fictions and empty phrases, and so reveal relevant, active forces' (Firth 1981: 195). Regardless of how applied anthropology came to be recognised and exercised, the theory is that anthropological perspectives can highlight and help to overcome discursive gaps in ways that bring people together. In simple terms anthropologists in development can meaningfully stand within – and act as a bridge between – diverse actors and interests (Crewe and Axelby 2013). With this in mind, the applied stance combines traditional philosophies and methodologies with anthropological insights to assist and support decision-makers and actors of change in a thoughtful and respectful way. This may well speak to those who had and continue to advocate for knowledgeable, meaningful and locally sensitive frameworks to both enlighten and actively collaborate.

Social anthropology and participatory action research

With the anthropological position, methodological traditions and perspective in place I now turn to how this may be applied within SDP research. One solution and opportunity has already been suggested by SDP researchers in the form of participatory action research (PAR) (Burnett 2008; Darnell and Hayhurst 2011; Sherry *et al.* 2017). Although this has not always been connected with social anthropology I suggest it can and should. PAR involves 'collecting data involving those affected by a problem in a collaborative effort which is then directed toward actions to alleviate the root cause of the problem' (Schensul *et al.* 2015). This form of transformative research is directed towards structural, operational or policy changes; and 'it is conducted by affected groups; and in the process, it brings about change in individual-level capacity, power, influence and voice' (ibid.: 191). Social transformation therefore becomes a process of research, education and action (see Hall 1981). The overarching ethical principles of PAR speak to issues of power inequality, hearing the voices of silenced and democratising science and research. Importantly in the context of SDP and development more broadly, this not only connects to the challenges local populations face in the context of development programming and everyday life but the political and neocolonial nature of SDP research. In relation to SDP and PAR, Darnell and Hayhurst argue that 'sport offers a critical hub for re-thinking and re-practicing the politics of development in support of decolonisation (Darnell and Hayhurst 2011: 193). The advocation, methodological framework and context all seem to connect effortlessly, so how can social anthropology contribute to this approach? And what are the implications?

One of the primary objectives of this chapter is to stress the importance of cultural context, the everyday realities of local populations, knowledge production through voices and personal reflection and the experiences and belief systems of individuals intimately and actively positioned in the SDP process (at any level). Social anthropological embedded within a PAR approach provides opportunities for decolonisation as well as rich, embodied and immersed ethnographic work. As with all research pursuits this is not without challenge or critical commentary. For example, it has been argued that participatory research methodologies used within development contexts may operate to exclude certain social categories from involvement in the research process while also limiting the kinds of issues which the research can address (see Mosse 2001). The intricacies involved in any PAR design needs to account for multiple voices, perspectives, social groupings, cultural exchanges and power structures to avoid the almost inevitable exclusion of 'some'. I may propose here that fieldwork, long-term engagement and immersion in multi-spaces is a necessity of achieving meaningful, ethical and impactful change or transformation and this is PARs most significant connection/advocation to and for social anthropology. In this respect, PAR also offers a new dynamic to social anthropology in the form of extending beyond cultural brokerage and translation. Often anthropologists speak of difficulties of exiting the field or guilt. Potentially a form of action of giving back may relieve some of these personal and ethical anxieties.

The notion of mutual learning underpins social anthropology within a PAR research design. Personal and political values and agendas are always embedded in the decisions ethnographers and anthropologists make and respond to (Green 2006; Schensul *et al.* 2015). This is a point of reference and awareness; it is inevitable and arguably heightened by the sense of personal commitment and investment required in ethnography and PAR research. With the cautions in place, it is useful to consider some key indicators for PAR that have emerged from anthropological experiences, Schensul *et al.* highlight nine key indicators, including: the reduction of imbalances in political power, economic resources, access and environmental constraints, as well as, the co-constructing of research, and enhancing the ability of marginalised populations to access, utilise and conduct research that addresses their needs and aspirations (Schensul *et al.* 2015: 193). Academics in the field of SDP have been quick and justified in their critical appraisal of the sector from multiple perspectives, which provides a number of opportunities for social anthropology and PAR. The continued absence of effective and meaningful monitoring and evaluation assessment of SDP practices maybe one appropriate theme for social anthropology and PAR to consider (see Coalter 2010).

Anthropologist Cora Burnett demonstrated the role of PAR utilised as a sport development impact assessment tool in the context of a two sports programmes implemented in South Africa. The results of the comparative study highlighted the role of informed and knowledgeable researchers on contextual issues positioned as essential for interpretation and the potential application of results. Importantly, Burnett's paper demonstrates the positive influence of rich knowledge embedded in PAR in influencing sustainability and 'local penetration' of sport for development projects and the implementation of a needs-based service (Burnett 2008). I propose here that PAR in the absence of social anthropology and its associated methodologies may feed into the critiques of exclusion, bias, cultural slippage and power imbalances. Yet, the natural relationship between the two may construct an effective, ethical, legitimate, credible and democratised research framework.

Social anthropology and participation social interaction research

Does participation always need to seek change? For some time, scholars have debated and continue to distinguish participatory research from action research. Principally, the resistance emerges from the idea that participatory research is more focused on learning for the purpose of discovering silenced voices and repositioning power imbalances in a wide range of contexts; while action research is more focused on social action, policy reform or other types of social or systemic change (see Kindon *et al.* 2007). Fundamentally the stance researchers adopt is a choice influenced by politics, access, ethics and personal preference. As noted in the above section the notion of change and the position of researchers as change agents is an uncomfortable stance for some which is embedded in historical narratives of neocolonialism, power dynamics between the researcher and the researched and the questioning of purpose within the realm of knowledge production.

I argue here that social anthropologists and ethnographers are often consumed with the complexities of in-the-field identity, constructing roles and managing knowledge and expertise with 'playing the clown' (Eriksen 2001: 25). The defining boundary between participatory research and action research is intent to change versus unintended consequences of knowledge exchange, reciprocity and interaction. One possibility for those uncomfortable with the objective of action is 'participatory social interaction research' (PSIR). According to Collison and Marchesseault,

> PSIR is a form of participatory research that centralizes, prioritizes and situates sporting interventions and development through the experiences and daily lives of participants. PSIR seeks not to change behaviour or practice but aims to gain deeper insights and understandings of local populations, culture and experiences through and beyond the participation of SDP.
>
> *Collison and Marchesseault 2018: 228*

The three founding principles of PSIR state: (a), that the objective to take action creates social boundaries, carries expectations and feeds into neoliberal and complex historical and post-conflict baggage; (b), PSIR allows the researcher to organically integrate into alien cultural and social systems which lead to authentic relationship building thus presenting oneself as neutral; and (c), PSIR prioritises the everyday lives and experiences of the participants of SDP and knowledge is always situated according to local populations and the recipients of SDP (Collison and Marchesseault 2018: 228). But how is this achieved?

To answer this question, I turn briefly to David Marchesseault's examination of SDP in Rwanda and my own research in Liberia. Without any intention of creating change or indeed arriving with a fixed agenda, the pursuit of research was centred on the initial commitment to long-term fieldwork, immersion and employing an anthropological lens to explore and contextualise SDP activity and local experiences of SDP programmes. Be it personal choice, a natural affinity for participation or having the privilege of time and space or allowing for flexibility and evolving opportunities for interaction, both researchers found themselves participating 'with' SDP participants in the context of their everyday lives and SDP pursuits. In Rwanda, Marchesseault found himself cycling the famous hillsides of East Africa with Team Rwanda, embodying their everyday, inclusive of their training regimes and life off the bicycle (Marchesseault 2016). In Liberia, I found myself coaching a community football team created and financed by international religious and philanthropic agencies with the objective of youth social and moral development (Collison 2016). The use of sporting skill in this context was specifically applied, organically and unintentionally, to enhance social interaction and constructing a role 'within' which transcended the boundaries of SDP programmes. Immersed in the act of SDP and with the participants in their homes and communities, PSIR allowed the researchers to discover embodied and social experiences which contextualised their realities, culture, social positions and the transferable (if any) impacts of SDP on their lives. The notion of applying one's skills in the field as a strategy to establish perspective, purpose and position, while creating a balanced exchange through shared interests is the central act of PSIR. PSIR is a physical and literal understanding of research 'with' participants instead of 'on' them.

Evans-Pritchard (1974: 79) argues that 'to understand a people's thought one has to be able to think in their symbols'. Through PSIR, field researchers are allowed and forced into worlds of meaning and symbols that ultimately provide researchers with nuanced and rich descriptions of participants' lived experiences from within, outside and around SDP. Participatory Research broadly and PSIR more specifically naturally connects to social anthropology by virtue of social and cultural exploration and the priority given to local voices, immersion and positionality as an outsider–insider. This contrasts with PAR which, in the absence of social anthropology, confirms and sustains outsider status for the researcher. As with any methodological approach, PSIR has its limits and challenges.

The most significant challenge is establishing a 'way in' to create opportunities to transition from passive to active within the fieldwork process. Yet there are endless possibilities within and outside of sport, from officiating, volunteering, coaching, recreational participation in sport, attendance to community events or gatherings are a few examples. Once a role is established and begins to evolve, *time* becomes the critical factor to effectively dilute outsider identity and construct social interaction, cultural translation and interpretation of the symbolic and social meanings and impact of SDP participation. Time, cultural slippage and local barriers to social interaction (language, distrust, local resistance to 'others') are all significant threats to the PSIR framework. Of course, there is always the local expectation of *action* to manage within the context of development and aid, associated with outsiders. Here I would suggest that time, familiarity and commitment to people and community helps to manage such expectations. Yet the depth of knowledge production, thick description, interpretation of social and cultural systems and the importance placed on those at the receiving end of policy agendas and SDP allows for important accounts of experience and impact which may, in turn, allow for an enhanced humanistic approach to examining organisational practices and programming.

Conclusion

For some time, academics have exposed and called for richer accounts of SDP experiences, the need to hear local and silenced voices and the tensions within global North reporting, which lacks credible social and cultural understanding beyond immediate spaces of organisational practice. Arguably we have become accustomed to 'thin descriptions' of SDP work and experiences. That's not to criticise the notable work of my colleagues, peers and those that have influenced my passion for research in the sector, but such reflections have become regular sources of debate and frustration. For example, it has been suggested that 'grassroots practitioners' knowledge, and in particular young, female Africans' knowledge, is rarely considered as part of the evidence base of sport for development and is often dismissed in favor of knowledges emanating from the Global North' (Nicholls *et al.* 2011: 250). Despite evidence of some cultural commentary within case study research, cultural context needs to exceed the historical, social and ethnic narratives and background that directs development programming from afar. An anthropological perspective goes beyond this by providing deeper understandings of the beliefs and meanings that local populations place on actions, words and their everyday realities.

In this chapter I have suggested why and how social anthropology can provide an important perspective and lens to speak to the challenges associated with SDP research and how the discipline can advance our current understandings of its practice, purpose and impact. From the perspective of social anthropology, it is important to remember that any account of SDP ultimately refers to people, place and programming. But this chapter argues that reference is not enough nor adequate: cultural context, social systems, everyday realities, personal experiences and transitions of movement, thought and behaviour within and beyond the spaces of SDP activity are vitally important. Fundamentally, any discussion of SDP needs to recognise both people(s) and culture in the process of inquiry. As an anthropologist, I would suggest this needs to be the entry point of any investigation. The exception to this of course is the use of sport, or indeed SDP, to access the everyday and local populations; but this needs to go beyond the entry point of sport and its facilitators.

PAR and PSIR are both potential methodological options to enact an anthropological perspective. Through the pursuit of participation, culturally specific origins of perspective, approach and behaviours can be explored. In the absence of an anthropological lens, however, this approach may be deemed as narrow and restricted by physical space, types of voice and the realities of the marginal, targeted, decision-makers and practitioners. A deeper inquiry, immersion and, if possible, embodiment responds to these limitations and allows for description, interpretation, reflection and analysis that exceeds the immediate, the superfluous and the distraction often presented by the performance and participation of sport itself. I will also take this final opportunity to expose another missing voice from research, and that is the often-silenced voice of the researcher. The 'I' and 'my' interpretive and reflective stance is arguably an important source of knowledge production and part of the cultural translation needed in SDP research. It is often the individuals, charismatic leaders, or social groups that capture our fieldwork experience and it is in the description and narratives of these individuals and groups that fieldwork comes to life for the reader. The researchers' lived experience in the field, voice and personal belief system and reflections are part of the research process, yet there continues to be resistance to explore and expose these. Reciprocity in voice is a further extension of what social anthropology and its methodological intricacies can contribute to SDP research.

Despite the challenges associated with participation and the objective of change or the personal standpoint of interaction and social reciprocity, participation with an anthropological perspective may be the answer to those of us unable to commit to traditional exploration over a prolonged period of time. SDP and social anthropology naturally connect, which has been demonstrated through significant work cited in this chapter and by anthropologists working in the field of development.

References

Amit, V. (ed.). (2003). *Constructing the Field: Ethnographic Fieldwork in the Contemporary World*. London: Routledge.

Blanchard, K. (1985). Sports studies and the anthropology of sport. *American Sport Culture: The Humanistic Dimensions*. Lewisburg, PA: Bucknell University Press.

Burnett, C. (2008). Participatory action research (PAR) in monitoring and evaluation of sport-for-development programmes: Sport and physical activity. *African Journal for Physical Health Education, Recreation and Dance, 14*(3), 225–239.

Carter, T. (2002). On the need for an anthropological approach to sport. *Identities: Global Studies in Culture and Power, 9*(3), 405–422.

Chawansky, M. (2015). 'You're juicy': Autoethnography as evidence in sport for development and peace (SDP) research, *Qualitative Research in Sport, Exercise and Health, 7*(1), 1–12.

Clifford, J. (1992) Traveling cultures. In L. Grossberg, C. Nelson and P. A. Treichler (eds), *Cultural Studies*. New York & London: Routledge, pp. 96–116.

Coalter, F. (2010). The politics of sport-for-development: Limited focus programmes and broad gauge problems? *International Review for the Sociology of Sport, 45*(3), 295–314.

Collison, H. (2016). *Youth and Sport for Development: The Seduction of Football in Liberia*. London: Palgrave MacMillan.

Collison, H. and Marchesseault, D. (2016). Finding the missing voices of sport for development and peace (SDP): Using a 'participatory social interaction research' methodology and anthropological perspectives within African developing countries. *Sport in Society, 5*(9), 1–17.

Crewe, E. and Axelby, R. (2013). *Anthropology and Development: Culture, Morality and Politics in a Globalised World*. Cambridge: Cambridge University Press.

Culin, S. (1903). American Indian games (1902). *American Anthropologist, 5*(1), 58–64.

Darnell, S. C. and Hayhurst, L. M. (2011). Sport for decolonization: Exploring a new praxis of sport for development. *Progress in Development Studies, 11*(3), 183–196.

Dyck, N. (ed.). (2000). *Games, Sports and Cultures*. Oxford: Berg.

Dyck, N. (2003). Home field advantage? Exploring the social construction of children's sports. *Constructing the Field*. London: Routledge, pp. 40–61.

Eriksen, T. H. (2001). *Small Places, Large Issues: An Introduction to Social and Cultural Anthropology (2nd edn)*. London: Pluto.

Eriksen, T. H. (2017). *What is Anthropology?* London: Pluto.

Escobar, A. (1991). Anthropology and the development encounter: The making and marketing of development anthropology. *American Ethnologist, 18*(4), 658–682.

Evans-Pritchard, E. (1974). *The Nuer: A Description of the Modes of Livelihood and Political Institutions of a Nilotic People*. New York: Oxford University Press.

Firth, R. (1981). Engagement and detachment: reflections on applying social anthropology to social affairs. *Human Organization*, 40(3), 193–201.

Firth, R. (1990). Encounters with Tikopia over sixty years. *Oceania*, 60(4), 241–249.

Geertz, C. (1973). Thick description: Toward an interpretive theory of culture. *The Interpretation of Cultures*, New York: Basic, pp. 3–30.

Green, M. (2006). International development, social analysis … and anthropology? *Applications of Anthropology: Professional Anthropology in the Twenty-first Century*, 23(2), 110–123.

Gupta, A. and Ferguson, J. (1997) Discipline and practice: 'The field' as site, method, and location in anthropology. In A. Gupta and J. Ferguson (eds), *Anthropological Locations. Boundaries and Grounds of a Field Science*. Berkeley, CA & London: University of California Press, pp. 1–46.

Hall, B. L. (1981). Participatory research, popular knowledge and power: A personal reflection. *Convergence*, 14(3), 6.

Hammersley, M. and Atkinson, P. (2007). *Ethnography: Principles in Practice (3rd edn)*. London & New York: Routledge.

Hastrup, K. and Hervik, P. (eds) (1994a). Introduction. *Social Experience and Anthropological Knowledge*. New York & London: Routledge, pp. 1–27.

Hayhurst, L. M. (2009). The power to shape policy: Charting sport for development and peace policy discourses. *International Journal of Sport Policy*, 1(2), 203–227.

Kay, T. (2009). Developing through sport: Evidencing sport impacts on young people. *Sport in Society*, 12(9), 1177–1191.

Kidd, B. (2008). A new social movement: Sport for development and peace. *Sport in Society*, 11(4), 370–380.

Kindon, S., Pain, R. and Kesby, M. (eds) (2007). *Participatory Action Research Approaches and Methods: Connecting People, Participation and Place*. London: Routledge.

Layton, R. (1997). *An Introduction to Theory in Anthropology*. Cambridge: Cambridge University Press.

Lesser, A. (1933). *The Pawnee Ghost Dance Hand Game: A Study of Cultural Change* (Vol. 16). New York: Columbia University Press.

Maanen, J.V. (1988). *Tales of the Field: On Writing Ethnography*. Chicago: University of Chicago Press.

Malinowski, B. (1945). *The dynamics of Culture Change: An Inquiry into Race Relations in Africa*. New Haven, CT: Yale University Press.

Marchesseault, D. (2016). The Everyday Breakaway: Participant Perspectives of Everyday Life Within a Sport for Development and Peace Program. Available at: https://tspace.library.utoronto.ca/handle/1807/76481.

Mooney, J. (1890). The Cherokee ball game. *American Anthropologist*, 3(2), 105–132.

Mosse, D. (2001). Social research in rural development projects. *Inside Organizations. Anthropologists at Work*. Oxford & New York: Berg.

Nicholls, S., Giles, A. R. and Sethna, C. (2011). Perpetuating the 'lack of evidence' discourse in sport for development: Privileged voices, unheard stories and subjugated knowledge. *International Review for the Sociology of Sport*, 46(3), 249–264.

Okely, J. (1992) Anthropology and autobiography: Participatory experience and embodied knowledge. In J. Okely and H. Callaway (eds), *Anthropology and Autobiography*. ASA Monographs 29. London & New York: Routledge, pp. 1–28.

Pink, S. (ed.). (2006). *Applications of Anthropology: Professional Anthropology in the Twenty-First Century* (Vol. 2). Oxford: Berghahn.

Roberts, J. M., Arth, M. J. and Bush, R. R. (1959). Games in culture. *American Anthropologist*, 61(4), 597–605.

Sahlins, M. (1999). What is anthropological enlightenment? Some lessons of the twentieth century. *Annual Review of Anthropology*, 28(1), i–xxiii.

Sands, R. R. (2002). *Sport Ethnography*. Champaign, IL: Human Kinetics.

Schensul, J. (2013). Community-based research organizations: Co-constructing public knowledge and bridging knowledge/action communities through PAR. In S. Beck and C. A. Maida (eds), *Public Anthropology in a Borderless World*. New York: Berghahn.

Schensul, S. L., Schensul, J. J., Singer, M., Weeks, M. and Brault, M. (2015). Participatory methods and community-based collaborations. *Handbook of Methods in Cultural Anthropology*, 2, 185–212.

Schnegg, M. (2014). Epistemology: The nature and validation of knowledge. In, H. R. Bernard and C. C. Gravlee (eds), *Handbook of Methods in Cultural Anthropology*. Lanham, MD: Rowman and Littlefield.

Sherry, E., Schulenkorf, N., Seal, E., Nicholson, M. and Hoye, R. (2017). Sport-for-development: Inclusive, reflexive, and meaningful research in low-and middle-income settings. *Sport Management Review*, *20*(1), 69–80.

Spaaij, R. (2012). Beyond the playing field: Experiences of sport, social capital, and integration among Somalis in Australia. *Ethnic and Racial Studies*, *35*(9), 1519–1538.

Tylor, E. B. (1879). The History of Games. Available at: https://en.wikisource.org/wiki/Popular_Science_Monthly/Volume_15/June_1879/The_History_of_Games.

20

SDP and sport psychology

Andrew M. Guest

Introduction

The language and the goals of Sports for Development and Peace (SDP), like the language of sports itself, are often very psychological. Programs claim to build confidence and self-esteem, they target behavioral and personality traits identified as life skills, they aim to facilitate healthy child and youth development, they work to reduce prejudice and discrimination, they aspire to promote mental health and wellness, and they proclaim a wide range of other individualized and psychological goals. The United Nations Office on Sport for Development and Peace, for example, describes the role of sport for the UN in largely psychological terms: sport 'can make a difference where other means have failed. Sport provides a forum to learn skills such as discipline, confidence, and leadership, and it teaches core principles such as tolerance, cooperation, respect, and the value of effort' (United Nations Office on Sport for Development and Peace n.d.). Ironically, however, and with some notable exceptions (e.g. Blom *et al.* 2015; Schinke *et al.* 2016), psychologists themselves have not been regularly involved with or included in SDP initiatives.

One recent review of academic literature on sport for development, for example, identified the top 10 journal outlets for academic work on SDP and none were from sport psychology – most were from either the sociology of sport or sport management (Schulenkorf *et al.* 2016). Yet, when the review identified the 11 theoretical frameworks most frequently employed in SDP research, over half have significant psychological dimensions: positive youth development, social learning theory, identity theory, social cognitive theory, social inclusion theory, and the social education model. This SDP paradox of heavily psychological goals, concepts, language, and theory contrasted with relatively little contribution from psychologists begs an obvious question: why are sport psychologists largely missing from the action?

One reason for the relative dearth of sport psychologists involved in SDP is the complicated nature of sport psychology as a field. Much of what is usually called sport psychology is primarily focused on mental skills for performance enhancement in elite sports contexts. One recent review of 795 articles in mainstream sport psychology journals, for example, found almost no research on SDP – instead topics such as motivation and performance anxiety seem to dominate the field (Lindahl *et al.* 2015). Even research on youth development in sports contexts comprised only about 21 of 795 articles in the review. In general, even outside of SDP contexts, researchers and practitioners associated with sport psychology tend to focus on high-level sport performance more than issues of mental health, community development, or grassroots sport – the types of psychological issues that might be more relevant in international development work.

Sport psychology as a field has also tended to be dominated by Western approaches and perspectives from the global North. This is starting to change, and there have been several recent calls for more inclusive and reflexive cultural perspectives in sport psychology (e.g. Schnike *et al.* 2012; Ryba *et al.* 2013; Blodgett *et al.* 2015). In fact, in 2016 the International Society of Sport Psychology put forward a position stand on 'social missions through sport and exercise psychology' that explicitly promoted a need for culturally sensitive and reflexive sport psychology as a potential contributor to SDP (Schinke *et al.* 2016). Yet, other major sport psychology academic journals including *The Sport Psychologist*; *Psychology of Sport and Exercise*; *Sport, Exercise, and Performance Psychology*; and the *Journal of Clinical Sport Psychology* have published virtually nothing in the last five years that relates directly to international development.

Ultimately, the contrast between the relative prevalence of psychological concepts in SDP theory and the relative absence of psychologists in SDP practice may be best explained by the realities of what it means to do sports and development work on the ground. I have written elsewhere about children participating in SDP programs whom I have met in places such as Angolan refugee camps (Guest 2013a). One participant, pseudonymously called Diego, was a seven-year-old boy without functioning legs who also happened to be an avid soccer player (simply using his hands to bat the ball and move around the field according to a set of adaptive rules created and tacitly agreed to entirely by his peer group). Diego's family lived in extreme poverty, housed in a hut made of sticks, mud, and old UN tarps and subsisted largely on donated food and bartered goods. Yet, despite the massive structural obstacles Diego faced, he displayed the type of psychological adaptability and resilience that so often characterizes children in marginalized communities (e.g. Masten 2015). Watching Diego joyfully engage in his daily games of pickup soccer, and competently navigate his challenging day-to-day tasks, it was hard to think that Diego's primary developmental needs were improved life skills, better self-esteem, or other psychological traits. Instead, it seemed clear that Diego's development depended heavily upon access to the types of external assets available in communities that allow possibilities for individual social mobility: functioning schools, living wage jobs, decent healthcare, and safe places to live, work, and play.

Using sport psychology in SDP, in other words, is risky. If not done thoughtfully and through collaboration, psychological perspectives can individualize poverty and oversimplify global inequality. When done well, however, psychology has significant contributions to make and perspectives to offer that can improve the SDP movement. In what follows, this chapter will explore examples of both the potential and the complications of sport psychology in SDP contexts. The intention is not to provide a comprehensive review, but instead to offer targeted examples of how psychology relates to several themes in SDP work: positive youth development, health education, and peacebuilding and prejudice reduction. Following brief discussions of each of those areas, the chapter will also discuss promising directions for future contributions of sport psychology to SDP. While sport psychology can apply to a wide variety of SDP domains (including, for example, gender issues and disability sport – which are also dealt with elsewhere in this handbook), the underlying themes of this chapter should be relevant regardless of domain: sport psychology can best serve the SDP movement by being culturally sensitive, empirically informed, and collaborative.

Positive youth development and life skills

The psychology most often employed in SDP endeavors derives from a mix of both performance enhancement sport psychology and broader psychological theory – a mix most evident in efforts to employ a positive youth development perspective. The broad approach, which has become popular in psychology as a whole in recent decades (e.g. Larson 2000), evolved in response to a sense that psychology often focused too much on deficit models redressing pathology and deviance and not enough on asset models attentive to well-being and strength building. One prevalent positive youth development scheme, for example, specifically identifies both internal assets – such as positive values and a commitment to learning – and external assets – such as constructive ways to use time and supportive school climates – that youth programs can help to build to promote healthy development and psychological well-being (Scales and Leffert 2004). Much of this work has also been situated in programs that facilitate youth development through arts, music, service, sports, and other related activities. Partially because of the broad popularity of sports in youth culture, there has been particular interest in what is now often called 'sport-based youth development' as an avenue to employ positive youth development theory (e.g. Holt 2016).

The sport-based youth development approach also tends to emphasize building life skills as a central concern that occasionally harkens back to the idea of sport building character. One oft-cited discussion of building life skills through sports programs, for example, defines life skills as 'those internal personal assets, characteristics, and skills such as goalsetting, emotional control, self-esteem, and hard work ethic that can be facilitated or developed in sport and are transferred for use in non-sport settings' (Gould and Carson 2008: 60). Though sport programs using this life-skills approach have been more common in North America and the global North than in international sports and development efforts, international organizations such as UNICEF have also made life-skill building central to global development efforts.

While the rhetoric of positive youth development and life skills has been very common among SDP practitioners, research examples applying the approach to international SDP have only gradually emerged. One example is a line of research that takes a particularly direct approach to using mental skills training techniques from sport psychology toward facilitating development with people ranging from Mexican gang members, to Argentine 'barrio' dwellers, to Botswanan youth coaches (Hanrahan 2011; Hanrahan and Ramm 2015; Hanrahan and Tshube 2016). While these applications and studies are useful in demonstrating the value of psychological skills training, they do leave open the question of how such training may relate to longer-term youth and community development. In an application with Mexican former gang members and drug users, for example, Hanrahan and Ramm (2015) found that sport-based psychological skills training on topics such as goal setting, imagery, and self-talk was effective in increasing participant happiness but they note that the initial happiness scores of individual participants already tended to be above average. As they explain:

> although the mean pre-test happiness scores of the former gang members were above the normative mean, the participants still represent a disadvantaged group. Just because they did not score below the norm for happiness before the intervention does not mean that they could not benefit from even higher levels of happiness. After all, it may be easier to increase the well-being of individuals in this population than it is to change socio-economic factors.
> *Hanrahan and Ramm 2015: 45*

While it is likely true that increasing happiness is easier than changing socio-economic factors, the question still remains as to whether improving already high levels of psychological well-being for disadvantaged groups serves to genuinely address development and inequality.

Other efforts to promote life skills and positive youth development in SDP settings have built on physical education theories such as Hellison's Teaching Personal and Social Responsibility (TPSR) model (Hellison 2011). Whitely *et al.* (2015), for example, undertook research in Kayamandi Township in South Africa with the explicit intent of trying to understand what life skills and competencies associated with sport might be most culturally relevant in the particular local context of Kayamandi. They found both similarities and differences in local understandings of competencies and life skills associated with sport when compared with conventional Western understandings. While, for example, Kayamandi residents emphasize the importance of familiar life skills such as leadership and goal setting, the most commonly discussed competency locally was '*Ubuntu*' defined as a multidimensional respect and caring for others. This effort to broaden and contextualize the definition of life skills related to sport offers a relatively rare but promising example of how SDP programs might employ more culturally sensitive versions of positive youth development.

As a final example of a positive youth development approach to SDP, Mandigo *et al.* (2016) offer a useful illustration through their work with physical education teachers in El Salvador. Also employing the TPSR model, this program began by working with physical education teachers-in-training to promote a life skills-based approach. Putting particular emphasis on preventing youth violence, the research tracked a variety of life skills-related outcomes for students over a three-year period. While results in some domains were mixed, the program did show positive effects in locally relevant skills such as nonviolent conflict resolution. Importantly, this effort also demonstrated the value of collaborating with schools and educators to implement SDP initiatives. The idea that SDP programs can offer sustainable and locally relevant life skills through short-term interventions of the type popular in sport psychology more broadly seems limited for international development work. But, the idea that sport psychology can offer ways of understanding and promoting life skills for ongoing and collaborative sport-based youth development efforts in international contexts holds significant promise.

Health promotion

Given the inherent physicality of sport, the idea of connecting physical health with participation in SDP programs has a broad intuitive appeal. But increasing physical activity by itself is rarely enough to justify targeted SDP interventions. Instead, most SDP programs oriented to health promotion try to connect sports with educational activities oriented to health knowledge. For these programs to succeed the mechanisms are necessarily psychological: shifting attitudes and behaviors through educational engagement involves both motivation and persuasion. Further, some well-known SDP programs are explicit in drawing on psychological theory in their program design. Grassroot Soccer, for example, draws on Bandura's Social Learning Theory as the foundation for its efforts to address HIV through athlete role models and interactive teaching associated with sports activities (Kaufman *et al.* 2013).

While this general idea has often been applied to HIV prevention, particularly in sub-Saharan Africa, the broad concepts of using athlete role models and engaging sports contexts as ways to convey health messaging also has a more general appeal. In conjunction with recent soccer World Cups, for example, FIFA developed a program called '11 for Health' that attempted to collaborate with national organizations to convey health messages ranging from the importance of treated bed nets in preventing malaria to the importance of handwashing for basic hygiene.

FIFA has collected evidence from programs in countries ranging from Brazil to Zimbabwe to suggest significant gains in health knowledge after 11 educational sessions of 90 minutes split between developing football skills and learning about health issues (e.g. Fuller *et al.* 2011; Fuller *et al.* 2015), though most of these studies did not include a comparison group receiving educational messages in non-sport contexts. These programs have also offered successful examples of collaborations in SDP between international sports organizations and national Ministries of Education along with NGOs and smaller sports organizations.

While improving health knowledge is always a good thing, one vexing issue that arises in related psychological literature is the complicated relationship between knowledge, attitudes, and behavior change. Put simply, it is not always the case that understanding health risks leads to behaving in ways that prevent risk. As one example from the broader psychological literature on adolescent development, research has made it clear that much adolescent risk-taking is based less on cognitive understandings of risk and more on the emotional rewards of risk-taking (Steinberg 2008). Thus, adolescents may know the health risks of smoking and drinking but still engage in those behaviors when in peer contexts that offer immediate rewards.

This distinction between knowledge and behavior may be particularly important in sport-based HIV prevention efforts. In an assessment of HIV prevention efforts through the Mathare Youth Sports Association in Kenya, for example, researchers found that teenage sport program participants exposed to information about the importance of condom use were somewhat more likely to use condoms during intercourse, but overall rates of condom use were still 'disturbingly low' (Delva *et al.* 2010). Consistent condom use was reported by only 23.2 percent of participants in the sports program. The participants, in other words, all had exposure to the knowledge about the importance of condom use, but the overwhelming majority did not translate that knowledge into behavior change.

The challenges of ensuring that the lessons of sport interventions transfer from knowledge to attitudes and behavior are also evident in the programs of Grassroot Soccer, which has been a leader in gathering evidence about the effectiveness of SDP programming. Following a 2013 literature review by Kaufman *et al.* on the effectiveness of sport-based HIV prevention interventions, which found generally positive effects on participant knowledge and self-reported behavior but a relatively low quality of research design, Grassroot Soccer initiated one of the rare large-scale randomized controlled trials of an SDP intervention to test its sport-based HIV prevention curriculum. This 'Goal Trial' study was undertaken in South African schools and involved the random assignment of thousands of adolescent schoolchildren to either the Grassroot Soccer sport-based HIV prevention program or a more general life orientation class. Though final results of the three-year study seem to not yet have been published, mid-trial results reported by Kaufman (2014) suggest that the sport-based program had a very positive effect on both HIV-related knowledge and HIV testing. But, surprisingly, the trial also found a deleterious effect for males on behaviors such as multiple sexual partners and the perpetration of intimate partner violence. As Kaufman (2014: 3) summarizes 'the midline results suggest the SBHP [sport-based HIV prevention] intervention was not effective in achieving its primary behavioural objectives but did improve HIV-related knowledge and HIV testing uptake among males'.

Grassroot Soccer has found success through randomized controlled trial research in other sport-based health interventions such as promoting male circumcision as a way of reducing HIV risk (Kaufman *et al.* 2016), and should be commended for their rigorous attention to evidence. Some of that evidence, however, illustrates the complexity of using sport to shift attitudes and motivate behavioral change. From a psychological perspective it is simply not enough to convey knowledge if the goal is to genuinely improve health as part of the broader development endeavor. Sport psychology may, therefore, best help initiatives interested in promoting health through sport by careful empirical attention to differences between knowledge and behavior while also collaborating toward addressing the broader structural inequalities that shape health outcomes.

Peacebuilding and prejudice reduction

The popular rhetoric of sports as a universal language and way to bring people together lends itself naturally towards efforts to break down barriers between groups. Of course, as commentators from George Orwell on have countered, sport also has a historical tendency to divide and reify artificial group identities. There is a large social psychological literature about this identity process, often descended from Tajfel's Social Identity Theory (1982). At its most basic level, this theory suggests that the human mind is primed to identify in-groups and out-groups in ways that are often automatic and superficial. Thus, for example, fans of rival professional sports teams who otherwise have much in common display a seemingly irrational enmity simply because of group affiliations marked largely by different colored jerseys. And, inversely, people who may not otherwise have much in common can sometimes bond through their participation on a team with shared goals that require collective effort. A significant number of SDP programs have arisen to try facilitating the seeming ease with which sport shapes human bonds towards broader developmental goals. While some of these programs are oriented towards diversity and inclusion around issues such as gender, race, and sexuality, at an international level many programs focus on mitigating regional and ethnic political conflicts. Though all these types of programs merit academic consideration and involve psychological dimensions, for the sake of example this chapter will focus on SDP programs oriented to peacebuilding and prejudice reduction.

As one example of such an initiative that draws explicitly on psychological theory, Tuohey and Cognato (2011) have described PeacePlayers International as a program where the theory of change is based on Allport's contact hypothesis. The program has offered basketball programs in regions identified as conflict zones including parts of South Africa, Northern Ireland, Israel and the West Bank, Cyprus, and New Orleans. The basketball teams attempt to bring people together from across group divides to work toward common sport goals using Allport's guidelines that contact across social groups can reduce prejudice when people engage in activities that are guided, when the groups have relatively equal status during their interactions, when there are realistic opportunities for meaningful interpersonal relationships, and when the activities are sanctioned by a recognized authorities. Tuohey and Cognato also draw on classic research in social psychology such as Muzafer Sharif's 'Robber's Cave' experiment, to emphasize that basketball can provide 'superordinate goals' that require individuals to work together in ways that serve a bonding function. Tuohey and Cognato report that when well-designed with local leadership, a balance of sports and educational content, long-term programming, along with careful monitoring and evaluation, PeacePlayers International programs have had success reducing prejudice and promoting peace (Tuohey and Cognato 2011).

Sport sociologist John Sugden has also been involved with related programs using soccer for peace in Northern Ireland and in Israel, and tends to be positive but a bit more circumspect about the effects of peacebuilding through sport. Sugden (2010 : 258) argues that while 'sport is intrinsically value neutral … under carefully managed circumstances it can make a positive if modest contribution to peace building'. Importantly, Sugden suggests this contribution comes mostly through a 'ripple effect' where small local programs necessarily interact with other micro and macro social and political forces. In other words, SDP programs based on contact theory and other psychological concepts primarily make contributions only as they collaboratively and intentionally connect with political and social systems in conflict zones.

Other sociological analyses of peacebuilding and prejudice reduction through SDP programs can be more explicitly critical. Donnelly, for example, describes the nature of sport in development as 'Janus-faced' and argues that

> employing sport in reconciliation initiatives is like playing with fire, and requires careful planning and a great deal of caution. It is possible, under carefully controlled circumstances, to accomplish a great deal of 'good' with sport, but the more destructive potential is always there.
>
> *Donnelly 2011: 74*

This critique resonates with other psychological literature on contact theory and social identity formation, suggesting that intergroup interactions can often inflame conflict as easily as they soothe tensions (e.g. Barlow *et al.* 2012). This may be particularly true in sport contexts where emotions run hot and there can be a tacit acceptance of degrees of aggression and hostility.

Though there is not an extensive academic literature about situations where SDP programs have inflamed intergroup tensions, likely at least partially because few programs would want such an outcome publicized, there are examples where peacebuilding and prejudice reduction through sport confronts pragmatic obstacles. Litvak-Hirsch and colleagues (2015), for example, describe a two-year study of the 'United Soccer for Peace' program in Israel designed to mitigate conflict between Jewish and Arab Israelis. While the program, focused on training coaches and based again on Allport's contact hypothesis, did have some modest success in shifting attitudes and in motivating participants to work for change, the program also confronted logistical challenges. At several sites, for example, groups that were initially balanced between Jewish and Arab participants ended up with all the Arab participants dropping out. While the researchers were not able to discern the exact reason why all the Arab coaches left, they speculate that hosting training sessions in predominantly Jewish areas, administering training primarily in Hebrew, and recruiting Arab coaches with limited sport backgrounds may have discouraged Arab participants. Whatever the specifics, using contact theory to reduce intergroup conflict in a setting where one group is unavailable for interaction, is an inherently futile effort. This example thus serves as a further reminder that the best designed psychological interventions can only produce developmental outcomes when other aspects of the social, political, and cultural context are carefully considered.

Future directions for sport psychology in SDP

As should be evident in the above examples, if sport psychology is to make constructive contributions to SDP endeavors, a primary theme will need to be collaboration. Psychological theories offer useful conceptual tools for designing and implementing SDP programs, and sport psychologists offer skills and knowledge that can enhance the developmental value of sport. But psychology as a field and sport psychology as a sub-discipline have not always been very good at accounting for culture and context. Further, psychology is an inherently individualizing endeavor. International development, in contrast, depends greatly on deep understandings of social, cultural, economic, and political contexts along with significant structural inequalities that limit opportunities regardless of individual merit. Fortunately, sport psychologists are beginning to develop schemes that involve both collaboration and cultural sensitivity in approaching SDP.

As one useful example, Blom *et al.* (2015) offered reflections on their experiences as scholars and practitioners with backgrounds in sport psychology undertaking international SDP programs in the *Journal of Sport Psychology in Action*. They offer the acronym RESPOND to conceptualize and operationalize ways of partnering with non-academic organizations undertaking sports and development work. The acronym suggests collaboratively developing '*relevant, empowering, sustainable partnerships* that promote local *opportunities, networks*, and *development*'. (Blom *et al.* 2015: 4) Such collaborations, particularly with organizations experienced in international development and with grassroots organizations already working in target communities, may allow sport psychology to avoid assumptions of deficiency in target communities and of the universality of particular psychological skills.

Likewise, I have suggested elsewhere that sport psychology might do well to frame its potential contributions to SDP more in relation to the skills of successful process consultation, and less in relation to the tools of performance enhancement (Guest 2013b). Effective sport psychology practice depends upon careful listening, ongoing reflexivity, and thoughtful assessment. Similarly, effective SDP practice depends upon understanding local needs, ongoing attention to program quality, and meaningful monitoring and evaluation. As such, sport psychology may be best able to contribute to SDP by combining a deep understanding of the dynamics of sport with practical skills that might complement and supplement the work of SDP and international development initiatives.

Such a contribution would also depend greatly on moving beyond the individualizing tendencies of sport psychology. While sport psychology is still largely focused on individual performance enhancement, the growing popularity of sport-based youth development programs that draw on psychological concepts and knowledge may offer opportunities to attend more carefully to communities and broader social change. As an example, Petitpas *et al.* (2016) recently called for more collaborative efforts between sport psychology initiatives and community-based sport and physical activity programs with a focus on North American contexts. This call included an emphasis on balancing traditional positive youth development foci with broader attention to 'community youth development'. The emphasis in a community youth development approach is on facilitating constructive relationships, tangible opportunities, and local ownership of development initiatives. In other words, the intention is to balance a focus on external and community-level assets with internal and psychological assets.

Working collaboratively with SDP initiatives, international development programs, other sport scholars, and local communities also offers important opportunities to be empirically informed and culturally relevant. How can SDP programs, for example, know whether the life skills they intend to promote are both needed and relevant in target communities? As noted earlier, and as emphasized by other sport psychology scholars (e.g. Whitely *et al.* 2015), one way to answer that question is to listen through reflexive research and collaborative needs assessments. In doing so, some scholars have raised questions about the popularity of common SDP program goals such as raising self-esteem in communities where that particular 'life skill' is not particularly deficient (e.g. Coalter 2010). Likewise, in my own work I have questioned the cultural relevance and relativity of both self-esteem and other popular life skills such as teamwork (Guest 2007; Guest 2008).

One other potentially promising way for sport psychology to work toward cultural relevance is to focus less on top-down programming and more on facilitating healthy developmental spaces for sports and play. As Lawson (2005) notes in offering a social work perspective on sports and development, 'in many parts of the world, awareness has grown about the need to do more than teach, coach, and counsel individuals and groups. There is an accompanying need to *create health-enhancing settings and environments*' (Lawson 2005: 144). This idea is also consistent with calls in the sport management literature for SDP programs to work towards creating safe spaces for sport and play that include psychological safety (Spaaij and Schulenkorf 2014). Such spaces might be particularly relevant in post-conflict and post-disaster settings, where SDP programs emphasizing mental health have grown popular though they are currently under-researched (Hamilton *et al.* 2016). In North American sport-based youth development research there is also a small literature on 'trauma-informed sports programming' (e.g. Bergholz *et al.* 2016) that may offer useful ways of integrating psychological approaches with sports and development. But that literature, as with so many of the potential applications of sport psychology in SDP, is still evolving and would benefit from further evidence, particularly if applied in diverse cultural settings.

Conclusion

So could a child such as Diego, a disabled boy in an Angolan refugee camp, really benefit from a psychological approach to SDP? At this point, the best answer is probably 'maybe'. Psychology as a field, and sport psychology as a sub-discipline, do offer useful theoretical foundations for SDP initiatives: positive youth development (along with the community youth development), social learning theory, the contact hypothesis, and other psychological concepts are regularly employed as guides for programs otherwise motivated largely by a belief in the pure power of sport. Further, a psychological orientation at its best should emphasize skills essential to quality SDP initiatives: careful listening and needs assessment, cultural sensitivity, and attention to reflexive process along with empirical evidence. If sport psychology were one part of collaborative efforts in communities such as Diego's, working together with local grassroots organizations, school systems, and/or other development scholars and programs to complement and supplement existing sports and play initiatives, these concepts and skills could be part of genuine development through sports. At the same time, however, sport psychology has sometimes been better at attending to elite performance enhancement than cultural sensitivity and social consciousness. Integrating psychology into SDP, as per psychology as a field, risks individualizing and pathologizing marginalized peoples and communities. Children such as Diego don't necessarily need their sports and play to be leavened with psychological intervention, but when done well quality SDP initiatives can benefit from being psychologically informed.

References

Barlow, F. K., Paolini, S., Pedersen, A., Hornsey, M. J., Radke, H. R., Harwood, J. Rubin, M. and Sibley, C. G. (2012). The contact caveat: Negative contact predicts increased prejudice more than positive contact predicts reduced prejudice. *Personality and Social Psychology Bulletin, 38*(12), 1629–1643.

Bergholz, L., Stafford, E. and D'Andrea, W. (2016). Creating trauma-informed sports programming for traumatized youth: Core principles for an adjunctive therapeutic approach. *Journal of Infant, Child, and Adolescent Psychotherapy, 15*(3), 244–253.

Blodgett, A. T., Schinke, R. J., McGannon, K. R. and Fisher, L. A. (2015). Cultural sport psychology research: Conceptions, evolutions, and forecasts. *International Review of Sport and Exercise Psychology, 8*(1), 24–43.

Blom, L. C., Judge, L., Whitley, M. A., Gerstein, L., Huffman, A. and Hillyer, S. (2015). Sport for development and peace: Experiences conducting US and international programs. *Journal of Sport Psychology in Action, 6*(1),1–16.

Coalter, F. (2010). Sport-for-Development Impact Study. A Research Initiative Funded by Comic Relief and UK Sport and Managed by International Development through Sport. Stirling, Scotland: University of Stirling.

Delva, W., Michielsen, K., Meulders, B., Groeninck, S., Wasonga, E., Ajwang, P., Temmerman, M. and Vanreusel B. (2010). HIV prevention through sport: The case of the Mathare Youth Sport Association in Kenya. *AIDS Care, 22*(8), 1012–1020.

Donnelly, P. (2011). From war without weapons to sport for development and peace: The Janus-face of sport. *SAIS Review of International Affairs, 31*(1), 65–76.

Fuller, C. W., Junge, A., Dorasami, C., DeCelles, J. and Dvorak, J. (2011). '11 for Health', a football-based health education programme for children: A two-cohort study in Mauritius and Zimbabwe. *British Journal of Sports Medicine, 45*(8), 612–618.

Fuller, C. W., Thiele, E. S., Flores, M., Junge, A., Netto, D. and Dvorak, J. (2015). A successful nationwide implementation of the "FIFA 11 for Health" programme in Brazilian elementary schools. *British Journal of Sports Medicine, 49*: 623–629.

Gould, D. and Carson, S. (2008). Life skills development through sport: Current status and future directions. *International Review of Sport and Exercise Psychology, 1*(1), 58–78.

Guest, A. M. (2007). Cultures of childhood and psychosocial characteristics: Self-esteem and social comparison in two distinct communities. *Ethos, 35*: 1–32.

Guest, A. M. (2008). Reconsidering teamwork: Popular and local meanings for a common ideal associated with positive youth development. *Youth and Society, 39*(3), 340–361.

Guest, A. M. (2013a). Cultures of play during middle childhood: Interpretive perspectives from two distinct marginalized communities. *Sport, Education and Society, 18*(2), 167–183.

Guest, A. M. (2013b). Sport Psychology for development and peace? Critical reflections and constructive suggestion., *Journal of Sport Psychology in Action, 4*(3), 169–180.

Hamilton, A., Foster, C. and Richards, J. (2016). A systematic review of the mental health impacts of sport and physical activity programmes for adolescents in post-conflict settings. *Journal of Sport for Development, 4*(6), 44–59.

Hanrahan, S. J. (2011). Working in the 'villas' of Buenos Aires: Cultural considerations. *Journal of Clinical Sport Psychology, 5*(4), 361–371.

Hanrahan, S. J. and Ramm, M. D. L. F. (2015). Improving life satisfaction, self-concept, and happiness of former gang members using games and psychological skills training. *Journal of Sport for Development, 3*(4), 41–47.

Hanrahan, S. J. and Tshube T. (2016). Training the trainers in Botswana. In J. G. Cremades and L. S. Tashman (eds), *Global Practices and Training in Applied Sport, Exercise, and Performance Psychology: A Case Study Approach.* New York: Routledge.

Hellison, D. R. (2011). *Teaching Personal and Social Responsibility Through Physical Activity.* Champaign IL: Human Kinetics.

Holt, N. L. (ed.) (2016). *Positive Youth Development Through Sport.* New York: Routledge.

Kaufman, Z. A. (2014). The GOAL Trial: Sport-Based HIV Prevention in South African Schools. Doctoral dissertation, London School of Hygiene and Tropical Medicine.

Kaufman, Z. A., DeCelles, J., Bhauti, K., Hershow, R. B., Weiss, H. A. *et al.* (2016). A sport-based intervention to increase uptake of voluntary medical male circumcision among adolescent male students: Results from the MCUTS 2 cluster-randomized trial in Bulawayo, Zimbabwe. *Journal of Acquired Immune Deficiency Syndromes, 72*: S297–S303.

Kaufman, Z. A., Spencer, T. S. and Ross, D. A. (2013). Effectiveness of sport-based HIV prevention interventions: A systematic review of the evidence. *AIDS and Behavior, 17*(3), 987–1001.

Larson, R. W. (2000). Toward a psychology of positive youth development. *American Psychologist, 55*(1), 170.

Lawson, H. A. (2005). Empowering people, facilitating community development, and contributing to sustainable development: The social work of sport, exercise, and physical education programs. *Sport, Education and Society, 10*(1), 135–160.

Lindahl, J., Stenling, A., Lindwall, M. and Colliander, C. (2015). Trends and knowledge base in sport and exercise psychology research: A bibliometric review study. *International Review of Sport and Exercise Psychology, 8*(1), 71–94.

Litvak-Hirsch, T., Galily, Y. and Leitner, M. (2016). Evaluating conflict mitigation and health improvement through soccer: A two-year study of Mifalot's 'United Soccer for Peace' programme, *Soccer and Society, 17*(2), 209–224.

Mandigo, J., Corlett, J. and Ticas, P. (2016). Examining the role of life skills developed through Salvadoran physical education programs on the prevention of youth violence. *Journal of Sport for Development, 4*(7), 25–38.

Masten, A. S. (2015). *Ordinary Magic: Resilience in Development.* New York: Guilford.

Petitpas, A., Van Raalte, J. and France, T. (2016). Facilitating positive youth development by fostering collaboration among community-based sport and physical activity programs. *The Sport Psychologist, 31*(3), 1–21.

Ryba, T. V., Stambulova, N. B., Si, G. and Schinke, R. J. (2013). ISSP position stand: Culturally competent research and practice in sport and exercise psychology. *International Journal of Sport and Exercise Psychology, 11*(2), 123–142.

Scales, P. C. and Leffert, N. (2004). *Developmental Assets: A Synthesis of the Scientific Research on Adolescent Development.* Minneapolis, MN: Search Institute.

Schinke, R. J., McGannon, K. R., Parham, W. D. and Lane, A. M. (2012). Toward cultural praxis and cultural sensitivity: Strategies for self-reflexive sport psychology practice. *Quest, 64*(1), 34–46.

Schinke, R. J., Stambulova, N. R., Lidor, R., Papaioannou, A. and Ryba, T. V. (2016). ISSP position stand: Social missions through sport and exercise psychology. *International Journal of Sport and Exercise Psychology, 14*(1), 4–22.

Schulenkorf, N., Sherry, E. and K. Rowe (2016) Sport for development: An integrated literature review. *Journal of Sport Management, 30*(1), 22–39.

Spaaij, R. and Schulenkorf, N. (2014). Cultivating safe space: Lessons for sport-for-development projects and events *Journal of Sport Management, 28*(6), 633–645.

Steinberg, L. (2008). A social neuroscience perspective on adolescent risk-taking. *Developmental Review, 28*(1), 78–106.

Sugden, J. (2010). Critical left-realism and sport interventions in divided societies. *International Review for the Sociology of Sport, 45*(3), 258–272.

Tajfel, H. (ed.) (1982) *Social Identity and Intergroup Relations.* Cambridge: Cambridge University Press.

Tuohey, B. and Cognato, B. (2011). PeacePlayers International: A case study on the use of sport as a tool for conflict transformation. *SAIS Review of International Affairs, 31*(1), 51–63.

United Nations Office on Sport for Development and Peace. (n.d.). Achieving the objectives of the United Nations through sport. Available at: www.un.org/sport/content/resources/factsheets (accessed 4 February 2017).

Whitley, M. A., Hayden, L. A. and Gould, D. (2016). Growing up in the Kayamandi Township: II. Sport as a setting for the development and transfer of desirable competencies. *International Journal of Sport and Exercise Psychology, 14*(4), 305–322.

21

SDP and sport management

Jon Welty Peachey

Introduction

The sport for development and peace (SDP) field has seen remarkable growth, perhaps no more so than within the past two decades. With its roots in the ancient Olympic Games when the advent of the Games brought a temporary halt to wartime actions, and more recent initiatives to assist wounded veterans adjusting back into society after World War I (Burnett 2001), SDP has attracted policy-makers, practitioners, and scholars from a variety of disciplines due to its perceived potential to evince positive development-related outcomes at the individual, community, national, and international levels. Within the past two decades, in fact, hundreds if not thousands of SDP-related organizations have emerged around the globe targeting various development-based agendas with their programming (Schulenkorf *et al.* 2016). This proliferation of SDP organizations and SDP policy from non-governmental organizations (NGOs) and government entities has also captured the attention of scholars from across various social science disciplines, such as sociology, development studies, business management, and sport psychology. Within the past 10 years in particular, however, there has also been a growing body of SDP scholarship initiated by sport management scholars which has advanced SDP theory and praxis in important ways. This scholarship has focused on a number of key areas, such as theory and program design (Lyras *et al.* 2011; Schulenkorf 2012), SDP policy and governance (Coalter 2010; 2013), SDP program and intervention outcomes (Sherry 2010; Welty Peachey *et al.* 2013a), management and leverage of SDP events (Welty Peachey *et al.* 2015b; Schulenkorf 2016), partnerships in SDP (MacIntosh *et al.* 2016; Sherry and Schulenkorf 2016), and organizational capacity building (Svensson and Hambrick 2016). Other areas, such as leadership and volunteer management in SDP (Welty Peachey *et al.* 2015c; Welty Peachey and Burton 2016), have also begun to emerge. Critically, sport management scholars also continue to engage with the question of 'What is potentially unique about managing SDP organizations, particularly in contrast to managing other forms of sport-based organizations?'

Overall, the key contribution of sport management to the SDP field has been to bring a managerial focus to the design, implementation, and evaluation of programs and initiatives, and to examine the management of SDP organizations in ways that may differ from managing other sport (or non-sport) organizations. The purpose of this chapter, then, is to examine key areas in which the sport management discipline has (or can) contribute to advancing scholarship and praxis in SDP. To do so, the chapter offers six contributions that sport management can make to the study of SDP: theory, program design, and outcome assessment; event management; volunteer management; inter-organizational partnerships; organizational capacity building; and leadership of SDP programs and initiatives. The claim is not that these are the only areas in which sport management contributes to SDP, but the six areas do illustrate important connections between the discipline of sport management and the SDP sector. Throughout, research and advances associated with these key contributions are reviewed, and challenges discussed. The chapter concludes with remarks on salient avenues where sport management can advance future SDP scholarship and practice.

Contribution #1: Theory, program design, and outcome assessment

The first contribution sport management can make to the SDP field is to advance the development of theoretical frameworks related to SDP program design and outcomes. Here, sport management can help to address the 'black box' of SDP, which is that the processes and mechanisms through which SDP programs can potentially achieve impact are not known (Coalter 2013). Questions to be asked are: How do SDP interventions and programs achieve targeted outcomes? What are the component parts of these programs, and which components are related to which outcomes? These important questions are directly related to the management of SDP programs. Sport management scholarship has examined outcomes of SDP programs and how these outcomes may be related to program design, particularly with regards to the efficacy of sport-based interventions in facilitating social inclusion and social capital for marginalized and disenfranchised individuals (Sherry 2010; Sherry and Strybosch 2012; Welty Peachey et al. 2013a). This research, and other work as a collective, shows that if designed and managed well, sport has the potential to achieve positive outcomes (Schulenkorf 2012; Schulenkorf et al. 2016).

One of the first theoretical frameworks addressing this black box from a sport management perspective is Sport for Development Theory (SFD Theory) (Lyras and Welty Peachey 2011). SFD Theory suggests that there are five components which should underpin an SDP program and initiative, regardless of context. These are (1) impacts assessment; (2) organizational; (3) sport and physical activity; (4) educational; and (5) cultural enrichment. The impacts assessment component suggests that SDP programs should have valid and well-designed monitoring and evaluation schemes. From an organizational standpoint (the second component), bottom-up (local stakeholder and participant involvement) and top-down managerial and design processes should be employed. The sport and physical activity component suggests that these activities must be strategically designed to match targeted outcomes, and that new and non-traditional sports should be activated when possible. Educational activities (the fourth component) such as guest speakers and topic discussions should complement the sport programming, along with cultural enrichment activities (the fifth component) such as music, art, and dance. SFD Theory is predicated on a sports-plus model, where sport is seen as an essential tool for achieving targeted outcomes when complemented with other non-sport activities and programs to enhance outcome attainment (Coalter 2010). Within SFD Theory, sport is adapted and modified to fit the target population and its needs, and packaged with educational and cultural components to best achieve specified outcomes. Some sport management work utilizing SFD Theory has shown that while the gestalt of sport, education, and the cultural arts working in tandem is critical to achieving outcomes, specific components are also related to specific outcomes. For instance, Welty Peachey and colleagues (2015a) tapped SFD Theory to examine the World Scholar-Athlete Games (WSAG), a large SDP event which brings together the youth of the world every four years using sport, education, and the cultural arts to work at fostering understanding and peace. Here, it was found that the team-based sport environment was important for reducing prejudice, while the educational component was critical for increasing change agent self-efficacy of participants (their belief that they have the efficacy to make a positive difference in society).

Similar to SFD Theory, the theoretical underpinnings of SDP programs and events to achieve long-term sustainability has also been conceptualized by Nico Schulenkorf (2012) with his Sport-for-Development (S4D) framework. This holistic and flexible framework is meant to be a guide for examining the use of sport programs and events to attain positive social impact and sustainable social outcomes across contexts and communities. It begins with a change agent who has a vision for the program or event, who then actively works with local communities to foster participation, engagement, preparation, and organization of the project sensitive to local contextual differences and needs. The S4D project can then bring about social impact and experiences, which can be leveraged toward long-term social outcomes.

Other theory from sport management has focused on integrating micro- and macro-level change in order to facilitate robust and rigorous program design, implementation, and evaluation (Massey *et al.* 2015). These authors argue that systems theory is an avenue to think through how micro-level change can possibly lead to broader, macro-level change and outcomes, since typically there is a largely unfounded assumption that micro-level change automatically brings about macro-level change. For instance, many SDP programs target outcomes at the individual (micro) level, such as enhanced social capital or increased self-esteem, with the assumption this individual-level change will then lead to change at the societal level. The systems theory approach emphasizes the interconnectedness of a system (e.g. the dynamic interactions between foreign aid, war economy, social inclusion through sport, and levels of peace) to reduce the isolation of SDP organizations and the need to increase partnerships through a multidisciplinary emphasis. They posit that this systems approach will help integrate micro-level programming with macro-level goals to enhance organizational sustainability. In essence, a focus on interconnectedness will link potential individual (micro) level outcomes to broader societal change.

Sport management scholars have also contributed their thoughts to evaluation theory of SDP programs and initiatives. Baker *et al.* (2015) have described how empowerment evaluation can contribute to effective SDP program design and management. They articulated that power in evaluation should be shifted to staff and program participants, placing evaluation in the control of stakeholders who are implementing and managing the program. This will promote the ability of the SDP organization to advance social justice, self-determination, and capacity building through increased program ownership and investment, which can lead to greater sustainability of the organization. One pronounced problem in the SDP sector is that organizations are often short-lived due to a variety of external and internal factors such as an unstable economic climate, political turmoil, or lack of managerial, entrepreneurial, financial, or evaluation skills necessary for the organization to thrive (Coalter 2013). In response, empowerment evaluation could be one avenue to provide organizational capacity and skill sets to local stakeholders who can then manage programs more effectively and efficiently.

A common thread in the above work is the critical need to examine the programmatic structures, mechanisms, components, management, and evaluation schemes that can provide guidance for designing, implementing, and evaluating SDP programs and events for optimal effect. While this theoretical work is highly important, it also presents a major challenge, in that scholars have wrestled with the idea of whether or not there can, or even should be, an overall theory of program design and evaluation that fits every SDP program (Schulenkorf and Spaaij 2015). SDP programs and events are highly contextual and localized, with communities and cultures having disparate needs and many differences in cultural norms and values. This wide disparity makes it potentially problematic to consider a 'one size fits all' theory about how SDP programs can achieve targeted outcomes and sustainability. Nevertheless, the above work is important and helps to shape the ongoing dialogue about the mechanisms and processes through which SDP programs can contribute to a social development agenda (Schulenkorf and Spaaij 2015).

Contribution #2: Event management and SDP

A second area in which sport management can make a contribution to SDP is in exploring various facets of events and event management within SDP programs. Some SDP programs administer special events, such as tournaments and festivals, to augment year-round programming. A good example is the Street Soccer program run in various countries. These year-round programs utilize Street Soccer to help individuals suffering from homelessness make positive changes in their lives, and then hold a showcase event, such as the Homeless World Cup or the Street Soccer USA Cup, to bring together teams of homeless people to compete in soccer tournaments once a year (Sherry 2010; Welty Peachey et al. 2013a). Other SDP events are one-off or special events, not connected to a year-round programming effort. Examples include the WSAG described earlier, which is held every four years, but does not have intermediate programming (Welty Peachey et al. 2015a).

SDP events can make important contributions to community development, as research has shown that they may 'contribute to building of community networks and social capital, the celebration and enhancement of cultural traditions, the opportunity to develop community spirit and pride, and the acquisition of new (management) skills' (Schulenkorf 2016: 629). Schulenkorf (2016) provides a helpful framework for understanding the contribution of special events to SDP programs. He posits that special events contribute to the ongoing work of SDP organizations and initiatives by creating new interest and excitement among stakeholders, reconnecting community stakeholders to the goals and mission of the broader SDP program, leveraging partnerships to help achieve the mission of the SDP initiative, and providing opportunities to develop and shape managerial and organizational capacity of local organizers.

Clearly, events can play a positive role in the development agenda of SDP organizations, but the potential positive outcomes are predicated on their strategic design, implementation, and management (Chalip 2006; Welty Peachey et al. 2015b; Schulenkorf 2016). An SDP event will not achieve its potential impact unless it is strategically designed and managed. This is where the concept of social leverage of events comes into play (Chalip 2006; O'Brien and Chalip 2008). O'Brien and Chalip (2008) have theorized a number of strategies and tactics event organizers and communities can use to help achieve social objectives through events. They argue that liminality (a liminoid, in between space created by events) and communitas (a sense of community and celebration engendered at events) can be leveraged to enhance social development agendas in communities and lead to positive lasting change for participants. Based on this concept of social leverage, Welty Peachey and colleagues (2015b) explored the potential leverage of the Street Soccer USA Cup for social capital development in its homeless participants. They found that the Cup was able to strategically leverage liminality and communitas to enhance social capital development through aligning the event with the targeted social issue of homelessness, aligning values and the subcultures of soccer and homelessness, increasing length of visitor stays, and facilitating engagement with the issue of homelessness (O'Brien and Chalip 2008; Welty Peachey et al. 2015b).

In terms of event impact, Sherry (2010) found that the Homeless World Cup was effective at enhancing both bonding (relationships with similar others) and bridging (relationships with dissimilar others) forms of social capital development among homeless people through the reciprocal relationships formed with other participants and volunteers at the event, which were then leveraged by participants to make positive changes in their lives. Similarly, two separate studies by Welty Peachey and colleagues found that the Street Soccer USA Cup and the WSAG were effective at enhancing social capital development among volunteers with these events, by bonding with similar volunteers for idea sharing and by bridging with individuals different from themselves to break down stereotypes and motivate for future social work upon returning home (Welty Peachey *et al.* 2013b; Welty Peachey *et al.* 2015c). In addition to social capital, other work has found that SDP events can help reduce prejudice and foster understanding between disparate individuals and communities which are in conflict (Schulenkorf *et al.* 2011; Welty Peachey *et al.* 2015a).

While this event-focused scholarship has made a significant contribution, events do have inherent challenges related to their efficacy. From a managerial standpoint, time and effort must be given to the strategic leverage of these events in order for them to be able to contribute effectively and efficiently to the ongoing mission of SDP organizations. In organizations often strapped for time, staff, and volunteers, giving the requisite time necessary to carefully craft these leveraging strategies can be problematic, particularly as SDP practitioners are often focused on the exigencies of the here and now and running programs on a shoestring budget (Schulenkorf *et al.* 2011; Welty Peachey *et al.* 2015b). In turn, if events are not strategically leveraged for community and social development and artfully crafted to fit within the ongoing program suite of the SDP organization, their unique contributions to development agendas will be mitigated.

Another challenge related to SDP events is in ascertaining their potential long-term impact on participants and communities. Participants in these SDP events are often difficult to track over time as they may 'disappear' at any stage upon returning from an event and contact may be lost (Welty Peachey *et al.* 2013a). This means that it is challenging to determine the long-term impact of an event without follow up communication with participants, months or even years later. Nevertheless, despite these challenges, sport management and events have made a considerable contribution to the conceptual and empirical understanding of how SDP initiatives can be best designed and managed in order to pursue development agendas.

Contribution #3: Volunteer management and SDP

Volunteers are often an indispensable aspect of the sport industry, providing economic efficiencies for sport organizations by helping to minimize staff costs and by generating innovative ideas (Cuskelly 2008). Volunteers are vitally important to the success of SDP organizations, as most of these organizations worldwide are smaller, employ limited staff, and rely on the backbone of volunteers to carry out their programming (Welty Peachey *et al.* 2014). As such, a third contribution of sport management to the SDP field is in helping to articulate sound volunteer management policies and strategies, particularly with regards to recruitment and retention.

When there is high turnover of volunteers in SDP organizations, this can impact long-term program success and viability. An understanding of volunteer motivation and retention factors is critical for SDP organizations, as they will be better able to craft recruitment and retention strategies to obtain qualified volunteers, keep them satisfied with work routines and other benefits, and ultimately, retain them over the long-term (Welty Peachey *et al.* 2013c). In a study on volunteer motivation and retention factors with the WSAG, using the functionalist approach to volunteer motivation (Clary and Snyder 1999), it was found that the strongest initial motivator for SDP volunteers was 'values alignment', or a belief in the mission and goals of the organization; volunteers wished to be associated with these values and make a contribution to the mission (Welty Peachey *et al.* 2014). Other initial motives of these volunteers included socialization with others, gaining an understanding of world issues, career advancement, and self-enhancement. Interestingly, 'love of sport', which has been identified as a strong motive in individuals to volunteer with sport-based organizations (Bang *et al.* 2009), did not emerge as a significant motive for volunteers at this SDP event. Volunteers then remained involved with the WSAG and volunteered for subsequent iterations of the event when their initial motives were satisfied. However, another volunteer motivation study with the Street Soccer USA Cup found that in addition to values alignment being a strong initial motivator, 'love of sport' (Bang *et al.* 2009) was a key motive (Welty Peachey *et al.* 2013c).

In addition to motivation and retention, sport management work can contribute to the exploration of how to manage SDP programs so as to bring about positive outcomes for volunteers. While the majority of SDP work has focused on outcomes for participants in the programs (Schulenkorf *et al.* 2016), there is a growing interest in how SDP initiatives may impact other key stakeholders, such as staff, community members, and volunteers. With regards to volunteers, as mentioned previously, a study on Street Soccer USA Cup volunteers revealed that volunteering fostered social capital development by enhancing awareness and understanding about the plight of the homeless, building community and relationships with individuals suffering from homelessness, enhancing passion to work in the social justice field, and developing self-satisfaction through a 'feel good' mentality (Welty Peachey *et al.* 2013b). Both bonding and bridging social capital were important outcomes for volunteers. Similarly, a study on volunteer impact with the WSAG revealed volunteers experienced social capital development through building relationships, learning, and enhanced motivation to work for social change and reciprocity (Welty Peachey *et al.* 2015c). These studies, collectively and from a management standpoint, indicate that SDP organizations should strategically design volunteer orientations, programs, and opportunities such that positive outcomes can be realized for these important stakeholders, in addition to actual participants in the initiatives. Challenges remain, however, as individuals have a proliferation of volunteer opportunities with various charitable and non-profit organizations, and attracting and retaining volunteers can be incredibly difficult since SDP organizations are often recruiting from the same human resource base (i.e. typically younger individuals interested in sport and social justice). As research has demonstrated that the relationships formed by SDP program leaders and volunteers contribute to positive change in program participants, perhaps more so than sport participation itself (Coalter 2013), recruiting and retaining qualified volunteers, who work intimately with program participants, becomes even more crucial.

Contribution #4: Inter-organizational partnerships and SDP

The majority of SDP organizations must engage in inter-organizational partnerships in order to be successful in achieving their mission. These partnerships can take a variety of forms, but often include partnering with local, regional, and national governments and government agencies, NGOs at the community, national, and international levels, community-based organizations, professional sport teams, the corporate sector, and educational institutions, among others. Inter-organizational partnerships enable organizations to 'address societal issues, accomplish tasks, and reach goals that fall outside the grasp of any individual entity working independently' (Woodland and Hutton 2012: 366). However, forming, managing, and sustaining partnerships can be incredibly difficult, and often comes with a host of challenges. As such, a fourth key contribution of sport management to the SDP field is in identifying strategic and managerial foci to assist SDP organizations with managing these partnerships more effectively in order to optimize their goals and missions (Macintosh *et al.* 2016; Sherry and Schulenkorf 2016).

SDP organizations face many common challenges when attempting to form and sustain different kinds of partnerships. These can include skepticism on behalf of partners about sport's viability as a development mechanism (Coalter 2010; Sherry and Schulenkorf 2016); competition with other SDP organizations for the same funding source and partnership opportunity (Coalter 2010); mission drift, where the SDP organization is pulled off course by the demands of the partner (Coalter 2010; Sherry and Schulenkorf 2016); unequal power dynamics in the partnership that privilege the partner and place it in a hierarchal position over the SDP organization (Nicholls and Giles 2007); and implementation and logistical challenges (Svensson and Hambrick 2016), among others.

Importantly, though, scholars have suggested strategies and tactics to help address these challenges, enabling the SDP organization to manage its partnership process more effectively. It is important for the SDP organization to build strong relationships and networks with partners, focusing on the people aspect of the partnership, and communicating continuously with the partner (Babiak 2007). This strategy can enhance trust and legitimacy, help lessen skepticism about sport as a development tool, and address unequal power relation issues. In a recent study with 29 SDP organizations from around the world with varied missions and foci, for instance, SDP practitioners in every organization highlighted the importance of taking time to develop strong relationships with potential and current partners (Welty Peachey *et al.* 2018). It is also critical to identify a cause champion (an individual who is supportive of the SDP organization's mission) within the partnering organization who can aid in partner negotiations and communication (Frisby *et al.* 2005). SDP organizations must clearly articulate benefits to the partner, and just not focus on what the potential partnership will do for the SDP organization. The partner should be involved in the design, implementation, and evaluation of the SDP initiative to help facilitate buy-in, as was the case in Papua New Guinea with the League Bilong Laif SDP program when the researchers involved local partners in all facets of the design and evaluation of the initiative (Sherry and Schulenkorf 2016). The SDP organization must also know itself and what it can or cannot do, staying centered on its goals so as not to be pulled off kilter by the demands of the partner (Svensson and Hambrick 2016). Thus, sport management has contributed to understanding the nature of partnerships in the SDP space, and more importantly, helped to articulate strategies and tactics that SDP organizations can employ when navigating the complex terrain of partnerships.

Contribution #5: Organizational capacity and SDP

Related to partnerships, sport management scholars have also contributed to the SDP sector by examining the challenges of building organizational capacity in SDP organizations as well as strategies for doing so (Doherty *et al.* 2014; Svensson and Hambrick 2016). Organizational capacity encompasses dimensions of human resources, financial management, external relationships, internal structures and process, and organizational development (Hall *et al.* 2003), and is a prerequisite for organizations in achieving sustainability. Unfortunately, within the SDP field, organizations are often 'woefully underfunded, completely unregulated, poorly planned and coordinated, and largely isolated from mainstream development efforts' (Kidd 2008: 376). To move the field forward, it is critical that SDP organizations develop, implement, and sustain effective and efficient structures and processes to achieve sustainability (Schulenkorf *et al.* 2014). It is in this area where sport management can be helpful to the SDP field.

For instance, Svensson and Hambrick (2016) examined the organizational capacity challenges and strategies of a small, non-profit SDP organization based in the US but running programs in East Africa. They found that this organization faced a plethora of human resource, financial, and structural capacity constraints that hindered its ability to effectively carry out its mission. The management of power dynamics also emerged as a critical challenge in building organizational capacity, which hampered sustainability efforts of the organization. To help surmount these challenges, it was recommended that SDP organizations adopt a flexible and nimble managerial strategy to quickly respond to changing environmental parameters, and to strategically balance the desire for revenue diversification with focusing on a more limited number of key revenue generating opportunities due to potential lack of capacity to sustain diverse programming. While sport management scholars have wrestled with the theoretical aspects of program design in SDP to best achieve targeted outcomes (Lyras and Welty Peachey 2011; Schulenkorf 2012), it is also recommended that scholars and practitioners adopt a more comprehensive and holistic approach to their work that includes focus on programmatic, organizational, and environmental factors influencing SDP efforts (Svensson and Hambrick 2016). As mentioned earlier, SDP practitioners often lack specific training in business and managerial skill sets which would enable them to most effectively guide and develop organizational capacity and sustainable SDP organizations. Passion for and a belief in the 'power' of sport for social change and development can only sustain an organization for so long. Thus, it is imperative for SDP practitioners to acquire these business, management, and entrepreneurial skill sets to most effectively develop capacity in their organizations, while being mindful of the neocolonial heritage of much of these neoliberal educational offerings. Carefully crafted and culturally sensitive sport management programs can perhaps provide this training and understanding.

Contribution #6: Leadership and SDP

Finally, but not least, sport management can contribute to the SDP sector by pushing forward conversations about what effective leadership could or should look like in SDP. Is the type of leadership necessary to effectively guide and steward SDP organizations different from the leadership required in other forms of sport organizations or non-profits? There has been some initial conceptual work in this regard, particularly focusing on the applicability of servant leadership (Greenleaf 1977) within the SDP context. Servant leadership is focused on follower care and development, where the individual seeks to be a servant first (van Dierendonck 2011). This style of leadership could be highly effective in SDP organizations, due to its focus on care, nurture, and empowerment of followers (employees, volunteers, and participants in SDP programs), and as such, it could be invaluable in helping SDP organizations toward sustainability and outcome achievement (Welty Peachey and Burton 2016).

van Dierendonck (2011) outlined six characteristics of servant leadership: empowering and developing people, humility, authenticity, interpersonal acceptance, providing direction, and stewardship. SDP practitioners who embody these characteristics and who embrace servant leadership may be able to navigate the tension of building relationships and empowering followers with the business side of the organization in more astute and creative ways, given their focus on acceptance and relationship building, but also on stewardship of resources to achieve sustainability (Welty Peachey and Burton 2016). Developing a servant leadership mindset which translates into behavioral actions could also be useful for the viability and sustainability of SDP organizations. Of course, servant leadership is not the only form of leadership likely to be effective in SDP organizations. As Welty Peachey and Burton (2016) advocate, this form of leadership may need to be coupled with other leadership styles, such as authentic, transformational, and transactional, at various stages in the life cycle of the SDP organization to best steer the course forward.

Other sport management scholarship has examined the role of social entrepreneurship and its effectiveness in and with SDP organizations (Cohen and Welty Peachey 2015).

A social entrepreneur uses his or her entrepreneurial experience and acumen in an effort to contribute to society in a meaningful fashion without expecting profits or publicity (Shaffie *et al.* 2012). A traditional entrepreneur is associated with financial gains and business acumen, while social entrepreneurs are often judged by social returns, where profitability is important but not the only goal (Shaffie *et al.* 2012). Just as business entrepreneurs transform industries and maximize profits, social entrepreneurs act as change agents and attempt to maximize their outreach. In the one empirical investigation of social entrepreneurship in the SDP space, it was found that a young woman who began a Street Soccer team in Sacramento, California, had a number of traumatic life events that influenced the development of her social entrepreneurial mindset, and she leveraged her entrepreneurial gifts to optimize fundraising, partnerships, and community networking to enhance the effectiveness and sustainability of her Street Soccer program (Cohen and Welty Peachey 2015). One challenge, however, is that SDP practitioners often lack the leadership and entrepreneurial training to bring to bear within their organizations in order to create the policies, organizational cultures, and human resource strategies necessary to optimize their organization's potential. It is in this space that sport management can continue to contribute to discussions about effective and culturally sensitive leadership within SDP.

Conclusion

It has been the intent of this chapter to provide an overview of key contributions that the sport management discipline can make to the study and practice of SDP. As has been shown, sport management has furthered theory and conversation around a number of salient areas in SDP, all with the goal of improving the long-term efficacy of initiatives and programs. Each of these key contributions also comes with its associated challenges, and it will be valuable going forward for sport management scholars and practitioners to continue to wrestle with these challenges and to propose strategies for mitigating them, while also engaging in new scholarship and praxis to advance the field.

Specifically, continued work is needed on theory development and program design which is sensitive to local context and culture. If a one size fits all theory is inadvisable (Schulenkorf and Spaaij 2015), then how can theory and program design best capture local context and nuances to ultimately serve program participants and development agendas more effectively and efficiently? More engagement is also needed with the contribution of events to the SDP field. What are the most effective strategies for synthesizing one-off events with ongoing SDP programming? What other leveraging strategies can be deployed to optimize the role of SDP events in local communities for long-term development? Additional work in inter-organizational partnership formation and development is also called for, particularly with regard to understanding perceptions and workings of partnerships from the perspectives of the external partner (i.e. the NGO or government entity) and participants in the SDP programs. Do these partnerships enhance the outcomes for participants?

The sport management discipline should also continue to examine leadership in the SDP space, and can make a strong contribution by investigating how leadership is connected to participant and development outcomes. Along these lines, sport management scholars can investigate the types of organizational forms, structures, and cultures which might be most effective in achieving development aims, particularly when targeting disenfranchised and marginalized populations. These forms, structures, and organizational cultures may be distinctly different from what is common and from what works in other types of sport organizations or non-profit entities.

In summary, the intersection between sport management and SDP is critical for the continued growth of the field and for helping SDP practitioners manage and lead their organizations with foresight, business savvy, and effective, culturally sensitive leadership. The discipline of sport management, alongside other academic disciplines, can help to provide the legitimacy, credibility, and managerial skill set SDP organizations need to astutely design and carry out effective, long-term programming. Sport management students may also find fulfilling careers working in SDP. Sport management scholars, practitioners, and students are encouraged to think creatively about how they may become involved with and contribute to this exciting and important field.

References

Babiak, K. (2007). Determinants of interorganizational relationships: The case of a Canadian nonprofit sport organization. *Journal of Sport Management, 21*(3), 338–376.

Baker, R., Baker, P., Atwater, C. and Andrews, H. (2015). Sport for development and peace: A program evaluation of a sport diplomacy initiative. *International Journal of Sport Management and Marketing, 16*(1/2), 52–70.

Bang, H., Alexandris, K. and Ross, S. D. (2009). Validation of the revised volunteer motivations scale for international sporting events (VMS-ISE) at the Athens 2004 Olympic Games. *Event Management, 12*(3–4), 119–131.

Burnett, C. (2001). Social impact assessment and sport development. *International Review for the Sociology of Sport, 36*(1), 41–52.

Chalip, L. (2006). Towards social leverage of sport events. *Journal of Sport Tourism, 11*(2), 109–127.

Clary, E. G. and Snyder, M. (1999). The motivations to volunteer. *Current Directions in Psychological Science, 8*(5), 156–159.

Coalter, F. (2010). The politics of sport-for-development: Limited focus programmes and broad gauge problems. *International Review for the Sociology of Sport, 45*(3), 295–314.

Coalter, F. (ed.) (2013). *Sport for Development: What Game Are We Playing?* New York: Routledge.

Cohen, A. and Welty Peachey, J. (2015). The making of a social entrepreneur: From participant to cause champion within a sport-for-development context. *Sport Management Review, 18*(1), 111–125.

Cuskelly, G. (2008). Volunteering in community sport organizations: Implications for social capital. In M. Nicholson and R. Hoye (eds), *Sport and Social Capital*. Oxford: Elsevier.

Doherty, A., Misener, L. and Cuskelly, G. (2014). Toward a multidimensional framework of capacity in community sport clubs. *Nonprofit and Voluntary Sector Quarterly, 43*(2), 124–142.

Frisby, W., Reid, C., Millar, S. and Hoeber, L. (2005). Putting 'participatory' into participatory forms of action research. *Journal of Sport Management, 19*(4), 367–386.

Greenleaf, R. K. (1977). *Servant Leadership: A Journey into the Nature of Legitimate Power and Greatness*. New York: Paulist Press.

Hall, M. H., Andrukow, A., Barr, C., Brock, K., de Wit, M., Embuldeniya, D., et al. (2003). *The Capacity to Serve: A Qualitative Study of the Challenges Facing Canada's Nonprofit and Voluntary Organizations*. Toronto, ON: Canadian Centre for Philanthropy.

Kidd, B. (2008). A new social movement: Sport for development and peace. *Sport in Society, 11*(4), 370–380.

Lyras, A. and Welty Peachey, J. (2011). Integrating sport for development theory and praxis. *Sport Management Review, 14*(4), 311–326.

MacIntosh, E., Arellano, A. and Forneris, T. (2016). Exploring the community and external-agency partnership in sport-for-development programming. *European Sport Management Quarterly, 16*(1), 38–57.

Massey, W., Whitley, M., Blom, L. and Gerstein, L. (2015). Sport for development and peace: A systems theory perspective on promoting sustainable change. *International Journal of Sport Management and Marketing, 16*(1/2), 18–35.

Nicholls, S. and Giles, A. R. (2007). Sport as a tool for HIV/AIDS education: A potential catalyst for change. *Pimatisiwin – A Journal of Aboriginal and Indigenous Community Health, 5*(1), 51–85.

O'Brien, D. and Chalip, L. (2008). Sport events and strategic leveraging: Pushing towards the triple bottom line. In A. Woodside and D. Martin (eds), *Tourism Management: Analysis, Behavior and Strategy*. Cambridge, MA: CABI.

Shaffie, F., Yusof, A., Abdullah, W., Ahmad, W. and Bahari, A. (2012). Social Entrepreneurship: An Overview. Paper presented at the 2nd Annual Summit on Business and Entrepreneurial Studies, Sarawak, Malaysia.

Schulenkorf, N. (2012). Sustainable community development through sport and events: A conceptual framework for sport for development projects. *Sport Management Review*, *15*(1), 1–12.

Schulenkorf, N. (2016). The contributions of special events to sport for development programs. *Journal of Sport Management*, *30*(6), 629–642.

Schulenkorf, N., Sherry, E. and Rowe, K. (2016) Sport for development: An integrated literature review. *Journal of Sport Management*, *30*(1), 22–39.

Schulenkorf, N. and Spaaij, R. (2015). Commentary: reflections on theory building in sport for development and peace. *International Journal of Sport Management and Marketing*, *16*(1/2), 71–77.

Schulenkorf, N., Sugden, J. and Burdsey, D. (2014). Sport for development and peace as contested terrain: Place, community, ownership. *International Journal of Sport Policy and Politics*, *6*(3), 371–387.

Schulenkorf, N., Thomson, A. and Schlenker, K. (2011), Intercommunity sport events: Vehicles and catalysts for social capital in divided societies. *Event Management*, *15*(2), 105–119.

Sherry, E. (2010). (Re)engaging marginalized groups through sport: The homeless World Cup. *International Review for the Sociology of Sport*, *45*(1), 59–71.

Sherry, E. and Schulenkorf, N. (2016). League Bilong Laif: Rugby, education and sport-for-development partnerships in Papua New Guinea. *Sport, Education and Society*, *21*(4), 513–530.

Sherry, E. and Strybosch, V. (2012). A kick in the right direction: Longitudinal outcomes of the Australian Street Soccer Program. *Soccer and Society*, *13*(4), 495–509.

Svensson, P. G. and Hambrick, M. E. (2016). 'Pick and choose our battles': Understanding organizational capacity in a sport for development and peace organization. *Sport Management Review*, *19*(2), 120–132.

van Dierendonck, D. and Nuijten, I. (2011). The servant leadership survey: Development and validation of a multidimensional measure. *Journal of Business Psychology*, *26*(3), 249–267.

Welty Peachey, J., Borland, J., Lobpries, J. and Cohen, A. (2015b). Managing impact: Leveraging sacred spaces and community celebration to maximize social capital at a sport-for development event. *Sport Management Review*, *18*: 86–98.

Welty Peachey, J., Bruening, J., Cohen, A., Lyras, A. and Cunningham, G. (2015c). Examining social capital development among volunteers of a multinational sport-for-development event. *Journal of Sport Management*, *29*(1), 27–41.

Welty Peachey, J. and Burton, L. (2016) Servant leadership in sport-for-development and peace: A way forward. *Quest*. Advance online publication, doi:http://dx.doi.org/10.1080/00336297.2016.1165123.

Welty Peachey, J., Cohen, A., Borland, J. and Lyras, A. (2013b). Building social capital: Examining the impact of Street Soccer USA on its volunteers. *International Review for the Sociology of Sport*, *48*(1), 20–37.

Welty Peachey, J., Cohen, A., Borland, J. and Lyras, A. (2013c). Exploring the initial motivations of individuals to volunteer with a sport-for-homeless initiative. *International Journal of Sport Management*, *14*: 103–122.

Welty Peachey, J., Cohen, A., Shin, N. and Fusaro, B. (2018). Challenges and strategies of building and sustaining organizational partnerships in sport for development and peace. *Sport Management Review, 21*, 160–175.

Welty Peachey, J., Cunningham, G., Lyras, A., Cohen, A. and Bruening, J. (2015a). The influence of a sport for development event on prejudice and change agent self-efficacy. *Journal of Sport Management*, *29*(3), 229–244.

Welty Peachey, J., Lyras, A., Borland, J. and Cohen, A. (2013a). Sport for social change: Investigating the impact of the SSUSA Cup. *ICHPER-SD Journal of Research*, *8*(1), 3–11.

Welty Peachey, J., Lyras, A., Cohen, A., Bruening, J. and Cunningham, G. (2014). Exploring the motives and retention factors of sport-for-development volunteers. *Nonprofit and Voluntary Sector Quarterly*, *43*(6), 1052–1069.

Woodland, R. H. and Hutton, M. S. (2012). Evaluating organizational collaborations: Suggested entry points and strategies. *American Journal of Evaluation*, *33*(3), 366–383.

Part III
Themes and issues in SDP

22
SDP and gender

Karen Petry and Friederike Kroner

Introduction

The self-determination of women and girls is a basic objective of development-based measures. Yet this relates not just to the participation of girls and women but rather to their equality. Sport and movement-based projects have the capacity to shatter stereotype expectations and to call socio-cultural role behaviour into question. This should also go hand in hand with the goal of enhancing the participation of women and girls in public life, for in many countries women and girls tend to be marginalised within society, they are denied access to education and violence against them is trivialised.

The notion of the concept of 'Sport and Development' has emerged only recently and sport has lately become an integral part of socio-economic development agendas worldwide (Beutler 2008; Kidd 2008; Coalter 2010). Yet, sport as an engine for development is commonly deployed by an ever-expanding range of local, national and international actors comprising sports associations, multinational corporations, non-governmental organisations, development agencies and governments (Levermore 2008a, 2008b; Spaaij 2009b; Giulianotti and Armstrong 2011; Hartmann and Kwauk 2011). Its recent emergence rests on the notion that common economic policies have failed to succeed in developmental achievements (Levermore and Beacom 2009). The growing recognition of the need for new approaches and actors has led to a recent increase of sport as an actor for social change. Political claims and initiatives such as the United Nations' Millennium Development Goals, the appointment of the United Nations' first Special Advisor on Sport for Development and Peace in 2001, the 2005 proclaimed International Year of Sport and Physical Education, the Sport for Development and Peace International Working Group as well as sporting initiatives such as the Olympic Aid programme and other sporting initiatives were launched (Beutler 2008; Kidd 2008; Coalter 2010).

Two main trends can be observed in the current and predominant discussions. First, there is a strong belief that sport might indeed be making a critical contribution to development objectives and to gender equality in particular; and second, substantial criticism does exist directly linked to this optimistic assumption (Donnelly *et al.* 2011). In the first instance, sport is instrumentalised and it is believed that sport encompasses gender equality, health, peace and other social issues while addressing traditional sport ideologies of discipline, confidence, tolerance, leadership, social capital and respect (Coalter 2008). But as Coalter (2006) points out, such projects do not stop where traditional objectives such as increased participation, development of sporting skills and fun and recreation end; they actually go one step further. Beyond those, it is supposed that sport may yield social and economic change in various forms (Kidd 2008; Levermore 2008b; Guest 2009; Coalter 2010).

Supported by the international community, broad policy statements and the sports community itself, it is assumed that sport has the potential to fuel change and to address objectives such as empowerment of girls and women, gender equality as well as gender-based violence, inter alia, by harnessing the popular appeal and inherent properties of sport (Giulianotti 2004; Lawson 2005; Beutler 2008; Fokwang 2009; Kay 2009; Kay and Bradbury 2009; Spaaij 2009a; Vermeulen and Verwell 2009; Darnell 2010; Giulianotti and Armstrong 2011). Lyras and Peachy (2011: 1) describe

> the use of sport to exert a positive influence on public health, the socialisation of children, youths and adults, the social inclusion of the disadvantaged, the economic development of regions and states, and on fostering intercultural exchange and conflict resolution.

However, these overly positive claims, in particular concerning gender effects, have to be treated with some caution. Although the extent of evaluation and impact studies has increased, many authors critically mention that there is still a serious gap in research and verification entailing a lack of conceptualisation, monitoring, evaluation, methodological considerations, organisation and structure of the sport and development area (Coalter 2006; Levermore 2008b; Spaaij 2009b; Coalter 2010; Donnelly *et al.* 2011; Hartmann and Kwauk 2011). Moreover, Skinner *et al.* (2008) as well as Darnell and Hayhurst (2011) and Mwaanga and Adeosun (2016) criticise the fact that sport is often imposed on communities using a top-down approach without recognising relevant cultural contexts or gender practices.

Hence, based on rather anecdotal evidence, there is less understanding of the mechanisms by which sport might promote gender equality and empowerment of girls and women and a great number of unanswered questions and a crucial lack of research in the context of this sport-related '*incredibly complex social intervention*' (Donnelly *et al.* 2011: 592).

The role of gender in the development context

The issue of gender is featured largely in the history of development policy. During the 'UN-Decade for Women' (1975–1985), gender analyses gained momentum in terms of political scope for action and research (Meier 2005). The 1995 Beijing Conference, which 189 countries participated in, subsequently laid the foundations for a serious international debate about gender policy. According to Handy and Kassa (2004), gender equality plays a key role in adopting a holistic and sustainable approach to social and economic development. Studies have shown that better education and empowerment of girls and women reduce poverty, promote health and family, reduce the birth rate and lead to better human resources (Tembon and Fort 2008). The first 'women in sport' movement emerged in 1990. However, this was characterised by an elitist western approach and focused little on development goals (Saavedra 2005). In 1994, the International Working Group on Women and Sport (IWG) was set up with the initial objective of promoting the participation of women in sport and physical activities globally with a view to accomplishing development goals (Meier 2005).

After Namibia hosted the 2nd World Conference on Women in Sport in 1998, and the *Windhoek Call for Action* was published, the advocacy organisation African Women in Sport Association (AWISA), which is based in Namibia, was founded to support African sportswomen.

The term 'gender and development' (Touwen 1996) emerged from the analytical concept 'women in development' owing to the fact that the gender balance is deeply rooted in social structures. This means that prospects, roles and competencies of women and men need to be taken equally into consideration. In the past few years, the sport and gender debate has moved away from 'gender equity in sport' towards 'sport for gender equity'. Instead of merely promoting the participation of women in sport, the aim is to define gender equity as the goal for international sport-for-development initiatives (Saavedra 2005). This indicates that the specific needs of girls and women need to be seen and taken into account in a cultural context.

The adoption of the Sustainable Development Goals (SDGs) signalled the replacement of the Millennium Development Goals (MDGs) in September 2015, introducing a new, global development agenda. Whereas the narrowly defined MDGs were oriented specifically to emerging economies and developing countries, the goals and measures defined in the 2030 Agenda for Sustainable Development also apply to industrialised countries. This lends universal importance to the SDGs and fosters cooperation among all the relevant actors. Despite the universal nature of the new Agenda, it is intended to create greater scope for adjustments to regional demand. In a participatory consultation process, 17 SDGs and 169 associated targets were defined. In #37 of the final results document of the United Nations on the 2030 Agenda for Sustainable Development 'Transforming our World: The 2030 Agenda for Sustainable Development', sport is also highlighted as an important enabler of sustainable development, with particular emphasis on its growing contribution to the realisation of development and peace, health, education and social inclusion. SDG 5 explicitly refers to the aspect of gender ('Achieve gender equality and empower all women and girls') while calling for equal opportunities for women and girls in all areas. It mentions a number of legal violations that tend to affect girls and women in particular, violence, forced marriage and female genital mutilation. Other important goals include ensuring women's full and effective participation and equal opportunities for leadership at all levels of decision-making in political, economic and public life. Fortunately, several of the targets include women's rights and mention the issue of gender equality.

The situation of girls and women around the globe

In many countries around the world, the constitution bans all forms of discrimination and safeguards gender equity. In most countries, Ministries of Gender Equality and Child Welfare have been established and a National Gender Policy is available in local languages. Despite these official efforts, women and girls around the globe continue to face discrimination and inequalities. First, women tend to be greatly underrepresented in the government and media coverage, and more women are economically inactive than men. Furthermore, women tend to run the household in many countries and, for example, the number of women who are pregnant under the age of 20 or are widows is particularly high in rural areas in African countries. Hence, women and girls tend to spend their leisure time resting and "recharging their batteries". Williams (2003) reinforces this by saying that if girls have any free time, they tend to spend it on household work because they are used to traditional gender divisions.

Even though the enrolment and retention rate of boys and girls in schools is roughly the same in some countries, female learners are more likely to not complete their education due to teenage pregnancies, economic pressures from family members or early marriages. Although many countries around the globe have adopted modern constitutions which guarantee equal rights, day-to-day life is governed mainly by traditional laws. Many administrative bodies are male-dominated; women are more exposed to crimes such as rape and sexual abuse, have limited access to education, and are restricted to household responsibilities (Saavedra 2003; Pelak 2005;

Agergaard and Botelho 2014; Nauright 2014; Ogunniyi 2014). In many African countries, in particular, the traditional assumptions about 'gender role, socialization and occupation of separate spheres [are] still visible' (Shehu 2010: xii).

Apart from the gendered division of household labour, many active women face stigmas and harassment. There are a lot of initiatives at national and departmental level aimed at protecting women's rights. For example, the South African Government, among others, has ratified the Convention on the Elimination of All Forms of Violence against Women (CEDAW). However, progressive legislation continues to have very little impact on outcomes for women.

Recent research indicates the need for further gender-based violence prevention and proves the effectiveness of girls' clubs in this field. ActionAid research (2013) showed that girls' clubs have positive effects on girls' knowledge, confidence, attitudes and practices in managing violence and inequality. Open discussion on intimacy enables girls to break their silence on taboos around sex and sexual violence, and to change their own reporting practices. In addition, according to the research, girls' increased confidence has been reflected in their mothers' capacity to speak out on violence and gender inequality.

In these difficult environments, girls also face challenges based on cultural assumptions about women's and girls' roles in their culture. There are a few sporting activities that have been tailored to girls for leisure purposes and leadership development.

The general potential of sport for gender equality in the development context

There are a number of approaches that can be taken regarding the potential sport has for accomplishing gender-specific development goals. On the one hand, sport has the potential to enhance the status of women and to foster empowerment (Meier 2005; Kay 2009). On the other hand, however, it is not easy to eliminate deep-rooted, hegemonic gender relations through sport (Saavedra 2009).

According to Campbell et al. (2009), it seems paradoxical to deal with the issue of gender in the context of sport since the organisation of sport is informed by hegemonic masculinity, through which the gender divide and the unequal power balance continue to be strengthened. In this regard, Meier (2005) confirms that women are underrepresented at all levels of sport in large parts of the world. Owing to the fact that women's participation in sport is frequently considered to be 'unfeminine', these women are putting their femininity at risk. Furthermore, women participating in sport frequently face obstacles such as socio-economic, socio-cultural and infrastructure-related barriers, safety problems, lack of female role models, as well as male and female ideals, which are part and parcel of sport (Meier 2005; Pelak 2006).

Studies from southern Africa ascertained that the main obstacles to women participating in sport are gendered beliefs, attitudes and cultural barriers, financial problems and lack of leisure time, limited access and resources to materials and sporting infrastructure, as well as absence of non-material support such as media coverage and public support (Saavedra 2003; Pelak 2005).

In turn, participation in sport can also offer women and girls a safe space without violence (Jeanes and Magee 2014). Studies show that women feel empowered by sports participation, and experience increased socio-economic mobility as well as physical freedom of expression (e.g. Engh 2010; Hayhurst 2013; Sikes and Jarvie 2014), like working outside the home or the ability to travel.

A review of SFD literature undertaken by Schulenkorf et al. (2017) includes 437 articles and shows that only 3 per cent of the research studies published between 2000 and 2014 include a gender perspective (Schulenkorf et al. 2017: 182). Twenty per cent of the literature was classified as multidisciplinary, which means it may cover a gender topic. Nevertheless, the authors of the literature review state that 'the advancement of access and rights for girls and women were also inadequately covered in the literature identified' (Schulenkorf *et al.* 2017: 187). It is worthwhile noting, however, that 92 per cent of the researchers were from North America, Europe and Australia (ibid.: 188).

Sport as a tool for empowering women and girls – myths or truth?

Fair access to healthcare and education are the most important prerequisites for reducing gender-specific inequalities and changing socio–cultural gender norms. Other important starting points are equal opportunities in respect of social participation and equal opportunities for leadership at all levels of decision-making in political, economic and public life. As a tool, sport can play a supporting role – if the empowerment of women takes place at the individual, the structural as well as the cultural level.

At the individual level, sports education programmes are particularly suitable for enhancing access to education for girls. Furthermore, physical activity promotes the physical and emotional well-being of women and girls. Because of the physical nature of sport, it can also be used to address gender-sensitive issues such as sexual and reproductive health. The knowledge imparted gives women and girls more control over their bodies and lives. This helps to lower the rate of teenage pregnancies, thereby prolonging the school attendance of girls. Boys and men should also be integrated appropriately into this process and be encouraged to reflect critically on sexuality, HIV/AIDS and traditional role models.

At structural and cultural levels, organisations working with sport facilitate the participation of girls and women in civil society. Saavedra (2005) argues that the participation of girls and women in sport could lead to a universal, transformative process that frees young girls and women from traditional values and can change general 'ideas of normality' in relation to gender and the gender balance. Beutler (2008) added that social settings can be changed when women prove their sporting ability and call traditional views into question. Meier (2005) confirms that sport has the capacity to promote education, networking and social skills in order to build social skills and to strengthen empowerment of women. What is more, providing information about health, bodily functions, illnesses, hygiene and legislation helps young girls and women to gain control over their own lives. On the other hand, she criticises the fact that the majority of studies in this area have been conducted in western countries and are, by and large, gender neutral. Kay (2009) highlights the fact that young women from India who participated in special sports programmes managed not only to improve their physical and emotional health but also to enhance their status and respect within the family and the community.

However, Campbell *et al.* (2009) hold the view that a holistic empowerment of women needs to go hand in hand with a shift in power between men and women. Men, in particular, would need to abandon their claim to power for the benefit of women. Campbell says it is clearly evident that this task is difficult to implement for sport-for-development programmes. Meier (2005) and Saavedra (2009) claim that persons who lose their position of power are strongly opposed to sport-for-development initiatives, which has the potential to disempower women even further within the community. This often happens through initiatives that have a limited understanding of the complex social structures of societies (Darnell 2007; Saavedra 2009; Darnell and Hayhurst 2011). But gender-specific sports programmes can also have unintended negative consequences, for instance owing to neocolonial views that have not been sufficiently explained (Donnelly *et al.* 2011). Willis (2000: 844) raises the question of 'whether sport in the Global South can provide a unique opportunity to break down patriarchal structures, leading towards more equality'.

If so, a way of thinking is needed that departs from cultural, gender-specific stereotypes (Meier 2005). A large number of northern and western sociologists have confirmed that sport reflects the cultural values and social norms of society. In Iran, for instance, girls are prohibited from playing on public sports grounds, whereas in Côte d'Ivoire it is normal for them to do so and is actually encouraged by society. In order to implement sustainable sport projects as part of the promotion of gender equality, the special socio-cultural and socio-economic parameters therefore need to be taken into account. In this context, Coalter (2013) explains that the issue of gender depends on deep-felt convictions and attitudes and that it is not yet clear to what extent sport-for-development programmes can bring about change. Meier (2005) also confirms that it is difficult to measure the direct impact sport has on the empowerment of women.

Research, mostly from the global north, reveals that sportswomen are insulted by using negative stereotypes to disparage them, like telling them they look masculine or unsexy or labelling them as lesbians, especially in football (Engh 2010; Ogunniyi 2014).

Football as a tool of empowerment of women and girls

Some development initiatives focus on general physical education; others concentrate on special sports, mainly on football. Many of those initiatives aim to increase the access of women and girls to football, to provide information, for example about HIV, and to foster life skills, thereby working towards gender equality.

The great interest in football must undoubtedly be seen in the global context of a male-dominated world of sport. Meanwhile, it could be argued that the area of 'Sport for Development' is solely 'Football for Development'. Literature reveals that football has great developmental potential and is therefore a popular tool for many development projects all over the world. Research especially in the field of personal development and HIV/AIDS education through football confirms its positive impact (e.g. Tobisch and Preti 2010; Šafaříková 2012; 2013). As such, the 'competitive, participatory, team-based, and communicative aspects of the game' (Khan 2010: 6) are used to deliver knowledge and develop a range of life skills.

The international governing body of football, FIFA, is the main supporter of football development projects in a lot of countries. Its campaign '20 Centres for 2010' within the 2010 FIFA World Cup was launched in 2007 to build 20 community-based Football For Hope centres in sub-Saharan Africa with a view to approaching young people and combining football with health education (Geddes 2010). FIFA also supports football for development initiatives such as Streetfootballworld or Grassroot Soccer. Further examples of football-based development programmes in sub-Saharan Africa include Coaching for Hope, PlaySoccer and TackleAfrica, to name just a few. All of them initiate community-based football projects and aim to drive social change. Nevertheless, only few football-based programmes, such as Moving the Goalposts Kilifi in Kenya or Galz and Goals in Namibia, approach girls and women directly. An interview with a successful Namibian female footballer, who belongs to the Himba tribe, gave to the FIFA World magazine discloses typical barriers encountered by girls who want to play football. She said that most Himba people think sport is not important at all; only educated people understand the meaning of sport (Crowe 2010). Many tribes like the Himba have traditional customs and rules, for instance that girls should marry very young and have many children, or that girls are not allowed to raise their legs like when jumping (ibid.). Hence, it is prohibited for women and girls to play football in a community. Many girls around the globe play without the approval of their community or have to give up their passion for football. The number of women who play football and manage teams is still very small compared to men (Williams 2003). Female coaches are also rare; most coaches are male and train both men's and women's teams.

There is little research focusing on women and football in the SDP sector. Research topics range from sponsorship and violence to career opportunities for elite players (Williams and Chawansky 2013). Football is still generally considered to be a male-only sport and female participation is not the norm. FIFA's Financial Assistance Programme, for instance, donates $1 million to national associations to improve grassroots development, of which a mere 4 per cent is to be used for women's football (Saavedra 2003).

It is important to convey football in a gender-sensitive way, not in terms of different techniques or tactics, but in terms of analysing preconditions for girls and boys which depend on their backgrounds. Girls who have been raised according to traditional stereotypes are not used to taking up space, raising their voice or using their bodies to fight. It is difficult, especially for girls' teams, to find educated female coaches/assistants who have trained as a coach.

Female coaches can have a lasting impact on girls and sport through their way of training. For instance, female players tend to feel more secure if they are trained by women, and parents are more inclined to let their daughters be trained by female coaches. At the same time, female coaches are important role models for girls. This could increase their motivation to become coaches themselves one day.

The following aspects should also be taken into consideration when planning and implementing measures: 'Successful initiatives need to include factors such as types of, and venues for, sporting activities, safety requirements for women and girls, leadership roles, the need for positive images or the requirement for specific recruitment strategies' (DEZA 2005: 54).

Conclusion and general future directions

Societal or traditional practices in many countries around the globe still foster gender inequality. Besides equal opportunities for girls and women concerning education and employment, gender-based violence, HIV/AIDS infections, health care and early pregnancy are urgent issues.

Furthermore, women often receive no support from their families to participate in sport (Jeanes and Magee 2014). Besides these cultural norms and expectations, women's sport is also neglected in terms of media coverage, facilities and material resources (Saavedra 2003; Pelak 2005; Nauright 2014).

Burnett (2009) argues that developmental actions have to refer to individual and cultural meanings, and thus have to be interpreted in relation to respective social contexts. In cases where cultural identity and traditions are compromised, conflicts and political instability may surface and in turn severely impair individual development. Lastly, social participation is the overall presupposition for development, so that all other requirements and conditions can occur. Therefore, empowerment and participation of girls and women are commonly regarded as key components, and development is generally considered to be an active process of participation.

'The SDP sector [sport for development and peace] is moving into a new phase,' stated Giulianotti (2014: 15). But what does this mean for the gender debate in the SDP discourse? The future concept of gender equality has to be based on the principles of building a learning environment for all partners within a development cooperation process. The post-2015 development agenda should have a broader approach with wider definitions of global learning in all geographical directions around the world (Petry and Runkel 2016). The global northern, western, eastern or southern patterns of gender equality should become part of a global learning perspective. The term 'global learning' is more related to the debate of sustainable education and it is based on the principle of a global responsibility for both women and men. Global learning in the area of gender equality is possible at all levels, from the individual to the international, and is related to a democratic approach of partnership. It is already part of the SDGs and of the post-2015 Agenda, including the following target for SDG 4:

by 2030, ensure that all learners acquire knowledge and skills needed to promote sustainable development … gender equality, promotion of a culture of peace and non-violence, global citizenship, and appreciation of cultural diversity and of culture´s contribution to sustainable development.

United Nations 2014

References

ActionAid International. (2013). Stop Violence Against Girls in School. A cross-country analysis of change in Ghana, Kenya and Mozambique. Available at: www.actionaid.org/sites/files/actionaid/svags_review_final.pdf (accessed 18 December 2016).

Agergaard, S. and Botelho, V. (2014). The way out? African players' migration to Scandinavian women's football. *Sport in Society, 17*(4), 523–536.

Beutler, I. (2008). Sport serving peace and development: Achieving the goals of the United Nations through sport. *Sport in Society, 11*(4), 359–369.

Burnett, C. (2009). Engaging sport-for-development for the social impact in the South African context. *Sport in Society, 12*(9), 1192–1205.

Campbell, C., Gibbs, A., Nair, Y. and Maimane, S. (2009). Frustrated potential, false promise or complicated possibilities? Empowerment and participation amongst female health volunteers in South Africa. *Journal of Health Management, 11*(2), 315–336.

Coalter, F. (2006). Sport in development: Process evaluation and organizational development. In Y. van den Auweele, C. Malcolm and B. Mulders (eds), *Sport and Development*. Leuven: Lannoo Campus, pp. 149–162.

Coalter, F. (2008). Sport-in-development: Development for and through sport? In M. Nicholson and R. Hoye (eds), *Sport and Social Capital*. Oxford: Elsevier, pp. 39–67.

Coalter, F. (2010). The politics of sport-for development: Limited focus programmes and broad gauge problems. *International Review for the Sociology of Sport, 45*(3), 295–314.

Coalter, F. (2013). *Sport for Development*. Oxford: Routledge.

Crowe, K. (2010). Die Himba-Gladiatorin. *FIFA World*, (Mai), 42–45.

Darnell, S. C. (2007). Playing with Race: Right to play and the production of whiteness in development through sport. *Sport in Society, 10*(4), 560–579.

Darnell, S. C. (2010). Power, politics and 'sport-for development and peace: Investigating the utility of sport for international development. *Sociology of Sport Journal, 27*(1), 54–75.

Darnell, S. C. and Hayhurst, L. (2011). Sport for decolonization: Exploring a new praxis of sport for development. *Progress in Development Studies, 11* (3), 183–196.

DEZA (Direktion für Entwicklung und Zusammenarbeit). (2005). *Sport für Entwicklung und Frieden*. Bern: DEZA.

Donnelly, P., Atkinson, M., Boyle, S. and Szto, C. (2011). Sport for development and peace: A public sociology perspective. *Third World Quarterly, 32*(3), 589–601.

Engh, M. H. (2010). Football, empowerment and gender equality: An exploration of elite-level women's football in South Africa. In J. Shehu (ed.), *Gender, Sport and Development in Africa: Cross-cultural Perspectives on Patterns of Representations and Marginalization*. Dakar: Codesria, pp. 63–78.

Fokwang, J. (2009). Southern perspective of sport-in-development: A case study of football in Bamenda, Cameroon. In R. Levermore and A. Beacom (eds), *Sport and International Development*. Basingstoke: Palgrave MacMillan, pp. 198–218.

Geddes, M. (2010). Zentren der Hoffnung. *FIFA World*, (June/ July), 28–29.

Giulianotti, R. (2004). Human rights, globalization and sentimental education: The case of sport. *Sport in Society, 13*(7), 355–369.

Giulianotti, R. (2014). Sport for Development and Peace Policy Options in the Commonwealth. In O. Dudfield (ed.), *Strengthening Sport for Development and peace. National Policies and Strategies. Commonwealth Secretariat*. London: Commonwealth Secretariat, pp. 13–24.

Giulianotti, R. and Armstrong, G. (2011). Sport, the military and peacemaking: History and possibilities. *Third World Quarterly*, *32*(3), 379–394.

Guest, A. (2009). The diffusion of development-through-sport: Analysing the history and practice of the Olympics Movement's grassroots outreach to Africa. *Sport in Society*, *12*(10), 1336–1352.

Handy, F. and Kassa, M. (2004). Women's Empowerment in Rural India. Paper presented at the ISTR conference, Toronto, Canada, July 2004.

Hartmann, D. and Kwauk, C. (2011). Sport and development: An overview, critique and reconstruction. *Journal of Sport and Social Issues*, *35*(3), 284–305.

Hayhurst, L. (2013). Girls as the 'new' agents of social change? Exploring the 'Girl Effect' through sport, gender and development programs in Uganda. *Sociological Research Online*, *18*(2), 1–12.

Jeanes, R. and Magee, J. (2014). Promoting gender empowerment through sport? Exploring the experiences of Zambian female footballers. In N. Schulenkorf and D. Adair (eds), *Global Sport-for-Development: Critical Perspectives*. Basingstoke: Palgrave Macmillan, pp. 134–154.

Kay, T. (2009). Developing through Sport: evidencing sport impacts on young people. *Sport in Society*, *12*(9), 1177–1191.

Kay, T. and Bradbury, S. (2009). Youth sport volunteering: Developing social capital? *Sport, Education and Society*, *14*(1), 121–140.

Khan, N. (2010). Using Football for HIV/AIDS Prevention in Africa. Football for an HIV-free Generation. Available at: www.grassrootsoccer.org/wp-content/uploads/F4_HIV_Report.pdf (accessed 12 January 2017).

Kidd, B. (2008). A new social movement: Sport for development and peace. *Sport in Society*, *11*(4), 370–380.

Lawson, H. A. (2005). Empowering people, facilitating community development, and contributing to sustainable development. The social work of sport, exercise and physical education programs. *Sport, Education and Society*, *10*(1), 135–160.

Levermore, R. (2008a). Sport in international development: Time to treat it seriously? *The Brown Journal of World Affairs*, *14*(2), 55–56.

Levermore, R. (2008b). Sport: A new engine of development? *Progress in Development Studies*, *8*(2), 183–190.

Levermore, R. and Beacom, A. (eds) (2009). *Sport and International Development*. Basingstoke: Palgrave MacMillan.

Levermore, R. and Beacom, A. (2012). Reassessing sport-for-development: Moving beyond 'mapping the territory'. *International Journal of Sport Policy and Politics*, *4*(1), 125–137.

Lyras, A. and Peachy, J. W. (2011). Integrating sport-for-development theory and praxis. *Sport Management Review*, 1–16.

Mwaanga, O. and Adeosun, K. (2016). The critical participatory paradigm and its implications. In Y. Vanden Auweele *et al.* (eds), *Sport Ethics in the 21st Century*. London & New York: Routledge, pp. 190–198.

Meier, M. (2005). Gender Equity, Sport and Development- Working Paper. Available at: http://assets.sportanddev.org/downloads/59__gender_equity__sport_and_development.pdf (accessed 20 December 2016).

Nauright, J. (2014). African women and sport: The state of play. *Sport in Society*, *17*(4), 563–574.

Ogunniyi, C. (2014). Perceptions of the African women's championships: Female footballers as anomalies. *Sport in Society*, *17*(4), 537–549.

Pelak, C. F. (2005). Negotiating gender/race/class constraints in the new South Africa: A case study of women's soccer. *International Review for the Sociology of Sport*, *40*(1), 53–70.

Pelak, C. F. (2006). Local-global process: Linking globalisation, democratisation and the development of women's football in South Africa. *Africa Spectrum 41*(3), 371–392.

Petry, K. and Runkel, M. (2016). The concept of development and the sport related (future) approach. In Y. Vanden Auweele, *et al.* (eds), *Sport Ethics in the 21st Century*. London & New York: Routledge, pp. 208–216.

Saavedra, M. (2003). Football feminine – development of the African game: Senegal, Nigeria and South Africa. *Soccer and Society*, *4* (2–3), 225–253.

Saavedra, M. (2005). Women, Sport and Development. Available at: http://assets.sportanddev.org/downloads/56__women__sport_and_development.pdf (accessed 20 December 2016).

Saavedra, M. (2009). Dilemmas and opportunities in gender and sport in development. In R. Levermore and A. Beacom (eds), *Sport and International development*. Basingstoke: Palgrave Macmillan, pp. 124–155.

Šafaříková, S. (2012). The influence of football on the personal development of children in Uganda. *Journal of Human Sport and Exercise*, 7(1Proc), 173–177.

Šafaříková, S. (2013). *The Influence of Sport and Physical Activities on Youth Development within the Context of Developing Countries (The Kids League, Uganda)*. Palacky University in Olomouc, Olomouc. Available at: http://theses.cz/id/e1lzl4/disertace_final_1_4.pdf (accessed 20 January 2017).

Schulenkorf, N., Sherry, E. and Rowe, K. (2017). Global sport-for-development. In N. Schulenkorf and S. Frawley (eds), *Critical Issues in Global Sport Management*. London & New York: Routledge, pp. 176–191.

Shehu, J. (2010). Introduction. In J. Shehu (ed.), *Gender, Sport and Development in Africa: Cross-cultural Perspectives on Patterns of Representations and Marginalization* (ix–xiv), Dakar: Codesria.

Sikes, M. and Jarvie, G. (2014). Women's running as freedom: development and choice. *Sport and Society, 17*(4), 59–74.

Skinner, J., Zakus, D. and Cowell, J. (2008). Development through sport: Building social capital in disadvantaged communities. *Sport Management Review, 11*(3), 253–275.

Spaaij, R. (2009a). Sport as a vehicle for social mobility and regulation of disadvantaged urban youth: Lessons from Rotterdam. *International Review for the Sociology of Sport, 44*(2–3), 247–264.

Spaaij, R. (2009b). The social impact of sport: Diversities, complexities and contexts. *Sport in Society, 12*(9), 1109–1117.

Tobisch, C. and Preti, D. (2010). *The Role of Football in HIV Prevention in Africa*. Brussels: Koning Boudewijnstichting; Swiss Academy for Development.

Tembon, L. and Fort, L. (2008). *Girls Education in the 21st Century: Gender Equality, Empowerment, and Economic Growth*. Washington, DC: World Bank.

Touwen, A. (1996). *Gender and Development in Zambia, Empowerment of Women Through local Non-Governmental Organisation*. Groningen: Rijksuniversiteit.

United Nations. (2014). Sustainable Development. Available at: https://sustainabledevelopment.un.org/focussdgs.html (accessed 15 December 2016).

Vermeulen, J. and Verwell, P. (2009). Participation in Sport: Bonding and bridging as identity work. *Sport in Society, 12*(9), 1206–1219.

Williams, J. (2003). Women's football – An international comparison. *A Game for Rough Girls? A History of Women's Football in Britain*. London: Routledge, pp. 148–180.

Williams, J. and Chawansky, M. (2013). Namibia's brave gladiators: Gendering the sport and development nexus from the 1998 2nd World Women and Sport Conference to the 2011 Women's World Cup. *Sport in Society, 17*(4), 550–562.

Willis, O. (2000). Sport and development: The significance of Mathare Youth Sports Association. *Canadian Journal of Development Studies, 21*(3), 825–849.

23
SDP and peace[1]

Tom Woodhouse

If football embraces the relentless uncertainty of play, it also holds fast to the generosity, universalism and egalitarianism of play. When we play power games, we are not playing at all, for we have crossed into the realm of instrumentalism, self-interest, manipulation and inequality. Play can encompass none of these. Indeed, play that does not descend into bullying is necessarily democratic. Play rests on consensus, negotiation and turn-taking. It recognises the virtues and limits of collaboration and competition. Too much of the former and you have an oligarchy; too much of the latter and you have a war of all against all. Play, like democracy, is open to revision, responsive to change and necessarily open-ended. The future is never closed. How could it be?

Goldblatt 2007: 910

This opening quotation from David Goldblatt aptly encapsulates the significance of the topic of this chapter – the relationship between sport, peace and conflict.[2] The SDP sector has expanded dynamically and creatively in recent years, occupying and engaging an ever-widening circle of academics, policy-makers, practitioners, and media analysts and commentators. Academic fields as diverse as sport science, history, sociology, anthropology, economics, politics and international relations, global and cultural studies, international development, psychology, management and marketing, medicine, education, law, philosophy, and gender studies have all engaged with analysis of sport in their areas of concern. Yet, given the prominent usage of the word 'peace' in the labelling of the sector, the connections and relationships between sport and peacemaking is rarely acknowledged in the academic field of peace research and conflict resolution. There are of course notable exceptions, and this work is acknowledged and summarised below. Still, much of the literature that connects sport and peace has been produced by specialists whose orientation and perspective come from fields outside peace and conflict research – from sociologists, historians, and international relations and development specialists especially.

This relative neglect in peace research is surprising, given that many of the great charismatic peace leaders have used the passion generated by sport to successfully mobilise support for their campaigns. Probably the best known of these is Nelson Mandela, who used the game of rugby union and the universal following it had among white people in South Africa, to engage the black and white communities in support of the peaceful transformation of the apartheid regime.

The story is well known and the subject of a major film, *Invictus*, based on a book by Carlin (2008). Korr and Close (2008) have also shown how football was used as a support for physical and psychological survival and to sustain the struggle against apartheid by Mandela and his fellow prisoners on Robben Island. Perhaps even more towering as an icon of nonviolence, but less well known for his association with sport, there are also well founded claims that Gandhi organised football teams (Passive Resisters Soccer Clubs) in Pretoria, Johannesburg and Durban in pursuit of his *satyagraha* principles and in his campaign for civil liberties, during his time as a young lawyer in South Africa in the early years of the twentieth century.[3]

The boxer Muhammad Ali, one of the most well-known sporting personalities of all time, has left as his enduring legacy not only his unparalleled record and skills as a fighter, but his endowment of the Muhammad Ali Institute of Peace and Justice at the University of Louisville in the USA. In the case of football FIFA, the world governing body, was nominated (unsuccessfully) for the Nobel Peace Prize in 2001; Jules Rimet, who founded the football World Cup, was nominated (also unsuccessfully) for the award in 1956; and Philip Noel Baker, a Labour politician who won a silver medal in athletics for the British Olympic Team at the 1920 Games, also facilitated the tour of Moscow Dynamo to play matches against four British clubs in a goodwill tour in 1945. Noel Baker won the Nobel Peace Prize in 1959 for his pioneering work on disarmament and peace research (Hough 2008: 1287–1288).

From these brief introductory examples (and many more could be offered) it is clear that sport has an impact in a variety of ways outside of its own boundaries.[4] A survey conducted on behalf of the UK-based charity Comic Relief, which funds many SDP projects, divided the main areas of SDP activity and specialization in the UK into the following six groupings: policy; socio-cultural issues; education; strategic and organisational development; communications and technology, and Olympism and peace. The Olympism, peace and conflict resolution dimensions were the least developed.

> The area of 'human rights and conflict resolution' is only represented by 4 per cent of researchers, and as this is an explicit theme in the strategies of a number of grassroots organizations, this seems rather sparse, and may be an area in which the sector may wish to deploy additional research activity.
>
> *Cronin 2011: 32*

This is a clear reflection and measurement of the lack of knowledge transfer between sport and peace research.

This chapter sets out to suggest that while sport is currently seen as a marginal concern at best by peace researchers, the transfer of knowledge between peace research/conflict resolution and the SDP sector can have positive gains for evolving theory, policy and practice in both fields. Following this introduction, the chapter is organised in three sections. The first, 'Knowledge transfer and peace culture: Expanding the field', surveys existing work on the connections between peace and sport and uses an approach to peace theory, derived from Elise Boulding. This approach argues for peace as an evolutionary capacity, developed in a wider theory of change than dominant narratives and frameworks in peace and conflict theory, and within which sport can be situated. The second section, 'Spaces for sport in peace research', maps the way in which sport might be inserted as more of a core concern in peace and conflict research, using a spatial model provided by Galtung. The third section, 'Time to change the playing field: Methodologies and future research and challenges',[5] suggests ways in which established and emerging peace and conflict research and training methodologies might enhance the development of both theory and practice in the SDP sector.

Peace culture and knowledge transfer: expanding the sport and peace field

In the recent literature which has sought to connect research on sport with peace research, the work of two leading analysts, Darnell and Giulianotti, helps to formulate a robust survey of the current state of knowledge and an understanding of the sport-peace frameworks within which continued knowledge transfer would be beneficial. Darnell (2014) has analysed the relationship between the peace movement and sport historically. He shows how the peace movement recognised and informed the organisation of sport from at least the nineteenth century, but identifies a concern or a tension evident in the relationship between peace movements and sport and the way this has shifted during the twentieth century and the early years of this century. In the twentieth century, he argues, the peace movement had 'oppositional and resistive political goals' – against militarism, nationalism, colonialism and hegemonic forms of international relations. Peace movements remained oppositional and resistive to militarism, nuclear armaments, military coalitions and warfare for much of the past century and continue to operate in resistive mode post 9/11, and also in the current era of weakening neoliberal international institutions, re-emergent nationalisms and international terrorism. However, Darnell points to a shift in the nature of the relationship between peace and sport, away from political resistance to violence and militarism, in favour of a 'paradigm shift from a culture of war to a culture of peace, a shift promoted in part by the designation by the UN of 2000 as the Year of the Culture of Peace' (Darnell 2014: 100–101). A culture of peace has been defined by the UN as 'a set of values, attitudes, modes of behaviour and ways of life that reject violence and prevent conflicts by tackling their root causes, to solve problems through dialogue and negotiation among individuals, groups and nations' (Ramsbotham *et al.* 2016: 406).

This shift to a culture of peace paradigm applied to the sport-peace movement relationship has its critics. Indeed, the critique runs back to the origins of the field of peace research itself, when its foundational theories were dismissed as based on a naïve set of socio-psychological models. In this view, the impact of peace research and peace studies was to serve as an instrument of pacification, ignoring or concealing existing power structures, failing to take sides or to resist the forces of global militarism, exploitation and oppression. While the debate is a complex and continuing one, in essence the accusation is that peace research ignored structures of control and domination and prioritised methodologies that attempted only to change behaviours and attitudes, leaving oppressive structures untouched.[6]

The response to this critique from peace researchers has been to insist that peace research has an emancipatory objective, based on developing a reflexive transformational paradigm which depends on careful systemic analysis of deep-rooted conflict and its causes; on uncovering the structural and institutional failures of governance to meet basic human needs; and on transforming 'either-or' antagonism into a recognition that violent conflict is a systemic problem that can only be solved jointly. It is a paradigm that prioritises evolutionary processes of peacemaking based on problem-solving and related communication methodologies which are interdisciplinary, transcultural and cosmopolitan (Ramsbotham *et al.* 2016: ch. 19).

The idea of peace as an evolving cultural capacity emerged in peace research after 1945 when pioneering academics in the field reflected on the failures of peace movement campaigns to prevent or to stop both the First and the Second World Wars. The failure of the peace movement to prevent war was also regarded as a failure of the discipline of international relations. Peace and conflict research emerged after 1945 to build knowledge in the academies about how to evolve cultures and institutions of conflict prevention and peacebuilding. The field developed initially in Northern Europe, America and the UK, and is now institutionalised worldwide.

> Two main objectives were characteristic of this new field. The first was the effort to identify the conditions for a new world order based on conflict analysis, conflict prevention and problem-solving. The second was the effort to mobilise and inspire ever-widening and inclusive constituencies based on the promotion of the values of non-violent peacemaking. Putting these two dimensions of activity together, peace research and conflict resolution emerged as an enterprise that was normatively associated with the promotion of peace at three levels: first, through a radical reformation of world political systems; second, through the promotion of an inclusive anti-war and pro-peace politics; and, third, through the fashioning of methodologies and processes that provided the opportunity to move through the politics of protest towards a proactive peacemaking project. This proactive peacemaking project was concerned to address the behavioural, attitudinal and structural/objective elements of Galtung's well-known conflict triangle. It also aligned conflict resolution not only with the negative peace goals of preventing war and containing violent conflict, but, crucially, with the even more challenging task of building a positive emancipatory peace, in which individuals and groups would be able to pursue their life-goals non-violently in ways of their own choosing.
>
> *Ramsbotham et al. 2016: 39*

In this idea of peace, while resistive politics has played a part and will continue to do so, it is the contention of this chapter that the culture of a peace model provides a more robust normative and analytical framework within which to develop and apply the policy outcomes and practical implications of the sport-peace relationship. The culture of peace idea was interpreted pedagogically and conceptually in a creative way to provide a wider agenda for peace research by one if its pioneers, Elise Boulding, who acknowledged the importance of institution building in peacemaking, but also stressed the power of imagination, creativity and human desire in creating what she called a 'global civic culture'. Boulding identified three 'modes of knowing': the cognitive/analytic, the emotional/affective, and the intuitive. In a world increasingly governed by science and technology, the cognitive/analytic mode has come to dominate and the emotional/affective and intuitive modes have become relatively less used. For Boulding, it was important to find ways of 'freeing the other modes for action by developing the skills of the imagination' (Boulding 1990: 95).

This pedagogic framework provides a strong signal for academic peace research to engage with the cultural and artistic dimensions of conflict resolution, expressed in popular culture, in art, theatre and music, and also in sport as a universal expression of popular culture. These creative and expressive areas of human activity provide access to a powerful source of peacebuilding energy and passion that is not always apparent in the formalised processes of political conflict resolution. At the same time, creative conflict resolution both nourishes and defines the emergence of a culture of peace.

Returning to Darnell's analysis, the culture of peace model has come to encapsulate much of the activity of current peace research and practice, and the study of the institution of sport has also shown how sport has become more comfortably associated with the culture of peace model than with resistive politics of peace movements. Giulianotti, in another landmark article, has traced the development of sport as a peacemaking tool in the historical expansion of the SDP sector. His approach outlines three stages of growth: Phase 1 – sport, colonisation and 'civilisation', which lasted from the late eighteenth to the mid-twentieth century; Phase 2 – sport, nationalism, post-colonialism, from the 1940s to the 1990s; and Phase 3 – a continuation of the 1990s to date, but which has witnessed a maturation and institutionalisation of the SDP sector as a focus for development and peace, 'with the emergence of transnational SDP institutions such as the Sport and Development platform in Switzerland, Peace and Sport in Monaco, Right to Play in Toronto, and streetfootballworld in Berlin'. (Giulianotti 2011: 209–211).

Giulianotti proceeds to outline three models of SDP projects based on an analysis of projects which focus primarily on peacemaking: model 1, Technical SDP; model 2, Dialogical SDP; and model 3, Critical SDP. The social heuristics of each model are outlined in detail but in essence models 2 and 3, the dialogical and the critical, closely reflect the objectives and methods of transformative conflict resolution established in the field of peace research by theorist practitioners ('pracademics') such as Elise Boulding in her future workshops (Woodhouse and Santiago 2012); Adam Curle in his reflexive mediation and his idea of peacebuilding from below (Woodhouse and Lederach 2016); John Paul Lederach in his distinction between prescriptive and elective training methodologies and his advocacy of the use of moral imagination in supporting peaceful transformation (Lederach 1999; 2005); and Wolfgang Dietrich in his recent work on transrational peace theory and elicitive conflict mapping (Dietrich 2014). While none of these pioneers and innovators of peace thinking and practice have applied their work directly to the sport–peace interface, they have constructed frameworks and understandings which are rich in their potential to cross over to the peace work of the SDP sector and to enhance the methodologies of Giulianotti's three models – the technical, the dialogical and the critical.

In the next section, 'Spaces for sport in peace research' we use a model drawn from Galtung to map the way in which sport might be inserted as a more core concern in peace and conflict research. The concluding section, 'Time to change the playing field: Methodologies and future research and challenges', suggests ways in which established and emerging peace and conflict research methodologies, along with the development of theoretical innovation, might be developed and applied to peace and sport to enhance both the elicitive models of Giulianotti (the dialogical and the critical especially) and the relevance of the four 'spaces' to encourage more engagement by peace researchers in the SDP sector.

Spaces for sport in peace research

From its inception, peace and conflict research took a wide-ranging definition of the kinds of conflict with which it should be concerned (Ramsbotham *et al.* 2016: Ch.1). Analysis and resolution had to embrace all levels of conflict: intra-personal (inner conflict), inter-personal, inter-group (families, neighbourhoods, social and ethnic affiliations), international, regional, global and the complex interplays between them. Galtung added to this list the level of ecology – the relationship between people, planet and nature. From this multi-level analysis, Galtung (founder of one of the first and most influential peace centres, the Peace Research Institute, Oslo, and the *Journal of Peace Research*) suggested that relationships which produce peace or violence are formed in four 'spaces': personal relationships (the human space); the social space of societal constructions (broadly, culture, politics, economy); the global space of world systems (international politics); and the ecological space (the relationship of people to the planet or to nature). He adds to these four spaces the dimensions of time and culture (Galtung 1996).

In this section, we review work on sport and peace which ranges across these spaces, first as a way of making visible how what is already being done fits into the holistic/multi-level model of Galtung; and second, how, presented in this way, the model will look familiar to peace researchers. For the sake of brevity, the review is based primarily on examples of case studies of football. To start at the global space, we have already mentioned the work of Hough (2008) who shows how, counter to the prevailing negative view of the sport in regard to internationalist and democratic values (which emphasises hooliganism, intensifying rivalries between nations and, for many people during this era of economic hardship, obscenely high income for top sports personalities), football has the capacity and universal appeal to act as a normative progressive force in its ability to contribute to international peace and security. Examples include assisting rapprochement in international diplomacy, and within and across divided communities; peacekeeping; nation building and providing a safe outlet for national rivalries; and, contributing to global human rights norms through the consistent application of Article 3 of FIFA's statues, the anti-discrimination rule. In this global space of international relations there is an obvious need to be cautious about over-stating claims and Hough recognises this, concluding with the reasonable claim that while football cannot stop a war it has exceptional capacity to bring nations together and to contribute to the process of communication, which is fundamental to peace at any level. Remaining in the global space, some brief comments on peacekeeping may help make the case for the positive impact of sport-football in the international security architecture of the UN.

The case of peacekeeping, mentioned by Hough, provides an opportunity to reflect on the positive role of sport in one of the most successful mechanisms available to the international community for ending war and sustaining peace post-conflict. Both Woodhouse and Giulianotti have written on the use of sport in peacekeeping missions. Woodhouse (2010) explores the idea of culture as a contributory factor in the emergence of new forms of what he terms 'cosmopolitan peacekeeping'. He draws on Robert Rubinstein's concept of the 'root metaphor' that legitimised early peacekeeping operations through a process of what Rubinstein calls 'cultural inversion', in which the UN and its peacekeeping operations represent and adopt the symbols and rituals of a pacific global order, which are opposites or inversions of state-based militarism. Legitimacy with host governments and civilian populations is a key challenge for the deployment of peacekeeping missions and Woodhouse argues that current (cosmopolitan) peacekeeping can be legitimised through new root metaphors that use the creativity of popular culture in favour of an emergent global peace culture.

Sport is a pre-eminent example of popular culture, and in 2006 the Department of Peacekeeping Operations, the UN Office on Sport Development and Peace and the International Olympic Committee (IOC) formed a partnership to use sport in the peace-making framework of UN peacekeeping operations. Three missions were chosen as locations for pilot sport and peace projects – namely the UN Mission in the Democratic Republic of Congo (MONUC), the UN Operation in Côte d'Ivoire (UNOCI) and the UN Mission in Liberia (UNMIL). Some examples of these pilot projects will suffice to indicate how sport has been used in peacekeeping and post-conflict peacebuilding. In the MONUC mission, Peace Games were held to support an atmosphere of peace and reconciliation around the elections of July and August 2006. In Liberia, UNMIL organised a sport for peace programme in March and April 2007. In Côte d'Ivoire, the UNOCI peacekeeping mission has promoted a very active sport-based peacebuilding programme since 2006. This included activities during the 2006 football World Cup, when it provided opportunities for viewing of matches on widescreens throughout the country, during which peace messages and information about the mandate of the peacekeeping mission were delivered. UNOCI staff attempted also to 'sensitize the population on the purpose of sport for peace in countries in crisis or out of it; to encourage the population to get involved in crisis solving; and confirm the rallying role of sport'.[7] Also, international sports events are organised within multinational contingents to enhance mutual understanding among personnel. Significantly, and in view of the theme and argument of this chapter, one of the main events that inspired this development in peacekeeping was the very positive role played by Didier Drogba, the captain of the international football team, as a peacemaker in brokering a ceasefire in the civil war in the Côte d'Ivoire (Woodhouse 2010; 2016).

Giulianotti and Armstrong (2011) have also recognised this new role for sport in peacekeeping. Referring to fieldwork in Bosnia and Liberia, and to the role of the Conseil Internationale du Sport Militaire, they suggest that

> sport-based peacemaking interventions provide the military with a new kind of institutional function, and fresh ways of building positive social links to civilian populations. However, such engagement is only possible if full dialogical engagement between civilians and peace-keeping forces is established, in which the military adapt their practices to suit the local cultural context.
>
> *Giulianotti and Armstrong 2011: 379*

This sensitivity to local cultural context has been a primary driver of peace and conflict research and in the case of peacekeeping is reflected in the work of Curran (2016), who applies methods derived from conflict resolution theory to examine the training programmes and needs of peace-keeping personnel, in a way that supports both the dialogical and critical models of Giulianotti – an illustration of the potential value added from knowledge exchange between the sport and peace science fields.

The majority of projects in the SDP sector take place within the personal and social spaces of Galtung's model. We deal with the personal and societal spaces together here because in practice many projects deal with personal life skills (communication, confidence building, team work, ethics and values, motivation and so on) which are valuable in themselves but also a pre-requisite for engagement with social inclusion and social cohesion programmes. There is also a developing literature within this space which traces and analyses the growing extent of the use of sport for peace work. For football, recent literature and programmes have been described and analysed by Lea-Howarth (2006) within a framework of evaluation based on familiar concepts of peacebuilding as defined by Galtung, Lederach and others. Using case studies of grassroots foot-ball for peace projects based in Sierra Leone (World Vision International Youth Reintegration Training and Education for Peace), Israel (Football4Peace), Liberia (Bosco United Sports Association) and Bosnia Hercegovina (Open Fun Football Schools, Balkans and the Middle East), he concludes that, while much of the literature on peacebuilding agrees with the desir-ability of peacebuilding from below, practical ways of engaging in this process are often lacking.

Sport and football provides one important and still underused practical entry point for conflict resolvers and a dimension of activity that is transcultural and universal in its appeal.[8] Specifically in relation to peace and conflict resolution promotion, the Foundation of Football Club Barcelona has launched its 'FutbolNet' programme to teach the skills of dialogue, medi-ation and conflict resolution. FutbolNet is a project that attempts to educate children and young people via the promotion of the positive values that come from playing sport. Since 2011/12, the FC Barcelona Foundation has developed this programme in Barcelona and around Catalonia, and the project has been extended internationally through alliances with, among others, the Lionel Messi Foundation in Argentina, the Cruyff Foundation, the Rafa Marquez Foundation in Mexico, the Instituto Projecto Neymar Jr and the Inter-American Development Bank in Brazil (Foundation FC Barcelona 2016). The programme is based on a series of rules that produce social interaction between those taking part – it obliges them to understand one another and use the tools available to resolve conflicts. One of the main features is the absence of a referee who is replaced by a 'teamer', (in some variants a mediator), a figure who accompanies the participants in the game without intervening. FutbolNet was inspired and developed from experiences in Colombia (in the context of the long conflict there and following the murder of the footballer Andes Escobar) and also via the organisation streetfootballworld, which developed the original methodology of dialogue and mediation applied through football (Gannett 2014). There are now many examples and case studies where football is used in peacebuilding and as a tool for strengthening social cohesion and social inclusion, in the flourishing football foundation and football in the community projects run, for example, by most professional clubs in the professional English football leagues (Woodhouse 2014; Woodhouse and Antin 2017). These areas in particular – the personal and societal spaces – are rich in potential for further collaboration between sports and peace researchers to look at the benefits of crossover research on methodologies, monitoring and evaluation, classification typologies, in-depth case studies, and even, eventually, theories of change.

The fourth space is Galtung's ecological space – the relationship between people, planet and nature. In relation to sport and ecology, peace research, despite a strong concern with climate change, conflict and peace ecology, is largely silent. The importance of the topic for sport researchers, and the degree to which it is charted in detail by Courchesne-O'Neill (2015), shows how there has been an increasing concern with the environment within the Olympic Movement. The ecological impact of sport is a relatively new field where again there is productive space and opportunity for collaborative research between sport and peace researchers. One cameo case study may suffice here to illustrate emerging good practice. The English Northern League club side Forest Green Rovers, already claiming the distinction of having the first organic pitch in the world, announced plans in 2015 to build a new stadium set within an EcoPark, which would be environmentally sustainable with all energy generated on site so the facility would be either carbon neutral or carbon negative (*The Times*, 4 November 2016). This is clearly a small and perhaps insignificant example in itself, but climate change as a generator of conflict, and strategies to counter this, is becoming a main theme in academic peace research (Ramsbotham *et al.* 2016: ch. 12) and given the recognised and often negative impact of sporting mega-events on the environment (Courchesne-O'Neill 2015), this fourth space is another productive area for collaborative work.

Time to change the playing field: methodologies and future research and challenges

This chapter has argued the need for greater involvement of peace researchers in sport research. While the case for collaboration is strong, there is also a concern for a more critical orientation to research on SDP generally, especially in response to the concerns of those who, like Coalter (2013), warn against exaggerated claims made about the effectiveness of programmes. Sanders (2016), has written about the need to recognise the limitations of SDP projects. His call, that it is 'time to change the playing field', refers to the need to avoid 'sports evangelism' and to explore a better understanding of how sport can help to foster social change by tackling the structural causes of poverty, inequality and, in relation to the 'peace' content of SDP, of violence. This is partly a challenge of methodology – the development of practices, processes and skills in designing and evaluating research and programme impacts critically and reflexively. Darnell has cautioned against over-reliance on positivist-quantitative approaches that tend to be top down, mechanistic, and to subjugate local knowledge. He calls for innovative and imaginary approaches to social change through sport, in the same way that Giulianotti identifies his dialogical and critical models of SDP activity, which are cooperative, multi-method, participatory and critically reflexive.

Peace research and conflict resolution has much to offer in this area, including conflict modelling (escalation, de-escalation and complementarity processes), conflict data collection, problem-solving workshops, game theory, elicitive methodology and elicitive conflict mapping, cross-cultural, hybrid and transrational peace theory, dialogue processes, mediation skills and models, future imaging workshops, data-sets of peace structures, post-conflict peacebuilding, and more (Ramsbotham *et al.* 2016: chs 2 & 3). Many of these models and methods are designed to enable and empower the emergence of peace cultures and peace structures as part of broader processes of social change, in which sport can play a part. Looking ahead, and especially for younger peace researchers looking for fresh challenges, it is indeed a good time to enlarge the playing field for peace researchers and sport. As Goldblatt observed, in the quote noted at the head of this chapter, 'The future is never closed. How could it be?'

Notes

1   Thanks to Yolanda Antin of the Foundation of FC Barcelona for her helpful comments and for information about FutbolNet and the community programmes of FFCB.
2   In one of the early texts which defined conflict studies, Anatol Rapoport (1960) argued that a more systematic understanding of conflict would enable fights, in which opponents tried to destroy each other, to be transformed into games, where differences can managed in a framework of accepted rules; and games can be transformed into debates, the most productive mode of conflict management.
3   See Football History: FIFA World 22 October 2010. Available at: www.fifa.com/news/y=2010/ m=10/news=mahatma-gandhi-football-legend-1322010.html. *Satyagraha* was the name given to the movement started by Gandhi based on the principles of truth and nonviolence.
4   There are a number of accounts of the connections between football, national politics, international relations, war and conflict. See for example Burns (2006), Foer (2006), Goldblatt (2007), Kuper (2003), Riordan (2008), Shobe (2008), Zanotti *et al.* (2015).
5   I am grateful to Sanders (2016) from where the phrase 'Time to change the playing field' is taken.
6   For a summary of this critique of peace research see Ramsbotham *et al.* (2016: 476–486).
7   Woodhouse (2010: 495).
8   For early and innovative work on this from the perspective of sociology, see Sugden (2010). Also a group of young scholars working within peace research, including Cardenas (2013), Dilliway (2013), Lea-Howarth (2006), Lucheva (2011) and Oxford (2012).

References

Boulding, E. (1990). *Building a Global Civic Culture: Education for an Interdependent World*. New York: Syracuse University Press.
Burns, J. (2006). *Barca: A People's Passion*. London: Bloomsbury.
Cardenas, A. (2013). Peace building through sport? An introduction to sport for development and peace. *Journal of Conflictology*, 4(1), 24–33.
Carlin, J. (2008). *Invictus: Nelson Mandela and the Game that Made a Nation*. London: Penguin.
Coalter, F. (2013). *Sport-for-Development: What Game Are We Playing?* London: Routledge.
Cronin, O. (2011). *Comic Relief Review, Mapping the Research on the Impact of Sport and Development Interventions*. London: Comic Relief.
Courchesne-O'Neill, S. (2014). Sport and the environmental movement. In J. Harvey, J. Horne, P. Safai, S. Darnell, and S. Courchesne-O'Neill (eds), *Sport and Social Movements: From the Local to the Global*. London: Bloomsbury, pp. 114–136.
Curran, D. (2016). *More than Fighting for Peace? Conflict Resolution, UN Peacekeeping, and the Role of Training Military Personnel*. Berlin: Springer.
Darnell, S. (2014). Sport and the global peace movement. In J. Harvey, J. Horne, P. Safai, S. Darnell and S. Courchesne-O'Neill (eds), *Sport and Social Movements: From the Local to the Global*. London: Bloomsbury, pp. 93–113.
Dietrich, W. (2014). A brief introduction to transrational peace research and elicitive conflict transformation. *Journal of Conflictology*, 5(2), 48–57.
Dilliway, S. (2013). Sport and Peace: To What Extent Can Sports Programs Contribute to Building Peace in East Africa, MA Thesis, University of Bradford, UK.
Foer, F. (2006). *How Football Explains the World: An Unlikely Theory of Globalisation*. London: Arrow.
Foundation FC Barcelona. (2016). *Annual Report*, 2015/2016. Barcelona.
Galtung, J. (1996). *Peace by Peaceful Means: Peace and Conflict, Development and Civilisation*. Oslo, Norway: PRIO.

Gannett, K.R, Kaufman, Z., Clark, M. and S. McGarvey, T. (2014). Football with three 'halves': A qualitative exploratory study of the Football3 Model at the Football for Hope Festival 2010. *Journal of Sport for Development, 2*(3), 47–59.

Giulianotti, R. (2011). Sport, peacemaking and conflict resolution: A contextual analysis and modelling of the sport, development and peace sector. *Ethnic and Racial Studies, 34*(2), 207–228.

Giulianotti, R. and Armstrong, G. (2011). Sport, the military and peacemaking: History and possibilities. *Third World Quarterly, 32*(3), 379–394.

Goldblatt, D. (2007). *The Ball is Round: A Global History of Football*. London: Penguin.

Grix, J. and Lee, D. (2013). Soft power, sports mega-events and emerging states: The lure of the politics of attraction. *Global Society, 27*(4), 521–536.

Hough, P. (2008). 'Make goals not war': The contribution of international football to world peace. *The International Journal of the History of Sport, 25*(10), 1287–1305.

Korr, C. and Close, M. (2008). *More than Just a Game: Football v. Apartheid*. New York & London: Collins.

Kuper, S. (2003). *Ajax, The Dutch, The War: Football in Europe During the Second World War*. London: Orion.

Lea-Howarth, J. (2006). Sport and Conflict: Is Football an Appropriate Tool to Utilise in Conflict Resolution, Reconciliation or Reconstruction? MA thesis, University of Sussex, UK.

Lederach, J. P. (1999). *The Journey toward Reconciliation*. Scottdale, PA: Herald.

Lederach, J. P. (2005). *The Moral Imagination: The Art and Soul of Building Peace*. Oxford: Oxford University Press.

Lucheva, D. (2011). Sport in Peace-Building: Another Toolkit Burden or an Agent of Positive Change? MA Thesis, University of Bradford, UK.

Oxford, S. (2012) Sport for Development and Peace; Gender as the Missing Link, MA Thesis, University of Bradford, UK.

Ramsbotham, O., Woodhouse, T. and Miall, H. (2016) *Contemporary Conflict Resolution* (4th edn). Cambridge: Polity.

Rapoport, A. (1960). *Fights, Games and Debates*. Ann Arbor, MI: Michigan University Press.

Riordan, J. (2008). *Comrade Jim: The Spy Who Played for Spartak*. London: Fourth Estate.

Sanders, B. (2016). An own goal in sport for development: Time to change the playing field. *Journal of Sport for Development, 4*(6), 1–5.

Shobe, H. (2008). Place, identity and football: Catalonia, Catalanisme and football club Barcelona, 1899–1975. *National Identities, 10*(3), 329–343.

Sugden, J. (2010). Critical left-realism and sport interventions in divided societies. *International Review for the Sociology of Sport, 45*(3), 258–272.

Woodhouse, T. (2010). Peacekeeping, peace culture and conflict resolution. *International Peacekeeping, 17*(4), 486–498.

Woodhouse, T. (2014). A case study of football in the community initiatives in England. In C. Solanes (ed.), *Deporte y Resolution de Conflictos*, Barcelona: Open University of Catalunya.

Woodhouse, T. (2016). Sport as a peacebuilding tool: More than a game – sport and conflict resolution. *Peace in Progress 27*, May issue. Online journal of the Catalan International Institute for Peace (ICIP). Available at: www.icip-perlapau.cat/numero27/articles_centrals/article_central_1/.

Woodhouse, T. and Antin, Y. (2017). Building Bridges. Sport for Community Development and Conflict Resolution. Text of a lecture delivered at the University of Barcelona, January 2017.

Woodhouse, T. and Lederach, J. P. (2016). *Adam Curle Radical Peacemaker*. Stroud: Hawthorn.

Woodhouse, T. and Santiago, I. (2012). Elise Boulding: New voices in conflict resolution. *Journal of Conflictology, 3*(2), 4–12.

Zanotti, L., Stephenson, M. Jr and Schnitzer, M. (2015). Biopolitical and disciplinary peacebuilding: Sport, reforming bodies and rebuilding societies. *International Peacekeeping, 22*(2), 186–201.

24
SDP and disability

P. David Howe

When we are exploring sport, development and peace (SDP) programmes across the globe issues surrounding the involvement of people with impairment are complex. Even in the 'developed world' provision of sport and leisure opportunities for individuals with impairment (those who are disabled by society) are more restrictive than for members of the mainstream population. In order to properly explore the use of SDP programmes for people with impairment it is vital to understand how these individuals are being treated globally. Some have argued that people with impairment are marginal in the participation in society (Tisdall 2003) and this is a situation that is even more stark in the context of sport (Howe and Silva 2018). Increasing numbers of people are aware of the Paralympic Games and the opportunity it provides for high-performance sporting opportunities for impaired individuals disabled by society. However, before we get into further detail I believe it is important to say a brief word about terminology.

In this chapter I follow the nomenclature advocated by those who follow what is commonly called to social model of disability; following the thinking of the historical materialist Oliver (1990) who highlights the inextricable connection between the modes of production and the centripetal orientation of society around values and ideologies that engender disability. I see the limiting structure and attitudes of societies as disabling to people who are considered different in terms of physical, psychological or sensory ability. Impairment for Oliver (1990) was considered to be a biological/physical manifestation, while the social causality of disability was redirected from the individual to society and its organization. It was the causality that was at stake for Oliver in the definitional process, one that could only be fulfilled by people with a disability. For example, the contested and changing lexicon of disability saw the eradication of the word handicap.[1] Therefore, an understanding of how society 'defines' itself is important. Oliver (1990: 2) states 'human beings give meanings to objects in the social world and subsequently orientate their behaviour towards these objects in terms of the meanings given to them'. It is logical then that negative connotations of disability will result in the direction of negative behaviour and attitudes towards anyone considered to be disabled. Government policy should tackle the social oppression at the heart of disability rather than disability being perceived to be an individual's problem. In other words, '[d]isability as a category can only be understood within a framework which suggests that it is culturally produced and socially structured' (Oliver 1990: 22). Thus, the historical and cultural relativism of disability needs to be considered when we explore the impact of SDP programmes on people with impairment. Following Oliver, we can see how the Gramscian concept of hegemony links social structuration and ideology engendering disability in society.

> The hegemony that defines disability in capitalist society is constituted by the organic ideology of individualism, the arbitrary ideologies of medicalization underpinning medical intervention and personal tragedy theory underpinning much social policy. Incorporated also are ideologies related to concepts of normality, able-bodiedness and able-mindedness.
>
> *Oliver 1990: 44*

The product of Oliver's theorizing was inculcated in the social model which stands in opposition to the disabling society and its disabling ideologies. Oliver states that the social model 'is about nothing more complicated than a clear focus on the economic, environmental and cultural barriers encountered by people who are viewed by others as having some form of impairment' (Oliver 2009: 47). The social model is a simple and effective tool that identifies the social injustices of society. For the purposes of this chapter, therefore, we need to be mindful that while globally the world refers to impaired populations as disabled and therefore the title of this chapter is appropriate I would urge students and scholars alike to help rid society of disability in part by celebrating difference by acknowledging impairment.

Like so many of the social issues that are highlighted throughout this volume on SDP – disability cannot be explored in isolation. In order to help frame disability in relation to SDP we need to highlight explicitly the marginal status of impaired populations by articulating them through the lens of human rights. At this stage the chapter now turns to look at international legislation surrounding the concept of human rights that has already been addressed in this volume (see chapter 12) but it is needed to further critically explore the relationship between disability and sport.

Human rights and disability

Human rights are principles that are regularly used to highlight the wrong being done to an individual on the basis of an infringement of a basic need that is considered inherently 'natural'. The concept of 'natural rights' that should govern humanity comes originally from the work of philosopher John Locke in the seventeenth century (Locke [1689] 1970) and while human rights are not seen to be 'natural' today there is a sense in the discourse surrounding discussions of rights that there is something in all human societies that leads us to believe in inherent basic rights (Donnelly 1985; Freeman 2002). However, philosophers remind us that a 'right' can only be achieved as the end result of a moral argument and not as a premise for the discussion in the first place. Following Harris

> when it is said that someone has a right to something, that just means that in all circumstances of the case she should not be hindered in or prevented from doing or achieving something. And if it is asked why she should not be hindered, the answer is *not* 'because she possesses something called a right which has been independently established or "discovered"' but simply because there are good moral reasons why it is wrong to hinder her.
>
> *Harris 1985: xvi*

In other words, for the purpose of this chapter rights should not be seen as an object or a thing an individual possesses but an entitlement that is the result of a moral or legal argument. As a result, the Universal Declarations of Human Rights of the United Nations (UN) was designed to highlight that all people should be treated with respect. This statute should not be seen as an answer to human rights violations but rather as a marker that they have and do occur. After all the UN is not a utopian body but a political one and since its Declaration was written there have been thousands of examples of the existence of gaps between the ideology associated with the establishment of universal human rights and the lived reality. As Freeman suggests 'It is *politically* important that human rights have been codified in international and national law, but it is a mistake to believe that the legalization of human rights takes the concept of politics out' (Freeman 2002:10, Freeman's emphasis).

UN human rights legislation is *not* intended to impose a legal obligation upon nation states but as a set of guidelines that are seen as universally good behaviour. In other words, the Universal Declaration of Human Rights outlined what the UN felt were 'moral and political principles that could make a *prima facie* plausible claim to universality' (Freeman 2002: 36). The claims for universality are laid out in Article 2 which states that we are all entitled to freedoms 'without distinction of any kind, such as race, colour, sex, language, religion, political or other opinion, national or social origin, property, birth or status'. To reinforce this statement Article 7 states that all are equal before the law and are entitled to equal protection of the law without discrimination. While implementation of human rights was designed to eliminate human wrongs such as political oppression and racism it is important that their implementation follows on from the development of a just society (Donnelly 1985). A just society is of course an ideal and

> International human-rights law is the product of political power, pragmatic agreement and limited moral consensus. It has no deeper theoretical justification. Verbal agreement on general principles may conceal disagreement on the meaning and policy implications of those principles.
>
> *Freeman 2002: 60*

Western societies continue to place a great deal of importance on human rights. Yet international expectation that all societies will act in the same way towards their citizens is problematic. The development of both the Vienna Declaration of 1993 on minority rights and the more recent Convention on the Rights of Persons with Disabilities (CRPD) of 2006 attest to the fact that human rights are not understood universally. In effect rights exist in a hierarchy from local customs – national and international laws – it is normal for individuals or groups to seek resolution at the more local level to try to resolve problems. Yet it is the state (or rather those states who signed up to these statutes) that has the obligation towards human rights which leave the way open for unseen violations in the corporate world for example or within the more private sphere of the family.

Parasport and the SDP sector

The establishment of the SDP sector was largely a result of the violation of human rights in various segments in society and the need to use sport for a greater good in order to help eliminate or limit violations (Giulianotti 2004). To date, however, there has been very little attention paid to the use of sport as a vehicle for the empowerment of impaired populations in the context of the developing world. Work adopting anthropological approaches (see Ingstad and Whyte 1995; 2007) has highlighted the value of investigating the role impairment plays in often limiting the opportunity to participate in wider society. Tisdall (2003) has gone so far as to question the need to get people suffering from disability actively engaged in a culture of participation.

To this end this is one of the lofty goals of the International Paralympic Committee (IPC) to empower the athletes that engage in high-performance parasport. While the dictum of the IPC 'Empower, Inspire, Achieve' is a useful marketing tool whether engagement for most with high-performance sport can be disempowering (Purdue and Howe 2012a). Elsewhere it has been argued there is a tension between the celebration of the sporting ability of an elite athlete with an impairment and their potential value as a role model to people within the so-called disabled community. The tension between these two roles might be articulated in the express 'Paralympic paradox' which is a tension created by the representation of a Paralympian as either an impaired athlete or an athlete (with a disability). This concept is a useful tool in actively critiquing the images perpetuated in both mainstream and parasports (Purdue and Howe 2012b).

Within the SDP sector there have been occasional attempts to highlight the importance of engagement with the disabled community directly. Good examples of this type of engagement can be seen in the work of Chappell (2005) who emphasizes the use of sport as a vehicle for the potential empowerment of casualties of war, and Forber-Pratt *et al.* (2013) who highlight the use of parasport as useful in the development of opportunity for people with impairments. More specifically, Forber-Pratt (2015) highlights how parasport may be seen as a vehicle for social change in Bermuda and Ghana. However, to date the amount of high-quality research which specifically focuses upon what might be called adapted physical activity in the context of SDP is rather limited. There are a number of non-governmental organizations (NGOs) who have the improvement of the lives of people with impairment. A notable example is APAID.

> Adapted Physical Activity International Development (APAID) is a Dutch-French initiative started in February 2008. Its aim is to enhance quality of life of people with disabilities in developing countries through sports. APAID assists well-established local and international sport and development organizations in the implementation of sport projects for individuals with disabilities.[2]

For the vast majority of SDP organizations, whether they are NGOs or local grassroots organizations, the social problems that they are trying to address often mean that marginal groups such as impaired people who suffer from disability are often forgotten. In this regard it is important to the work of Martha Nussbaum, particularly the capabilities approach that has utility in context of the SDP sector (Darnell and Dao 2017) as well as within the field of adapted physical activity (Silva and Howe 2012).

Theorizing disabilities absent presences: Nussbaum's capability approach

In order to address the concerns of all individuals (including those suffering from disability), I turn to Nussbaum who has developed a theory of capabilities that is as universal as possible while being culturally sensitive to the quality of life of individuals (Nussbaum 2006; Malhotra 2008). These capabilities are designed to act as a litmus test for the quality of life of individuals motivating moral action because of the shared vulnerability of the human species. As Nussbaum suggests

> [t]he capabilities approach is a political doctrine about basic entitlements, not a comprehensive moral doctrine. It does not even claim to be a complete political doctrine, since it simply specifies some necessary conditions for a decently just society, in the form of fundamental entitlements of all citizens.
>
> *Nussbaum 2006: 155*

Nussbaum uses the case of the disabled population in part because this segment of global society is absent from more conventional understandings of justice as triumphed by Rawls (1971) in his influential The Theory of Justice. Rawlsian 'justice as fairness' is not appropriate for the achievement of social justice for marginalized groups according to Nussbaum where a capabilities approach evaluates the individual in question in relation to a list related to the quality of life similar to the list outlined in international human rights conventions such as living a full life, bodily health, freedom of movement and affiliation. Also included are abstract capabilities related to the senses of imagination and the capability for reason (Nussbaum 2006: 76–78). 'Capability can be regarded as a combination of an individual's personal characteristics (such as age or physiological impairment), [a] basket of purchaseable goods [as a measure of their standard of living] and the individual's environment in the broadest sense' (Malhotra 2008: 85). In other words, a person's quality of life should be determined by the relationship between the physical and social environment and what their standard of living equates to in an individual context.

It is important in the context of the capability approach adopted by Nussbaum to highlight the struggle for disability rights that led to the establishment of the social model of disability (Oliver 1990) previously discussed. The response by the United Nations to the polemic of various human rights groups against the claims of universalism and the problems associated with cultural imperialism was the establishment of the Vienna Declaration of 1993 that included a number of special categories, such as women, children, minorities, Indigenous people, disabled persons, refugees, migrant workers, the extremely poor and the socially excluded. There is a need to recognize these holders of human rights because these groups are more prone to human rights violations than the majority and they can get lost in the 'universality' of human rights that can so easily, if not checked, drift towards ideologically inappropriate cultural imperialism (Freeman 2002). To further solidify the case, in 2006 the CRPD placed the spotlight on the disabled community and included Article 30, which includes suggestions of the right to participate in cultural life including sport. The problem with disability specific conventions is that it singles out 'the disabled' as a group that are in need of being helped. Many people with impairments, including a high proportion of those involved in sport, do not require or accept their status as universally vulnerable people.

The documents such as the CRPD, revered and celebrated by some who fight in disability rights circles, inherently lack the clout that disability activists with impairment often wish they had. For example, one of the capabilities Nussbaum highlights is the right to play, and it is fair to assume we would all agree with that requirement for a good life. Yet by signing up to international agreements, the state is placing the burden of proof of rights infringements upon the individual. In most nations for example the rights of Paralympians in receiving equal treatment, in terms of financial and medical support compared to Olympians (Friedman and Norman 2009), is regularly infringed upon. If this sort of imbalance impacts upon equal rights for Paralympians, more marginalized people with impairment may not have the opportunity to exercise the right to play or engage in sport.

In spite of this inequity MacIntyre (1999) reminds us that *all* human beings are vulnerable, in fact we are dependent rational animals, and this being the case we should as a species be more adaptable to a common good.

> [H]ow much is involved in allegiance to a conception of the *common good* that requires both the virtues of the independent practical reasoner and the virtues of acknowledged dependence. For this is a good common to the very young and to the very old, as well as to mature adults, to the paraplegic and to the mentally backward as well as to the athlete

and to those engaged in intellectual enquiry, a good that has regard to every vulnerability to which out animal identity and our animal nature, as well as our specifically human condition expose us.

MacIntyre 1999: 165–166, emphasis added

It is in the pursuit of a common good that the Universal Convention for Human Rights and its various latter day 'offspring' were developed although clearly there are major problems with their implementation in practice.

In a sense human rights in individual nations need to be balanced with other values social order, and even among human rights there can be conflicts. Yet the social case for human rights and the protection of vulnerable populations (e.g. the impaired by social institutions) that can in turn pose a threat. Stammer (1999) suggests that we examine power relations and focus upon the impact of institutions and social movements and their role in the distribution of it rather than simply exploring the legal formalization of rights. In this respect the SDP sector has a role to play through the development of a universalizing ethos. Unfortunately, the SDP sector has lately become commercialized, which traditionally has been subversive with respect to human rights, in much the same way as democracy where the will of the those individuals with economic power are advantaged. The problem is that '[t]he Universal Declaration is based on the assumption that individual human rights, including the prohibition of discrimination and the right to practice one's culture, are sufficient to protect cultural minorities' (Freeman 2002: 114). This is problematic in so far as the political theory of liberal democracy has *not* been designed historically to solve the problems of cultural minorities, such as the disabled in part, because the classical construction of democracy presupposed a culturally unified people. One of the ways that protection of minority groups has been articulated in the past is through the 'sport for all' movement, the last iteration having been Article 30 of the CRPD.

'Sport for all'

Looking at inequitable treatment of people within the realm of sport the United Nations Educational Scientific and Cultural Organisation (UNESCO) established the International Charter of Physical Education and Sport in 1978 which stated in Article 1 that the practice of physical education and sport is a right for all. Human rights are also mentioned in relation to sport as a key element within the Olympic Charter which means they are even believed to be of concern at the high-performance end of the sporting spectrum. Because of the high profile concern for human rights related to sport issues of injustice, this seems to be a stepping off point for talking about the poor treatment of individuals with impairment in a sporting context (Howe 2012). Successful NGOs have lofty goals that celebrate the importance of physical activity and sport in the development agenda few mention disability specifically. One of the most successful organizations, Right to Play established in 2000, states on its website, 'We use the power of play to educate and empower children to overcome the effects of poverty, conflict and disease in disadvantaged communities.'[3] While statements such as this do not exclude young people that suffer from disability, the reality of SDP programmes is that they largely focus upon mainstreamed young males (Collison *et al.* 2016). The tradition of sport being primarily a male pursuit, with a long history underlined by hegemonic masculinity, makes the recruitment of marginalized others, including the disabled, difficult.

The reality, therefore, is that 'sport for all' while a laudable goal it is extremely hard to achieve in practice. It is certainly not solely the responsibility of the NGOs to change minds of local people to the significance of 'sport for all'. One culture difficulty related to SDP is that sport is predominately a western construct. As such the promotion of sport over traditional body cultures may lead to decline of important traditions that may be just as good for people's quality of life as the practice of sport. More research needs to be done on traditional body culture in order to ascertain whether or not these contexts are better for those individuals who are marginalized in the practice of western sport. Whatever the case, the elevation of sport over other forms of physical education (used in the broadest sense) globally may not be considered a good thing in non-western contexts. Access to and availability of sports programmes for the impaired populations in the west has been increasing but much of the development can be seen as rhetoric – that is part of the 'tick-box culture' that is at the heart of the CRPD. Previously I have suggested that

> there is also an assumption, by policy-makers and the public alike, that Paralympic sport is synonymous with the spectrum of disability sport opportunities and this is hindering the expansion of participation and the idea of equality in sport for [dis]abled people.
>
> *Howe and Silva 2018:126*

The lure of high profile parasport is a draw to nations where SDP programmes are prevalent, but this is often at the expense of more grassroots developments. One of the big difficulties is that all too often programmes are not integrated to include people that are suffering from disability (Bruun 1995; Devlieger 1995) and as a result the expectation that sporting activities should include these people, while admirable in somewhat misguided. That being said, following the rehetoric of the CRPD the target, both at home and abroad, should be seen as an inclusive sport system.

Integrated or inclusive sport

All too often terms such as integration and inclusion are used interchangeably, but in the diverse cultural contexts that are central to SDP we need to be mindful of the different meaning (Shuttleworth and Kasnitz 2006). Within the interdisciplinary field of disability studies there has been criticism of the concept of integration since it implies to some that the impaired populations are required to change in order to join the mainstream (Northway 1997). Oliver (1996) has gone so far as to suggest that integration is based on concepts of normality. In other words, the concept of integration requires members of the disabled community to adopt an 'able' disposition in order to become members of the mainstream. Because of its shortcomings Oliver dismisses integration as being heavily laden with policy rhetoric and sees the term inclusion, because of its association with politics as more appropriate (Oliver 1996; Northway 1997). Inclusion means that members of the disability community have a choice in whether to fully embrace the mainstream.

> [E]quality (defined as 'the participation and inclusion of all groups') may sometimes be best achieved by differential treatment. This does mean that if oppressed groups so choose they can opt for groups-specific recognition in policy and provision, since within an inclusive approach difference would be accepted or included as a natural part of the whole.
>
> *Northway 1997: 166*

Following these debates there has been a shift within the literature on disability from the dichotomy of integration/segregation to another where inclusion/exclusion are seen as a more politically appropriate way to advocate the acceptance of the impaired populations. It is possible, however, to see integration as a literal intermixing that entails the culture of both groups adapting to a new cultural environment. In other words, integration is 'a multifaceted and difficult process, which although it could be defined at a policy level rhetoric, [is] much less easy to define in reality' (Cole 2005: 341). The difficulty when exploring the success of integration policies is that the balance between the philosophical position and the reality (in this case a cultural sport environment) is not always clear. Simply exploring the policy landscape means that any interpretation is devoid of explicit cultural influences though all policy is a cultural artefact. This being said, the aim of integration is to allow people with impairment to take a full and active role within society. The ideal would be

> [a] world in which all human beings, regardless of impairment, age, gender, social class or minority ethnic status, can co-exist as equal members of the community, secure in the knowledge that their needs will be met and that their views will be recognised, respected and valued. It will be a very different world from the one in which we now live.
>
> *Oliver and Barnes 1998: 102*

What we need to do in SDP sector is determine to what extent integration is actually possible. Of course, elite sport can never be completely integrated because we don't all have elite sporting bodies and certainly this is one of the pitfalls of the relatively high profile of Paralympic sport (Howe and Silva 2018). In order to fully understand the success or failure of integration within SDP at a time when human rights concerns and/or violations are regularly drawn to our attention it is important to begin to get a sense of the culture of sport for the disabled globally. This is an onerous task and one that both SDP experts and students like to engage in. The pursuit of sport and leisure is a human right that is well articulated in the CRPD and it is hoped that all SDP programmes will take the opportunity to be more inclusive in the future.

In this chapter I have highlighted the need to explore the SDP sector with specific reference to populations that suffer from disability. Those individuals who are impaired in some way are often seen as marginal within society and certainly within the context of sporting provision. Scholars and students with interest in SDP need to be mindful of human rights-based legislation such as the CRPD which many countries around the globe have signed. The UN charter gives rights to people with impairments who suffer disability, including the right to engage in physical activity and sport. As researchers, however, we need to be mindful of the specific cultural contexts in which SDP programmes are being implemented. In order to properly embrace global cultural diversity, we could be engaging in the use of the capabilities approach as articulated by Nussbaum (2006), which places the individual at the heart of understandings of social justice. A capability-informed assessment of SDP programmes (Darnell and Daos 2017) would no doubt be fruitful. In the field of adaptive physical activity (APA) the implementation of the capabilities approach is clearly paramount.

> Because the idea of capability includes not only the actual realizations but also the opportunities/alternatives available, working toward capabilities expansion can potentially increase people's freedom to pursue the type of life they value, thus enhancing empowerment and self-determination. In practical terms, capabilities' development values individual's personal views of meaningfulness, what is incompatible with imposed goals retrieved from APA manuals and with prescriptive ideas of 'acceptable' bodies, movement, and physical activity.
>
> *Silva and Howe 2012: 38*

The philosophy surrounding the 'sport for all' movement required us to be of individual needs that the capabilities approach is so useful in bringing to our attention but the social world in not organized in a clearly defined mater. Layering of culture around concepts such as disability is never clear cut and the implementation of the CRPD is not a simple undertaking (Bickenbach 2009).

There should be an expectation that NGOs think through the planning of their SDP programmes in order to include 'sport for all' opportunities. However, the implementation of programmes on the ground is far from simple. Marginalized individuals should be included, wherever possible, but the reality is that these people must be encouraged by family and friends to attend organized SDP events. Even the best practitioners in the SDP sector cannot provide an inclusive programme if diverse bodies are not physically present. In other words, this chapter is a call for those working and researching in the SDP sector to be mindful of the needs of people with impairments when exploring opportunities to enhance their daily lives through active engagement in sport.

Notes

1   The word handicap has fallen out of favour in the debates for English speakers, however, it is still considered appropriate in the French language.
2   www.beyondsport.org/organisations/a/adapted-physical-activity-international-development-apaid-netherlands/.
3   www.righttoplay.com/Learn/ourstory/Pages/What-we-do.aspx.

References

Bickenbach, J. E. (2009). Disability, culture and the UN convention. *Disability and Rehabilitation*, *31*(14), 1111–1124.

Bruun, F. J. (1995). Hero, beggar, or sports star: Negotiating the identity of the disabled person in Nicaragua. In B. Ingstad and S. Reynolds-Whyte (eds), *Disability and Culture*. London: University of California Press, pp. 196–207.

Chappell, R. (2005). Sport in Namibia conflicts, negotiations and struggles since independence. *International Review for the Sociology of Sport*, *40*(2), 241–54.

Cole, B. A. (2005). Good faith and effort? Perspectives on educational inclusion. *Disability and Society*, *20*(3), 331–344.

Collison, H, Giulianotti, R., Howe, P. D. and Darnell, S. (2016). The methodological dance: Critical reflections on conducting a cross-cultural comparative research project on 'sport for development and peace'. *Qualitative Research in Sport, Exercise and Health*, *8*(5), 413–423.

Darnell, S. and Dao, M. (2017). Considering sport for development and peace through the capabilities approach. *Third World Thematics: A TWQ Journal*, *2*(1), 23–36.

Devlieger, P. (1995). Why disabled? The cultural understanding of physical disability in an African society. In B. Ingstad and S. Reynolds Whyte (eds), *Disability and Culture*. Berkeley, CA: University of California Press, pp. 94–106.

Donnelly, J. (1985). *The Concept of Human Rights*. London: Croom Helm.

Forber-Pratt, A. J. (2015). Paralympic sport as a vehicle for social change in Bermuda and Ghana. *Journal of Sport for Development*, *3*(5), 35–49.

Forber-Pratt, A. J., Scott, J. A. and Driscoll, J. (2013). An emerging model for grassroots Paralympic sport development: A comparative case study. *International Journal of Sport and Society*, *3*(1), 55–67.

Freeman, M. (2002). *Human Rights: An Interdisciplinary Approach*. London: Routledge.

Friedman, J. L. and Norman G. C. (2009). The Paralympics: Yet another missed opportunity for social integration. *Boston University International Law Review*, *27*(2), 345–366.

Giulianotti, R. (2004). Human rights, globalisation and sentimental education: The case of sport. *Sport and Society: Culture, Commerce, Media, Politics*, *7*(3), 355–369.

Harris, J. (1985). *The Value of Life: An Introduction to Medical Ethics*. Routledge: New York.

Howe, P. D. (2012). Children of a lesser god: Paralympics and high-performance sport. In J. Sugden and A. Tomlinson (eds), *Watching the Olympics: Politics, Power and Representation*. London: Routledge, pp. 165–181.

Howe, P. D. and Silva, C. F. (2018). The fiddle of using the Paralympic games as a vehicle for expanding [dis] ability sport participation. *Sport and Society: Culture, Commerce, Media, Politics, 21*(1), 125–136.

Ingstad, B. and Reynolds–Whyte, S. (1995). (eds), *Disability and Culture*. Berkeley, CA: University of California Press.

Ingstad, B. and Reynolds–Whyte, S. (2007). *Disability in Local and Global Worlds*. Berkeley, CA: University of California Press.

Locke, J. ([1689] 1970). *Two Treaties of Government*. Cambridge: Cambridge University Press.

MacIntyre, A. (1999). *Dependent Rational Animals: Why human Beings Need the Virtues*. Open Court: Chicago.

Malhotra, R. (2008). Expanding the frontiers of justice: Reflections on the theory of capabilities, disability rights, and the politics of global equality. *Socialism and Democracy, 22*(1), 83–100.

Northway, R. (1997). Integration and inclusion: Illusion or progress in services in services for disabled people. *Social Policy and Administration, 31*(2), 157–172.

Nussbaum, M. C. (2006). *Frontiers of Justice: Disability, Nationality, Species Membership*. London: Belknap Harvard.

Oliver, M. (1990). *The Politics of Disablement*. London: Macmillan.

Oliver, M. (1996). *Understanding Disability: From Theory to Practice*. Basingstoke: Macmillan.

Oliver, M. (2009). *The Politics of Disablement: Critical Texts in Social Work and the Welfare State* (2nd edn). London: Macmillan.

Oliver, M. and Barnes, C. (1998). *Social Policy and Disabled People: From Exclusion to Inclusion*. London: Longman.

Purdue, D. E. J. and Howe, P. D. (2012a). Empower, inspire, achieve: (Dis)empowerment and the Paralympic games. *Disability and Society, 27*(7), 903–916.

Purdue, D. E. J. and Howe, P. D. (2012b). See the sport, not the disability? – Exploring the Paralympic paradox. *Qualitative Research in Sport and Exercise, 4*(2), 189–205.

Rawls, J. (1971). *The Theory of Justice*. Cambridge, MA: Harvard University Press.

Silva, C. F. and Howe, P. D. (2012). Difference, adapted physical activity and human development: Potential contribution of capabilities approach. *Adapted Physical Activity Quarterly, 29* (1), 25–43.

Shuttleworth, R. P. and Kasnitz, D. (2006). Cultural context of disability. In G. L. Albrecht (ed.), *Encyclopaedia of Disability*. London: SAGE, pp. 330–335.

Stammer, N. (1999) Social movements the social construction of human rights. *Human Rights Quarterly, 21*(4), 980–1008.

Tisdall, E. T. M. (2003). A culture of participation. In S. Riddell and N. Watson (eds), *Disability, Culture and Identity*. Harlow, UK. Pearson Education, pp.19–33.

25

SDP and volunteering

Nicolien van Luijk, Shawn Forde and Liv Yoon

Introduction

In a recent call for commentaries relating to volunteering within Sport for Development and Peace (SDP), Paul Hunt (2016), the editor of the Platform on Sport and Development website, stated that:

> People volunteer for a wide variety of reasons, whether to advance in their careers, fill their time or respond to the needs of an organisation and the people it supports. Volunteer work is crucial to many non-profit organisations … Volunteers can be crucial in providing extra support to organisations with few staff and high workloads, leading to improved services for those that benefit from their projects. But the relationship between development and volunteerism is complex.
>
> *Hunt 2016: 3–4*

This complexity is reflected in the social science literature on volunteering. For example, Rochester, Ellis Payne, and Howlett (2010) explain that a particular and dominant understanding of voluntary action within the United Kingdom, North America, and other 'western' societies, has formed over the last several decades, which can limit broader discussions relating to the role and purpose of volunteering. Rochester *et al.* (2010) note that the dominant understandings of voluntary action tend to position volunteering as a form of philanthropy, through 'gifting' one's time, that is often targeted towards marginalized or disadvantaged populations. Further, it is often assumed that volunteers take on specific roles, similar to employed positions, within large government and non-government organizations (NGOs) that oversee and mediate the process. This understanding of voluntary action has been described as the 'non-profit paradigm' (Lyons *et al.* 1998), which has helped to solidify a volunteer industry that aims to structure and professionalize the process of volunteering. Importantly, Rochester *et al.* also argue that this dominant paradigm often overlooks volunteering as a form of mutual aid, volunteering as activism, and volunteering as leisure. By contrast, understanding different conceptions of volunteering can lead to more dynamic understandings of what constitutes and counts as volunteering, the values that underpin volunteering, and the meanings and importance of volunteering to both individuals and societies.

Scholars also point out that this narrowed understanding of volunteering has resulted in a lack of critical engagement with the concept. For example, in introducing a new journal titled *Critical Studies in Voluntary Action*, Rochester (2015) highlights three shortcomings with the dominant perspective on voluntary action. First, he notes that most research draws on organizational theory and management literature to address problems of efficiency found in a particular type of volunteering. Second, volunteers themselves are often understood as unpaid workers who should therefore be managed the same as paid employees. Third, it is often taken for granted that voluntary action within society complements the work of government. These shortcomings are also emphasized by scholars who argue that neoliberal ideologies (discussed below), that currently dominate the global political and economic environment, influence the practices of volunteering, resulting in the professionalization of volunteering, as well as a focus on volunteering as service delivery rather than advocacy or activism (Lacey and Ilcan 2006).

In contrast to this dominant, neoliberal perspective, a critical approach to voluntary action has emerged that goes beyond the logic of the market to focus on examining 'mutual aid groups; advocacy and campaigning organizations; informal and non-bureaucratic collective action, and other kinds of civil society organizations'. (Rochester 2015: para. 4) In doing so, this critical approach attempts to resist the 'infiltration of the culture and behaviours of the market into the non-market parts of our society and reassert the idea that voluntary action embodies/expresses important and distinctive values that are not compatible with a market society' (ibid.).

Although the scholars mentioned above are concerned with voluntary action in general, their arguments also apply to the field of SDP. There has been important critical work in recent years that has challenged the dominant ideologies that underpin SDP and the place of volunteers within SDP (e.g. Darnell 2012); however, there is also a growing amount of research in SDP, drawing from management perspectives, that focuses on issues relating to organizational capacity and volunteer motivations, retentions, and benefits (Welty Peachey *et al.* 2013a; 2013b; 2014; Smith *et al.* 2014). Much like the sport sector in general, this research has typically focused on the individual level, investigating the behaviours of, and benefits accrued to, volunteers, as well as organizational and institutional factors such as volunteer retention and performance management (Wicker 2017). We do not argue that this research is not worthwhile or important, but it illustrates Rochester *et al.'s* argument that, over time, conceptions of what constitutes voluntary action have become rather limited and even taken for granted. Therefore, in this paper, we seek to expand the understanding of what it means to volunteer, specifically within the SDP sector, with the overall goal of promoting a broader definition of what volunteering could look like. In building this argument, we begin by outlining literature relating to volunteering within international development studies and SDP. Here, we consider critical perspectives on volunteering and use this literature to set the stage for questioning our own volunteer experiences in SDP. Within these discussions of our experiences, we each raise questions that challenge the dominant 'non-profit paradigm' of volunteering, while considering what could be done differently in terms of SDP and volunteering. In doing so, we aim to generate a discussion that broadens understandings of volunteering within SDP, while reflecting on how the sector's reliance on volunteers impacts its conceptualization and goals.

Volunteering in development

In this section, we review previous literature that offers a critical perspective on the role of volunteers within the international development sector generally, and within SDP more specifically. We then bring these literatures together in critical consideration of the place and use of volunteers within international development and the meanings of volunteering in the current political climate. In so doing, we ask, what are the potential consequences of volunteering, as outlined by previous researchers? In turn, how can this knowledge be incorporated into discussions of our own volunteer experiences?

Volunteering and international development

International development is a concept that has a long-contested history and has been studied in much detail over the past 40 years. It can be broadly defined as: 'the organized intervention in collective affairs according to a standard of improvement' (Nederveen Pieterse 2001: 3). Although development interventions have had beneficial outcomes, they have also been open to criticism, particularly in relation to their impacts upon intended recipients. SDP organizations and their goals are closely linked to the international development sector, with SDP initiatives promoting the use of sport to achieve goals of international development.

Many international development initiatives have made use of volunteers and, similar to the SDP sector, have arguably relied on volunteers to perform many of their daily functions (Lacey and Ilcan 2006). Researchers have suggested that international volunteering is often the purview of relatively privileged individuals, who use such experiences to build their sense of 'global citizenship' and gain access to social capital (Baillie Smith and Laurie 2011; Morgan 2013). While volunteering may indeed be a necessary and useful complement to achieving the goals of international development, it has also been necessary to critically examine volunteering and the impacts it has on international development processes. In turn, critical discussions of volunteering within international development and within SDP have tended to focus on the power relations embedded therein.

In particular, researchers have worked to critique the concepts of volunteering in international development by highlighting western and colonialist assumptions that are often embedded within these interventions. For example, postcolonial critiques problematize views of the world, 'particularly the homogenizing of the South into the "Third World", and … the unacknowledged and unexamined assumptions at the heart of western disciplines that are profoundly insensitive to the meanings, values, and practices of other cultures' (McEwan 2009: 120–121). While a full discussion of these critiques is beyond the scope of this chapter, such arguments point to the power structures that influence the ways in which volunteering occurs within development spaces and organizations. This has led scholars like Hayhurst (2011) to adopt a feminist postcolonial approach to examining SDP interventions targeting girls and women in the global South, drawing attention to development interventions which 'seem benevolent and perhaps relatively harmless on the surface' (Hayhurst 2011: 545), but can unwittingly play a role in continuing global inequalities.

Indeed, many SDP interventions are still operated by organizations from the global North and intended to achieve development goals in the global South (Tiessen 2011). Research has found that such SDP interventions often align with dominant approaches to development 'that take place in hegemonic relations in which privileged groups (nations, citizens, corporations) maintain a position of benefit and accruement over others' (Darnell 2010: 57). In this context, researchers have utilized Said's (2003) concept of Orientalism – which challenged the European construction of the world and its 'others', and called into question the differences between the Orient (the East) and the Occident (the West) – to articulate ways in which SDP may reinforce particular knowledges over others (see Darnell 2014). Central to such discussions has been the concept of 'Whiteness'. Whiteness, often culturally invisible, constitutes a 'symbolic form of authority' (Kothari 2006: 9) and serves as the standard to which all other races are compared and deemed 'inadequate', which perpetuates the image of the 'helpless cultural other' (Heron 2007). For SDP volunteers, Whiteness can offer 'a subject position of benevolence, rationality and expertise' in opposition to 'marginalized, unsophisticated and appreciative bodies of colour' (Darnell 2007: 560). As such, the concept of race is often a silent one in SDP volunteering, but one that nevertheless can have significant impacts on the ways in which volunteering systems and programs are structured and implemented.

With these critical insights in mind, the next section examines how the current political and cultural climate has also impacted volunteering, and considers some further issues worthy of attention in SDP volunteer initiatives and/or research.

Volunteering in the current political climate

The broader political, economic and social environment affects the act of volunteering. This was discussed above in acknowledging power relations within many international development interventions and practices. This section takes the discussion a step further by considering literature that argues for critical reflection regarding the influence of neoliberal ideologies on international volunteering initiatives. While only a few SDP researchers have examined volunteering in this manner (see Darnell 2012), there is a wealth of research that has considered how neoliberalism – as the dominant political ideology – has influenced volunteering more broadly and the impact this has on communities.

Neoliberalism is a theory of political economics that promotes the freedom of the market above all else. Harvey (2005) suggests that neoliberalism 'proposes that human well-being can best be advanced by liberating individual entrepreneurial freedoms and skills within an institutional framework characterized by strong private property rights, free markets, and free trade'. Neoliberal policies have resulted in the withdrawal of social welfare programs and social health policies, decreases in public education funds, weakening of labour unions, exploitation of workers, increases in the power of corporations, deregulation of the market, greater global 'free' trade policies, increased market competition, and much more (Peck 2010). Some scholars have also posited the concept of neoliberalism as a 'technology of governing "free subjects"', which is not inherently linked to a specific political agenda (Ong 2007: 4). Neoliberalism thus governs individuals, encouraging them to be responsible citizens. Both of these conceptualizations of neoliberalism are important for analysing experiences of volunteering in SDP.

Within this discussion, it is reasonable to question the assumption that non-profit and voluntary institutions can and/or do reject market ideologies and encourage civic engagement because they are outside of the influence and logic of the market (Devereux 2008). Eikenberry (2009) argues that neoliberal ideology permeates beyond the market and that this ideology is often just as prevalent in non-profit volunteer organizations. We do not argue here that volunteering *necessarily* promotes neoliberal ideologies; in fact, volunteering has a long history associated with socialist and liberal democratic societies. However, we do acknowledge that volunteering can promote neoliberal ideologies, both intentionally and unintentionally. For example, volunteer-based organizations have had to find a way to attract volunteers in a society that encourages a focus on the individual; as a result, more and more organizations focus on promoting the benefits of volunteering *for the volunteer*, rather than for the broader community (Morgan 2013). This further speaks to the importance of critically examining volunteer work within the current political climate, and considering whether and how volunteering might challenge neoliberal ideologies.

From this perspective, while volunteering is often seen as a moral and benevolent activity, its consequences are not automatically positive. Indeed, some researchers have argued that some types of volunteering benefit the volunteer more than the intended beneficiaries, potentially increasing social inequalities rather than working to minimize them (Coote 2011). In Vrasti's (2013: 3) ethnographic work with individuals involved in what is called volunteer tourism, she came to the conclusion that short-term international volunteering 'helps young adults from the Global North assume a type of political subjectivity that, in its fidelity to neoliberal injunctions, embodies a new normative ideal'. Similarly, for Holdsworth (2015), the drive to accumulate volunteer experiences is often tied to securing employment and a safe future for the volunteer. This 'cult of experience' serves to privilege a homogenized set of experiences that particular volunteers are then able to market and leverage for their own benefit. These different analyses show how volunteering has become a product of social or economic capital for the volunteer and may have little to do with the intended recipients of volunteer programs themselves.

Other researchers acknowledge that while volunteering may benefit the community volunteers are embedded in, within the current neoliberal climate, the type of volunteering practised tends to focus on individual behavior modification rather than broad social change (Dean 2015). Increasingly, volunteer opportunities take the place of service delivery and move away from advocacy work (Lacey and Ilcan 2006). Even in SDP, some scholars have argued that the majority of organizations focus on changing individual circumstances rather than promoting broad institutional change for entire communities and generations (Black 2010; Darnell 2010; Hartmann and Kwauk 2011).

In sum, in a neoliberal climate, non-profit organizations are increasingly encouraged or even required to demonstrate productivity, including in the ways they recruit volunteers. This individualization has turned volunteering into something of a transaction that is useful to an individual for achieving something else – like obtaining a job. As Dean (2015) explains, 'the very notion of altruistic volunteering, giving one's time without an economic rationale, has been challenged' (p. 144). This is especially important to reflect upon when discussing international volunteering, where short-term opportunities are still the norm (Tiessen and Heron 2012). In turn, it raises the question of whether volunteering in SDP represents a limited view of what volunteering 'can' be, and calls for critical attention to be paid to the goals and focus of SDP initiatives, as well as the broader political climate in which SDP organizations understand and define volunteering.

In the personal reflections that follow, we comment on the kinds of issues raised here. Our intent is not simply to draw conclusions from our individual experiences, but also to encourage conversations about what it means to volunteer in SDP. While we recognize the limitations of using anecdotal incidents as data, we also concur that case studies can provide opportunities for an evaluation of context, interactions, and social processes (Flyvbjerg 2006). Each of our three experiences were situated in different contexts. First, Forde discusses a local 'in-the-field' setting in southern Africa, asking who benefits from volunteering. Second, van Luijk reflects on her experiences working as an unpaid intern and considers how volunteering within this setting may perpetuate global inequalities rather than work to minimize them. Finally, Yoon writes about running a Canadian university club for a prominent SDP NGO and questions whether those in volunteering might be the ones who benefit from global hierarchies and structures.

Who benefits from volunteering in SDP?

My own experience of volunteering in SDP has had a persistent impact on my writing and research about SDP. I spent one year in Lesotho, working on an HIV/AIDS project as the 'Football and Life Skills' coordinator. My role within the project was to coordinate workshops with local soccer coaches, facilitated by coaches from the UK. Through these workshops, local coaches became familiar with a coaching manual that focused on how to include HIV/AIDS education into their coaching sessions with youth in their communities. Following the workshops, I was responsible for mentoring and monitoring the coaches. One of the lingering questions that I continue to think about is: who actually benefited, and continues to benefit, from my experience? For Vrasti (2013), in order to think through who benefits from volunteering in such a way, we should focus on how we, as political subjects, are (re)produced through international voluntary activities. Therefore, as a way to assess who benefited from my experience, I aim to think through the subject positions that I took up during my placement, and continue to take up since its conclusion.

The organization I worked with had particular metrics relating to outcomes, which were then reported back to donors, such as: how many local coaches were reached, how many workshops were offered, and how many youth the coaches were able to reach? Further, in my role of monitoring and mentoring the coaches, I had to devise a way to evaluate and certify the coaches based on their understanding and implementation of the HIV/AIDS coaching manual. In this way, my role as coordinator was to manage and take account of the local coaches' actions and achievements. As described earlier, this accounting is typical of neoliberal forms of development that reduce social relations and the concept of development to numbers. As a result, I was more often concerned with delivering and reporting on project outcomes (recruiting coaches, hosting workshops, and distributing resources) than I was with engaging with participants and exploring potentially different ways of delivering sport and HIV/AIDS education.

In some ways, this is an overly cynical representation of my time in Lesotho. At the time, I did not feel like a manager or an accountant. I felt like I was forming meaningful relationships, some that continue to this day, and that I was working with the local coaches in ways that would benefit them and their communities. However, even after my volunteer placement, I have arguably taken up a 'neoliberal' subject position that allows me to benefit, disproportionately, from my volunteering. In research articles, grant applications, lectures, conference presentations, and book chapters, I have been able to package my experiences in ways that arguably lend my work some legitimacy or uniqueness, and make myself marketable within the field of SDP and academia more broadly. Following Holdsworth (2015), I continue to participate in the 'cult of experience' into which youth are increasingly socialized.

With that in mind, and motivated by both Vrasti's (2013) and Holdsworth's (2015) critical injunctions, I have tried to move beyond asking myself 'who benefits' from volunteering, and to start to ask how people can open themselves up to new experiences that potentially challenge the status quo? With an interest in physical activity, health, and international development, I took up a volunteer/work position with a SDP organization doing HIV/AIDS prevention activities in southern Africa. I now wonder if there were other ways that I could have engaged, or other experiences I could have sought out. What if, instead of volunteering with an NGO, I decided to use my body to take part in marches, occupations, or demonstrations that aimed to raise awareness of, and hold governments to account, for how they fund and address health and education? In order to consider these alternative approaches, as Hartmann and Kwauk (2011: 296) argue, I would have had to '[interrogate] the relations of power underlying sport-based interventions as well as [my] own assumptions about sport and development'. Following Hartmann and Kwauk, taking on this critical perspective and conception of sport as a potential space for the development of critical consciousness might have caused me to reject taking up a position as a volunteer and as a deliverer of development, and instead encouraged me to acknowledge my own place and complicity within an unequal world, and to seek out different ways of addressing these inequalities. This is not to say that taking an alternative approach would necessarily have had a greater impact, or would have done more in terms of facilitating social change, but in a small way it might have contributed to a needed shift from 'using sport to change the individual toward using sport to challenge the common-sense notions and relations of power' (Hartmann and Kwauk 2011: 298).

Here, I have focused on my time volunteering in SDP, and how I have used that experience. In addition, to think through who benefits from volunteering we also have to consider who is able to take on particular volunteering experiences. These experiences may range from positions that offer small stipends, like mine in Lesotho, to positions such as the one described next, which are unpaid or for which volunteers even pay for the experience.

SDP, volunteering and elitism

In 2013, I worked as an unpaid intern at a large international development institution for three months. Before I began my internship, my critical reflections were based on the personal sacrifices that I was being asked to make and what this meant for potential, future, and paid job opportunities. In thinking about future job prospects, it made me nervous that there were many volunteer opportunities in SDP but few paid opportunities. As I began my internship position, these critiques did not change; however, I also began to see how the unpaid internship and volunteer industry was having an impact on the SDP sector more generally. Specifically, my attention was drawn to the way(s) in which elitism plays a role in these positions and how this affects how we do our work and what kind of work we do.

By elitism, I am referring to the relatively small group of privileged people who are eligible for these unpaid positions through their ability to fulfill the desired requirements, such as specific educational training, social connections, and access to adequate finances. These requirements rule out the vast majority of individuals around the world, specifically those who do not have access to these resources. This creates a system wherein these positions reproduce the structure and idea that only a certain group of people (i.e. the 'elite') have the ability or even the 'right' to work as interns.

Researchers have pointed out that much of the SDP movement has adopted ideologies that are embedded with culturally imperialistic tendencies, that focus on what western individuals and groups can offer the rest of the world (Tiessen 2011). From my experience, these neo-imperial tendencies are influenced not only by the goals of SDP organizations, but also by their operations, including a heavy reliance upon volunteers and unpaid interns as labour. Put simply, the use of volunteers serves to perpetuate certain ideologies and separations among those who are able to volunteer and those who are to be 'volunteered for'.

The social class and birth origins of volunteers are not the only issues that limit the potential of SDP programs. What comes with these unpaid positions – almost necessarily – is high turnover rates. Volunteers serve for short periods of time and usually leave before they begin to see the impacts of a program or policy (of which the goals are usually much longer term). This approach limits interns' abilities to reflect critically upon the sustainability of a program and how it may or may not have an intended impact. I was privy to this in the organization I worked for. Six months was the maximum amount of time an intern was allowed to work, and nearly half of those who worked at the organization were interns. The turnover was continuous and the need to create programs and systems that adapted to this was obvious. For example, while there was an acknowledgement that evaluation of the programs and partnerships with program recipients was necessary, every attempt at creating evaluations had stalled, and finally it was accepted that evaluations could not be adopted in this short-term working environment. This further accentuated the gap between the volunteer and 'the volunteered for'; not only were we separated by privilege but we were also limited in our ability to build sustainable connections with communities who were impacted by our development programs.

Given this, while there is an increasing (and important) acknowledgement of the need for SDP programs to be reflective and bring in broader perspectives and ideologies, it is difficult for any of these recommendations to be incorporated without a restructuring of how the SDP sector relies on volunteers. From my experience, this reliance of unpaid short-term interns to perform the everyday work of this organization had a negative impact on being able to consider broader, and more marginalized, perspectives because the pool of potential candidates necessarily came from already privileged positions and because we lacked the ability to reflect on the overall goals of the organization due to high turnover rates. Further contributing to this lack of connection was the focus on how we, as interns, could use these positions to build our own social capital. Upon reflection, this could be a reaction to lack of remuneration, however, it also highlights that volunteers often enter these positions as a way to 'gain experience' rather than as an act of benevolence, itself a hallmark of a neoliberal climate (Holdsworth 2015).

It is also worth asking whether or not the goals of SDP are compromised by the consistent use of volunteer labour? By this I mean to ask: if our goals are equitable development, what does it mean for us to rely on unpaid volunteers who often come from an elite homogenous group of people? Furthermore, how do goals of equitable development correspond with a reliance on using unpaid labour? Are we perpetuating the systems of inequality that SDP organizations ostensibly seek to change? This discussion is continued in the next section, through questions about the popularization of volunteering 'abroad', and whether this fetishizes those for whom SDP programs are designed.

Volunteerism benefits from orientalism/hierarchy

From 2012 to 2013, I was part of a Canadian university chapter of a prominent SDP organization. At the beginning of the school year, the 'executive' team of the organization set up a booth advertising 'who we are and what we do', in an attempt to recruit new members. Many of the students with whom we engaged had already heard of the organization and had an idea of what the organization does – namely, sport and recreation programs run by volunteers (as well as 'celebrity-status' athletes) in underprivileged areas, both domestically and around the world. However, the questions we were most often asked were: 'Do I/we get to go [volunteer] abroad with this club?' Many were quick to leave our booth when we answered: 'no, but we have partnerships and programs at several schools in neighbourhoods around here.' Only a handful of students stayed to listen more about our local programs. In the end, four new students joined and volunteered for after-school activities at local schools, but none of them returned the following year.

Upon reflection, during my time with the organization, we did not question the dominant, imperialistic sense of 'development' (McEwan 2009; Hayhurst 2011; Tiessen 2011). This could be seen, for example, in the pictures we used as promotional material. Photos taken from the official website of the organization portrayed (mostly white) westerners in their early twenties 'helping' and/or posing with young, smiling (mostly black) children. The places in these photos were clearly and explicitly outside of North America, including sceneries of dust-swept horizons, rubble, and makeshift shelters. Against this backdrop, which perpetuates the image of the 'helpless cultural other' (Heron 2007), there was a strong desire displayed by Canadian university students for volunteering abroad, more so than in nearby locations domestically or local neighbourhoods. Particularly on North American (or 'one-third' world [Hayhurst 2011: 533]) university campuses, the allure of volunteering abroad – at least within the SDP context – was much stronger and more attractive than doing the same activities in 'our own backyard'.

The allure of the 'foreign' in SDP raises important questions about the dominant portrayals of the supposed 'beneficiaries' of SDP, portrayals that may influence how people perceive what it is like to volunteer within the SDP sector and the implications of doing so. It also asks us to think about how the subject position of the 'benevolent' and 'evangelistic' first-world volunteer may be inspired and privileged. Tiessen (2011) claims that SDP is laden with culturally neocolonial, imperialistic tendencies; it is possible that such roots of SDP may be (unintentionally) reflected and reproduced through the structures of volunteer-led SDP initiatives like the one described here.

In this way, if the concept of the underdevelopment of others derives mostly from perceived differences, it is upon these interpreted differences that volunteering in SDP is often founded and secured. Whether or not these prospective Canadian university student volunteers intentionally subscribed to the notion of the 'exotic foreign other', the hierarchical structures, neocolonial discourses, and evangelistic imagery embedded and promoted by the organization made it more difficult to avoid neocolonial approaches to volunteering.

Reflecting on this experience, when faced with questions about the availability of programs abroad, I found myself making a case for why local areas 'need just as much help', but in so doing I nonetheless reproduced the rhetoric of 'we the benevolent' and 'they the needy'. My arguments were underlined by hierarchy and, ultimately, it was my discomfort with this hierarchy that eventually led me to walk away from SDP initiatives altogether. I am not necessarily proud of this reaction, which could be interpreted as apathetic, and my intention here is not to criticize those with noble desires to help others. However, the ways in which international volunteerism connects to and reproduces hierarchies in racial relations is one that warrants further critical attention, especially when imagining a broader understanding of volunteering within SDP.

Conclusion

We opened this chapter arguing that the discussions of volunteering within SDP are predominantly situated within the 'non-profit' paradigm. We first delineated literature on the growing role of volunteers in international development then focused on the role of volunteers in SDP specifically. We connected the two bodies of literature by considering research that examines the reasons for the growth of both demand and supply for volunteering roles and the implications of this state of affairs – namely, the proliferation of neoliberal ideologies and the increasing demand for individuals to differentiate themselves competitively. In this way, and perhaps due to the challenges posed by the current political-economic context, volunteering has shifted from the benevolent, altruistic notion of 'giving one's time without an economic rationale' to yet another mechanism through which to gain experience that can be rendered as capital – what Holdsworth (2015) calls the 'cult of experience'.

Drawing from our own volunteering experiences in SDP-related initiatives, we have attempted to ask uncomfortable questions of who really benefits through volunteering, who has the choice to volunteer their time and resources, and what assumptions about 'us' and 'them' make volunteering not only possible, but attractive? We suggest that the conjecture that western volunteers will facilitate development elsewhere in the world through the 'power of sport' implicitly (and perhaps inevitably) creates an unrealistic and unjust power dynamic (Darnell 2010). Simply put, dominance creates a need for benevolence, sustaining itself in often cyclical terms.

With these arguments in mind, further studies could benefit from examining the challenges to the notion of volunteering posed by the current political context, researching the so-called typical volunteer experiences (e.g. local volunteer work) as well as understudied forms of volunteering, and comparing cases of SDP initiatives with alternative means of (mutual) aid, such as community-based, cooperative models of social and economic exchange.

References

Baillie Smith, M. and Laurie, N. (2011). International volunteering and development: Global citizenship and neoliberal professionalisation today. *Transactions of the Institute of British Geographers*, *36*(4), 545–559.

Black, D. R. (2010). The ambiguities of development: implications for 'Development through sport'. *Sport in Society*, *13*(1), 121–129.

Coote, A. (2011). Big society and the new austerity. In M. Stott (ed.), *The Big Society Challenge*. Thetford: Keystone Development Trust Publications.

Darnell, S. C. (2007). Playing with race: Right to play and the production of whiteness in 'development through sport'. *Sport in Society*, *10*(4), 560–579.

Darnell, S. C. (2010). Power, politics and 'sport for development and peace': Investigating the utility of sport for international development. *Development*, *27*(1), 54–75.

Darnell, S. C. (2012). *Sport for Development and Peace: A Critical Sociology*. London: Bloomsbury.

Darnell, S. C. (2014). Orientalism through sport: Towards a Said-ian analysis of imperialism and 'sport for development and peace'. *Sport in Society*, *17*(8), 1000–1014.

Dean, J. (2015). Volunteering, the market, and neoliberalism. *People, Place and Policy*, 9(2), 139–148.

Devereux, P. (2008). International volunteering for development and sustainability: Outdated paternalism or a radical response to globalisation? *Development in Practice*, *18*(3), 357–370.

Eikenberry, A. (2009). Refusing the market: A democratic discourse for voluntary and nonprofit organizations. *Nonprofit and Voluntary Sector Quarterly*, *38*(4), 582–596.

Flyvbjerg, B. (2006). Five misunderstandings about case-study research. *Qualitative Inquiry*, *12*(2), 219–245.

Hartmann, D. and Kwauk, C. (2011). Sport and development: an overview, critique, and reconstruction. *Journal of Sport and Social Issues*, *35*(3), 284–305.

Harvey, D. (2005). *Neoliberalism: A Brief History*. Oxford: Oxford University Press.

Hayhurst, L. M. C. (2011). Corporatising sport, gender and development: Postcolonial IR feminisms, transnational private governance and global corporate social engagement. *Third World Quarterly*, *32*(3), 531–549.

Heron, B. (2007). *Desire for Development: Whiteness, Gender, and the Helping Imperative*. Waterloo: Wilfrid Laurier University Press.

Holdsworth, C. (2015). The cult of experience: Standing out from the crowd in an era of austerity. *Area*. Published Online First 20 May 2015, doi:10.1111/area.12201.

Hunt, P. (2016). Call for articles: The role of volunteers in sport and development. Available at: www.sportanddev.org/en/article/news/call-articles-role-volunteers-sport-and-development (accessed 1 February 2017).

Kothari, U. (2006). An agenda for thinking about race in development. *Progress in Development Studies*, *6*(1), 9–23.

Lacey, A. and Ilcan, S. (2006). Voluntary labor, responsible citizenship, and international NGOs. *International Journal of Comparative Sociology*, *47*(1), 34–53.

Lyons, M., Wijkstrom, P. and Clary, G. (1998). Comparative studies of volunteering: What is being studied. *Voluntary Action*, *1*(1), 45–54.

McEwan, C. (2009) *Postcolonialism and Development*. New York: Routledge.

Morgan, H. (2013). Sport volunteering, active citizenship and social capital enhancement: What role in the 'big society'? *International Journal of Sport Policy and Politics*, *5*(3), 381–395.

Nederveen Piertse. J. N. (2001). *Development Theory: Deconstructions/Reconstructions*. London: SAGE.

Ong, A. (2007). Neoliberalism as a mobile technology. *Transactions of the Institute of British Geographers*, *32*(1), 3–8.

Peck, J. (2010). *Constructions of Neoliberal Reason*. Oxford: Oxford University Press.

Rochester, C. (2015). Critical thinking about voluntary action and its history. *Voluntary Action History Society*. Available at: www.vahs.org.uk/2015/02/critical-thinking-about-voluntary-action-and-its-history

Rochester, C., Paine, A. E., Howlett, S. and Zimmeck, M. (2010). *Volunteering and Society in the 21st Century*. London: Palgrave Macmillan.

Said, E. W. (ed.) (2003). Preface. *Orientalism – 25th Anniversary Edition*. New York: Vintage.

Smith, N. L., Cohen, A. and Pickett, A. C. (2014). Exploring the motivations and outcomes of long-term international sport-for-development volunteering for American millennials. *Journal of Sport and Tourism*, *19*(3–4), 299–316.

Tiessen, R. (2011). Global subjects or objects of globalization? The promotion of global citizenship in organizations offering sport for development and/or peace programs. *Third World Quarterly*, *32*(3), 571–587.

Tiessen, R. and B. Heron (2012). Volunteering in the developing world: The perceived impacts of Canadian youth. *Development in Practice*, *22*(1), 44–56.

Vrasti, W. (2013). *Volunteer Tourism in the Global South: Giving Back in Neoliberal Times.* New York: Routledge.

Welty Peachey, J., Cohen, A., Borland, J. and A. Lyras (2013a). Building social capital: Examining the impact of street soccer USA on its volunteers. *International Review for the Sociology of Sport*, *48*(1), 20–37.

Welty Peachey, J., Cohen, A., Borland , J. and Lyras, A. (2013b). Exploring the initial motivations of individuals to volunteer with a sport-for-homeless initiative. *International Journal of Sport Management*, *14*(1), 103–122.

Welty Peachey, J., Lyras, A., Cohen, A., Bruening, J. E. and Cunningham, G. B. (2014). Exploring the motives and retention factors of sport-for-development volunteers. *Nonprofit and Voluntary Sector Quarterly*, *43*(6), 1052–1069.

Wicker, P. (2017). Volunteerism and volunteer management in sport. *Sport Management Review*, *20*(4), 325–337.

26

SDP and social capital

James Skinner, Geoff Woolcock and Arthur Milroy

Introduction

The issues facing humanity and development today are complex, heightened by an increased presence of globalization. Displacement triggered by long-term conflicts has a considerable knock on effect impacting on millions of people's basic physical, economic and social needs. Poverty in all its forms remains one of the world's greatest challenges and although the number of those living in extreme poverty has been reduced by more than half from 1.9 billion in 1990 to 836 million in 2015, there are still far too many people struggling to survive for the most basic of human needs. According to the United Nations Development Programme (UNDP), there are more than 800 million people still living on less than $1.25 a day and lacking access to clean drinking water (Milroy 2016).

Chronic and catastrophic disease remains some of the main factors pushing households from poverty into deprivation. AIDS is the leading cause of death among adolescents in sub-Saharan Africa, while the UNDP report that non-communicable diseases equate to 63 per cent of all deaths worldwide. Great strides have been made in efforts to reduce preventable child deaths, but new HIV infections are increasing in hard-to-reach areas resulting in people becoming excluded or marginalized.

This exclusion and inequality is another global development issue on the rise, particularly among minority groups, women and the disabled. Discriminatory legislation and mind-sets are restricting numerous groups of people, while disabled and women populations also experience exclusion. It has been well documented by IMF that income inequality is also growing, with the richest 10 per cent earning up to 40 per cent of total global income. Reducing this gap, the stigmas attached to discrimination and promoting true gender equality are crucial to accelerating sustainable development (Milroy 2016).

Peace, stability and human rights are too important elements in sustainable development and allow for real action to take place. We are living in a world that is becoming increasingly divided and while some countries enjoy prolonged periods of peace and prosperity, others seemingly encounter endless conflict and violence. Fighting brings insecurity and a destructive impact on a country's development and there is a need to take measures to protect those who are most at risk. But the role sport can play is significant, with a unified acknowledgement of the meaningful and lasting impact it can have on tackling these problems on a global scale. Sport has historically had an important role in cultures and societies, in the forms of competitive sport, physical activity or general play. It holds a universal popularity stretching to all corners of the world, with much of this enjoyment stemming from the rewarding and entertaining aspects that sport has for participants, spectators and organizers (Milroy 2016).

This popularity is evident through mega events. In 2006, an estimated 715.1 million people viewed the FIFA World Cup Final, while 7.5 million spectator tickets were made available for the Rio 2016 Olympic Games. Sport has the ability to connect people, irrespective of social, cultural or political background, and major sporting events are just one of the ways to do this. Its popularity and global coverage makes sport a great communication platform for public education and social mobilization. Opportunities for worldwide exposure can promote values of fair play, and teachings through the media, sporting roles models and goodwill ambassadors can reach millions. Valuable skills such as teamwork, cooperation and respect can be learned and instilled in people young and old during sport and physical activities. It has the ability to empower, motivate and inspire while helping people believe in their abilities and showcase their accomplishments. Similarly, sporting programs on local, national and international levels give people of all ages the opportunity to do this, as sport is inclusive and hold no barriers. As such, sport is a versatile and flexible developmental tool commonly associated with having the capacity to contribute to positive social capital in communities (Milroy 2016). Within the context described above, this chapter debates the role of sport as an enabler for development, and the key role it can play in achieving positive social capital. In this sense, the chapter explores the use of sport as a vehicle for development and its potential to bring people together from different economic, social and cultural backgrounds to foster greater social cohesion and cultural tolerance through facilitating the development of social capital.

Sport for development

Although sport was first used in the 1920s to achieve developmental related objectives it was not until 2002 that the United Nations Secretary-General summoned a task force to evaluate how sport may be more intimately allied to the United Nations structure. The aim of the task force was to develop more efficient and logical use of sport in achieving development and humanitarian objectives (Edwards and Skinner 2006). The task force was empowered to: 'establish an inventory of existing sport for development programs, identify instructive examples, and encourage the United Nations system to incorporate sport into their activities and work toward achieving the Millennium Development Goals (MDGs)' (United Nations Inter-agency Task Force on Sport for Development and Peace, 2003: 1).

The Task Force brought together bureaus with previous experience of using sport as a means for repatriation, human rights, health and environmental issues. The Task Force was co-chaired by Adolf Ogi, the Special Advisor to the Secretary-General on Sport for Development and Peace, and the Executive Director of UNICEF. The committee submitted its report in March 2003 with recommendations for an increased role of sport to help achieve the MDGs by: (1) improving public health; (2) boosting education performance; (3) redressing discrimination among girls, the disabled and the elderly; (4) encouraging tolerance and respect for others; (5) bridging social, cultural and ethnic divisions; (6) supporting local economic development and job creation; (7) healing deep psychosocial wounds among victims of war and other abuse; and (8) more effective communication of the broad United Nations agenda (Edwards and Skinner 2006).

Following submission of the report the United Nations General Assembly Resolution 58/5 entitled: 'Sport as a Means to Promote Education, Health, Development and Peace', the positive values of sport and physical education were recognized. This Resolution in November 2003 proclaimed 2005 as the International Year of Sport and Physical Education (IYSPE), and invited governments, the United Nations system and international sporting organizations such as the IOC and FIFA to use sport and physical education as a tool in global development. The United Nations hoped that the IYSPE 2005 would generate a sustainable impact beyond 2005 and

Table 26.1 Key sport for development and peace initiatives

1978	UNESCO (United Nations Educational Scientific and Cultural Organisation) General Conference adopts the International Charter of Physical Education and Sport
1997	Heads of State and Government of the European Commission focus special attention on sport during the Amsterdam treaty negotiations
2001	UN Secretary-General Kofi Annan appoints Mr. Adolf Ogi (former President of the Swiss Confederation) as the first Special Advisor on Sport for Development and Peace to enhance the network of relations between UN organizations and the sports sector
2002	The UN Secretary-General convenes the UN Inter-Agency Task Force on Sport for Development and Peace to review activities that involve sport within the UN system
2003	First International Conference on Sport and Development, Magglingen, Switzerland AND First Next Step conference: 'International Expert Meeting on Development in and through Sport', Amsterdam, the Netherlands
2004	Roundtable forum: Harnessing the Power of Sport for Development and Peace, Athens, Greece, which laid the cornerstones for establishing the Sport for Development and Peace International Working Group (SDPIWG) creating a new policy framework for the use of sport for development and peace
2005	International Year of Sport and Physical Education (IYSPE) 2005 is proclaimed by the General Assembly of the United Nations
2005	The Sport for Development and Peace International Working Group (SDPIWG) is formed; Second Magglingen Conference on Sport and Development, Magglingen, Switzerland; Second Next Step conference, Livingstone, Zambia; Commonwealth Advisory Body on Sport (CABOS) established
2007	Third conference 'Next Step', Windhoek, Namibia; European Commission publishes a White Paper on Sport stating it will promote the use of sport as a tool for development in international development policy
2008	IOC and the UN agree on an expanded framework for action to use sport to reach the goals of the UN; UN Secretary-General Ban Ki-Moon establishes a trust fund on Sport for Development and Peace
2009	First UN-IOC Forum on Sport for Development and Peace held in Lausanne, Switzerland
2010	sportanddev highlights Sport and Development at the 2010 FIFA World Cup
2012	Meeting of experts (including sportanddev) in Sport and Development held at the Commonwealth Secretariat to develop guidelines on Sport for Development and Peace to be used throughout the Commonwealth
2013	The 67th United Nations General Assembly proclaims that 6 April is to be observed as the 'International Day of Sport for Development and Peace'
2014	A Sport for Development and Peace International Working Group (SDP IWG) Thematic Meeting was held in Geneva, Switzerland on addressing gender-based violence in and through sport

encourage all members and sports networks to start shifting their thinking from the '*development of sport*' to '*development through sport*'. Sport was therefore viewed by the United Nations as having the ability to develop new frontiers and become the universal remedy for political and human catastrophes. Table 26.1 illustrates some of the key sport for development and peace initiatives

Defining social capital

There is an emergent empirical justification that social capital contributes substantially to the sustainable development of communities (Hill 2005). Its popularity stems from the ability to provide a universal solution to how societies can bond together in order for individuals to act collectively towards common goals and economic accomplishment (Ostrom 1994). The most recent and cited thinking about social capital can be attributed to Bourdieu (1986), Coleman (1988) and Putnam (1993; 2000). There are theories few and far between that have developed into renowned explanations of what constitutes social capital.

Bourdieu (1986) suggests capital can exhibit itself in three essential forms: (1) economic capital, which is instantly exchangeable into cash and may be established in the shape of estate entitlements; (2) cultural capital, which is transformable, in selected circumstances, into economic capital and may be established in the configuration of educational diplomas; and (3) social capital, comprised of social bonds and understandings, that is transformable, in particular settings, into economic capital. Bourdieu specifically characterizes social capital as affiliation in a consortium that bestows every one of its participants with the support of the combined capital, or alleged qualification that enables those members to recognize. For Coleman (1988) social capital is described by its purpose, not as a lone being, however, as a multiplicity of assorted individuals possessing mutual binary features made up of a particular facet of social configurations, and they simplify specific behaviours of actors, either business or individuals, inside the framework or network, where honesty and reliability is assumed and exchange is able to transpire effortlessly, that in its nonexistence would not be achievable. Putnam (1993), however, refers to social capital as characteristics of social configuration, understood as trust (in beings and organizations), norms (mutually beneficial standards), and networks (of public/political appointment), as well as participation (membership in volunteer groups), that are capable of bettering the effectiveness of the general public by enabling harmonized proceedings in order to realize sought after objectives. Yet later, Putnam (2000) makes reference to norms of mutual benefit and trustworthiness that arise from relationships or networks midst individuals.

Perhaps Putman's (2000) most significant contribution to the discourse of social capital is his reference to bonding and bridging capital. Putman suggests that 'bonding social capital' occurs when people with similar backgrounds, values and interests enter into relationships and collaborate together to achieve shared goals. These associations, according to Putnam, are inward looking, close knit and tend to reinforce exclusive and homogenous identities. However, he suggests that although social capital is relational, its influence on communities is most profound when relationships are among heterogeneous groups. Heterogeneity of social connections promotes linkages with diverse groups and across a broad range of resources or opportunities (Narayan and Cassidy 2001). Putman suggests 'bridging social capital' has the potential to forge these connections. It connects people from different backgrounds (e.g. races, neighbourhoods, clubs, religions and socio-economic classes), both within the entity and with outside groups, to work together for the benefit of the broader community. These networks and ties are outward looking and comprise people from different social locations. Based on this view, it can be argued that individuals who are connected through bridging capital have a greater range of associates, greater opportunities for broader community engagement, and wider opportunities for social and economic advancement (Frank and Yasumoto 1998; Paxton, 1999, Skinner *et al.* 2008a). Bridging social capital is therefore not only essential for enhancing social cohesion but also for improving a community's overall ability to build capacity; that is, to be able to adapt to the onset of shifting demographics and economic dislocation bought on by globalization, and restrict the dissolution of socially and culturally identifying institutions such as community sport organizations (Putnam 2000; Skocpol and Fiorina 1999; Skinner *et al.* 2008a).

Extending the work of Putnam, Woolcock (2001) identified the concept of 'linking social capital'. This plays an important but different role to bonding and bridging capital as these are concerned with horizontal social relationships as opposed to linking capital which is concerned with vertical connections between the different levels of social strata. These vertical connections can include individuals from entirely outside the community and provide 'further opportunities for access to wider networks and the potential to leverage a broader range of resources' (Coalter 2007a: 547). Linking capital is therefore important because it can play a role in the exchange of power, wealth and status among social groups (Portes and Landolt, 2000; Putnam 2000) from different hierarchical locations in society. Linking social capital has specific policy implications for the social inclusion agenda, although it is Putnam's (2000) notions of bonding and bridging capital that are discussed most often in policy applications to sport (Field 2003).

Sports role in generating development and social capital

Sport is frequently advocated as the glue that holds communities together (Barnes 1998) – although this view is largely based on a traditional and normative view of sport. Cairnduff (2001) suggests that sport can assist in creating communities with high levels of positive social capital which in turn and can make them more resilient to negative outcomes as a result of economic, social and cultural changes. This support exists despite the limited supportive research specifically targeted towards the relationship and role of sport in the creation of social capital.

When looking at the available research on sport and social capital it becomes obvious that most studies have been conducted in sporting club environments within highly developed countries. There is a dearth of empirical studies that look at the generation of social capital around Sport for Development (SFD) initiatives in a developing world context and only limited evidence suggests that active involvement in SFD can help people to establish new friendships, networks or links, which add to the overall stock of social capital. Hence, the organization of, and participation in, sport projects may provide a superordinate goal for people and groups. Investigating the potential of sporting events in facilitating social relations and social development, Misener and Mason (2006) suggested that short-term interventions can also provide 'fresh spaces' that bring communities together through participation, planning, volunteering and spectating. However, no empirical investigation was conducted to support these claims and the question remains what role short-term initiatives (e.g. sporting events or SFD projects) can truly play in the creation of social capital.

The relationship between social capital and sport has attracted increasing research attention in recent years (Dyreson 2001; Jarvie 2003; Collins 2003; 2005; Blackshaw and Long 2005; Brown 2006; Seippel 2006; Sharpe 2006; Coalter 2007a; Harvey *et al.* 2007; Nicholson and Hoye 2008; Skinner *et al.* 2008a; Hoye and Nicholson 2009; Zakus *et al.* 2009). Hoye *et al.* (2015) note that many of these efforts have focused on conceptualizing the potential links between social capital and sport. However, social capital and its related concepts have been used to explain, justify and legitimize instrumental sport policies, yet the link between sport and social capital is often simply assumed, without strong empirical evidence (Nicholson and Hoye 2008). Sport's relatively unquestioned role in developing social capital, as articulated by various national governments, appears to be based on long-held assumptions and generally accepted affirmations of the value of sport; however, the mechanisms for how sport delivers such outcomes is largely unknown.

Hoye *et al.* (2015) note that in response to this lack of evidence, there is an increasing amount of empirical research now being reported that has attempted to test the relationship between sport and aspects of social capital (see Tonts 2005; Atherley 2006; Bradbury and Kay 2008; Long 2008; Numerato 2008; Persson 2008; Zakus *et al.* 2012; Lock *et al.* 2013). Many of these studies, however, have utilized aggregated social survey data and have tended to use participation data as a proxy for social capital and/or have not separated associations with sport as against non-sport involvement (Coalter 2007). Hoye *et al.*'s (2015) survey of social connectedness and sport concluded that while their study had provided evidence about whether involvement in sport influences people's sense of social connectedness, important unanswered questions remain: does heightened social connectedness facilitate one's entry into sport involvement (rather than the other way around) and if there is indeed something special about being involved in sport that fosters people's social connectedness, what is it?

Oliver's (2014) PhD on the power of sport to build social bridges and overcome cultural barriers found that sport is not the magic bullet to 'cure all' social ills that some people assume. In fact, in many cases sport reaffirms existing power structures that cause discrimination and inequality. However, participation in and through sport can help processes of belonging, trust and inclusion; and if managed correctly, sport can be an excellent medium for encouraging awareness and valuable public debate on wider social issues. This thesis investigated the nature, effects and consequences of policies, programs and systems that have been put in place to encourage inclusive, non-discriminatory environments across a number of different sports in Australia. This research certainly highlighted the significant contribution that sportspeople, events and campaigns have made to enhancing social networks and furthering awareness and debate on wider social, physical and health issues but that sport alone cannot achieve social goals or solve complex issues. It is the participants (e.g. players, coaches and administrators) who are the heart and soul of sporting organizations, at both grassroots and elite levels, who hold the key to what sport is capable of delivering.

Although social capital can be created everywhere individuals bond for the intention of accomplishing a mutual good, yet it is most influential when developed by and through officially established community organizations, including community sport organizations. People who had frequently engaged in activities in their community are more likely to possess high social capital and be well connected within their community, to trust individuals, and to have a good feeling about life (Leonard and Onyx 2004). This strengthens a sense of belonging and the motivation to establish mutual objectives for the community (Meikle-Yaw 2006). Community belonging is a non-tangible benefit of sport, although complicated to measure. Collins and Kay (2003) perceive sport as supplying benefits such as healthier self-esteem, community identity and unity, and also as being able to encourage community pride and ownership. They believe this demonstrates a compelling link between sport and significant assets like community unity, identity and pride. Closely connected to these assets are the components of social capital (Cox 1995).

Coalter, however, suggests there is a 'conflict between developing sport *in* communities and developing communities *through* sport' (Coalter 2007a: 552; author's emphasis) and that these are two different projects and processes. In the end, a viable path to manage at the heart of sport, and how sport is developed. The focus must be at the community level, on viable sport policy goals, and on ways to structure and operate strong developmental gains. Coalter argues that we do not have enough theoretically informed empirical evidence to make judgements on the role sport and sport clubs as the main delivery point of social policy and in the development of social capital.

The cautionary words of Coalter (2007a) raise questions of directionality (sport builds social capital, social capital aids sport, or a reciprocity exists). While there is currently little direct evidence that sport contributes to social capital through fostering development, sport does have substantial social value (Skinner *et al.* 2008a). This lack of empirical evidence should not undermine the importance of the potential for development through sport. For example, if done correctly sport can assist in building community capacity. Banks and Shenton (2001) describe community capacity building as:

> Development work that strengthens the ability of community organisations and groups to build structures, systems, people and skills so that they are better able to define and achieve their objectives and engage in consultation and planning, manage community projects and take part in community partnerships and enterprises. It includes aspects of training, organisational and personal development and resource building, organised in a planned and self-conscious manner, reflecting the principles of empowerment and equality
>
> *Banks and Shenton 2001: 289–290*

The focus on development of a 'developmental approach' raises the question as to what types of organization/s are best placed to deliver developmental outcomes. Examples exist of traditional sport clubs, local government and a range of community/social development and NGO organizations all attempting to deliver developmental outcomes through sport. This begs the question, is one type of organization best placed or do they all have a role to play? While some sport clubs may have this ability, it is unlikely that the majority would consider development their role. That said, a broad array of positive community networks and relationships can be developed through engagement with sport. This engagement can create opportunities that can foster social inclusion and community development, which in turn, can assist in building high levels of positive social capital.

While many community service organizations (COs) find it difficult to measure impact, the exception here is measurement of inputs and outputs by participant-based member organizations, primarily community-funded COs, such as sporting clubs and community arts organizations. A strong body of evidence demonstrates the benefits of such COs in terms of community benefits (such as social cohesion), social benefits (such as development of social networks) and economic benefits (such as increased employment and social enterprise), and clear opportunity exists for individual skill development (ASC 2009). The provision of sporting infrastructure (an output) for example, is likely to lead to community benefits due to the high use of sporting facilities in Australia and the evidence-based link between increased physical activity and increased well-being (health benefits, socialization). This was clearly the case in the Centre for Sport and Social Impact (at La Trobe University) who found in a survey of over 1,600 football clubs in Victoria, Australia that

> the social return on investment for an average community football club indicates that for every $1 spent to run a club, there is at least $4.40 return in social value in terms of increased social connectedness, well-being, and mental health status; employment outcomes; personal development; physical health; civic pride and support of other community groups.
>
> *Centre for Sport and Social Impact*

Similar numbers emerged from a like-minded study in the UK (Fujiwara *et al.* 2014) that commissioned researchers from the London School of Economics to undertake analysis and develop the evidence base on the social impacts of cultural engagement and sport participation, and to estimate the monetary values for those impacts. Social impacts were considered in four areas: health, education, employment and economic productivity, and civic participation. The social benefits of culture and sport participation were wide ranging and this research found several statistically significantly associations: sports participants were 14 per cent more likely to report good health than non-participants, which produced a cost saving to the government of £97 per person. Generally, sports participants were not more likely to go on to further education than non-sports participants. However, among the sports variables, there was a statistically significant relationship for persons associated with swimming, they were 7 per cent more likely to seek further education; Unemployed persons who participate in sport were 11per cent more likely to have looked for a job during the past four weeks; and sports participants are 3 per cent more likely to be frequent volunteers and (on average) donate £25 more per person to charities than non-participants. However, these impacts depend upon gender and age.

This interest in sport and social capital's capacity to ignite civic renewal was the trigger for Delaney and Keaney (2005) analysing data from a large number of existing statistical studies from both British and international surveys. Their research compared levels of sports participation in the United Kingdom with that of other European Union countries, and explored links between sports participation and social capital. These researchers suggest that sport has an important role to play in the civil renewal agenda particularly because of its ability to foster social capital. They identify three ways that this can be achieved. First, through the social activity and membership of sports clubs. Second, it can be achieved when sports groups create networks that extend beyond the participants themselves, for instance among groups of parents or supporters of a local team, or volunteers who help run an activity. Third, it can be achieved when bonds between different groups of people are created. For instance, between supporters of a national, regional or local sports team. In other words, sport can help build shared identities.

Another thread of critique questioning the authenticity of global sporting brands backing SDP was taken up by Hayhurst and Szto (2016) arguing that

> although Nike claims that it is promoting social change through sport, it continues to use the 'marketplace as a driver' of this change and subsequently accepts the axiomatic discourses and structures of private authority, therefore conforming to existing global governance norms.
>
> *Hayhurst and Szto 2016: 538*

Spaaij and Westerbeek (2010) make a compelling case too arguing that through acting on their social responsibilities directed at internal and external constituents, sport business organizations can make contributions to the creation and transference of bonding, bridging and linking social capital but also show that sport business organizations aim to exploit opportunities in different markets for social capital that, in one way or another, will advance their business objectives.

Concluding comments

During the last two decades, there has been a concerted effort to remobilize sport as a vehicle for broad, sustainable social development, especially in the most disadvantaged communities in the world (Kidd 2008). Sport, sports organizations and other institutions included in the delivery of sport, can perform a crucial function in delivering this objective and in doing so help create social capital and improve the quality of life for individuals (Skinner *et al.* 2008a; Zakus *et al.* 2009).

To participate in sport is to participate in social interactions of commonality and trust. Commonality and trust are main components of social capital. Sport is inherently geared towards building social and community capital due to its organizational nature. Teams have players (team-mates), coaches, managers, referees, opponents and facilitators for sport to transpire. Specifically, participants are instructed on how to interrelate and behave within sport and societal boundaries. Sport teams, competitions and leagues are all systems of interactions. Developing lifelong friendships and significant networks due to involvement in sports is frequently claimed (Zakus *et al.* 2009). The necessity for working collaboratively to accomplish results, of anticipating in response to what an individual contributes into the sporting endeavour builds a mutual relationship. Sport is therefore capable of acquiring the vital mutual components of social capital.

Despite these claims of the positive benefits sport can bring to communities, some researchers have argued that sport spaces are sites of conflict and contestation between different ethnic groups and can inhibit development outcomes. Macdonald and Skinner (2001) note the latent ethnic tensions between rival soccer clubs in Australia. The traditional organization of soccer clubs along ethnic lines has also served to marginalize the game from the mainstream Australian sporting imagination (Skinner *et al.* 2008b). Moreover, the Cronulla beach riots of 11 December 2005 were widely depicted as race or ethnic riots between Middle-Eastern (Lebanese/Muslim) and Anglo youth (Poynting 2006). By contrast, Seippel (2006) suggests that social networks developed through sport strengthen communities, further various individual and social competencies, and generate social integration. One could also point to the success of policies adopted by the Brisbane El Salvadorian soccer club to increase levels of cultural understanding and cooperation. Political Football (2001) reports on how soccer connected the Brisbane, 'Tiger 11' team comprised entirely of Afghanistan asylum seekers (12–20 age range) to the Australian community. Bunde-Birouste (2007) writes of the integrating powers of soccer for recently arrived refugees in Sydney. Similarly, Playing for Success (2007) reports on improvements in literacy, numeracy and computer competency for boys and girls (ages 9–14) involved in education programs developed by soccer clubs in partnership with local education authorities in the UK.

The Studies on Education and Sport and Multiculturalism Report (2004: 1) notes that the importance of cultural diversity 'has grown as the processes of globalization have accelerated and extended the flows of cultures and peoples'. In particular, the report noted that sport has the potential to: (1) promote social integration for young people; (2) offer a common language and a platform for social democracy; (3) enhance understanding and appreciation of cultural differences and contribute to the fight against prejudices; and (4) reduce levels of social exclusion of immigrant and minority groups (ibid.). This is because sport is an activity common to all cultures and hence provides a non-threatening way to engage people. This lends itself to realising developmental outcomes including participating as volunteers, development of organizational skills and gaining confidence to play an active role in local communities. Frequently, through the playing of sport, future leaders are identified, and if mentored, could possibly play an array of more formal leadership roles from team captain, president of a club, community advocate to political representation. Communities would benefit from a pool of leaders from diverse cultural and religious backgrounds with diverse perspectives and visions to respond to new social, economic and environmental challenges.

It is clear that as a recognized enabler for development, sport can have a key role to play in achieving positive social capital. A strong foundation of social capital has many benefits including the development of social networks, the creation of common bonds between disparate groups and the establishment of social norms. In this sense, the use of sport as a vehicle for development has the potential to bring people together from different economic, social and cultural backgrounds and foster greater social cohesion and cultural tolerance through facilitating the development of social capital. The challenge moving forward is to provide greater empirical evidence to support this hypothesis and provide evidence to support significant investment by governments in sport for development initiatives.

References

Atherley, K. M. (2006). *Sport, Localism and Social Capital in Rural Western Australia*. Crawley: The University of Western Australia.

Australian Sports Commission (ASC). (2009). Study into the Contribution of the Not For Profit Sector. Preliminary Submission to the Productivity Commission. September. Available at: https://www.acoss.org.au/images/uploads/ACOSS_submission_-_PC_Study_into_the_Contribution_of_the_Not_for_Profit_Sector.pdf.

Banks, S. and Shenton, F. (2001). Regenerating neighbourhoods: A critical look at the role of community capacity building. *Local Economy*, *16*(4), 286–298.

Barnes, S. (1998). Could Sport and Recreation Opportunities be the Glue Which Holds Rural Communities Together. Paper presented at ISA XIV World Congress of Sociology, Montreal. 26 July – 1 August 1998.

Blackshaw, T. and Long, J. (2006). What's the big idea? A critical exploration of the concept of social capital and its incorporation into leisure policy discourse. *Leisure Studies*, *24*(3), 239–258.

Bourdieu, P. (1986). The forms of capital. In J. G. Richardson (ed.), *Handbook of Theory and Research for the Sociology of Education*. New York: Greenwood, pp. 241–253.

Bradbury, S. and Kay, T. (2008). Stepping into community? The impact of youth sport volunteering on young people's social capital. In M. Nicholson and R. Hoye (eds), *Sport and Social Capital*. Oxford: Butterworth-Heinemann, pp. 285–316.

Brown, K. M. (2006). The position of Australian community sporting organisations in the third sector: Membership profiles, characteristics and attitudes. *Third Sector Review*, *12*(2): 17–39.

Bunde-Birouste, A. (2007). Football United: Refugee Soccer Development Program, Available at: www.sphcm.med.unsw.edu.au/SPHCMWeb.nsf/page/RefugeeSoccer?Open.

Cairnduff, S. (2001). *Sport and Recreation for Indigenous Youth in the Northern Territory*. Canberra: ASC.

Coalter, F. (2007). Sports clubs, social capital and social regeneration: 'Ill-defined interventions with hard to follow outcomes'? *Sport in Society*, *10*(4), 537–559.

Coleman, J. (1988). Social capital in the creation of human capital. *American Journal of Sociology*, *94*, S95–120.

Collins, M. and Kay, T. (2003). *Sport and Social Exclusion*. London: Routledge.

Cox, E. (1995). *A Truly Civil Society*. Sydney: ABC Books.

Delaney, L. and Keaney, E. (2005). Sport and Social Capital in the United Kingdom: Statistical Evidence from National and International Survey Data. Economic and Social Research Institute, Institute for Public Policy Research, Dublin.

Dyreson, M. (2001). Maybe it's better to bowl alone: Sport, community and democracy in American thought. *Sport in Society*, 4(1), 19–30.

Edwards, A. and Skinner, J. (2006). *Sport Empire*. Aachen: Meyer and Meyer Sports.

Field, J. (2003). *Social Capital*. London: Routledge.

Frank, K. A. and Yasumoto, J. Y. (1998). Linking action to social structure within a system: Social capital within and between subgroups. *American Journal of Sociology*, *104*(3), 642–686.

Fujiwara, D., Kudrna, L. and Dolan, P. (2014). *Quantifying the Social Impacts of Culture and Sport*. Department for Culture, Media and Sport, UK.

Hayhurst, J. M. L. and Szto, C. (2016). Corporatizating activism through sport-focused social justice? Investigating Nike's corporate responsibility initiatives in sport for development and peace. *Journal of Sport and Social Issues*, *40*(6), 522–544.

Hill, S. B. (2005). Social ecology as a framework for understanding and working with social capital and sustainability within rural communities. In A. Dale and J. Onyx (eds), *A Dynamic Balance: Social Capital and Sustainable Community Development*. Vancouver: UBC Press, pp. 48–68.

Hoye, R. and Nicholson, M. (2009). Social capital and sport policies in Australia: Policy transfer in action. *Public Management Review*, *11*(4), 441–460

Hoye, R., Nicholson, M. and Brown, K. (2015). Involvement in sport and social connectedness. *International Review for the Sociology of Sport*, *50*(1), 3–21.

Jarvie, G. (2003). Communitarianism, sport and social capital: 'Neighbourly insights into Scottish sport'. *International Review for the Sociology of Sport, 38*(2), 139–153.

Kidd, B. (2008). A new social movement: Sport for development and peace. *Sport in Society, 11*(4), 370–380.

Leonard, R. and Onyx, J. (2004). *Social Capital and Community Building: Spinning Straw into Gold.* London: Janus.

Lock, D., Filo, K., Sotiriadou, P., Zakus, D., Skinner, J., Wicker, P. and Kunkel, T. (2013). *Social and Economic Value of Basketball in Queensland.* Basketball Queensland.

Long, J. (2008). Sport's ambiguous relationship with social capital: The contribution of national governing bodies of sport. In M. Nicholson and R. Hoye (eds), *Sport and Social Capital.* Oxford: Butterworth-Heinemann, pp. 207–232.

Macdonald, R. and Skinner, J. (2001). The long and winding road. *The Sport Management Association of Australia and New Zealand Newsletter, 2*(2), 21–2.

Meikle-Yaw, P. A. (2006). *Democracy Satisfaction: The Role of Social Capital and Civic Engagement in Local Communities.* Mississippi: Mississippi State University.

Milroy, A. (2016). Sport as an Effective Tool for Social Development and Peace. Speech written for Mr Wilfred Lemke, Special Advisor to the United Nations Secretary-General on Sport for Development and Peace.

Misener, L. and Mason D. S. (2006), Creating community networks: Can sporting events offer meaningful sources of social capital? *Managing Leisure, 11*(1), 39–56.

Narayan, D. and Cassidy, M. F. (2001). A dimensional approach to measuring social capital: Development and validation of a social capital inventory. *Current Sociology, 49*(2), 59–102.

Nicholson, M. and Hoye, R. (eds) (2008). *Sport and Social Capital.* Oxford: Elsevier Butterworth-Heinemann.

Numerato, D. (2008). Czech sport governing bodies and social capital. *International Review for the Sociology of Sport, 43*(1), 21–34.

Oliver, P. D. (2014). The Power of Sport: Building Social Bridges and Breaking down Cultural Barriers. PhD thesis. Curtin University, AU. Available at: http://hdl.handle.net/20.500.11937/535 (accessed 19 June 2018).

Ostrom, E. (1994). Constituting social capital and collective action. *Journal of Theoretical Politics, 6*(4), 527–562.

Paxton, P. (1999). Is social capital declining in the United States? A multiple indicator assessment. *American Journal of Sociology, 105*(1), 88–127.

Persson, T. H. (2008). Social capital and social responsibility in Denmark: More that gaining public trust. *International Review for the Sociology of Sport, 43*(1), 35–52.

Playing for Success. (2007). The Sports Factor, Interview Transcript on ABC Radio National, 9 February. Available at: http:///www.abc.net.au/rn/sportsfactor/stories/2007/1842264.htm.

Political Football. (2001). The Sports Factor, Interview Transcript on ABC Radio National, 2 November. Available at: www.ausport.gov.au/fulltext/2001/sportsf/s406401.htm.

Poynting, S. (2006). What caused the Cronulla riot? *Race and Class, 48*(1), 85–92.

Portes, A. (1998). *Social Capital: Its origins and applications in modern sociology. Annual Review of Sociology, 24*(1), 1–12.

Portes, A. and Landolt, P. (2000). Social capital: Promise and pitfalls of its role in development. *Journal of Latin American Studies, 32*(2), 529–547.

Putnam, R. (1993). *Making Democracy Work: Civic Traditions in Modern Italy.* Princeton, NJ: Princeton University Press.

Putnam, R. (2000). *Bowling Alone: The Collapse and Revival of American Community.* New York: Simon & Schuster.

Skocpol, T. and Fiorina, M. P. (eds.) (1999). *Civic Engagement in American Democracy.* Washington, DC: Brookings Institution Press.

Seippel, Ø. (2006). Sport and Social Capital. *Acta Sociologica, 49*(2), 169–183.

Skinner, J., Zakus, D. and Cowell, J. (2008a). Development through sport: Building social capital in disadvantaged communities. *Sport Management Review. 11*(3), 253–275.

Skinner, J., Zakus, D. and Edwards, A. (2008b). Coming in from the margins: Ethnicity, community support, and the rebranding of Australian Soccer. *Soccer and Society, 9*(3), 394–404.

Spaaij, R. and Westerbeek, H. (2010) Sport business and social capital: A contradiction in terms? *Sport in Society, 13*(9), 1356–1373.

Studies on Education and Sport and Multiculturalism Final Report (2004). *Institute of Sport and Leisure Policy.* Loughborough University.

Tont, M., (2005). *Competitive sport and social capital in rural Australia*. The University of Western Australia; Crowley, WA.

Woolcock, M. (2001). The place of social capital in understanding social and economic outcomes. *Canadian Journal of Policy Research*, *2*(1), 11–17.

Zakus, D., Skinner, J. and Edwards, A. (2009). Sport and social capital in Australia. *Sport and Society*, *12*(7), 986–998.

Zakus, D. H., Skinner, J. and Ogilvie, J. (2012). Measuring Social Capital in Queensland Rugby Clubs. A paper presented to the International Sociology of Sport Association Conference, Glasgow, Scotland.

27

SDP and health

Non-communicable diseases

Henry Dorling and Oscar Mwaanga

Introduction

There is now no doubt that we are currently facing a generational pandemic of inactivity and obesity. Much research has shown that this problem has not only contributed to engineer physical activity (PA) out of our lives but also created a new proliferation of non-communicable diseases (NCDs) such as diabetes, heart disease and cancer. The World Health Organization (WHO) in their 'Global Action Plan for the prevention and control of non-communicable diseases' report gives a stark assessment of the problem; 'The global burden and threat of non-communicable diseases constitutes a major public health challenge that undermines social and economic development throughout the world' (WHO 2013: 7).

In particular, an increase in childhood NCDs indicate a worrying trend which does not seem like being halted. The age of inactivity means that children and adults are ecologically engineered towards sedentary activities to entertain themselves as opposed to physically active methods, which in turn leads to weight gain and illness. The discourse that permeates around sedentary society is one which has grown exponentially in recent times. Numerous studies have concluded that NCDs can be attributed to inactivity and obesity and that the issue is becoming more and more prevalent, particularly in young people (Zieff 2011; Nike Inc. 2012; Mandic *et al.* 2012).

Statistics and economic costs

Within the current discourse and debate around obesity, sedentarism and NCDs, statistics and economic analysis are central. Accordingly, NCDs and associated conditions afford some tremendous costs to UK society and represent a significant economic strain on health services across the world too.

The WHO Global Action Plan for the prevention and control of NCDs estimates that '36 million deaths, or 63% of the 57 million deaths that occurred globally in 2008, were due to non-communicable diseases, comprising mainly cardiovascular diseases (48% of non-communicable diseases), cancers (21%), chronic respiratory diseases (12%) and diabetes (3.5%)' (WHO 2013: 7). Baker (2017) in a recent UK Government obesity briefing paper stated that 63 per cent of adults are obese or overweight with 22 per cent of 4–5 year old children and 34 per cent of 10–11 year old children obese or overweight. The NHS in England spent £5.1 billion on treating obesity and overweight related ill health in 2014/15 with indirect costs totalling nearly £47 billion per year (HM Government UK 2016). Dobbs *et al.* (2014) for The McKinsey Global Institute estimated that this is a greater burden on the UK's economy than armed violence, war and terrorism. Ding *et al.* (2016) report that physical inactivity cost global health care systems about US$3.8 billion worldwide in 2013. The estimated direct cost of physical inactivity to the NHS is £1.06 billion (Department of Health 2011). These estimates are also reported to be conservative in nature and probably represent a small proportion of actual costs. It is important to underline then, that the economic burden of physical inactivity could be enormous.

Policy landscape

There is a plethora of attempts to define the main arguments framing this discourse around NCDs and their causes. It has become one of the main social and political ideological debates and has become influential and of importance in many areas of society. Robertson (1998 in Zieff *et al.* 2009: 155) comments that, 'health discourses … emerge and take root in a society because they are congruent with the prevailing social, political, and economic context within which they are produced'. This can be seen in the UK where recent turbulent political and economic times have contributed to government policy, NHS schemes and many different charities emerging as front runners in tackling the rooted issues and causes of NCD prevalence with somewhat limited successes. In particular, the UK Government has been an advocate of policy-led interventions; however, their policy cycles have fluctuated to date, which is indicative of the challenges around implementing and sustaining PA policy in a difficult political climate, which in turn leads to the reduced opportunity for the profiling of active lifestyles (Milton and Bauman 2015).

Policy-makers in the UK have attempted to address the issues at varying levels. The government have recently published an obesity strategy (HM Government 2016) which purports to look at ways in which this problem can be tackled. After publication it was roundly criticised for lacking any decisive action and stated itself that it was merely a starting point for a conversation rather than the final word for action. Many labelled it disappointing with overemphasis on the importance of identifying those that are obese rather than strategies that may address it. The strategy does, however, recognise that this is a complex and multifaceted problem and highlights physical activity as a clear and effective method to reduce obesity rates. With nearly a third of children aged 2–15 overweight or obese this is clearly an issue that needs policy interventions. As Houlihan (1997) explains, sport and policy is now inextricably linked in most industrial countries across a wide and diverse range of areas.

The Sport England strategy 'Towards an Active Nation' was also published in 2016. The emphasis here shifted from promoting sport specific participation levels to the importance of being physically active through a number of lifestyle choices and interventions. Environments such as schools, health organisations and community settings have been suggested as focal points to target this policy shift. This seems a positive move and one that could halt the upward trend of obesity, inactivity and NCDs. However, the picture at this level is complex and ever-changing with a variety of factors to consider such as demographics, socio–economic status, localised funding, and more individualised areas such as motivation, family circumstance, attitudes and awareness. This seems to be where their policy falls down as it fails to recognise and understand what is needed for whom, in what circumstances and why. Sport England announced £88 million to go to National Governing Bodies (NGBs) of sport in order to facilitate this potentially ground breaking work. However, it is hard to see the evidence base from which this decision has come. NGBs have been at the centre of intervention delivery in UK sport for development for a long time with limited evidence of participation increases or improvement in social issues. It begs the question: is it not logical to fund a partnership between organisations such as 'UKActive' or 'Exercise Works!' who have more experience in PA promotion and delivery and not Sport England or NGB's whose focus on sport specific activity is what we are trying to shift away from? Otherwise it may be a case of doing the same thing over again and expecting different outcomes.

Recent studies emanating from the US, where arguably the crisis is at its most potent, have shown that there seems to be no correlation between increased physical activity levels and a decrease in obesity and NCDs (Dwyer-Lindgren *et al.* 2013). This seems to suggest that the problem is far more difficult to impact than may have first been assumed with factors such as location, demographics, unemployment and access to health care considered. If this is true, policy developments such as those detailed above may really struggle to have any influence at all, and if they are to succeed, must address the issues and needs of communities at a truly grassroots level.

Vested interest groups and their response

Sport for Development and Peace (SDP) as a field has responded in the way it knows best through the utilisation of sport-based interventions that have attempted to address and identify some of the major causes of NCDs. All interventions in the sector employ sport and physical activity as a method to do so, and many look to sedentary behaviour-based projects. However, sport and physical activity alone may not be enough to ward off the effects of sedentary behaviours, (Bailey *et al.* 2012; Dwyer-Lindgren 2013). Metcalf *et al.* (2012: 345) state that, 'the small increase in physical activity that emerges from formal interventions seems insufficient to improve the body mass/fat of children'. As a result, promotion of nutritional awareness and the long-term health effects of inactivity should also be noted. Any interventions should look to promote reduced sedentary behaviour alongside more traditional lifestyle behaviours such as increased moderate to vigorous physical activity and dietary change (Wilmot *et al.* 2012). Bailey *et al.* (2012: 2) cite social factors as just as positive an influence on health-related problems as the physical activity itself. They comment that, 'the social relationships developed within physical activity settings, as well as the values embedded within them, are as potent in realising the impressive (and distinctive) range of outcomes as is the physical activity itself'.

Another area that has been claimed to be able to make a difference as a part of the bigger response is school-based sport and physical education. The Designed to Move report (Nike Inc. 2012) indicates that the school environment is accessible, and provides undoubted opportunity for regular, structured play, physical education, physical activity and sports. Schools have an enormous impact on the course of people's lives and on society, with some clear and strengthening links regarding early physical activity interventions and the impact they have on the potential of suffering from NCDs in later life. Children are not just simply active naturally and need the help and support of an environment such as the school, with teachers, parents and carers all having a crucial role to play in developing healthy habits early on in life (All-Party Parliamentary Group on A Fit and Healthy Childhood 2016). Kirk (2005: 251) suggests that quality early learning experiences develop 'perceptions of competence that underlie the motivation that is vital to continuing participation', linking to the importance of a lifelong involvement in physical activity. It would therefore seem essential that the school is viewed as an important vehicle through which PA can be integrated into daily life and strategies that allow for this area are developed (Dobbins *et al.* 2013).

Schools, however, form only a small micro-focused part of a much larger response to this problem which has come from other vested interest groups and organisations. There are many multifaceted determinants and inequalities relating to this area. Addressing physical inactivity and the root causes of NCDs is complex and requires a holistic, multilevel approach rather than focusing solely on localised community and behavioural processes (Lyn 2010; Noar and Mehrotra 2011).

The United Nation's Millennium Development Goals (MDGs) (UN MDGs n.d.) were a coordinated response by the UN to attempt to address significant global issues with clearly defined and quantifiable targets. Sport was seen as a major contributor to the achievement of these goals and as such has often been mentioned as a prominent part of plans across many MDG interventions.

The Sustainable Development Goals (SDGs) retain a similar overarching reliance and belief in the 'power' of sport with organisations calling on its potential to positively affect a number of the goals including areas such as health and well-being, gender equality, employment, peace and justice. As the United Nations Development Programme (UNDP) say, the potential success of the SDGs are predicated on 'the growing contribution of sport … in its promotion of tolerance and respect and the contributions it makes to the empowerment of women and of young people, individuals and communities' (UNDP 2016). Indeed, the Commonwealth Secretariat has also stated in their recent analysis of SDP and its contribution to the SDGs that it recognises sport as an important enabler of sustainable development (Dudfield and Dingwall-Smith 2015). They do, however, acknowledge the limitations of SDP to address these global targets due to the need for many more evidence-based programmes, more training, better safeguarding and clearer links to broader outcomes and stakeholders.

Although it should be acknowledged that this view of sport and its potential to address international development challenges through its influence within the MDGs and SDGs is commendable, it is with some apprehension that one could say whether it has truly met or influenced these targets in any significant way, and its claims have been at best broad and inflated. Evidence is still sparse and nuanced often with individual case studies used to demonstrate success. There has seemed to be an obsession with proof that things work and no focus on the mechanisms at play deep in the ecology of these international interventions. Burnett (2015: 387) makes reference to the problems around 'proof of effect' whereby donors utilise narrow objectives to achieve and justify investments in projects that make little tangible difference and lead from a lack of critical discourse. As Mwaanga and Adeosun (2017b: 2) state, 'superficially sport is seen to be a benevolent social institution, which carries with it myths of modernity and progress.'

The Commonwealth's response to this has been interesting. It has critically examined the use of SDP and asked several notable questions. The implicit complexity of many development challenges is a noteworthy paradox alongside the claim of sport as a singular tool to address the many issues in this area. Coalter (2010) reminds us that too often sport is used as a narrow focus solution to address very broad gauge problems. The Commonwealth go on to say that,

> for sport to make a positive contribution to national development agendas, interventions must be well planned, effectively implemented and robustly monitored and evaluated … (with) the need to base the use of sport as a tool for development on a set of clear principles that connect sport-based approaches to the development areas and policy domains they aim to contribute to.
>
> *Dudfield and Dingwall-Smith 2015: 76*

In other words unless sport development interventions are clear in their intentions, are not overly ambitious in their objectives and can evaluate their worthiness in an effective way the sector will find it difficult to develop and actually make a difference. Particularly in addressing NCDs, sport can be seen too often as a panacea, which in itself begins to create problems.

The current position of SDP

This evangelical style approach to SDP has existed for a number of years alongside an overly Eurocentric style of development which has seemingly widened the global North–South divide in international sport development terms. A hegemonic relationship has existed within these environments meaning that the privileged groups still maintain a 'position of benefit and accruement over others' (Darnell 2010: 57). This has arguably led to imbalanced voices from within the sector, which has led to a lack of awareness of the key mechanisms at play from both a global North and global South perspective. This imbalance has meant that development has been problematic with views and ideas often in conflict with each other. Most development ideals have demonstrated a binary outlook, which is where societies have attempted to move from a clear start point to a definite end point or in other words 'a traditional society which develops into an advanced, modern society' (Kingsbury *et al.* 2008: 23). This theory of modernisation, if applied to the SDP movement, can be seen to have an assumptive effect whereby 'in SDP policy circles the meaning of the concept of development is often assumed and rarely critiqued' (Mwaanga in Hylton 2013: 326). In turn this means that there has been a lack of awareness around localised need and its reliance on a linear and homogenous outlook with clear failings of development in this manner. As Mwaanga (in Hylton 2013: 330) states, this style of SDP activity, 'can only lead to partial individual empowerment, particularly as root causes of underdevelopment … are never addressed'. In relation to NCDs this can mean potential problems when trying to influence change or show improvements.

Intervention at scale has been an issue in SDP for a long time. Localised research-based programmes have had reasonable success, however, there seems to have been much more difficulty to effect any sort of change on a societal level. There have been efforts to try and map interventions to prevailing social issues to help in their success; however, the main criticism is that on a bigger scale it is very hard to pigeonhole the behaviours of large numbers of people, and virtually impossible to show any sort of commonality with and between interventions. In the recent series on physical activity and health in the *Lancet*, Andersen *et al.* (2016: 1256) indicate that 'activity interventions that have shown effectiveness in laboratory or community settings need to be embedded into multiple sector systems that include public health practitioners, stakeholders, and policy makers'. This seems simply not to have happened as the clear issues around context and its influence on individuals and their needs have just not been appreciated. Mwaanga and Adeosun (2017a: 7) add to this by referring to the importance of the 'people within the local context using sport innovatively as a tool, whose transformed (or untransformed) lives is the paramount measure of authenticity in SDP interventions'. In other words local voices need to be privileged more effectively to ensure SDP programmes and projects that target health are a success for those they are intended for.

Mathie and Cunningham (2011) refer to the transformative power of asset-based models in development. This type of development is when a community or organisation looks to build upon what already exists to make things better and more aligned with local need or can exploit an existing resource or advantage in a community (Haines in Phillips and Pittman 2009). It encapsulates areas such as sustainable livelihoods, the enhancement of capacity and agency, citizenship and the role of multiple stakeholders (Mathie and Cunningham 2011). This can therefore create an empowering feeling and development can potentially be much more effective. When looking at SDP one can see the overarching model is of deficit-based development, that is, programmes and projects that look to fill a void or develop a particular area that has been identified as being lacking in some way within a community or existing programme. In other words, the target group must demonstrate some form of inadequacy before being eligible for assistance. This can create unrealistic expectations about how sport can help to 'fill' these often significant social and societal deficits and as such the evangelical approach is borne out. SDP is thus seen as universal and presumed to have the power to overcome inequality (Darnell in Dudfield 2014). The potential of utilising assets to build development potential in communities and society is huge particularly if one looks to PA and non-sport populations as the drivers. However, the challenge is to employ this approach effectively within the already existing needs based, problem solving paradigm (Mathie and Cunningham 2011).

The failure of the clear conceptualisations of SDP is also crucial as to whether projects are successful or not. Sport interventions have often been based on assumptions and used in a more traditional environment to tackle areas such as crime, anti-social behaviour and unemployment. This sport focus has meant that often those attracted to the project have not engaged with the idea of using it to address the social issues but merely to play more sport; and assumptions have been made by practitioners 'that participation in sport automatically contributes to transferring socially desirable or character attributes such as self-discipline, teamwork and respect' (Mwaanga and Adeosun 2017a: 5). Although a good first step, sport is 'not sufficient for creating positive health-related, educational or social outcomes' (Haudenhuyse *et al.* 2012: 3). As a result the expected behaviour change or improvement in social issues has not been observed and the project has suffered from a lack of sustainability. As Spence and Lee (2003: 8) indicate, although 'interventions often alter individual behaviour initially, it is likely that enduring social and environmental factors shape return to previous sedentary behaviour once the intervention is over'. This indicates the need for a more wide-ranging and societally acceptable perspective which centres on more embedded physical activity as potential interventions.

The main voices in the sector acknowledge that this area 'requires a multisectoral approach, to foster preventative action, behavioural change and therefore improved quality of life' (Dudfield and Dingwall-Smith 2015: 25); it therefore seems prudent to think about how we can shift focus to a more embedded and realistic method of addressing the prevailing issues as 'increased participation in sport and physical activity are a major and necessary contributor to these changes' (Dudfield and Dingwall-Smith 2015: 25).

A move from sport for development towards physical activity for health

SDP has emerged as a credible movement utilised by a number of organisations as an interventionist tool to nurture peacemaking across divides and to address a wide variety of issues (Giulianotti 2011). Kidd (2011) reflects on SDP as a well-known approach to social interventions consisting of an array of proclamations, endorsements programmes and organisations. Indeed the Commonwealth Secretariat states that, 'increased participation in sport … should form an important part of national public health strategies' (Dudfield and Dingwall-Smith 2015: 25). The work so far by a number of organisations and stakeholders is mobilising sport towards the goals of development and peace which suggest more congruence in the efforts by policy-makers, stakeholders and civil society to gain the benefits afforded through sport both social and political (Darnell in Giulianotti 2015).

Kidd (2008) indicates that the SDP movement has been in part a response to athlete activism and idealist responses to major societal and social ills with Beutler (2008) showing clear evidence that systematic and coherent use of sport can make an important contribution to public health within a range of diseases as well as peacebuilding and conflict resolution.

However, the overarching concept of SDP could be argued as a contested term and one to which some sectors of society and communities nationally and internationally struggle to relate. The use of structured sport with the SDP movement still suffers from a lack of evidence discourse, which although addressed at a micro-level in part, on a wider societal macro-level there is still a lack of awareness about what works for whom, in what circumstances and why. Darnell *et al.* (2016) call for a move towards critical perspectives on international development in SDP as the way forward.

There is still a tendency for it to be viewed as a panacea for good rather than a significant structure within which development and peacebuilding activities can be framed. Sport is not an essential force for, or tool of, international development but rather a social, cultural and political phenomenon and institution with significant implications for development and peace (Darnell and Black 2011).

Sport still harbours feelings of positive values and the promotion of cohesion and is often talked of as a common language through which many diverse communities can experience change and development. From this there seems to have been an issue around the mythopeic status of sport (Coalter 2007) and the idea that it is a 'magic bullet' to cure all ills. Clearly this is not the case and more current developments have started to show an awareness of this. Moreover, 'sport' as a concept to address social issues has started to become less prominent, as awareness of the need to demonstrate more empathy towards a community and of what works for whom and in what circumstances as a development tool has become more conspicuous, depowering the idea of structured sport as the answer. This softer approach to development has taken the focus away from traditional politicised endeavours in development and more towards a focus on the people and how this related commonality may be explored and promoted.

This approach can be termed as a move towards the use of PA as opposed to a more sport specific focus, which creates a more accessible and realistic target for those involved. The notion of a more physical activity-related development position has the ability to utilise a less impenetrable interface, in particular for those who experience social issues where the use of traditional sport may not be the answer. Too often sport for development can be accused of assumptions around what is thought to work to involve communities and participants within a project. The use of physically active events and action utilising less traditional sporting mediums has started to be realised as a more effective way to engage people in particular contexts. Physical activities such as pilates, yoga, walking, cycling and dance have seen a rise in their use. In addition, within health promotion there has been a policy shift towards the use of more 'Physical Activity for Health' which has proven to be more popular to a wider diverse population and indeed more effective to embed into everyday healthy behaviours. Research around this area related to the dose-response relationships between PA and diseases such as diabetes, cancer and heart disease has shown positive relationships between the amount and type of PA and the likelihood of a significant reduction in the risk of these diseases (Kyu *et al.* 2016). In particular Smith *et al.* (2016) found a particular relationship between a reduction in diabetes and leisure time physical activity. In addition, the study found that the greatest relative benefits could be found at low levels of activity therefore if the findings of this study can be interpreted directly within the context of the PA for Health discourse it may be surmised that low-level leisure time physical activity can be an essential factor for addressing NCDs more generally. As a public health style intervention this could be argued to be more cost-effective and realistic to embed into everyday life. The Commonwealth Secretariat even recommends 'public health stakeholders to embed prevention as a key pillar of public health policy, and in doing so, prioritise increasing physical activity as an important public health goal' (Dudfield and Dingwall-Smith 2015: 27).

As such this could promote a move away from sport specific reactive interventions based on a deficit style model and more towards a prevailing societal-level intervention incorporating a pro-active asset-based model which could have the chance to become more influential and effective in addressing NCDs and their root causes and issues.

This could then lead to effectively addressing the unique set of circumstances that could help steer a community towards a more focused public health outlook which includes active working relationships with the many and varied community and institutional stakeholders. The complexity of such arenas may limit the possibilities of integration within residing and competing discourses, meaning traditional sport-focused interventions may lack the awareness of specific contextual factors. However, this may be the key to unlocking the potential of such facilitations and, as a result, more effectively address NCDs and their related complications. In particular, working with young people could yield the most favourable longer-term benefits for society as a whole. As Kohl and Murray (2012: 208) indicate, 'the emphasis for young adults should be on health, fitness and behaviours that can be adopted and maintained into adulthood.'

Conclusion

The landscape is not straightforward and there remain many challenges to overcome, with the area still in the relatively early stages of understanding. As Zieff (2011: 121) recognises, 'effective tools for determining community and population needs and interest in physical activity are currently in formative stages'. Long-term problems around NCD's are multifaceted and need to be tackled in many forms. As Burkhardt and Brennan indicate,

> Public health is likely to be dominated by the obesity and physical activity agenda for many decades to come. As a society we have engineered physical activity out of our lives and now face the challenges of how to encourage people to stay active enough to maintain their health.
>
> *Burkhardt and Brennan 2012: 159*

Donnelly *et al.* state that, two related trends seem apparent:

> The first is a clear belief that, under certain circumstances, sport may make a useful contribution to work in international development and peacebuilding; the second is that criticisms of it are frequently constructive, intended to support the work of practitioners in the field by outlining the limitations of what may be achieved through sport, and under what circumstances.
>
> *Donnelly et al. 2011: 589*

They go on to argue that in order for the sector to move forward there needs to be more engagement with practitioners in the field. More attempts are needed to privilege and strengthen community and grassroots voices, which in turn become a part of the process which can then integrate change and development into their lives. This seems to be a useful summary of the current climate from which one can start to frame an alternative view.

The prevalence of NCDs is one of the major global issues of our lifetime and there is no doubt that sport and physical activity can play a role in addressing the associated issues. At this point it could be argued that the SDP movement although active in this field, has done little to halt the increase in and associated effects of a number of NCDs. More traditional sport development programmes utilising the 'power' of sport have seen some success in raising awareness of these diseases and their effects but the evidence for a significant difference in changing people's behaviours and attitudes towards this area is less than convincing. A move towards physical activity for health may be one way in which the issues could be addressed more significantly. Interventions can be less stand-alone and more embedded into the life of individuals and communities in wider and non-sport populations. A move away from more sport-focused activities may help to allow some perspectives to be broadened and activity that leads to positive health outcomes to be part of everyday life.

Intervention at an early age may help to develop a motivation to be more consistently part of physical activity through the life course and schools can play a huge role in this. Already in UK primary schools we are seeing examples of external companies delivering physical activity, physical education and health-related programmes in an attempt to influence and educate young people. Schools are seeing the need to be proactive and look at community asset-based methods to help address issues. Early age interventions will also have more of a chance of being influential through the life course where habits can be formed and behaviour change proven much more effectively. Of course, this concept is not straightforward and will come with challenges.

The move towards PA to address NCD prevalence may be seen as a weak response. Sport is the embodiment of a strong, muscular and combative solution and as such the less belligerent tendency of PA for Health may be seen as less effective. It is a disruption to the norm and as a result there may be a difficulty to accept it as an effective intervention strategy. Reductionist doctrine still prevails with a lack of knowledge, resources and funding also a factor (Weiler and Stamatakis 2010). However, the potential for it to be integrated into everyday life and to become part of normalised behaviour seems to set it apart in its potential to make some serious health-related advancements. Schools are becoming more aware of the need to make their environment more activity biased via school wide PA promotion, more time on PE, and employing more physically active teaching and learning methods, utilising programmes such as EduMove which promotes education through embedding enjoyable physical activity and movement in classrooms and around the school (edumove.co.uk). Communities are enjoying more exposure to less traditional activities such as yoga, dance, parkour or walking groups to address health-related issues all of which is an attempt to position itself as a viable alternative to SDP to redress the current epidemic of NCDs and the associated costs. If a move towards physical activity for health can become accepted and used to address the multifarious and complex issues detailed in this chapter, then there may be a claim for finally advancing and moving this area forward.

References

All-Party Parliamentary Group on a Fit and Healthy Childhood (2016). *A Report by The All-Party Parliamentary Group on A Fit and Healthy Childhood*: Physical Education.

Andersen, B., Mota, J. and Di Pietro, L. (2016). Update on the global pandemic of physical inactivity; Comment. For the Lancet Physical Activity Series 2. *Lancet, 388*(10051), published online 27 July.

Bailey, R., Hillman, C., Arent, S. and Petitpas, A. (2012). Physical activity as an investment in personal and social change: The human capital model. *Journal of Physical Activity and Health, 9*(8), 1053–1055.

Baker, K. (2017). Obesity Statistics Briefing Paper No. 3336, January 2017. House of Commons Library.

Beutler, I. (2008). Sport serving development and peace: Achieving the goals of the United Nations through sport. *Sport In Society, 11*(4), 359–369.

Burkhardt, J. and Brennan, C. (2012). The effects of recreational dance interventions on the health and well-being of children and young people: A systematic review. *Arts and Health: An International Journal for Research, Policy and Practice, 4*(2), 148–161.

Burnett, C. (2015). Assessing the sociology of sport: On sport for development and peace. *International Review for the Sociology of Sport, 50*(4–)5, 385–390.

Coalter, F. (2007). *A Wider Social Role for Sport: Who's keeping the score?* London: Routledge.

Coalter, F. (2010). The politics of sport–for–development: Limited focus programmes and broad gauge problems? *International Review for the Sociology of Sport*, *45*(3), 295–314.

Darnell, S. (2010). Power, politics and 'sport for development and peace': Investigating the utility of sport for international development. *Sociology of Sport Journal*, *27*(1), 54–75.

Darnell, S. and Black, D. (2011). Mainstreaming sport into international development studies. *Third World Quarterly*, *32*(3).

Darnell, S., Chawansky, M., Marchesseault, D., Holmes, M. and Hayhurst, L. (2016). The state of play: Critical sociological insights into recent 'sport for development and peace' research. *International Review for the Sociology of Sport*, *39*(1), 1–19.

Department of Health. (2011). Start Active, Stay Active: Report on Physical Activity in the UK. UK Government: Department of Health. Available at: https://assets.publishing.service.gov.uk/government/uploads/system/uploads/attachment_data/file/216370/dh_128210.pdf (accessed 24 May 2018).

Ding, D., Lawson, K. D., Kolbe-Alexander, T. L. *et al.* (2016). The economic burden of physical inactivity: A global analysis of major non-communicable diseases. *Lancet*, *388*(10051), 1311–1324.

Dobbins, M., Husson, H., DeCorby, K. and LaRocca, R. L. (2013). School-based physical activity programs for promoting physical activity and fitness in children and adolescents aged 6 to 18. *Cochrane Database of Systematic Reviews*, *2*, CD007651.

Dobbs, R., Sawers, C., Thomson, F., Manyika, J., Woetzel, J., Child, P., McKenna, S. and Spatharou, A. (2014). Overcoming Obesity: An Initial Economic Analysis. Discussion Paper. McKinsey Global Institute, November.

Donnelly, P., Atkinson, M., Boyle, S. and Szto, C. (2011). Sport for development and peace: A public sociology perspective. *Third World Quarterly*, *32*(3), 589–601.

Dudfield, O. (ed.) (2014). *Strengthening Sport for Development and Peace National Policies and Strategies*. London: Commonwealth Advisory Body on Sport and Commonwealth Secretariat.

Dudfield, O. and Dingwall-Smith, M. (2015). *Sport for Development and Peace and the 2030 Agenda for Sustainable Development*. London: Commonwealth Secretariat.

Dwyer-Lindgren, L., Freedman, G., Engell, R., Fleming, T., Lim, S., Murray, C. and Mokdad, A. (2013). Prevalence of physical activity and obesity in US counties, 2001–2011: A road map for action. *Population Health Metrics*, *11*(1), 1–11.

Giulianotti, R. (2011). Sport, peacemaking and conflict resolution: A contextual analysis and modelling of the sport, development and peace sector. *Ethnic And Racial Studies*, *34*(2), 207–228.

Giulianotti, R. (ed.) (2015). *Routledge Handbook of the Sociology of Sport*. London & New York: Routledge.

Haudenhuyse, R., Theeboom, M. and Nols, Z. (2012). Sports-based interventions for socially vulnerable youth: Towards well-defined interventions with easy-to follow outcomes? *International Review for the Sociology of Sport*, *36*(1), 41–57.

HM Government (UK). (2016). Childhood Obesity: A Plan for Action. Available at: https://www.gov.uk/government/publications/childhood-obesity-a-plan-for-action (accessed 25 May 2018).

Houlihan, B. (1997). *Sport Policy and Politics; a comparative analysis*. London & New York: Routledge.

Hylton, K. (ed.) (2013). *Sport Development Policy, Process and Practice* (3rd edn). London & New York: Routledge.

Kidd, B. (2008). A new social movement: Sport for development and peace. *Sport In Society*, *11*(4), 370–380.

Kidd, B. (2011). Cautions, questions and opportunities in sport for development and peace. *Third World Quarterly*, *32*(3), 603–609.

Kingsbury, D., McKay, J., Hunt, J., McGillivray, M. and Clarke, M. (2008). *International Development Issues and Challenges*. Basingstoke: Palgrave Macmillan.

Kirk, D. (2005). Physical education, youth sport and lifelong participation: The importance of early learning experiences. *European Physical Education Review*, *11*(3), 239–255.

Kohl, H. and Murray, T. (2012), *Foundations of Physical Activity and Public Health* Human Kinetics Champaign, IL

Kyu, H., Bachman, V., Alexander, L., Mumford, J., Afshin, A. *et al.* (2016). Physical activity and risk of breast cancer, colon cancer, diabetes, ischemic heart disease, and ischemic stroke events: Systematic review and dose-response meta-analysis for the Global Burden of Disease Study. *BMJ*, *354*(3857). Available at: www.ncbi.nlm.nih.gov/pubmed/27510511 (accessed 25 May 2018).

Lyn, R. (2010). Physical activity research: Identifying the synergistic relationships between individual, social and environmental factors to promote active lifestyles. *Health Education Research*, *25*(2), 183–184.

Mandic, S. Bengoechea, E. G., Stevens, E., Leon de la Barra, S. and Skidmore, P. (2012). Getting kids active by participating in sport and doing it more often: Focusing on what matters. *International Journal of*

Behavioural Nutrition and Physical Activity, 9(86). Available at: https://ijbnpa.biomedcentral.com/articles/10.1186/1479-5868-9-86 (accessed 25 May 2018).

Mathie, A. and Cunningham, G. (2011). Who is driving development? Reflections on the transformative potential of asset-based community development. *Canadian Journal of Development Studies, 26*(1), 175–186.

Metcalf, B., Henley, W. and Wilkin, T. (2012). Effectiveness of intervention on physical activity of children: systematic review and meta-analysis of controlled trials with objectively measured outcomes (EarlyBird 54). *BMJ*, 345(e5888), 16 October.

Milton, K. and Bauman, A. (2015). A critical analysis of the cycles of physical activity policy in England. *International Journal of Behavioral Nutrition and Physical Activity, 12*:8, 15 July.

Mwaanga, O. and Adeosun, K. (2017a). Decolonisation in practice: A case study of the kicking AIDS out, programme development Jamaica. *The Journal of Sport for Development*, 4 December.

Mwaanga, O. and Adeosun, K. (2017b). Reconceptualising sport for development and peace (SDP) from a critical reconsideration of Nelson 'Madiba' Mandela's view of sport. *The Journal of Sport Society, Commerce and Culture* (in press).

Nike Inc. (2012). *Designed to Move – A Physical Activity Action Agenda*.

Noar, S. and Mehrotra P. (2011). Toward a new methodological paradigm for testing theories of health behavior and health behavior change. *Patient Education and Counseling, 82*(3), 468–474.

Phillips, R. and Pittman, R. (eds) (2009). *An Introduction to Community Development* (2nd edn). London & New York: Routledge.

Smith, A. D., Crippa, A., Woodcock, J. et al. (2016). Physical activity and incident type 2 diabetes mellitus: A systematic review and dose–response meta-analysis of prospective cohort studies. *Diabetologia, 59*(12), 2527–2545.

Spence, J. and Lee, R. (2003). Toward a comprehensive model of physical activity. *Psychology of Sport and Exercise, 4*(1), 7–24.

Sport England. (2016). Towards an Active Nation. Available at: www.sportengland.org/media/10629/sport-england-towards-an-active-nation.pdf (accessed 25 May 2018).

UNDP. (2016). Sport for SDGs: A journey from Khartoum to Rio de Janeiro. *Our Perspectives*. United Nations Development Programme. Available at: www.undp.org/content/undp/en/home/blog/2016/8/19/Sport-for-SDGs-a-journey-from-Sudan-to-Rio-de-Janeiro-.html (accessed 14 January 2017).

UN MDGs. (n.d.). Available at: www.un.org/millenniumgoals/aids.shtml (accessed 15 January 2017).

Weiler R. and Stamatakis, E. (2010). Physical activity in the UK: A unique crossroad? *British Journal of Sports Medicine, 44*(13), 912–914.

Wilmot, E. G., Edwardson, C. L., Achana, F. A., Davies, M. J., Gorely, T. et al. (2012). Sedentary time in adults and the association with diabetes, cardiovascular disease and death: Systematic review and meta-analysis *Diabetologia, 55*(11), 2895–2905 14 August.

World Health Organization. (2013). Global Action Plan for the Prevention and Control of Non-Communicable Diseases 2013–2020. Available at: www.who.int/nmh/events/ncd_action_plan/en/ (accessed 25 May 2018).

Zieff, S. (2011). Increasing physical activity for health one cultural critique at a time. *Quest, 63*(1), 118–129.

Zieff, S. and Veri, M. (2009). Obesity, health, and physical activity: Discourses from the United States. *Quest, 61*(2), 154–179.

28

SDP and health

HIV/AIDS

Pete Beeley, Ben Sanders and Chris Barkley

This chapter seeks to chart the evolution of a sport-based approach to tackling the HIV and AIDS epidemic, in the context of various social complexities and shifting priorities within the wider adolescent health field. An overview of the epidemic is provided, along with how priorities have changed in the last decade, before a more detailed case study analysis of Grassroots Soccer is undertaken, in order to understand how one organization has sought to respond to the changing external circumstances through adaptive strategies, new approaches, and a set of universal principles that have remained consistent over time.

The evolution of the HIV and AIDS response

HIV and AIDS is one of the most serious global public health issues of our time, particularly affecting the developing world. Globally, it is estimated that 78 million people have now been infected and 35 million people have died as a result of AIDS-related illnesses (UNAIDS 2017a). While it was in the USA in the early 1980s, that the first immune deficiency–related deaths were widely documented, it was in sub-Saharan Africa where the virus would eventually have the most profound effect. In 1986, there were just over 2,000 reported cases of AIDS in Africa but by 1999, HIV and AIDS had become the number one cause of death on the continent (WHO 1999). Africa is now home to around 25 million people living with the virus (UNAIDS 2017a).

Despite this, HIV and AIDS remain both preventable and treatable. Though there is not yet a cure or vaccine for the virus, over the last 30 years there has been marked progress in controlling this complex epidemic and addressing its social determinants. Since 2000, there has been an annual reduction in new HIV infections in children and adults, and since 2016, 19.5 million people living with HIV were accessing highly effective anti-retroviral therapy (ART) (UNAIDS 2017a). This represents almost half of the population of people living with HIV. One of the greatest success stories has been in the prevention of mother to child transmission with 77 per cent of pregnant women accessing the treatment to prevent the transmission of HIV to their children, reducing infant mortality from AIDS significantly. The number of AIDS-related deaths peaked in 2005 at around 1.9 million and dropped to 1 million in 2016 (UNAIDS 2017a). Most recently, science has shown that starting treatment as early as possible has the dual benefit of keeping people living with HIV healthy and preventing HIV transmission by making the virus undetectable, and therefore untransmittable (UNAIDS 2017b). This finding led to UNAIDS' 90-90-90 targets, which have become a central pillar of the global quest to end the AIDS epidemic. The 90-90-90 global goals are: 90 per cent of people living with HIV know their status, 90 per cent of them are on ART and 90 per cent of those on treatment are virally suppressed by 2020.

Testing is much faster and more accessible than it was previously, and many countries with high prevalence of HIV now operate 'universal test and treat' programs, which means that anyone testing positive for HIV will receive treatment immediately whether in need or not. We have also come to understand that the AIDS epidemic is about *location* and *population*. In 2012, the President's Emergency Plan for AIDS Relief (PEPFAR) pivoted on a data-driven approach that strategically targets geographic hotspots and key populations to maximize impact of its investments and aims to halt transmission in high-incidence areas. Key populations, those most at-risk of contracting or transmitting the virus, such as men who have sex with men, sex workers, and people who inject drugs are now being supported with more intensive programming including treatment as prevention. Launched in 2014, PEPFAR 3.0 describes itself as doing the 'right things' in the 'right places' at the 'right times'; stating that 'we need to go where the virus is – targeting evidence-based interventions for populations at greatest risk in areas of greatest HIV incidence' (United States Government 2014). So today we are much clearer on which interventions have the greatest impact on reducing HIV incidence.

Despite the progress and a greater understanding of what works, major challenges remain in the HIV epidemic, including the significant costs associated with preventing and treating such an unprecedented burden of disease. Most concerning though is the fact that one age group in particular, adolescents, continue to be disproportionately affected. AIDS is the leading cause of death for adolescents (age 10–19) in Africa and the second leading cause of death among adolescents globally. In fact, adolescents remain the only group in which AIDS-related deaths are not dropping – they have in fact tripled since 2000 (UNICEF 2017).

Furthermore, about half of adolescents (age 15–19) living with HIV are in six countries: South Africa, Nigeria, Kenya, India, Mozambique, and Tanzania. Adolescent girls have a significantly higher risk of HIV infection than boys of the same age. In South Africa, for example, adolescent girls account for 800 new HIV infections per week, and are eight times more likely to contract HIV than their male counterparts (Shisana *et al.* 2014).

As a result, those working with adolescents in the HIV and AIDS space are seeing a major shift in what is understood to be most effective both in terms of reaching the most at-risk and marginalized adolescent populations, but what also represents the most efficient investments considering the finite resources available to fight the disease. Since the HIV and AIDS epidemic began in the early 1980s, the world has shifted in its understanding of the virus and how we respond. The outbreak of the epidemic resulted in an *emergency* response which focused on getting services and information as fast as possible to those affected. The response is now transitioning to looking at HIV as one issue within an array of health risks, challenges, and opportunities that face young people. The World Health Organization in particular, now lists HIV and AIDS as just one of 11 emerging health priorities for adolescents (World Health Organizations 2014).

The emergence of sport-based HIV prevention

Amid nearly four decades of the AIDS response, new and innovative prevention strategies were sought to stop the spread of a virus that had become increasingly hard to control. One such approach, which emerged in the early 2000s, was the use of sport-based HIV prevention (SBHP).

The emergence of SBHP was aligned to the growth of the wider SDP sector which as seen elsewhere in this book, consisted of organizations addressing social issues through the use of sport and wider support services. In the case of SBHP, organizations such as Mathare Youth Sports Association, Kicking AIDS Out, Right to Play, Grassroot Soccer and various transnational and national sports governing bodies established sport-based programming that focused on integrating aspects of HIV and AIDS prevention. Many of these programs were based on the simple premise that sport could attract large numbers of young people and then be combined with health messages, services, and education programs. While positive outcomes were achieved in certain cases, some academics critiqued the evangelist approach assuming the power of sport, with little consideration for any unintended or even harmful consequences. SDP organizations, while doing work that was compelling and enjoyable for young people, often lacked the concrete evidence needed to show development-related outcomes for their work (Coalter 2010).

In 2012, a systematic review of the effectiveness of SBHP interventions found strong evidence that well-designed and well-implemented SBHP interventions can 'reduce stigma and increase HIV-related knowledge, self-efficacy, reported communication and condom use by roughly 20–40%' (Kaufman et al. 2012). However, the study also found no evidence that such approaches can reduce HIV, sexually transmitted infections, or unintended pregnancy rates. A further outcome of the study found that there were insufficient high-quality and rigorous evaluations of such approaches to be able to demonstrate this kind of impact, nor 'to compare the relative effectiveness and cost-effectiveness of SBHP interventions to other HIV prevention interventions' (Kaufman et al. 2012) – something which is essential for SBHP and indeed the wider SDP sector to do in order to continue to demonstrate relevance and impact. Further studies on SBHP have been conducted since this systematic review, but few have addressed this pertinent question. In addition, few have sought to examine how SBHP approaches need to evolve in order to align with the public health sector's shift to a focus on a broader and more integrated range of sexual and reproductive health and rights (SRHR) challenges that young people face.

The evolution of sport-based HIV prevention

Grassroot Soccer is one example of an SBHP organization that has evolved considerably over the last 15 years to respond to the changing epidemic and the needs of its program user-groups. In order to achieve maximum impact, Grassroot Soccer has broadened its focus from strictly HIV and AIDS prevention to improving adolescent health. This is demonstrated by the following three key evolutions in its work and approaches for young people.

From HIV to integrated HIV and SRHR

Recent studies have shown that the incorporation of a broader SRHR approach, while also looking at young people as a whole and considering the social determinants of their health, will lead to better health outcomes, including in the HIV and AIDS epidemic. Multiple and compounding social and structural norms around the sexual lives of adolescents as well as gender and service inequality, create challenging barriers to improving young people's sexual and reproductive health and rights (Stackpool-Moore et al. 2017). Therefore, focusing on a singular issue such as HIV prevention does not recognize young people's broader sexual context and needs. A shift to an integration of broader SRHR issues is predicted to have a greater impact on multiple health outcomes for adolescents, including reducing the rate of new HIV incidences, as outlined by UNAIDS in their 2020 strategy, stating that a core pillar of its reduction strategy is 'combination prevention, including comprehensive sexuality education,

PERCENTAGE OF GIRLS WHO DO NOT JUSTIFY VIOLENCE
Fewer girls justify violence against girls both age groups

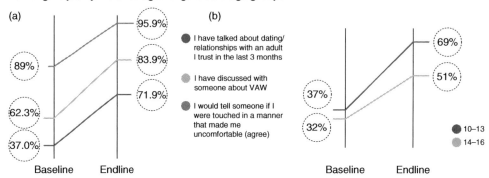

Figures 28.1a and 28.1b Percentage of female Grassroot Soccer participants justifying and reporting violence in Soweto, South Africa
VAW – violence against women

economic empowerment and access to sexual and reproductive health services for young women and adolescent girls and their male partners in high-prevalence locations' (UNAIDS 2016). The International HIV/AIDS Alliance highlight 14 key areas where HIV and sexual and reproductive health services should be integrated to ensure a more appropriate and effective response (International HIV/AIDS Alliance 2010). As such, Grassroot Soccer has evolved to focus on the intersectionality and integration of adolescent health issues, and programming that is needed to adequately respond to the variety of health challenges young people face. This focus includes the creation of an enabling environment for adolescent sexual and reproductive health education, which features youth empowerment, creation of safe spaces, peer-focused programs, schooling, parental engagement, community mobilization, mentoring, and positive role modelling, working with boys and men to promote gender-equitable norms, as well as meaningful youth participation in program design, implementation and research (Savenmyr *et al.* 2015).

One critical area of success achieved so far has been a greater focus on gender-based violence prevention (including physical, sexual, emotional and economic forms of violence) which is widely recognized as a structural driver of the HIV epidemic. Research has shown that HIV and AIDS programs that address gender and power in relationships are five times more likely to be effective than those that do not (Jewkes and Morrell 2010). As a result, Grassroot Soccer has deliberately incorporated discussion and reflection about gender norms and attitudes in all of its programs in order to challenge and transform harmful gender norms. The use of soccer, a male-dominated sport in sub-Saharan Africa, is particularly important as girls engaging in this medium are given an opportunity to challenge existing binaries. Results from a longitudinal study conducted with the Human Sciences Research Council and International Centre for Research on Women, showed that female participants at Grassroot Soccer were less likely to accept violence, and more likely to disclose incidents of violence when they do occur (see Figures 28.1a and 28.1b). Qualitative research also indicated that some girls participating in Grassroot Soccer programs chose to leave abusive relationships and had developed greater self-efficacy (Sanders *et al.* 2017).

From a focus on knowledge and behaviour change communication towards promoting and facilitating access to health services

Through the use of pre- and post-surveys, Grassroot Soccer and its implementing partners around the world have shown consistent increases in knowledge about HIV risk factors, improved knowledge and communication around HIV and SRHR issues and services, improved gender-equitable norms, reduced HIV stigma, and improved attitudes towards people living with HIV (Grassroot Soccer 2016). This has been complimented by external evaluations, including a number of randomized control trials (RCTs), which have shown that Grassroot Soccer participants are more likely to have higher knowledge levels and more desirable attitudes than their counterparts. However, while changes in knowledge and attitudes are important, these do not necessarily translate into behaviour change.

In line with the increased biomedical focus and 90-90-90 targets of the global HIV sector, Grassroot Soccer has sought to improve linkage to services among its adolescent participants to ensure they can access and adhere to critical HIV and SRHR services. Grassroot Soccer has moved further along the adolescent continuum of care by increasing the demand for sexual and reproductive health services and access to such services through youth-friendly clinical service providers. This approach acknowledges that while education and information is an important first step, it is also important to build an adolescent's capacity to identify, access, and adhere to health services. In the places where those services aren't available and/or accessible to adolescents, Grassroot Soccer has also sought to fill those gaps or to advocate for improved availability, accessibility, and quality of these services. Examples of this have included HIV testing, where studies have shown that Grassroot Soccer participants are more likely to test for HIV (see Figure 28.2), and deeper support programs to cater to the needs of HIV positive youth, in order to ensure adherence to treatment and care.

In addition, two RCTs conducted in Bulawayo, Zimbabwe, demonstrated that Grassroot Soccer male participants were 2.5 to 5 times more likely to uptake voluntary male medical

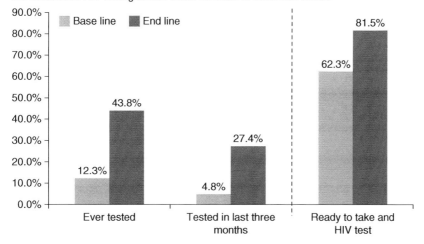

HIV testing among participants
3 × increase in HIV testing as well as an increase in readiness to test

Figure 28.2 Uptake of, and readiness for, HIV testing among Grassroot Soccer female participants in Soweto, South Africa

circumcision (VMMC) than their counterparts. VMMC has been recognized as a cost-effective means to prevent HIV and AIDS, as it reduces the likelihood of a man contracting the virus through sexual intercourse by up to 60 per cent (Kaufman *et al.* 2016). A process evaluation also demonstrated that the coach–participant relationship, including clinic accompaniment and follow-up, were major reasons for a participant choosing to uptake VMMC (DeCelles *et al.* 2016). In this intervention, the implementing coach is also circumcised, tying back to the idea of relatable role models and peer mentor methodology as effective ways to engage youth.

From working directly with young people in communities to scaling through partnerships

Many within the SDP sector have recognized their limitations when it comes to service provision and development expertise. As such, many actors form high-value partnerships to help them meet the complex health and development needs of young people. Partnerships have always been a key driver of growth and high-quality programming at Grassroot Soccer, allowing the organization to expand its approach through partners to hundreds of communities in over 40 countries. Grassroot Soccer's partnership approach has allowed it to reach more rural and at-risk populations with a wider spectrum of integrated HIV and SRHR programming. Grassroot Soccer has positioned itself uniquely within the public health sector to be able to forge strong partnerships to achieve great scale and impact through targeted and tailored replication of its youth-centred methodology. This involves creating value chains or models that combine respective strengths of partners to offer a platform of integrated, easily accessible, youth-friendly health services for adolescents. A key factor in the success of the program is leveraging the unique attraction of sport to bring together communities, government agencies, and private sector in innovative and sustainable partnerships.

The emergence of some universal principles

While Grassroot Soccer and other organizations using SBHP have undoubtedly evolved over the past 15 years, many of the underlying tenets have remained the same. These principles remain remarkably universal and transferable to a broader range of issues and, in the case of Grassroot Soccer, three principles in particular have underpinned, and indeed facilitated, a shift to a broader focus on adolescent health.

Play-based learning can improve cognition and build crucial life skills

Knowledge plays an important role in integrated HIV prevention efforts and is often a precondition to behaviour change. Yet the UNAIDS 2016 Prevention Gap Report highlighted that two thirds of young people still do not have correct and comprehensive knowledge of HIV (UNAIDS 2016).

At Grassroot Soccer, learning through play, is typified by the 'gamification' of key health messages and use of sport metaphors to help young people experience new concepts and learn in a fun and interactive way. Young people might dribble through cones that represent risky sexual behaviours, juggle balls that represent the challenges they face; or take penalties of varying difficulty to represent barriers to achieving their goals. Activities often follow a progression where new challenges, messages, and metaphors are introduced incrementally. Learning comes through discovery of information rather than delivery, and the discussion that leads to that discovery yields improved attitudes and communication skills that are essential for the successful adoption of healthy behaviours.

Community-based youth role models are available and are highly effective educators

Grassroot Soccer and various other SBHP programs are founded on the premise that young people are more likely to adopt healthy behaviours if those behaviours are modelled by people who they respect and can relate to. The use of role models and peer educators is supported by social learning theory, which suggests that, '[p]eople develop stronger belief in their capabilities and more readily adopt modelled ways if they see models similar to themselves solve problems successfully with the modelled strategies, than if they see the models as very different from themselves' (Bandura 1986). While Grassroot Soccer initially engaged local professional players in Bulawayo, Zimbabwe as role model coaches, the program has now expanded to include young people (usually age 18–25) in this coach role, who often have greater access to, and knowledge of, local communities. This shift was justified by research that shows that the 'age, sex, and status [of the role model], the type of problems with which they cope, and the situation in which they apply their skills', should be as close to the participant's own circumstances as possible (Bandura 1990). Grassroot Soccer coaches are old enough to command respect from, but young enough to relate to, participants. With a small amount of training and guidance, coaches are able to use their role model status as a tool to help them as educators and facilitators.

Intentionally maximizing the value of relationships is the key to impact

Adult-adolescent connectedness has emerged as a foundational part of adolescent health and well-being (Sieving *et al.* 2017), including sexual and reproductive health outcomes for youth (Markham *et al.* 2010). Collectively, research findings provide evidence that strong, positive relationships with parents and other caring adults protect adolescents from a range of poor health-related outcomes and promote positive development. Furthermore, relationship quality is directly linked to the development of social skills in youth (Sieving *et al.* 2017). The use of sport and play naturally fosters the building of relationships among young people and SBHP is often then used as a platform to ensure adolescents can build relationships with mentors too. In the case of Grassroot Soccer, the organization has been able to isolate, and then train coaches in, the critical components of an effective youth-friendly, mentor approach. These components are made up of five core techniques that help coaches to maximize the impact of their relationships with young people.

Praise
The benefits of praise are widely understood, though often underestimated, on young people's intrinsic motivation (Henderlong and Lepper 2002), but this is also affected by the way in which praise is given, the subject on which it is offered, and the person delivering it.

Grassroot Soccer coaches are trained to provide specific and behaviour-based praise to participants for their efforts rather than achievements. Targeted, data-driven and specific praise has been understood, alongside the concept of corrective feedback (and role modelling) to be a powerful driver of self-efficacy, which is an indicator for improved behaviour. While evidence that low self-esteem can lead to increased risky sexual behaviour is well documented (Goodson *et al.* 2006), studies focusing on self-efficacy in relation to HIV and AIDS have found that increased self-efficacy can lead to increased treatment adherence, better psychosocial functioning, and a lower likelihood of missing scheduled appointments (Johnson *et al.* 2007).

Personal connections

Although sport often provides a youth-friendly and engaging environment, we cannot assume that coaches have the skills needed to build effective mentor relationships with young people, especially where taboo and sensitive topics such as HIV are involved. As such, Grassroot Soccer trains coaches to be more conscious about how relationships are built, engaging naturally and intentionally during activities and down time. Coaches are trained to build personal connections through techniques as simple as maintaining eye contact, appropriate physical contact and getting to know a young person's name and story, and in return are taught to share their own 'Coaches Story', wherein they provide a real and honest account of their own struggles with health and sexuality, immediately creating relatability and a sense of equality.

Grassroot Soccer has conducted a number of mixed methods studies which under-score the impact of a close personal relationship between a coach and a participant. Insights show that well trained coaches can provide a valuable and unique communication point for participants to ask sensitive questions, that the coach–participant relationship has an effect on girls' attitudes and decision making and participants felt comfortable opting to take an HIV test at these events due to support and role modelling from their coaches (Hershow *et al.* 2015).

Furthermore, the personal connections between coaches and participants have led to many disclosures of violence and abuse that allow coaches to refer participants to appropriate pro-tective and psychosocial support services.

Safe space

Coaches are trained to immediately create a 'safe space' for participants through various culture-setting activities and to ensure that they maintain this space throughout the intervention. A safe space is an environment that encourages players to honestly and openly discuss sensitive, personal, and challenging issues among themselves and with their coaches without fear of judgement or persecution. This means going beyond their physical safety and the physical environment, and considering the atmosphere that young people experience during an intervention. When discussing sexual issues such as HIV and AIDS, being intentional with safe space is a critical factor in helping young people reflect, discuss, share their experiences and disclose potentially very sensitive information. It must be noted that this definition of safe space should be seen as distinct from physical safety and child safeguarding procedures that should already be in place for an organization working with young people.

Vital conversations

Coaches are trained to maximize their time with young people by fostering and seeking out vital conversations. A vital conversation is the free and natural sharing and debate of thoughts, ideas, or opinions that have the potential to change one's attitude, behaviour, or even well-being. This means not only providing young people with information but encouraging players to speak freely, to debate with each other, to laugh, to argue, and to reflect on the information they receive. This places greater emphasis on skills such as communication, listening, and critical thinking rather than memorization of information. In order to foster vital conversations, coaches are armed with challenging questions that they pose throughout the course of an intervention that are sure to arouse discussion and debate. For example, a coach may ask whether or not it is a boy's job to help with cleaning in the home, thereby stimulating a deeper discussion about gender roles and norms.

Providing accurate information

Coaches are trained to provide complete and accurate information about HIV and AIDS, and when they do not have information to help young people to find it. When it comes to HIV, AIDS, and sexual and reproductive health, young people need accurate information upon which to discuss, reflect and ultimately act. It has been noted that enhanced biological understanding of HIV, AIDS and human sexuality can help adolescents to identify flaws and misconceptions about health and disease, and to detect practical situations in which negotiation skills should be applied (Keselman *et al.* 2004). And while it is true that HIV *awareness* is high across many communities Grassroot Soccer work in, HIV *knowledge* is not. And knowledge, although only one small piece, still plays an important role in how Grassroot Soccer understands change to happen.

Recommendations

Moving forward, the experience of Grassroot Soccer and others using SBHP approaches, as well as the shifting external environment, provides a number of recommendations for future SBHP work.

First, there is a need to develop more *differentiated programs* that account for the needs and characteristics of specific populations, particularly those at highest risk. Many SBHP organizations now offer a range of programs that respond to the unique needs and drivers of HIV risk among different populations and different community contexts. So rather than an HIV education program for youth, we may find an HIV and SRHR program for early adolescent girls in densely populated urban communities with high rates of teenage pregnancy and school drop-out. Such focus is vital and may help SDP actors avoid the problem of 'seeking to solve broad gauge problems via limited focus interventions' (Coalter 2010).

Second, we need to further clarify how *SBHP activities contribute, align, or integrate* into broader strategies to achieve national, bilateral, and multilateral targets. This includes the shift towards an integration of HIV with SRHR and broader public health issues, and the modes of direct service delivery and achieving scale through partners. New types of partnerships are needed in SBHP, especially as the AIDS response requires a *rapid scale up* of core interventions. Such an approach accords closely with the advice and recommendations of UNAIDS:

> Closing gaps in service coverage requires intensified efforts to convince men to reject harmful versions of masculinity, and to reach and empower women and girls, young people and key populations, to enhance their agency and to ensure their human rights are respected and protected. Addressing stigma, discrimination and human rights violations at all levels through the creation of a protective and empowering legal environment and strong rule of law is an imperative for both the AIDS response and the wider 2030 Agenda for Sustainable Development.
>
> *UNAIDS, 2017*

Third, there is need to establish or strengthen measurement systems that demonstrate progress towards these targets, including adopting outcomes and indicators from national, bilateral, and multilateral frameworks. Many SBHP organizations have had to define success in terms of biomedical outcomes. While the move to more accountability and cost–effectiveness is welcomed, there is a natural tension between the biomedical outcomes and the difficulty in measuring the value of prevention, which relates to many of the theories that underpin the SDP sector. It seems clear that SBHP has the potential to improve learning, skills acquisition, social support, and trusted mentor relationships that may translate into safe sexual behaviours but also transfer to other health and social domains. However, outcomes in these areas may get ignored by donor agencies using strictly HIV and AIDS-related measures of success and cost-effectiveness, again reinforcing the importance of a more integrated approach to HIV.

Conclusion

The landscape of the HIV and AIDS response has changed dramatically over the last 35 years. The scale of the epidemic remains extremely high, but we have a much greater understanding of what works and what doesn't, as well as a clear pathway towards ending the epidemic. Despite all this, one group that continues to suffer disproportionately, are adolescents. Grassroot Soccer is one organization that has sought to respond to this evolving landscape and continued challenges, by broadening its strategic focus and integrating its work across the wider spectrum of adolescent health and development. This included a shift from focusing on the single issue of HIV to a broader consideration of SRHR, a move from a program focused on knowledge, to a more comprehensive focus on building young people's assets to access critical health services, and improving the quality and availability and youth-friendliness services through direct provision or high-value partnerships.

These changes have been underpinned by a number of principles that have proven to be remarkably consistent across 15 years of delivery experience in multiple contexts. The play-based learning curriculum, delivered by a community-based role model who has been trained to intentionally maximize the value of the mentor relationship, has been found to be demonstrably effective and universal in its application. Without these, Grassroot Soccer might have struggled to transition to a focus on broader adolescent health. The challenge for Grassroot Soccer and indeed for other SBHP organizations ahead, is to continue to evolve with the changing landscape of what works and what young people need, while continuing to demonstrate the impact, reach, ability to scale, and cost-effectiveness, of sport-based HIV prevention, or perhaps more appropriately now, sport-based adolescent health promotion.

References

Bandura, A. (1986). *Social Foundations of Thoughts and Action: A Social Cognitive Theory*. Englewood Cliffs, NJ: Prentice Hall.

Bandura, A. (1990). Perceived self-efficacy in the exercise of control over aids infection. *Evaluation and Program Planning*, *13*(1), 9–17.

Coalter, F. (2010). The politics of sport-for-development: Limited focus programmes and broad gauge problems? *International Review for the Sociology of Sport*, *45*(3), 295–314.

DeCelles, J., Hershow, R. B., Kaufman, Z. A., Gannett, K. R., Kombandeya, T., Chaibya, C., Ross, D. A. and Harrison, A. (2016). Process evaluation of a sport-based voluntary medical male circumcision demand-creation intervention in Bulawayo, Zimbabwe. *Journal of Acquired Immune Deficiency Syndromes* (1999) *72*(Suppl. 4), S304–308.

Goodson P., Buhi, E. R. and Dunsmore, S. C. (2006). Self-esteem and adolescent sexual behaviours, attitudes, and intentions: A systematic review. *Journal of Adolescent Health*, *38*(3), 310–9.

Grassroot Soccer. (2016). Research Report. Available at: www.grassrootsoccer.org/wp-content/uploads/2016/04/original-grs_research_report_2016_web_version.pdf (accessed 1 August 2017).

Henderlong, J. and Lepper, M. (2002). The effects of praise on children's intrinsic motivation: A review and synthesis. *Psychological Bulletin*, *128*(5), 774–795.

Hershow R. B., Gannett, K., Merrill, J., Kaufman, B. E., Barkley, C., DeCelles, J. and Harrison, A. (2015). Using soccer to build confidence and increase HCT uptake among adolescent girls: A mixed-methods study of an HIV prevention programme in South Africa. *Sport in Society*, doi:10.1080/17430437.2014.997586.

International HIV/AIDS Alliance. (2010). Integration of HIV and Sexual and Reproductive Health and Rights: Good Practice Guide. Available at: www.aidsalliance.org/assets/000/000/416/507-Good-Practice-Guide-Integration-of-HIV-and-Sexual-and-Reproductive-Health-and-Rights-(Black-_-White)_original.pdf?1405586797 (accessed 1 August 2017).

Jewkes, R. and Morrell, R. (2010). Gender and sexuality: Emerging perspectives from the heterosexual epidemic in South Africa and implications for HIV risk and prevention. *Journal of the International AIDS Society, 13*(1), 6. Available at: http://doi.org/10.1186/1758-2652-13-6.

Johnson, M. O., Neilands, T. B., Dilworth, S., Morin, S. F., Remien, R. H. and Chesney, M. A. (2007). The role of self-efficacy in HIV treatment adherence: Validation of the HIV treatment adherence self-efficacy scale (HIV-ASES). *Journal of Behavioral Medicine, 30*(5), 359–370.

Kaufman, Z. A., DeCelles, J., Bhauti, K., Hershow, R. B., Weiss, H. A., Chaibva, C. *et al.* (2016). A sport-based intervention to increase uptake of voluntary medical male circumcision among adolescent male students: Results from the MCUTS 2 cluster-randomized trial in Bulawayo, Zimbabwe. *Journal of Acquired Immune Deficiency Syndromes, 72*(Suppl. 4), S292–8.

Kaufman, Z. A., Spencer, T. S. and Ross, D. A. (2012). Effectiveness of sports-based HIV prevention interventions: A systematic review of the evidence. *AIDS and Behaviour,* doi 10.1007/s10461–012–0348–1.

Keselman, A. D., Kaufman R. and Patel V. L. (2004). 'You Can Exercise Your Way Out of HIV' and other stories: The Role of Biological Knowledge in Adolescents' Evaluation of Myths. Unpublished paper, Laboratory of Decision Making and Cognition, Department of Biomedical Informatics, Columbia University.

Markham, C. M., Lormand, D., Gloppen, K. M., Peskin, M. F., Flores, B., Low, B. and House, L. D. (2010). Connectedness as a predictor of sexual and reproductive health outcomes for youth. *Journal of Adolescent Health, 46*(3 Suppl.), S23–41.

Masters, A. (2015). Corruption in sport: From the playing field to the field of policy. *Policy and Society, 34*(2), 111–123.

Sanders, B., Barkley, C., Advani, N., Banciu, R., Das, M., Cooper, A. and Moolman, B. (2017). Changing the Game for Girls: Encouraging Results from a Longitudinal Study of a Soccer-Based HIV and SGBV Prevention Program for Adolescents in South Africa. Paper presented to the 8th SA AIDS Conference, ICC Durban, 13–15 June 2017.

Shisana, O., Rehle T., Simbayi L. C., Zuma, K., Jooste, S., Zungu, N., Labadarios, D. and Onoya, D. (2014). *South African National HIV Prevalence, Incidence and Behaviour Survey 2012.* Cape Town: HSRC Press.

Sieving, R. E, McRee, A. L., McMorris, B. J., Shlafer, R. J., Gower, A. L., Kapa, H. M. *et al.* (2016). Youth–adult connectedness: A key protective factor for adolescent health. *American Journal of Preventative Medicine, 52*(3S3), 275–278.

Stackpool-Moore, L., Bajpai, D., Caswell, G., Crone, T., Dewar, F., Gray, G. *et al.* (2017). Linking sexual and reproductive health and rights and HIV services for young people: The link up project. *Journal of Adolescent Health, 60*(2), 3–6.

Svanemyr, J., Amin, A., Robles O. J. and Greene, M. E. (2015). Creating an enabling environment for adolescent sexual and reproductive health: A framework and promising approaches. *Journal of Adolescent Health, 56*(1), 7–14.

UNAIDS. (2016). Prevention Gap. Page 10. Available at: www.unaids.org/en/resources/documents/2016/prevention-gap (accessed 1 August 2017).

UNAIDS. (2017a). Fact Sheet July 2017. Available at: www.unaids.org/sites/default/files/media_asset/UNAIDS_FactSheet_en.pdf (accessed 1 August 2017).

UNAIDS. (2017b). Ending AIDS: Progress towards the 90-90-90 Targets. Joint United Nations Programme on HIV/AIDS, Geneva. Available at: www.unaids.org/sites/default/files/media_asset/Global_AIDS_update_2017_en.pdf (accessed 1 August 2017).

UNICEF. (2017). Adolescents and Young People. Available at: https://data.unicef.org/topic/hivaids/adolescents-young-people/# (accessed 1 May 2017).

United States Government, Department of State. (2014). PEPFAR 3.0: Controlling the epidemic: Delivering on the promise of an aids-free generation. A/GIS/GPS.

World Health Organization. (1999). The World Health Report. Available at: www.who.int/whr/1999/en/whr99_en.pdf?ua=1 (accessed 1 August 2017).

World Health Organization. (2014). Health for the World's Adolescents: A Second Chance in the Second Decade. Department of Maternal, Newborn, Child and Adolescent Health'. Geneva, Switzerland. Available at: http://apps.who.int/adolescent/second-decade/files/1612_MNCAH_HWA_Executive_Summary.pdf (accessed 1 August 2017).

29

SDP and education

Ashleigh M. Huffman, Sarah J. Hillyer,
Alicia Malnati and Carolyn Spellings

Introduction

As recognized by the United Nations in the declaration of the Global Goals, individuals around the world are facing serious social, economic, and health challenges (United Nations 2015). Whether it is hunger, obesity, poverty, gender equality, violence, or environmental sustainability, people are looking for answers to social issues plaguing the global landscape. Educational institutions can play a unique role in international development agendas, particularly in the sport-based academic disciplines. As noted by the United Nations, sport is a low-cost, high-impact tool to resolve global socio-political problems (Right to Play 2008). This concept, known as Sport for Development and Peace (SDP), has sparked a wellspring of newly created sport-based development programs around the world, including more than 700 internationally registered SDP organizations (Hartmann and Kwauk 2011; SportandDev 2015). As the field of SDP continues to grow, the demand for greater academic contribution in the forms of training and research increases – in essence, a professional-ization of the field (ISDPA 2010). This demand calls for faculty willing to create new courses and embrace new pedagogical methods and research techniques to properly equip the next gener-ation of SDP practitioners and scholars. The purpose of this chapter is to explore the unique role higher education can play in the growth of SDP and to offer a framework for educators seeking to implement SDP courses within the academic curriculum.

SDP and the academy

Through the adoption of the United Nations Millennium Development Goals and subse-quent Global Goals campaign[1] (United Nations 2015), audiences worldwide are being asked to problem-solve and engage in local challenges. Educational institutions are no exception. Despite being leaders in research and knowledge creation, colleges and universities are noticeably absent from community-based discussions. Labeled as detached, ivory towers, higher education has historically been viewed as aloof and elite – rooted in, but not a part of the community – and therefore, not a part of community discourse or solutions (Butin 2010).

In an attempt to rectify this disconnect, colleges and universities have begun to engage in service to local and global communities. In fact, membership in Campus Compact, the national coalition for community engagement, has increased from three institutions in 1985 to more than 1,100 institutions in 2016 (Davis 2011; Compact 2016). In 2011, Ira Harkavy, University of Pennsylvania professor and founding director of the Netter Center for Community Partnerships, said, 'You would be hard-pressed to point to any other educational reform effort in higher education that has made that kind of movement in that amount of time. It has been a tremendous explosion of [service-learning] activity' (Davis 2011: 1). As a result of increased involvement, universities have established community-based partnerships in fields ranging from social work to architecture to education (Compact 2016). Service-learning classes have also been developed with hundreds of hours logged in the name of community engagement (Compact 2016).

The field of higher education is experiencing a transformation, most notably in the encouragement of faculty members to use creative and engaging pedagogies that promote diverse learning opportunities and global understanding (Butin 2010). With this type of institutional support, faculty and staff have the backing to develop classes that enable students to critically engage with course material and take ownership of the learning process (Butin 2010). For educators committed to student-centered learning and high-quality research, this new approach contributes to the movement of developing innovative methods of knowledge creation that are vital to understanding and serving local and global populations. This promising movement may even allow educators to redefine what it means to be knowledgeable, conscientious, and ultimately, educated (Freire 1970).

Despite the seemingly natural relationship between the hands-on philosophies of service-learning and the kinesthetic nature of sport, the connections between the two in higher education are rare (Miller and Nendel 2011). Currently, few academic institutions are engaged in SDP efforts (Bouzou 2015) and fewer still offer practical sport-based service-learning opportunities (Bruening *et al.* 2014). Despite SDP being recognized as an academic field in 2003 (Meier 2008), only two Master's degree programs in the world are dedicated to its study (Bouzou 2015). Although sport has been validated as a transformative tool to advance development, promote equity, create harmony and demonstrate goodwill, the academy has yet to fully embrace it as a viable and valuable mechanism for international development (Darnell 2013; Bouzou 2015). For the field of SDP to grow, it must have the support of educational institutions.

At this pivotal juncture, SDP must move away from the anecdotal space of 'sport is good' and into a legitimate and globally recognized profession (Coalter 2007; ISDPA 2010). This professionalization of the field requires a shift in the way SDP scholars think about the field (Darnell 2013) and train future sports leaders (Welty Peachy and Burton 2016). It requires exposure to sport as a vehicle not only for elite performance but transformative social change. It requires faculty willing to engage in global agendas, community discourse, and critical pedagogies, firmly taking advantage of the current higher education landscape and world trends. It requires administrative support of innovative teaching methods that challenge students to think differently about their world and their role in it. It requires a tenure and promotion system that recognizes the time-intensive nature of community-based teaching and applied research. In short, professionalization of SDP requires teamwork.

Throughout this chapter, we will analyze the intersections of SDP with pedagogy and research. We will draw upon the works of educational theorists Dewey (1938) and Freire (1970) to provide clear, guiding philosophies for successful SDP implementation in higher education. We will refer to the SDP literature and our own experiences as practitioners, researchers, and academicians to inform our understanding of SDP in practice. We will also expound on the ways SDP and higher education partnerships can be mutually beneficial in research and evaluation.

Lastly, we will introduce our own Theory of Empowerment for Social Change as a framework for incorporating SDP into educational spaces with the hopes of growing and professionalizing the field.

SDP and pedagogy

Although SDP is new to the academy, service-learning has been used as a method of teaching for decades, most notably tracing its roots to 'the father of service-learning', educational reformist and philosopher John Dewey (1938). Dewey radically challenged the notions of universal education, asking academicians to abandon rote habits and produce spaces for students to think creatively. He argued that real learning stems from experience and is motivated by personal connections to social problems. He called for a more active and experiential engagement where the classroom connects thinking, feeling, and doing, or the cognitive, affective, and kinesthetic domains (Dewey 1938). When reflecting on the Global Goals and the needs of local communities, this philosophy of experiential learning aligns well with collaborative, real-world problem-solving. It is also a natural fit for teaching the tenets of SDP.

As we analyze the current state of SDP, programmatically and in the literature, we see the need for sound research, thoughtful curriculum, and reflexive and innovative programs (Huffman 2011). We also recognize the need for reducing neocolonial control, a common criticism of the field (Giulianotti 2011; Darnell 2013), and replacing it with shared power, greater empathy and cultural awareness, enhanced communication skills, sustainable project management, and transformational leadership (Huffman 2011). To see SDP programs that reflect those skills and values, we must create educational programs that teach those skills and values. As Gilbert and Bennett (2012) noted in their work, *Contemplating a Moral World*, we must:

> Produce quality teachers and coaches who are culturally aware and have the ability to deliver [SDP] programmes in areas of extreme poverty, disaster, and danger … and to see more students taking master's and PhD degrees in the area (especially gender issues) so that they are better informed before taking time to go into the field and support change.
>
> *Gilbert and Bennett 2012: 500*

Incorporating sport-based service-learning into the academic curriculum is one way to achieve these desired outcomes.

Although there are a number of ways to implement service-learning programs into higher education courses, for the purposes of this chapter, we will highlight only one, the Freirean model, because it successfully offers 'the intellectual tools necessary to inform conceptually sound SDP programmes' (Spaaij and Jeanes 2013: 443). Based on the works of Brazilian educator Paulo Freire, the classroom is a place where learning is found in the process and the product. In these spaces, students should be seen as viable, intelligent beings, not passive recipients of information. Classrooms provide space for the co-creation of knowledge and the development of critical awareness through action and reflection (Freire 1973). Classrooms become environments where 'students learn to question answers rather than merely answer questions … where learners experience education as something they do, not as something done to them' (Spaaij and Jeanes 2013: 445). As advocated by Freire, this type of critical consciousness raising, the process by which people move from a position of unquestioning acceptance of the social order to a critical perspective on it, takes place in reality, in community, and in the lived experiences of human beings (Freire 1973).

Combining the philosophies of Freire and Dewey, sport-based service-learning initiatives hold the necessary power to achieve SDP objectives and demonstrate great value to the community and the students. Research reveals that when implemented in line with Dewey and Freire's philosophies, service-learning can: (1) increase student motivation for learning; (2) bridge theory and practice; (3) enhance conflict resolution and communication skills; (4) improve self-efficacy and confidence; (5) increase students' desire for a more equitable society; (6) reduce negative stereotypes; (7) increase cultural awareness; (8) heighten understanding of personal and social responsibility; (9) increase commitment to leadership and civic duty; (10) increase empathy and understanding of diversity; and (11) improve goal setting and project management (Eyler and Giles 1999).

By engaging in courses that move curriculum into community spaces, students are less likely to metabolize information in an academic vacuum. Information learned through traditional pedagogies – read, write, regurgitate – is 'inert knowledge', which Eyler and Giles (1999) refer to as the difference in knowing 'what' vs knowing 'how'. Studies reveal that this type of knowledge can almost never be applied when the same problems or scenarios exist outside of the classroom (Eyler and Giles 1999). This kind of textbook knowledge is also what often leads to interventionist SDP approaches. Having no shared lived experience or understanding of community needs, well-intentioned and well-educated people create programs based on information they consume through their own filters of socio-economics, race, gender, ability, and nationality. By offering sport-based service-learning courses taught with a critical lens, higher education has the potential to produce SDP leaders who are less likely to operate as interventionists and more likely to serve as reflexive collaborators.

SDP and research

It is well-documented that SDP is a burgeoning academic field, and as such, lacks the research and evidence needed to solidify a place on international agendas (Coalter 2013; Darnell 2013). Despite many case studies that conclude sport's importance in development and peacebuilding, the lack of continuity in theory and practice makes it difficult to enter global impact discussions (Coalter 2013; Darnell 2013). Throughout SDP literature, there is a ubiquitous call for more research and enhanced monitoring and evaluation efforts (Jeanes and Lindsey 2014). However, the calls are often to prove program success in an effort to sway funders and influence policy. As Donnelly *et al.* (2013: 592) contends, 'SDP needs a healthy dose of normal science' with descriptive research and evaluation methods and critical analyses of claims making and social reproduction. Now, more than ever, sound research from a trained, diligent, and critical perspective is needed to advance and professionalize the field (Kidd 2011; Darnell 2013).

For many SDP practitioners, the task of evaluation can be daunting. However, as Richards *et al.* (2013) notes, 'SFD organizations must "evaluate or perish"', which is why the intersection of SDP and higher education is so important. For practitioners, research concepts that are often overwhelming – monitoring, analysis, and reporting – are the very essence of the academic process. The concept 'publish or perish' has driven academia since the inception of the tenure and promotion system, which makes educators adept at theorizing, analyzing, and communicating results. Working with SDP organizations not only gives academicians opportunities to solve real-world issues, but also data to develop new theories and instruments.

As SDP practitioners come to understand the importance of evidence-based results for participants, volunteers, stakeholders, and donors, the search for trained evaluation consultants becomes momentous. According to Gilbert and Bennett (2012: 496), 'Guidance from any university would be good in supporting research into programmes of "sport, peace, and development" and the employment of graduates with statistical knowledge and general research skills is now becoming more and more important'. For higher education institutions, providing skills to students that make them more employable is a vital piece in the economic puzzle.

An additional benefit to SDP organizations partnering with higher education is the abundance of scholars familiar with reliable and valid measurement techniques. From sociology and psychology to public health and environmental studies, educators trained in parent disciplines can apply scales and proven methods of inquiry to sport for development and peace settings, which thereby gives credence to sport in broader conversations. For example, scholars versed in Pierre Bourdieu's (1986) theory of social capital may use it to qualitatively assess inclusion, networks, and social gains of participants in SDP programs. Psychologists familiar with Albert Bandura's work (1980) may use his validated scales to evaluate perceived self-efficacy as the basis for measuring life skills development in youth.

In order to advance and professionalize the field, it is important for research to move beyond the halls of academia and into the communities in which they are situated. With sport's emergence as a non-state actor in international development and the proliferation of social movements within the academy, SDP and higher education are uniquely positioned to address global challenges (Darnell 2013). Ultimately, an SDP–academic partnership allows for increased theoretical and methodological rigor and a more engaged, socially responsible delivery of programs, both necessary to advance the field (Donnelly *et al.* 2011). This unification of theory with practice, or praxis, is the basis upon which the Theory of Empowerment for Social Change emerged.

The theory of empowerment for social change

The Theory of Empowerment for Social Change is grounded in more than 20 years of fieldwork and 11 years of research. Drawing upon a broad range of disciplines, including sociology, psychology, education, pedagogy, social work, and public health, the theory combines literature with experience, including rigorous evaluation of SDP programs, SDP university courses, and SDP case studies. The theory has been applied in a variety of settings, including sport-based service-learning classes, after-school programs, international exchanges, development and peacebuilding programs, and mentorship curricula.

Epistemologically, we, the authors of this paper, are academic-practitioners, meaning our experiences are grounded in both the academic realm of undergraduate teaching and evidence-based research as well as the practitioner realm of fieldwork, community assessment, and collaborative training programs for global community sports leaders. In our role at the University of Tennessee, we have melded our academic and 'nonprofit' worlds to form the Center for Sport, Peace, and Society. As a result, we have a unique perspective on the macro trends associated with higher education and the SDP movement.

Throughout our explanation of the Theory of Empowerment for Social Change, we will refer to students and participants, which means undergraduate students in our service-learning courses or international participants engaged in our Better World SDP training programs. To date, we have worked with more than 300 undergraduate students and 500+ international participants from 72 countries using this curriculum. Philosophically, we see the 'classroom' as the world around us and understand that the intersections of sport and education may take place in the academy but may also take place on a soccer field in Brazil. Therefore, we put forth the Theory of Empowerment for Social Change as educator-practitioners who live in both worlds and understand the need to answer the ever-elusive question: How? How can we implement sport-based development and educational programs that produce empowered individuals who, in turn, collaborate with others to produce social change? That is what this theory seeks to explain.

Expose

We have found that the first step in the empowerment process[2] for social change is creating awareness or elevating the consciousness of individuals through exposure to new ideas, information, and ways of thinking (Freire 1970). Without the knowledge and lens in which to view societal challenges, it is difficult to understand the systemic and often invisible ways in which power is perpetuated. For us, exposure requires active listening. Students in our courses are encouraged to ask questions that challenge norms and assumptions, reflect deeply on the world around them, and then listen to the ideas put forth by their peers. We ask students to consider the individual challenges they face and to think broadly about how those challenges manifest themselves in society. This methodology of 'exposure' is rooted in the ideas of Dewey (1938) that encourage educators to stimulate enlightenment by asking students to draw upon their own passions and curiosities to connect cognitive knowledge with affective intelligence. Ultimately, this neural connection of head and heart produces greater learning and helps students move closer to empowerment, action, and social change.

Within SDP, similar issues exist. As noted by Giulianotti (2011), most SDP programs operate top-down, emphasizing a more prescriptive method of intervention rather than an organic, community-driven one. As a result, participants have very little input in the actual knowledge learned; rather they are told of the issues as seen through the eyes of granting agencies or sponsors. As Lyras and Welty Peachey (2011) contend, this power dynamic is diametrically opposed to the very essence of SDP programming, particularly those programs that advocate for human rights, equality, and the empowerment of underserved populations. Moreover, this approach also typically leads to limited investment by community members to serve as advocates, trainers, or educators. At best, these 'intervention' programs have the power to increase the knowledge of an individual but often lack the momentum needed to produce change at the societal level. Additionally, as Spaaij and Jeanes (2013) suggest,

> the existing pedagogical approaches utilized in SDP initiatives do not go far enough: they provide at best raised levels of knowledge and skills for individual participants, but as presently designed, they are often not capable of initiating profound social transformation at any (localized) structural or community level.
>
> *Spaaij and Jeanes 2013: 451*

To create profound societal change, the secondary portion of exposure is rooted in the ideas of bell hooks and engaged pedagogy. Within her writings on education, hooks (1994) speaks of an exposure that calls educators to reveal themselves as human – self-actualized beings with vulnerabilities and fallacies. hooks advocates for a classroom that cares for and respects the souls of her students, as individuals with complex lives, not as humans on an educational assembly line. To create such deep connections and alter the power dynamics in the room, both educators and students must be committed to mutual vulnerability (Berry 2010). Vulnerability allows for the authentic self to emerge. As hooks states,

> Engaged pedagogy does not seek simply to empower students. Any classroom that employs a holistic model of learning will also be a place where teachers grow and are empowered by

the process. That [shared] empowerment cannot happen if we refuse to be vulnerable while encouraging students to take risks.

hooks 1994: 21

For us, exposure in SDP programs and in higher education means creating a learning environment where openness, emotional safety, and active listening are at the forefront. As facilitators, we use music, humor, art, dancing, and our own stories of vulnerability to expose ourselves as human. We invite our students to do the same, to peel back their layers of protection and perfection so that we can start our discussions from a place of authenticity. This requires an environment that is safe, a place that allows trust to grow, and promotes feelings of family or team. As noted by Holley and Steiner (2005: 50), a classroom becomes a safe space when students feel 'secure enough to take risks, honestly express their views, and share and explore their knowledge, attitudes, and behaviors'. To create safety and empathy, we position ourselves as leaders who have failed and succeeded. We share our own stories freely. We encourage students to understand leadership as a process not an outcome. Through facilitated activities, we ask students to focus on the life moments that have molded and shaped their journey and the strengths and skills that have allowed them to persevere. Creating a safe space for people to learn, grow, and see themselves as leaders is the foundation for successful empowerment and, ultimately, social change.

Equip

Upon laying the groundwork for empowerment through exposure, as defined by active listening, vulnerability, and safe spaces, our theory asserts that the second phase of the empowerment process is to equip. In simple terms, 'to equip' means to offer resources, networks, tools, and strategies that aid students in their quest to address social or political issues. Through facilitated activities, we help students see themselves as leaders and understand that leadership is not a title, but a choice and a behavior. This approach is also reflected in empowerment and social change literature from Drechsler and Jones, Jr (2012: 401) who state, 'self-empowerment is based on the personal awareness that you can be "a" leader even if you are not "the" leader'. When working with participants in an SDP program, it is common for them to see the professor, instructor, or coach as a leader but fail to see that in themselves. If they do see themselves as leaders, it is often under the guise of leading by example, not necessarily with intention or a clear goal. For any SDP program or social change course to be successful, it is important for everyone participating to see themselves as leaders, influencers, and ultimately, change agents.

The equipping process is about cultivating individuals and giving them the tools, resources, and networks they need to establish a sense of leadership self-efficacy (Bandura 1995). According to Drechsler and Jones, Jr (2012: 406), 'Leadership self-efficacy has an impact on choices individuals make. If a person has confidence that she can make a difference with a cause or as a leader, she is more likely to get involved'. For profound societal transformation to take place, SDP programmers must be willing to train participants to see themselves as leaders and give them the tools necessary to act. This is the multiplier effect, where the empowerment of one leads to the transformation of many. For SDP programmers and professors, this empowerment stands in direct opposition to our survival instincts – if we train the community to address their own needs, we will work ourselves out of a job. But that, in and of itself, is the very essence of social change.

Specifically, during this phase, we equip students by asking reflective questions that allow them to identify the challenges they see in the world and work collaboratively as leaders to develop solutions. Through facilitated activities, we ask students to reflect on their passion, platform, and purpose:

- What are your greatest passions? What challenges do you see around those passion points?
- Who does your current platform allow you to reach? Who are your spheres of influence?
- How does this course or program help you achieve your purpose? How can we use this experience to help you create action towards your goals?

After answering these questions, we challenge them to discover who else is working in similar spaces and how they can create partnerships to move their goals forward. We offer frameworks for program design, monitoring and evaluation, and potential sources of funding or expertise. We shepherd the process, not the product, and assist in ways that encourage students to take ownership of the world around them. Much like Spaaij and Jeanes (2013: 453) contend, 'educators working in the field of SDP ... should not arrive with a pre-packaged curriculum that assumes that every group of participants only needs to learn certain core life skills or competencies. Rather, they [should be] prepared to share this kind of information, if participants name these concerns as areas of need in their own lives'. In this way, we allow students to drive the content while we provide the structure.

Engage

In the third phase of our Theory of Empowerment for Social Change, we ask students to engage in stimulated plans of action using structured curriculum activities, community outreach, and mentorship. As facilitators, we shift the classroom into the community and engage in processes of observation-action-reflection. After observing, interviewing, researching, and investing in community life, we challenge students to move from idea formation to streamlined plans of actions by answering the questions, 'who, what, when, where, why, and how?' Our goal for students in this phase is to put thoughts on paper and to share those thoughts with as many audiences as possible, including community partners, stakeholders, beneficiaries, donors, mentors, policy-makers, and campus or government officials.

The engage phase is an ongoing circle of dialogue in which students refine, revise, and reflect on their plans of action, while always ensuring that their mission is congruent with the needs of the community and their own passions. Throughout this phase, we offer guidance, support, and mentorship and help students reconnect to one another and to their goals. For a one-semester course, this may mean ten weeks of action and reflection (e.g. serving in the community on Tuesday and reflecting in the classroom on Thursday). For a one-month SDP program, it may mean front-loading the curriculum in the first week and community engagement and reflection in weeks two, three, and four. This process of observation-action-reflection is referred to by Freire (1970) as 'praxis' and is the foundation for social change.

Freire identifies praxis as the combination of theory, practice, reflection and action. Breunig (2005: 111) goes on to describe praxis as, 'an abstract idea (theory) or experience that incorporates reflection with the idea or experience and then translates it into purposeful action'. Praxis is part of the transformative learning process in which students come to understand their own assumptions about the world and to how to take action based on that understanding (Ross-Gordon et al. 2015). As Freire and Macedo (1987) assert, praxis is the difference in reading the words and reading the world.

Often times, courses in higher education highlight SDP in the form of one chapter or one week's discussion – typically within sport and globalization – piquing student curiosity but not fully engaging them in the work of SDP. Therefore, students are merely reading words, not engaging the world, and unfortunately, as a result, are not trained to do the work effectively and in collaboration with the community. Rather, as Spaaij and Jeanes (2013: 454) suggest, 'One way in which SDP programs can facilitate an authentically dialogical process is by introducing a preliminary phase during which educators spend time in the community' to establish local knowledge and engage the people they seek to serve. The engage phase is this preliminary phase and allows students to better understand the needs of the community while also creating a sense of agency. Successful program design, delivery, and evaluation are established in the engage phase.

Entrust

The last phase in the Theory of Empowerment for Social Change is to entrust. We entrust that students will take what they have learned and implement it in the real world. We entrust that they will become advocates for equality and social change and will be viewed as collaborative leaders who have more questions than answers. As facilitators, we also entrust that graduates of our programs will not be silent; rather, they will share what they have learned with family, friends, teammates, coaches, colleagues, and administrators and will therefore create change at the personal, community, and policy levels.

In order to assess student learning, we measure the 'entrust' phase using quantitative and qualitative methods. As Gilbert and Bennett (2012: 494) state, 'We need positive proof that all [SDP] programs which are undertaken are achieving some aims and objectives and achieving positive results.' To successfully silence the critics and bring unity to the field, we must provide proof of delivery. Therefore, by using a mixed methods approach for our SDP programs, we assess empowerment and development through a lens of: pre-test/post-test, 3-, 6-, and 12-month post-program interviews, and 6- and 12-month quantitative tracking sheets measuring action plan progress, new partnerships, volunteers, initiatives, awards/promotions, and funding. With our students, we assess using a pre-test/post-test coupled with qualitative interviews before and after course completion. We informally track their progress throughout the next year and continue to include them in community outreach.

For the future, we seek to formalize peer mentorship programs so students who graduate from our courses can become mentors to the next generation of leaders. As facilitators, we understand the importance of connection and the establishment of a support network, so we want to continue involving alumni of our programs. Social change can be exhausting and thankless work, and we have found this connection of current students with past participants to be vital in driving the cycle forward. Shared experience, allegiance to one another, and accountability to the group becomes its own external factor for stimulating social change. As noted by Ross-Gordon *et al.* (2015), belonging to a group of learners is the cornerstone of transformative education. Those who belong, who are serving and learning in community together, are more likely to take risks, to experiment, to collaborate, to support, to reflect, and to continue in dialogue. For a program to sustain itself, it needs a network of supporters and a pipeline of learners.

Conclusion

Upon conclusion, the future is ripe to introduce SDP into the academy. By involving the scholars and students in SDP work, we move one step closer to creating a more unified, strategic, and evidence-based approach to international development and peacebuilding through sport. Together, scholars and practitioners can collaborate on theory development, research, pedagogy, and evaluation techniques. Moreover, educators can teach students how to become community-minded leaders by ensuring that reflexivity and collaboration are integral aspects of their social change efforts. As professors, it is our job to fuel the next generation, to equip them for a world that does not yet exist, and to inspire them to contribute to that world in a positive way. We hope that our Theory of Empowerment for Social Change provides a tangible method for educators, in the classroom and on the sports field, to train future generations of leaders to use sport for equality and change.

Notes

1   A set of 17 goals proposed by the United Nations to promote economic growth, social inclusion, and environmental protection.
2   We define empowerment as 'the process of becoming stronger and more confident, especially in controlling one's life and claiming one's rights' not as 'the giving of power or authority to another' (English Oxford Living Dictionary, 2017). Like Darnell (2013) and others, we seek to reduce neocolonialism and the white horse mentality of the global North by working collaboratively with students and participants in a mutual, reflexive, and reciprocal way.

References

Bandura, A. (1995). Exercise of personal and collective efficacy in changing societies. In A. Bandura (ed.), *Self-Efficacy in Changing Societies*. Cambridge: Cambridge University Press.

Bandura, A., Adams, N. E., Hardy, A. B. and Howells, G. N. (1980). Tests of the generality of self-efficacy theory. *Cognitive Therapy and Research*, 4(1), 39–66.

Berry, T. R. (2010). Engaged pedagogy and critical race feminism. *Educational Foundations*. Summer–Fall: 19–26.

Bourdieu, P. (1986). The forms of capital. In J. Richardson (ed.), *Handbook of Theory and Research for the Sociology of Education*. Westport, CT: Greenwood.

Bouzou, J. (2015). Peace through Sport Engineers on the Rise. Available at: www.peace-sport.org/opinion/peace-through-sport-engineers-on-the-rise/ (accessed 30 January 2017).

Breunig, M. (2005). Turning experiential education and critical pedagogy theory into praxis. *Journal of Experiential Education*, 28(2), 106–122.

Bruening, J. E., Peachey, J. W., Evanovich, J. M., Fuller, R. D., Coble Murty, C. J., Percy, V. E., Silverstein, L. A. and Chung, M. (2015). Managing sport for social change: The effects of intentional design and structure in a sport-based service learning initiative. *Sport Management Review*, 18(1), 69–85.

Butin, D. (2010). *Service-Learning in Theory and Practice: The Future of Community Engagement in Higher Education*. New York: Palgrave Macmillan.

Campus Compact. (2016). Campus Compact. Available at: http://compact.org/who-we-are/our-coalition/membership/members/ (accessed 30 January 2017).

Coalter, F. (2007). *A Wider Role for Sport*. London: Routledge.

Coalter, F. (2013). *Sport for Development: What Game Are We Playing?* London: Routledge.

Davis, H. A. (2011). Rapid rise of service learning. *Penn Current*, 5 May: Available at: https://penncurrent.upenn.edu/2011-05-05/research/rapid-rise-service-learning (accessed 1 December 2016).

Darnell, S. C. (2013). *Sport for Development and Peace: A Critical Sociology*. London: Bloomsbury Academic Press.

Dewey, J. (1938). *Experience and Education*. New York: Collier.

Donnelly, P., Atkinson, M., Boyle, S. and Szto, C. (2011). Sport for development and peace: A public sociology perspective. *Third World Quarterly*, 32(3), 589–601.

Drechsler, M. J. and Jones, W. A. Jr. (2012). Becoming a change agent. In S. R. Komives and W. Wagner (eds), *Leadership for a Better World: Understanding the Social Change Model of Leadership Development*. San Francisco: Jossey-Bass.

Eyler, J. and Giles, D. E. (1999). *Where's the Learning in Service-Learning?* San Francisco: Jossey-Bass.

Freire, P. (1970). *Pedagogy of the Oppressed*. New York: Continuum.

Freire, P. (1973). *Education for Critical Consciousness*. New York: Continuum.

Freire, P. and Macedo, D. (1987). *Literacy: Reading the Word and the World*. South Hadley, MA: Bergin and Garvey.

Gilbert, K. and Bennett, W. (2012). Contemplating a Moral World. In K. Gilbert and W. Bennett (eds), *Sport, Peace, and Development*. Illinois: Common Ground.

Giulianotti, R. (2011). Sport, peacemaking and conflict resolution: A contextual analysis and modeling of the sport development and peace sector. *Ethnic and Racial Studies, 34*(2), doi:10.1080/01419870.2010.522245.

Hartmann, D. and Kwauk, C. (2011). Sport and development: An overview, critique, and reconstruction. *Journal of Sport and Social Issues, 35*(3), 284–305.

Holley, L. C. and Steiner, S. (2005). Safe space: Student perspectives on classroom environment. *Journal of Social Work Education, 41*(1), 49–64.

hooks, b. (1994). *Teaching to Transgress: Education as the Practice of Freedom.* New York: Routledge.

Huffman, A. M. (2011). Using Sport to Build Community: Using Service-Learning with Iraqi Refugees. PhD. Knoxville, Tennessee: University of Tennessee.

International Sport for Development Association (ISDA). (2010). ISDA Power of Sport Call to Action. Available at: www.sportanddev.org/sites/default/files/downloads/isdpasummitcall_to_action_.pdf (accessed 15 December 2016).

Jeanes, R. and Lindsey, I. (2014). Where is the evidence? Reflecting on monitoring and evaluation within sport-for-development. In K. Young and C. Okada (eds), *Sport, Social Development and Peace: Research in Sociology of Sport*, Bingley, UK: Emerald Group.

Kidd, B. (2011). Cautions, questions and opportunities in sport for development and peace. *Third World Quarterly, 32*(3), 603–609.

Lyras, A. and Welty Peachey, J. (2011). Integrating sport-for-development theory and praxis. *Sport Management Review, 14*(4), 311–326.

Meier, M. (2008). Monitoring and Evaluation in Disaster Settings. Available at: www.icsspe.org/documente/Monitoring_and_Evaluation_in_the_Disaster_Setting_-_Marianne_Meier.pdf (accessed 6 October 2010).

Miller, M. P. and Nendel, J. D. (eds) (2011) *Service-Learning in Physical Education and Related Professions: A Global Perspective.* Sudbury, MA: Jones and Bartlett.

Richards, J., Kaufman, Z., Schulenkorf, N., Wolff, E., Gannet, K., Siefken, K. and Rodriquez, G. (2013). Advancing the evidence base of sport-for-development: A new open-access, peer reviewed journal. *Journal for Sport for Development, 1*(1), 1–3.

Right to Play. (2008). Harnessing the Power of Sport for Development and Peace: Recommendations to Governments. Available at: www.righttoplay.com/moreinfo/aboutus/Documents/Sport%20For%20Dev%20(Summary)%20-%20ENG.pdf (accessed 1 December 2016).

Ross-Gordon, J., Gordon, S., Alston, G., Dawson, K. and Van Aacken, C. (2015). Efforts to transform learning and learners: The first decade of innovative doctoral program. *Journal of Thought, 49*(1–2), 52–70.

Spaaij, R. and Jeanes, R. (2013). Education for social change? A Freirean critique of sport for development and peace. *Physical Education and Sport Pedagogy, 18*(4), 442–457.

Sportanddev.org (2015). Available at: www.linkedin.com/company-beta/15183917/?pathWildcard=15183917 (accessed 18 January 2017).

United Nations Global Goals. (2015). Available at: www.globalgoals.org (accessed 15 December 2016).

Welty Peachy, J. and Burton, L. (2016). Servant leadership in sport for development and peace: A way forward. *Quest, 69*(1), 125–139.

30

SDP and positive youth development[1]

Nicholas L. Holt, Colin J. Deal, Kurtis Pankow,
Shannon R. Pynn and Helene Jørgensen

Sport remains one of the most popular organized activities for youth in contemporary society. For example, 77 percent of Canadians aged 5–19 years old participate in some form of organized sport (Canadian Fitness and Lifestyle Research Institute 2016). There is a great deal of (often unsubstantiated) rhetoric about using 'the power of sport' to produce positive developmental outcomes (Coakley 2016). Research shows that merely participating in sport does not necessarily produce positive outcomes for individuals, families, or communities. Indeed, some adolescents report experiencing negative peer interactions and inappropriate adult behaviors in sport (Hansen *et al.* 2003). We view sport as an educational context that can, when structured and delivered in appropriate ways, provide children and adolescents with opportunities to accrue positive developmental outcomes.

Realizing the benefits of sport participation requires an understanding of the processes and interactions that produce (or limit) the attainment of positive outcomes. The positive youth development (PYD) approach offers a way to cut through the rhetoric surrounding sport by examining questions such as *what works, for whom, and under what circumstances?* (Holt *et al.* 2013). More specifically, PYD is an asset-building approach to youth development research and practice that emphasizes enhancing strengths and developing potential in all youth (Lerner 2017). Programs designed to promote PYD typically include (a) positive and sustained relationships between youth and adults, (b) activities that build life skills, and (c) opportunities for youth to use life skills as both participants and leaders in community activities (Lerner 2004). Programs that incorporate these features may target a variety of PYD-type outcomes, including but not limited to bonding, resilience, competence, self-determination, self-efficacy, positive identity, opportunities for prosocial involvement, and prosocial norms (Catalano *et al.* 1998).

The purpose of this chapter is to provide an introduction to the area of PYD through sport. We begin by conceptualizing PYD and then provide a brief overview of PYD theories and some related research. We then present a case study, describing the emergence of a PYD research program based on our work in the Child and Adolescent Sport and Activity lab at the University of Alberta in Edmonton, Alberta, Canada. This case study is intended to illuminate some of the key findings and issues associated with PYD through sport (for other reviews, also see Weiss and Wiese-Bjornstal 2009; Holt 2016; Holt, Neely *et al.* 2017). We conclude by reflecting on some of the robust findings contained within the body of literature and considering some future directions for PYD through sport research.

Understanding positive youth development

PYD is an 'umbrella term' rather than a singular construct or theory. It is used in both research and practice, and tends to focus on the adolescent period of development. Adolescence is marked by significant changes in emotional, cognitive, social, and physical domains. Historically, due to the sometimes turbulent nature of these changes, adolescence was conceptualized as a time of 'storm and stress' during which youth were viewed as 'problems to be managed' (Roth et al. 1998). This became known as a deficit-reduction approach, whereby youth development meant, in practical terms, protecting individuals from engaging in undesirable behaviors (Scales et al. 2000). However, the deficit-reduction approach fails to capture that successful youth development entails more than simply avoiding undesirable behaviors. PYD emerged from dissatisfaction with the deficit-reduction approach (Damon 2004).

PYD is, therefore, a means of facilitating optimal development, which can be defined as preparing individuals to 'lead a healthy, satisfying, and productive life, as youth and later as adults, because they gain the competence to earn a living, to engage in civic activities, to nurture others and to participate in social relations and cultural activities' (Hamilton et al. 2004: 3). Rather than having few problems, adolescents who are fully prepared to enter adult society possess a range of emotional, behavioral, cognitive, and social strengths (Lerner et al. 2003) and take an active role in their development (Larson 2006).

The PYD perspective originated in developmental psychology and has increasingly been used in the context of sport (Holt 2016). Applying PYD to sport, Holt and colleagues offered the following definition:

> PYD through *sport* is intended to facilitate youth development via *experiences* and *processes* that enable participants in *adult-supervised programs* to gain *transferable personal and social life skills*, along with *physical competencies*. These skill and competency outcomes will enable participants in youth sport programs to *thrive* and *contribute to their communities*, both now and in the future.
>
> *Holt et al. 2016: 231, italics in original*

Theoretical underpinnings

Most contemporary models of PYD reflect principles of the bioecological systems theory (Bronfenbrenner and Morris 1998). This theory is based on four main concepts and dynamic relationships between the concepts, known as the process–person–context–time model. Process refers to reciprocal interactions between people and their immediate environments. Person is the individual characteristics of people that influence their social interactions. Context involves five interconnected systems, which range from more proximal 'microsystems' to more distal 'macrosystems'. Microsystems are the patterned activities, roles, and interpersonal relations a person experiences in a specific setting. The more distal macrosystems include public policy, governments, and economic systems. Time is conceptualized at three levels: micro-time (specific episodes in proximal processes), meso-time (which extends over days, weeks, or years), and macro-time (shifting expectancies in a culture within and across generations).

From this bioecological systems theoretical perspective, individuals interact with various different types of social contexts, which can include, for example families, peer groups, sport teams, schools, and communities. These interactions are bi-directional, which means that individuals both influence, and are influenced by, the social contexts with which they interact (Lerner 2017). For example, adolescent athletes on a sport team influence the social relationships on their team and are also influenced by the social relationships on their team. Athletes are influenced by their coach, and through their behaviors they can influence the coach. Therefore, long-term developmental changes are thought to be a consequence of the dynamic relations that occur between individuals and the multiple social contexts with which they interact. Hence, PYD is about creating mutually beneficial relations between people and their social contexts (Lerner 2017).

Conceptual approaches

Several conceptual approaches to PYD have been put forward in the developmental psychology literature and adapted for sport. For instance, Lerner *et al.* (2011) presented a model of PYD based on five indicators known as the 5Cs of PYD (confidence, competence, positive connections, character, and caring). Higher rates of PYD (i.e. the 5Cs) are hypothesized to decrease the likelihood of youth engaging in risk/problem behaviors and increase the likelihood of youth engaging in 'contribution'. Contribution is the 6th C of PYD and refers to contributions adolescents make to self, family, community, and civil society. It should be noted that the 5Cs measurement model of PYD has not been supported in studies with athletes (e.g. Jones *et al.* 2011), and sport psychology researchers have argued that a 4Cs approach (whereby the Cs represent competence, confidence, connection, and character) may better represent PYD in sport (Côté *et al.* 2010).

Benson (1997) and colleagues at the Search Institute in Minneapolis identified 40 developmental assets that are considered to be the qualities and characteristics of programs and individuals that foster optimal youth development. It is hypothesized that youth in possession of more assets will be more likely to experience more positive developmental outcomes than youth with fewer assets (Benson 1997). Research in sport has shown that the asset of empowerment predicts enjoyment in sport, whereas support and positive identity assets predict reduced burnout (Strachan *et al.* 2009).

Larson and colleagues' domains of learning experiences have also been used to study PYD. Dworkin *et al.* (2003: 20) defined growth experiences as 'experiences that teach you something or expand you in some way, that give you new skills, new attitudes, or new ways on interacting with others'. Growth experiences can be measured using the YES 2.0 (Hansen and Larson 2005), which has six positive domains (identity experiences, initiative experiences, basic skills, positive relationships, teamwork and social skills, and adult networks/social capital) and five negative domains (stress, negative influences, social exclusion, negative group dynamics, and inappropriate adult behavior). This measure has been adapted for sport via the creation of the YES-Sport (MacDonald *et al.* 2012) and university sport experience survey (Rathwell and Young 2016).

Sport-specific approaches to PYD through sport

Sport psychology researchers have also presented models of PYD specifically designed for sport. For instance, Fraser-Thomas *et al.* (2005) proposed an applied sport programing model of PYD incorporating Benson's (1997) developmental assets model, the National Research Council and Institute of Medicine's (2002) eight setting features, and the developmental model of sport participation (Côté 1999; Côté *et al.* 2003). Côté *et al.* (2014) proposed the personal assets framework (PAF). The PAF considers personal factors (i.e. personal engagement in activities), relational factors (i.e. quality relationships), and organizational environments (i.e. appropriate social and physical settings). The interaction of these three dynamic elements constitutes a specific sport experience (e.g. in games or practices) that generates changes in athletes' personal assets (confidence, competence, connection, and character) when repeated over time. Several other models have also been presented (e.g. Petitpas *et al.* 2005; Gould and Carson 2008; Hodge *et al.* 2016; Holt, Neely *et al.* 2017; Pierce *et al.* 2017). Thus, overall, it is clear that PYD through sport is a rapidly expanding area of research with growing empirical and conceptual support.

A model of positive youth development through sport

Holt, Neely, *et al.* (2017) recently presented a grounded theory model of PYD through sport based on a synthesis of previous qualitative studies. It is intended to expand current knowledge by detailing the types of interactions that occur within sport programs (e.g. on a sport team). Sport programs are therefore conceptualized as a microsystem (García Bengoechea 2002) within a series of broader ecological systems, such as family, community, and society. Individuals directly influence, and are influenced by, their experiences within microsystems. Hence, this grounded theory model focuses on experiences that occur in the microsystem of youth sport, and how these experiences can lead to PYD. The model also considers the characteristics of participants who enter sport programs such as along demographic (e.g. gender, ethnicity, and socio-economic status) and individual difference variables (e.g. traits and dispositions). These factors may influence the ways in which individuals acquire PYD outcomes through their involvement in sport.

The microsystem aspect of the model begins with the PYD climate created by peers, parents, and other adults. A mounting body of evidence shows that strong peer relationships (e.g. Fraser-Thomas and Côté 2009), autonomy-supportive or authoritative approaches to parenting (e.g. Holt *et al.* 2009), and mastery-oriented approaches to coaching (e.g. Smith *et al.* 2007) have been associated with promoting PYD. The model then deals with the processes through which PYD outcomes may be acquired. Two processes are proposed. The first, an implicit process, suggests that it is possible for PYD outcomes to be gained through an implicit process if a suitable PYD

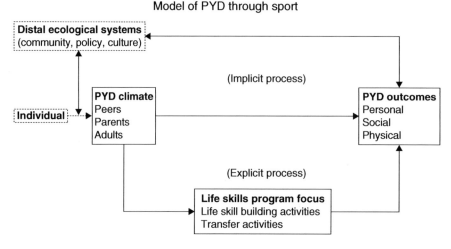

Figure 30.1 Model of PYD through sport
Reprinted with permission from Holt, Neely *et al.* (2017)

climate is in place (the arrow linking PYD climate and PYD outcomes in Figure 30.1). The explicit learning process suggests a mechanism for explicit learning of PYD outcomes if there is a life skills program focus (i.e. life skills building activities and transfer activities). Life skills are physical, behavioral, or cognitive skills that are required to deal with the demands and challenges of everyday life (Hodge and Danish 1999). They must be transferable to other life domains (Papacharisis *et al.* 2005). The explicit learning process is represented by the arrows linking PYD climate to life skills program focus to PYD outcomes in Figure 30.1. By gaining PYD outcomes, youth will be able to thrive and contribute to their communities (the arrow linking PYD outcomes back to distal ecological systems).

The grounded theory model of PYD through sport includes five hypotheses. These hypotheses have yet to be tested, and they are intended to provide a guide for future research. The hypotheses are: (a) distal ecological systems and individual factors influence PYD through sport, (b) a PYD climate (based on relationships between athletes and peers, parents, and other adults such as coaches) can produce PYD outcomes (i.e. through implicit processes), (c) PYD outcomes can be attained if a life skills program focus (involving life skill building activities and transfer activities) is in place (i.e. through explicit processes) and in the presence of a PYD climate, (d) the combined effects of a PYD climate *and* a life skills focus will produce more PYD outcomes than a PYD climate alone, and (e) gaining PYD outcomes in and through sport will facilitate transfer and enable youth to thrive and contribute to their communities.

Case study: tracing the emergence of a PYD research program

We now turn our attention to describing the emergence of a PYD research program based on our work in the Child and Adolescent Sport and Activity lab at the University of Alberta. We use this case study to illustrate some key issues associated with PYD through sport. In the early- to mid-2000s there was little PYD research in sport (although it should be noted there is a rich legacy of strength-based research in youth sport that predates the PYD movement; see Weiss 2016). There was also a small body of sport research examining life skills, which are a feature of PYD programs (Lerner 2004). Our earliest research involved examining what life skills people can learn through their participation in sport.

First, in an ethnographic study with a well-respected coach of a high school soccer team, we examined whether and how youth learned life skills through their involvement on the team (Holt *et al.* 2008). The coach had a philosophy that focused on building relationships with the student–athletes and involving them in decision-making. The student–athletes reported learning about initiative (e.g. learning to set realistic goals and take responsibility for oneself), respect, and teamwork/leadership. Teamwork/leadership was the only skill that student–athletes thought directly transferred to other domains (e.g. school). We observed little direct teaching of these life skills. Rather, the structure created by the coach provided opportunities to demonstrate initiative; student–athletes were punished or reprimanded if they failed to show respect (e.g. to opponents or a referee), and they appeared to be producers of their own teamwork/leadership experiences.

In another study, we examined how people learn life skills through their involvement in competitive sport by conducting interviews with 40 young adults who played sport during adolescence (Holt *et al.* 2009). An underpinning feature of the results was that social interactions were central to how the participants learned life skills through participating in sport. For example, social skills were learned through interactions with peers and these skills retained meaning in the participants' adult lives, which echoed results of the high school study (i.e. Holt *et al.* 2008) in that participants were producers of their own experiences and social skills transferred to other contexts. Participants' parents used sport to reinforce values and work ethic. Their coaches emphasized hard work and teamwork but also had some negative influences on participants' experiences (e.g. by overemphasizing winning or engaging in too much negative communication). Overall, these findings reinforced the idea that sport can provide an educational context for acquiring life skills, and highlighted that interactions with key social agents are crucial components of how people learn life skills through their involvement in sport.

Around 2009–2010, Nick met with the principal of an elementary/junior high school in an inner-city area of Edmonton. The principal explained that many of her students had disadvantaged backgrounds and, often, chaotic family environments. She was committed to using sport and physical education to enrich the students' learning experiences. Hence, this school seemed to have a PYD-type of focus and it became the impetus for the next phase of our work in PYD through sport.

Before entering the school to engage in research, we more broadly examined some of the benefits and challenges associated with sport participation among children and parents from low-income families (Holt *et al.* 2011). Parents and children reported that sport participation was associated with a range of personal and social developmental benefits (e.g. relationships with coaches, making new friends, teamwork and social skills, emotional control, confidence, discipline, improved academic performance). However, parents also reported several remaining barriers and constraints that restricted the extent to which their children could remain engaged in sport and gain sustained developmental benefits. These included time management and scheduling demands, as well as ongoing financial barriers, especially in terms of maintaining their children's involvement in sport as they improved (because sport participation – in Canada at least – tends to become more expensive as youth reach higher levels of performance).

Simultaneously, we conducted a year-long study within the inner-city elementary/junior high school that used a PYD-type of approach in sport and physical education. The first study examined physical activity opportunities in the inner-city neighborhood itself (Holt *et al.* 2009). Whereas the neighborhood was highly 'walkable' and included multiple play spaces, safety concerns restricted children's access. Indeed, the children were rarely allowed to play outdoors alone, but the accompaniment of a family member facilitated their engagement in physical activity. We found that adult-supervised programs were important, but agencies faced staffing problems that served to limit the opportunities they could provide to the children in the inner-city neighborhood. Hence, the school itself appeared to play an important role in the neighborhood in terms of providing programming for children.

We then focused on assessing the possibilities for promoting PYD through the program offerings within the school itself, specifically in terms of physical education classes, intramural sports, and the school's competitive sport teams (Holt *et al.* 2012). Data were collected via individual interviews with eight teachers and 59 children from the aforementioned school. In physical education classes, the importance of a specialist physical education teacher who established clear boundaries during lessons, while providing children with perceptions of choice, was apparent. Children enjoyed intramural sports, but there were few attempts to create an appropriate developmental atmosphere during these sessions. In fact, some negative student interactions were observed during intramurals (e.g. students not coping well with losing, damaging equipment, not listening to the referee, swearing at the referee and at each other, and pushing). In contrast, coaches of the competitive sport teams used several techniques to promote positive social interactions and respect, which included prioritizing student development above winning, sharing personal experiences, emphasizing peer support, and having students sign behavioral 'contracts' at the start of the season. The most notable student outcomes associated with PYD related to fostering empathy and social connections. Hence, this study highlighted contextual factors across programs that helped promote PYD, which included the developmental orientation of physical education classes and the life skills focus of the sport teams. Intramurals were seen as being fun, but the lack of a developmental structure or life skills focus seemed to impair the acquisition of PYD outcomes in this context.

With a better understanding of the specific need for programs in certain inner-city areas (Holt *et al.* 2009), financial barriers (Holt *et al.* 2011), program context factors that facilitate PYD (Holt *et al.* 2012), and the social interactions that appear central to the acquisition of life skills (Holt *et al.* 2008; Holt, Tamminen *et al.* 2009), we launched a three-year research program that used a participatory action research approach to create a sport-based after-school program for children attending elementary schools in low-income areas of Edmonton (Holt *et al.* 2013). This program, called TRY-Sport, was created through two broad 'action' phases. Following collaboration and consultation with key stakeholders, the first action phase involved the creation and delivery of a multi-sport program in two schools. Semi-structured interviews were then conducted with 28 children and two teachers to evaluate program content and benefits. Analysis revealed that the program provided children with new opportunities and helped them to learn social and personal life skills, and also provided directions for improving the program.

In the second action phase, a revised version of TRY-Sport was delivered to 35 children (grades K-3). TRY-Sport used three sports (soccer, basketball, and volleyball) and required minimal equipment that was already available in the schools. The goals of the program were to teach fundamental movement and sport skills (in soccer, volleyball and basketball) and three life skills (teamwork, leadership, and confidence). The name TRY-Sport was chosen because of the 'tri' focus (three sports, three life skills) and to emphasize that the program was an opportunity for children to 'try' sports. Evaluation of this second action phase, based on interviews with 14 children and three teachers, revealed some of the difficulties encountered such as over-estimating children's skill level, and challenges with students' listening and behavior. Strengths were the pedagogical approaches to creating optimal challenges and encouraging children to use their imaginations, the value of children learning fundamental movement and sport skills, and the explicit focus on life skills.

There was some variation in the extent to which the children learned life skills. Most children were able to provide specific examples of teamwork they had learned in TRY-Sport. Confidence was a life skill the children had difficultly expressing, but the teachers provided some insights that they witnessed children growing in confidence. Leadership was particularly difficult for the children to understand and/or express. It appeared to be the most poorly articulated component of the TRY-Sport program. There were, nonetheless, examples of some of these life skills transferring into other areas of the children's lives, such as in the classroom and at home. TRY-Sport has since been adapted and delivered in other program contexts, including a basketball program in the Mathare area of Nairobi, Kenya and recreational and sport programs in other parts of Alberta.

PYDSportNET

Despite the burgeoning PYD literature, we found that policies, programs, and practices in youth sport are rarely informed by research evidence (Holt *et al.* 2016). In response to this challenge, we recently created PYDSportNET (positive youth development through sport network), a knowledge translation project designed to enhance the use of research evidence to promote PYD through sport (Holt, Camiré *et al.* 2017). Knowledge translation is a dynamic and iterative process that involves interactions between researchers and knowledge users to improve the application of knowledge to provide more effective policies, programs, and practices (Graham *et al.* 2006).

The PYDSportNET project is based on Graham *et al.'s* (2006) knowledge-to-action (KTA) framework, which has two interconnected components: knowledge creation and the action cycle. We first synthesized existing knowledge (which is known as 'second generation knowledge creation' in the KTA framework) by completing a meta-study of qualitative research examining PYD through sport to produce the grounded theory model (Holt, Neely *et al.* 2017), which was described earlier in this chapter. We created 'third generation knowledge' via the development of a series of 'knowledge products' designed to present information in clear, concise, and user-friendly ways. These knowledge products have included infographics and an online magazine for parents titled *The Sport Parent* (issuu.com/thesportparent), supported by a website (positivesport. ca) and Twitter account (@PYDSportNET).

The second component of the KTA framework is the action cycle, which is a process leading to the implementation or application of knowledge. PYDSportNET has been focused on the initial stages of the action cycle (i.e. working with stakeholders on problem identification and knowledge identification/selection). One study was conducted with 21 representations of Canadian National Sport Organizations to explore factors associated with the use of research evidence (Holt, Pankow, Camiré *et al.* 2018) and a second study was conducted via interviews with 60 representatives of Canadian Provincial Sport Organizations to examine their perceptions of important topics for future youth sport research (Holt, Pankow, Tamminen *et al.* 2018). These studies focus on the early stages of the action cycle, and in the future we will focus on implementing and applying knowledge in sport contexts, and evaluating its effects.

Conclusion

In this chapter we provided an overview of key theories and conceptual approaches to PYD through sport. We then presented a case study describing the emergence of one PYD research program. The body of research reviewed herein suggests that sport can be used to promote PYD among different populations (children, adolescents, and even young adults) and in a range of different contexts (e.g. high school sport, competitive sport, after-school programs, and recreational sport). Participants' experiences within such contexts can be shaped to promote PYD. Relationships between youth and caring adults, as well as among program participants themselves, are critical. Strong peer relationships, autonomy-supportive or authoritative approaches to parenting, and mastery-oriented approaches to coaching are important 'ingredients' for promoting PYD with youth sport microsystems. Opportunities for participants to produce their own experiences, experience leadership, learn life skills, and take initiative are also important principles for promoting PYD. Yet, the delivery of specific PYD approaches can vary; intentional curriculum-based approaches can be effective, but so too can more implicit approaches that focus on creating a PYD climate.

PYD is a vibrant area of research and there are several issues that must still be addressed by researchers. For example, little is known about how life skills transfer actually works. Research in cognitive psychology (e.g. Frensch and Rünger 2003) and motor learning (e.g. Rendell *et al.* 2009) regarding implicit and explicit learning may be helpful for shedding more light on transfer. The hypotheses proposed in the model of PYD through sport (Holt, Neely *et al.* 2017) may provide some directions for future research, particularly with regard to implicit and explicit learning. It will also be important to learn more about how individual factors contribute or detract from PYD. Furthermore, examining how the interaction of individual and contextual factors influence PYD remains an important area of future research. Another issue concerns the effects of PYD; what types of 'contributions' do people with high levels of PYD make to sport and their communities? A fundamental assumption is that gaining positively developmental outcomes will enable individuals to make contributions to themselves, others, and communities more broadly (Lerner 2017). However, it remains unclear whether people who experience PYD through sport are more likely, for example, to coach or volunteer with sport programs or give back to their communities in other ways.

In the future, we expect to see increased adoption of PYD research internationally, which may reveal more information about contextual factors that influence the promotion of PYD through sport (e.g. Reverdito *et al.* 2017). Finally, we see opportunities for using some of the theoretical and conceptual approaches to PYD in the sport for development literature more broadly to shed light on the person-context interactions that produce, or limit, the attainment of positive developmental outcomes. Given the enduring popularity of sport in contemporary society, it behooves researchers to reject rhetoric about the power of sport and, instead, strive to understand what features of sport programs 'work' across different types of contexts. Such evidence will ultimately help ensure that youth sport programs more consistently and effectively help individuals to attain positive developmental outcomes through their sustained participation in youth sport.

Note

1   The writing of this chapter was supported by a Partnership Development Grant from the Social Sciences and Humanities Research Council of Canada awarded to Nick Holt.

References

Benson, P. L. (1997). *All Kids Are Our Kids: What Communities Must Do To Raise Caring and Responsible Children and Adolescents.* San Francisco, CA: Jossey-Bass.

Bronfenbrenner, U. and Morris, P. A. (1998). The ecology of developmental processes. In W. Damon and R. M. Lerner (eds), *Handbook of Child Psychology: Theoretical Models of Human Development.* Hoboken, NJ: Wiley.

Canadian Fitness and Lifestyle Research Institute. (2016). Bulletin 2: Participation in Organized Physical Activity and Sport. Ottawa, ON. Available at: www.cflri.ca/document/bulletin-2-participation-organized-physical-activity-and-sport-0.

Catalano, R. F., Berglund, M. L., Ryan, J. A. M. *et al.* (1998) Positive Youth Development in the United States: Research Findings on Evaluations of Positive Youth Development Programs. Available at: http://aspe.hhs.gov/hsp/PositiveYouthDev99/chapter2.htm.

Coakley, J. (2016). Positive youth development through sport: Myths, beliefs, and realities. In N. L. Holt (ed.), *Positive Youth Development Through Sport.* London: Routledge.

Côté, J. (1999). The influence of the family in the development of talent in sport. *The Sport Psychologist, 13*(4), 395–417.

Côté, J., Baker, J. and Abernethy, B. (2003). From play to practice. In J. L. Starkes and A. Ericsson (eds), *Expert Performance in Sports: Advances in Research on Sport Expertise,* Champaign, IL: Human Kinetics.

Côté, J., Bruner, M. W., Erickson, K. *et al.* (2010). Athlete development and coaching. In J. Lyle and C. Cushion (eds), *Sport Coaching: Professionalism and Practice.* Oxford, England: Elsevier.

Côté, J., Turnidge, J. and Evans, M. B. (2014). The dynamic process of development through sport. *Kinesiologia Slovenica, 20*: 14–26.

Damon, W. (2004). What is positive youth development? *The Annals of the American Academy of Political and Social Science, 591*(1), 13–24.

Dworkin, J. B., Larson, R. and Hansen, D. (2003). Adolescents' accounts of growth experiences in youth activities. *Journal of Youth and Adolescence, 32*(1), 17–26.

Fraser-Thomas, J. L. and Côté, J. (2009). Understanding adolescents' positive and negative developmental experiences in sport. *The Sport Psychologist, 23*: 3–23.

Fraser-Thomas, J. L., Côté, J. and Deakin, J. (2005). Youth sport programs: An avenue to foster positive youth development. *Physical Education and Sport Pedagogy, 10*(1), 19–40.

Frensch, P. A. and Rünger, D. (2003). Implicit learning. *Current Directions in Psychological Science, 12*(1), 12–18.

García Bengoechea, E. (2002). Integrating knowledge and expanding horizons in developmental sport psychology: A bioecological perspective. *Quest, 54*(1), 1–20.

Gould, D. and Carson, S. (2008). Life skills development through sport: Current status and future directions. *International Review of Sport and Exercise Psychology, 1*(1), 58–78.

Graham, I. D., Logan, J., Harrison, M. B. *et al.* (2006). Lost in knowledge translation: Time for a map? *Journal of Continuing Education in the Health Professions, 26*(1), 13–24.

Hamilton, S. F., Hamilton, M. A. and Pittman, K. (2004). Principles for positive youth development. In S. F. Hamilton and M. A. Hamilton (eds), *The Youth Development Handbook: Coming of Age in American Communities*. Thousand Oaks, CA: SAGE.

Hansen, D. M. and Larson, R. (2005). The Youth Experience Survey 2.0: Instrument Revisions and Validity Testing. Unpublished manuscript, University of Illinois at Urbana-Champaign. Available at: http://web.aces.uiuc.edu/youthdev/UnpublishedManuscriptonYES2111%20(2).doc.

Hansen, D. M., Larson, R. W. and Dworkin, J. B. (2003). What adolescents learn in organized youth activities: A survey of self-reported developmental experiences. *Journal of Research on Adolescence, 13*: 25–55.

Hodge, K. and Danish, S. (1999). Promoting life skills for adolescent males through sport. In A. M. Horne and M. S. Kiselica (eds), *Handbook of Counseling Boys and Adolescent Males: A Practitioner's Guide*. Thousand Oaks, CA: SAGE.

Hodge, K., Danish, S., Forneris, T. *et al.* (2016). Life skills and basic psychological needs. In N. L. Holt (ed.), *Positive Youth Development through Sport* (2nd edn). London: Routledge.

Holt, N. L. (ed.) (2016) *Positive Youth Development through Sport* (2nd edn). London: Routledge.

Holt, N. L., Camiré, M., Tamminen, K. A. *et al.* (2017). PYDSportNET: A knowledge translation project bridging gaps between research and practice in youth sport. *Journal of Sport Psychology in Action*, doi:10.1080/21520704.2017.1388893.

Holt, N. L., Cunningham, C.-T., Sehn, Z.L. *et al.* (2009). Neighborhood physical activity opportunities for inner city children and youth. *Health and Place, 15*: 1022–1028.

Holt, N. L., Deal, C. J. and Smyth, C. L. (2016). Future directions for positive youth development through sport. In N. L. Holt (ed.), *Positive Youth Development through Sport* (2nd edn). London: Routledge.

Holt, N. L., Kingsley, B. C., Tink, L. N. *et al.* (2011). Benefits and challenges associated with sport participation by children and parents from low-income families. *Psychology of Sport and Exercise, 12*: 490–499.

Holt, N. L., McHugh, T.-L. F., Tink, L. N. *et al.* (2013). Developing sport based after school programs using a participatory action research approach'. *Qualitative Research in Sport, Exercise and Health, 5*(3), 332–355.

Holt, N. L., Neely, K. C., Slater, L. G. *et al.* (2017). A grounded theory of positive youth development through sport based on results from a qualitative meta-study. *International Review of Sport and Exercise Psychology, 10*(1), 1–49.

Holt, N. L., Pankow, K., Camiré, M. Côté, J., Fraser-Thomas, J., MacDonald, D., Strachan, L. and Tamminen, K. (2018). Factors associated with using research evidence in national sport organisations. *Journal of Sports Sciences, 36*(10), 1111–1117.

Holt, N. L., Pankow, K., Tamminen, K. A. Strachan, L., MacDonald, D. J., Fraser-Thomas, J., Côté, J. and Camiré, M. (2018). A qualitative study of research priorities among representatives of Canadian provincial sport organizations. *Psychology of Sport and Exercise, 36*, 8–16. doi:10.1016/j.psychsport.2018.01.002.

Holt, N. L., Sehn, Z. L., Spence, J. C. *et al.* (2012). Possibilities for positive youth development through physical education and sport programs at an inner city school. *Physical Education and Sport Pedagogy, 17*(1), 97–113.

Holt, N. L., Tamminen, K. A., Black, D. E. *et al.* (2009). Youth sport parenting styles and practices. *Journal of Sport and Exercise Psychology, 31*(1), 37–59.

Holt, N. L., Tink, L. N., Mandigo, J. L. *et al.* (2008). Do youth learn life skills through their involvement in high school sport?' *Canadian Journal of Education, 31*(2), 281–304.

Jones, M. I., Dunn, J. G. H., Holt, N. L. *et al.* (2011). Exploring the '5Cs' of positive youth development in sport. *Journal of Sport Behavior, 34*(3), 250–267.

Larson, R. (2006). Positive youth development, willful adolescents, and mentoring. *Journal of Community Psychology, 34*(6), 677–689.

Lerner, R. M. (2004). *Liberty: Thriving and Civic Engagement among American Youth*. Thousand Oaks, CA: SAGE.

Lerner, R. M. (2017). Commentary: Studying and testing the positive youth development model: A tale of two approaches. *Child Development, 88*(4), 1183–1185.

Lerner, R. M., Dowling, E. M. and Anderson, P. M. (2003). Positive youth development: Thriving as the basis of personhood and civil society. *Applied Developmental Science, 7*(3), 172–180.

Lerner, R. M., Lerner, J. V., von Eye, A. *et al.* (2011). Individual and contextual bases of thriving in adolescence: A view of the issues. *Journal of Adolescence, 34*(6), 1107–1114.

MacDonald, D. J., Côté, J., Eys, M. *et al.* (2012). Psychometric properties of the youth experience survey with young athletes. *Psychology of Sport and Exercise, 13*: 332–340.

National Research Council and Institute of Medicine. (2002). *Community Programs to Promote Youth Development*, Washington, DC: National Academy Press.

Papacharisis, V., Goudas, M., Danish, S. *et al.* (2005). The effectiveness of teaching a life skills program in a sport context. *Journal of Applied Sport Psychology, 17*(2), 247–254.

Petitpas, A. J., Cornelius, A. F., Van Raalte, J. L. *et al.* (2005). A framework for planning youth sport programs that foster psychosocial development. *The Sport Psychologist, 19*(1), 63–80.

Pierce, S., Gould, D. and Camiré, M. (2017). Definition and model of life skills transfer. *International Review of Sport and Exercise Psychology, 10*(1), 186–211.

Rathwell, S. and Young, B. W. (2016). An examination and validation of an adapted youth experience scale for university sport. *Measurement in Physical Education and Exercise Science, 20*(4), 208–219.

Rendell, M. A., Masters, R. S. W. and Farrow, D. (2009). The paradoxical role of cognitive effort in contextual interference and implicit motor learning. *International Journal of Sport Psychology, 40*(4), 636–647.

Reverdito, R. S., Galatti, L. R., Carvalho, H. M. *et al.* (2017). Developmental benefits of extracurricular sports participation among Brazilian youth., *Perceptual and Motor Skills, 124*(5), 946–960.

Roth, J., Brooks-Gunn, J., Murray, L. *et al.* (1998). Promoting healthy adolescents: Synthesis of youth development program evaluations. *Journal of Research on Adolescence, 8*: 423–459.

Scales, P., Benson, P., Leffert, N. *et al.* (2000). Contribution of developmental assets to the prediction of thriving among adolescents. *Applied Developmental Science, 4*: 27–46.

Smith, R. E., Smoll, F. L. and Cumming, S. P. (2007). Effects of a motivational climate intervention for coaches on young athletes' sport performance anxiety. *Journal of Sport and Exercise Psychology, 29*: 39–59.

Strachan, L., Côté, J. and Deakin, J. (2009). An evaluation of personal and contextual factors in competitive youth sport. *Journal of Applied Sport Psychology, 21*(3) 340–355.

Weiss, M. R. (2016). Old wine in a new bottle: Historical reflections on sport as a context for youth development. In N. L. Holt (ed.), *Positive Youth Development through Sport* (2nd edn). London: Routledge.

Weiss, M. R. and Wiese-Bjornstal, D. M. (2009). Promoting positive youth development through physical activity. *President's Council on Physical Fitness and Sports. Research Digest, 10*: 1–8.

31

SDP and youth in the global North

Laura Kelly

It has been argued that contemporary definitions and practices of 'Sport for Development and Peace' must be located in their historical context to be properly understood. As Giulianotti (2011: 209) notes, sport 'has functioned as a highly important socio-cultural and political-ideological tool in shaping Global North-South relations, particularly in circumstances defined by immense power inequalities'. This chapter will show how SDP provision in the global North also reflects power relationships and inequalities, including those relating to age, class, gender, 'race'/ethnicity, and place. While there are examples of programs aimed at reconciliation following military conflict in the North (for example, Sugden 2010), much activity focuses on individual or community development rather than peacemaking.[1] A related focus on social integration, social cohesion, and intercultural understanding is observable. Within the European Union, for example, sport has been presented as a tool to promote 'young people's engagement and involvement in society', to help 'steer away from delinquency' (European Commission 2007: 6), and as a means of promoting 'economic and social cohesion and more integrated societies' (European Commission 2007: 7, see also Becker *et al.* 2000; Council of the European Union 2010).

Numerous studies of the social benefits of sport have been commissioned to support policy development in other more economically developed countries: for example, the United States (Witt and Crompton 1996; 2002); Canada (Reid *et al.* 1994); Australia (Morris *et al.* 2003; Atherley 2006); and New Zealand (New Zealand Institute of Economic Research, Inc. 2000). This proliferation of activity suggests policy-makers in the global North share considerable confidence in the capacity of sport and sports-based programs to address their national social policy concerns. As Coakley (2011: 307–308) summarizes, the claims made in relation to young people fall into three major categories: personal character development and 'positive youth development'; preventing crime and reforming 'at-risk' populations; and fostering 'social capital' to encourage occupational success, civic engagement, and social integration (i.e. the role of sport in promoting 'social inclusion'). This apparent consensus should be treated with appropriate caution when reviewing the international literature; research findings may translate to different national contexts, but this cannot be assumed due to differences in the cultural and policy environments in which programs are located, as well as potential diversity in provision.

This chapter is divided into four sections. The first considers the historical emergence of youth services that aim to use sport to achieve social goals, with a focus on Britain and North America. The second provides a schematic overview of more recent provision in the global North, tracing the movement towards and away from state-supported universal leisure provision in the context of broader changes to welfare regimes. In so doing, it introduces the targeted, problem-oriented sports-based interventions that often characterize SDP activities in the North. The third section analyses key claims made about this work with young people: that sports-based interventions can develop character, prevent youth crime and promote social inclusion. The chapter concludes by reflecting on possible future directions for research.

Nineteenth-century origins

Ideas of social development and social control have historically been intertwined in sports-based youth provision. In nineteenth-century Britain, concerns that urban life was detrimental to the physical and moral health of the industrial workforce led reformers to advocate for forms of 'rational recreation'. Supported by legislation, educational institutions and parks were established to discourage drinking and gambling, prevent disorder, and safeguard the health of the working class (Coalter *et al.* 1988). The newly defined problem of 'juvenile delinquency' also reflected concerns about the corrupting effect of urban life. Reformers on both sides of the Atlantic established philanthropic institutions intended to 'save' children from damaging social influences and 'reform' those deemed already 'dangerous' (Platt 1969). They also intervened directly in working-class neighbourhoods. As Holt suggests in his history of British sport:

> 'Youth', by which commentators usually meant inner-city working-class boys, was defined as a 'social problem' towards the end of the nineteenth century and efforts were made to direct the energies of what came to be called 'adolescence' into acceptable channels. The traditional institutions of youth with their licensed revels had gone, and new forms of control were required … sport soon came to play an important part in the strategy of counter-attraction.
>
> *Holt 1992: 138*

The 'games cult' that had first thrived in elite public schools embedded ethical and ideological assumptions that are inextricably linked with modern sport (Mangan 1981; Giulianotti 2004). Popularized by mid-Victorian literature and exported globally as a tool of empire (e.g. MacAloon 2008), so-called muscular Christianity extended existing understandings of Christian manliness to emphasize the role of athleticism in the development of moral character and good citizenship.

Such ideas had particular domestic influence in the public school missions, the university settlements and the Boys' Clubs that grew from them. As Russell and Rigby (1908: 115), in their classic account of *Working Lads' Clubs*, explain, organized games were regarded 'not only as an end in themselves, but as one of the most valuable of all aids in the training of character'. It was assumed they gave 'youths of the poorer classes' […] 'some conception of the meaning of *esprit de corps* and fair play' (Russell and Rigby 1908: 4, 19–20). Games thus supported the main educational goal of a club: to 'civilise its members'. This was understood to mean teaching: 'self-respect and self-control, decency in manners and speech, cleanliness, obedience and order', as well as fostering social instincts and widening interests (ibid.: 20; see also Springhall 1977). Clubs were shaped by conservative understandings of gender, as well as class. Despite developing enthusiasm for sport in girls' public schools (McCrone 1984), working girls' clubs focused on preparing members for their future role as wives and mothers. Critical scholars have queried why there was little working-class resistance to philanthropic services that consolidated class divisions. Drawing comparisons with increased state regulation of education following the Chartist upsurge of the 1830s and 1940s, Davies (1986) has argued that the British labour movement's lack of interest in developing its own services may help explain why state intervention in the sector remained minimal until the mid-twentieth century. The principle of voluntary participation also meant young people could opt out, assuming they were willing to forgo the recreational benefits.

In North America, where the 'playground movement' used recreation to discourage 'delinquency' and encourage the assimilation of immigrant populations (Cavallo 1981), Donnelly and Coakley similarly note:

> The double-edged sword of recreation provision is … evident here, with the achievement of recreation space and programmes being won at the cost of cultural loss (something, it should be pointed out, that has been embraced by many immigrant parents, especially in previous generations, who wanted their children to be 'Canadian' or 'American').
>
> *Donnelly and Coakley 2002: 5*

The expansion of universal education in the nineteenth century had consolidated the construction of 'youth' as a separate life stage to 'childhood' and 'adulthood'. Theories of 'adolescent' development (for example, Hall 1904) soon characterized this life stage as a period of 'storm and stress', where the character of the future adult is shaped. Social commentaries and practice reports about the 'youth problem' were disseminated across North America, Europe and European colonies, encouraging similar services and international youth movements (Hendrick 1990; Park 2007). These voluntary responses also laid the foundations for state-provided youth services, which developed in many countries as welfare states consolidated in the twentieth century (for example, Dunne *et al.* 2015). As the next section explores, contemporary sports-based interventions can be understood to reflect a broader movement away from public provision and back towards more fragmented and targeted youth and recreation services.

From 'sport for all' to a 'social problems industry'

State sport policies are also relevant to the study of SDP provision, particularly in relation to recreational facilities and the encouragement of mass participation. The European Sport for All Charter (Council of Europe 1975) institutionalized the idea that European Union Member States should protect the right of every individual to participate in sport. The revised European Sport Charter maintains a commitment to ensuring that all citizens have opportunities to take part in sport (Council of Europe 2001), although the implementation of this principle in national policy frameworks is not straightforward. Heinemann (2005) explored this issue by considering the mutual interconnections between welfare states and sport systems in six European countries: Denmark, the UK (focusing on Great Britain), Germany, France, Italy, and Spain. Despite acknowledging differences in approaches to broader welfare provision, he argues that there are some surprisingly similar trends observable in European countries, which together undermine opportunities for mass participation and the capacity of national governments to guarantee 'sport for all':

> Among these are: (a) progressive withdrawal from sport on the part of the state, at least as a provider of sport opportunities, often observed as decreasing financial support; (b) advancing decentralisation, i.e. the shift of sport responsibility from the central to the local level; (c) expansion of sport suppliers across the borders of the voluntary sector, i.e. a wider

spectrum of institutional arrangements; and lastly (d) increasing application of new public management to sport, in order to administer waning financial support more efficiently.

Heinemann 2005: 188

The Canadian and Australian governments have also maintained a rhetorical commitment to mass participation but decentralized responsibility for sport policy, with funding allocations skewed towards elite sport development (Green 2007). Countries with a commitment to low welfare spending have often tended to view the provision of general opportunities for sports participation as a matter for the market and not the state. As Hartmann (2016: 25) notes, the United States 'has never had a real rhetoric for or commitment to sport for its own sake at least in terms of recreation and participation for the masses'.

Pitter and Andrews' (1997) concept of a 'social problems industry' is significant in understanding recent changes to sport and leisure provision in the United States, and beyond. Funding for recreation facilities had formed part of an official response to American inner-city social problems until the 1970s, but federal and public disinvestment meant the poor were left 'underserved' by patchy, unaffordable private provision and a 'shrinking pool' of public services. They argue that subsequently, and particularly from the 1990s, underserved youth became the focus for a new kind of welfare, where 'public groups seek out private financial support for initiatives directed toward ameliorating the many social problems faced by the underserved living in America's urban environments' (Pitter and Andrews 1997: 86). Mixed economies of welfare now exist across Europe, Australasia and North America, as national governments adopt strategies of decentralization, contractualization and marketization, which disrupt existing welfare institutions and hierarchies (for example, Newman 2005). As Green (2009: 125) summarizes, a mix of methods enables this 'arms-length' form of government: 'decentralisation, collaboration, partnerships – all coordinated by a state more concerned with "steering" (guiding, shaping, leading) than "rowing" (intervening at the operational level of policy delivery)'. The decline of welfare bureaucracies has also encouraged new hybrid organisations, which share features of more than one sector: public, private or third/voluntary. SDP provision commonly reflects this hybridity.

Hartmann (2001; 2016) has conducted detailed research on Midnight Basketball, the program Pitter and Andrews (1997) used to represent the new paradigm of service provision in the United States.[2] Introduced by G. Van Standifer, a former town manager in the late 1980s, Midnight Basketball attracted national attention in 1989, when funds from the Chicago Housing Authority were matched by a grant of $50,000 from the US Department of Housing and Urban Development. Standifer's program had three core components: it targeted young men aged between 17 and 21 years; no game could begin before 10 p.m.; and two uniformed police officers were present and visible at each game. The model outlined by the Chicago Housing Authority aimed to develop this by using sport as a 'hook' to engage participants in extra 'components', which came to include elements such as 'life skills training and conflict resolution, drug prevention, educational counseling, and job training' (Hartmann 2001; Hartmann and Depro 2006: 184).

Coalter (2007: 71) has termed this kind of approach 'plus-sport', to distinguish from traditional sport development or 'sport-plus' approaches. 'Sport-plus' programs emphasize goals such as increased participation in sport and skills development; 'plus-sport' initiatives prioritize social, educational and health goals, and conceive sport primarily as a 'hook' to promote participation in programs. The concept of 'social inclusion' has become established in international policy discourse and frameworks as a shorthand to refer to multiple dimensions of social, economic and political participation, which intersect traditional policy domains (for example, Council of the European Union 2010). Collins and Haudenhuyse (2015: 6) use the terms 'inclusion in sports' and 'inclusion through sports' to echo the distinction between: (a) sport-plus/sport-development, where inclusion implies opportunity to participate in sport; and (b) plus-sport/sport-for-development, where inclusion implies the improvement of participants' position across multiple domains, such as education, employability, housing, health, leisure. The next section explores the claims commonly made about the potential of SDP provision to achieve these goals.

Current research agendas

The claims made about the benefits of youth sports participation and involvement in targeted sports-based interventions fall into three major categories: personal development; crime prevention or reduction; and the promotion of 'social inclusion' and 'social integration'. In terms of the first claim, the benefits of youth sports participation are an established topic within sport studies. More recently, developmental psychologists have become interested in sport as a new terrain for the application of broader theories of Positive Youth Development (or PYD). Such approaches speak directly to the assumptions about adolescent development discussed at the start of this chapter. As Holt suggests:

> The tendency to view adolescence as a period of storm and stress was associated with a deficit-reduction approach, whereby researchers examined ways to prevent and/or reduce the problems adolescents may encounter. Over the past 15 years a new version of adolescent development has emerged; this vision has been labeled positive youth development (PYD).
>
> *Holt 2008:1*

Various frameworks have been proposed (see Fraser-Thomas *et al.* 2005 for discussion in relation to sport), which are linked by a belief in youth's capacity for change and a concern to understand and shape contexts that nurture the agentic participation of young people in their own development. In focusing on young people's potential, PYD is described as a 'strength-based' or 'asset-building' paradigm, in contrast to a 'deficit-reduction' approach. It has been argued that sport has the potential to contribute to young people's development in several areas: (1) physical health; (2) psychosocial development and the development of life skills such as cooperation, discipline, leadership, and self-control; and (3) motor skills and sporting performance. However, youth sport programs currently tend not to produce 'outstanding results' in these areas (Côté *et al.* 2008: 34).

As Coakley (2011: 309–310) summarizes, the research literature suggests that benefits do not automatically follow from sports participation, but rather depend on multiple factors, including: the type of sport played; orientations and actions of peers, parents, coaches, and program administrators; norms and culture associated with particular sports or sports experiences; socially significant characteristics of sport participants; material and cultural contexts under which participation occurs; social relationships formed in connection with sport participation; meanings given to sport and personal sport experiences; the manner in which sport and sport experiences are integrated into a person's life; and the changing definitions and interpretations of sport experiences that occur during the life course. As the PYD literature also acknowledges, sport may even be damaging in developmental terms, for example in the case of sports that encourage early specialisation. Here, participants may be more at risk of overuse injuries, eating and body image disorders, drop-out, and burnout (Fraser-Thomas *et al.* 2005; Côté *et al.* 2008).

The potential for positive and negative impacts to co-exist has also been observed by scholars interested in sport and youth crime prevention/reduction. Key mechanisms identified by the literature include 'diversion' (offering a physical alternative or stimulating interest in a new activity), 'deterrence' (due to the physical presence of adults such as sports coaches) and (prosocial) 'development'. The last mechanism is broad. It can encompass the theories of youth development outlined above, but also ideas of social inclusion and empowerment, since sport is often conceptualized as a 'hook' for attracting participants to programs that aim to address health, welfare, and educational problems (Hartmann 2003; Crabbe 2007). Nichols and Crow (2004), following Brantingham and Faust (1976), also distinguish between three levels of intervention: primary, secondary, and tertiary. Drawing examples from UK programs, they suggest the former operates at the level of the community and focuses on the reduction of neighbourhood disadvantage (for example, the Youth Justice Board Program, Splash). Secondary crime reduction targets 'at-risk' individuals identified as likely to commit crime (for example, the Fairbridge Program). Tertiary interventions work with young people within the criminal justice system, with the intention of preventing recidivism (for example, the West Yorkshire Sports Counselling Program). They argue that these mechanisms can apply to programs at all levels, and that understanding the intended mechanism could support more effective evaluation. Other studies have made specific recommendations about program size and organization, including the benefits of smaller groups, informal structures, and the encouragement of social relationships over competition (see Ekholm 2013 for discussion).

The relationship between high school sports participation and 'delinquency' is of long-standing interest to US sociologists of sport (Schafer 1969). Hartmann and Massoglia (2007) draw on longitudinal data to argue that the effects of involvement in high school sport are bifurcated – since sports participation is negatively associated with some deviant or criminal behaviours (e.g. shoplifting), but positively associated with others (e.g. drunken-driving) – and also enduring (relationships were observed at age 30 in their sample). Male-dominated sporting cultures can also be associated with violence and sexual assault (e.g. Messner and Sabo 1994). Assessing the impact of targeted sports-based programs is also challenging, due in part to the extent and quality of evaluation, but also to difficulties disaggregating the effects of specific interventions. Ekholm (2013: 98–102) in a recent review of the international literature on sport and crime prevention similarly argues that several main findings emerge, including: (1) there is nothing essential about sport that makes it suitable for crime prevention; (2) studies tend not to support a direct causal relationship; (3) various possible causal mechanisms have been proposed; (4) maximizing the possible impact of sport on youth crime has implications for the organization of sport programs; and (5) sport can also generate crime.

Sport scholars have also drawn on sociological and criminological theories as part of their attempts to evaluate sport as a vehicle for youth crime prevention or reduction. This includes theories of 'criminality' (i.e. why individuals become involved in crime), such as those proposed by mid-twentieth century US sociological theorists Cohen and Sutherland (Schafer 1969) and, more recently, the predictive 'risk factors' derived from developmental criminology (Farrington 2000; see, for example, Nichols 2007). Desistance research that aims to understand why people *stop* offending (for example, Maruna 2001; Laub and Sampson 2003) has also had an impact. Recent work has considered sports-based interventions with young men in custodial institutions (Parker *et al.* 2014; Van Hout and Phelan 2014) and drawn attention to the role of sport in establishing new routines and new prosocial identities, and facilitating access to broader supportive structures that promote desistence. More critical scholars have drawn on approaches that problematize 'race', gender and class/inequality to explore complexity in patterns of lawbreaking among young people, particularly the ways in which dynamic social identities, social relationships and power relationships shape complex social conditions in which individual conflict with the law is located (Hartmann 2001; Blackshaw and Crabbe 2004). In relation to Midnight Basketball, Hartmann (2001: 364) argues that the program 'served as a symbolic means by which racial stereotypes about risk, fear, and crime were reinforced and legitimated, with different possibilities to be certain, but united around beliefs about the risk and nature of risk posed by African American young men'. In so doing, the program obscured their disproportional marginalization and, in denying the role of white privilege, established the 'social problems' associated with dein-dustrialization and welfare retrenchment as 'racial problems' stemming from individual deficits.

Such accounts intersect with a third major priority for SDP provision in the global North: the role of sport in promoting 'social inclusion' and 'social integration', and developing 'social capital'. Fuller accounts of these related terms and their relationship to national and supranational policy agendas can be found elsewhere (for example, Becker *et al.* 2000; Donnelly and Coakley 2002; Collins and Kay 2014). Bailey (2005: 74) highlights: 'a broad shift from viewing social inclusion via urban regeneration largely in economic terms … to one which places more emphasis on people and the development of "social capital"' – in other words, the enhancement of social networks, civic engagement and community mobilization. As noted above, the idea of 'inclusion through sports' implies the improvement of participants' position across multiple domains, such as education, employability, housing, health, and leisure (Collins and Haudenhuyse 2015). Becker *et al.* (2000), in their report for the European Commission, explore the extent to which sport can promote intercultural understanding and the social and professional integration of young people in European Member States. The team conducted interviews and organizational visits to iden-tify 'best practice' in case study countries. There are also many positive accounts of the potential of sports-based programs to support these goals in other countries, for example in the reviews listed in the introduction. However, as Long *et al.* (2002) explore, evaluation in this field must be approached with caution: projects delivered in disadvantaged areas are not necessarily working with the socially excluded, while work with socially excluded groups can deliver benefits to individuals without promoting social inclusion. In other words, and as the next section explores, inclusion may require challenging the social, economic, and political processes associated with exclusion, and not only supporting excluded groups.

Future directions

Research on sport as a vehicle for youth and social policy objectives has flourished in recent years. This research is increasingly international in scope. Sport-focused issues of the open-access journal *Social Inclusion* (Haudenhuyse and Theeboom 2015 and Haudenhuyse 2017), for example, attracted contributions from the UK, Canada, Sweden, Belgium, Denmark, the Netherlands, the USA, Japan, and Australia, some of which involved fieldwork in additional countries. International collaborations are also increasingly common. This should advance existing knowledge by encouraging comparative research that analyses differences, as well as similarities, between national contexts.

The subfield is also extending its critical analyses of programs and the experiences of participants. A body of critical research draws upon (post)Foucauldian debates to locate sports-based interventions within historically specific articulations of power and rule – specifically, within the context of 'neoliberal' or 'advanced liberal' modes of governance (Foucault 1991; Rose and Miller 1992; Dean 2010). It has been suggested that SDP provision contributes to neo-liberal strategies of 'responsibilization', involving the reconfiguration of citizen-state relationships in a context of welfare retrenchment, market-led reform in formerly public services, and the promotion of notions of active citizenship and community mobilization. Authors have argued that increasingly conditional and targeted services position 'risks' associated with structural inequalities as amenable to individual-level intervention, assuming that 'role models' (i.e. SDP staff) can guide participants in a process of self-transformation that leaves them equipped to self-govern and navigate uncertain futures (Spaaij 2009; Hartmann and Kwauk 2011; Kelly 2013;

Ekholm 2017, see also Haudenhuyse *et al.* 2012). Analyses of 'governmentality' have been influential in many policy-focused fields, and a growing cross-disciplinary body of empirical work is exploring how strategies of responsibilization are realized – or not – in interactions between participants and professionals (see Juhila *et al.* 2017 for discussion). SDP researchers interested in supporting genuinely 'transformative' alternatives to forms of provision that reproduce inequality must therefore engage with the practice as well as the politics of SDP (Hartmann and Kwauk 2011; Darnell *et al.* 2016).

The project of 'de-colonizing the SDP research space and SDP more generally' (Darnell *et al.* 2016: 14) involves questioning power relations in academic collaborations, and collaborations between researchers and practitioners, as well as the dominant discourses perpetuated in sport and social policy. This project is central to the analysis of provision in the global North as well as the South, since the contribution of sport to assimilative nationalism is intertwined with the history of targeted interventions sketched above (Donnelly and Coakley 2002). Research deploying critical theoretical frameworks highlights how this legacy is reflected in contemporary attempts to use sports-based programs as a vehicle to 'integrate' postcolonial diasporas in multicultural societies, or to assist with the resettlement of young people from refugee backgrounds (for example, Jeanes *et al.* 2014). Other forms of power relation are also problematized. As Collison *et al.* (2017: 225) note, 'youth tends to present itself as a masculine term'. References to 'young people' within policy and research in the global North can conceal a gender imbalance across participants in SDP provision, as well as generally lower female participation rates in sport (Collins and Kay 2014). This unequal access has encouraged programs specifically intended to promote girls' access to sport, but critical analysis goes further: to problematize male power and dominance in sport, to explore its intersection with other forms of privilege and subordination (e.g. in relation to 'race'/ ethnicity, class, sexuality, ability, etc.), and to propose alternatives. Programs targeting other marginalized groups, such as disabled young people, also offer a site for rich, intersectional analyses of experiences and processes of exclusion, as well as assessments of the extent to which these initiatives facilitate inclusion or support. Future work is likely to further engage with these themes.

Notes

1 The term SDP is increasingly applied to activities in the global North as well as the global South. Authors focused on the North have historically tended to use other terms, including programs for 'at-risk' youth, youth development programs, and sports-based interventions. A range of terms are therefore used in this chapter to refer to programs in which the social benefits of sport are emphasised.
2 Although paradigmatic in its funding arrangements and its use of sport 'as a hook', Midnight Basketball differs from many youth programs due to its focus on young adults, rather than school-age young people.

References

Atherley, K. M. (2006). *Sport and Community Cohesion in the 21st Century: Understanding Linkages Between Sport, Social Capital and the Community*. Leederville: Western Australia Department of Sport and Recreation.

Bailey, R. (2005). Evaluating the relationship between physical education, sport and social inclusion. *Educational Review*, 57(1), 71–90.

Becker, P., Brandes, H., Kilb, R., Opper, E., Stolz, H. J., Vestweber, K., Eifrig, M. and Jeglitza, M. (2000). Study on Sport as a Tool for the Social Integration of Young People. No. 1999-0458/001-001 SVE – SVE4ET. Homburg, GOPA-Consultants.

Blackshaw, T. and Crabbe, T. (2004). *New Perspectives on Sport and 'Deviance': Consumption, Performativity and Social Control*. Abingdon: Routledge.

Brantingham, P. J. and Faust, F. L. (1976). A conceptual model of crime prevention. *Crime and Delinquency, 22*(3), 284–296.

Cavallo, D. (1981). *Muscles and Morals: Organized Playgrounds and Urban Reform, 1880–1920*. Philadelphia: University of Pennsylvania.

Coakley, J. (2011). Youth sports: What counts as 'positive development?', *Journal of Sport and Social Issues, 35*(3), 306–324.

Coalter, F. (2007). *A Wider Social Role for Sport: Who's Keeping the Score?* Abingdon: Routledge.

Coalter, F., Long, J. and Duffield, B. S. (1988). *Recreational Welfare: The Rationale for Public Leisure Policy*. Aldershot: Gower.

Collins, M. and Haudenhuyse, R. (2015). Social exclusion and austerity policies in England: The role of sports in a new area of social polarisation and inequality?' *Social Inclusion, 3*(3), 5–18.

Collins, M. and Kay, T. (2014) *Sport and Social Exclusion, 2nd Edition*. Abingdon: Routledge.

Collison, H., Darnell, S., Giulianotti, R. and Howe P. D. (2017). The inclusion conundrum: A Critical account of youth and gender issues within and beyond sport for development and peace interventions. *Social Inclusion, 5*(2), 223–231.

Council of Europe. (1975). *The European Sport for All Charter*. Strasbourg, Council of Europe/Committee for the Development of Sport.

Council of Europe. (2001). *The European Sports Charter (Revised)*. Brussels: Council of Europe.

Council of the European Union. (2010). *Conclusions of 18 November 2010 on the Role of Sport as a Source and Driver for Active Social Inclusion (Official Journal 3.12.2010 C326/5–7)*. Brussels: Council of the European Union.

Côté, J., Strachan, L. and Fraser-Thomas, J. (2008). Participation, personal development and performance through youth sport. In N. L. Holt (ed.), *Positive Youth Development through Sport*. London: Routledge.

Crabbe, T. (2007) Reaching the 'hard to reach': Engagement, relationship building and social control in sport based social inclusion work. *International Journal of Sport Management and Marketing, 2*(1–2), 27–40.

Darnell, S., Chawansky M., Marchesseault, D., Holmes, M. and Hayhurst, L. (2016). The state of play: Critical sociological insights into recent 'sport for development and peace' research. *International Review for the Sociology of Sport*. First published online: 11 May 2016. Available at: https://doi.org/10.1177/1012690216646762.

Davies, B. (1986). *Threatening Youth: Towards a National Youth Policy*. Milton Keynes: Open University Press.

Dean, M. (2010). *Governmentality: Power and Rule in Modern Society (2nd edn)*. London: Sage.

Donnelly, P. and Coakley, J. (2002). *The Role of Recreation in Promoting Social Inclusion*. Toronto, ON: Laidlaw Foundation.

Dunne, A., Ulicna, D., Murphy, I. and Golubeva, M. (2015). *Working with Young People: The Value of Youth Work in the European Union*. Brussels: European Commission.

Ekholm, D. (2013). Research on sport as a means of crime prevention in a Swedish welfare context: A literature review. *Scandinavian Sport Studies Forum, 4*: 91–120.

Ekholm, D. (2017). Sport-based risk management: Shaping motivated, responsible and self-governing citizen subjects. *European Journal for Sport and Society, 14*(1), 60–78.

European Commission. (2007). *White Paper on Sport, COM(2007)391 Final*. Brussels: European Commission.

Farrington, D. P. (2000) Explaining and preventing crime, *Criminology, 38*(1), 1–24.

Foucault, M. (1991). Governmentality. In G. Burchell, C. Gordon and P. Miller (eds), *The Foucault Effect: Studies in Governmentality*. Chicago: University of Chicago Press.

Fraser-Thomas, J. L., Côté, J. and Deakin, J. (2005). Youth sport programs: an avenue to foster positive youth development. *Physical Education and Sport Pedagogy, 10*(1), 19–40.

Giulianotti, R. (2004). Human rights, globalization and sentimental education: The case of sport. *Sport in Society, 7*(3), 355–369.

Giulianotti, R. (2011). Sport, peacemaking and conflict resolution: A contextual analysis and modelling of the sport, development and peace sector. *Ethnic and Racial Studies, 34*(2), 207–228.

Green, M. (2007). Olympic glory or grassroots development?: Sport policy priorities in Australia, Canada and the United Kingdom, 1960–2006. *The International Journal of the History of Sport, 24*(7), 921–953.

Green, M. (2009). Podium or participation? Analysing policy priorities under changing modes of sport governance in the United Kingdom. *International Journal of Sport Policy and Politics, 1*(2), 121–144.

Hall, G. S. (1904). *Adolescence: Its Psychology and its Relations to Physiology, Anthropology, Sociology, Sex, Crime, Religion, and Education (Vols I and II)*. New York: D. Appleton and Co.

Hartmann, D. (2001). Notes on midnight basketball and the cultural politics of recreation, race and at-risk urban youth. *Journal of Sport and Social Issues, 25*(4), 339–371.

Hartmann, D. (2003). Theorizing sport as social intervention: A view from the grassroots. *Quest, 55*(2), 118–40.

Hartmann, D. (2016). *Midnight Basketball: Race, Sports, and Neoliberal Social Policy,* Chicago, IL: University of Chicago Press.

Hartmann, D. and Depro, B. (2006). Rethinking sports-based community crime prevention. *Journal of Sport and Social Issues, 30*(2), 180–196.

Hartmann, D. and Kwauk, C. (2011). Sport and development: An overview, critique, and reconstruction. *Journal of Sport and Social Issues, 35*(3), 284–305.

Hartmann, D. and Massoglia, M. (2007). Re-assessing high school sports participation and deviance in early adulthood: evidence of enduring, bifurcated effects. *The Sociological Quarterly, 48*(3), 485–505.

Haudenhuyse, R. (2017). Sport for social inclusion: Questioning policy, practice and research. *Social Inclusion, 5*(2), 85–90.

Haudenhuyse, R. P. and Theeboom, M. (2015). Sport for social inclusion: Critical analyses and future challenges. *Social Inclusion, 3*(3), 1–4.

Haudenhuyse, R. P., Theeboom, M. and Coalter, F. (2012). The potential of sports-based social interventions for vulnerable youth. *Journal of Youth Studies, 15*(4), 437–454.

Heinemann, K. (2005). Sport and the welfare state in Europe. *European Journal of Sport Science, 5*(4), 181–188.

Hendrick, H. (1990). *Images of Youth: Age, Class and the Male Youth Problem 1880–1920,* Oxford: Clarendon Press.

Holt, N. L. (ed.) (2008). Introduction: Positive youth development through sport. *Positive Youth Development through Sport.* Abingdon: Routledge.

Holt, R. (1992). *Sport and the British: A Modern History.* Oxford: Clarendon Press.

Jeanes, R., O'Connor, J. and Alfrey, L. (2015). Sport and the resettlement of young people from refugee backgrounds in Australia. *Journal of Sport and Social Issues, 39*(6), 480–500.

Juhila, K., Raitakari, S. and Hall, C. (eds) (2017) *Responsibilisation at the Margins of Welfare Services.* Abingdon: Routledge.

Kelly, L. (2013). Sports-based interventions and the local governance of youth crime and antisocial behaviour. *Journal of Sport and Social Issues, 37*(3), 261–283.

Laub, J. H. and Sampson, R. J. (2003). *Shared Beginnings, Divergent Lives: Delinquent Boys to Age 70.* Cambridge, MA: Harvard University Press.

Long, J., Welch, M., Bramham, P., Hylton, K., Lloyd, E., Bowden K. and Robinson, P. (2002). *Count Me In: The Dimensions of Social Inclusion through Culture and Sport.* Leeds: Leeds Metropolitan University.

MacAloon, J. J. (ed.) (2008). *Muscular Christianity in Colonial and Post-Colonial Worlds.* Abingdon: Routledge.

Mangan, J. A. (1981). *Athleticism in the Victorian and Edwardian Public School: The Emergence and Consolidation of an Educational Ideology.* Cambridge: Cambridge University Press.

Maruna, S. (2001). *Making Good: How Ex-convicts Reform and Rebuild their Lives.* Washington, DC: American Psychological Association.

McCrone, K. E. (1984). Play Up! Play Up! And Play the Game! Sport at the Late Victorian Girls' Public School. *Journal of British Studies, 23*(2), 106–134.

Messner, M. A. and Sabo, D. (1994). *Sex, Violence and Power in Sports.* Freedom, CA: Crossing.

Morris, L., Sallybanks, J. and Willis, K. (2003). *Sport, Physical Activity and Anti-social Behaviour in Youth (No. 49).* Canberra: Australian Institute of Criminology.

Newman, J. (ed.) (2005). *Remaking Governance: Peoples, Politics and the Public Sphere.* Bristol: Policy Press.

New Zealand Institute of Economic Research, Inc. (2000). *The Government's Role in Sport, Fitness, and Leisure.* Wellington: NZIER.

Nichols, G. (2007). *Sport and Crime Reduction: The Role of Sports in Tackling Youth Crime.* London: Routledge.

Nichols, G. and Crow, I. (2004). Measuring the impact of crime reduction interventions involving sports activities for young people. *The Howard Journal of Criminal Justice, 43*(3), 267–283.

Park, R. J. (2007). 'Boys' clubs are better than policemen's clubs': Endeavours by philanthropists, social reformers, and others to prevent juvenile crime, the late 1800s to 1917. *The International Journal of the History of Sport, 24*(6), 749–775.

Parker, A., Meek, R. and Lewis, G. (2014). Sport in a youth prison: Male young offenders' experiences of a sporting intervention. *Journal of Youth Studies, 17*(3), 381–396.

Pitter, R. and Andrews, D. L. (1997). Serving America's underserved youth: Reflections on sport and recreation in an emerging social problems industry. *Quest, 49*(1), 85–99.

Platt, A. M. (1969). *The Child Savers. The Invention of Delinquency.* Chicago: University of Chicago Press.

Reid, I., Tremblay, M., Pelletier, R. and MacKay, S. (1994). *Canadian Youth: Does Activity Reduce Risk? An Analysis of the Impact and Benefits of Physical Activity/Recreation on Canadian Youth-at-Risk.* Ottawa: Canadian Parks/Recreation Association.

Rose, N. and Miller, P. (1992). Political power beyond the state: Problematics of government. *The British Journal of Sociology, 43*(2), 173–205.

Russell, C. E. B. and Rigby, L. M. (1908). *Working Lads' Clubs.* London: Macmillan.

Schafer, W. E. (1969). Participation in interscholastic athletics and delinquency: A preliminary study. *Social Problems, 17*(1), 40–47.

Spaaij, R. (2009). Sport as a vehicle for social mobility and regulation of disadvantaged urban youth: Lessons from Rotterdam. *International Review for the Sociology of Sport, 44*(2–3), 247–64.

Springhall, J. (1977). *Youth, Empire and Society: British Youth Movements, 1883–1940.* London: Croom Helm.

Sugden, J. (2010). Teaching and playing sport for conflict resolution and co-existence in Israel. *International Review for the Sociology of Sport, 41*(2), 221–240.

Van Hout, M. C. and Phelan, D. (2014). A grounded theory of fitness training and sports participation in young adult male offenders. *Journal of Sport and Social Issues, 38*(2), 124–147.

Witt, P. A. and Crompton, J. L. (eds) (1996). *Recreation Programs that Work for At-risk Youth: The Challenge of Shaping the Future.* State College, PA: Venture.

Witt, P. A. and Crompton, J. L. (eds) (2002). *Best Practices in Youth Development in Public Park and Recreation Settings,* Ashburn, VA: National Recreation and Park Association.

32

SDP and action sports

Holly Thorpe, Nida Ahmad and Neftalie Williams

Introducing action sports for development and peace (ASDP)

To date, most research related to SDP studies has focused on evaluating, contextualizing and critiquing governmental and non-governmental (NGO) programmes that employ traditional competitive sports (i.e. soccer, basketball) to improve the health and well-being of disadvantaged groups and communities. The growth of action sports programmes for youth development, or local youths' own engagement with informal or action sports (i.e. skateboarding, surfing, parkour) in contexts of (re)development, however, have garnered considerably less attention (for exceptions see Thorpe and Rinehart 2013; Wheaton 2013; Friedel 2015; Thorpe 2016a). Since the mid and late 1990s, action sports participants have established non-profit organizations and movements relating to an array of social issues, including health (e.g. Surf Aid International – a non-profit humanitarian organization dedicated to improving the 'health, well-being and self-reliance of people living in isolated regions', particularly in popular surfing locations in Indonesia; see Thorpe and Rinehart 2013), education (e.g. Skateistan – co-educational skateboarding schooling in Afghanistan, Cambodia and South Africa; see Thorpe and Chawansky 2016), environment (e.g. Surfers Environmental Alliance [SEA]; Surfers Against Sewage [SAS] – an environmental campaign group with a mission to rid the UK coastline of sewage; see Laviolette 2006; Wheaton 2007), female empowerment (e.g. Wahine on Waves – a New Zealand organization aimed at providing girls and young women with safe and supportive opportunities to learn to surf); and anti-violence (e.g. Surfers for Peace – an informal organization aimed at bridging cultural and political barriers between surfers in the Middle East).[1]

There is considerable variation within such action sport-related non-profit organizations and social campaigns. Some ASDPs can be broadly categorized within the SDP sector since they use participation in action sports such as snowboarding, skateboarding or surfing as an 'interventionist tool to promote peace, reconciliation, and development in different locations across the world' (Giulianotti 2011: 50). For many others, while the physical act of surfing or snowboarding plays an important role in uniting members of these groups and inspiring potential donors, the action sport is not directly being used as an interventionist tool. Rather, action sport participants establish these organizations utilizing pre-existing structures and connections within and across local, national and global sporting cultures and industries to raise awareness and fundraise for issues they deem to be socially significant. While some of these organizations remain at the grassroots level and are relatively unknown beyond the local community or outside the action sport culture, others are gaining recognition from mainstream social justice and humanitarian organizations for their innovative efforts and creative strategies to facilitate change in local and global contexts.

While ASDP organizations are a relatively new topic of scholarly investigation, a few researchers are drawing on psychological theories and concepts to explain humanitarian and empathetic responses among action sport participants (see Wymer *et al.* 2008; Brymer and Oades 2009). Yet such approaches have tended to oversimplify, decontextualize and romanticize the relationship between action sport participation and activism. Arguably, recent work by sociologists and cultural geographers offers greater insight into the nuances and contradictions operating within and across these organizations and the broader social context in which they emerge (see e.g. Laviolette 2006; Wheaton 2007; Thorpe and Rinehart 2013; Thorpe 2015; 2016a). This chapter focuses on the work of the latter to provide an overview of foundational research on this topic, and the latest developments in research on ASDP initiatives around the world.

Adopting a critical development perspective, it is important to note that many ASDPs are underpinned by the same assumptions as other sport for youth development programmes. To date, the founders of most ASDP organizations have typically been action sport enthusiasts (rather than experienced humanitarian/aid workers) who became inspired to create change when they observed poverty and inequalities during their sport-related travel (see Thorpe and Rinehart 2013). In other words, action sport enthusiasts from high-income countries (HIC) have founded most ASDP initiatives in low- and middle-income countries (LMIC). Thus, action sports-related programmes similarly share critiques of neocolonialism facing other SDP organizations. Indeed, much like the 'sport evangelists' discussed by Coakley (2011), some ASDP leaders, staff and volunteers uncritically assume that action sport participation will automatically have a positive impact on 'personal character development, reforming 'at-risk' populations, and fostering social capital leading to future occupational success and civic engagement' (Coakley 2011: 308; also see Coalter 2007). Some ASDP also adopt the 'dominant vision' described by Hartmann and Kwauk (2011: 288), that is, they target marginalized young people with the aim of 'equipping them with the tools of self-improvement and management', but in so doing are 'recalibrating identities', bringing them in line with the values of the organizers and various other stakeholders (ibid.: 292). Yet other ASDPs are working to adopt what Hartmann and Kwauk (2011) term an alternative, 'interventionist approach' with the aim of contributing to 'more fundamental change and transformation' beyond the individual (ibid.: 284).

The value of ASDP

In this section we suggest that action sports offer the potential for developing different skills and learning opportunities than the sports typically used in SDP programmes (Thorpe 2015; 2016a). In contrast to organized sports such as soccer and basketball, most action sports are not based on head-to-head competition (although competitions are popular among elite performers), thus offering opportunities for youth to gain a sense of achievement without having to compete against, and beat, another opponent. Rather, participants can learn alongside one another and gain a sense of accomplishment based on their own skill development. For example, a novice skateboarder can get much satisfaction and joy from simply standing on the board and rolling a few feet along a flat surface; an intermediate skateboarder in the same space might be filled with pride when he/she successfully 'ollies' (jumps) the board a few inches off the ground; whereas an advanced skateboarder might get a sense of achievement from a 360-degree 'ollie'. When appropriately supported, action sports offer ample opportunities for individual empowerment through skills mastery (e.g. coordination, balance), as well as valuable social skills (e.g. communication, sharing of social space, understanding difference).

Many traditional sports require referees to control the play and discipline the players. Most action sports, however, are self-regulating, and thus participants often quickly develop an implicit understanding of the cultural etiquette for sharing the space. There is also a celebration of play, self-expression and creativity in the use of space and movement in many action sport cultures, which may offer unique opportunities for skill development, communication and respect between participants in developing nations or war-torn communities. According to Sharla Nolan, one of the co-founders of Skateistan, skateboarding is 'a fantastic tool for communication': 'We get kids from all different ethnicities building relationships with each other. So we've got Hazera kids with Tajik kids' skateboarding together (cited in *Skateistan*: The Movie). Arguably, many current SDP youth programmes could be redesigned to provide more opportunities for shared experiences based on non-competitive achievement that respect individual differences, celebrate creative self-expression and embrace peer-mentoring rather than hierarchical coach-athlete relationships in competitive environments that clearly distinguish the winners and losers and those with power/knowledge and those without.

In contrast to many traditional, organized sports that were designed by men for men, most action sports developed in a different gender context. As such, (western) women have been active participants from very early in the development of many action sports, thus offering opportunities for alternative gender relations (Thorpe and Olive 2016). While most traditional sports divide men and women into two separate and distinct groups, in many action sports, girls, boys, men and women often share the same space (e.g. the waves, a skateboard park, an indoor climbing facility), participating alongside friends and/or family members from both sexes and of varying ages and ability levels. Moreover, many action sports (e.g. skateboarding, parkour) do not so explicitly privilege the male body (e.g. speed, upper body strength, physical force) as sports such as rugby, ice hockey or American Football. Rather, the gender-neutral traits of balance, coordination, personal style and the creative use of space are highly valued within action sport cultures, such that boys and girls do not need to be separated in the learning experience (although, in some cultural context it might be inappropriate) and can learn to respect one another and enjoy participating together.

Arguably, well-designed and critically considered action sports programmes can offer a valuable contribution to the SDP movement by offering empowering learning experiences, encouraging self-expression, creative thinking and developing a different set of physical and social skills among youth from different socio-economic and cultural backgrounds. Of course, such development outcomes are not automatic based on the type of sport being utilized, and thus we cannot assume simple distinctions between ASDP and SDP organizations. Developing in a different historical context and underpinned by a different set of cultural values, however, action sport cultures may offer something unique to the SDP community. Wheaton's (2013) analysis of skateboarding among street children in (post-apartheid) South Africa, suggests that the 'newness' of skateboarding was an important factor in its appropriation by young, black South Africans because 'it represented a rejection of the traditional colonial sports of rugby and cricket' (Wheaton 2013: 108). Founder of Skateistan, Oliver Percovich makes a similar observation in regard to the potential for girls skateboarding participation in Afghanistan, explaining: 'lots of sports here are seen as for boys [but] skateboarding was too new to be related to gender' (personal communication 2011).

While action sports may not be entrenched with the same histories of exclusion, marginalization and inequality as many traditional sports, it would be a mistake to romanticize action sports as offering a panacea for the field of SDP. As various sociologists of sport have shown, action sport cultures are often dominated by upper-middle-class young, white, males whom tend to embrace risk-taking and hedonistic lifestyles. Indeed, not dissimilar from many traditional sports, action sport cultures are often hierarchically organized, with forms of sexism, homophobia and racism present particularly among fratriarchal groups (see Thorpe and Olive 2016). The key point here is that it is not necessarily the type of sport that distinguishes programmes for youth development, but rather the educational and pedagogical vision underpinning such programmes (Hartmann and Kwauk 2011: 287). Thus, it is only when critically developed and appropriately supported that ASDPs can provide empowering learning experiences that encourage self-expression and creative thinking and can develop a different set of physical and social skills among children and youth of both sexes and from varying ability levels and socio-economic and cultural backgrounds.

Key issues in ASDP

In the final section of this chapter we provide insights into some key issues within the field of ASDP and current literature emerging on the topic. In particular, we critically discuss the implications of the 'Girl Effect' in action sports programmes, the increasing use of action sports for 'cause marketing' and diplomacy, and recent calls for paying greater attention to grassroots action sports initiatives, youth agency and creativity in local contexts.

The Girl Effect in ASDP: the need for postcolonial feminisms

Over the past decade, we have seen the emergence of informal and formal action sport for development and peacebuilding (ASDP) programs focused on girls and women's empowerment in contexts of poverty, conflict and systemic disadvantage. For example, Waves of Freedom proclaims to use surfing as 'a tool for gender engagement and gender equity across cultures' and to create 'self-empowered individuals who are active agents of change in their communities and beyond'. Easkey Britton, an Irish professional big-wave surfer, founded this female-focused ASDP after she became the first woman to surf in Iran. In her own words, 'I see surfing as a great leveller, a sport that Iranian women could claim as their own and use to empower themselves' (Britton 2014: 1). A similar example is the Bangladesh Surfer Girls Project which provides scholarships to orphaned and disabled girls selected from women-headed households in Bangladesh, and offers 'child friendly quality education and sports and cultural training opportunities' to help 'prepare the girls for a better life as independent women' (cited in Thorpe and Chawansky 2016: 140). In 2013, the organization offered 54 scholarships, with three surfing trips included in their curriculum. However, to critically understand the growth of, and operations within, such initiatives, it is important to locate them within the broader context of the 'Girl Effect' in development.

Since the mid-2000s, there has been a 'turn to girls' and a 'girl powering' of development (Koffman and Gill 2013). Originally coined by Nike Foundation in 2008, the 'Girl Effect' has become a key development discourse taken up by a wide range of governmental organizations, charities, and non-governmental organizations (NGOs). Underpinning this movement is the belief – endorsed by an alliance of multinational corporations, charity and NGO leaders and governmental representatives – that 'when given the opportunity, women and girls are more effective at lifting themselves and their families out of poverty, thereby having a multiplier effect within their villages, cities, and nations' (Shain 2013: 2). Adopting a post-structuralist, post-colonial and feminist critique, Koffman and Gill (2013 : 84) illustrate how the Girl Effect discourse 'articulates notions of girlhood, empowerment, development and the Global North/ South divide'. In so doing, they reveal its

> selective uptake of feminism and how it yokes discourses of girl power, individualism, entre-preneurial subjectivity and consumerism [together with] rhetorics of 'revolution' in a way that – perhaps paradoxically – renders invisible the inequalities, uneven power relations and structural features of neoliberal capitalism that produce the very global injustices that the Girl Effect purports to challenge.
>
> *Koffman and Gill 2013: 86*

In the subtle shift from women to girls, Sensoy and Marshall (2010) refer to the 'newly emergent discursive strategies that construct first world girls as the saviours of their "Third World" sisters' as 'missionary girl power' (Sensoy and Marshall 2010: 296). As various SDP scholars have explained, many SDP initiatives are including girl-focused programs to latch onto this current cultural moment (Chawansky and Hayhurst 2015) and many of the sensibilities of the Girl Effect are evident in such projects (Hayhurst 2014). As McDonald (2015) argues, too many 'sport for girls development' programmes assume a 'taken-for-granted liberatory character' focusing on 'sport's allegedly progressive role in supporting gender equality' without considering the complexities of creating long-term, sustainable changes for the lives of girls and women in local contexts (MacDonald 2015: 1). Continuing, she cites the work of Wilson (2011), who suggests that the focus on girls agency and 'women's ability to make decisions and choices', has had the result of 'largely shift[ing] attention away from both material structures of power and gendered ideologies' (Wilson 2011: 317 cited in McDonald 2015: 9).

Arguably, many of these critiques apply to ASDP initiatives aimed at 'empowering' girls and women in LMIC's through surfing, skateboarding, snowboarding and other action sports. As Thorpe and Chawansky (2016) argue, many such programmes give little consideration of the broader forms of religious, cultural, national, and international power relations operating on and through girls and women's bodies, or local girls and women's own culturally specific forms of agency. Despite the best of intentions, as Sensoy and Marshall (2010: 308) remind us the processes and results of such activism 'can be tangled, complex, and reinforce the very power relations that these groups had meant to challenge'.

The politics of girl-focused ASDP programmes, and media coverage of their activities, demand a 'close examination of who represents whom, for what purposes and with what results' (Sensoy and Marshall 2010: 309). Some women involved in such projects are highly reflexive of their involvement, and critical of how their initiatives may be interpreted, consumed, even co-opted, by HIC's. For example, Farhana Huq, co-founder of the Bangladesh Surfer Girls Project and Brown Girl Surf organization, demonstrates an acute awareness of the problematic tendency for those from HIC's to uncritically (re)produce images of girls from LMIC's participating in action sports that offer culturally complex, and thus somewhat intriguing, images. However, they are essentially presenting these 'brown girls' as the 'exotic other[s]' (Said 1979, cited in Carmel, 2014) on boards, as Huq notes:

> There's always a lot of hype when people discover girls are surfing in such a poor region. All of a sudden, the western world wants to come in and help everyone. While well intended, sometimes surfing is confused with being an answer to helping people overcome systemic poverty … So it's great there are pictures of under-resourced girls popping up on surfboards, but we have to ask, then what?

Here Huq demonstrates a critical understanding of the power relations and ethics involved in the representation of girls and young women from the global South and the challenges of creating long lasting social change in local contexts. Thorpe and Chawansky (2016) have revealed similar critical understandings among the international female staff of Skateistan. According to Thorpe and Chawansky (2016), the international female staff of Skateistan are embracing Wilson's (2014) notion of the 'middle walker' as they demonstrate the ability to be 'sensitive to the problems with and potential of SDP' and actively negotiate the 'very meanings of the terms that are the foundations of SDP the field' (Wilson 2014: 23–24).

Yet such a level of awareness is not apparent across all female-focused ASDP initiatives, many of who continue to assume positions as 'the saviours of their "Third World" sisters' (Sensoy and Marshall 2010: 296) and utilize potent imagery of 'brown' girls 'popping up on surfboards' (or other action sport equipment) to help garner international attention and support for their organizations, while simultaneously raising their own public profiles as passionate activist philanthropists (Wilson 2011). As Sensoy and Marshall (2010) suggest, if we view such initiatives and representations as 'a political text mired in its social context and tied to historically bound colonial discourses and material power relations, then we can ask a different set of questions around "whom do activists represent and how far the right to represent extends" (Ignatieff 2001: 10)' (Sensoy and Marshall 2010: 309). Building upon the work of critical development and SDP scholars (i.e. Hartmann and Kwauk 2011), and particularly those engaging with feminist postcolonial theory (i.e. Hayhurst 2016), there is important work to be done that revisits the implicit assumption that global North women providing access for girls and women from the global South to participate in action sports can lead to improved gender relations, female empowerment, and to healthier and happier lives.

The rise of action sports for philanthropy and diplomacy

Following the trend of transnational corporations (i.e. the Nike Foundation) involvement in development issues more broadly, international businesses and governmental agencies are also increasingly utilizing action sports for the purposes of 'cause marketing' and diplomacy, respectively (see Thorpe 2014; 2016a; also see O'Connor 2016). In this section we briefly discuss both trends with some critical commentary on how such initiatives are being appropriated and interpreted in local contexts. Transnational corporations are increasingly co-opting and commercializing youth action sporting participation in sites of disaster and conflict. For example, in 2015 the American-based denim corporation Levi-Strauss announced that it would donate NZ$180,000 towards the building of a community skatepark in the small coastal Christchurch village of Sumner (population estimated at <4000) – a community significantly impacted by the earthquakes of 2011, with cliff collapses and rock-falls extensively damaging and destroying houses and community infrastructure. Despite having the best of intentions, this is an obvious case of 'cause marketing', and part of the broader Levis global campaign that has included building skateparks in Bolivia and India, and recently in Pine Ridge Indian reservation in South Dakota. While Levis funds the building of each of the skateparks, once built they become the responsibility of the local skateboarding community to manage and maintain. For their investment, Levis produces short videos of the building process with affecting narratives of the challenging lives of local youth. These videos are then posted and shared widely across the Internet with very little Levis branding, except for a subtle logo at the end of the videos. During interviews by the first author with those involved in the Levis global campaign, some openly admitted this campaign as an attempt to 'get the corporate stink off' the company as it continued to try to break into the difficult skateboarding industry (interviews, December 2015). Yet all involved in this campaign also strongly believed that the building of these skateparks offered something valuable to local youth, and discussed the predominantly positive responses to their initiatives from both local communities and the broader skateboarding culture. In contrast to their building projects in LMICs (i.e. Bolivia, India), however, they acknowledged that similar skatepark building projects in the global North with much tighter regulations of land access and usage are considerably more complicated, with post-disaster Christchurch – a city 'overwhelmed with bureaucracy and red-tape' (interviews, December 2015) – their most difficult project to date (see Thorpe 2016b).

Similarly, in 2011 Red Bull built the 'Mississippi Grind River Barge', a floating skatepark, which travelled 1,705 miles from Minnesota's Twin Cities to New Orleans, hosting four skateboarding competitions and various performances for communities along the way. Upon the completion of the journey, Red Bull had intended to donate the obstacles from the barge skatepark to the city of New Orleans to be placed in a public skate space, but ultimately the city could not accept the offer due to the cost of finding and establishing an appropriate site (Rice 2012). Another example was the DEWeezy indoor skateboard park that opened (briefly) in New Orleans on the seventh anniversary of Hurricane Katrina. The skatepark was opened with support of Mountain Dew, rapper Lil Wayne and the Make It Right Foundation; designed to 'echo the landscape of the Lower Ninth Ward', the skatepark was intended to become a 'beacon of hope and a rebirth for the community' (Fleming 2012). However, local skateboarders expressed concerns about the top-down approach adopted by the founders of the DEWeezy skateboard park, and were sceptical of the motives of corporate investors, such as Mountain Dew and Lil Wayne:

> the story they were trying to tell is how Mountain Dew built a skatepark to save New Orleans, but it's not even open to the public yet … Now all the local skaters hate Lil Wayne for being involved in such a superficial project.
>
> *local New Orleans skateboarder, cited in Thorpe 2016b*

Such examples suggest the need for more research that considers different strategies of 'cause marketing' and what Naomi Klein (2007) refers to as 'disaster capitalism' in the field of ASDP – with some offering more longer-term investments than others – and how local youth make meaning of different approaches to corporate investment and 'cause marketing' in geographies of (re)development.

Some governmental agencies are also recognizing the potential of action sports for the purposes of development and diplomacy. For example, the United States Department of State, Sports United division, recently worked with long-time skateboarder, photographer, lecturer and PhD candidate (and third-author) Neftalie Williams to develop a short skateboarding programme for refugees in the Netherlands. 'Meet and Play' was a programme designed by Sports United Office with the aim to use skateboarding as a tool for cultural and sport diplomacy, with a dual target audience of (1) Syrian refugee youth, granted asylum in the Netherlands, and (2) Dutch children in secondary school. The programme took place in March 2016, and included skateboarding classes for both young refugees and Dutch nationals run by Williams, with the support of local grassroots community members and the international skateboarding community. Running alongside the physical demonstrations and activity sessions was a lecture-based educational campaign for students and staff of International School of Eindhoven who then joined the team to co-produce an engaging, inclusive learning environment for both young recent immigrants and Dutch nationals.

Grassroots ASDP initiatives: rethinking top-down models of development

While recognizing the potential of such governmental and corporate-sponsored programmes for making a valuable and unique contribution to the SDP movement, we also express caution. As Thorpe (2016b) has argued elsewhere,

> before governmental agencies, SDP organisations or action sport enthusiasts from the Global North jump on the 'bandwagon' and start implementing action sport programmes in at-risk or developing communities, it is first necessary to take a closer examination of the informal sporting participation already occurring within local contexts.
>
> *Thorpe 2016b: 555*

In the remainder of this section we offer a brief case study of the development of a grassroots parkour group in Gaza to highlight the need to move beyond top-down models of development, and consider the unique forms of agency, creativity and resourcefulness being developed by local youth themselves (Thorpe and Ahmad 2015; Thorpe 2016b).

Parkour reached Gaza in 2005 (shortly after the withdrawal of the Israeli army and the dismantling of Israeli settlements), when unemployed, recent university graduate Abdullah watched the documentary Jump London on the Al-Jazeera documentary channel in his over-crowded family home in the Khan Younis refugee camp. He promptly followed this up by searching the Internet for video clips of parkour, before recruiting Mohammed to join him in learning the new sport. Continuing to develop their skills, they soon found parkour to be so much more than a sport, 'it is a life philosophy' that encourages each individual to 'overcome barriers in their own way' (cited in Shahin 2012). To avoid conflicts with family members, local residents and police, members of PK Gaza (the name chosen by the group) sought out unpopulated spaces where they could train without interruption. Popular training areas included cemeteries, the ruined houses from the Dhraha occupation, UNRWA (United Nations Relief and Works Agency) schools, and on the sandy hills in Nusseirat, formerly an Israeli settlement now deserted in the centre of Gaza City. The latter is particularly meaningful for the youth who proclaim that by practising parkour in the space, 'we demonstrate that this land is our right' (Mohammad, interview, January 2013).

As part of the younger generation of technologically savvy Gazan residents, the founders of PK Gaza are explicitly aware of the potential of the Internet for their parkour practices, and also for broader political purposes. 'We started filming ourselves with mobile phones and putting the videos on YouTube', explains Mohammed, and they have continued to develop more advanced filming techniques using borrowed cameras and editing the footage on a cheap computer (interview, January 2013). Social media sites such as Facebook, Instagram and YouTube are key spaces for interaction and dialogue with youth beyond the confines of the Gaza strip. In so doing, 'we contribute very significantly to raising international awareness of what is happening in Gaza. We offer video clips, photographs and writings related to the situation in which we live in the Gaza strip and deliver the message to all the people's that's watching online that there are oppressed people here', proclaimed Mohammed (interview, January 2013).

While raising awareness of the conditions in Gaza and offering a temporary escape from the harsh realities of everyday life, the PK Gaza team strongly advocates the socio-psychological benefits of their everyday parkour experiences. They proclaim the value of parkour for their resilience and coping with the frustrations, fears, anxieties and pains of living in the Khan Younes refugee camp. As Abdullah explains, 'I have witnessed war, invasion and killing. When I was a kid and I saw these things, blood and injuries, I didn't know what it all meant … this game [parkour] makes me forget all these things' (cited in Sorcher 2010). As the following comments from Gazan psychologist, Eyad Al Sarraj (MD) suggest, some medical and health professionals also acknowledge the value of such activities for young men living in such a stressful environment:

> Many young people in Gaza are angry because they have very few opportunities and are locked in. An art and sports form such as free running gives them an important method to express their desire for freedom and allows them to overcome the barriers that society and politics have imposed on them. It literally sets them free.
>
> *cited in Shahin 2012:17*

Such observations are supported by a plethora of research that has illustrated the value of physical play and games for resilience in contexts of high risk and/or ongoing physical and psychological stress (e.g. refugee camps), and the restorative value for children and youth who have experienced traumatic events (e.g. natural disaster, war, forced migration; see, e.g. Orayb 2005; Berinstein and Magalhaes 2009).

In sum, the brief case of PK Gaza reveals how some youth are engaging with action sport initiatives as critical resources within situations and systems where their specific needs, opinions and actions are often marginalized. Indeed, this group of youth has appealed for 'safe' indoor training spaces to train themselves and their next generation, but their calls continue to go unanswered. Arguably, such examples of grassroots youth engagement with action sports in sites of development should prompt those of us working in SDP to consider: How many other calls might we be missing when we begin with the assumption that 'our' forms of SDP programmes are going to be (part of) the answer for local youth? What might we learn about the needs, struggles and strategies of local youth when we create space for their voices and experiences before we start imagining, planning and implementing what 'we' believe are the most effective approaches for creating change in 'their' lives?' (Thorpe 2016b).

Conclusion

In this chapter we have provided an overview of the growth of ASDP organizations and initiatives around the world, and discussed the value that well-designed and supported non-competitive action sports can bring to development programmes. Alongside the rapid growth in action sport-focused NGOs has been a surge of academic interest in this field, particularly among graduate and postgraduate students, and established researchers in the field of sociology of sports. We have signalled some of the emergent themes in the field, including the need to think critically about the growth in the Girl Effect in ASDP, the involvement of transnational corporations and governments, and the need to consider local, youth-led grassroots initiatives. Other emerging areas of academic interest include the ways ASDP organizations are adopting and integrating monitoring, evaluation and learning methods into their programmes in culturally specific ways, the ways ASDP organizations are using social media in their campaigns and the ethics and risks of representing their participants in digital spaces (Thorpe, Hayhurst and Chawansky, 2018), the experiences of ASDP volunteers, and the efforts by Muslim women to negotiate their own space in action sports and ASDP initiatives. We are excited for the ongoing growth and development of the field of ASDP, and see much potential for the next generation of researchers to build upon some of the foundational research with new lines of critical questioning and interdisciplinary innovations in theory, method and practice.

Note

1   For an interactive global map of more than 200 ASDP organizations and initiatives, see www. actionsportsfordev.org

References

Berinstein, S. and Magalhaes, L. (2009). A study of the essence of play experience to children living in Zanzibar, Tanzania. *Occupational Therapy International, 16*(2), 89–106.

Britton, E. (2014). Into the Sea and Beyond the Veil in Iran. *Maptia.* Available at: https://maptia.com/easkey/stories/into-the-sea-and-beyond-the-veil-in-iran (accessed 26 April 2015).

Brymer, E. and Oades, L. (2009). 'Extreme sports: A positive transformation in courage and humility', *Journal of Humanistic Psychology, 49*(1), 114–126.

Carmel, D. (2014). Creating waves of social change with brown girl surf. *Time Travel Plans.* Avaiable at: www. timetravelplans.net/surfer-girls-brown-girl-surf/ (accessed 14 April 2015).

Chawansky, M. and Hayhurst, L. M. C. (2015). Introduction girls, international development and the politics of sport. *Sport in Society, 18*(8), 877–881.

Coakley, J. (2011). Youth sports: What counts as 'positive development'? *Journal of Sport and Social Issues, 35*(3), 306–324.

Coalter, F. (2007). *A Wider Social Role for Sport: Who's Keeping the Score?* Abingdon: Routledge.

Fleming, R. (2012). Lil' Wayne Opens Skatepark in NOLA. Available at: http://xgames.espn.go.com/skateboarding/article/8436813/lil-wayne-opens-deweezy-skatepark-new-orleans-ninth-ward (accessed 15 October 2012).

Friedel, S. (2015). *The Art of Living Sideways: Skateboarding, Peace and Elicitive Conflict Transformation.* Wiesbaden: Springer.

Giulianotti, R. (2011). The sport, development and peace sector: A model of four social policy domains. *Journal of Social Policy, 40*(4), 757–776.

Hartmann, D. and Kwauk, C. (2011). Sport and development: An overview, critique and reconstruction. *Journal of Sport and Social Issues, 35*(3), 284–305.

Hayhurst, L. M. C. (2014). The 'Girl Effect' and martial arts: Social entrepreneurship and sport, gender and development in Uganda. *Gender, Place and Culture, 21*(*3*), 297–315.

Hayhurst, L. M. C. (2016). Sport for development and peace: A call for transnational, multi-sited, post-colonial feminist research. *Qualitative Research in Sport, Exercise and Health, 8*(5), 424–443.

Klein, N. (2007). *The Shock Doctrine: The Rise of Disaster Capitalism,* New York: Metropolitan Books.

Koffman, O. and Gill, R. (2013). The revolution will be led by a 12-year-old girl: Girl power and global biopolitics. *Feminist Review, 105*(1), 83–102.

Laviolette, P. (2006). Green and extreme: Free-flowing through seascape and sewer. *Worldviews, 10*(2), 178–204.

McDonald, M. (2015). Imagining neoliberal feminisms? Thinking critically about the US diplomacy campaign, 'empowering women and girls through sports'. *Sport in Society, 18*(8), 909–922.

O'Connor, P. (2016). Skateboard philanthropy: Inclusion and prefigurative politics. In K. J. Lombard (ed.), *Skateboarding: Subcultures, Sites and Shifts.* New York: Routledge.

Orayb, S. (2005). The Forgotten Children of Albaqa'a: Children's Play in a Palestinian Refugee Camp', Unpublished thesis. University of British Columbia [online]. Available at: http://circle.ubc.ca/bit-stream/handle/2429/16203/ubc_2005-0109.pdf?sequence=1 (accessed 10 July 2013).

Rice, J. (2012). Red bull barge park floats in limbo. *ESPN.com.* Available at: http://espn.go.com/action/skateboarding/story/_/id/7484117/red-bull-barge-nola-park-floats-limbo (accessed 5 April 2016).

Said, E. (1979) *Orientalism.* New York: Vintage.

Sensoy, Ö. and Marshall, E. (2010). Missionary girl power: Saving the 'third world' one girl at a time. *Gender and Education, 22*(3), 295–311.

Shahin, M. (2012). Free running Gaza. *Saudi Aramco World.* Available at: www.saudiaramcoworld.com/issue/201206/free.running.gaza.htm (accessed 12 February 2013).

Shain, F. (2013). The girl effect: Exploring narratives of gendered impacts and opportunities in neoliberal development. *Sociological Research Online, 18*(2), 9.

Sorcher, S. (2010). Palestinian Parkour. *The New York Times.* Available at: www.nytimes. com/video/2010/10/13/world/middleeast/1248069141234/palestinian-parkour.html (accessed 9 December 2012).

Thorpe, H. (ed.) (2014). Transnational connections and transformation: Action sport for development and peace building. *Transnational Mobilities in Action Sport Cultures*. Houndmills: Palgrave Macmillan.

Thorpe, H. (2015). Natural disaster arrhythmia and action sports: The case of the Christchurch earthquake. *International Review for the Sociology of Sport, 50*(3), 301–325.

Thorpe, H. (2016a). Action sports for youth development: Critical insights for the SDP community. *International Journal of Sport Policy and Politics, 8*(1), 91–116.

Thorpe, H. (2016b). 'Look at what we can do with all the broken stuff!' Youth agency and sporting creativity in sites of war, conflict and disaster. *Qualitative Research in Sport, Exercise and Health, 8*(5), 554–570.

Thorpe, H. and Ahmad, N. (2015). Youth, action sports and political agency in the Middle East: Lessons from a grassroots parkour group in Gaza. *International Review for the Sociology of Sport, 50*: 678–704.

Thorpe, H. and Chawansky, M. (2016). The 'girl effect' in action sports for development: The case of the female practitioners of Skateistan. In H. Thorpe and R. Olive (eds), *Women in Action Sport Cultures: Identity, Politics and Experience*, Houndmills: Palgrave Macmillan.

Thorpe, H. Hayhurst, L. and Chawansky, M. (2018). The girl effect and 'positive' representations of sporting girls of the global south: Social media portrayals of Afghan girls on skateboards. In K. Toffoletti, H. Thorpe and J. Francombe-Webb (eds), *New Sporting Femininities*. Houndmills: Palgrave Macmillan.

Thorpe, H. and Olive, R. (2016). *Women in Action Sport Cultures: Identity, Politics and Experience*. Houndmills: Palgrave Macmillan.

Thorpe, H. and Rinehart, R. (2013). Action sport NGOs in a neo-liberal context: The cases of Skateistan and Surf Aid International, *Journal of Sport and Social Issues, 37*(2), 115–141.

Wheaton, B. (2007). Identity, politics, and the beach: Environmental activism in 'surfers against sewage'. *Leisure Studies, 26*(3), 279–302.

Wheaton, B. (ed.) (2013). Globalisation, identity and race: Lifestyle sport in post-apartheid South Africa. *The Cultural Politics of Lifestyle Sports*. London: Routledge.

Wilson, K. (2011). 'Race', gender and neoliberalism: Changing visual representations in development. *Third World Quarterly, 32*(2), 315–331.

Wymer, W., Self, D. and Findley, C. (2008). Sensation seekers and civic participation: Exploring the influence of sensation seeking and gender on intention to lead and volunteer. *International Journal of Non-profit and Voluntary Sector Marketing, 13*(4), 287–300.

33

SDP and homelessness

Emma Sherry and Angela Osborne

Introduction

Increasingly, sport is identified as a viable method through which to address issues of social marginalization. Although the evidence is contentious, and causal links between sport participation and social inclusion difficult to identify, the use of sport in support of beneficial outcomes for participants continues to gain momentum internationally.

This chapter examines the relationship between sport and one particular aspect of social marginalization: homelessness. It aims to provide a thematic analysis of evaluations of sport-for-development interventions aimed at homeless populations. The chapter discusses sport and homelessness through five key areas of focus: (1) defining homelessness, (2) understanding homelessness as social exclusion, (3) connecting homelessness and sport interventions, (4) critical considerations, and (5) conclusions and future directions.

Defining homelessness

Definitions of homelessness vary slightly across the world; however, vulnerability of accommodation is the common thread. According to the Australian Bureau of Statistics (2012):

> When a person does not have suitable accommodation alternatives they are considered homeless if their current living arrangement:
> a) is in a dwelling that is inadequate; or
> b) has no tenure, or if their initial tenure is short and not extendable; or
> c) does not allow them to have control of, and access to space for social relations.

Homelessness is a significant societal issue; globally, it is estimated there are 1.6 billion people living in inadequate housing, and a further 100 million people with no form of housing at all (HWC 2015). Homeless populations potentially experience a complex array of issues that necessitate addressing community reintegration, social cohesion, anti-social behavior, poor mental health, and drug and alcohol rehabilitation, among others, often requiring an integrated approach to service delivery (Sherry and O'May 2013). High incidences of poor mental and physical health have been noted in homeless populations (Sherry 2010; Randers *et al.* 2012; Sherry and O'May 2013), as have substance abuse (Biswas-Diener and Diener 2006; Magee 2011; Sherry and O'May 2013) and encounters with the legal system (Sherry 2010; Curran *et al.* 2016). Important to note, however, is that homeless populations also perceive personal strengths, enjoy activities and experiences considered otherwise 'normal', and view their housing status as a consequence of a range of factors, and not primarily constitutive of identity. Tweed, Biswas-Diener and Lehman (2012) adopted a strengths-based approach in their community psychology research with homeless people and found participants perceived many personal strengths, including 'social intelligence, kindness, persistence, authenticity, and humor' (Tweed *et al.* 2012: 481). Individuals experiencing homelessness therefore have a sense of identity founded on aspects other than their vulnerable housing (Parsell 2010). The homeless people in Biswas-Diener and Diener's (2006: 199) examination of subjective well-being 'reported surprisingly high satisfaction with domains related to the self, including morality, intelligence, and physical appearance'.

Notably, sport proficiency was also cited as positively influential on perceptions of personal strengths and identity by homeless people in Tweed *et al.*'s (2012) study. Neale, Nettleton and Pickering's (2012) research with heroin-users, some of whom were also homeless, examined sport participation and found that having aspects of a 'normal' life, including participation in sport, remained meaningful to marginalized and disenfranchised groups. This finding was confirmed in a study by Thomas, Gray and McGinty (2012: 780) that found 'keeping safe, being positive and feeling good, connecting with others, and the ability to participate in "normal" life were the key contributors of subjective wellbeing'. As expressed by a homeless participant in Parsell's (2010: 181) research, 'homeless is what I am, not who I am'.

Homelessness as social exclusion

Homelessness is a particularly acute form of social exclusion. Barry (2002: 27) identified that there are

> obvious material conditions that have to be satisfied to avoid social exclusion. The most basic is a place to live: those with 'no fixed abode' (whether sleeping rough or moving between shelters and hostels) are excluded from most forms of participation.

Homelessness, then, often equates to social exclusion.

Defined by Barry (2002: 14–15), an individual is socially excluded if:

a) he or she is geographically resident in a society; but
b) for reasons beyond his or her control, he or she cannot participate in the normal activities of citizens in that society; and
c) he or she would like to so participate.

Social exclusion can manifest in many ways, including unequal access to educational, occupational, political opportunities; it also manifests in access to sport and recreation. Sport has a long history of exclusion, both in terms of performance through the inherent competitive nature many sport practices, and through socio-demographic indicators such as gender, ethnicity, social class, and sexuality. This exclusion can also extend to socio-economic indicators through limited access to sport participation due to membership fees, equipment, transport, and requirement to pay for coaching and competition. At the same time, participation in sport can promote social inclusion and social mobility for marginalized individuals as a consequence of its support of connections between various groups and social networks (Skinner *et al.* 2008; Spaaij

2009). Social networks established and expanded through sport participation are often valuable in fostering social inclusion and helping individuals reintegrate into society by feeling part of the community and developing a sense of belonging (Sherry 2010; Sherry and Strybosch 2012; Thomas *et al.* 2012; Welty Peachey *et al.* 2013a).

Such discussions of homelessness and social exclusion often turn to the issue of social capital, which has become an important concept in the study of sport and SDP. Bourdieu (1986: 48) defined social capital as 'the aggregate of the actual or potential resources which are linked to a durable network of more or less institutionalized relationships and mutual acquaintance and recognition'. According to Bourdieu, social capital is unevenly distributed; social capital is predicated on access to resources, and is used to secure position. Bourdieu's conceptualization is focused on actors engaged in struggle and is skeptical about altruistic actions free from the constraints of individual interests. Cultural capital, also unevenly distributed, is defined by Bourdieu as the cultural goods, knowledge, experience, education, competencies, and skills that an individual possesses and that confer power or status in society.

For Coleman (1994), social capital is a more universal resource, rather than a positional good, property, or asset belonging to a social class. It is defined as 'the set of resources that inhere in family relations and in community social organization and that are useful for the cognitive or social development of a child or young person' (Coleman 1994: 300). Coleman's theory posits social capital as a way to explain how individuals cooperate through social processes – social structure and social relationships, which originate in free choice – in order to further individual self-interests.

By contrast, social capital is defined by Putnam (2000) as:

> properties of social life – such as trust, norms and networks – which promote and make it possible to achieve certain goals…like all forms of capital, social capital is productive in the sense that it makes it possible to achieve certain goals which would not have been achievable in its absence.
>
> *Putnam 2000:.167*

In Putnam's theory, there is less emphasis on kinship relations and instrumentalism, and more on social capital as a public good that binds communities together; it views social capital as the 'features of social organization such as networks, norms, and social trust that can facilitate coordination and cooperation for mutual benefit' (Putnam, 1995: 66). The theory posits that when personalized, generalized, and institutionalized trust is developed, social networks can be created, providing the potential for reciprocity to occur. Greater social solidarity and better social cohesion is theorized to emerge from increased social connectedness, particularly through the mechanisms of bonding, bridging, and linking.

Specifically, *bonding social capital* refers to social networks between homogenous groups, such as family, neighbors, or close friends. The close interaction and familiarity between individuals provides resources which they use to cope with their situations. *Bridging social capital* occurs when relationships are developed with individuals who differ from oneself and one's immediate group; these social ties and bonds may be looser and more diverse in nature providing the potential to leverage a broader range of resources than can be accessed through bonding social capital alone. *Linking social capital* refers to relationships developed with people entirely outside individuals' communities; these vertical relationships link individuals from differing social strata. The breadth of this network provides yet greater potential to more effectively leverage resources and obtain greater access to economic and material wealth, as well as cultural capital.

This discussion of social capital is important because programs seeking to harness the power of sport to re-engage disadvantaged and socially excluded people – often designed with a view to developing social capital among such populations – have proliferated in recent years. Associated with this has been a shift toward neoliberal policy frameworks – as opposed to those of the welfare state – to deliver social services, including in the area of sport. As a result, 'private–public partnerships, tax advantages (and expectations) for corporate social responsibility (CSR) and the reduction of social solidarity become key aspects of the new institutional framework' (Skinner et al. 2008: 254). Funding is often scarce and highly competitive and program organizers are required to demonstrate program efficacy according to funding regimes – which may vary over time (Schulenkorf and Adair 2014). Examples of sport interventions aimed at homeless populations that have emerged in this context include: street soccer (Sherry 2010; Magee 2011; Sherry and Strybosch, 2012; Welty Peachey et al. 2013a; Curran et al. 2016); softball (Burling et al. 1992); hockey (Holt et al. 2015; Scherer et al. 2016); physical activity (Gregg and Bedard 2016); and dance (Knestaut et al. 2010). Overall, evaluations of such programs have resulted in identification of common themes pertinent to the use of sport interventions with homeless people. The next section offers a thematic analysis of these outcomes and also discusses issues, and challenges relevant to sport-for-development interventions in homeless populations.

Homelessness sport interventions

Programs designed and developed to engage homeless populations often use sport as a 'hook' and draw on a range of sports and physical activities as the foundational activities around which the program is constructed. Such interventions do not seek to improve participants' proficiency in the activity but are more often focused on social transformation. In the case of interventions targeting homeless populations, the development of social capital is typically implicated in program objectives.

The most common example of sport programs designed for and delivered to people experiencing homelessness are the street soccer programs delivered across the globe in association with the Homeless World Cup. These programs are delivered through various non-governmental organizations and charities, such as The Big Issue, and are targeted at a grassroots level with a focus on community participation. Many of these programs are also associated with social support programs including housing, health and safety. Another example of a program for the homeless community is Back on My Feet, which develops running programs for residents of homeless facilities across the USA, and aims to cultivate participants' commitment to run three days per week during a 30-day period. Once participants have completed this initial phase, they are moved into the Next Steps program, which provides education and employment support.

Evaluations of these kinds of sport programs for homeless populations have revealed several areas in which interventions have had an impact. Participants have reported improved health and self-esteem, increased connectedness and improved social networks, reductions in anti-social and harmful behaviors, and some success in addressing issues of unemployment and homelessness. Each of these findings is discussed here.

Improved health

A commonly reported outcome emerging from evaluations of SFD interventions with homeless populations is that individuals feel fitter and more physically capable (Sherry 2010; Magee 2011; Randers et al. 2012; Sherry and Strybosch 2012; Curran et al. 2016; Gregg and Bedard 2016). Better sleep, reduced stress, and better mental health have also been reported as a result of participation in sport and physical activity programs (Knestaut *et al.* 2010; Sherry and Strybosch 2012; Sherry and O'May 2013). For example, a participant in Sherry and Strybosch's (2012) research with the Community Street Soccer Program (CSSP), the weekly session run by The Big Issue (2017) around Australia, from which national representatives for the Homeless World Cup team are drawn, summarized the impact participation had on his mental health: 'You haven't got time to be depressed if you have to chase a man and a ball' (Sherry and Strybosch 2012: 503). Participants reported using sport participation as a coping strategy to deal with situations that would previously have caused a relapse into substance abuse or been a source of significant stress or mental health issues (Magee 2011; Sherry and O'May 2013; Curran *et al.* 2016). Participation has also been cited as representing a positive distraction (Sherry 2010) or something to look forward to (Holt *et al.* 2015). The requirement to be immersed in the immediate activity has also been singled out as beneficial for managing mental health problems (Sherry and Strybosch 2012) and relieving stress (Knestaut *et al.* 2010).

Programs have also been found to provide structure (Burling 1992; Sherry 2010; Curran *et al.* 2016) around which homeless individuals can begin to organize (Holt *et al.* 2015), and even access mental and physical health support (Sherry 2010; Sherry and O'May 2013 ; Curran *et al.* 2016). Participation in a regular event which includes social interactions and responsibilities has been cited as a positive outcome of participation, as a participant in Curran *et al.*'s study articulated:

> I'd only sit around or get myself into trouble again if I wasn't coming here. ... I've made some good mates, before this I just f★★★★★' sat in every, day ... all day. It was depressin' but now I've got something to look forward to and I'm loads fitter.
>
> *Curran et al. 2016: 19*

Enjoying improved health and fitness has in turn been consistently linked to improved self-esteem (Sherry 2010; Sherry and Strybosch 2012; Welty Peachey *et al.* 2013a; Curran *et al.* 2016).

Self-esteem

Increased self-esteem is another commonly cited outcome of participation. Individuals in a range of interventions reported feeling more confident (Sherry and Strybosch 2012), having a renewed sense of pride (Sherry 2010; Welty Peachey *et al.* 2013a), positive psychosocial development (Curran *et al.* 2016), and increased belief in their abilities (Cohen and Welty Peachey 2015). Increased masculine capital – competence in traditionally masculine behaviors, providing masculine credit – stemming from sanctioned physicality was cited as positively influential on self-esteem in Holt, Scherer and Koch's (2015) study with homeless veterans attending a floor hockey program in Canada. Improvements in technical skills and perceived sport competence have also been reported as a source of pride, impacting positively on participants' self-esteem (Magee 2011; Sherry 2010), and providing some confirmation of the mediating effects of sport participation on self-esteem (Sonstroem 1997). Participants attending the Homeless World Cup in Sherry's (2010) and Sherry and Strybosch's (2012) research reported high levels of self-satisfaction after being selected for the Australian team. Welty Peachey *et al.*'s (2013a) US street soccer participants likewise reported improvements in self-esteem.

However, Magee and Jeanes' (2011) research provided a counterpoint to these positive outcomes; their study of the experiences of the Welsh HWC team revealed that, although there were positive outcomes for some team members, several experienced a detriment to their self-esteem as a result of humiliating defeats on the field. Differing approaches to team composition and differing access to resources, in concert with varying international approaches to engaging in the HWC – such as prioritizing competitive aspects – led to an uneven competition in which less-skilled and less well-resourced teams were disadvantaged, resulting in reductions of the self-esteem of the Welsh players (Magee and Jeanes 2011). Still, defeats and challenges do not necessarily result in reduced self-esteem, as Burling's (1992) research with a softball team comprised of homeless men demonstrated. That study found that dealing with the disappointments and challenges 'on the softball diamond' (Burling, 1992: 412) encouraged participants to deal with challenging situations by 'provid[ing] support and feedback for trying new coping strategies' (ibid.). Overall, the competitive nature of sport, and its ability to discourage participation and/or build resilience among participants, is an important topic across the SFD research. As noted above, the focus and design of the program or event, and the associated supports available for participants affects the participant experience and opportunities for personal growth through the activity. As a result, at all times the design of programs and initiatives need to clearly focus on the desired developmental outcomes, rather than the sport activity itself.

Social networks

The development of social networks is arguably the most influential aspect of sport participation, leading to positive outcomes for program participants, particularly in developing social capital. Participants in sport interventions aimed at homeless people commonly cite making friends (Sherry 2010; Magee 2011; Welty Peachey et al. 2013a) and having improved social networks as positive outcomes (Sherry and Strybosch 2012; Sherry and O'May 2013; Holt et al. 2015; Curran et al. 2016). For example, participants in Knestaut and colleagues' (2010) dance program described the program's impact in terms of providing a sense of purpose, founded largely on the social interactions enjoyed in the movement class. The men in Curran et al.'s (2016) study were classified as hard to reach' (HTR), a term 'often used within the health sector when referring to individuals who find it difficult to engage in physical activity (PA) and/or positive health behaviours, or who do not access the allied health services that are available to them' (Curran et al. 2016: 15). The study evaluated a 12-week sport intervention delivered by Everton Football Clubs' Football in the Community (FitC) scheme, part of a national program of men's health delivered in/by English Premier League (EPL) football clubs, attended by men living in homeless shelters and/or recovering from substance misuse (Curran et al. 2016). Attendance at the program was hampered by factors originating in individuals' complex forms of disadvantage; however, the authors note that community-based sport interventions endorsed by professional sports properties are well positioned to engage HTR populations, evidenced by many participants seeking to continue their engagement. Despite participants' individual challenges in attending, the study 'identified specific psychosocial effects of engaging in a Football in the Community programme, most notably, the development of structure, social interaction and social capital amongst the participants' (Curran et al. 2016: 20).

Similarly, homeless veterans attending a weekly floor hockey program in Holt et al.'s (2015: 528) research cited 'being part of a group' and relationships formed with one another as key positive outcomes of participation, and largely therapeutic in terms of self-esteem and developing a sense of connectedness. Holt et al. (2015) found that participants developed relationships with support staff that facilitated asking for help in a manner that was culturally and socially appropriate. This was engendered through the program by providing an opportunity for the participants to build trust, which was seen to be particularly important for participants who may be distrustful of institutions. Increased social connectedness and the development of increased social capital as a result of regular social interaction can also have positive impacts in other life spheres, including seeking treatment for harmful behaviors (Sherry and Strybosch 2012; Holt *et al.* 2015).

Reduction in harmful behaviors

A reduction in harmful behaviors has also been noted as a positive outcome of participation in sport for homeless people. As mentioned previously, homeless participants commonly experience a range of disadvantage; these co-morbidities are exacerbated by a lack of permanent safe accommodation (Sherry 2010; Magee 2011; Curran *et al.* 2016). Participation in sport interventions has been cited as influential in reducing harmful behaviors (Sherry 2010; Magee 2011; Sherry and Strybosch 2012; Sherry and O'May 2013). Participants in soccer-based interventions all described positive movement toward cessation of harmful behaviors, including reduction in smoking and substance abuse, and in some cases, seeking treatment in detox facilities (Sherry 2010; Magee 2011; Sherry and Strybosch 2012; Sherry and O'May 2013). Burling's (1992) research was aimed at preventing relapse with substance-addicted homeless veterans; participants in that softball program were almost twice as likely to remain abstinent post-program as the non-participant cohort, and they relapsed far less frequently. As previously mentioned, participation has also been reported as representing a distraction from stressful experiences, an alternative avenue for coping with difficult situations (Burling 1992; Knestaut *et al.* 2010; Sherry and Strybosch 2012). Further, the desire to live up to expectations, and not to let the team down, was an important factor in such abstinence decisions, further underscoring the influence and importance of social connectedness on positive program outcomes.

Long-term impacts

In addition to helping develop social networks, sport interventions' success in assisting individuals to transcend their situation often requires providing connections with support services dealing with specific issues. For example, mental and physical health and social welfare agencies were involved with street soccer sessions in Sherry and colleagues' (2010; 2012; 2013) and Welty Peachey *et al.*'s (2013a) research, as they were in Holt *et al.*'s (2015) hockey sessions, and Curran *et al.*'s (2016) FitC sessions, all of which provided participants with immediate access to key sources of aid. Engagement with such services is an essential aspect of sport programs, as program attendees commonly experience difficulty accessing psychosocial support (Curran *et al.* 2016). The provisions of such, in the context of a safe environment, have been shown to be effective in preparing participants for the future. To provide an illustrative, if singular, example, Cohen and Welty Peachey's (2015: 111) narrative enquiry examining a Street Soccer USA (SSUSA) participant's journey from 'participant to cause champion' demonstrated the important impact that participation in sport intervention programs targeting homelessness can make. Through participation in the intervention and engagement with social support services, the participant was empowered to consider a different future, to consolidate her personal strengths, and to forge a future in championing the cause of street soccer.

Providing a safe space in which to forge social connections is also argued to be foundational in successful sport-for-development programming (Spaaij and Schulenkorf 2014). 'Conceptualized as a multidimensional process that involves physical, psychological/affective, sociocultural, political, and experimental dimensions' (Spaaij and Schulenkorf 2014: 633), the provision of a safe environment, in which individuals engage in experiences and activities routinely enjoyed by the wider population, is a key preliminary factor in affecting social transformation. Using Chalip's (2006) social leverage theory, Welty Peachey *et al.* (2015) analyzed SSUSA Cup events to determine the extent to which they were appropriate environments in which to achieve social transformation. They assessed events' liminality – defined as a conceptual space and time in which individuals are transitioning from one state of being into another, and the 'in-between' moments which hold the potential for change – and *communitas* – defined as an unstructured state in which individuals share equal status and common experiences. They found that the sport intervention was successful in cultivating liminality and *communitas* and foundational to the accrual of social capital (Welty Peachey *et al.* 2015). Providing a safe space (Spaaij and Schulenkorf 2014) that includes ready access increases the likelihood of engagement with such drug treatment supports (Sherry and O'May 2013). Therefore, sport interventions can become a potential site in which to build on existing personal strengths, consider the construction of alternative identities (Harris 2011), and aspire to alternative futures (Appadurai 2004).

Critical considerations

With all of this research in mind, it is important not to overstate the positive results that such interventions are able to achieve. Despite evidence of positive movement toward healthier decision-making (Sherry 2010; Magee 2011; Sherry and Strybosch 2012; Sherry and O'May 2013), comparatively high levels of substance abuse and other harmful behaviors are still noted in many post-program participant cohorts. Indeed, the limited ability of sport-for-development programs to address the underlying causes of homelessness and individuals' disadvantage, and the potential for such interventions to simply act as a form of social control rather than an avenue for social mobility, are criticisms of such interventions (Spaaij 2009; Coalter 2010; Magee and Jeanes 2011; Coakley 2015). Moreover, uncritical programming risks reproducing inequities if it lacks consideration of structural constraints and prioritizes competition and winning over other development goals, such as participation and inclusion (Magee 2011; Magee and Jeanes 2011). Concerns have also been raised about the limited effectiveness of interventions that are aimed at improving the experiences of individuals without addressing the issues which underpin their disadvantage (Coalter 2010; Magee and Jeanes 2011; Coakley 2015). Indeed, several scholars argue that a focus on the micro – the individual – fails to affect lasting change, as the structures and power relations that constrain individuals' social mobility remain relatively untouched (Coalter 2010; Magee and Jeanes 2011; Coakley 2015).

Nonetheless, sport interventions' capacity to generate positive micro-level outcomes for individual participants has been confirmed by numerous evaluations of sport interventions, and there is some evidence to suggest that at the micro-level, interventions can achieve some longevity. The homeless veterans attending the softball program in Burling's (1992) research, for example, remained in treatment for much longer than the non-participant group and were far less likely to relapse into substance abuse. Similarly, Scherer *et al.* (2016: 185) demonstrated how a Canadian sport-for-development program 'served as a communal "hub" within a network of social solidarity and as a crucial site for marginalized individuals to negotiate, and, at times, resist conditions of precarious labor'. Their analysis used the radical philosophy of Hardt and Negri (2009) to argue that participation in the weekly floor hockey program represented a resistance to the constraints of the status of homelessness itself. Their study also demonstrated how the program became a site in which participants exchanged information about the labor market, sometimes providing information about available work. More commonly, and more influentially, however, participants engaged in human interaction that consolidated their individual sense of worth as members of the labor force. Having experienced exploitative employer practices, participants in Scherer *et al.*'s (2016) research were highly cognizant of the inequities they faced in the labor market and the ways in which a reduction in social solidarity has become a key aspect of 'the new institutional framework' (Scherer *et al.* 2016: 254) of the current neoliberal context (Skinner *et al.* 2008). In response, sport-based programming became a valuable site for these men to reassert their sense of self as valuable members of the labor force through social interaction. As a result, Scherer *et al.* (2016) argued that sport interventions can become 'spaces where even the most marginalized can creatively explore a "wide range of productive activities inside and outside wage relations" [Hardt and Negri 2009: xi], "not in an isolated or independent way but in the complex dynamic with the resistance of other bodies" [Hardt and Negri 2009: 31]' (Scherer *et al.* 2016). In other words, the sport program represented a site for developing social solidarity.

Similar small acts of social solidarity, that served as a form of resistance, and which occurred outside institutional frameworks, were found in Sherry *et al.*'s (2010; 2012) research. Several participants found employment through connections they had made in the CSSP, and several more reported having found accommodation with people they'd met through the program. Although a long way from achieving full social inclusion, these small movements toward the development of increased social capital, achieved through participation in sport-for-development settings, suggest that such programming can be effective in changing individuals' lives.

Conclusion and future directions

This chapter has provided a thematic analysis of evaluations of sport-for-development interventions aimed at homeless populations. The research literature suggests that sport interventions can provide homeless individuals with a safe space in which they can establish and extend social networks, engage in health-promoting physical activity in a social setting, receive practical and social support from service providers, experience personal transformations, and even begin to imagine different futures. In these ways, sport interventions can provide sites in which participants negotiate and resist their social exclusion and begin to develop social capital. Research examining how to leverage these individual, micro-level outcomes to achieve ongoing, lasting change would therefore be valuable. In addition, there is space for the development of appropriate metrics by which to measure program impacts and determine areas of efficacy, particularly in terms of sustainability. Improved ability to demonstrate program efficacy would also be a boon for service providers seeking funding, particularly in the contemporary climate of increased pressure to justify government and donor spending and the context of private–public partnerships in service delivery.

That said, the development of programs addressing the needs of those who are socially marginalized should include a multidisciplinary or interdisciplinary approach to programming and research in order to deal with the complexity of social disadvantage that such populations potentially experience. *Multidisciplinarity* occurs when different disciplines or sectors join to work on a common problem, but split apart again unchanged when the work is complete. *Interdisciplinarity* involves the combining of two or more sectors or disciplines into one project, creating something new by thinking across boundaries. There is space for both in the study of sport and homelessness.

It is also worth noting that the most commonly used sport in homelessness interventions remains football (soccer); research examining the use of other sports would be useful because even though programs using football are not gender-exclusive, football is often perceived as a masculine sport (Holt *et al.* 2015), suggesting that there may be unexplored potential with the use of other, less male-dominated sports. Further, while football enjoys high status as the global sport, Holt *et al.* (2015) and Scherer *et al.* (2016) argued that the selection of the national sport, in those instances hockey, was positively influential on program outcomes. International research examining the use of national sports could offer insights into belonging as expressed through participation in mainstream, national sports. Lastly, existing research with homeless populations has demonstrated definitively that homeless people perceive personal strengths (Tweed *et al.* 2012) and a sense of identity founded on aspects other than their vulnerable housing (Parsell 2010). Studies examining the role sport plays in the development and establishment of personal and social identity and how to leverage this for long-term sustainability would make a welcome contribution to the field.

References

Australian Bureau of Statistics. (2012). 4922.0 – Information paper – A statistical definition of homelessness, 2012 Available at: www.abs.gov.au/ausstats/abs@.nsf/Latestproducts/4922.0Main%20Features22012?o pendocumentandtabn.

Appadurai, A. (2004). The capacity to aspire: Culture and the terms of recognition. In V. Rao and M. Walton (eds), *Culture and Public Action*. Palo Alto, CA: Stanford University Press, pp. 59–84.

Barry, B. (2002). Social exclusion, social isolation, and the distribution of income. In J. Hills, J. L. Grand, and D. Piachaud (eds), *Understanding Social Exclusion*. Oxford: Oxford University Press, pp. 4–29.

Biswas-Diener, R. and Diener, E. (2006). The subjective well-being of the homeless and lessons for happiness. *Social Indicators Research, 76*(2), doi:185. 10.1007/s11205-005-8671-9.

Bourdieu, P. (1986). The forms of capital. In S. Baron, J. Field, and T. Schuller (eds), *Social Capital – Critical Perspectives*. Oxford: Oxford University Press, pp. 83–95.

Burling, T. A., Seidner, A. L., Robbins-Sisco, D., Krinsky, A. and Hanser, S. B. (1992). Batter up! Relapse prevention for homeless veteran substance abusers via softball team participation. *Journal of Substance Abuse, 4*(4), 407–413, doi:10.1016/0899-3289(92)90047-2.

Chalip, L. (2006). Towards social leverage of sport events. *Journal of Sport and Tourism, 11*(2), 109–127, doi:10.1080/14775080601155126.

Coakley, J. (2015). Assessing the sociology of sport: On cultural sensibilities and the great sport myth. *International Review for the Sociology of Sport, 50*(1), 402–406, doi:10.1177/1012690214538864.

Coalter, F. (2010). The politics of sport-for-development: Limited focus programmes and broad gauge problems? *International Review for the Sociology of Sport, 45*(3), 295–314, doi:10.1177/1012690210366791.

Cohen, A. and Welty Peachey, J. (2015). The making of a social entrepreneur: From participant to cause champion within a sport-for-development context. *Sport Management Review, 18*(1), 111–125, doi:10.1016/j.smr.2014.04.002.

Coleman, J. S. (1994). *Foundations of Social Theory*. Cambridge, MA: Belknap Press.

Curran, K., Drust, B., Murphy, R., Pringle, A. and Richardson, D. (2016). The challenge and impact of engaging hard-to-reach populations in regular physical activity and health behaviours: An examination of an English Premier League 'football in the community' men's health programme. *Public Health, 135*, 14–22, doi:10.1016/j.puhe.2016.02.008.

Gregg, M. and Bedard, A. (2016). Mission impossible? Physical activity programming for individuals experiencing homelessness. *Research Quarterly for Exercise and Sport, 87*(4), 376–381, doi:10.1080/02701367.2016.1233314.

Hardt, M. and Negri, A. (2009). *Commonwealth*. Cambridge, MA: Belknap Press.

Harris, A. (2011). Constructing clean dreams: Accounts, future selves, and social and structural support as desistance work. *Symbolic Interaction, 34*(1), 63–85, doi:10.1525/si.2011.34.1.63.

Holt, N. L., Scherer, J. and Koch, J. (2015). Using masculine capital to understand the role of a sport program in the lives of men from a Western Canadian inner city. *Journal of Sport and Exercise Psychology, 37*(5), 523–533, doi:10.1123/jsep.2015-0109.

HWC. (2015). Global Homelessness Statistics. Available at: www.homelessworldcup.org/homelessness-statistics/.

Knestaut, M., Devine, M. A. and Verlezza, B. (2010). 'It gives me purpose': The use of dance with people experiencing homelessness. *Therapeutic Recreation Journal, 44*(4), 289–301.

Magee, J. (2011). Disengagement, de-motivation, vulnerable groups and sporting inclusion: a case study of the Homeless World Cup. *Soccer and Society, 12*(2), 159–173, doi:10.1080/14660970.2011.548353.

Magee, J. and Jeanes, R. (2011). Football's coming home: A critical evaluation of the Homeless World Cup as an intervention to combat social exclusion. *International Review for the Sociology of Sport, 48*(1), 3–19, doi:10.1177/1012690211428391.

Neale, J., Nettleton, S. and Pickering, L. (2012). Heroin users' views and experiences of physical activity, sport and exercise. *International Journal of Drug Policy, 23*(2), 120–127, doi:10.1016/j.drugpo.2011.06.004.

Parsell, C. (2010). 'Homeless is what I am, not who I am': Insights from an inner-city Brisbane study. *Urban Policy and Research, 28*(2), 181–194, doi:10.1080/08111141003793966.

Putnam, R. (1995). Bowling alone: America's declining social capital. *Journal of Democracy, 6*(1), 65–79, doi:10.1353/jod.1995.0002.

Randers, M. B., Petersen, J., Andersen, L. J., Krustrup, B. R., Hornstrup, T., Nielsen, J. J., … Krustrup, P. (2012). Short-term street soccer improves fitness and cardiovascular health status of homeless men. *European Journal of Applied Physiology, 112*(6), 2097–2106, doi:10.1007/s00421-011-2171-1.

Scherer, J., Koch, J. and Holt, N. L. (2016). The uses of an inner-city sport-for-development program: Dispatches from the (real) creative class. *Sociology of Sport Journal, 33*(2), 185–198, doi:http://dx.doi.org/10.1123/ssj.2015-0145.

Schulenkorf, N., and Adair, D. (eds). (2014). *Global Sport-for-Development: Critical Perspectives.* Basingstoke: Palgrave Macmillan.

Sherry, E. (2010). (Re)engaging marginalized groups through sport: The Homeless World Cup. *International Review for the Sociology of Sport, 45*(1), 59–71, doi:10.1177/1012690209356988.

Sherry, E., Karg, A. and O'May, F. (2011). Social capital and sport events: Spectator attitudinal change and the Homeless World Cup. *Sport in Society, 14*(1), 111–125, doi:10.1080/17430437.2011.530015.

Sherry, E. and O'May, F. (2013). Exploring the impact of sport participation in the Homeless World Cup on individuals with substance abuse or mental health disorders. *Journal of Sport for Development, 1*(2), 1–11. Available at: https://jsfd.files.wordpress.com/2013/10/jsfd-sherry-at-al-2013.pdf.

Sherry, E. and Osborne, A. (2011). A tale of two events? Media analysis of the Melbourne 2008 Homeless World Cup. *Media International Australia incorporating Culture and Policy, 140*(97–106).

Sherry, E. and Strybosch, V. (2012). A kick in the right direction: longitudinal outcomes of the Australian Community Street Soccer Program. *Soccer and Society, 13*(4), 495–509, doi:10.1080/14660970.2012.677225.

Skinner, J., Zakus, D. H. and Cowell, J. (2008). Development through sport: Building social capital in disadvantaged communities. *Sport Management Review, 11*(3), 253–275, doi:http://dx.doi.org/10.1016/S1441-3523(08)70112-8.

Sonstroem, R. J. (1997). The physical self-system: A mediator of exercise and self-esteem. In K. R. Fox (ed.), *The Physical Self: From Motivation to Well-being* Champaign, IL: Human Kinetics, pp. 27–58.

Spaaij, R. (2009). Sport as a vehicle for social mobility and regulation of disadvantaged urban youth: Lessons from Rotterdam. *International Review for the Sociology of Sport 44*(2–3), 247–264, doi:10.1177/1012690209338415.

Spaaij, R. and Schulenkorf, N. (2014). Cultivating safe space: Lessons for sport-for-development projects and events. *Journal of Sport Management, 28*(6), 633–645, doi:10.1123/jsm.2013-0304.

The Big Issue. (2017). Community Street Soccer Program. Available at: www.thebigissue.org.au/community-street-soccer/about/.

Thomas, Y., Gray, M. and McGinty, S. (2012). An exploration of subjective wellbeing among people experiencing homelessness: A strengths-based approach. *Social Work in Health Care, 51*, 780–797, doi:10.1080/00981389.2012.686475.

Tweed, R. G., Biswas-Diener, R. and Lehman, D. R. (2012). Self-perceived strengths among people who are homeless. *Journal of Positive Psychology, 7*(6), 481–492, doi:10.1080/17439760.2012.719923.

Welty Peachey, J., Borland, J., Lobpries, J., and Cohen, A. (2015). Managing impact: Leveraging sacred spaces and community celebration to maximize social capital at a sport-for-development event. *Sport Management Review (Elsevier Science), 18*(1), 86–98, doi:10.1016/j.smr.2014.05.003.

Welty Peachey, J., Cohen, A., Borland, J. and Lyras, A. (2013b). Building social capital: Examining the impact of Street Soccer USA on its volunteers. *International Review for the Sociology of Sport, 48*(1), 20–37, doi:10.1177/1012690211432068.

Welty Peachey, J., Lyras, A., Borland, J. and Cohen, A. (2013a). Street Soccer USA Cup: Preliminary findings of a sport-for-homeless intervention. *ICHPER – SD Journal of Research in Health, Physical Education, Recreation, Sport and Dance, 8*(1), 3–11. Available at: http://eric.ed.gov/?id=EJ1013804.

34

SDP and forced displacement

Ramón Spaaij and Sarah Oxford

Introduction

> Being involved in football, even as a spectator, helped me settle as an immigrant and in fact helped me assimilate. I also believe that football has played a similar role in other refugees' stories. As I mingle with the old-timers who came here as refugees and with the new arrivals from Africa, the Middle East and Asia; together they bring football in their baggage and use it as a tool of survival.
>
> *Murray 2014*

People with refugee backgrounds have long been actively involved in sport from the grassroots to the elite level. The late Les Murray's journey to becoming the face of football (soccer) in Australia is a case in point. His journey began as an 11-year-old boy fleeing with his family from their home near Budapest, Hungary, in 1956. Murray (then known as László Ürge) and his family fled across the Austrian border and spent the next six months in refugee camps. The family would eventually resettle in Australia. He recalls how adjustment to life in Australia was not easy for his family – the challenges of starting again in a new country, learning a new language, and understanding and adjusting to different social expectations and attitudes (Murray 2006). In Australia, Murray continued his love for the game he had played as a child in Hungary; a game that, at the time, was a minority sport in Australia. He has played a major role in popularizing football in Australia as a media commentator, presenter and producer. He was appointed the Special Broadcasting Service's (SBS) Head of Sport in 1996 and served in this role until 2006, when he returned to sports journalism to become SBS Sport's editorial chief.

Les Murray's opening quote reflects his passionate commitment to football as a positive force in the lives of refugees and asylum seekers. He argues that

> for many young asylum seekers and refugees, football is a source of hope and a way for them to start healing from the traumas of the refugee experience. It helps give them a sense of purpose and belonging, as well as an opportunity to practice English and socialize with other children.
>
> *Murray 2014*

This belief resonates with the language of organizations and activists in the sport for development and peace (SDP) sector that have been delivering projects to refugees in conflict zones and refugee camps as well as in countries of resettlement. For example, in recent years global stakeholders in sport, such as the International Olympic Committee and FIFA, have been convening with leaders in the development sector and settlement services, as well as with multinational corporations, to identify how sport can be better used to support refugees and other displaced persons around the world. These initiatives come at a time when forced displacement is at a record high. By the end of 2015, 65.3 million individuals were forcibly displaced worldwide as a result of persecution, conflict, generalized violence or human rights violations (United Nations High Commissioner for Refugees [UNHCR] 2016).

Critically, Murray's experience illustrates how refugees' private troubles are, to paraphrase C. Wright Mills, divisive public issues. Murray's biography points to the multilevel barriers that people with refugee backgrounds may face both in sport and in the resettlement process more broadly; issues which are well documented in recent academic research (Correa-Velez *et al.* 2013; Spaaij 2013; 2015). As Warren St John's (2007; 2009) critically acclaimed account of the Fugees football team in Clarkston, Atlanta, vividly demonstrates, refugees find both hope and hostility on the sports field, including resentment and vitriol levelled at them by some opposing teams and local residents (see also Dukic *et al.* 2017). These accounts suggest that, as former United Nations Secretary-General Ban Ki-moon observes, the 'refugee crisis' is 'not just a crisis of numbers; it is also a crisis of solidarity' (United Nations 2016).

Recent manifestations of the politicized and divisive nature of the 'refugee crisis' are manifold, ranging from Europe's attempts to regulate the mass movement of more than one million refugees and migrants across its borders, to US President Donald Trump's executive order blocking refugees from entering the United States, and Australia's controversial offshore detention policy (e.g. Farrell 2016). In the Australian context, Murray confesses feeling

> bewildered and disenchanted by how my fellow refugees are being treated today. Current policies and attitudes are so far-removed from the welcome I remember receiving [...] and certainly don't reflect the generous spirit of most Australians whom I've come to know. [He believes that] current rhetoric and policies [only] cultivate fear and xenophobia, [and that] it's time to intervene.
>
> *Murray 2014*

Murray further signals his dissatisfaction with the dominant representation of refugees as problematic subjects of a policy encouraging conformity and assimilation (Leach and Zamora 2006). He instead portrays refugees as agents with potential who make vital social, cultural and economic contributions to their countries of resettlement. Murray (2014) notes that, 'we can all play a part in this by first understanding that refugees are not a threat and that, on the contrary, they enrich our culture and build our nation, as so much historical evidence shows'.

The life stories of Les Murray, members of the Fugees, and other people with refugee backgrounds who participate in and contribute to sport, raise important questions for SDP research, policy and practice. What participation opportunities does the SDP sector provide to refugees and other displaced persons? What are the assumptions that underpin these initiatives? To what extent, and how, does the SDP sector succeed in addressing barriers and facilitators to refugee participation and well-being? This chapter will critically examine contemporary SDP programs and research in this area to address these questions. In order to achieve this objective, we will draw upon multiple sources including biographical accounts such as Murray's, contemporary academic literature, and our own primary research on the intersections of sport and forced displacement in global North and global South settings (see also Spaaij 2012; 2013; 2015; Dukic *et al.* 2017; Oxford 2017; Oxford and Spaaij 2017).

We recognize that the SDP sector's engagement with refugees and internally displaced persons (IDPs) is not confined to the global South. Rather, it also incorporates myriad 'sport/exercise for inclusion' and refugee settlement initiatives in global North settings (Guerin *et al.* 2003; Amara *et al.* 2004; Olliff 2008; Hashimoto-Govindasamy and Rose 2011; Ha and Lyras 2013; Nathan *et al.* 2013; Jeanes *et al.* 2015; Whitley *et al.* 2016). We define 'refugee' as someone who is unable or unwilling to return to their country of nationality owing to a well-founded fear of being persecuted for reasons of race, religion, nationality, membership of a particular social group, or political opinion (UNHCR 2010). IDPs are those who are forced to flee their homes but who remain within their country's borders.

This chapter first provides an overview of SDP initiatives that work with refugees and IDPs. It then critically examines existing SDP initiatives in relation to the aforementioned questions. Following this discussion, we present an illustrative case study based on the second author's ethnographic fieldwork with a development program in Colombia that seeks to engage IDPs through sport. In the final section, we reflect on the main themes and findings, and propose issues for future research on SDP and forced displacement.

Mapping the field

This research, although not exhaustive, provides an exploratory synopsis of the diverse and numerous SDP initiatives catering to refugees and IDPs. Two websites were used to map and take stock of SDP initiatives that explicitly aim to engage this target group: the International Platform for Sport and Development (www.sportanddev.org) and Beyond Sport (www.beyondsport.org). Both online platforms provide a virtual space for the SDP community to network and share resources. The first has 532 registered organizations and the latter 2,158 registered projects. From this sample of SDP organizations and projects, we identified 29 organizations and projects that explicitly focused on refugees and IDPs. The websites of these SDP initiatives were thematically

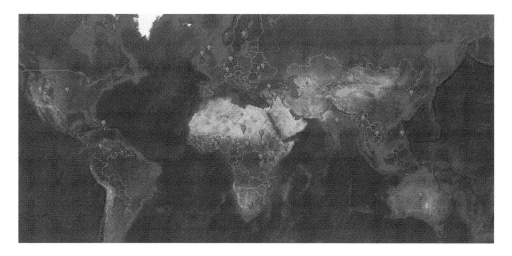

Figure 34.1 Map of SDP initiatives working with refugees and IDPs (May 2017)

analysed for variables including geographical location, donor location, target population, primary objective, sports offered, educational focus and descriptive language.

Figure 34.1 shows the countries and contested territories where the 29 refugee-focused SDP initiatives operated at the time of writing (May 2017). The initiatives are diverse in size, structure and application. Fourteen organizations work in multiple locations. For example, Capoeira4refugees operate across 200 refugee camps and communities in 21 countries, and Right to Play work with more than one million children in 20 countries. Ten initiatives employ programs in Western nations. This number may reflect staff access to the English language and/ or technology enabling their inclusion on the two examined websites, rather than a dominance of Western-based initiatives. Two initiatives include corporations that collaborate with UN agencies to fundraise and provide equipment. Last, there are seven grassroots no-governmental organizations (NGOs) established by individuals who experienced conflict personally as either an aid worker or displaced person. Examples of these programs include the Tegla Loroupe Peace Foundation in Kenya, a circus and arts program in Cambodia, and Reclaim Childhood in Jordan.

The locations of the SDP initiatives listed expose where major humanitarian crises have occurred or are ongoing. For example, many organizations operate in multiple locations in Jordan, Israel, the West Bank and the Gaza Strip, reflecting the large numbers of people fleeing Syria, but also the long-term refugee status of many Palestinians (UNRWA 2016). The primary stated objectives of the initiatives in this region include providing a fun activity, social networking, building life skills, teaching resilience and empowerment. In addition, there are relatively large numbers of both refugee camps and SDP initiatives in Central and Eastern Africa – a repercussion of the conflict in the Central African Republic, the ongoing conflict in and rebuilding of South Sudan, and the long term instability affecting inhabitants of the Democratic Republic of Congo, Rwanda, Burundi and Somalia. SDP initiatives in these areas seek to promote peace/ healing, social integration, teamwork and leadership, as well as overcoming boredom. Initiatives in the United Kingdom, Australia, Sweden, Germany and the United States created in response to the arrival of refugees who have fled predominantly Syria, Iraq and Afghanistan promote anti-racism, community integration and social inclusion programs, as well as scholastic support.

Although most of the SDP initiatives' stated objectives are fairly generic, it is possible to discern thematic groupings. More than one-third of the listed programs prioritize education and life skills, with almost the same number (and perhaps many of the same organizations) also working towards peacebuilding and community development. Subsequent themes include health and well-being, recreation and play, and intercultural exchange and tolerance. Additionally, a few Western-located initiatives work to tackle xenophobia and anti-immigration sentiment among the host population. Sports associated with educational themes include capoeira, football, climbing, cricket, basketball, table tennis, taekwondo, play/games and circus/arts.

Akin to the SDP sector in general, the website descriptions of the 29 SDP initiatives are mostly framed by fashionable positive terms that focus on the initiatives' transformative goals, such as empowerment, resilience and social integration. In contrast, a few initiatives market their work with grave words and phrases describing the participants such as trauma, poor, misery, suffering, at risk. This language use appears to reflect the aforementioned dominant representation of refugees as problematic subjects including cultural misrecognition associated with an equation of refugee difference and marginality with deficit and lack. The problematic nature of this deficit discourse is well documented in various fields of study, including refugee studies (Horst 2006); education (Roy and Roxas 2011; Keddie 2012); and increasingly in SDP research (e.g. Spaaij 2011; Schulenkorf and Spaaij 2015). For example, educational research shows that the discourse employed by educators towards refugee families is often grounded in a deficit-based paradigm that creates missed opportunities for connecting with parents and students by blaming them rather than evaluating the lack of education provided to refugee families in how to 'do school' in their new country (Roy and Roxas 2011). In SDP research, it has been argued that this deficit model can lead practitioners to try to identify and fix problems and solve issues for, rather than *with*, participants. There have been calls for an alternative paradigm, that of asset-based development, where communities are supported to design programs around their own needs, strengths, resources and autonomy (Schulenkorf and Spaaij 2015; Misener and Schulenkorf 2016). Within this context, Hashimoto-Govindasamy and Rose (2011) argue that it is critical that any initiatives to address refugees' (re)settlement needs and difficulties are sustainable and aim to empower participants and 'promote their existing strengths and resilience techniques' (ibid.: 107). There is thus an opportunity for the SDP sector and researchers to learn from refugees and IDPs about how they perform these qualities (Evers 2010).

A limitation of the methodology we used to take stock of SDP initiatives that cater to refugees and IDPs, namely thematic analysis of two online SDP platforms, is that it does not indicate how the objectives and framing of initiatives evolve over time. A noteworthy trend is the growth in sport-based programs whose objectives include the prevention of radicalization and violent extremism, within the context of growing concerns about the impact of refugee arrivals on national security, such as the belief that terrorists may gain entry to Western nations disguised as refugees. This trend suggests the othering of refugees not just in terms of deficit and lack, but in terms of *threat* and *security risk*. For example, in Belgium, the Netherlands, Australia and elsewhere, martial arts and football programs have been introduced to assist Muslim immigrants and refugees in fostering positive social relationships and a sense of belonging, which, it is believed, will build resilience against risks of radicalization and violent extremism (e.g. Johns *et al.* 2014; Rutter 2016).

The need for community-based programs focused on sports, the arts and music in order to promote resilience to violent extremism is frequently flagged (Grossman *et al.* 2016). Moreover, sports are now being used in a few prison-based de-radicalization programs as a platform for engagement and rehabilitation through personal growth and mutual trust (Barkindo and Bryans 2016). Within this context, the rise of anti-radicalization on the SDP agenda may present an opportunity for SDP organizations to attract public funding and visibility; yet, it risks dehumanization of refugees in the process, potentially adding to the creation of 'suspect communities' (Breen-Smyth 2014; Kundnani 2014). Furthermore, it could exacerbate ideological and practical tensions between SDP organizations and donors (Oxford 2017). The former's desire to contribute to human and social development can be at odds with the national security agenda of donors such as law enforcement or criminal justice agencies. We have personally observed this tension in our conversations with existing projects in this area. In at least two instances (in the Netherlands and in Australia), the organizers were reluctant to brand their program as an anti-radicalization intervention due to fear of community backlash and because they believed it would turn away the target population. For this reason, the projects are publicly promoted as initiatives that focus on empowerment, resilience, education, employability and social integration, even though they are funded by government agencies with the specific purpose of contributing to the prevention of radicalization and violent extremism. The forms of regulation and social control that operate in these programs are thus strategically and discursively concealed from public view.

In the remainder of this chapter, we move beyond this broad overview of SDP initiatives targeting refugees and IDPs to present an illustrative case study of a development program in Colombia. This case study is based on ethnographic research conducted by the second author in 2015 and 2016.

Supporting IDPs in Colombia through sport and play

Lasting nearly 60 years, Colombia's internal conflict, which included government forces, guerrillas and paramilitary groups, was the longest running armed conflict in the Western hemisphere. Since 1985, more than 5.5 million Colombians have registered with the national government as victims of conflict (Revista Semana 2016). Most internally displaced Colombians fled from rural to urban environments in search of two things: 'the security of being anonymous to avoid being targeted again; and access to public services that are inaccessible in their home municipalities' (COHA 2015). The trauma experienced by these citizens coupled with their stigmatization has resulted in IDPs choosing anonymity, leading the UNHCR to dub Colombia's forced displacement an 'invisible crisis'. In a joint evaluation, the International Committee of the Red Cross and the World Food Programme found IDP living conditions to be harsh:

> the average monthly income of an internally displaced family represents a little over 41 percent of the official minimum wage, equivalent to US$63 dollars. Of this amount, displaced people spend 58 percent on food, 6 percent on health, and just 3 percent on education
>
> *WFP 2015*

Many IDPs therefore rely heavily on local assistance provided by NGOs and the Catholic Church (Vidal Lopez *et al.* 2011).

The SDP organization VIDA (a pseudonym) works in marginalized communities throughout Colombia – neighborhoods where sexual and domestic violence and teen pregnancy are critical issues that assist in reproducing poverty, and where residents live in insecure and overcrowded housing and commonly experience chronic stress leading to high levels of depression (Pallitto and O'Campo 2005). VIDA does not explicitly note that they work with refugees and IDPs in its reports; however, the communities in which they work have high proportions of IDPs as residents. VIDA manages sport-based development community programs throughout Colombia. Responding to the diversity of Colombia's geography and people, VIDA draws from multiple methodologies to create their own pedagogical approach. In VIDA, children play together on a regular basis (two days a week) and are taught values such as tolerance and respect. Sport is applied as a strategy to recruit participants, but also to encourage ludic play in their routine schedule. A variety of sports or games are offered at each location depending on what is popular, socially acceptable, and suggested by participants. Sometimes players are organized by gender or age, but often, players are integrated. VIDA hires coaches, social workers, and psychologists to support participants on and off the field. Parents are required to register their children, but VIDA does not regulate attendance. By design it rewards participants for being self-motivated and attending on their own accord.

VIDA aims to improve children's lives and to transform vulnerable communities through sports/play, education and health. Prominent themes in its projects are combatting violence, promoting tolerance and encouraging social inclusion. A key component of its mission is enrolling and supporting children in education. Young participants have access to after-school tutoring led by youth leaders, and after one year of engagement, participants qualify to participate in a school support program that includes educational supplies (e.g. notebooks, book bag) and academic scholarships. Selected participants are also provided with opportunities to experience life outside of their enclave through national and international travel to sports-based festivals, science-focused competitions, SDP/NGO conferences and professional football games (e.g. FIFA World Cup, Premier League).

Daniela is an 18-year-old leader who has taken advantage of VIDA's programs and was identified as a 'model leader' by staff members. Born in Venezuela, at a young age she fled with her family to Panama before settling in Colombia. She credits VIDA for her current self-discipline, academic success and positive attitude:

> A large part of my life was changed through football. When I arrived at the foundation, I got here and they made me a part [of the organization]. They put new ideas in my mind, they put new concepts and life projects and everything started to change. From that time, I didn't see the world like before. Before I was a really violent child, from the street. I didn't spend time at home. I didn't want to study and so I arrived here and they gave me a new concept of what life was and what my future would hold. And well, at that time, I began to understand and I began to study. I am well behaved with everything that I have to do.
>
> *Daniela, personal communication*

Yuliza, an 18-year-old female leader made a similar statement, recognizing behavioural changes in relation to her commitment to VIDA:

> My experience has been very good because since I joined the foundation I learned a lot because I used to be one of the girls who fought all the time. I treated everyone badly, they couldn't even look at me because I would hit them and here they helped me, I'm not like that anymore.
>
> *Yuliza, personal communication*

Both quotations display proclamation of personal transformation and an active embodiment of VIDA's values. VIDA seeks to create a supportive community for residents who have experienced trauma. Participants commonly endorsed VIDA as their family and a positive community resource. Due to VIDA's stability in relation to the local context and extensive community networks, it lends itself to support the community in a variety of ways beyond their stated mission. For example, parents are invited and encouraged to attend monthly seminars that relate to the topics children are studying. VIDA hosts medical specialists and affordable clothing sales. And, basic infrastructure (e.g. phone lines, field) is maintained and updated. Staff member, Julio, spoke about VIDA's efforts to support the community:

> Before we trained on a field where VIDA made necessary adjustments to make it work. There was a mountain in front and sewage drained onto the field, so we flattened the earth to open ditches around the field … That space was recovered for the community not only for VIDA.
>
> *Julio, personal communication*

It is recognized that VIDA's efforts are influential in the community, but the common rhetoric of self-change coupled with values, as captured in Daniela and Yuliza's quotations, is potentially problematic. In what seemed to be automated and cursory responses, VIDA employees and participants alike proudly asserted that VIDA impacts the community because of values. All 22 interlocutors directly associated with VIDA mentioned the word 'values' a total of 73 times in their interviews. Underpinning these statements is a conceptual dichotomy between good and bad behaviour and an assumption that following the 'good' path will result in opportunity, if not a life-changing trajectory. This is seen again with Daniela when comparing children inside the program to those outside:

> Children in the street do not have the support, they do not have that person to tell them, 'Don't say this, don't say that.' Children come here and they are influenced with values like

respect, honesty, all those types of values. And I think that through that they are educated and they are being better people.

Daniela, personal communication

In a similar vein, Yuliza considers integration and opportunity through assimilation to be connected to success: 'Here [in the program] you can learn values, you pass your free time instead of being in the street, doing things like taking drugs or robbing people.' Thus, we see here further illustrations of the forms of regulation and social control that operate in SDP initiatives (Spaaij 2009; Hartmann and Kwauk 2011). Only when discussing personal and sometimes painful experiences did interlocutors bypass the argument that values remedy social inequalities such as racism, sexism and classism to address the double standards and social stigma frequently accepted as normal.

A common concern when analysing VIDA and other SDP organizations is the underpinning assumption of the deficit-based paradigm – that children and young people must first change themselves or be changed in order to assimilate into a specific non-threatening mould accepted by society (or those in power) before they can then become change-makers. Terms signifying regulation and social control, such as 'empowered', 'good citizen', 'healed', 'leaders', and 'confident', are commonly found on the websites of the 29 listed organizations. But when participants adopt specific values and embody qualities of the 'good, active citizen', we must ask: will they then be capable and equipped to change the oppressive and intersectional structures (e.g. patriarchy, class system, structural racism, poor educational system) that caused them to need to participate in the program to begin with?

This is not to argue that VIDA is unneeded, but rather to highlight the limitations of the program, and to call attention to the fact that the most stigmatized and marginalized in society are not being applauded for their resilience and creativity, but rather are being identified as 'deficit citizens' and then socialized and taught to conform to the dominant culture that oppresses them. In VIDA there were a few exemplar cases of participants who became leaders and not only assimilated into the 'good citizen' promoted by VIDA, but who have taken advantage of the organization's offerings. At each location, leaders spoke proudly of their travel opportunities and some had even begun attending university or a work-focused tertiary program. Leaders who reaped these rewards were the exception, and not the rule, and it is too early to know the extent of their benefit. Other participants benefited from having cultivated a local social support system and taking advantage of access to supportive employees, but even when they subscribed to VIDA's value system, their life varied little from their parents' because of the structures that shape their lives, such as the government enforced class system, the Catholic church and local gangs and paramilitary groups. Single mother of a previous player and IDP, Daniela Maria, appreciated VIDA for the 'new atmosphere in the community' and for the support they had provided her and her daughter over the last decade, but she did not connect VIDA to macro-social change. When asked if she believed her daughter's life is different from her own or if the social inequalities such as sexism, had changed since VIDA's inception, she replied, 'No'.

Conclusion

The global attention on refugees and internally displaced persons in politics, media and civil society is reflected in the SPD sector's variegated attempts to engage and support this target population through its programs. Existing initiatives are geographically dispersed and diverse in their objectives and approaches. They have been providing tangible outcomes for refugees and IDPs in areas such as access to sport and play, education, health and well-being, life skills and community capacity building. In this chapter, we have discussed some of the underlying assumptions on which SDP initiatives that work with refugees and IDPs are built, with specific reference to the existence of a deficit-based paradigm that associates refugee difference and marginality with deficit and lack, as well as threat and security risk. The latter is reflected in, for instance, the emergence of SDP initiatives whose objectives include the prevention of radicalization and violent extremism, within the context of growing concerns about the impact of refugee arrivals and immigrants on national security.

Many of the SDP initiatives addressed in this chapter operate in volatile and resource-scarce settings where daily challenges can become dire and troubleshooting the norm. Although for participants and staff daily programming may feel isolated from macro-structures, this is not the case. SDP organizations are embedded within the broader fields of business, politics and development. Moreover, it is vital that these organizations compete for funding. In this position, they are encouraged – potentially at the cost of discontinuation – to adapt to the prevailing and dominant discourse. The game of survival is not then limited to the refugee alone, but includes the SDP initiative. Flexible wording and marketing that targets wealthier, donor audiences may appear distant from on-the-ground programing, albeit when words and labels are connected to marginalized individuals and groups, a risk of (re)confirming social stigmas and (re)producing negative stereotypes is created. The implications of this risk are limitless as social identifiers such as race, religion and class can be embedded within these words and images, creating a multi-pronged socially constructed barrier that challenges the participant's agency. There is a need for critical reflection on the implications of this issue, for example in relation to risks to the (perceived) legitimacy of SDP initiatives and the potential dehumanization of refugees. More broadly, this chapter suggests the need for a philosophical shift in SDP programs from a deficit-based model to an asset-based approach that recognizes, values and supports refugees and IDPs' strengths and resources as well as the social, cultural and economic contributions they make to society.

From the analysis presented in this chapter, a number of questions for future research can be identified. How might an asset-based approach to SDP and forced displacement be conceived and fostered? How can the needs and aspirations of refugees be met and community resilience be strengthened without resorting to deficit-based or threat-based approaches? And, how can the SDP sector and researchers learn from, and accommodate, refugees and IDPs' intimate knowledge of resilience, agency and autonomy (Evers 2010)? These questions, we argue, have applicability beyond initiatives that work specifically with refugees and IDPs. They are, indeed, vital to the future development of the SDP sector more broadly and to its capacity to contribute to the kinds of human and social development that Les Murray was a passionate advocate for.

References

Amara, M., Aquilina, D., Argent, E., Betzer-Tayar, M., Green, M., Henry, I., Coalter, F. and Taylor, J. (2004). *The Roles of Sport and Education in the Social Inclusion of Asylum Seekers and Refugees: An Evaluation of Policy and Practice in the UK*. Loughborough: Institute of Sport and Leisure Policy, Loughborough University and University of Stirling.

Barkindo, A. and Bryans, S. (2016). De-radicalising prisoners in Nigeria: Developing a basic prison based de-radicalisation programme. *Journal for Deradicalization*, 7(1), 1–25.

Breen-Smyth, M. (2014). Theorising the "suspect community": Counterterrorism, security practices and the public imagination. *Critical Studies on Terrorism*, 7(2), 223–240.

Correa-Velez, I., Spaaij, R. and Upham, S. (2013). 'We are not here to claim better services than any other': Social exclusion among men from refugee backgrounds in urban and regional Australia. *Journal of Refugee Studies*, 26(2), 163–187.

Council on Hemispheric Affairs [COHA] (2015). Colombia's 'Invisible Crisis': Internally Displaced Persons. Available at: www.coha.org/colombias-invisible-crisis-internally-displaced-persons/ (accessed 1 July 2016).

Dukic, D., McDonald, B. and Spaaij, R. (2017). Being able to play: Experiences of social inclusion and exclusion within a football team of people seeking asylum. *Social Inclusion*, 5(2), doi:10.17645/si.v5i2.892.

Evers, C. (2010). Intimacy, sport and young refugee men. *Emotion, Space and Society*, 3(1), 56–61.

Farrell, P. (2016). UN human rights office calls on Australia to end offshore detention. *The Guardian*, September 17, 2016. Available at: www.theguardian.com/australia-news/2016/sep/17/un-human-rights-office-calls-on-australia-to-end-offshore-detention (accessed 3 February 2017).

Grossman, M., Peucker, M., Smith, D. and Dellal, H. (2016). *Stocktake Research Project: A Systematic Literature and Selected Program Review on Social Cohesion, Community Resilience and Violent Extremism 2011–2015*. Melbourne: Community Resilience Unit, Department of Premier and Cabinet, State of Victoria.

Guerin, P., Diiriye, R. O., Corrigan, C. and Guerin, B. (2003). Physical activity programs for refugee Somali women: Working out in a new country. *Women and Health*, 38(1), 83–99.

Ha, J. and Lyras, A. (2013). Sport for refugee youth in a new society: The role of acculturation in sport for development and peace programming. *South African Journal for Research in Sport, Physical Education and Recreation*, 35(2), 121–140.

Hartmann, D. and Kwauk, C. (2011). Sport and development: An overview, critique, and reconstruction. *Journal of Sport and Social Issues*, 35(3), 284–305.

Hashimoto-Govindasamy, L. S. and Rose, V. (2011). An ethnographic process evaluation of a community support program with Sudanese refugee women in western Sydney. *Health Promotion Journal of Australia*, 22(2), 107–112.

Horst, C. (2006). *Transnational Nomads: How Somalis Cope with Refugee Life in the Dadaab Camps of Kenya*. Oxford: Berghahn Books.

Jeanes, R., O'Connor, J. and Alfrey, L. (2015). Sport and the resettlement of young people from refugee backgrounds in Australia. *Journal of Sport and Social Issues*, 39(6), 480–500.

Johns, A., Grossman, M. and McDonald, K. (2014). More than a game: The impact of sport-based youth mentoring schemes on developing resilience toward violent extremism. *Social Inclusion*, 2(2), 57–70.

Keddie, A. (2012). Pursuing justice for refugee students: addressing issues of cultural (mis)recognition. *International Journal of Inclusive Education*, 16(12), 1295–3110.

Kundnani, A. (2014). *The Muslims are Coming! Islamophobia, Extremism, and the Domestic War on Terror*. London & New York: Verso.

Leach, M. and Zamora, A. (2006). Illegals/*Ilegales*: Comparing anti-immigrant/anti-refugee discourses in Australia and Spain. *Journal of Iberian and Latin American Research*, 12(1), 51–64.

Misener, L. and Schulenkorf, N. (2016). Rethinking the social value of sport events through an asset-based community development (ABCD) perspective. *Journal of Sport Management*, 20(3), 329–340.

Murray, L. (2006). *By the Balls: The Rags to Riches Memoir of a Football Tragic*. Melbourne: Random House Australia.

Murray, L. (2014). Soccer gives refugees a sporting chance. *The Sydney Morning Herald*, 20 June 2014. Available at: www.smh.com.au/comment/soccer-gives-refugees-a-sporting-chance-20140618-zse77.html (accessed 29 March 2015).

Nathan, S., Kemp, L., Bunde-Birouste, A., MacKenzie, J., Evers, C. and Shwe, T. A. (2013). 'We wouldn't of made friends if we didn't come to Football United': The impacts of a football program on young people's peer, prosocial and cross-cultural relationships. *BMC Public Health*, 13(1), 1–16.

Olliff, L. (2008). Playing for the future: The role of sport and recreation in supporting refugee young people to 'settle well' in Australia. *Youth Studies Australia*, 27(1), 52–60.

Oxford, S. (2017). The social, cultural, and historical complexities that shape and constrain (gendered) space in an SDP organisation in Colombia. *Journal of Sport for Development*.

Oxford, S. and Spaaij, R. (2017). Critical pedagogy and power relations in sport for development and peace: Lessons from Colombia. *Third World Thematics: A TWQ Journal*, doi:10.1080/23802014.2017.1297687.

Pallitto, C. and O'Campo, P. (2005). Community level effects of gender inequality on intimate partner violence and unintended pregnancy in Colombia: Testing the feminist perspective. *Social Science and Medicine*, 60(10), 2205–2216.

Revista Semana. (2016). Proyecto Víctimas. Available at: www.semana.com/especiales/proyectovictimas/index/index.html#cifras (accessed 5 May 2016).

Roy, L. and Roxas, K. (2011). Whose deficit is this anyhow? Exploring counter-stories of Somali Bantu refugees' experiences in 'doing school'. *Harvard Educational Review*, *81*(3), 521–542.

Rutter, T. (2016). Sport and extremism: 'If young people are excluded, they're easier to radicalise'. *The Guardian*, 24 October 2016. Available at: www.theguardian.com/public-leaders-network/2016/oct/24/football-boxing-extremism-young-people-excluded-radicalise-brussels (accessed 21 February 2017).

Schulenkorf, N. and Spaaij, R. (2015). Reflections on theory building in sport for development and peace. *International Journal of Sport Management and Marketing*, *16*(1/2), 71–77.

Spaaij, R. (2009). Sport as a vehicle for social mobility and regulation of disadvantaged urban youth: Lessons from Rotterdam. *International Review for the Sociology of Sport*, *44*(2), 247–264.

Spaaij, R. (2011). *Sport and Social Mobility: Crossing Boundaries*. London: Routledge.

Spaaij, R. (2012). Beyond the playing field: Experiences of sport, social capital and integration among Somalis in Australia. *Ethnic and Racial Studies*, *35*(9), 1519–1538.

Spaaij, R. (2013). Cultural diversity in community sport: An ethnographic inquiry of Somali Australians' experiences. *Sport Management Review*, *16*(1), 29–40.

Spaaij, R. (2015). Refugee youth, belonging and community sport. *Leisure Studies*, *34*(3), 303–318.

St John, W. (2007). Refugees find hostility and hope on soccer field. *The New York Times*, 21 January 2007, p. A1. Available at: www.nytimes.com/2007/01/21/us/21fugees.html (accessed 12 January 2013).

St John, W. (2009). *Outcasts United*. London: Fourth Estate.

United Nations. (2016). Refugee crisis about solidarity, not just numbers, Secretary-General says at event on global displacement challenge. Press release SG/SM/17670-REF/1228, 15 April 2016. Available at: www.un.org/press/en/2016/sgsm17670.doc.htm (accessed 17 April 2016).

UNHCR. (2010). *Convention and Protocol Relating to the Status of Refugees*. Geneva: United Nations High Commissioner for Refugees.

UNHCR. (2016). *Global Trends: Forced Displacement in 2015*. Geneva: United Nations High Commissioner for Refugees.

UNRWA. (2016). *UNRWA in Figures 2016*. Jerusalem: United Nations Relief and Works Agency for Palestine Refugees.

Vidal López, R., Atehoróa Arrendondo, C. & Salcedo, J. (2011). The Effects of Internal Displacement on Host Communities. Bogotá: Brookings Institution-London School of Economics Project on Internal Displacement.

WFP. (2015). Colombia | WFP | United Nations World Food Programme – Fighting Hunger Worldwide. Available at: http://web.archive.org/web/20150409220744/www.wfp.org/countries/colombia /overview (accessed 23 February 2017).

Whitley, M. A., Coble, C. and Jewell, G. S. (2016). Evaluation of a sport-based youth development programme for refugees. *Leisure/Loisir*, *40*(2), 175–199.

35

SDP and the environment

Simon C. Darnell

Introduction

Since the early 2000s, sport has increasingly been institutionalized within international development, with organizations from the United Nations (UN) to the International Olympic Committee (IOC) touting the ability of sport to address a myriad of social ills. Recently, however, sport has also been connected to global strategies of sustainable development, including as a means to promote environmental protection and remediation in the face of impending challenges such as global climate change. This is illustrated within the Sustainable Development Goals (SDGs), the UN's primary development policy through the year 2030 which draws attention to the environment as a key aspect of development policy, and also outlines the specific contributions of sport to sustainable development (United Nations 2015).

The inclusion of sport within the SDGs and the 2030 development agenda marks the highest profile and most specific recognition to date of sport's potential contribution to sustainable development. This, in turn, highlights the increasing importance and significance of the environment in the burgeoning relationship between sport and international development. Indeed, the inclusion of sport within the SDGs was accompanied by conclusions from organizations like the then United Nations Office on Sport for Development and Peace (UNOSDP 2016) that sport can and should play a role in responding to issues of environmental sustainability:

> Sport can contribute to combating climate change, for instance through sport-based projects aimed at supporting the relief of communities and reconstruction of facilities in natural disaster recovery. It can also raise awareness on climate change by transmitting messages on its impacts and encourage action in this context.
>
> *UNOSDP 2016*

With this in mind, this chapter offers an assessment – historical, theoretical, and substantive – of the relationship between sport and environmental sustainability, particularly in the context of the growing SDP sector. In so doing, the chapter explores and advances three key ideas. First, given the challenge and significance of issues like climate change, environmental sustainability constitutes a central issue within international development, and may now be the *most* important development challenge and threat facing humanity in the twenty-first century and beyond. Second, while critical understandings and assessments of the relationship between sport and the environment are not new, they do provide important insights into sport's environmental track record, which in turn help to illustrate whether or not sport (at least in its current form) might effectively contribute to sustainable development on a global scale. Third, the efforts to institutionalize the SDP sector, and the significance of sport's inclusion in the SDGs and the 2030 Agenda, mean that the SDP sector will likely need to confront issues of environmental sustainability, and show itself to be focused on the environment, in order to stay relevant in the context of contemporary international development and global politics. Some of the ways in which sport and SDP might (re)imagine and (re) position itself to contribute to environmental sustainability are discussed.

International development and the environment

The significance of environmental issues within development processes and development studies is not new. Indeed, the environment has been considered of crucial importance in global politics and international development since at least the second half of the twentieth century. In 1972, the United Nations Conference on the Human Environment was held in Stockholm, Sweden. It led to the Stockholm Declaration, a statement comprised of 26 principles concerning the relationship between the environment and development, including the need to safeguard the world's natural resources and to support developing countries in their pursuit of environmental management and sustainability. It also led to the creation of the United Nations Environment Programme (UNEP), an agency within the UN system that advocates for environmentally sustainable human development.

Building on this, and recognizing the significance and persistence of the environmental challenges facing humanity, in 1983 the United Nations General Assembly lent its support, through the passing of a resolution, to the creation of the World Commission on Environment and Development (WCED), an arm's length organization designed to focus on the relationship between the environment and development and the problems posed therein. The WCED was led by the then Prime Minister of Norway, Gro Harlem Bruntland, and led to the publication of *Our Common Future*, also known as The Bruntland Report, in 1987. The Bruntland Report is seen as an important event in generating the notion of sustainable development, which it defined as 'development that meets the needs of the present without compromising the ability of future generations to meet their own needs' (United Nations 1987). For scholars and analysts of sustainable development, it was in The Bruntland Report that the idea 'received its most popular exposition' (Pearce *et al.* 1990: ix).

In turn, The Bruntland Report led to further significant events in global policy and politics, particularly within the UN system. The 1992 United Nations Conference on Environment and Development, held in Rio de Janeiro (and sometimes referred to as the Rio Summit or the Earth Summit), continued to draw attention to the seriousness of environmental issues facing humanity, and helped to solidify the importance of the environment and sustainability within development policies and practices. The Rio Summit was attended by many of the world's leaders, including heads of state and high profile members of global civil society. It subsequently led to the formalization of the United Nations Framework Convention on Climate Change, which in turn begat the 1997 Kyoto Protocol that set targets on greenhouse gas emissions, and the 2015 Paris Agreement on Climate Change. These were major milestones in the struggle to create and maintain a global framework for environmental sustainability.

Overall, these events demonstrate the extent to which the environment has been linked to the processes and politics of international development over the past several decades. They also illustrate the increasing attention paid to the environment and sustainability by the UN system, national governments, and civil society actors. There are several reasons why the environment has assumed such an important and growing position within the politics and policies of international development. First is that the problem of environmental degradation – and climate change in particular – has worsened, not improved since the middle of the twentieth century. A whole range of evidence exists to support this claim, much of which is summarized in the 2014 Summary Report of the Intergovernmental Panel on Climate Change (IPCC 2014). The report shows that mean global temperatures are now 1.0 degree Celsius higher than during the nineteenth century, the likely impacts of which are dire and far-ranging. These include threats to food security, direct and negative effects on population health, increases in poverty, and escalations in human displacement and refugee crises (Gough 2017). The IPCC Report concludes that climate change increases 'the likelihood of severe, pervasive, and irreversible impacts for people and ecosystems' (IPCC 2014). Such evidence forcefully demonstrates that humanity cannot ignore current environmental trends, particularly the challenges posed by a changing climate.

Second is that the environment is linked in some way to nearly all of the issues that are normatively and regularly recognized in the theory, practice and research of international development (and by extension those attended to in the SDP sector). These include issues such as health promotion, education, and gender empowerment. For example, eco-feminists have argued for years that women, and particularly poor women of colour living in the global South, are more likely to bear the brunt of ecological deterioration, particularly amid capitalist accumulation, resource extraction and/or exploitative labour, all of which contribute to environmental degradation (Mies and Shiva 1993). In turn, the ever-widening ecological footprint of industrialization restricts those with fewer resources to increasingly precarious positions socially, economically, and/or geographically. In this sense, and third, environmental issues are themselves revelatory of international development's geo-politics and political economy. While it has been the global North (and relatively powerful nation states, corporations, and citizens) who have tended to reap the most benefits from the industrial processes that have led to or exacerbated climate change, it is those in the global South who are most often left to bear the brunt of climate change's impacts, both sooner and more directly. Thus, for a number of years, the issues of environmental sustainability and sustainable development have been understood as more than simply technical and/or ecological, but also fundamentally rooted in justice and equity (Shue 1999).

From this perspective, the challenges of climate change and environmental sustainability bring into sharp relief the question of what should constitute the focus of development. Should sustainable development be about economic growth, and facilitating the success (material and discursive) of those who have traditionally been excluded from the benefits of the global economy? Or do environmental concerns mean that the pursuit of economic growth should be abandoned? And can the binary thinking implied in such questions be reconciled? Overall, the question of what is to be sustained, and how sustainability should be approached, is embedded in development processes, policies, and politics now more than ever. In turn, the different ways in which sustainability is conceptualized and approached are indicative of different development ideologies, politics, and policies (Redclift 2014).

Such contestability can be seen specifically in relation to the issue of climate change and debates about what to do in response to the threat it poses. While there have been calls to downsize economically and industrially in order to minimize or slow the impacts of climate change, there are also arguments in favour of focusing on adaptation and the adaptive capacity that is and will be required to survive amid a changing climate. Adaptation is defined as 'adjustment in natural or human systems in response to actual or expected climate stimuli or their effects, which moderates harm or exploits beneficial opportunities,' and connects to development in that both adaptation and development are 'concerned with social processes and issues of vulnerability, change and human agency' (Boyd 2014: 343).

Regardless of the proposed solution or response, there can be no question that climate change poses a problem for all stakeholders in the field of international development, including citizens, civil society actors, and policy-makers. Indeed, for some, climate change constitutes a 'super wicked problem' because time is running out to do something about it, there is no strong central authority to address it, those who cause the problem also seek to address it, and it regularly includes an irrational discounting of the future (Levin *et al.* 2012). Thus, responding to climate change may require not just new policies but even new epistemologies for policy creation and implementation. For example, while studies of the impact of climate change have tended to start from the use of modelling, by which scientific theories and data are used to assess how a radically changing climate will impact people, Gough (2017: 23) suggests that studying the impact of climate change should also be concerned with issues of social vulnerability and inequality, particularly 'starting from the local development context in which climate change occurs'. It is in this way that the environment and critical climate studies can be seen to intersect with development and development studies. For those interested in SDP, the next question is how does sport connect to these increasingly connected relationships between development and the environment? The next section offers an initial foray into this discussion by examining the relationship between sport and the environment, and sport's rather poor environmental track record to date.

Sport and the environment

Researchers have been examining the relationship between sport and the natural environment for decades. One of the earliest and best known assessments of this relationship is David Chernushenko's 1994 text *Greening Our Games,* in which he outlined steps that sport managers could take to limit the negative impact of major sporting events on the natural environment. Such calls were viewed as increasingly necessary given the deleterious effects of many sporting events on natural landscapes, impacts that were gradually subject to public outcry. While such concerns about environmental issues were raised about the hosting of the Olympic Games as far back as the 1964 games in Tokyo, the negative environmental impacts of the 1992 Winter Olympics in Albertville drew renewed attention to the importance of minimizing sport's environmental footprint. The subsequent 1994 Winter Olympics in Lillehammer Norway were dubbed 'The Green Games', and showed that sport organizations like the IOC could no longer ignore the environmental aspects of sport, or the damage caused by sports events (Cantelon and Letters 2000; Harvey *et al.* 2014). Eventually, this led to the recognition of the environment as a key consideration in choosing Olympic hosts, and the Olympic Charter was modified to include reference to the environment.

With that said, such attention – and its associated policy responses by organizations like the IOC – stopped well short of actually 'solving' the problem of sport's poor environmental track record and impact. Arguably, what occurred primarily were a series of strategic efforts to promote environmental sustainability in sport while leaving the key structures – and profits – of international elite sport intact and in place. For critical scholars such as Lenskyj (1998), this approach was evident in the 'corporate environmentalism' that took place within international sport at the beginning of the new millennium. As Lenskyj argued, the 2000 Sydney Olympics, which also claimed to be environmentally responsible, employed a corporate approach to sustainability in which the environment was worth protecting but only so long as it was deemed profitable to do so. From this perspective, the organizers of the Sydney Games promoted the event as 'green' while using the popularity of sport to deflect attention from actual environmental reforms and stewardship.

Similar critiques have continued in more recent analyses and assessments of the environmental effects and impact of sport, particularly within the 'greening' of sports like golf (see Millington and Wilson 2016) and the ongoing practice of 'greenwashing' sport, in which sport organizations and corporations attempt to market themselves as environmentally conscious and their products as sustainable (see Beder 1999; Miller 2017). In the former, efforts to reform the golf industry have been found to be grounded primarily in notions of ecological modernization, which seek technical solutions to environmental challenges but in ways that minimize interruptions to capitalist accumulation as much as possible. Ecological modernization proffers the idea that the issue and challenge of environmental degradation (in sport) is primarily a technical one, and that practical methods can and will be developed to achieve the goal of sustainability (Millington and Wilson 2016). At its most extreme, ecological modernization in sport has even led to claims that sport can *improve* the natural environment. Such rhetoric was seen at the 2016 Rio Olympics, where the return of golf to the Olympic program was positioned and celebrated as a way to secure the stewardship and maintenance of sensitive environmental sites, particularly through technologically advanced golf course design (Millington *et al.* 2018).

While the ostensible 'greening' of sports like golf continues, is it through the latter practice – greenwashing – where the sport sector has further sought to claim a position of environmental responsibility while avoiding any real changes to its governance, structures or profits (Miller 2017). Miller (2017: 2) argues that the greenwashing of sport occurs through two, inter-related processes: sport organizations themselves contribute to climate change through their significant carbon footprint, while simultaneously working to 'legitimize the harm they cause by promoting themselves as good environmental citizens'. This process is further exacerbated by the opportunity that sport affords to corporate polluters, such as petroleum companies and others who profit from extractive industries, but who strive to create positive images of themselves by and through their sponsorship of sport. This all adds up to a general complicity between sport and environmental degradation, and stands in rather direct opposition to the notion that sport might be organized in the service of sustainability.

Of course, despite this poor track record, it would be inaccurate to suggest that the world of sport is entirely devoid of environmental consciousness, or that sport organizations and actors have simply failed to make changes in support of sustainability. Indeed, it is important to acknowledge that often precisely because of its poor environmental track record, sport has been a site of environmental activism. Harvey *et al.* (2014), for example, have examined some of the overlaps between the sport sector and various social movements focused on the environment. They show that environmental organizations, notably Greenpeace, have focused on sport as an area for reform. At the same time, some activist organizations focused on environmental stewardship have emerged from sport itself. One of the best known of these groups is Surfers Against Sewage, established in Britain in 1990 over concerns about the polluting of local surfing spots. Since then, the organization has become involved in a broad range of environmental causes (see Wheaton 2007). In addition, groups such as the Global Network for Anti Golf Course Action formed in response to the environmental degradation caused by golf course construction and maintenance (Harvey *et al.* 2014). Each of these examples illustrate important connections between sport and environmental movements, and also demonstrate that the need for environmental sustainability is recognized within particular sections of the mainstream sport sector.

In sum, the importance of environmental sustainability within global sport is now recognized and discussed more than ever before, and it is even reasonable to suggest that there is an emerging environmental consciousness within sport. Indeed, it may be the case that sustainability as a concept has increasingly found its way into the sports industry, and has even re-shaped some of the structures, organizations and consumption practices of sports mega events like the Olympics (see Mol 2010). Still, there is a significant body of literature to show that powerful interests in sport continue to work to deflect attention away from sport's negative environmental impact, while attempting to build consent for the notion that sport is a net positive in relation to sustainability without making substantial or fundamental changes. This poses some important and challenging questions for the SDP sector. First, is it possible to *apply* sport to solving environmental challenges like climate change, particularly on a global scale? Second, is it necessary – or even possible – to reform sport in order to align it with environmental challenges as understood within sustainable development? Third, is there a place for environmentalism and environmental activism within the still evolving SDP sector? If so, what would this look like? The next section discusses some of these issues.

SDP and environmental sustainability

Despite (a) the development discourses attached to sport through the SDGs, (b) the growth of the SDP sector, and (c) the attention paid to environmental sustainability within the global sports industry, it is only recently that the environment has assumed any emphasis within the SDP sector. Further, it is still rare for SDP organizations to focus on environmental protection and remediation in their policies and programming. This lack of attention paid to the environment within SDP is particularly conspicuous given that UNEP used the popularity of sport in the 1990s to 'promote environmental awareness and respect for the environment among the public, especially young people', and established environmental guidelines for sporting events such as the Olympic Games (UNEP n.d.). These guidelines eventually informed the IOC's environmental mandate, including a commitment to 'encourage and support a responsible concern for environmental issues, to promote sustainable development in sport and to require that the Olympic Games are held accordingly' (IOC 2014).

To be fair, there have been some SDP organizations concerned with the environment. One of the best known is the Mathare Youth Sport Association (MYSA), a sport-based community development program operating since the 1980s in the Mathare slum on the outskirts of Nairobi, Kenya (see Willis 2000). Started by a Canadian development worker named Bob Munro, MYSA included an environmental mandate from its outset, by requiring youth football teams to participate in clean-up and removal of trash. Because of this, MYSA has always been notable for awarding points to teams based not only on their football performance, but also for their contributions to environmental clean-up in Mathare. The organization has received significant praise and attention for this work over the years, including coverage in the New York Times, and members of the club also attended the 1992 Earth Summit in Rio as guests of football legend Pele.

Still, the example of MYSA notwithstanding, issues of the environment, sustainability and climate change have arguably lagged behind other issues within the SDP sector, and at least have yet to assume a primary place of importance for many SDP actors and advocates. As a result, environmental sustainability remains somewhat secondary to what are understood to be the core SDP issues of gender empowerment, health promotion, and peace and reconciliation. Given this, there are a plethora of issues that need to be addressed in order for the SDP sector to embrace the importance and significance of sustainability and in turn to remain relevant within the current global development agenda. While not an exhaustive list, six of these issues are discussed here.

First is the issue of policy-making. Increasingly, policy decisions within the SDP sector – and questions of who makes SDP policy, in whose interests' policies are developed, and on what issues such policies can and should focus – have been the subject of critical scrutiny (see Hayhurst 2009). While the SDGs clearly provide a policy platform and agenda to increase the connections between environmentalism and development, it is still notable that the environment has yet to be taken up as directly as it could be within SDP policy. For example, in response to the 2030 Agenda, SDP advocates like the Commonwealth Secretariat have tended to focus on specific SDGs but *not* those SDGs that have an explicit environmental focus (see Lindsey and Chapman 2017). This is not altogether surprising, given many of the issues and challenges discussed in this chapter, but does highlight that opportunities remain to include environmental issues within the SDP policy agenda, and that significant work may be required to make this happen. Indeed, the wide range of issues captured within the SDGs presents a challenge to the SDP sector in terms of policy coherence (Lindsey and Darby 2018). This raises the question of whether it is possible for SDP to commit to the environment or whether this might detract from what has been, until now, the sector's main policy foci. No matter the response to this, it is reasonable to conclude that until such time as the environment is seen as a policy priority at high levels of SDP advocacy, it is unlikely to enjoy a significant position within SDP practice and programs.

Second is the need to recognize the place of sport and SDP within the specific and ongoing challenges of climate change, and amid the issues of risk and insecurity that climate change exacerbates. The point here is that the conventional or typical targets of SDP programs – often people living on the social and cultural margins within communities in the global South – are precisely those communities and populations who face the biggest risks and threats from climate change, particularly in regard to their natural environment, access to resources, and the sustainability of their livelihoods and lifestyles. As SDP programs continue to operate in such spaces, they will need to acknowledge and account for this increased impact and risk on already marginalized people. From this perspective, it would be ignorant at best (and disingenuous at worst) for SDP organizations to continue programming in the global South without acknowledging the threat of climate change and the ways in which it is already making life harder for many communities.

Third, and more specifically, there may be both a need and opportunity for SDP to engage in and support communities as they struggle to adapt to environmental threats in general and climate change in particular. Again, while it is important to recognize that focusing on adaptation is a contestable approach both politically and strategically, it cannot be denied that some level of adaptation is already happening, and (again) taking place primarily in the global South communities that SDP programs most typically target and in which they tend to operate. A question, then, is what role can sport and SDP play in supporting these adaptation processes? It may be, for example, in keeping with the general approach to SDP programming, that sport offers a hook or cultural form (Mwaanga 2010) in and through which to educate and train local communities to promote adaptation processes and better prepare to deal with climate change. It might also be that new sporting practices may emerge amid adaptation and change brought on by environmental challenges, which can themselves form the basis for SDP programs. At any rate, as global South communities adjust – in both their everyday practices and their longer term cultural forms – there may be a role for sport and SDP in supporting such new forms of, and approaches to, sustainable development.

A fourth issue facing the SDP sector as it relates to the environment is the ongoing importance of geo-politics and political economy. While the SDGs and 2030 Agenda clearly went some way to mainstreaming the notion of environmental sustainability and showing its broad policy relevance, the challenge of climate change – and what to do about it – remains firmly political and therefore contestable. These politics have several dimensions, including: debates over when and how to transition to a global economy that does not rely on fossil fuels; whether the global North has a political or ethical responsibility to lead the way in responding to climate change; and whether citizens have rights in demanding changes from government and corporations to ensure a sustainable future. Such issues are intensely political and often hotly contested, which means that for the SDP sector to engage with issues of environmental sustainability, it may need to become more directly engaged in environmental politics. To date, there has been a recurring and popular sense that SDP is, and even should be, politically neutral, or that one of the strengths that sport holds within international development is its broad and universal popularity that transcends political divides. However, given the issues discussed in this chapter, it is reasonable to contend that the environment may be an issue about which SDP organizations, advocates and policy-makers can no longer remain politically neutral. Indeed, to make a real contribution to the 2030 Agenda, SDP's champions may need to join current debates about how to position sport in support of environmental sustainability.

In turn, while sport may offer a platform from which to educate people about environmental issues, as discussed in this chapter sport is also firmly implicated in environmental politics and cannot claim a neutral role. The political implications of sport's poor environmental track therefore pose a significant challenge to the still burgeoning SDP sector; SDP advocates may need to be prepared to call for environmental reforms *within* the global sport sector in order to reposition sport in support of sustainability.

Fifth, and related, if the SDP sector is to make a commitment to environmentalism and recognize the importance of the environment in development, it may benefit from building connections and coalitions with sport-based activists and activist organizations that focus on the environment. For example, it is reasonable to suggest that activist organizations like Surfers Against Sewage could find productive synergies with the SDP sector if and when SDP shows itself to be interested in advocating for sport as a catalyst and champion for environmental sustainability. As Giulianotti (2011) has suggested, new social movements and radical NGOs with a commitment to social justice form one of the four ideal-types of SDP organizations (alongside private/commercial institutions, mainstream NGOs, and national and intergovernmental agencies), but are also arguably the least represented within the SDP sector given their overt politicization and demands for change. It may be, then, that the environment offers an issue around which New Social Movement organizations, radical NGOs, and social justice advocates can assume a greater role within the SDP sector.

Finally, and sixth, while the SDP sector has not always attended directly to issues of inequality and how to redress it, tending to focus more on notions of empowerment (Darnell 2012), the environment is one such issue where equality matters but also, crucially, in which all are implicated and by which all are threatened. Environmental sustainability may, therefore, offer a development topic and issue in and through which the SDP sector can build a sense of global solidarity that simultaneously recognizes unequal relations of power on an international scale. In this sense, there would appear to be some productive conceptual possibilities and opportunities in centering the environment within SDP rhetoric, policy, and practice. While issues such as HIV/AIDS prevention, post-conflict resolution, and even gender empowerment are ones that can be conceptually attached to *particular* communities and cultures, the scope and ubiquity of environmental issues and the challenge posed by climate change is such that it cannot be considered an issue only for underdeveloped countries or communities. The environment might therefore offer the basis for conceptualizing, structuring, and practicing SDP in ways that are more truly global.

Conclusion

This chapter has sketched out various ways in which: (a) environmental sustainability is an issue of international development, (b) sport has environmental impacts, often negative ones, and (c) the SDP sector faces challenges about how to prioritize environmental sustainability and remain relevant amid issues of sustainability, such as climate change. In concluding, it is reasonable to suggest that there are (at least) two main ways in which critical SDP scholars and researchers might engage with sustainability issues and the question of climate change.

The first is to study development inequalities and the ways in which they connect to, and are likely to be exacerbated by, environmental degradation. In this line of inquiry, a key question is what sport and SDP might offer to the challenge of sustainability and climate change as the pre-eminent development issues of the twenty-first century? Some initial thoughts around this issue have been proposed in this chapter, but are worthy of ongoing reflection as the SDP sector works to assert and maintain its position of relevance within international development structures and processes.

The second is to continue critical analyses of sport's environmental track record, and in turn contribute to political discussions (and even policy shifts) that might mitigate sport's negative influence on the environment. This may even lead to discussions about how to reorganize sport itself in support of sustainability. For example, what would a low-carbon sport industry look like, and how might it be organized? Key to such discussions will be moving beyond conceptualizations of sport as a discrete sub-field of global policy and politics and toward broader and deeper conceptualizations and analyses of sport that bring it more in line with the concept of global sustainability and the 2030 Agenda. This is no easy task. However, if the sport sector broadly, and the SDP sector in particular, are to live up to the promise of contributing to sustainability as claimed in the SDGs, then it will require a commitment to addressing the clear and present danger to humanity that is climate change and environmental degradation.

References

Beder, S. (1999). Greenwashing an Olympic-sized toxic dump. *PR Watch, 6*(2), 1–6.

Boyd, E. (2014). Climate change and development. In V. Desai, and R. Potter (eds), *The Companion to Development Studies* (3rd edn). London: Routledge, p. 341.

Cantelon, H. and Letters, M. (2000). The making of the IOC environmental policy as the third dimension of the Olympic movement. *International Review for the Sociology of Sport, 35*(3), 294–308.

Chernushenko, D. (1994). *Greening our Games: Running Sports Events and Facilities that won't Cost the Earth.* Ottawa: Centurion.

Darnell, S. (2012). *Sport for Development and Peace: A Critical Sociology.* London: Bloomsbury Academic.

Giulianotti, R. (2011). The sport, development and peace sector: A model of four social policy domains. *Journal of Social Policy, 40*(04), 757–776.

Gough, I. (2017). *Heat, Greed and Human Need: Climate Change, Capitalism and Sustainable Wellbeing.* Cheltenham: Edward Elgar.

Harvey, J., Horne, J., Safai, P., Darnell, S. and Courchesne-O'Neill, S. (2014). *Sport and social movements: From the local to the global.* London: Bloomsbury Academic.

Hayhurst, L. M. (2009). The power to shape policy: Charting sport for development and peace policy discourses. *International Journal of Sport Policy, 1*(2), 203–227.

IOC. (2014). IOC plays a key role at first ever UNEA. Available at: www.olympic.org/news/ioc-plays-key-role-at-first-ever-united-nations-environment-assembly-unea.

IPCC. (2014). Summary Report of the Intergovernmental Panel on Climate Change. Available at: http://ar5-syr.ipcc.ch/topic_summary.php.

Lenskyj, H. J. (1998). Sport and corporate environmentalism: The case of the Sydney 2000 Olympics. *International Review for the Sociology of Sport, 33*(4), 341–354.

Levin, K., Cashore, B., Bernstein, S. and Auld, G. (2012). Overcoming the tragedy of super wicked problems: Constraining our future selves to ameliorate global climate change. *Policy Sciences, 45*(2), 123–152.

Lindsey, I. and Chapman, T. (2017). *Enhancing the contribution of sport to the sustainable development goals.* London: Commonwealth Secretariat.

Lindsey, I. and Darby, P. (2018). Sport and the sustainable development goals: Where is the policy coherence? *International Review for the Sociology of Sport*. SAGE Journals, 22 January. Available at: http://journals.sagepub.com/doi/abs/10.1177/1012690217752651.

Mies, M. and Shiva, V. (1993). *Ecofeminism*. London: Zed Books.

Miller, T. (2017). *Greenwashing Sport*. Abingdon: Taylor & Francis.

Millington, B. and Wilson, B. (2016). *The Greening of Golf: Sport, Globalization and the Environment*. Manchester: Manchester University Press.

Millington, R., Darnell, S.C. and Millington, B. (2018). Ecological modernization and the Olympics: The case of golf and Rio's 'green' games. *Sociology of Sport Journal*. 35(1), 8–16.

Mol, A. P. (2010). Sustainability as global attractor: The greening of the 2008 Beijing Olympics. *Global Networks*, 10(4), 510–528.

Mwaanga, O. (2010). Sport for addressing HIV/AIDS: Explaining our convictions. *Leisure Studies Association Newsletter*, 85(March), 61–67.

Pearce, D., Barbier, E. and Markandya, A. (1990). *Sustainable Development: Economics and Environment in the Third World*. Routledge.

Redclift, M. (2014). Sustainable development. In V. Desai and R. Potter (eds), *The Companion to Development Studies* (3rd edn). London: Routledge, p. 333.

Shue, H. (1999). Global environment and international inequality. *International Affairs*, 75(3), 531–545.

UNEP. (n.d.). About UNEP, Sport and the Environment. Available at: www.unep.org/sport_env/about.aspx.

United Nations. (1987). Report of the World Commission on Environment and Development: Our Common Future. Available at: www.un-documents.net/our-common-future.pdf.

United Nations. (2015). Transforming our World: The 2030 Agenda for Sustainable Development. Available at: https://sustainabledevelopment.un.org/post2015/transformingourworld.

UNOSDP. (2016). Sport and Sustainable Development Goals. Available at: www.un.org/sport/content/why-sport/sport-and-sustainable-development-goals.

Wheaton, B. (2007). Identity, politics, and the beach: Environmental activism in surfers against sewage. *Leisure Studies*, 26(3), 279–302.

Willis, O. (2000). Sport and development: The significance of Mathare youth sports association. *Canadian Journal of Development Studies/Revue Canadienne d'Études Du Développement*, 21(3), 825–849.

36

SDP and coaching

Dean M. Ravizza

Introduction

If you ask athletes to describe their sport experiences, they often mention important coaches they have encountered along their timeline of participation. More so than most other individuals, the coach stands in a significant role within athletic competition. They are often referred to as leaders and shapers of young people whose coaching role extends well beyond the playing venue to one that intricately intertwines with life. Coaches are often credited with not just making better athletes, but making better people. Because coaches work intimately with children and youth who are at critical stages of development in their lives (Fraser-Thomas and Côté 2006; Côté and Fraser-Thomas 2007), they possess a unique opportunity to have a strong influence on young people.

The United Nations system and its Member States recognized the potential for these positive coach-related experiences to extend beyond merely a performance-related sports setting (United Nations 2003; for resolutions, see also www.un.org/wcm/content/site/sport/home). The field of Sport for Development and Peace (herein stated as SDP) emerged based on the growing understanding and reinforcement from supporting public resolutions from the Sport for Development and Peace International Working Group (2008) that sport programs are powerful vehicles for achieving broader goals, particularly in advancing development and peace agendas (United Nations 2003). The field has come to prominence within social policy agendas, university programming, sports management, web-based platforms (see www.sportanddev.org), and research outlets including the *Journal of Sport for Development* (Richards *et al.* 2013) to further evidence that SDP is a recognized sector aligned with broader development and peace goals. The role of sport aimed at social progress is further highlighted in the recent United Nations Declaration of the 2030 Agenda for Sustainable Development as an 'important enabler of sustainable development' (see UNOSDP n.d.) with great potential to address challenges outlined in each of the 17 Sustainable Development Goals (SDGs) as an integral part of the post-2015 Development Agenda (IOC 2015). At the field level, hundreds of programs[1] are leveraging the inherent opportunities presented through participation in sport for humanitarian responses, reconciliation and peacebuilding, rehabilitation and inclusion of persons with disabilities, civic engagement, advocacy and social change, awareness raising and education, and economic development (see UNESCO 2016 for country-specific applications). Despite strong advocacy for SDP, there is a critical need to examine the role of coaches who are on the frontlines of implementation to achieve important program outcomes.

The capacity for a coach to help navigate children and youth through the societal challenges being addressed by SDP programs is incalculable. Given their direct access to large numbers of children and youth and their potential to make positive impacts on their lives, coaches are in the unique position to facilitate the program objectives aimed at promoting a development agenda. This chapter seeks to utilize existing critical literature in SfPD to provide an understanding of the role of coaches in sport-based social interventions, their function within such programs, and their impact on achieving program objectives. The author provides reflexive accounts of long-term fieldwork, research, and programming in former conflict settings to further the understanding of the varied roles of coaches as part of community-based research and the subsequent design and implementation of SDP programs as a vector for reintegration and social inclusion of young survivors of war.

Coaches and sport for development and peace programs

When athletes reflect upon past sport experiences they often describe influential coaches as leaders, educators, advisors, and guides who develop sports skills, provide mentorship, and help navigate young athletes through life. Conversely, others speak of the deleterious effect of coaches on their sporting experiences; coaches who subsequently ignore the massive impact they have on athlete's lives for the sake of their own individual agenda. Participation in sports may provide a healthy outlet for children, but the hyper-competitive environment of organized sports puts children's minds and bodies at risk of physical and emotional stress (Moses 2015). By placing excessive demands on young athletes, coaches can push their young players toward feelings of stress and performance anxiety, a general sense of unhappiness, a push to other alternative and athlete-organized sports and games, and early exit from sports altogether (Coakley 2008). Concurrent to their central role of developing athletic skills and tactics within their sports, coaches may also contribute to the positive development of participants as human beings and citizens, teams as cohesive units, and broader community goals by mobilizing communities in shared social spaces around a team (ICCE 2012). Therefore, it is easy to comprehend the potential of sport to meet international development objectives and any tensions that may exist under the guidance of quality coaches.

Our understanding of coaches is complicated by the varying roles in which they are engaged within the existing scope of SDP programs. Beyond the title of coach, they are also referred to as mentors, instructors, and facilitators.[2] And, coaches are referred to as 'trainers' within an organization that adopts a *train-the-trainer approach* where coaches receive training and mentoring from experienced facilitators who build the capacity of coaches to deliver the program content themselves. The term 'coach' is used often by existing sports organizations seeking to further address a development agenda resembling what Coalter (2009) refers to as *Sport-Plus* programs. Meanwhile, a program aimed at increasing youth employment opportunities uses 'mentors' to enable the transferability of market-driven skills from a sport context to the workplace (*Plus-Sport*). The former combines the traditional coaching role with the facilitation of additional activities that meet the development aspect of their program while the latter uses sport, and subsequently the mentors, to motivate participants within a program designed to build their personal resources (Coalter 2009).

SDP programs, and the organizations sponsoring them, rely heavily upon coaches to facilitate activities in order to meet their aims. Coaches' backgrounds and experience vary drastically across the spectrum of SDP programming. Coaches from similar background experiences as program participants work as 'credible messengers' to deliver program content. Local implementing coaches understand the unique challenges the children and youth face within their communities, create positive relationships around sport, and further enhance the participant's receptivity to positive program messages (Baptiste *et al.* 2006). Using credible messengers within a SDP program returns resources and opportunity to communities whose lack of those two key elements feeds into higher rates of pervasive development issues. To further their role, programs should enlist their knowledge of local customs and cultures to strengthen the connection between these practices and program content. Regardless of the designated title, a coach's guidance as an external support is critical for positive growth (Petipas *et al.* 2005).

Research on coaches in sport for development programs

Coaching and coaching education is an increasingly important area of sports science. Looking at sport as a global institution, there is extensive quantitative and qualitative research on the role of coaches and their impact on athletes and sports programs. Rangeon *et al.* (2012) reported coach development as the lead topic of research with a strong focus on coach education, learning, and related developmental issues. The shift in focus from coaching behaviors as noted in previous similar analysis research (Gilbert and Trudel 2004: 91) to addressing coach development issues signaling a shift from 'developmental questions rather than mere behavioral observations', demonstrates a deeper quest for understanding dynamic processes for coach learning and development. Even with this expansive body of knowledge on coaches, and widespread calls to build a stronger SDP evidence base (Nicholls *et al.* 2011; Giles and Lynch 2012), there is only slight advancement toward understanding the impact of coaches within the SDP field despite the acknowledgment of their important role in achieving program outcomes and recent outlets dedicated to sharing this knowledge.

In an interesting study, Whitely and her colleagues (2013) explored South African SDP programs from the broad perspective of study participants instead of one particular program or organization. Through focus group discussions with coaches from a range of (Sport-Plus) programs, the authors sought to understand the realities of the sport settings, the experiences of coaches and young people in these underserved communities. This also included unpacking the necessary approaches needed when designing, implementing, and evaluating sport for development programs. Findings reflected positively on the coaches' belief that sport served as a significant tool for promoting positive development despite facing significant barriers that affect youth participation and desired program outcomes. Despite their beliefs, a lack of resources such as facilities, equipment, and funding present challenges to creating the safe, developmental spaces they desired, while a lack of transport and sport offerings within their communities impacted the accessibility to programs. From a development perspective, their findings suggested the effectiveness of the 'inclusion of an inside-up indigenous approach' (Whitley *et al.* 2013: 10) to understand and address community needs through local sports programs. When SDP programs adopt a top-down, outside-in, deficit-based approach (Giles and Lynch 2012), coaches and participants are vanquished to passive roles rather than active participants in identifying community needs and shaping programs, determining solutions, and providing input toward long-term, sustainable change. Coaches experiencing these tensions will struggle to see the value in their role thus reducing their program 'buy-in' and affecting the desired outcomes.

The voices of these coaches reflect their ability to provide unique insights into the strengths and challenges of a SDP program that may otherwise go unnoticed. Here, coaches move from being passive subjects whose interactions are studied through mere observations or quantitative surveys (Levermore 2011) to that of a critical voice highlighting program strengths and challenges therefore providing important contributions to overall program improvement. The field will continue to benefit from further research that not only observes and critiques coaching behaviors, but solicits their thoughts to provide further understanding of positive aspects and challenges to their experiences to advance the quality of SDP programming.

Critical reflections from post-conflict settings

Background

Practitioners and scholars have recently recognized the importance of sport and play for children and youths' resilience in geographies of war, conflict and disaster (Thorpe 2016), refugees in flight and resettlement (Jeanes *et al.* 2015; see also RCOA 2010), and the internally displaced as part of post-disaster interventions (Henley 2005; Valenti *et al.* 2012). Furthermore, field-based research continues to enhance the understanding of the uses of sport as a component of reintegration programming for former child soldiers (Dyck 2011, Ravizza 2012; 2016).

The following reflexive account of SDP experiences is a product of this author's long-term engagement in research, fieldwork, and programming in Northern Uganda during times of conflict and within the post-conflict setting. Since the height of the conflict in 2004, we sought to understand the uses of sport within various environments with an initial focus on rehabilitation and reintegration programs for children formerly associated with the Lord's Resistance Army (LRA). Outcomes from the extensive fieldwork and research yielded a grassroots programmatic effort to utilize sport as a means to resolve incidences of low-level conflict to build more inclusive post-conflict communities (Ravizza *et al.* 2012). In each phase, coaches played a critical role on multiple levels to enhance our understanding of the applications of sport in this complex humanitarian crisis.

Introduction and context

The long-running conflict between the LRA and Government (of Uganda) Forces created a large-scale humanitarian disaster including displacement of millions of citizens into internally displaced (IDP) camps. This forced coalescence of large groups of diverse citizens under harsh conditions contributed to issues of alcoholism and drug abuse, domestic and sexual violence, poor security, and lack of educational and economic opportunities. Additionally, thousands of children and youth[3] were abducted by the LRA and forced into a wide range of non-combative and combative roles causing significant threats to their psychological and emotional well-being. Sexual violence and the forced marriage of young girls to rebel group members proved to be a pervasive threat to their physical and emotional safety (McKay and Mazurana 2004). During the conflict, governmental agencies and non-governmental organizations (NGOs) worked in tandem to support the reintegration efforts of young abductees by creating amnesty protocols and holistic programs to foster an innocuous return to their communities.

In 2004, I began a post-doctoral internship in Uganda in cooperation with the United Nations International Children's Emergency Fund (UNICEF) and a large international SDP organization that operated in several locations within the country and throughout the immediate region. I worked closely between field offices to monitor and evaluate, and report challenges that created disconnects between program facilitation and outcomes. This meant traveling to program locations, and observing and conversing with program coaches. Throughout this formative year,

I documented a substantial number of challenges these coaches experienced that made their role difficult while also noting factors they described that enhanced programming outcomes. These experiences crystallized my decisions to pursue further fieldwork on the uses of sport as part of psycho-social programming for children and youth experiencing violence, particularly in areas of conflict.

Upon near completion of this post-doctoral experience, the director of the Gulu Support the Children Organization interim care center for former child soldiers – a transit point for recently returned children prior to family re-unification and community reintegration – requested me to work cohesively with center staff to integrate sports into their holistic reintegration program. The aims here were to capitalize on the inherent opportunities of sports to apply socially acceptable and structured patterns of behaviors for children coming from a social context in which violence was normalized to reinforce the value and strategies of non-violent conflict resolution. The staff prioritized this key theme given the significant stigma faced by former child soldiers as unconditional threats to peace in the very fragile communities to which they sought to return (Wessells 2006). I worked cohesively with center social workers who led the daily sport activities of football (soccer) for boys, netball for girls, and volleyball (mixed teams) to create localized opportunities for sport to meet the programming objectives. Social workers (with me as an active observer) facilitated activities by managing the equipment set-up and organizing and verbally supporting the participants while occasionally playing alongside them. Afterwards, we led group talk activities that centered on issues of non-violent resolution to low-level interpersonal conflicts using the sport context as the medium of discussion. Through their daily notations and central evaluation system, social workers noted a few incidences of conflict among returnees and, if applicable, the strategies they used to resolve these conflicts.

This case highlighted the expanded role of mental health professionals whose main tasks in the reintegration program intersected with facilitating sport programming as an appealing means to promote prosocial behaviors. Their involvement expanded the concept of 'the coach' by using sport as a psycho-social component within existing programming. Their involvement promoted expansive thought regarding the potential effectiveness of sport as part of the holistic reintegration program for the children and youth receiving services at the center.

From reintegration to peaceful play

Research on the uses of sport for reintegration and long-term social inclusion of former child soldiers is limited. To contribute to the evidence base, we began long-term field research with the support of the Government of Uganda (GoU) and funding from the United States Agency for International Development (USAID) Mission in Uganda. The aims of our research were to assess factors of sport to facilitate social reintegration of former child soldiers (boys and girls). The original field survey sample comprised of 442 children and youth from two (subsequently divided into four) conflict-affected districts to include nearly 100 former child soldiers. Our research in Northern Uganda indicated high participation rates of girls and boys, who did so mainly at schools revealing a gap in community-based programs. Former abductees were less likely to participate in sports than their non-abducted peers since they were less likely to return to school, needed to generate an income, and faced increased levels of social stigma. Boys and girls reported that borderline violence in sports was not acceptable and negotiation was a preferred method of resolving conflict in sport (Ravizza 2010; 2012). Local officials, community members, and my team determined that further investigations were necessary to understand more acute applications of sport that could support post-conflict recovery and development efforts.

Following this phase, our research included in-depth follow-up interviews with former child soldiers, key informant interviews and focus group discussions with community-based sport coaches, school-based sport teachers,[4] and members of the district communities. Each provided the team with valuable insights into the uses of sport as a means to achieve development objectives aligned with the government's Peace and Recovery Development Plan (GoU 2007), its connections to the reintegration process, and its value as a source of social inclusion. The outcomes of this phase yielded support for a community-based program using coaches within existing community and school-based sport programs as a means to socially support children and youth marginalized as a result of the conflict. The regional peacebuilding agenda utilized sports as a means to resolve conflicts of low-intensity that remained prevalent following the cessation of hostilities (Pham *et al.* 2007).

To begin this process, the regional District Sports Officers referred coaches and sport teachers to our research team for involvement in a series of participatory research workshops to learn about their localized attitude toward resolving conflict through sport. Because the initial research took place in their districts, I had already established a rapport with many of them. References at this phase were based on service to their respective communities, knowledge of community needs, and positive social status within their communities in addition to their success as a community-based coach. The inclusion of sport teachers was critical given our original research revealed school as a main sport venue, because the majority of schools remained operational during the conflict (Ravizza 2010). To ensure inclusiveness and to address issues across gender and disability, the participation of female coaches and coaches working with disabled athletes was emphasized. Some coaches played dual roles like school-based sport teachers who also coached as part of a district-wide volleyball association. While sport teachers received training in issues on key topics such as child protection through localized, school-based programs, many of the participant coaches had received varying levels of training on such topics through their local district and/or through specialized NGO-initiated workshops. Each coach participated in intensive workshops aimed at our understanding of acts of conflict in sport and ways to resolve those acts based on localized acceptable practices. Each workshop began with small-group qualitative research exercises called *Free Listing* (Weller and Romney 1988) to rapidly identify conflict-related behaviors in sports and strategies for resolution. For example, participants were posed a question in their native language in order to generate a list of responses for analysis. The initial list was based on the question: What causes conflict to happen among children in sport? Interviewers probed for multiple responses followed by a short description of each cause. Once the responses were recorded, a second question was posed in order to generate another list of responses. The second list of responses was derived from the question: How are conflicts in sports resolved? to explore the routine ways in which coaches and participants resolved conflict that occurred during sport activities. The most interesting, and perhaps unintentional, outcome of this phase was constructed by a group of coaches that centered on the topic of revenge. Here, a player engages in delayed retaliation by seeking out a specific time to do harm to another player. Labeled in the Acholi Luo dialect as *Gin Marac,* this behavior is the result of a past incident – often a direct result of the larger conflict – that caused harm to the player exacting revenge. For instance, a young male football (soccer) player encountered another who committed an act of violence against his family during the conflict. This was not at all uncommon given the large number of children and youth abducted into the LRA who perpetrated acts of violence against communities (Annan *et al.* 2006). Coaches described how a player is overtaken by emotion and anger, which resorts in marking the opposing player until an opportunity is presented to do them physical harm. This level of conflict illustrated an acute, often latent, effect of the long-standing conflict on both formerly abducted and non-abducted children and youth as recognized by coaches. These actions posed uncondi-tional threats to community peace through acts of violence during sports that can reduce a well-adjusted former child soldier to retaliate as a situational response, recreating the very hostile behaviors that were otherwise overcome (Wessells 2006; Ravizza 2012).

In addition to the free listing exercises and workshop activities, coaches and sport teachers were interviewed by research team members to further establish their attitudes toward using sport in this context. Among these, coaches felt that former child soldiers were frequently the catalyst of verbal and physical conflict-related behaviors and should be 'screened' prior to par-ticipating in sport. They also struggled with conceding that youth have the capacity to resolve their own conflict – it can only occur through the intervention of an adult – reflecting their own desire to function in a deficits capacity. These findings were critical to reaching the program objectives and played out during the initial implementation phase within the conflict-affected region.

Peaceful play 'in the field'

In a shift from empirical data to program conception, workshop participants confirmed their interpretations of conflict in sport and strategies for resolution. The use of local language was critical to avoid any interpretive pitfalls that may cause coaches to seek out suitable direct equiva-lent translations that may not be there (Lambert 2006). As a result, we created the Peaceful Play program (Ravizza *et al.* 2012) which described four varying levels of conflict in sport based on localized definitions and strategies for resolution.

Three other levels of conflict accompanied the aforementioned level of *Gin Marac* or seeking revenge. *Telle* described a disagreement involving two opposing views about a particular play or call after which a decision is made for immediate resolution. *Cero Lok*, depicted an extension of a disagreement that is beyond an immediate resolution and where further consultation is needed for the conflict to be resolved. Finally, coaches demonstrated how a player may physically retaliate against an opponent following unintentional strong physical contact or a verbal incident (*Kero/Teko me Kom*). Since former child soldiers often experienced peer provocation, transfer strategies were discussed and described as opportunities to expand the potential of sport to create meaningful social change in their communities.

From coaching to monitoring, evaluation, and learning

As part of our monitoring, evaluation, and learning components (MEL), the field team conducted bi-weekly field visits to coaches and sports teachers at their respective sites. During these visits, a period of discussion ensued between the field team and coaches following each observational period. It was during this time that coaches further constructed their views of the conflicts that were occurring in sport and the potency of their strategies to resolve them. Our field visits revealed that under the guidance of sport teachers and coaches, children and youth utilized dialogue, referring to existing rules, and seeking outside assistance when appropriate to resolve conflicts consistent within their operant cultural belief systems. Coaches gradually shifted from their initial attitudes of children's inability to resolve conflict by working directly with youth to resolve conflict independent of their intervention, thus capitalizing on their sense of agency and reflecting the coach–participant partnership for which we had aimed. One female coach spoke to how she began to 'draw back' from wanting to intervene thus allowing her participants to resolve their conflicts peacefully using the strategies she taught them. This enriched the idea of the co-education of coaches and youth to further understand program content and its intersection with political and social constructs that influence outcomes (Hartmann and Kwauk 2011).

Through continued interaction and reflective thought, coaches no longer viewed former child soldiers as sources of conflict any differently than their non-abducted peers. This allowed them to demonstrate their readied abilities to resolve conflict peacefully. For instance, one male football coach articulated his adamant belief that former child soldiers provoked conflict and needed counseling prior to participation in sport from the outset. After several weeks of program monitoring, he reported no incidences of conflict in which former child soldiers engaged and cited examples of them seeking to resolve disagreements and arguments using program strategies.

The process of constructing the levels of conflict in sport and strategies for resolution with the community coaches yielded a deeper understanding of the ideals and potential for sport in this context not made possible had we attempted to create a program based solely on research outcomes and perceived needs of the community. This reflexive account of our previous fieldwork and research illuminates the capacity of coaches to play key informant roles in the construction and facilitation of programming based on community needs and localized customs. This supports the critiques of SDP programming by researchers who advocate for placing a strong consideration on 'local practices, local knowledge, the sociocultural and political–economic contexts as well as the needs and desires of communities themselves' (Hartmann and Kwauk 2011: 294). Therefore, the importance of understanding the values, attitudes, and beliefs of the coaches to further the understanding of sport as an opportunistic way to contribute to positive social change is necessary (Blom *et al.* 2015).

Failing to also understand the conflict-related experiences of the coaches would be failing to recognize such implications on their social relationships and how that affects program delivery and outcomes. A coach who experienced violence, either directly or indirectly, at the hands of a former child soldier could easily harbor resentment toward them, seek to prevent their participation, reproduce conditions of marginalization within the group, and reinforce community stigma, therefore underscoring the very message coaches are intended to impart through a SDP program. It is important to note the coaches' undeniable desire to maximize their role as members of the (sporting) community to contribute within their capacity to build more inclusive communities as a larger investment in regional peace and security. This investment is likely to pay off when coaches see the potential and receive the support necessary to pursue such opportunities to contribute to the overall stability of the region.

Conclusions

There is a strong societal belief that sport-based approaches can contribute to international development and peacebuilding objectives. However, this becomes untenable without careful consideration of the coaches tasked in the involvement of meeting such objectives. Our understanding of the role of the coach within the SDP field is complicated by their varying experiences within a wide range of programming. What we do know is they play a critical role in achieving the desired prosocial outcomes and effects. Yet, even with this knowledge, their role is often supplanted as a localized resource to support program planning, implementation, and critical feedback. This chapter provided only a glimpse into the role of coaches in SDP programs supported with findings and reflections from fieldwork, research, and program development in one localized context. It will take the field to convene as a community of learners to provide more detailed examples through research and practical experiences that can broaden our contextual understanding of coaches and how best to utilize them as an important resource partner. Future research should involve well-thought descriptions of the role of coaches in SDP programs, pose critical questions that support theoretical and practical applications, and provide systematic examination of and alongside coaches within their programmatic contexts.

The challenges faced by coaches who are involved in SDP programs are multiple, complex, and varied across ethnic cultures, gender, and communities. In order to meet these challenges, we must develop partnerships that build the evidence base and test locally driven and feasible sport interventions. We have a lot to learn from local people, how they respond to adversity, conflict, health-risk behaviors, and other societal issues. Coaches can enlighten us to a number of local processes that must not be displaced, but built upon to create sustainable, localized sport interventions that can further confirm the role of sport in meeting an international development agenda. And, most importantly, in providing the systems of support for the children and youth to thrive within the communities in which the coaches live and support.

Notes

1   At this writing, the Platform registers 957 organizations listed as one of the following: NGO/non-profit (690), business corporations (83), university/research (40), international organizations (37), government agencies (12) and sport clubs/federations (95). The Platform does not recognize some programs sponsored by country governments such as the Global Sports Mentoring Program, a main component of the Empowering Women and Girls through Sports Initiative, under the Sports Diplomacy Division in the United States Department of State.
2   For the purpose of this chapter, the author completed a systematic review of SDP programs in order to identify the key word (coach) or a suitable substitute. A list of potential synonyms to the key word was generated. Any terms found through the review not matching those previously generated were added to the list. The review started with programs listed on the International Platform as 'Non-Profit Organization/Charity/NGO/INGO'. Program weblinks and search engines provided opportunity to review for coach or coach-related terminology in program literature. Programs not listed on the website, but either known to the author, represented within International Working Groups, or mentioned in SDP literature, were also included in this review because some programs have not made the official connection to the Platform, and many grassroots programs have limited internet capacities to support an online presence.
3   Annan, Blattman and Horton (2006) in their Survey of War-Affected Youth (SWAY 1) estimated 66,000 children and youth were abducted by the LRA for periods of a couple of days to over ten years resulting in an inability to account for those unreturned. Accessed at: http://chrisblattman.com/projects/sway/
4   Sport teachers is a localized term describing those employed by schools to run daily sporting activities. Some activities take place during the school day, while some take place after school. Sport teachers are often accompanied by a 'sport prefect' or student assistant during activity time.

References

Annan, J., Blattman, C. and Horton, R. (2006). Survey of War-Affected Youth I: The State of Youth and Youth Protection in Northern Uganda. Available at: http://chrisblattman.com/projects/sway/ (originally accessed 10 July 2007 from www.swayuganda.org).

Baptiste, D. R., Bhana, A., Petersen, I., McKay, M., Voisin, D., Bell, C. and Martinez, D. D. (2006). Community collaborative youth-focused HIV/AIDS prevention in South Africa and Trinidad. *Journal of Pediatric Psychology*, 31(9), 905–16.

Blom, L., Gerstein, L., Stedman, K., Judge, L., Sink, A. and Pierce, D. (2015). Soccer for peace: Evaluation of in-country workshops with Jordanian coaches. *Journal of Sport for Development*, 3(4), 1–12. Available at: https://jsfd.org/ (accessed 10 July 2016).

Coakley, J. J. (2008). *Sport in Society: Issues and Controversies* (10th edn). New York: McGraw-Hill.

Coalter, F. (2009). Sport-in-development: accountability or development? In R. Levermore and A. Beacom (eds), *Sport and International Development*. Basingstoke, UK: Palgrave MacMillan.

Côté, J. and Fraser-Thomas, J. (2007). The health and developmental benefits of youth sport participation. In P. E. Crocker (ed.), *Sport Psychology: A Canadian Perspective*. Toronto: Pearson Education Canada.

Dyck, C. (2011). Football and post-war reintegration: Exploring the role of sport in DDR processes in Sierra Leone. *Third World Quarterly, 32* (3), 395–415.

Fraser-Thomas, M. and Côté, J. (2006). Youth sports: Implementing findings and moving forward with research. *Athletic Insight, 8* (3), 12–27.

Gilbert, W. and Trudel, P. (2004). Analysis of coaching science research published from 1970–2001. *Research Quarterly for Exercise and Sport, 75*(4), 388–399.

Giles, A. R. and Lynch, M. (2012). Postcolonial and feminist critiques of sport for development. In R. J. Schinke and S. J. Hanrahan (eds), *Sport for Development, Peace and Social Justice*, Morgantown, WV: Fitness Information Technology.

Government of Uganda. (2007). Peace and Recovery Development Plan for Northern Uganda 2007–2010. Available at: www.opm.nulep.org/documents/../441_8bb769bc0f0e094989a08e0f9629cbd4 (original copy accessed 15 June 2008).

Hartmann, D. and Kwauk, C. (2011). Sport and development: An overview, critique and reconstruction. *Journal of Sport and Social Issues, 35*(3), 284–305.

Henley, R. (2005). Helping Children Overcome Disaster Trauma Through Post-Emergency Psychosocial Sports Programs. Working Paper, Swiss Academy for Development.

International Council of Coaching Excellence (ICCE). (2012). *International Sport Coaching Framework.* Champaign, IL: Human Kinetics.

International Olympic Committee (IOC). (2015). The Contribution of Sport to the Sustainable Development Goals and the post-2015 Development Agenda. Available at: www.sportanddev.org/en/article/publication/ (accessed 8 December 2015).

Jeanes R., O'Connor, J. and Alfrey, L. (2015). Sport and the resettlement of young people from refugee backgrounds in Australia. *Journal of Sport and Social Issues, 39*(6), 480–500.

Lambert, J. (2006). A values-based approach to coaching sport in divided societies: The football for peace coaching manual. In J. Sugden and J. Wallis (eds), *Football for Peace. The Challenges of using Sport for Co-Existence in Divided Societies.* Aachen: Meyer and Meyer.

Levermore, R. (2011). Evaluating sport-for-development: Approaches and critical issues. *Progress in Development Studies, 11*(4), 339–353.

McKay, S. and Mazurana, D. (2004). *Where Are the Girls? Girls in Fighting Forces in Northern Uganda, Sierra Leone and Mozambique: Their Lives During and After War.* Montreal: International Center for Human Rights and Democratic Development.

Moses, G. (2015). Competitive youth sports and the rise of overuse, burnout, and career-ending injury. *PIT Journal, Cycle 6.* Available at: http://pitjournal.unc.edu/article/competitive-youth-sports-and-rise-overuse-burnout-and-career-ending-injury (accessed 8 August 2016).

Nicholls, S., Giles, A. R. and Sethna, C. (2011). Perpetuating the 'Lack of Evidence' discourse in sport for development: Privileged voices, unheard stories and subjugated knowledge. *International Review for the Sociology of Sport, 46*(3), 249–264.

Petipas, A., Cornelius A., Van Raalte J. and Jones, T. (2005). A framework for planning youth sport programs that foster psychosocial development. *The Sport Psychologist, 19*(1), 63–80.

Pham, P., Vinck, P., Stover, E., and Moss, A., Wierda, M. and Bailey, R. (2007). *When the War Ends: A Population Survey on Attitudes About Peace, Justice, and Social Reconstruction in Northern Uganda.* Berkley, CA: Human Rights Center, U. of California. Available at: (https://escholarship.org/uc/item/8m56w3jj#page-2).

Rangeon, S., Gilbert, W. and Bruner, M. (2012). Mapping the world of coaching science: A citation network analysis. *Journal of Coaching Education, 5*(1), 83–113.

Ravizza, D. M. (2010). The uses of sport for children in armed conflict. *Journal of Sport Science and Physical Education, Sport and Globalization issue, 59*(1), 14–20.

Ravizza, D. M. (2012). We don't play war anymore: The role of sport in the reintegration of former child soldiers in northern Uganda. In W. Bennett and K. Gilbert (eds), *Sport, Peace, and Development.* Champaign, IL: Common Ground.

Ravizza, D. M. (2016). Sport and the reintegration and social inclusion of former child soldiers. *Peace in Progress*, Sport and Peacebuilding Issue, 27: 8–10. Available at: www.icip-perlapau.cat/numero27/portada.

Ravizza, D. M., Matonak, E., Okot, G. and Achan J. (2012). *Peaceful Play: Strategies for Resolution to Conflict in Sport,* Salisbury, MD: Bosserman Center for Conflict Resolution.

Refugee Council of Australia (RCOA). (2010). The Role of Sport in Assisting Refugee Settlement. Sydney: Author. Available at: www.refugeecouncil.org.au/sport-recreation/ (accessed 8 August 2017).

Richards, J. Kaufman Z., Schulenkorf N., Wolff E., Gannett K., Siefken K. and Rodriguez G. (2013). Advancing the evidence base of sport for development: A new open-access, peer-reviewed journal. *Journal of Sport for Development*, *1*(1), 1–3. Available at: https://jsfd.org/ (accessed 10 July 2016).

Sport for Development and Peace International Working Group (SDPIWG). (2008). *Harnessing the Power of Sport for Development and Peace: Recommendations to Governments*, Toronto: Right to Play (Secretariat).

Thorpe, H. (2016). 'Look at what we can do with all the broken stuff!' Youth agency and sporting creativity in sites of war, conflict and disaster. *Qualitative Research in Sport, Exercise, and Health*, *8*(5), 554–570.

United Nations Education, Scientific, and Cultural Organization (UNESCO). (2016). The Power of Sport Values. Available at: http://unesdoc.unesco.org/images/0024/002443/244344m.pdf (accessed 8 August 2016).

United Nations Inter-agency Task Force on Sport for Development and Peace. (2003). *Sport for Development and Peace: Towards Achieving the Millennium Development Goals*, New York: UNESCO.

United Nations Office for Sport for Development and Peace (UNOSDP). (n.d.). *Sport and Sustainable Development Goals*. Available at: www.un.org/sport/content/why-sport/sport-and-sustainable-development-goals (accessed 23 October 2015).

Valenti, M., Vinciguerra, M. G., Masedu, F., Tiberti S. and Sconci, V. (2012). A before and after study on personality assessment in adolescents exposed to the 2009 earthquake in L'Aquila, Italy: Influence of sports practice. *BMJ Open*. Available at: http://bmjopen.bmj.com/content/2/3/e000824.short (accessed 10 July 2016).

Weller, S. and Romney, A. (1988) *Systematic Data Collection*. Newbury Park, CA: SAGE.

Wessells, M. (2006). *Child Soldiers: From Violence to Protection*, Cambridge, MA: Harvard University Press.

Whitely, M. A., Wright E. M. and Gould, D. (2013). Coaches' perspectives on sport-plus programmes for underserved youth: An exploratory study in South Africa. *Journal of Sport for Development*, *1*(1), 1–13. Available at: https://jsfd.org/ (accessed 10 July 2016).

Part IV

SDP in national and regional contexts

37
Africa
SDP and sports academies

Paul Darby, James Esson and Christian Ungruhe

Introduction

Within mainstream migration studies, there is a voluminous literature on migration-development interactions and outcomes (cf. De Haas 2010). As this Handbook reveals, there is also a significant and growing body of research on the relationships between sport and development. Falling between these two canons of academic work is a smaller literature which has explored the intersections between sports migration and development in the global South (Darby 2000; Bale 2004; Klein 2014; Esson 2015a). Much of this work has focused on football migration from the African continent, particularly West Africa, and has acknowledged that football academies, defined as facilities or coaching programs designed to produce talent predominantly for export, are pivotal in this process (Darby *et al.* 2007).

Recent scholarship has shown how aspirations to migrate and the academies that seek to facilitate this articulate with varying forms of social and economic development in complex ways, and produce more heterogeneous outcomes than were previously observed (Darby 2013a; Dubinsky and Schler 2017). This chapter explores these articulations in relation to football in Africa, predominantly Ghana where academies have become increasingly visible. While African football is the focus of the chapter, this discussion speaks to wider debates on the migration-development nexus in the context of sport, namely the tension between sport development, the commodification of sporting talent, and aspirations to develop an individual through sport and thereby enact wider social development.

We begin by positioning the academic, media and policy discourses concerning football academies within wider polemicizing on the migration-development nexus. After briefly accounting for the typologies of football academies in Africa, we then concentrate on Ghana, a context where all three authors have undertaken considerable ethnographic field research examining various aspects of what has become a culture of football migration. The chapter examines the relationship between migration, football academies and development via the following four themes: the shifting role of academies in relation to national development agendas; academies as vehicles for development; their contribution to local and national sport development; and the role of family in decision-making around the pursuit of transnational mobility through football. We conclude by outlining two key areas for future research that will extend debates over football academies vis-à-vis the migration (in sport)-development nexus.

The migration-development nexus and sports academies in the global South

The inclusion of a migration-specific and several migration-related targets in the United Nations Sustainable Development Goals, published in 2015, has firmly entrenched migration in the mainstream development agenda. However, conceiving of migration and migrants as levers or engines of development is not new. The emigration of both the highly skilled and unskilled from the global South to the North and the impact of this process on development in sending countries has long vexed politicians, economists, policy-makers and academics alike. In the second half of the twentieth century, conflicting intellectual paradigms rooted in neo-classical and neo-Marxist perspectives vied for primacy in the migration research and policy communities. Migration was painted as a zero-sum game involving either gains or drains, winners or losers, a cause for optimism or pessimism. Optimists argued that capital could be accrued by donor nations through remittances, the (assumed) return of migrants and associated brain circulation, rising wages and transnationally minded diasporas, all of which could drive development. Pessimists on the other hand, depicted skilled migration as an extractive process characterized by the haemorrhaging of valuable resources abroad, underdevelopment, a deepening of poverty and global inequality, and damaging socio-cultural impacts in sending societies (De Haas 2010).

Similar fault-lines are observable when considering the relationship between development and the production (in academies) and migration of elite sportsmen and women from the global South. For example, Alan Klein's pioneering research on the presence of Major League Baseball academies in the Dominican Republic has illustrated that these facilities have not only contributed to the stagnation of Dominican baseball but have also promoted American cultural hegemony in the region (Klein 1991). At the same time however, the Dominican response to this process and the subsequent development of the academy 'system' has seen local development gains being captured (Klein 2009; 2014). Arbena (1994) has also noted the mixed impact of facilities or training programmes designed to enable sports migration from Latin America, particularly in football. Likewise, Bale and Sang's (1996) study of Kenyan running has shown that the growth of a system for producing elite Kenyan middle-distance runners has been characterized variously by processes of development and underdevelopment, exploitation, dependency and resistance.

The last two decades have witnessed an increasingly acrimonious debate on the consequences and developmental impact of the migration of African football players and the academies that have sprung up around the continent. This debate has played out in the game's corridors of power, in media circles, between politicians and in both European and African courts. On one side are optimists who argue that the migration of African footballers provides the sort of exposure to elite leagues and salaries that not only contribute to the development of football in the continent, but that also allow individuals to become upwardly socially mobile. These micro-related impacts, it is argued, are broadened through the reinvestment of financial and intellectual capital back into the continent. Others vehemently disagree, painting the loss of Africa's football resources to Europe as evidence of uneven global development and neocolonialism. This latter view was perhaps expressed most caustically by Sepp Blatter, the former president of the Fédération Internationale de Football Association (FIFA) who described those European clubs involved in the recruitment of African labour as 'neocolonialists' who 'engage in social and economic rape by robbing the developing world of its best players' (*Financial Times* 2003).

Issues of 'development' have also featured in academic scholarship on the mobilities of African players. Early research was strongly influenced by historical structuralist approaches that sought to expose how the uneven relations of power between actors in the global South and

North respectively shaped African football more generally (see Darby 2002), and the migration of players specifically (Darby 2000; Bale 2004). These macro-structural, neo-Marxist-informed studies tended to produce analyses that often reduced African football players to commodities, bought and sold in international markets and controlled by European clubs and institutions (cf. Poli 2006a). According to this perspective, opportunities for capturing developmental gains from transnational football migration in sending countries were limited. While arguably able to articulate general trends in world football, this approach perpetuated a problematic understanding of African football institutions, African football players and their families as relatively powerless and passive actors within the football industry and concealed migration-development interactions at the micro- and meso-level.

As part of a broader shift in the sports migration literature that positions athletes as the central unit of analysis (Carter 2013), recent research on the mobility of African players and the role of academies therein has accounted for the perspectives and experiences of actual and aspiring football migrants (Darby 2013a; Engh and Agergaard 2015; Esson 2015b; Ungruhe and Büdel 2016; Ungruhe and Esson 2017), including those whose mobility can be described in terms of human trafficking (Esson 2015c). There has also been recent work exploring the varying degrees of agency at play within football academies, particularly how both players and family members engaged in decision-making around entering and how players experienced residing in and exiting an academy as part of a broader process of athletic mobility (Van der Meij and Darby 2017). This meso-level research locates individual players within larger aggregates, particularly the family but also peer groups, communities and a whole host of social institutions, and illustrates how these actors engage with the player and inform their understandings of how best to develop their careers (see also Ungruhe 2017). Combined, this work shows that the pursuit of spatial mobility through football is closely linked to aspirations for social mobility, personal development and self-actualization and the search for routes through which to meet intergenerational obligations towards family and the wider social environment (e.g. peers). Football academies have increasingly become pivotal in all of this and have come to function as sites where migration-development interactions and football intersect.

Football academies: insights from Africa

Football academies have come to secure a central place in Africa's export-oriented football industry. As demand for highly skilled but cheap football labour in Europe has accelerated since the late 1990s, the presence of these facilities around the continent, but particularly in West Africa, has increased. Echoing the pessimistic perspective on migration-development interactions, academies have been implicated as part of an unseemly scramble for young, malleable athletes and have been variously described by senior African football administrators and journalists as 'farms', 'a terrible thing' and as sites where young players are 'groomed' for export, leaving domestic leagues 'bereft of talent' (Hayatou 1999; Maradas 2001). However, it is clear from our research in Ghana that academies are also considered by external and local actors not only as crucial in the production and export of talented footballers but as institutions that contribute to the development of football locally and that also impact, albeit modestly, on other development agendas (Darby 2013a; Dubinsky and Schler 2017). Before detailing how these competing perspectives play out in Ghana (and neighbouring countries), it is important to add some additional context on African football academies.

African football academies vary in terms of approaches, infrastructure and type of ownership. Predominantly, while they share a common goal of producing African players for the European market and making profit, some foster additional educational aims and community development.

Darby *et al.* (2007) identified the following typology of African football academies, and it is possible to see how this typology maps onto trends in Ghana.

Type 1: Academies organized and run by professional African club sides or African national federations, which operate in a manner similar to those that exist in other parts of the world. In Ghana, a good example of this is the residential centre of excellence in Accra operated by the Ghanaian Football Association (GFA). Similarly, Liberty Professionals FC has gained renown in recent years for their success in producing young players for the professional game in Europe.

Type 2: Afro-European academies, which involve either a partnership between an existing academy and a European club, or an arrangement whereby a European club takes a controlling interest in an African club and then either subsumes the club's existing youth structures or establishes new ones. For example, in the late 1990s, Ajax Amsterdam invested €6 million in a 51 per cent stake in the then Premier League Club, Obuasi Goldfields.

Type 3: Private, corporate-sponsored academies or charities, which have well-established foundations and operate with the support and sponsorship of private individuals, usually former high-profile African players, national football federations, the corporate sector or on a charitable basis. The most notable example of the latter in Ghana is the Right to Dream Academy, a non-profit venture established in 1999 with internationally recognized facilities and educational and vocational training schemes.

Type 4: Improvised academies, which are set up on an ad hoc basis and involve unqualified staff and basic facilities. These academies provide a loosely structured football education and are typically not affiliated with the GFA.

Empirical evidence suggests that African football academies are more fluid than can be accounted for via a typology, and in nations renowned as exporters of football talent each form of academy can be found (Darby *et al.* 2007). Notably, the form and function of football academies change over time and in line with developments taking place both within the football industry and wider society. Accordingly, a brief historical detour is illustrative of the landscape in which Ghanaian football academies have emerged and operate in the interstices between sport, migration and development.

Football academies, national development and Bosman

Following independence from colonial rule in 1957, Ghana's first president Kwame Nkrumah sought to implement a programme of socialist reform in line with the era's dominant belief in the state as the guiding force behind development. This involved implementing 'developmental state policies', such as maintaining a large public sector and providing universal healthcare and education. In addition, President Nkrumah saw sport, especially football, as having the capacity to aid the national development process by mobilizing Ghanaians around a shared identity (Darby 2013b). The Nkrumah government embarked on an intensive process of what would now be viewed as state-led 'sport development', by which we mean 'programmes designed to assist those engaged in organized sport – athletes, coaches, officials, administrators – and to strengthen the infrastructure of facilities and institutions within which organized sport takes place' (Kidd 2008: 371). As part of this approach, the Ghanaian government invested in footballing infrastructure for youth competitions known locally as 'Colts' football. Sport development at this level was not commercially motivated, and only a handful of players migrated abroad to play football. When senior players did migrate, it was tied to furthering sport development initiatives in Ghana such as improving coaching techniques (Darby 2010). Moreover, because education was considered a prerequisite for individual social mobility, which would enable national development, sport development initiatives were used as a means to engage youth in formal schooling, for example through the 'Academicals' system, which involved secondary school students competing at local to national level (Esson 2016).

Following the military coup that ended Nkrumah's reign in 1966, sport development initiatives associated with the former president were either reversed or allowed to stagnate. Moreover, the introduction of neoliberal economic policies by way of an International Monetary Fund inspired Structural Adjustment Program during the 1980s led to a severe decrease in public expenditure. Sport development suffered as a consequence and state support for Colts football diminished significantly. Despite this, Ghanaian players performed exceptionally in the FIFA World Youth Championships and were crowned champions in 1991 and 1995. Meanwhile, in an era where mainstream development explicitly rejected calls for structural change through 'developmental state policies' and instead championed a suite of ideas usually bracketed together under the banner of neoliberalism, attempts were made to professionalize football in line with prevailing neoliberal philosophies. The Ghanaian Amateur Football Association (GAFA) became the Ghanaian Football Association (GFA) and firmly established itself as a private body, and clubs were encouraged to diversify their revenue streams and adopt business-like structures (Pannenborg 2010). It was also during this era that the Bosman ruling was enforced which led to increasing relaxation of foreign player restrictions in professional European football and meant that clubs could increasingly sign players outside the EU (Frick 2009).

The passing of the Bosman ruling is significant for sport development and labour migration in relation to football academies in Ghana and many other African countries, as well as those located in South America, for two reasons. First, it contributed to wages in European professional football rising substantially. Therefore, in addition to their value on the field, it is argued that demand for young players from African academies increased because clubs could make significant savings by paying African players less than their counterparts from elsewhere (Poli 2006a; 2006b). For example, European clubs signed several members of Ghana's World Youth Championships winning teams and it was during this time that accounts of young African football players being exploited within the football industry began to appear in academic research and media reportage (Donnelly and Petherick 2004). Second, African players were recruited from academies at an early age as part of a speculative strategy, oriented around maximizing profits through onward sales (Poli, 2010). This development increasingly resulted in media allegations of human trafficking and exploitation of minors. As a consequence, FIFA introduced regulations in 2001 that banned international transfers of minors (with some exceptions). However, this has not reversed the trend of the increasing commodification of young football talent.

In Ghana, this coming together of macroeconomic development policies built on neoliberal principles, coupled with the success of the Ghanaian youth team in international tournaments, and the passing of the Bosman ruling, coalesced to fundamentally transform the way that sport and player development were operationalized within football more broadly and in academies specifically. In sum, there has been a shift away from the explicit framing of sport development, football academies and player migration as part of national development projects, to an understanding of football academies as sites for identifying, developing and commodifying sporting talent to be traded on the international transfer market to generate profits. In the discussion that follows, we examine how this shift has impacted on African football migration and the academies that seek to facilitate it, in relation to broader processes of social and economic development at the micro- and meso-level.

Sport development and the commodification of talent

The commodification of athletic skills and attributes via the academy system is not unique to Ghana or men's football, and is rather emblematic of a global football industry that makes use of transnational labour. Individual success stories abound, however, most players in Africa who are recruited by academies remain in their 'home' country, with only a relatively small number obtaining opportunities to play football abroad (Poli, 2010). The potential to make a profit by transferring a player abroad has proved a catalyst for the emergence of a variety of academies as outlined above. Yet, the question remains if there is a long-term contribution for sport development through these new institutional arrangements that appear to foreground the commodification of athletic skill and labour mobility. We can see this tension between sport development and the commodification of athletic skill via the academy system unfolding in Ghana and other African countries.

The case of the Ivorian academy ASEC Mimosas is often described as a template for talent and sport development. While it has produced a number of players who have embarked on successful international careers, it has also contributed to the success of the Ivorian national team, particularly since the 1990s after the academy was professionalized. Players like Romaric, Kolo Touré and Yaya Touré are some of the outstanding graduates of the academy who made careers in European football and were part of Côte d'Ivoire's winning squad at the African Cup of Nations in 2015. In addition, ASEC Mimosas has won several Ivorian championships and the African Champions League in 1998. Hence, the academy has contributed to the improvement of national football as well as producing talent for the export market. The example of Red Bull Ghana provides a counter to this success story. In 2008, the energy drinks company invested several million euros in a facility in Ghana's Volta Region. The academy teams did not take part in official youth leagues and refrained from engaging with the local game for many years due to a view that it would be counter-productive to their players' development. However, as a result of failing to produce enough players for the parent club in Austria or for sale on the international market, Red Bull terminated their Ghanaian academy project in 2014. Still, Red Bull Ghana did produce several players who have graduated from the academy to the domestic Ghanaian league and they also sponsored a local amateur side and provided equipment and technical support. Hence, the sport development impact of the academy is visible in West African football today, although on a relatively modest level.

In general, as these two cases reveal, professional academies' approaches to talent production primarily follow sportive and economic goals that contribute to the commodification of players; yet their efforts to contribute to local sport development may differ significantly. In the next section, we elaborate further on the nexus between academies and their contribution to social development in Ghana, particularly by focusing on players' individual aspirations and family dynamics therein.

Academies and social development: individual aspirations and family dynamics

There is evidence, although limited, to indicate that elite academies set up by European teams have used the rubric of corporate social responsibility to signal their potential for broader development impacts on Ghanaian society. The former Fetteh Feyenoord Academy, sponsored by its partner club based in Rotterdam, provided peer education around HIV/AIDS in partnership with UNICEF, and Red Bull Ghana provided infrastructure for fresh drinking water in neighbouring villages and donated equipment to a hospital (Darby, 2013a). Moreover, other, private-owned academies promote the idea of local and cultural development by taking a cosmo-politan approach to education (Dubinsky and Schler 2017). Some private/corporate-sponsored academies go further, and attempt to contribute to wider development agendas by up-scaling individual benefits to the broader community and societal level through encouraging trainees to take part in community projects and entrepreneurial activities in African contexts. Meanwhile, a range of academies provide employment for local coaches, teachers and construction workers, and support the activities of a whole plethora of local micro-businesses (Darby 2013a).

Yet, it is perhaps not through these initiatives that football academies and social and economic development intersect most profoundly. Many young boys from underprivileged backgrounds now view football academies as sites enabling them to become agents of development through cultivating opportunities to migrate. The belief that migration and development are interrelated now constitutes a dominant narrative within wider cultural meanings of mobility circulating within Ghana (Collins *et al.* 2013; Martin *et al.* 2016). Thus, while many academy prospects are keen to migrate to play at a higher level and progress their careers (Darby 2013a), the desire to migrate is not reducible to football-related aspirations solely. Moreover, and as touched upon above, successive Ghanaian governments have adopted neoliberal reform, and in a society devoid of state welfare the belief that football offers a means to earn an income is appealing because it tallies with prevailing ideologies that encourage people to be self-sufficient and instrumental. An ironic outcome of this situation, given that one of the touted developmental benefits of attending an elite academy is the provision of a quality education, is that a football career is now seen as a way to sidestep a formal education system argued to lead to either unemployment or employment in the informal economy (cf. Rolleston and Oketch 2008; Esson 2016).

The increasing involvement of former professional players and the professionalization of academies gives hope to today's budding talents, but the experience of being released by an academy or concluding their training without obtaining a transfer overseas, and the loss of status and sense of shame that this elicits, also feeds into a renewed belief that with effort, luck and reli-gious faith, they will eventually migrate and make it as a professional player (Esson 2015b). Often, this belief is misplaced and serves to prolong the pursuit of social and economic development both for the individual concerned and their family (Van der Meij and Darby 2016). This point is a good example of how the conceptual shift from a macro- to a meso-level of analysis has led to research that understands the academy player as being situated within larger aggregates, particu-larly the family but also peer groups, communities and a whole host of social institutions, and a concomitant realization that these actors engage with the player and inform their understandings of how best to develop their careers.

Families are often pivotal to decisions around the migration (or otherwise) of football-playing family members to an academy, a point that was until recently neglected in the wider literature. For example, due to societal norms where Ghanaian children and youth are taught to show deference to their elders, and given that most of these players are minors, i.e. under the age of 18, they rarely make these decisions on their own. Van der Meij and Darby (2017) have been instructive in addressing this oversight by introducing the work of scholars such as Hein De Haas (2010), who are working on the migration-development nexus, to discussions about football academies. More specifically, they have advocated De Haas' (2012) call for migration decisions to be understood as part of broader attempts by households to diversify their income streams and overcome constraints to improve their life chances in their places of origin. Here, the decision to pursue a transnational football career is often made as part of a household livelihood strategy, with football increasingly seen by Ghanaian families as a way to improve their limited socio-economic prospects.

The route to success in football is highly competitive and very few will succeed (Ungruhe and Büdel 2016; Ungruhe 2017). There are no guarantees that a period of extended, often residential, training at an academy will allow players to gain social mobility via a sustained career abroad. This points to a divergence between the expectations of players and their family members and the reality for most, which is a future characterized by 'involuntary immobility', whereby there is a discrepancy between their desire to migrate through football and their ability to do so. Thus, for the majority, the pursuit of a career in the game abroad and a player's (and family members) investment in their academy training frequently results in costs rather than developmental gains. While the education that some of the more structured academies provide may off-set some of these costs, most players who fail to move overseas on conclusion or termination of their academy training remain committed to the pursuit of football-related mobility, and this can compound their difficulties in terms of potentially acquiring social mobility in other ways.

It is perhaps not a coincidence that in a context where academies are seen as vehicles for generating an income and helping one's family attain social mobility, but competition for opportunities to do so is fierce, there have been numerous documentaries and journalistic pieces about human traffickers and clubs exploiting the aspirations of young African would-be transnational professional footballers (McDougall 2008; *Soccer's Lost Boys* 2010; Hawkins 2015). On the one hand, these accounts have drawn attention to cases where after handing over money to an intermediary, a young African player obtains a contract or trial with a club, but it is of an exploitative nature akin to modern slavery. Or, where alleged interest from a foreign club is a sham and, the intermediary takes his fee but abandons the player once they arrive in a destination country. On the other hand, these accounts depict young Africans through a lens of powerlessness and desperation via an uncritical 'escape from poverty discourse' (Van der Meij and Darby 2017). Moreover, there is often an implicit assumption that creating more academies of a better standard and improving the wider football infrastructure will limit the desire to migrate, and thereby reduce the exposure of young African players to individuals seeking to exploit them. In both cases attention is diverted away from the broader structural conditions, highlighted above, that funnel youth into the football industry in the first place.

Conclusions and future research agendas

This chapter illustrated how attempts at social development through sport in general, and football academies in particular, are rarely individual projects, but are rather grounded in wider social processes and discourses, including understandings of migration and development as interlinked. We demonstrated how football academies can and do interact with these processes and discourses to produce advantageous outcomes. Yet the chapter also highlighted how calls for the creation of more elite football academies, as part of sport development and/or sport for development agendas, ignores how the professionalization of football, including the rise in elite academies, reproduces aspirations among individuals, families, communities and a whole host of social institutions to achieve social development through the commodified and transnationally mobile professional athlete. Given football's predilection for a profit-driven speculative strategy (Agergaard and Ungruhe 2016), it is somewhat understandable that clubs would view having a ready supply of aspirational youthful talent as an advantage not a hindrance. However, this chapter qualifies this perception by showing how these aspirations, and the people they are tied to, will invariably exceed the capacity of the professional football industry to accommodate all would-be professional players. Consequently, the numbers who will unsuccessfully invest in a football career through the academy system will increase.

Concern regarding professional football's inability to accommodate young would-be professional players brings us to the first key area in need of further research; specifically, longitudinal methodological studies that examine the post-academy trajectories of young players who are released by their club. For example, as documented above, existing research has observed a strong migratory disposition among trainees in African football academies, and has noted how this disposition relates to broader social narratives and understandings of development through spatial mobility. Yet comparatively little is known about 'the social dynamics and agency at play when players' academy training concludes without them becoming internationally mobile' (Van der Meij *et al*. 2016: 186) – an oversight that is particularly troubling since African footballers frequently face precarious career transitions and challenging livelihoods after having ended their career (Agergaard and Ungruhe 2016).

There is also a need for research capable of conceptualizing regulations and policy responses that enable young people and wider society to benefit from development through sport, while also ensuring that young people are protected from abuse and exploitation by sporting institutions and/or associated individuals. This conceptual clarity is needed given that, for example, FIFA regulations, the United Nations Convention on the Rights of the Child (UNCRC), and the Sustainable Development Goals appear at odds with each other when applied to young African players at football academies. This incompatibility is evident if one looks at the ban on international transfers involving minors. The ban was introduced by FIFA to protect children from harmful practices that surround player recruitment, including human trafficking and modern slavery, and thereby corresponds with key principles of the UNCRC and SDGs. This chapter has shown how harmful practices continue to thrive despite the ban, and at the same time some young players are denied the opportunity to migrate and pursue a career in football under circumstances that might prove beneficial in relation to other key principles of the UNCRC, such as the child's right to an adequate standard of living (Article 27), and the Sustainable Development Goals regarding quality education. The Ghanaian case is particularly illustrative here, as research indicates that if a European club with the infrastructure to train and educate a player to a high standard were to try and recruit a talented young Ghanaian, it is likely that the player (and his family) would be keen to take this opportunity to potentially improve their life chances. Problematically, this attempt at development through migration would most likely contravene the ban on the international transfer of minors. Further research is therefore needed to untangle this conceptual and regulatory quagmire.

References

Arbena, J. (1994). Dimensions of international talent migration in Latin American Sports. In J. Bale, and J. Maguire (eds), *The Global Sports Arena: Athletic Talent Migration in an Interdependent World*. London: Cass, pp. 99–111.

Agergaard, S. and Ungruhe, C. (2016). Ambivalent precarity: Career trajectories and temporalities in highly skilled sports labor migration from West Africa to Northern Europe. *Anthropology of Work Review*, 37(2), 67–78.

Bale, J. (2004). Three geographies of African footballer migration: Patterns, problems and postcoloniality. In G. Armstrong, and R. Giulianotti (eds), *Football in Africa*. Hampshire, Palgrave, pp. 229–246.

Bale, J. and Sang, J. (1996). *Kenyan Running: Movement Culture, Geography and Global Change*. London: Cass.

Carter, T. F. (2013). Re-placing sport migrants: Moving beyond the institutional structures informing international sport migration. *International Review for the Sociology of Sport*, 48(1), 66–82.

Collins, R., Esson, J., O'Neill Gutierrez, C. and Adekunle, A. (2013). Youth in motion: Spatialising youth movement(s) in the social sciences. *Children's Geographies*, 11(3), 369–376

Darby, P. (2000). The new scramble for Africa: African football labour migration to Europe. *The European Sports History Review*, 3, 217–244.

Darby, P. (2002). *Africa, Football and FIFA: Politics, Colonialism and Resistance.* London and Portland, OR: Frank Cass.

Darby, P. (2010). 'Go Outside': The history, economics and geography of Ghanaian football labour migration. *African Historical Review, 42*(1), 19–41.

Darby, P. (2013a). Moving players, traversing perspectives: Global value chains, production networks and Ghanaian football labour migration. *Geoforum 50,* 43–53.

Darby, P. (2013b). 'Let us rally around the flag': Football, nation-building, and the Pan-Africanism of Kwame Nkrumah's Ghana. *The Journal of African History, 54*(2), 221–246.

Darby, P., Akindes, G. and Kirwin, M. (2007). Football academies and the migration of African football labor to Europe. *Journal of Sport and Social Issues, 31*(2), 143–161.

De Haas, H. (2010). Migration and development: A theoretical perspective. *International Migration Review, 44*(1), 227–264.

De Haas, H. (2012). The migration and development pendulum: A critical view on research and policy. *International Migration, 50*(3), 8–25.

Donnelly, P. and Petherick, L. (2004). Workers' playtime? Child labour at the extremes of the sporting spectrum. *Sport in society, 7*(3), 301–321.

Dubinsky, I. and Schler, L. (2017). The Mandela soccer academy: Historical and contemporary intersections between Ghana, Lebanon, and the West. *The International Journal of the History of Sport, 33*(15), 1730–1747.

Engh, M. H. and Agergaard, S. (2015). Producing mobility through locality and visibility: Developing a transnational perspective on sports labour migration. *International Review for the Sociology of Sport, 50*(8), 974–992.

Esson, J. (2015a). You have to try your luck: Male Ghanaian youth and the uncertainty of football migration. *Environment and Planning A, 47*(6), 1383–1397.

Esson, J. (2015b). Escape to victory: Development, youth entrepreneurship and the migration of Ghanaian footballers. *Geoforum, 64*, 47–55.

Esson, J. (2015c). Better off at home? Rethinking responses to trafficked West African footballers in Europe. *Journal of Ethnic and Migration Studies, 41*(3), 512–530.

Esson, J. (2016). Football as a vehicle for development: Lessons from male Ghanaian Youth. In N. Ansell, N. Klocker and T. Skelton (eds), *Geographies of Global Issues: Change and Threat.* Singapore: Springer, pp. 1–18.

Frick, B. (2009). Globalization and factor mobility: The impact of the 'Bosman-Ruling' on player migration in professional soccer. *Journal of Sports Economics, 10*(1), 88–106.

Hawkins, E. (2015). *The Lost Boys: Inside Football's Slave Trade.* London: Bloomsbury.

Hayatou, I. (1999). Interview with Issa Hayatou. *Soccer Africa* (October), 16–19.

Kidd, B. (2008). A new social movement: Sport for development and peace. *Sport in Society, 11*(4), 370–380.

Klein, A. (1991). *Sugarball: The American Game. The Dominican Dream.* New Haven, CT: Yale University Press.

Klein, A. (2009). The transnational view of sport and social development: The case of Dominican baseball. *Sport in Society, 12*(9), 1118–1132.

Klein, A. (2014). *Dominican Baseball: New Pride, Old Prejudice.* Philadelphia: Temple University Press.

Maradas, E. (2001). Human traffic. *African Soccer, 66*: 8–9.

Martin, J., Ungruhe, C. and Häberlein, T. (2016). Young future Africa-images, imagination and its making: An introduction. *AnthropoChildren, 6*(May), 1–18.

McDougall, D. (2008). The scandal of Africa's trafficked players. *The Observer.* Available at: www.guardian.co.uk/football/2008/jan/06/newsstory.sport4.

Pannenborg, A. (2010). Big men, big gains? The involvement of African club officials in the transfer of players. *African Historical Review, 42*(1), 63–90.

Poli, R. (2006a). Migrations and trade of African football players: Historic, geographical and cultural aspects. *Africa Spectrum, 41*(3), 393–414.

Poli, R. (2006b). Africans' status in the European football players' labour market. *Soccer and Society, 7*(2–3), 278–291.

Poli, R. (2010). African migrants in Asian and European football: Hopes and realities. *Sport in Society, 13*(6), 1001–1011.

Rolleston, C. and Oketch, M. (2008). Educational expansion in Ghana: Economic assumptions and expectations. *International Journal of Educational Development 28*(3), 320–339.

Ungruhe, C. (2017) Mobilities at play: The local embedding of transnational connections in West African football migration. *International Journal for the History of Sport, 33*(15), 1767–1785.

Ungruhe, C. and Büdel, M. (2016). Im Spiel bleiben. Ethnologische Perspektiven auf Fußballmigrationen aus Afrika, *Zeitschrift für Ethnologie 141*(1), 81–99.

Ungruhe, C. and Esson, J. (2017). A social negotiation of hope. Male West African youth, 'waithood' and the pursuit of social becoming through football. *Boyhood Studies, 10*(1), 22–43.

Van der Meij, N. and Darby, P. (2017). Getting in the game and getting on the move: Family, the intergenerational contract and internal migration into football academies in Ghana. *Sport in Society*, *20*(11), 1–18.

Van der Meij, N., Darby, P. and Liston, K. (2016). 'The downfall of a man is not the end of his life': Navigating involuntary immobility in Ghanaian football. *Sociology of Sport Journal*, *34*(2), 183–194.

38

Belgium

Community sport in Flanders

Reinhard Haudenhuyse, Evi Buelens, Pieter Debognies,
Veerle De Bosscher, Inge Derom, Hebe Schaillée, Marc Theeboom,
Jasper Truyens, Jikkemien Vertonghen and Zeno Nols

Introduction

The purpose of this chapter is to give a short overview of the sport-for-development (SfD) field in Belgium, with a specific focus on community sports in Flanders (Belgium). Belgium is constitutionally divided into three 'language communities' (Flemish/Dutch, French and German) with separate responsibilities for several matters, such as education, culture and sport (De Knop *et al.* 1996). Flanders is the northern, Dutch speaking part of Belgium. In Belgium, the Flemish community and the French and German speaking communities have separate sport policies at each level, from local to national (including three separate ministers of sport). Apart from the Olympic Committee (BOIC), whose main task is to select athletes for the Olympic Games, there is no national (federal) policy or structure for sport, nor are there expenditures on sport at federal level. Although Flanders is a prosperous region, societal challenges concerning, for example, social exclusion, marginalization and poverty are also present in 'developed' high-income countries (Currie-Alder 2016; Svensson *et al.* 2016). Unlike some other developed countries, such as Norway or Australia, Belgium (including Flanders), has no specific international SfD policy, nor does it have any SfD-projects in developing low-income countries directly funded by the Flemish government. In Flanders (and Belgium in general) sport remains largely absent in the policy domain of international development and cooperation. The concept of SfD is rarely used in Flanders. Instead, terms such as 'social integration' or 'social inclusion' are more commonly used in combination with sport. Nonetheless, sport in Flanders has been considered a vehicle for development, both in relation to personal and broader societal issues. For example, the Policy Plan of Sport 2014–2019 of the Flemish Government states that:

> The Flemish Government recognizes that sport has an important social role and that it contributes to the fitness and health, the overall well-being and the social cohesion and the inclusion of disadvantaged groups.
>
> *Flemish Government 2014: 12*

Specifically, in relation to young people (who still remain the main target group of SfD programs), sport is recognized as an opportunity to actively engage youth in a leisure context that covers participation in sport activities, as well as education, employment and training, community leadership and healthy lifestyle activities (Haudenhuyse *et al.* 2012). Although there are groups of young people (e.g. young people living in poverty, young women with a non-western background) who are less likely to partake in organized sports, it has been argued that sport practices seem to provide rich contexts for attracting young people from disadvantaged socio-economic background (Haudenhuyse *et al.* 2012). Such instrumental views on sports are, however, not new. There is a long history of viewing sports, as part of a physical education curriculum and broader pedagogical offensive, to achieve a variety of outcomes relating to the individual and the wider community (Bailey *et al.* 2009; Darnell 2016). Historically, the focus has regularly been on educating and socially 'elevating' low and working-class youth, who were often perceived as underdeveloped, in need of education, at-risk of doing crime (Kidd 2008). This underlying view, although more recently disguised in 'fancy' new concepts such as empowerment or positive youth development, can still be considered as the underlying core idea of SfD policies, practices and programs. This SfD core idea sits very comfortably within a neoliberal policy discourse in which individuals and communities are seen as agents of their own development, requiring as Darnell (2016: 433) argued: 'individuals to conform to, rather than resist, the dominant structures and logic of social and economic life.' Although the SfD rhetoric often claims to address broad issues, for example, crime prevention, poverty alleviation, school drop-out, empowerment or community development, Coalter (2015) stated that most programs have an essentially individualistic perspective.

Conceptualizing sport for development

According to Darnell (2016) SfD falls into several broad categories, namely: (i) social issues; (ii) health; (iii) education; (iv) economic development; and (v) peace and reconciliation. This largely corresponds how Lyras and Peachey (2011: 311) define SfD, as: 'the use of sport to exert a positive influence on public health, the socialization of children, youth and adults, the social inclusion of the disadvantaged, the economic development of regions and states, and on fostering intercultural exchange and conflict resolution.' Such definitions and (often overlapping) categorizations remain, however, very broad and vague. Kruse (2006, quoted in Coalter 2015) stated that the concept of SfD remains open for several interpretations. As a consequence, to date there is no agreed SfD definition, but rather SfD is a 'fluid' concept. One way to orient SfD is by positioning it on the spectrum of 'development-of-sport' and 'development-through-sport'. Inspired by Houlihan and White (2002), the Sport and Society Framework in Figure 38.1

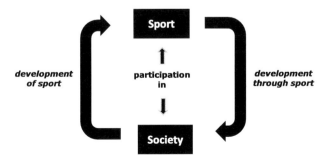

Figure 38.1   Sport and Society Framework

shows two interrelated dimensions: on the left side 'development-of-sport' and on the right side 'development-through-sport'.

Pieterse (2001, quoted in Black 2010) defined development as the organized intervention in collective affairs according to a standard of improvement. This definition can be applied to development-of-sport as well as development-through-sport. Development-of-sport broadly covers 'collectively funded' interventions (e.g. policies, programs and practices) with the end-goal of developing sport-related outcomes. Notions of inclusion in sport, sport-for-all and sport-for-sport's-sake can be situated here. The main objective is to get people participating (developing, performing) in sport. Referring to Pieterse's definition, it is not clear, however, what an agreed upon standard of improvement in terms of sport participation would be? For example, what could be viewed as 'acceptable' increases of sport participation (or elite sport performance) on a national or community level in relation to policy-based interventions promoting sport participation? Nor is it clear which levels of sport participation on a national/community level could be viewed as 'desirable' or 'socially just' (60 per cent, 80 percent or...)? Development-through-sport (or sport-for-development) covers interventions in which sport is seen as a vehicle for generating a broad array of wider societal outcomes. Inclusion through sport, sport-for-good, sport-for-change, sport-plus and plus-sport are common terms that fall under this dimension. Here, the main purpose is to improve the participation and position of (often disadvantaged) people in society, and this from the assumption that sport participation can meaningfully and effectively facilitate general participation in society, in terms of, for example, education, employment, health care or housing. An additional assumption is that the existing societal institutions, such as schools, the labour market and organized sports, are inherently beneficial, supportive and useful for everybody, and in particular disadvantaged groups. What an acceptable standard of improvement would be regarding this dimension is again not clear. For example, how many people should be lifted out of poverty through a sport-based intervention?

Challenging assumptions

The above formulated assumptions have been challenged (Haudenhuyse *et al.* 2012; Coalter 2015; Coakley 2016). First, the fact that individuals or communities are members of a target population perceived in need of 'development', does not necessarily mean that they want 'developmental' programs (Rossi *et al.* 2004) and that they are uniformly underdeveloped or deficient (Coakley 2016; Nols *et al.* 2017). Second, we cannot unconditionally assume that groups that are excluded from society and its mainstream institutions (including sport), will simply and unidimensionally benefit from their inclusion in sport when a society has excluded and marginalized them in the first place. It is for such reasons that Coalter (2015) suggested that various aspects of social inclusion (e.g. stable income, available transport, proper housing conditions) more likely precede sport participation, and not the other way around. Third, we need to acknowledge that sport is very much part of (an exclusive) society and does not exist in a social vacuum in which, as Coakley (2015) puts it, sport somehow possesses an inherent mythopoeic purity and goodness. This raises questions about using sport as a vehicle for inclusion or 'development'. In this context it is relevant to refer to Ziai (2013), who critically argued that numerous practices that have been carried out in the name of 'development', have not improved (but rather deteriorated) the human condition, implying that notions of 'development' should not be considered as inherently positive.

Black (2010) argued that development can be on the one hand a constraining and oppressive process and, on the other, an emancipatory and liberating one that can create new opportunities for disadvantaged groups and communities. Coakley (2016) and others (e.g. Burnett 2015) have indicated that linking individual development to the broader community and mobilizing power to promote progressive social change, equality and social justice, has never been a central concern for SfD programs. One of the underlying reasons might be that many SfD programs are often produced and constrained by a dominant logic of neoliberalism (Darnell 2016). In the next sections, we will explore such issues with one of the SfD pioneers in Flanders; namely the community sport movement. Within this movement, we can see the duality and fluidity of development-of-sport on the one hand, and development-through-sport on the other. After the description of community sport field in Flanders, three community sport for development (CSfD) cases will subsequently be discussed to illustrate different approaches and organizational settings. We will also try to position these cases in the Sport and Society Framework (Figure 38.1).

Community sports for development (CSfD) in Flanders

The European Sport for All Charter, adopted in 1976 by the Council of Europe and later renamed into the European Sport Charter, provides a common set of principles for all sport policies in European member states. The Charter Article 1.1 and 4.1 state that:

> measures shall be taken to ensure that all citizens have opportunities to take part in sport and where necessary, additional measures shall be taken aimed at enabling […] disadvantaged or disabled individuals or groups to be able to exercise such opportunities effectively.
>
> *Council of Europe 2001*

Defenders of this social movement that originated in the 1960s, aimed to shift the long-standing focus within sports from performance (i.e. competition and competence) towards participation more broadly. More inclusive and democratic participation in sport was viewed in relation to the generated health benefits and the social integration effects for both the individual and society. In the late 1970s, Flanders was one of the regional pioneers in implementing a sport-for-all policy in Europe (De Knop *et al.* 1996). Over the past 40 years, Flemish sport policy has been characterized, among other things, by a growing recognition of the importance to regard sport as a separate policy arena. This resulted in appointing for the first time a specific Flemish Minister of Sport in 1999. There has also been a shift from a broad sport promotional strategy towards an approach of targeting specific groups. Since the early 1990s, specific community sport programs have been set up in Flanders to stimulate participation among socially excluded groups in general and youth in particular. These (often small-scaled) community sport initiatives – primarily situated within the youth welfare sector – regarded sport as a means for facilitating social inclusion and contributing to the well-being of participants (De Knop and Walgrave 1992). From the late 1980s until 2000, the philanthropic King Baudouin Foundation has played a major role in optimizing efforts for using sport as a means of integration and directing the attention of other sport actors in Flanders to the need for a community SfD approach in reaching out to socially deprived youth (De Knop and Walgrave 1992). The Foundation's first initiative was a street football campaign in collaboration with the Royal Belgian Football Federation (Theeboom and De Maesschalck 2006). Their aim was to improve social integration of underprivileged migrant youth through the organization of accessible street football competitions in deprived urban areas. As the range of areas to organize the competitions became larger (i.e. public parks, squares, beaches, etc.), its name changed to *community football* in 1992. Two years later, its name changed to *community ball* as other ball sports were included (i.e. basketball and volleyball). In 2001, the Flemish government started to support the program and renamed it *community sports*, since more sports were included. In addition, the *Flemish Community Sport Secretariat* was installed. Illustrative for the initial focus of community sports on youth, the secretariat was initially installed as the regional umbrella organization of municipal youth services. Later on, it moved to the umbrella organization of municipal sport services. The secretariat's (recently renamed as the Community Sports Expertise Centre) main tasks include knowledge exchange, supporting local initiatives, communication and information sharing as well as research. As a result, local sport services of (especially) larger municipalities and cities became more involved in the organization of community sport initiatives as they increasingly regarded disadvantaged people in general, and youth in particular, as a specific target group within their sport policy (Theeboom *et al.* 2010).

Mainstreaming community sports

Since the 1990s, local governments (municipalities) have also started to recognize the potential of sport from a broader social welfare perspective in various aspects of their policy. This resulted, for example, in a shift in local sport policies with community sport initiatives being organized. In Flanders, the organizational format of such community sport initiatives was (and is) characterized by its flexible organization. In this format, a number of local structures (e.g. youth, prevention, welfare) work together in providing highly accessible sport activities, often with the use of – albeit a small number – paid professionals. It is also characterized by the fact that the organizational format and subsidizing policy framework are seen as distinctly different from those of traditional membership-based voluntary-based sport clubs. As a consequence, within the current sport policy legal framework, sport clubs cannot be considered as community sports (Haudenhuyse and Theeboom 2015), even if clubs formulate developmental goals in relation to specific target groups in the community.

While the majority of Flemish municipalities still use their community sport programs to stimulate sport participation among its population as part of their sport-for-all policy, cities and larger municipalities in Flanders are also claiming to use it for social inclusion of specific (mostly disadvantaged) target groups. The underlying reasons are likely related to the concentration and high visibility of societal problems, such as poverty, migration and crime, and the availability of specific social community organization in larger cities. Especially within larger cities, sport has become, to an increasing extent, part of other municipal policy domains such as youth, education and social welfare. The main reason why such non-sport actors have started to use sport from a social and developmental perspective – often with regard to specific target groups – can be related to the fact that sport is known to attract many (young) people.

To date, an overall policy vision of community SfD at the Flemish level is however still missing, together with a common community sports 'vocabulary' and 'grammar'. Vocabulary in the sense that there is a lack of formulated common goals of what community sport is and needs to do. Grammar in the sense that there is no evidence-based framework in relation to how community sport can contribute in promoting social inclusion or development. It has furthermore been indicated that there is a lack of a scientific base and an incapability of making tangible the wider social outcomes that community sport claims to strive towards.

The 'what works' mantra

Both in and beyond Flanders, the scientific knowledge base of community sports – and specifically using sport as a tool for social inclusion – is weak. Collins (2014) stated that, for example, there is still little research that can claim to explain how sport contributes to social inclusion. There is, however, a growing body of literature in the domain of critical SfD research, underlining the view that sport-based interventions need to be more clearly conceptualized in terms of *inputs* (the used human, social, physical, cultural, political, economic resources), *throughputs* (what is being done with used resources and how it is done), *outputs* (what is being accomplished with used resources) and *outcomes* (to what concrete consequences have such accomplishments led for those involved) (e.g. Coalter 2007). It is believed that this will contribute in creating better and more effective SfD interventions. Coakley (2011) also emphasized the need for these insights as this could provide organizations, policy-makers and practitioners a better, more theory-based and fundamental understanding of how sport participation is related to various forms of personal, social and community development. It is, however, questionable, and to date not empirically proven, whether a focus on positivism and a pragmatic preoccupation in finding 'what works' (Currie-Alder 2016) effectively contributes to sport practices that can help in improving the human condition of communities and individuals. Currie-Alder (2016: 20) argued that for mainstream development studies:

> The questions asked and the nature of explanation shifted from describing historical patterns of social transformation, towards identifying causal mechanisms linking specific interventions and their outcomes. […] a pressure to demonstrate the 'value' of publicly funded scholarship, pushed the field towards more realist and positivist methods and epistemology.

One of the consequences is also the adaption of smaller-scale units of analysis (i.e. individuals, programs), instead of broader units (i.e. communities, countries). Such statements also resonate with the SfD research field (*see* Darnell *et al.* 2016).

Integration: participation paradigm shift

The incapability to 'prove' that community sports can contribute to social inclusion and development, together with the mainstreaming of CSfD initiatives within local municipal (sport) services and the expansion of the target group beyond non-participating disadvantaged youth, have paved the way for a paradigm policy shift (Haudenhuyse and Theeboom 2015). The original sport-for-integration philosophy that was ingrained in the first community sport initiatives, has gradually shifted towards a more 'sport-for-sport's-sake' philosophy (Haudenhuyse and Theeboom 2015), where the main focus is on maximizing accessibility for non-participating groups in the community.

The often taken-for-granted belief about the inherent transformative and positive developmental power of sport has also contributed to such a paradigm shift, in which it is often uncritically assumed that participation in itself will contribute to the processes of social inclusion. Illustrative of this is what Green (2008: 132) formulated: 'the belief that sport builds character is so ingrained that neither providers nor participants feel it necessary to do anything more than to provide opportunities.' The consequence is that social inclusionary and developmental objectives and the ways and conditions in which community sports can effectively contribute to achieving such objectives, are less clearly formulated. Therefore, if we would position the current municipal CSfD field in Flanders within the Sport and Society Framework (Figure 38.1), it would rather be situated in the left hand-dimension, the development-of-sport. However, it is important to stress that, although the community SfD field of the late 1980s and early 1990s explicitly aimed at the social and cultural integration of migrant youth (often children of migrant workers who lost their jobs after the closing of the mines and related heavy industries in Belgium), the focus was largely on the individual level. The rationale was mainly to intervene in young people's lives with the aim of, as Coakley (2016) noted 'keeping them out of trouble'. Linking community sport participation to the larger community, with the aim of taking action and promote social, political and economic change (Coakley 2016), was not on the agenda. The aim was, in other words, neither to empower disadvantaged young people nor to enable them to intervene in and change the social conditions that made them target groups in the first place. The integration-participation paradigm shift, however, does not necessarily mean that local community sport practices do not aspire to go *beyond sport*.

While there is a diversity of community sport programs and contexts in Flanders where sport is used as a social instrument for disadvantaged youth, it is interesting to note that the terminology used to describe the aims of most of these programs is very similar. Besides referring to the provision of a meaningful and enjoyable leisure activity, most of these initiatives indicate to aim for social inclusion. To illustrate the multifarious community SfD field in Flanders, we describe three CSfD practices that are situated in different sectors and societal fields (i.e. civil society, state and/or market). The cases are all examples of CSfD initiatives that have emerged mainly outside the context of local municipal sport services. As such settings are not institutionalized within municipal sport services, we could expect that they are less likely to be narrowly focused on sport-for-sport's-sake policy ends.

Case 1: Molenbeek's Brussels Boxing Academy

Brussels Boxing Academy (BBA) is a sport-for-development practice in Brussels that is supported by the non-profit youth welfare work organization *D'Broej* (The Brussels Organization for the Emancipation of Youth). The general aim of D'Broej is to offer young people from disadvantaged neighbourhoods a 'positive space' to develop their talents and strengthen their position in society. D'Broej tries to contribute to the individual and collective emancipation of children and young people by providing leisure activities in cooperation with eight neighbourhood practices, of which BBA is one. Since D'Broej works closely with other civil society organizations, BBA can be situated within civil society. D'Broej is funded by the Flemish Community Commission (the representative of the Flemish authorities in the Brussels-Capital Region), but has a high degree of autonomy.

Many of the young people who come and practise boxing at BBA live in the poorest areas of Brussels with a high population density, hardly any green areas, a high unemployment rate, high levels of school drop-out and bad housing conditions. Approximately 500 young people – of which one third are girls – are registered as BBA members, most being between 6 and 25 years old.

Supported by D'Broej, BBA is run by four professionals and a large team of volunteers. The specific aim of BBA is to make children and young people more resilient and to provide them with skills, attitudes and knowledge to help develop their personality (e.g. identity, self-esteem, responsibility) and strengthen their position in society. Apart from recreational and competitive boxing, BBA supports young people by helping them with school assignments. Whenever needed, the organization also helps with looking for educational and job opportunities. In addition, BBA organizes activities to broaden the experiences and relationships of their members (e.g. go mountain hiking or setting up a theatre piece around boxing).

Within the Sport and Society Framework (Figure 38.1), BBA can be situated mostly on the right because they work on the development of young people, trying to strengthen their position and influence political agendas on how sport can be used as a means *beyond* 'controlling' young people. The fact that a sport club (BBA) is embedded within a youth welfare organization is what makes BBA a rather unique case in Belgium. In 2017, they received the Human Rights Prize of the Belgian Human Rights Organization, which recognizes the societal value of BBA.

Case 2: Coca-Cola's Street Action

The Street Action project across different municipalities in Flanders (e.g. Ronse, Duffel, Boom) was organized by the umbrella organization of Flemish local sport services (ISB vzw) and financed by the Coca-Cola Foundation (2012–2014). The main funding came from a private commercial partner, making it unique in Flanders. A funding prerequisite for each individual program was the coordination by the municipal community sport service and the collaboration with one or more social partners (e.g. youth welfare work, social or youth service). As a result, the organizers of each program included both a sport and social partner organization.

The aims of Street Action were to increase the sport participation of disadvantaged youth and promote sustainable volunteering in sport among 12 to 18-year-olds in disadvantaged situations. 'Ownership' could be seen as one of the main themes. For this, youngsters were encouraged to become regularly involved in the organization of the community sport offer in their own neighbourhood in order to develop their 'human capital'.

Buelens (2016) analysed the first eight 'pilot' municipalities in which it ran from 2012 and onward. This analysis showed that most programs experienced difficulties in attracting youngsters in the first place and understandably also difficulties in encouraging them to become involved as volunteers. It turned out that the main reason why these programs were not able to go beyond attracting and retaining youth as mere participants, was simply because program providers did not fully recognize the distinction between what Coalter (2007) has referred to as necessary and sufficient conditions. There were only two programs that were able to achieve volunteer engagement from youngsters through satisfying sufficient conditions. Interesting to note is that these two municipalities were both collaborating with a youth work organization.

A key sufficient condition here was the organization of a specific youth animator training course for the target group which consisted of 60 hours of training and was followed by an apprenticeship of 60 hours as well. During and after this course, youngsters were actively encouraged to take on responsibilities in the design and provision of the community sport offer and were guided by one or more professionals from the local sport and/or social partners and the youth work organization. In sum, 18 youngsters participated in the two programs.

Data analyses from in-depth interviews with organizers and focus groups with youngsters from the eight pilot municipalities indicated that youngsters in the programs developed their human capital (i.e. personal and intra-personal competences) through informal and experiential learning only when they felt valued and recognized. By focusing on becoming involved as a volunteer, the programs seemed to implicitly aim for a more critical approach to youth development. Although not all types of volunteering can be referred to as critical, the fact that youngsters were encouraged to organize their own (sport) activities, a setting was created where they experienced that through their volunteer involvement, they can change things in their own neighbourhoods (e.g. more disadvantaged children and youngsters having a joyful leisure time by participating in a community sport offer) and even feel that they are making a meaningful contribution to society in general. Furthermore, by making use of self-reflection techniques among youngsters, they were able to critically reflect on their own situation and progress. As a result, within the Sport and Society Framework, Street Action can be situated on the right sight, namely striving for development of vulnerable youngsters through (volunteering in) sport.

Case 3: Fight and Dance project

In 2007 'Jeugd en Stad' (in short JES, literally: 'Youth and City') a social-profit youth welfare work organization operating in three of the largest urban areas in Belgium (i.e. Brussels, Ghent and Antwerp), was commissioned by the Flemish Minister for Sport to develop the pilot project 'Sport in Large Cities'. The project was financed through the Participation Decree (18/01/2008), which is complementary to and supportive of the existing independent sector specific decrees and policies in the fields of culture, youth and sport. Specifically, by anchoring some cross-sectoral collaborative practices with innovative projects that can increase participation rates of disadvantaged individuals, this decree adds supportive measures intended to structurally embed policy attention to target groups that are underserved in the aforementioned (independent) domains.

The 'Fight and Dance' project (Antwerp), was one of the two pilot projects organized by JES (see Schaillée 2016). The two types of sport (i.e. kick- and Thai boxing and urban dance styles) were chosen because of their popularity among the target group (i.e. young people in socially vulnerable positions). This project can be situated at the intersection between the state and civil society because it was funded by grants awarded by the Flemish government and implemented by the non-profit youth welfare work organization JES. The aim of the project was not only to improve the accessibility (of mostly recreational) organized sports for disadvantaged youth, but also to provide participating youth with opportunities to develop skills, attitudes and to gain knowledge that can contribute to their personal and social development, as well as to strengthen their position in society.

Apart from the regular training sessions that were delivered by mainly volunteer sport coaches, professionals of JES provided participating youth with additional social contexts to broaden their learning experiences and relationships (e.g. volunteer opportunities, instructor courses, teambuilding activities). Most young people involved in this project grew up in poor and densely populated areas of Antwerp. Many of these young people had a (non-western) immigrant background, were in lower educational tracks (i.e. technical or vocational secondary education) and lived in challenging family situations (e.g. single-parent households, many resident family members). The project was run by three professional youth welfare workers. One professional youth welfare worker was responsible for the overall coordination and the two-remaining professional youth welfare workers were each responsible for one sport-related trajectory (i.e. kick- and Thai boxing versus urban dance).

The 'Fight and Dance' project is a unique case in Flanders because of its cross-sectoral collaborations. For instance, for the kick- and Thai boxing trajectory, collaborations were set up with four existing clubs. Similar collaborations were not possible for the urban dance trajectory because existing urban dance clubs appeared to be unable to reach the target group. It was, therefore, decided to create new urban dance initiatives at five different locations. At each location, collaboration with an external partner (e.g. school, cultural centre) was set up, in order to strengthen the sustainability. Within the Sport and Society Framework, the Fight and Dance project of JES can be situated on the right side because program providers worked on the personal and social development of young people and tried to strengthen young people's position in societal institutions.

Conclusion

To date, community sports in Flanders are, from a state, civil society and market perspective, seen as a 'jack of all trades' in terms of including a diversity of young people and increasingly other age groups, working towards a variety of 'claimed' social developmental objectives. Although the three described CSfD cases are different in many aspects, they all share the ambition to go beyond sport with the specific groups they work with. All three cases cover, as such, both dimensions of the Sport and Society Framework (Figure 38.1), namely development-of-sport and development-through-sport. However, in relation to the latter, although issues such as equality, social justice and social change, might be part of the (C)SfD rhetoric and formulated goals, it is remains difficult to ascertain if and how such issues are being addressed by the practices and their offered activities.

We can identify two reasons, among many others, that hinder a deeper understanding of the transformative potential of (C)SfD practices. The first reason is related to the fact that, as Darnell (2016) argued, (C)SfD initiatives are often produced and constrained by the logic of neoliberalism. The consequence is that although programs (such as the three cases described in this chapter) do seem to be concerned with promoting progressive equality, social justice and social change (Coakley 2016), they often adopt a fundamentally individualistic approach in how they work with (young) people in their sport contexts (Coalter 2015). Such approaches could be categorized under what Lawson (2005) called 'narrow empowerment', indicating the lack to go beyond the individual level. (C)SfD practices failing to incorporate wider structural dimensions, risk legitimating a reductive analysis of complex processes, by highlighting individual deficits and de-emphasizing structural inequalities (Kelly 2011; Haudenhuyse *et al.* 2012). This, as a consequence, disempowers SfD practices in addressing such broad social issues.

The second reason is related to narrow approaches in how (C)SfD practices are being studied and evaluated. As described in this chapter, current research is mainly focused on identifying causal mechanisms linking specific interventions and their outcomes (i.e. 'what works' mantra), and this often by using small units of analysis (i.e. individuals, programs). This is furthermore reinforced by ideological conceptions of policy-makers, funders and program providers about what counts as 'evidence' (and what not). Writing about mainstream development studies, but equally applicable to SfD studies, Currie-Alder (2016) identified two opposing trends. On the one hand, there is a well-established trend that embraces positivism in thinking and methods; and at the other hand, there is a much more recent trend towards a renewal of critical and more politicized social science that can challenge conventional thinking on SfD and defy the status quo of social inequalities (e.g. Hartmann and Kwauk 2011; Spaaij and Jeanes 2013; Darnell 2016; Darnell *et al.* 2016; Nols *et al.*, 2018). However, as Darnell and his colleagues (2016) have argued, such critical analysis is hindered by the mere fact that researchers in the SfD field have predominantly used less politicized social concepts and theoretical frameworks, such as social capital theory and positive youth development (Schulenkorf *et al.* 2016). Such frameworks, as Darnell *et al.* (2016: 6) have argued: 'tend to theorize development (through sport) as a process that can be successfully achieved if the correct or optimal tools, conditions, and processes are deployed or implemented'. More headway in the research field could be created by using theoretical frameworks and concepts based on political economy, governmentality, critical pedagogy, and other frameworks that are rooted in Marxist, feminist or anti-colonial perspectives (Darnell *et al.* 2016; Nols *et al.* 2017). Additionally, using more mesolevel units of analysis (e.g. community), the field could benefit from research that describes historical patterns of social transformation, providing more insights in how (C)SfD could help in improving the human condition of communities and individuals.

References

Bailey, R., Armour, K., Kirk, D., Jess, M., Pickup, I. and Sandford, R. (2009). The educational benefits claimed for physical education and school sport: an academic review. *Research Papers in Education, 24*(1), 1–27.

Black, D. (2010). The ambiguities of development: Implications for 'development through Sport'. *Sport in Society, 13*(1), 121–129.

Buelens, E. (2016). Exploring the Developmental Role of Volunteering in Sport for Youngsters in Socially Vulnerable Situations. SASO Series No. 10. Brussels: ASP/VUBPRESS.

Coakley, J. (2011). Youth sports: What counts as 'positive development?' *Journal of Sport and Social Issues, 35*(3), 306–324.

Coakley, J. (2015). Assessing the sociology of sport: On cultural sensibilities and the great sport myth. *International Review for the Sociology of Sport, 50*(4–5) 402–406.

Coakley, J. (2016). Positive youth development through sport: Myths, beliefs and realities. In N. Holt (ed.), *Positive Youth Development through Sport* (2nd edn). London: Routledge.

Coalter, F. (2007). *A Wider Role for Sport: Who's Keeping the Score?* London: Routledge.

Coalter, F. (2015). Sport-for-change: Some thoughts from a sceptic. In R. Haudenhuyse and M. Theeboom. *Sport for Social Inclusion: Critical Analyses and Future Challenges, Cogitatio, 3*(3), 19–23.

Collins, M. and Kay, T. (2014). *Sport and Social Exclusion.* London: Routledge.

Council of Europe (2001). European Sport Charter. Adopted by the Committee of Ministers on 24 September 1992 at the 480th meeting of the Ministers' Deputies and revised at their 752nd meeting on 16 May 2001.

Currie-Alder, B. (2016). The state of development studies: Origins, evolution and prospects. *Canadian Journal of Development Studies, 37*(1), 5–26.

Darnell, S. (2016). Sport, international development and peace. In: R. Giulianotti (ed.). *Routledge Handbook of the Sociology of Sport.* London: Routledge, p. 468.

Darnell, S. C., Chawansky, M., Marchesseault, D., Holmes, M. and Hayhurst, L. (2016). The state of play: Critical sociological insights into recent 'sport for development and peace' research. *International Review for the Sociology of Sport, 53*(2),1–19, doi:10.1177/1012690216646762.

De Knop, P., Vanreusel, B., Theeboom, M. and Wittock, H. (1996). Belgium. In P. De Knop, L. Engström, B. Skirstad and M. Weiss (eds), *Worldwide Trends in Youth Sport.* Champaign, IL: Human Kinetics.

De Knop, P. De and Walgrave, L. (1992). *Sport als Integratie. Kansen voor Maatschappelijk Kwetsbare Jongeren.* Brussels: Koning Boudewijnstichting.

Flemish Government. (2014). Policy Plan of Sport 2014–2019. Available at: www.vlaanderen.be/nl/publicaties/detail/beleidsnota-2014-2019-sport-1 (accessed 18 June 2017).

Green, C. (2008). Sport as an agent for social and personal change. In V. Girginov (ed.), *Management of Sports Development.* Oxford: Butterworth-Heinemann.

Hartmann, D. and Kwauk, K. (2011). Sport and development: An overview, critique, and reconstruction. *Journal of Sport and Social Issues, 35*(3), 284–305.

Haudenhuyse, R. and Theeboom, M. (2015). Buurtsport en sociale innovatie: Een tweede start voor buurtsport in Vlaanderen? In M. Theeboom, R. Haudenhuyse and J. Vertonghen (eds), *Sport en Sociale Innovatie: Inspirerende. Praktijken en Inzichten.*

Haudenhuyse, R., Theeboom, M. and Nols, Z. (2012). Sports-based interventions for socially vulnerable youth: Towards well-defined interventions with easy-to-follow outcomes. *International Review for the Sociology of Sport, 48*(4), 471–484.

Houlihan, B. and White, A. (2002). *The Politics Sport Development: Development of Sport or Development through Sport?* London: Routledge.

Kelly, L. (2011). Social inclusion through sports based interventions? *Critical Social Policy, 31*(1), 126–150.

Kidd, B. (2008). A new social movement: Sport for development and peace. *Sport in Society, 11*(4), 370–380.

Kruse, S. E. (2006). Review of kicking AIDS out: Is sport an effective tool in the fight against HIV/AIDS? (draft report to NORAD, unpublished).

Lawson, A. (2005). Empowering people, facilitating community development, and contributing to sustainable development: The social work of sport, exercise, and physical education programs. *Sport, Education and Society, 10*(1), 135–160.

Lyras, A. and Welty Peachey, J. (2011). Integrating sport-for-development theory and praxis. *Sport Management Review, 14*(4), 311–329.

Nols, Z., Haudenhuyse, R. and Theeboom, M. (2017). Urban Sport-for-Development Initiatives and Young People in Socially Vulnerable Situations: Investigating the 'Deficit Model'. *Social Inclusion, 5* (2), 210–222.

Nols, Z., Haudenhuyse, R., Spaaij, R. & Theeboom, M. (2018). Social change through an urban sport for development initiative? Investigating critical pedagogy through the voices of young people, *Sport, Education and Society,* DOI:10.1080/13573322.2018.1459536.

Pieterse, J. (2001). *Development Theory: Deconstructions/Reconstructions.* London: SAGE.

Rossi, P., Lipsey, M. and Freeman, H. (2004). *Evaluation: A Systematic Approach* (7th edition). Thousand Oaks, CA: SAGE.

Schaillée, H. (2016). More than just a game? The potential of programs to foster Positive Youth Development among disadvantaged girls. PhD thesis. Vrije Universiteit Brussel, Brussels: VUBPress.

Schulenkorf, N., Sherry, E. and Rowe, K. (2016). Sport for development: An integrated literature review. *Journal of Sport Management, 30*(1), 22–39, doi:10.1123/jsm.2014-0263.

Spaaij, R. and Jeanes, R. (2013). Education of social change? A Freirean critique of sport for development and peace. *Physical Education and Sport Pedagogy, 18*(4), 442–457.

Svensson, P., Hancock, M. and Hums, M. (2016). Examining the educative aims and practices of decision-makers in sport for development and peace organizations. *Sport, Education and Society, 21*(4), 495–512.

Theeboom, M., Haudenhuyse, R. and De Knop, P. (2010). Community sports development for socially deprived groups: A wider role for the commercial sports sector? *Sport in Society, 13*(9), 1392–1410.

Theeboom, M. and De Maesschalck, P. (2006). *Sporten om de hoek: een brede kijk op buurtsport in Vlaanderen. [Sport around the corner: a broad view on neighbourhood sport in Flanders].* Sint-Niklaas: Flemish Institute for Sport Management and Recreation Policy.

Ziai, A. (2013). The discourse of 'development' and why the concept should be abandoned. *Development in Practice, 23*(1), 123–136.

441

39

Cambodia

Reconciliation, hope and different ways of seeing

Kevin Young

Introduction

Cambodia represents a fascinating but complex case for the consideration of sport's role in wider processes of social development. Although on-the-ground sport-for-development programs are in place and relatively easy to identify, both their long-term impacts as well as sustained research efforts culminating in compelling published statements based upon them are far more difficult to identify. For instance, almost no empirically based work on Cambodian sport exists in the sub-discipline of the sociology of sport, and occasional reports based upon extant programs tend to be brief, descriptive, and uncritical. The scant scholarly research that does exist (e.g. Okada and Young 2011; Young and Okada 2016) provides clear pause for thought and points towards arguably contradictory conclusions. This paper summarizes the Cambodian sport-for-development scene, illustrating the author's experiences with various sport initiatives in the northern Cambodian community of Siem Reap. It begins by setting Cambodian Sport for Development and Peace (SDP) work in context.

Contextualizing Cambodia

Located on the southern tip of the Indochina peninsula in Southeast Asia, the Kingdom of Cambodia (formerly known as Kampuchea) has a modest population of approximately 15 million. By almost any measure, the country is extremely poor. Many Cambodians are agrarian and make their living as subsistence farmers and fieldworkers. The ethnic composition of Cambodia is strikingly homogeneous. More than 90 per cent of the population is ethnic Khmer (Vietnamese and Chinese represent the largest minority groups), and Khmer is also their official language. Buddhism is the predominant religion. The level of social indicators such as GNI (US$1,070 in 2015), literacy rate (approximately 74 per cent) and primary/secondary school enrolment ratio (approximately 45 per cent) are low even compared to other also poor countries in this region, although there have been some encouraging recent improvements (UNDP 2013).

Following centuries of turmoil and attempts by Vietnam and Thailand to vassalize the country, Cambodia's darkest political period occurred relatively recently. In the mid-late 1970s, under the Pol Pot/Khmer Rouge regime, extensive genocidal 'cleansing' occurred in a chaotic phase of military rule. Modelled on the so-called Great Leap Forward of Maoist China, cities, including the capital Phnom Penh, were evacuated and almost the entire population was forced to march into the countryside to work in manual labour camps. Clocks were turned back to 'Year Zero'. Approximately one third of Cambodians were killed (giving rise to the term 'The Killing Fields'), although the exact number of victims remains murky and disputed. Unofficial reports indicate that professionals such as lawyers, doctors, and teachers, as well as artists and athletes, were especially targeted because of their presumed power to influence the masses. Indeed, any persons considered 'intellectual' or 'threatening' suffered horrible cruelty in a context of wide-spread detention camps and torture. As Kaplan (1997: 406) has observed incredulously, 'eyeglasses were as deadly as the yellow star' since they were perceived as signifiers of dissent.

Although the Pol Pot regime ended in 1978 (Pol Pot himself died in 1998), civil war and social confusion continued throughout the 1980s, and ripple effects on social organization and quality of life endure to this day. The so-called Paris Peace Agreements were established in 1991 and the long road toward Cambodian revival began. While the lifestyles of ordinary Cambodians today continue to be modest by Western standards, economic growth hovers at a respectable 8 per cent per year. The garment and tourism sectors lead this growth, and Siem Reap (the loca-tion of the work reported below) accounts for a significant proportion of the national tourism income. However, even though the famous and tourist-drawing ruins of Angkor Wat are located there, poverty in this largely rural area is still more severe than in other provinces and living conditions can be harsh. In the current phase of post-genocidal peace and stability, about 53 per cent of residents in Siem Reap live below an already low poverty line set by the Cambodian government.

However, 'peace' and 'stability' are, of course, relative notions. The legacy of conflict lingers with millions of landmines scattered across the countryside (making Cambodia the third worst landmine topography on the planet after Afghanistan and Angola). Thousands of Cambodians are disabled without limbs and/or disfigured, as well as orphaned and forever saddened by the inhumane losses suffered under Pol Pot. In addition to widespread poverty, impartial reports have highlighted lack of political freedoms and high rates of political corruption. Indeed, where external perceptions of widespread social improvement are concerned (such as those often found in sources aimed at tourists and travellers, etc.), closer assessments remain more guarded. For evi-dence, look no further than Human Rights Watch's Southeast Asian Director, David Roberts, who characterizes Cambodia far more cautiously as a 'vaguely communist free-market state with a relatively authoritarian coalition ruling over a superficial democracy' (Roberts 2001), or the annual indexing of social factors such as the rule of law, criminal violence, and unequal appli-cation of law in various countries, where Cambodia ranks close to bottom and the worst in the region (e.g. Cuddy 2015). Despite the recent introduction of anti-corruption laws, corruption remains rampant throughout Cambodia, and there is an understandable lack of public trust in Cambodia's law enforcement system and in government institutions more generally (Doyle 2014). Unsurprisingly in such a context, the legacy of conflict also means that sport in any form remains fledgling and relatively unsophisticated. This, of course, is where Cambodian SDP work enters the picture.

Sport in Cambodia

Cambodian sport operates under the aegis of the Ministry of Education, Youth and Sport (MoEYS). Focusing on youth who, using an unfortunate local metaphor, are viewed as representing the 'work-horses' to lead the country into a more prosperous future, education is a high priority, and the importance of sport-related education is also increasingly emphasized.

However, the actual implementation of sport-related curricula has faced difficulties due to a chronic lack of human and material resources and a weak infrastructure. Individuals occupying roles such as administrative officers, teachers and coaches after the Pol Pot regime have been scarce, and the few persons in sport-organizing positions that do exist have struggled without basic educational materials and training opportunities. They have often had to work alone or in tiny cohorts, as detailed elsewhere (Young and Okada 2016).

In the Cambodian *Education Strategic Plan 2014–2018* from MoEYS (2014), physical education and sport were specifically earmarked as principal catalysts to improve health and contribute toward positive learning environments, as well as enhancing country-wide development on multiple levels. However, the plan was appropriately ameliorated by an inevitable dose of realism:

> The current challenges are lack of human resources in management, leadership, and organization for national and international champion competitions. There is a lack of infrastructure … and physical materials and equipment to train [for] … national and international competitions … and for managing and developing physical education and sport … In general … Cambodian sport in international competitions does not yet get good results.
>
> *MoEYS 2014: 46*

Although there are close to 400 primary and secondary schools, approximately 40,000 students, and 670 teachers in the province of Siem Reap, the total number of physical education teachers is surprisingly low (approximately 20). Since rigorous governmental support for sport cannot realistically be expected in a country lacking basic necessities, sport in the school system has gradually taken off as a private enterprise with minimal public sector support.

The meaning and relevance of sport in contemporary Cambodia has gradually changed over time. Football especially has boomed since the 2002 Korea/Japan FIFA World Cup. As Ota observed:

> Development of the capital city Phnom Penh is [moving] at a dizzy speed. At the same time, the number of foreign companies which have interests to invest in Cambodian football is increasing. Cambodian football is developing [and] running side-by-side [with] rapid recent economic development.
>
> *Ota 2012: 14*

Likewise, in the build-up to the 2014 World Cup, Ueda noted about football fans in Cambodia: 'It is not only in Brazil that soccer fans are getting heated up. Soccer is popular in Cambodia also, where they even have a professional league (commonly known as the C-League)' (Ueda 2014: 9).

Until the late 1990s, there were few leisure-time options in this mostly agrarian culture, and organized sport activity was rarely available due to lack of opportunity and, importantly, lack of cultural relevance except perhaps for in the capital city of Phnom Penh. However, there have been significant changes regarding sport and, most encouragingly, consistent and patterned systems of sport have sprung up in recent years throughout Cambodia. Today, while the sporting environment, sports opportunities and resources certainly remain basic, Cambodians have launched numerous sporting programs, albeit without the level of instruction, facilities or financial backing that are simply taken for granted in more developed countries. The number of private sport clubs (offering, for example, artificial football pitches, volleyball courts, and fitness facilities) is quickly increasing and, in some urban areas, it is now common for ordinary people to pay membership fees in order to participate. Today, it is fair to note that many Cambodians have come to recognize sport as a *preferred* aspect of their cultural lives, but hardly an *essential* component in a country still recovering from a turbulent past.

In terms of the actual practice of sport per se, volleyball and football are the most popular sports in Cambodia, with basketball, baseball, tennis and other sports (even including golf) gaining in popularity. As with all settings, the cultural legacy of folk games and forms of play also remains apparent in the organization of events such as boat and buffalo racing, Khmer boxing and wrestling, and the French pastime of pétanque (or *boules*). Depending on whose statistics one trusts, volleyball likely holds the place of *the* most popular sport by participation, but one of the most lauded sports in terms of real cultural significance is *pradal serey* (Cambodian freestyle kick-boxing). Germane to this study, there can be no doubt that using sport as one means of tackling conflict and encouraging social stability is very much on the radar of many Cambodian people.

SDP in Cambodia: exemplars and catalysts

The general picture: Cambodian SDP initiatives

As with other settings, Cambodian sport is encapsulated in and represented by the concrete practices of actual initiatives led not only by non-government organizations and non-profit organizations from various parts of the globe but also by actual on-the-ground leaders, both Cambodian and non-Cambodian. Although no official numbers are available, as of 2017 there are many SDP sport projects under way in Cambodia. Clearly, not all can be described here, but it seems important to summarize a few, along with their identified goals (which are picked up later in the paper):

- *Cambodian National Volleyball League, Disabled (CNVLD):* Christopher Minko, Secretary General of CNVLD, organizes events related to adaptive sports, and explains their benefits for the social re-integration of disabled people, especially landmine survivors, in the following way: 'Sport can generate a change in attitudes … it promotes values that are crucial in the process of collective socialization of the disabled individual'. According to Minko, sport for the disabled is a way to limit their social marginalization: 'They feel better physically and mentally.' 'Then we help them economically through a job search', he adds. The program is located throughout Cambodia but emphasizes provincial development. Among a long list of lofty objectives, four stand out: (i) to assist in socio-economic re-integration; (ii) to use sport as a tool for national reconciliation; (iii) to leverage various media to raise public awareness of disability and landmine issues; and (iv) to build accessible and multi-use sports facilities throughout Cambodia. Delivery and implementation partners include the Cambodian Ministry of Social Affairs Veterans and Youth Rehabilitation, the International Committee of the Red Cross, the National Olympic Committee of Germany, the Australian Agency for International Development, and the Swiss Academy for Development. (www.facebook.com/CNVLD2/posts/445240462153785).
- *Olympic Value Education Program (OVEP) and Sport for Tomorrow (SFT) Cambodia*: The University of Tsukuba, Japan in cooperation with the Japanese International Cooperation Agency (JICA) has sent students to Cambodia to undertake a 'Sport for Tomorrow' program. Linked to a non-profit organization – *Hearts of Gold* from Okayama – Japanese groups (often university students) have worked voluntarily with Cambodian physical education and sports development programs for many years in locations such as Phnom Penh, Sihanoukville, and Kratie. Cambodian university students from, for example, the Cambodian Mekong University, also

participate in programs aimed at providing opportunities for adaptive bodily play (e.g. blind games, seated volleyball, etc.) for young people (especially girls and women) with disabilities and amputations. Raising personal and social understanding, diversity and world peace are among identified objectives. Additional participating organizations include the National Olympic Committee of Cambodia (NOCC) and numerous Cambodian primary and secondary schools (www.sportanddev.org/en/event/ovep-x-sft-program-cambodia).

- *Globalteer Cambodia Sports Project*: Linked to the UK-registered charity Globalteer, beginning in 2009, the Siem Reap Junior Soccer League was established by a qualified soccer coach from the UK. Since then, the project has mushroomed and has offered over 1000 young Cambodians the opportunity to participate in sports activities. Once again aimed at both athletic participation and social integration and advancement possibilities, this program focuses not just on athletic competencies but also learning lessons regarding physical and emotional health, drug use and addiction, anti-social behaviour, and career development (www.globalteer.org/gallery. aspx?cambodia-sports-project).

The specific picture: Siem Reap research in focus

For several years, Chiaki Okada (from Osaka University) and I have been involved in empirically based research on the changing role of sport in Cambodia, and its possible connections to community development. Our main projects have essentially been two-fold: (i) qualitative fieldwork on an incipient sport initiative in the northern region of the country – the Siem Reap Hotel and Tourism Football League (SHTFL) (Okada and Young 2011); (ii) a life history study of a man who has been central in promoting sport as a vehicle for community development throughout Cambodia but especially in the Siem Reap area (Young and Okada 2016). These research interests have incorporated – indeed, methodologically speaking, they have *required* – the use of multiple techniques including observation, in-depth interviews with both individuals and groups, document analysis, questionnaire surveys, and life history 'narrativization'. The question is, what have we found?

In my view, and aware that there is no homogeneous consensus on these things (Berger 1977; Wilson 2014), it would be irresponsible to cavalierly report that our own informal 'impact assessment' shows that SDP initiatives are promoting post-conflict 'healing' and 'advancement' in Cambodia. Instead, our data offer up rather more contradictory results, and contain evidence *both* for what Donnelly and Young (1985) referred to as social reproduction and social transformation – for both hope *and* caution. For instance, we found clear evidence that establishing friendship, respect, and collegiality are certainly core *intended* outcomes of the SHTFL. To many readers, these may appear as simple, predictable, and even naïve motives. However, of real relevance for a culturally sensitive sociology of sport, Cambodia as a whole *and* the SHTFL specifically are beset with their own unique (post-conflict) experiences and problems where the uses of sport are concerned. The SHTFL is an intriguing cultural phenomenon in modern Cambodia where there remain relatively few opportunities for people to experience social integration except for work-related activities in the daily pursuit of making a living in an ongoing destitute country.

Reminiscent of a familiar theme in sport advocacy which is clearly not without its critics, the focal point of the discussions of the organizers of the SHTFL has consistently been about striking a balance between competitiveness and respect in Cambodian society, on and off the field of play. This always seemed to be at the heart of their discussions. Importantly, and as several of our respondents remarked, creating friendship in the SHTFL community as well as in the community more broadly carries the possibility of enhancing mutual understanding and inter-organizational cooperation. The invitation of school students and local residents to SHTFL games shows the SHTFL's commitment to encouraging personal networks among hotel staff members, between hotels, and among local residents. As several SHTFL representatives argued, when rival hotels enjoy close connections and exchange information and experience in such an informal and collegial way, the effectiveness of the tourism sector more broadly is enhanced, even though that efficacy is expressed in terms other than, say, annual revenues, and is admittedly difficult to quantify.

In his research on tourism in the Mekong area, Polladach (2010: 207) observed: 'An issue … that needs to be confronted is how income created by the tourism industry can be shared fairly to reduce poverty and make a healthier community.' In many of the developing countries, tourism development is typically owned, controlled and operated via foreign investment, and it is often the case that benefits to local residents are intangible, or worse. Although we certainly found evidence of conflict and struggle between elements of the Cambodian tourism industry and the local residents of Siem Reap, the SHTFL, to this point at least, shows genuine commitment to loftier motives aimed not at profit per se but at forms of mutual cooperation and respect among locals in the region, as ably summed up by a former player and executive house-keeper of one of the SHTFL hotels: 'We want to explain [to the] people in Siem Reap that we (the hotels) don't mean we want to earn by ourselves. We would like to contribute on the development of whole Siem Reap, for everyone'. Significantly, a leading figure in the SHTFL recently communicated this sentiment to me in terms of far loftier objectives and possibilities: 'Yes … sport seems to have played a very important role in helping Cambodia recover from a very difficult period in history'.

On the basis of our evidence to date, it seems reasonable to acknowledge that SHTFL activities, representing an alliance between local hotels and established civic organizations such as the provincial education office, underscore the *potential* of sport in strongly positive ways. But there are obvious checks and balances: the SHTFL, like much of Cambodian society more generally, opens up far more doors to males than females and remains patriarchal in this respect (a female 'version' of the league has been vaguely discussed but not seriously encouraged); like sport anywhere it is prone to exploitation and abuse (such as biased officiating); and we are aware that in time its still rather innocent goals might be impacted by the vicissitudes of power, finance, and corruption (such as violence on the field or cheating in the form of players being fielded by hotel teams they do not actually work for). But for the time being at least this modest initiative, embedded in both its own micro cultural setting and connected to the far broader principle of 'social development through sport', remains at an embryonic stage of its own life-course. When SHTFL committee members address the apparent paradox of competitiveness and friendship, they genuinely feel that they are pursuing an arena for the healthy co-existence of these two elements in a way that best fits local circumstances (Donnelly and Young 1985). Stated differently, and as Coalter (2005: 4) has remarked, 'developing sport in the community, it may also be possible to contribute to the development of communities through sport'.

The sociology of sport literature contains an entire early generation of largely functionalist sport studies taking for granted the positive outcomes of sport (one can see these mirrored in the four stated goals of the CNVLD described earlier). More recently and more critically, several notable studies underscore the possibility of friendship and integration through sporting activities (Coleman and Iso-Ahola 1993; Iso-Ahola 1996; Coalter 2005), and focus on cultivating fair and respectful value systems to allow communities to 'work' more efficiently (Coalter 2002; Ebbeck and Gibbons 2003). As with others, our Cambodian fieldwork leads us to acknowledge the *potentially* positive and integrative possibilities of sport as a tool of social development, but does not suggest that sport is so autonomous that it can make social problems magically disappear or new and better communities magically come to life. This is not the case with the SHTFL, nor indeed with Cambodian society more generally where, as we have seen, conditions such as poverty, social conflict and violence endure, despite the introduction of seemingly well-intended sport-related initiatives.

Of course, it is extremely difficult to evaluate the outcomes of sport in development sectors, especially when the targets are based on abstract characteristics and evaluated using 'outsider' instruments. These outcomes are often intangible, culturally specific, and/or take a long time to become evident and measure with accuracy. Indeed, Jeanes and Lindsey (2014) argue that evaluation considered this way is implausible and untrustworthy. In their words: '"absolute" understanding or "robust" evidence along global North lines simply is not possible'. I certainly understand this position but, like Sugden (2006) and others, have seen tangible evidence of integrity, purpose and impact in 'sport-for-development' work in Cambodia.

Through our research on the SHTFL – critically, designed *by* Cambodians *for* Cambodians, not by *outsiders* for Cambodians – we found that such 'outcomes' include personal and social friendship and cooperation, and the sprouting of spontaneous efforts for community development by members in the private sector. As the core values of sport (such as teamwork, cohesiveness, achievement, positive self-worth) reflect those of wider society (Sport for Development and Peace International Working Group 2007; 2008), SHTFL members regard 'sport' as a powerful tool to enhance local living conditions and circumstances via one of its key industries – tourism. Our Cambodian work does not necessarily mean that sport can be used as a 'development tool' successfully in all settings, or that it can simply be parachuted in from outside without the organizational input of locals. Indeed, our case study does not allow us to say with certainty that sport helps resolve social problems or, in fact, does anything more than 'living alongside' social problems as they continue to be struggled over by locals involved. But, on the other hand, our research, now over ten years in the making, does give us confidence that, as a concept and an organization, the SHTFL at the very least operates as a context in which social problems may be acknowledged, considered and addressed on a regular basis in respectful and healthy ways. For these reasons, we believe that exploring a fledgling sport initiative in a post-conflict and quickly developing setting such as Cambodia contains merit and meaning.

The second prong of our Cambodian work leads to similar conclusions but via a different methodological route than the largely ethnographic turn operationalized with the SHTFL. Specifically, it 'chronologizes' the various stages in the life of a man, now in his late 60s, who has been key in promoting sport as a vehicle for both sport and community development in Cambodia. Critically, Cambodia is a country where many formal, written, photographed, or aural accounts have been destroyed, and many people who could detail the history of Cambodian sport from different points of view have simply disappeared. Adopting a method of personal recollection, we have tracked the chronology of a human life – a *surviving* human life – that has strategically pursued sport as a catalyst to community development from childhood to the present and through often unimaginable human circumstances. Tapping biographical recollections that help us piece together a life sequence, our life history analysis (LHA) details the story of a man affectionately regarded as the 'father of sport' in a Cambodian province still deeply enmeshed in poverty, but that has overcome human terror at the hands of a genocidal political regime. Cambodian sport (especially football in the northwest province of Siem Reap), and Cambodian society more broadly, owes much to the committed efforts of Mr Ouk Sareth (Young and Okada 2016).

The contradictions of sport are acknowledged in the aforementioned paper. For instance, Sareth has faced numerous opponents over the years; persons and sometimes government officials who felt that his commitment to sport was misplaced, naïve or zealous, or simply that other areas of social reclamation were more important in a post-conflict society. Sareth acknowledges the diversity and complexity of social life, but always returned to defend sport and its possible benefits for the community. In many ways, one can understand the views of Sareth's critics, since his goals involve both the development of recreational sport for children as well as making Cambodia contenders on an international scale. Here, there is an obvious paradox between advocating for a democratic and participatory 'sport for all' model at the same time as promoting a clearly more hegemonic approach aimed at elite sport outcomes for mostly elite participants.

Given the difficulties faced by Cambodia over the past several decades, an insistence on competitive sport 'played properly' has understandably faced opposition from persons whose priorities lie elsewhere and are compelled by a more gradual rise back to elite sport competition. But Sareth continues to vie for a top-level Cambodian sports culture. For instance, he insists that sport is played on the best fields, with the best equipment, and under the best conditions possible: 'If you are going to play football, you have to play it properly. It is important to progress in the right way.' As trite as it sounds to people in the global North, he argues vehemently, for school children, for example, to wear comfortable and appropriate athletic apparel for sports, such as t-shirts and shorts rather than wearing their school uniforms. Of course, the elemental nature of this micro-struggle speaks volumes about the still relatively unsophisticated status of the entire Cambodian sport scene.

Sareth has also encouraged learning sport correctly in a technical sense, as well as with respect to the ethos of sportsmanship so familiar in other countries. In Cambodia, even today, one can frequently see people playing sport such as football without keeping rules (rules are often also ignored by referees during matches). But again, Sareth assiduously encourages the observance of the rules by all participants and officials: 'All persons must obey the rules. This way football will improve.' Needless to say, it is difficult to demand such codes of participation surrounded by severe poverty and limited resources. Although overly strict regulations may well exclude (or even repel) some people from playing, at the same time it could be one positive dimension towards the creation of an effective Cambodian sports culture. As a lifelong elite athlete and coach, Sareth is committed to a future where Cambodia can compete on national and international levels. As such, while he does not expect unrealistic things from children in schools who find pleasure in simply kicking or throwing a ball, his vision of 'sport development' for his country goes beyond recreational fun to consider a future where Cambodia is able to compete with the world's powerful nations: 'Football is important for our future,' he pleads. On this matter it is worth remembering that the modern hegemonic sporting environment is hardly problem-free, and using it as a model of for sport development does not always serve the recreational sport community well – especially in under-resourced, underdeveloped, and conflict regions.

In 2015, and in a discussion about 'development' held at the highest levels, a new agenda was established for Sustainable Development Goals (SDGs) – following the Millennium Development Goals (MDGs) – to be pursued in the next 15 years with 17 concrete targets. Since the MDGs started in 2000, sport has been recognized as a flexibly utilized and cost-effective tool in promoting peace and development. In the new SDGs agenda sport is expected to play a key role in accomplishing these development goals:

> Sport is also an important enabler of sustainable development. We recognize the growing contribution of sport to the realization of development and peace in its promotion of tolerance and respect and the contributions it makes to the empowerment of women and of

young people, individuals and communities as well as to health, education and social inclusion objectives.

UNOSDP n.d.

When viewing Ouk Sareth's approach from the standpoint of these sorts of principles (that is, taking the word 'development' to include strategic involvement in activities to pursue one's own happiness and philanthropically improve the lives of others, especially the disenfranchised), we can, indeed, claim that his life represents an exemplar of 'community development through sport'.

One strength of the life history prong of our Cambodian work is that it underlines the potential of an almost completely ignored qualitative method in sport-for-development research, especially in the context of monitoring and evaluation (M+E). Although scholars such as Kay (2009; 2012), Levermore (2008; 2011), Coalter (2013), Darnell (2014), Hayhurst (2014), and Jeanes and Lindsey (2014) have appropriately emphasized the importance of 'evidence-based' M+E, securing the validity of such 'evidence' in SDP fields remains difficult not least because the quality of evidence depends not only on external factors but on internal factors too. As Kay correctly points out: 'M+E procedures are shaped by funders' information requirements, emphasize external accountability, limit local program learning, compromise data quality and impose burdensome forms of data collection and reporting that undermine relationships' (Kay 2012: 904). Our argument is that LHA goes some way to help avoid these difficulties and to avoid, for instance, the potentially manipulative effect of funders and sponsors or even the imperialistic views of outsiders. Put very simply, one might not agree with Ouk Sareth's visions for sport, and one might see contradictions in his, at times, 'sport for all' and, at other times, 'elite model' approaches, but this is a local elder whose knowledge and influence run deep and who has played a seminal role in bringing sport out of an unspeakable abyss with absolutely no outside influence such as (global North) sponsors to steer or taint his view. His 'voice from the field' might not make sense to, or compel, all, and it might at times be contradictory, but it is categorically an *authentic* voice. The important scholarly lesson here is that it is entirely possible to combine novel methods with critical analyses of sport for development.

Many writers in the SDP area (such as Fred Coalter – 2002; 2005; 2013) have been vocal in calling for more robust evidence on the value of sport in the development process. Moreover, scholars such as Tess Kay (2009, 2012) have argued that *local* narratives should be at the forefront of our understanding and not dismissed as invalid or as 'soft' evidence. Our view is that life history approaches can add to the increasing calls for localizing SDP knowledge. Additionally, LHA, in principle at least and as implied above, seems to align well with the *de-colonizing agendas* that are also circulating extensively within SDP literature (see Darnell 2014; Hayhurst 2014). As a methodological approach, LHA enables the prioritizing of authentic local experiences, meaning that it could potentially make a significant contribution to de-colonizing agendas within SDP work.

Cambodian sport futures: hope and different ways of seeing

Even the most cursory glance at the recent history of Cambodia shows that this is a country that has been, quite literally, to hell and back. The harrowing practices of a genocidal regime in the form of the Khmer Rouge and the resulting deaths of millions in the 'Killing Fields' have not been, and will never be, forgotten. But there is abundant and encouraging evidence that long-suffering Cambodian people have turned a corner and are now in their second generation of post-genocide peace. It is difficult not to agree with Ranges (2010: 12) when he remarks on the current climate in Cambodia: 'There is a palpable hopefulness radiating from Cambodians

… National pride is on the rise with the Kingdom's re-emergence … on the world stage.' This hopefulness is being acted out on a number of cultural fronts, but one is certainly sport as the preceding discussion of country-wide sport-for-development initiatives clearly demonstrates.

But, for all of this, is there any truly compelling evidence that Cambodian sport-for-development programs are any more likely to reach their desired goals than anywhere else? The answer to this critical question must surely depend on what writer John Berger (1977) would call 'ways of seeing' and Brian Wilson (2014) refers to as 'negotiations' over making sense of SDP terrain. But, for me, the answer, simply stated, is 'not yet'.

While all of my research on Cambodian sport has, until recently, been conducted with my collaborator (e.g. Okada and Young 2011; Young and Okada 2014; 2016), as is often the case in collaborative research, we do not necessarily share exactly the same view on (or 'way of seeing') the impact and potential of sport in this Southeast Asian setting. Personally, as much as I would like Cambodian sport-for-development initiatives to meet their often lofty objectives in a country that unequivocally deserves civility, compassion, positivity, and support, my sociological training combined with what I have observed 'on the ground' in Cambodia and other countries (such as Kenya, Burundi, and Thailand) obliges me to recognize *both* the promise and limits of SDP projects. As such, in the Introduction to our edited anthology *Sport, Social Development and Peace* (Young and Okada 2014), I encouraged circumspection by 'acknowledging potential' but also 'respecting balance' (p. ix). I advance this same conclusion now by cautiously reporting on well-intended and promising Cambodian sport initiatives, but whose actual impacts (short or long term) on the communities in which they take part are often vague and unproven, and occasionally contradictory. Needless to say, this is not a judgement that can be made of Cambodian SDP initiatives alone, but likely of all constituencies where sport – socially constructed and imbued with power imbalances as it inescapably is – is viewed as a panacea for social problems far larger in size and scope than any soccer or baseball game, or indeed any one seminal figure, can realistically resolve.

References

Berger, J. (1977). *Ways of Seeing*. London: Penguin.

Coalter, F. (2002). *Sport and Community Development: A Manual*. Edinburgh: Sport Scotland.

Coalter, F. (2005). *The Social Benefit of Sport: An Overview to Inform the Community Planning Process*. Edinburgh: Sport Scotland.

Coalter, F. (2013). *Sport-for-Development: What Game are We Playing?* London: Routledge.

Coleman, D. and Iso-Ahola, S. E. (1993). Leisure and health: The role of social support and self-determination. *Journal of Leisure Research, 25*(2), 111–128.

Cuddy, A. (2015). Rule of law rank near bottom. *The Phnom Penh Post*. Available at: www.phnompenhpost.com/national/rule-law-rank-near-bottom (accessed 12 February 2017).

Darnell, S. (2014). Ethical challenges and principal hurdles in sport-for-development work. In K. Young and C. Okada (eds), *Sport, Social Development and Peace*. Bingley, UK: Emerald, 1–18.

Donnelly, P. A. and Young, K. (1985). Reproduction and transformation of cultural forms in sport: A contextual analysis of rugby. *International Review for the Sociology of Sport, 20*(1), 19–39.

Doyle, K. (2014). Cambodia's Culture of Impunity: What Price for Life? BBC News. Available at: www.bbc.com/news/world-asia-30324424 (accessed 12 February 2017).

Ebbeck, V. and Gibbons, L. S. (2003). Explaining the self-conception of perceived conduct using indicators of moral functioning in physical education. *Research Quarterly for Exercise and Sport, 74* (3), 284–291.

Hayhurst, L. (2014). Using postcolonial feminism to investigate cultural difference and neoliberalism in sport, gender and development programming in Uganda. In K. Young and C. Okada (eds), *Sport, Social Development and Peace*. Bingley, UK: Emerald: 45–65.

Iso-Ahola, S. E. (1996). Leisure-related social support and self-determination as buffers of stress-illness relationship. *Journal of Leisure Research, 28*(3), 167–187.

Jeanes, R. and I. Lindsey (2014). Where's the 'evidence'? Reflecting on monitoring and evaluation within sport-for-development. In K. Young and C. Okada (eds), *Sport, Social Development and Peace*. Bingley, UK: Emerald: 197–219.

Kaplan, R. D. (1997) *The Ends of the Earth: A Journey to the Frontiers of Anarchy*. New York: Vintage.

Kay, T. (2012). Accounting for legacy? Monitoring and evaluation in sport in development relationships. *Sport in Society, 15* (6), 888–904.

Kay, T. (2009). Developing through sport: Evidencing sport impacts on young people. *Sport in Society, 12*(9), 1177–1191.

Levermore, R. (2008). Sport: A new engine for development? *Progress in Development Studies, 8*(2), 183–190.

Levermore, R. (2011). The paucity of, and dilemma in, evaluating corporate social responsibility for development through sport', *Third World Quarterly, 32*(2), 223–241.

Ministry of Education, Youth and Sport of Cambodia (MoEYS) (2014). Education Strategic Plan 2014–2018. Available at: www.veille.univ-ap.info/media/pdf/pdf_1436325627550.pdf#search='Ministry+of +Education%2C+Youth+and+Sport+%282014%29+Education+Strategic+Plan+20142018' (accessed 12 February 2017).

Okada, C. and Young, K. (2011). Sport and social development: Promise and caution from an incipient Cambodian football league. *International Review for the Sociology of Sport, 47* (1), 5–26.

Ota, K. (2012). The recent situation of Cambodia professional football. *Cambodia Kuroma Magazine* (in Japanese) APEX Cambodia, *25*, 14.

Polladach, T. (2010). Pro-poor ethnic tourism in the Mekong: A study of three approaches in northern Thailand. *Asia Pacific Journal of Tourism Research, 14*(2), 201–221.

Ranges, T. (2010). *Cambodia*, Washington, DC: National Geographic.

Roberts, D. (2001). *Political Transition in Cambodia 1991–1999: Power, Elitism and Democracy*, Richmond, UK: Curzon.

Sport for Development and Peace International Working Group (2007). *Literature Reviews on Sport for Development and Peace*. Toronto: University of Toronto.

Sport for Development and Peace International Working Group (2008*). Harnessing the Power of Sport for Development and Peace: Recommendations to Governments*. Toronto: Sport for Development and Peace International Working Group.

Sugden, J. (2006). Teaching and playing sport for conflict resolution and co-existence in Israel. *International Review for the Sociology of Sport, 41*(2) 221–240.

Ueda, Y. (2014). 'C-league is sizzling hot!' *NyoNyom*, April/May, 9.

UNDP. (2013). Human Development Report 2013 (The Rise of the South: Human Progress in a Diverse World), New York: United Nations Development Program.

United Nations Office for Sport for Development and Peace (UNOSDP). (n.d.). Sport and Sustainable Development Goals. Available at: www.un.org/sport/content/why-sport/sport-and-sustainable-development-goals (accessed 11 April 2016).

Wilson, B. (2014). Middle-Walkers: Negotiating Middle Ground on the Shifting Terrain of Sport, Peace, and Development. In K. Young and C. Okada (eds), *Sport, Social Development and Peace*. Bingley, UK: Emerald: 19–45.

Young, K. and Okada, C. (2016). Engaging the field through retrospective methods: A Cambodian story. *Qualitative Research in Sport, Exercise and Health, 8*(4–5), 456–471.

Young, K. and Okada, C. (2014). Sport, social development and peace: Acknowledging potential, respecting balance. In K. Young and C. Okada (eds), *Sport, Social Development and Peace*. Bingley, UK: Emerald: ix–xxix.

40

Canada and Australia

SDP and Indigenous peoples

Audrey R. Giles, Steven Rynne, Lyndsay M. C. Hayhurst and Anthony Rossi

Introduction

This chapter discusses programs and policies under the banner of Sport for Development and Peace (SDP) aimed at Indigenous peoples in Canada and Australia. There is great diversity within and between Indigenous peoples in Canada and Australia. Importantly, within the country that is now known as Canada, there is a growing rejection of the term 'Aboriginal' to refer to Indigenous peoples (Canadian Broadcasting Corporation 2016). According to the Canadian Constitution Act, Aboriginal refers to three groups of people: First Nations, Métis, and Inuit. In this chapter, we use the term Indigenous unless we are referring more specifically to First Nations, Métis, or Inuit populations, or where 'Aboriginal' is used in an organization's name or an original quote. Within the area now known as Australia, we also use the term Indigenous to refer to Aboriginal peoples and Torres Strait Islanders. Torres Strait Islanders (descendants of the Indigenous people of the Torres Strait, between the tip of Cape York and Papua New Guinea) are distinct with respect to origin and culture, but are generally considered to be original inhabitants of Australia. Overall, there are passionate debates with respect to how Indigenous groups self-identify and are identified by others within Canada and Australia. These debates, though important, are beyond the scope of this chapter.

Though there has been a great deal of literature that explores and conceptualizes sport and SDP in relation to HIV/AIDS prevention (Nicholls *et al.* 2010; Njelesani 2011), environmental sustainability (Wilson and Millington 2013), gender equality (Saavedra 2009), and social entre-preneurship (Hayhurst 2013) in the global South, scholars have only recently started to extend studies of SDP to Indigenous peoples who live in First World countries such as Canada (Coleby and Giles 2013; Hayhurst and Giles 2013; Rovito and Giles 2013; Galipeau and Giles 2014; Hayhurst *et al.* 2015) and Australia (e.g. Cairnduff 2001; Beneforti and Cunningham 2002; Nelson 2009; Rossi *et al.* 2013; Rossi and Rynne 2014; Hayhurst *et al.* 2016).

With this in mind, in this chapter we examine SDP in Indigenous communities in Canada and Australia in order to further emphasize and broaden the understandings of where and how SDP takes place. Moreover, we seek to underscore the point that while SDP may have some merits, it is not necessarily relevant or valuable to Indigenous people in Canada and Australia. Indeed, while SDP has been positioned to have important social, political, and economic benefits for Indigenous people in Canada and Australia, we question the need for, and benefits of, such initiatives.

Comparing Canada and Australia

It is reasonable to consider SDP initiatives for Indigenous peoples in both Canada and Australia because of issues, both historical and contemporary, that bind the two countries through separate but related processes (Miller 1998). Canada and Australia are two of the 32 countries classified as 'high income countries' on the World Bank's Country and Lending Groups classification (World Bank 2016); this sets them apart from most sites where SDP is delivered (i.e. the global South). Nevertheless, Indigenous residents of Canada and Australia are over-represented among those who experience poverty, poor health status and outcomes, incarceration, and low life expectancy, particularly when compared to other segments of the overall population (Australian Bureau of Statistics 2010; Public Health Agency of Canada 2012; Brand *et al.* 2016; Aboriginal and Torres Strait Islander Social Justice Commissioner 2016; Reitano 2016).

These issues are tied to the history of colonialism in both countries (see Pearson 2009 for an Australian account and Loppie-Reading and Wien 2009 for the Canadian case). Indigenous peoples in both Canada and Australia were subjected to British colonial rule and then subsequent rule by the white, European majority. As a result, Indigenous peoples in Canada and Australia share a history of the state assuming guardianship over them, through the enactment of policies, regulations and control over nearly every aspect of Indigenous life (Wilson 2003). Among such racist policies, a prominent example is the recent past that Canada and Australia share with respect to the removal (often forcible) of Indigenous children from their families. Indigenous children were sent to boarding/residential schools where they were unable to practice traditional customs, language, or to be influenced by parents or family (Wilson 2003). More recently, both nations have instigated Royal Commissions into various aspects of Indigenous affairs (e.g. Aboriginal Deaths in Custody 1991 and Separation of Children from Parents 1997 in Australia; Royal Commission on Aboriginal Peoples 1996 and Truth and Reconciliation Commission (TRC) Canada (2015a; 2015b).

Canada and Australia are also both modern democracies, albeit marked by hierarchies of racial privilege (Fee and Russell 2007). Indigenous peoples of Canada and Australia were only able to vote recently (1960 in Canada, and 1965 for all of Australia) and continue to represent a small proportion of the entire population (i.e. less than 5 per cent in Canada and less than 3 per cent in Australia) (Australian Bureau of Statistics 2012). Despite this, in both countries there have been significant Indigenous political and cultural resurgences that have served to disrupt and even challenge the dominant national identities, such as the 'polite Canadian peacekeeper' and the 'egalitarian Australian mate' (Fee and Russell 2007: 192). Despite this resurgence, enduring challenges remain for Indigenous peoples in both Canada and Australia with respect to justice, health, education, land, and resources. These challenges are made similarly difficult to overcome in both countries where a neoliberal political economy has led to a retreat of the welfare state and proclamations of the end of the era of entitlement (Hayhurst and Giles 2013; Rossi and Jeanes 2016). This has serious implications for any form of support, including those related to sport.

It is also important to note that despite vast geographies in both countries, Indigenous populations are highly urbanized in both Canada and Australia. Around 70 per cent of Indigenous people live in urban settings (Australian Government 2011; Fredericks 2013). Not only that, the growth of the Indigenous Australian population in urban centres far outstrips that of Indigenous Australians in remote areas as well as non-Indigenous Australians in urban centres. However, this urban migration is somewhat different from similar trends globally with respect to duration of stay (i.e. Indigenous Australians who travel from remote areas to urban localities do not always stay there permanently), as well as reasons for, and peak periods of, migration (e.g. there was a period of 'return to country' when many of the historical policies of segregation were lifted as well as periods of 'forced' assimilation).

Similarly, according to the 2011 Canadian Census, urban-dwelling Indigenous peoples are the fastest growing segment of the Canadian population. Between 1996 and 2011, the urban Indigenous population increased from 49 per cent to 56 per cent of the overall Indigenous population in Canada. However, the population increase for urban Indigenous peoples has not been a result of large-scale out-migration from First Nations reserves, Métis settlements, and Inuit lands. Indeed, there has also been an increase in non-urban populations, too. These increases in population are due to a variety of factors: 'fertility rates, family formation or separation, changing patterns of identification, and through Bill C-31 of the Indian Act [through which some First Nations women reclaimed their previously stripped Indian status]' (Snyder and Wilson 2012: 2420–2421). Indigenous populations in Canada also show more mobility between rural/reserve and urban areas than do non-Indigenous Canadian due to a variety of push and pull factors, such as health, education, social, and economic factors (Snyder and Wilson 2012).

Despite the high proportion and increasing numbers of Indigenous peoples in urban settings in Australia and Canada, ideas still persist that Indigenous peoples live primarily in remote settings and that those who live in cities and towns are somehow 'less Indigenous'. This misrepresentation and stereotyping marginalizes the large and vibrant urban populations. It also can have negative implications for policy development and funding allocation, as funding, policies, and programs, including those in SDP, may neglect the unique needs of urban Indigenous populations.

Overall, we contend that the strong similarities between Canada and Australia –histories of settler colonialism, vast geographies, levels of state and non-state involvement in Indigenous affairs – enable complementary and comparative discussions concerning SDP in Indigenous communities. We now turn to public policies and state involvement in SDP in both Canada and Australia.

SDP and policy in Canada and Australia

Sport has historically offered many Indigenous peoples a reason to come together (Nelson 2009; Norman 2012; McHugh *et al.* 2015). That said, a prominent discourse that frames the apparent importance of sport to Indigenous peoples is the assumption that Indigenous people possess high levels of 'natural talent' or 'special gifts' for sport (Tatz 1987; Nelson 2009; Adair and Stronach 2011; Kidd 2013). This discourse can make SDP initiatives seem like a 'natural' fit, while emphasizing ability over hard work, training, effort, and intelligence. A different, but no less demeaning, discourse suggests that Indigenous sportspeople lack endurance, are lazy, show a reluctance to train, are mentally fragile, prone to violence, and in need of occupation to avoid a host of negative social behaviours like alcohol, drugs, teen sex, etc. (Tatz 1995; Maynard 2012). We suggest that these racist discourses have informed some SDP efforts aimed at Indigenous youth and propelled policy-makers and programmers to attempt to instil specific values and behaviours in targeted populations (Wane 2008; Adair and Stronach 2011; Maynard 2012).

These discourses need to be placed in historical context. Forsyth (2013) has noted that in the 1880s, restrictions were placed on Indigenous peoples' participation in traditional practices, such as the potlach and sun dance. There was a belief that the resulting gap in physical practices needed to be filled with productive, 'civilizing' activities for Indigenous peoples. As a result, both the church and state organized sport at Indian residential schools in order to control Indigenous people and their bodies, often under the guise of health and education. Indian residential schools were joint ventures between the government of Canada and the Anglican, Catholic, Presbyterian, and United Churches. First Nations, Inuit, and Métis young people were sent to these schools, which operated throughout most of Canada. Removed from their families and communities, and deprived of their culture, Indigenous children suffered abuse, and many died while attending residential schools.

The horrendous and far-reaching legacy of the Indian residential school system has received increasing attention in recent years. In particular, the Indian Residential Schools Truth and Reconciliation Commission (TRC) (2015a), established in 2008 and ended in 2015, labeled residential schools part of a 'cultural genocide', and identified what is needed for Canada and its Indigenous peoples to reconcile. The TRC issued 94 Calls to Action (2015b), of which five focused on sport. Indeed, two of the calls are strongly related to SDP. Number 8 calls for 'policies to promote physical activity as a fundamental element of health and well-being, reduce barriers to sports participation, increase the pursuit of excellence in sport, and build capacity in the Canadian sport system' (TRC 2015b: 2). Number 88 calls for ensuring stable funding for community sports programs that 'reflect the diverse cultures and traditional sporting activities of Aboriginal peoples ... An elite athlete development program for Aboriginal athletes ... Programs for coaches, trainers, and sports officials that are culturally relevant for Aboriginal peoples ... [and] anti-racism awareness and training programs' (TRC 2015b: 10). It is important to note that the TRC recommendations for sport came after Canada had been involved in international SDP policy-making and programming for a number of years, activity that rarely took account of the history of sport in Canada, or the history of sport for development aimed at Indigenous people (Nicholls and Giles 2007).

Similar to what occurred in Canada, the Australian Government adopted a highly paternalistic approach to engaging with Indigenous peoples, instituting a variety of severe restrictions to 'protect' Indigenous peoples in Australia in the run-up to federation in 1901. In effect, the government sought to control almost all aspects of Indigenous lives and lands. Similar to the Canadian context, churches and other religious entities acted as agents of the government, establishing missions and seeking to 'civilize' Indigenous Australians (Armitage 1995; Tatz 1995). Indigenous peoples in Australia were removed from their land, and denied the practice of traditional language and culture. Much of this was justified on the basis of the earlier declaration of *terra nullius* (that the land which had come to be known as Australia belonged to no one prior to English settlement) as well as on notions of racial superiority.

Also, similar to Canada, sport was included in policy and strategic approaches to dealing with Indigenous peoples in Australia. A key example emerged from the Royal Commission into Aboriginal Deaths in Custody (1987–1991), which found that Indigenous Australians should be afforded far greater access to sport and recreation. Implicit in this conclusion was that sport would reduce anti-social and criminal behaviour among Indigenous populations, as well as improve community cohesion. The result was the Australian Government's establishment of the Indigenous Sport Program through the Australian Sports Commission in 1993. Since the Royal Commission, research into diversionary strategies that incorporate sport has maintained some momentum in Australia (Rossi and Rynne 2014).

More recently, successive federal governments have prioritized policies aimed at Indigenous people. Building on the 2008 National Apology to Aboriginal and Torres Strait Islander Peoples, made by the then Labor Government, a long-term 'Closing the Gap' framework was developed and subsequently agreed to by the Council of Australian Governments. This agreement committed the Commonwealth, States and Territories to a range of investments related to redressing Indigenous disadvantage, specifically in relation to health outcomes, early childhood development, remote Indigenous housing, schooling, and remote service delivery. Accompanying this was the argument that sport is a valuable community development tool that can assist with improving Indigenous social and health outcomes (Rossi and Rynne 2014).

The recent Coalition Government in Australia moved to a somewhat different approach through its Indigenous Advancement Strategy. In the 2015–16 Budget, the federal government allocated AUS$4.9 billion over four years to the Indigenous Advancement Strategy (Australian Government 2015). While the government still reports on progress related to the Closing the Gap targets (Department of the Prime Minister and Cabinet 2017), the policy focus is on new program streams related to jobs, land and economy, children and schooling, safety and well-being, culture and capability, and remote Australia strategies. Notably, sport is positioned as an important component within this strategy and is prominent in the reporting of strategy pro-gress and outcomes. For example, in the most recent Closing the Gap report, sport featured in Chapter 4 Employment (i.e. an account of the Thursday Island Boat Club upgrade), Chapter 6 Healthy Lifestyles (i.e. an outline of the $13 million Indigenous Advancement Strategy resulting in 82 initiatives to increase participation in sport and active recreation), and Chapter 7 Strong and Safe Communities (i.e. description of family violence campaign connections with over 100 sporting teams).

Against this backdrop of history and policy, in the next section we look more closely at SDP programs aimed at Indigenous youth in Canada and Australia. We argue that Indigenous youth in both countries are often understood to be 'at-risk' and, as such, their bodies and minds are often the sites of SDP interventions.

SDP programs and indigenous youth

A multitude of SDP programs targeted towards Indigenous youth have been and are in operation throughout Canada. Here, we provide an overview of several of the larger ones. The Manitoba Northern Fly-In Sport Camp, which was established in 1986, was a predecessor for other programs that would follow its model of bringing recreation and sport professionals to rural and remote Aboriginal communities. One such program is Alberta's Future Leaders Program (AFLP). AFLP was established by the Alberta Sport, Recreation, Parks and Wildlife Foundation in 1996 due to a concern with Indigenous youth's over-representation in Alberta's justice system (Galipeau and Giles 2014). AFLP places pairs of mostly non-Indigenous college and university students, who are employed as 'youth workers' and 'arts mentors', on First Nations reserves, Métis settlements, and in inner-city locations throughout Alberta. During the summer months, these employees use sport, recreation, and the arts to develop Indigenous youth into future leaders and, in turn, improve their life trajectory (Galipeau and Giles 2014).

In recent years, Right to Play, a corporate-sponsored international SDP organization, has grown significantly in offering SDP in Indigenous communities throughout Canada. In partner-ship with local Aboriginal communities, its Promoting Life Skills in Aboriginal Youth (PLAY) program uses sport and recreation programming to attempt to improve the health, well-being, and leadership of First Nations youth. As with AFLP, funding comes from three sources: the communities that offer the programs, the provincial government, and private sponsors. Though it started in northern Ontario, PLAY is now offered by 88 First Nations communities and urban Indigenous organizations throughout Canada (Right to Play n.d.).

That said, SDP programs for Aboriginal youth are not only offered in the rural/remote con-text. Hayhurst *et al.* (2015) worked with participants of the Vancouver Aboriginal Friendship Centre Society's (VAFCS) Because We're Girls program. In the program, Aboriginal girls and young women in Canada's third largest city have the opportunity to take a leadership role in selecting and organizing physical activity and healthy eating programming. Hayhurst *et al.* (2015) found that despite the considerable barriers that the girls and young women had to overcome, they used the program as an opportunity to resist and challenge perceptions about their bodies, sporting abilities, lifestyles, and Aboriginal stereotypes in general.

In the Australian context, there is a similar array of programs making use of sport in targeting Indigenous youth. Among these programs, there is significant variation with respect to location and histories, sources and terms of funding, purpose and focus, and mode of operation. An example of a program focused on Indigenous girls is Role Models and Leaders Australia (RMLA). This private sector led non-governmental organization operates a Girls Academy program through high schools in Western Australia, the Northern Territory, and New South Wales, and provides leadership, sports, education, and employment training programs to 'assist Indigenous youth, who suffer from poverty, sickness, misfortune, or a disconnectedness from their community' (RMLA 2013: 554). The program focuses on young Indigenous women between the ages of 12 and 18 who 'experience poverty, sickness, misfortune or disconnectedness from their community' (RMLA 2015: para. 5). The program is based on the idea that the needs of Indigenous young women are often not met and, as a result, RMLA's main goal is to help them to 'achieve the necessary skills for further education, training and employment, and at the same time have the opportunity to improve their sporting and life skills' (RMLA 2014). In achieving these aims, young women are selected from communities to attend boarding (residential) colleges (although there are some local day-students) in major centres; at these schools, sport is positioned as a key component of the RMLA program. Specifically, sport is considered to be beneficial from a participation perspective, creating opportunities for participants to engage in 'healthy living practices' and develop new relationships. While there is some engagement in a variety of physical pursuits such as fitness programs and sporting carnivals, the primary focus is on basketball (Hayhurst *et al.* 2016).

An example of a program that targets young Indigenous males is the Clontarf Foundation (Clontarf). The focus of Clontarf is on improving education, employment, health, well-being, and life skills, as well as the sporting ability of young Indigenous males. From modest beginnings in 2000, Clontarf has developed more than 80 academies in schools across Western Australia (where the program originated), the Northern Territory, South Australia, New South Wales, and Queensland. With more than 4,700 Indigenous boys involved, the program aims to use sport (Australian Rules Football, Rugby League, Cricket) as a vehicle to motivate Indigenous youth to attend school and embrace the foundations' values and objectives. Upon graduation from school (and the program), graduates are given support in finding and maintaining employment. The funding model underpinning Clontarf programs involves equal support from federal government, state or territory governments, and the private sector (Clontarf 2016).

SDP in Indigenous communities and the need for a paradigm shift

Despite the popularity of SDP programs for Indigenous youth in Canada and Australia, there are nevertheless pressing issues that need to be addressed concerning these programs. To date, SDP programs in Indigenous communities have largely been imagined in very particular ways: pan-Indigenous, reactionary, deficit-based, and with donors exercising a great deal of control. We argue that there are important ways in which SDP in Indigenous communities in Australia and Canada can – and, in some cases, has already started to be – reimagined. A relevant example is the pilot and evaluation of an Australian Government-funded program called the Sports Demonstration Program. This was a comprehensive youth strategy for sport in remote regions of the Northern Territory of Australia that was aimed at diversion from 'at-risk' behaviours, improvement of life choices and outcomes, and strengthening youth service infrastructure through engagement in positive (sport) activities. Although there are paternalistic overtones to the project, key aspects of quality practice that were recognized/proposed included: greater local collaboration and involvement of personnel, building on previous developments and successes, realistic choices and consultation, a 'whole of community' focus, and a sport pathways approach to capacity building. As Rossi and Rynne (2014) reported, the level of success across the project was mixed. However, some of the communities within the project showed highly positive outcomes that included: increased sports participation especially by women and marginal groups (such as Indigenous people with diverse sexual identities), increased opportunities for leadership through coaching and officiating qualifications, and some opportunity for travel to other communities to play sport. Significantly, the more successful communities tended to be those where Indigenous leaders drove the initiative.

The lack of appreciation in SDP of the differences between and within Indigenous populations in both Canada and Australia is also an issue that needs attention. Pan-Indigenous approaches that fail to pay attention to important differences between cultures, resources, and locations can result in programs that fail to meet participants' needs. For example, Indigenous populations in urban centres are often much more heterogeneous than those in small communities (Peters 2006; Brand et al. 2016). Ensuring that programs are respectful and inclusive of all cultures thus poses an important challenge for programs offered in urban settings. At the same time, programs that are offered in rural and remote settings might struggle with access to resources that are more plentiful in urban environments, while access to the non-built environment provides those in rural and remote communities with opportunities for outdoor activities that might not be available to their urban counterparts. As a result, the uniform prescription of 'one size fits all' programming that fails to take into account important differences between and within Indigenous communities has significant limitations.

SDP programs that are offered to Indigenous peoples are also often reactionary in nature and put in place largely to respond to problems that have been identified – generally in a top-down fashion and largely by governments. Careful consultation and planning that is based on community members' needs and that responds to their self-identified priorities are not always the norm. As a result, programs are often deficit-based and involve a 'take it or leave it' approach to pre-packaged standardized programs. Further, Indigenous communities are often viewed as lacking the capacity to design and control their own programs. The ways in which this apparent lack of capacity is rooted in inequities that are the result of colonial policy (e.g. a lack of funding for Indigenous education and the need to use available human resources to address other urgent issues) is also rarely given attention.

Programs that meet Indigenous community members' self-identified needs, use a strengths-based approach, promote self-determination, and are designed and controlled by Indigenous peoples themselves would represent a paradigm shift within SDP. While some might argue that positive youth development is a strengths-based approach that is already in operation within SDP programs, the way in which these programs are entrenched in white societal ideals is often overlooked (Ginwright and Cammarota 2002). Rather than preparing youth for participation in Eurocentric education systems and competitive capitalism (Hayhurst et al. 2016), SDP programs designed and controlled by community members themselves may be able to play important roles in facilitating Indigenous activism and self-determination. The ability to control programming becomes all the more apparent when the focus shifts towards meeting Indigenous peoples' own goals rather than those of, for instance, the general public, neocolonial governments, and/or private enterprise. Thus, there is an opportunity to 'shift the gaze' away from pathologizing and objectifying Indigenous bodies as ones that must be targeted by interventions like SDP programs. Instead, non-Indigenous scholars can and should turn the gaze towards themselves (or, in the case of the authors of this chapter, ourselves) as well as the broader SDP sector in order to question how we might be complicit in the restricted choices and disadvantaged conditions that Indigenous peoples encounter.

Indeed, it is not appropriate for us as non-Indigenous scholars to make any definitive statements or concrete proposals regarding Indigenous SDP programs and the associated research agendas. Moreover, we acknowledge Indigenous populations have been involved in more research than most other populations throughout the world (and notably more often as the subject rather than the partner and driver of the research). However, we feel confident in our capacity to advocate for the need for Indigenous paradigms that can inform SDP and its associated research. In part, this is derived from the notion that quality and sustainability of such programs are likely to be derived from empowerment, self-determination, and through developing capabilities as a true(r) indicator of development (Nussbaum 2011).

Conclusion

In this chapter, we have noted that the similar histories of Indigenous peoples in Australia and Canada enables important comparison regarding SDP initiatives. In both countries (as well as others), SDP and Indigenous communities are often viewed as compatible, but in ways that may perpetuate harmful discourses and even hamper efforts for Indigenous emancipation and development based on self-determination. Moreover, the paternalistic, top-down, externally imposed and managed models that dominate much of the SDP landscape are arguably grounded in traditionally racist policy enactments in both countries.

Nevertheless, SDP programs aimed at Indigenous peoples have continued to proliferate and some are beginning to take alternative approaches. An ongoing reimagining of such SDP programs is needed if they are to become strengths-based, self-determined, and sensitive to Indigenous peoples' self-identified needs. There is a strong case to be made for increasing and improving community capacity building through SDP models that prioritize local design and management approaches. Further, associated research activities should be similarly founded in Indigenous paradigms where appropriate and, regardless of the approach, should engender significant local involvement regarding all aspects, from conception to dissemination to evaluation. Through careful strategy and in partnership with existing agencies, these approaches can, in turn, be scaled up.

Acknowledgement

The authors acknowledge funding of this research from the Social Sciences and Humanities Research Council of Canada.

References

Aboriginal and Torres Strait Islander Social Justice Commissioner. (2016). Social Justice and Native Title Report. Available at: www.humanrights.gov.au/sites/default/files/document/publication/AHRC_SJNTR_2016.pdf.
Adair, D. and Stronach, M. (2011). Natural-born athletes? Australian Aboriginal people and the double-edged lure of professional sport. In J. Long and K. Spracklen (eds), Sport and Challenges to Racism. London: Palgrave Macmillan. pp. 117–134.
Armitage, A. (1995). Comparing the Policy of Aboriginal Assimilation: Australia, Canada and New Zealand. Vancouver, Canada: UBC Press.

Australian Bureau of Statistics. (2010). The Health and Welfare of Australia's Aboriginal and Torres Strait Islander Peoples. Available at: www.abs.gov.au/AUSSTATS/abs@.nsf/39433889d406eeb9ca25706100 19e9a5/D059DE84AB99BE60CA2574390014BE51?opendocument.

Australian Bureau of Statistics. (2012). 3101.0 – Australian Demographic Statistics, Dec 2012. Available at: www.abs.gov.au/ausstats/abs%40.nsf/94713ad445ff1425ca25682000192af2/1647509ef7e25faaca25 68a900154b63?OpenDocument.

Australian Government. (2011). *Demographic, social and economic characteristics overview: Aboriginal and Torres Strait Islander people and where they live.* Canberra, Australia: Australian Bureau of Statistics.

Australian Government. (2015). Indigenous Advancement Strategy. Department of Prime Minister and Cabinet. Available at: www.dpmc.gov.au/indigenous-affairs/indigenous-advancement-strategy.

Beneforti, M. and Cunningham, J. (2002). *Investigating Indicators for Measuring the Health and Social Impact of Sport and Recreation Programs in Indigenous Communities.* Darwin, Australia: Australian Sports Commission and Cooperative Research Centre for Aboriginal and Tropical Health.

Brand, E., Bond, C. and Shannon, C. (2016). Indigenous in the city: Urban indigenous populations in local and global contexts. Available at: The University of Queensland: https://poche.centre.uq.edu.au/files/ 609/Indigenous-in-the-city%281%29.pdf.

Cairnduff, S. (2001). *Sport and Recreation for Indigenous Youth in the Northern Territory: Scoping Research Priorities for Health and Social Outcomes.* Darwin, Australia: Cooperative Research Centre for Aboriginal and Tropical Health and Australian Sports Commission.

Canadian Broadcasting Corporation. (2016). CBC Aboriginal Changes Name to CBC Indigenous. Available at: www.cbc.ca/news/indigenous/cbc-aboriginal-becomes-cbc-indigenous-1.3765790.

Clontarf Foundation. (2016). Clontarf Foundation Annual Report 2015. Available at: www.clontarf.org.au/ wp-content/uploads/downloads/2016/04/Clontarf-Foundation-2015-Annual-Report.pdf.

Coleby, J. and Giles, A. R. (2013). Discourses at work in media reports on Right to Play's 'Promoting Life-Skills in Aboriginal Youth' program. *Journal of Sport for Development, 1*(2), 1–14.

Darnell, S. (2010). Power, politics and 'Sport for Development and Peace': Investigating the utility of sport for international development. *Sociology of Sport Journal, 27*(1), 54–75.

Department of the Prime Minister and Cabinet. (2017). Closing the Gap (National Indigenous Reform Agreement). Available at: http://closingthegap.pmc.gov.au/.

Fee, M. and Russell, L. (2007). 'Whiteness' and `Aboriginality' in Canada and Australia: Conversations and identities. *Feminist Theory, 8*(2), 187–208, doi:10.1177/1464700107078141.

Forsyth, J. (2013). Bodies of meaning: Sports and games at Canadian residential schools. In *Aboriginal Peoples and Sport in Canada: Historical Foundations and Contemporary Issues.* Vancouver, Canada: UBC Press, pp. 15–34.

Fredericks, B. (2013). 'We don't leave our identities at the city limits': Aboriginal and Torres Strait Islander people living in urban localities. *Australian Aboriginal Studies, 1,* 4–16.

Galipeau, M. and Giles, A. R. (2014). An examination of cross-cultural mentorship in Alberta's future leaders program. In K. Young and C. Okada (eds), *Research in the Sociology of Sport.* Bingley, UK: Emerald, pp. 147–170.

Ginwright, S. and Cammarota, J. (2002). New terrain in youth development: The promise of a social justice approach. *Social Justice, 29*(4), 82–95.

Hayhurst, L. M. C. (2013). Girls as the 'new' agents of social change? Exploring the 'Girl Effect' through sport, gender and development programs in Uganda. *Sociological Research Online (Special Issue: Modern Girlhoods), 18*(2), 8.

Hayhurst, L. M. C. (2015). Sport for development and peace: a call for transnational, multi-sited, post-colonial feminist research. *Qualitative Research in Sport, Exercise and Health, 8*(5), 424–433, doi:10.1080/ 2159676X.2015.1056824

Hayhurst, L. M. C. and Giles, A. R. (2013). Private and moral authority, self-determination, and the domestic transfer objective: Foundations for understanding sport for development and peace in Aboriginal communities in Canada. *Sociology of Sport Journal, 30*(4), 504–519.

Hayhurst, L. M. C., Giles, A. R. and Radforth, W. (2015). 'I want to come here to prove them wrong': Examining a sport, gender and development program for urban Indigenous young women in Vancouver, Canada. *Sport in Society, 18*(8), 952–967, doi:10.1080/17430437.2014.997585.

Hayhurst, L. M. C., Giles, A. R. and Wright, J. (2016). Biopedagogies and Indigenous knowledge: Examining sport for development and peace for urban Indigenous young women in Canada and Australia. *Sport, Education and Society, 21*(4), 549–569, doi:10.1080/13573322.2015.1110132.

Kay, T. and Dudfield, O. (2013). The Commonwealth Guide to Advancing Development Through Sport. Available at: London: www.un.org/wcm/webdav/site/sport/users/melodie.arts/public/Commonwealth%20Secretariat_2013_The%20Commonwealth%20Guide%20to%20Advancing%20Development%20through%20Sport.pdf.

Kidd, B. (2013). In defence of Tom Longboat. *Sport in Society, 16*(4), 515–532.

Loppie-Reading, C. L. and Wien, F. (2009). *Health Inequalities and Social Determinants of Aboriginal Peoples' Health*. Prince George, Canada: National Collaborating Centre for Aboriginal Health.

McHugh, T.-L. F., Coppola, A. M., Holt, N. L. and Andersen, C. (2015). 'Sport is community': An exploration of urban Aboriginal peoples' meanings of community within the context of sport. *Psychology of Sport and Exercise, 18*, 75–84, doi:http://dx.doi.org/10.1016/j.psychsport.2015.01.005.

Maynard, J. (2012). Contested space – the Australian Aboriginal sporting arena. *Sport in Society, 15*(7), 987–996, doi:10.1080/17430437.2012.723368.

Miller, M. (1998). An Australian Nunavut – A comparison of Inuit and Aboriginal rights movements in Canada and Australia. *Emory International Law Review, 12*(2), 1175–1214.

Nelson, A. (2009). Sport, physical activity and urban Indigenous young people. *Australian Aboriginal Studies, 2*, 101–111.

Nicholls, S. and Giles, A. R. (2007). Sport as a tool for HIV/AIDS education: A potential catalyst for change. *Pimatisiwin: A Journal of Aboriginal and Indigenous Community Health, 5*(1), 51–85.

Nicholls, S., Giles, A. R. and Sethna, C. (2010). Perpetuating the 'lack of evidence' discourse in sport for development: Privileged voices, unheard stories and subjugated knowledge. *International Review for the Sociology of Sport, 46*(3), 249–264, doi:10.1177/1012690210378273.

Njelesani, D. (2011). Preventive HIV/AIDS education through physical education: Reflections from Zambia. *Third World Quarterly, 32*(3), 435–452, doi:10.1080/01436597.2011.573939.

Norman, H. (2012). A modern day corroboree – the New South Wales Annual aboriginal rugby league knockout carnival. *Sport in Society, 15*(7), 997–1013, doi:10.1080/17430437.2012.723370.

Nussbaum, M. C. (2011). *Creating capabilities: The human development approach*. Cambridge, MA: Harvard University Press.

Pearson (2009). *Up from the Mission : Selected Writings*. Melbourne, Australia: Black Inc.

Peters, E. (2006). *First Nations, Métis, and Inuit diversity in Canadian cities*. Montreal, Canada: Institute for Research on Public Policy.

Public Health Agency of Canada. (2012). The Chief Public Health Officer's Report on the State of Public Health in Canada. Available at: www.phac-aspc.gc.ca/cphorsphc-respcacsp/2012/chap-1-eng.php.

Reitano, J. (2016). Adult Correctional Statistics in Canada 2014/2015. Available at: www.statcan.gc.ca/pub/85-002-x/2016001/article/14318-eng.htm.

Right to Play. (n.d.). Our impact. Available at: www.righttoplay.com/canada/our-impact/Pages/.

Role Models and Leaders Australia (RMLA). (2015). Girls Academies. Available at: www.girlsacademy.com.au.

Role Models and Leader Australia (RMLA). (2013). Role Models and Leaders Australia. Available at: www.rolemodelsaustralia.com.

Rossi, T. and Jeanes, R. (2016). Education, pedagogy and sport for development: Addressing seldom asked questions. *Sport, Education and Society, 2*, 483–494, doi:10.1080/13573322.2016.1160373.

Rossi, T. and Rynne, S. (2014). Sport development programmes for Indigenous Australians: Innovation, inclusion and development, or a product of 'white guilt'? *Sport in Society, 17*, 1030–1045, doi:10.1080/17430437.2013.838355.

Rossi, A., Rynne, S. B. and Nelson, A. (2013). Doing whitefella★ research in blackfella★ communities in Australia: Decolonizing method in sports related research. *Quest, 65*(1), 116–131.

Rovito, A. and Giles, A. R. (2013). Youth development through recreation: Eurocentric influences and Aboriginal self-determination. In C. Hallinan and B. Judd (eds), *Native Games: Indigenous Peoples and Sports in the Post-Colonial World*. Bingley, UK: Emerald, pp. 183–203.

Saavedra, M. (2009). Dilemmas and opportunities in gender and sport-in-development. In R. Levermore and A. Beacom (eds), *Sport and International Development*. London: Palgrave Macmillan, pp. 124–155.

Snyder, M. and Wilson, K. (2012). Urban aboriginal mobility in Canada: Examining the association with health care utilization. *Social Science and Medicine, 75*(12), 2420–2424.

Tatz, C. (1987). *Aborigines in Sport*. Bedford Park, Australia: Lutheran Publishing House.

Tatz, C. (1995). *Obstacle Race: Aborigines in Sport*. Sydney: UNSW Press.

Truth and Reconciliation Commission of Canada (TRC). (2015a). Honouring the Truth, Reconciling the Future: Summary of the Final Report of the Truth and Reconciliation Commission of Canada.

Available at: www.trc.ca/websites/trcinstitution/File/2015/Findings/Exec_Summary_2015_05_31_web_o.pdf.

Truth and Reconciliation Commission of Canada (TRC). (2015b). Truth and Reconciliation Commission of Canada: Calls to action. Available at: www.trc.ca/websites/trcinstitution/File/2015/Findings/Calls_to_Action_English2.pdf.

Wane, N. (2008). Mapping the field of Indigenous knowledges in anti-colonial discourse: A transformative journey in education. *Race Ethnicity and Education*, *11*(2), 183–197, doi:10.1080/13613320600807667.

Wilson, S. (2003). Progressing toward an Indigenous research paradigm in Canada and Australia. *Canadian Journal of Native Education*, *27*(2), 161–178.

Wilson, B. and Millington, B. (2013). Sport, ecological modernization, and the environment. In D. L. Andrews and B. Carrington (eds), *A Companion to Sport*). Oxford, UK: John Wiley and Sons, pp. 129–142.

World Bank. (2016). World Bank Country and Lending Groups. Available at: https://datahelpdesk.worldbank.org/knowledgebase/articles/906519-world-bank-country-and-lending-groups.

41
Cuba
Revolutionary games

Robert Huish

Introduction

In late 1991, a cargo vessel departed the Soviet Union destined for Cuba; however, by the time it arrived in dock, the Soviet Union had dissolved. While the vessel was at sea 'the Hammer and Sickle' was struck from the Kremlin, taking with it the preferred trade agreement between the Soviet Union and Cuba. When the boat arrived in Havana Harbor after December 25, 1991 the Captain informed the longshoremen on the dock that the cargo would not be unloaded unless cash – US dollars to be precise – was handed over to the crew (Bain 2007). Cuba, a country that had dedicated close to 90 percent of its total exports to the Soviet Union in exchange for petroleum, machinery, and military assistance, had almost no foreign currency reserves (Zimbalist 1993; Cole 2002). Now, with its largest trading partner folded, and the new Russia not willing to accept checks, certificates of credit, sugar, or anything other than cash for trade, Cuba needed to reorient its political geography away from Moscow, and toward new partners in the Americas and throughout the global South (Ritter and Rowe 2002).

The dissolution of the Soviet Union was long predicted in Cuba (Bain 2007). In the mid-1980s, when Cuba's gross domestic product (GDP) growth all but stalled, President Fidel Castro declared a 'rectification of errors' campaign, meant to distance Cuba from any economic or social reforms taking place in Eastern Europe and the Soviet Union (Eckstein 1990; Hamilton 2002). This involved more 'made in Cuba' solutions to economic and social challenges, which ended up escalating tensions between the leaders in Moscow and Havana. Whereas Cuba had received tremendous economic support through the Soviet Union's 'Совет Экономической Взаимопомощи' (Council for Economic Assistance) since 1972, by 1991 leaders in Moscow rejected the idea of supporting the Cuban sugar industry at a time when they were making deep cuts within the Soviet Union itself (Bain 2007). Five-year trade agreements were reduced to one-year contracts in the Spring of 1991 (Bain 2005). In August, after a failed coup attempt in Moscow, Fidel Castro, and other Cuban leaders, began to openly criticize the Soviet leadership. In September, Soviet President Mikhail Gorbachev pulled out all Soviet military personnel from Cuba (Bain 2005). Four months later, fuel, commodities, medicines, and military assistance would no longer be sent to Cuba from the former Soviet Union, leading to a devastating loss of material goods, food, and energy. Named the 'Special period in the time of peace', Cuba's GDP collapsed by 35 percent in a year, and the country lost 88 percent of its foreign exports (Henken 2008). Rolling blackouts consumed the country. Medicine shortages were commonplace, and the average Cuban male lost 35 lbs in body weight (Huish 2013). It was in this time of economic and political chaos that Cuba turned to sport as one means of bolstering development at home, while also seeking new partnerships with other countries in the global South (Huish 2011). Thus, the place of sport in Cuba's development history requires particular attention, as it was used as a base for re-establishing regional connections, building domestic capacity, and even gaining hard currency for the country.

This chapter explores the various pursuits of sport for development in Cuba as grounded in nationalist commitments and notions of solidarity. Whereas elite sport achievement is often thought of as a demonstration of a nation's progress, Cuba's approach has been to use sport as a means to achieving development and progress. For Cuba, sport has been a method to build cooperation, to improve professional development within the country, to enhance health and well-being, and even to acquire hard currency and resources through trade. It is also a model grounded in the concept of 'solidarity', as opposed to frameworks of philanthropy, charity, and neoliberalism that have tended to dominate sport for development. What's more, Cuba has pursued international cooperation through sport in ways that have impacted over 100 nations worldwide. Such commitments to sport, for both domestic gains and for international cooperation, make Cuba an important national case study on the topic of sport for development.

A revolutionary approach to sport for development

The origins of Cuban nationalism began in the mid-nineteenth century, when, as a politically divided, and economically hobbled, Spanish colony, greater calls arose for independence and autonomy (Thomas 1971). Leading up to the Spanish capitulation in 1898, the Cuban nationalist movement adopted many 'American' (meaning both hemispheres and continents, not just the United States) influences in culture, philosophy, politics, and also sport (Pérez 1998). In Puerto Rico, Spain's 'other loyal little colony' (Thomas 1971), there was a long history of European-style sport influence that involved football, boliche (a rather chaotic equestrian sport that can be loosely associated with bowling), and bull fighting (Sotomayor 2016). While boliche was played in Cuba among Spanish soldiers, the Cuban nationalist movement adopted baseball as early as the 1860s. 'Cuban baseball games were used as nationalist rallying points to raise funds and support for the war movement led by Cuba's national hero, José Martí' (Huish 2011: 424). Landholders and workers alike embraced baseball with the belief that it promoted equity among players and broke away from the colonial hierarchies of the time (Pérez 1994; Echevarría 2001). While some assume that baseball arrived in Cuba from the 1898–1934 US military presence, there is considerable evidence to show that many mid-nineteenth century landholders formed baseball clubs for their workers, and even took the sport to other landholdings in the Caribbean, which explains why baseball clubs in British Honduras, Costa Rica, and the Dominican Republic were named after Cuban landholders and sugar plantations (Pérez 1994; Pope 1995).

In 1898, with the Spanish defeated, The United States oversaw the affairs of the Cuban government, first through an ad hoc military junta. After 1902, with the introduction of the 'Platt Amendment', a clause in the newly formed Cuban constitution giving the US powers over the Cuban government, more and more US influences found their way to Cuba (Thomas 1971). Schools in Havana were run in English, rather than Spanish, the US dollar was the adopted currency, and if labor movements challenged US business interests, the US Marines were called in. During this era, more 'American' sports came to Cuba. Baseball continued to expand in the cities, and boxing also grew in popularity. These sports, as Gems (2006) points out, were pressure cookers for racial and class tensions in Havana at the time. Catholics were pitted against Protestants. White sports teams and boxers would challenge blacks (Pérez 1999; Gems 2006). Tennis also arrived in Cuba in the affluent western parts of Havana and in some rural *latafundias* (large landholdings), but this was a leisure game of the elite, and not something available to the lower classes (Pachelli 2017).

In the pre-revolution era, from 1934–1959, sport increasingly became a forum for resistance against US influence (Pettavino and Pye 1994). Yet, baseball also became professionalized from the 1940s to the 1960s, with Cuban leagues closely connected to leagues in the United States, resulting in 135 Cuban players leaving for the United States to join the Majors (Huish 2011). It was a common practice, albeit not an expectation, that Cuba's top players would head to the US rather than build their careers in the lower-paying and, seemingly less prestigious Cuban leagues.

In January 1959, Fidel Castro ousted Fulgencio Batista from power which led to a radical change in Cuban society. The new Revolutionary government put tremendous emphasis on expanding public health and education programs, as well as fiercely promoting Cuban nationalism through key industries as well as culture. In 1961, the United States implemented the initial stages of the Cuban Embargo, with the passing of the Trading with the Enemy Act. The act prohibited most US business dealings with Cuba. This impacted sport immediately, as Major League Baseball clubs could not offer contracts to Cuban players. Cuban players would only be able to enter the Majors as free-agents, or to make it onto farm-teams based in the US.

At the same time, Cuba took the step of banning any private, professional sports clubs or associations, by either dissolving them or absorbing them into a nationalized network of professional athletes. For example, the Almendares, a baseball team in the Cuban professional league, which had played from 1878–1961, was folded with the nationalization of Cuban sport (Pérez 1994).

In its place, Cuba's newly minted Instituto Cubano de Deportes, Educación Física y Recreacion (Cuba's Ministry of Sport, Physical Education, and Recreation – INDER) established 'Los Industriales' team in the Serie Nacional de Béisbol (the Cuban National Series). The new team represented the industry workers in the suburban areas of Havana. Other teams were established to represent both the industries and regions of Cuba. Post-1961, Cuba prohibited privatized sport, and mandated that elite sport would be 'public' by nature (Carter 2001). At a high-political level, this was an attempt to make sport part of Revolutionary nationalism. In response to the flight of elite athletes, the Revolutionary government wanted to encourage 'professionalism in sport [that] could be congruent with nationalism, and that elite athletes could achieve moral and material compensation for their achievements within the nation, rather than going abroad' (Huish 2011: 424). It was a calculated attempt to create national identity through the symbolic value of nationalized sport.

Learning to win

This brief history shows the well-established presence of sport in Cuba, and illustrates some of the ways sport has been politicized as a means to further nationalist sentiment, independence, and resistance. However, in order for Revolutionary Cuba to encourage nationalist value through public sport, more needed to be done to popularize sport, and to make it accessible at the community level. INDER, in particular, was established to find opportunities to make organized sport, recreation, and physical education available for all Cubans, regardless of income or region. Schools across Cuba would participate in a program called the 'Junior Olympic Program' each year (Pettavino and Pye 1994). Today, the program continues and is meant to encourage wide participation in various sports, but also to identify early career talent for more advanced training in sport. While baseball is Cuba's national pastime, the Junior Olympics program has a wide range of team and individual sports that range from Olympic sports to chess. INDER was also tasked with providing opportunities for mass participation through a broader range of sport and recreation activities to the entire country. Fitness classes, and exercise programs were, and still are, organized at the community level, and exercise for seniors, often involving calisthenics and Tai Chi, are a common sight in public parks. Today, INDER claims that over 95 percent of Cubans have participated in some form of organized sport during their lives (Huish, 2011).

In addition, physical education in Cuba is mandatory from grade 2 up until university. INDER also organizes community-level sports programs for recreation and leisure. Between the physical education curriculum in schools and the semi-formal recreation and leisure activities, there are numerous opportunities for youth to pursue elite training, which is provided free by INDER. Unlike elite sport training in many countries in which private sector funding and coaching serve as the entry point into elite sport, Cuba views elite recruitment as the product of universal access to sport. This results in a highly nationalist discourse of the role of sport to society in Cuba, as 'INDER officials position elite performance as a representation of the potential, talent, strength, and health of the nation as a whole' (Huish and Darnell 2011: 149). Semantics aside, this wide populism in sport capacity has manifested into an enormous domestic capacity for elite sport excellence for Cuban athletes, coaches, and trainers (Bunck 2010). Cuba has some 99,000 professional athletes employed by INDER, in addition to close to 32,000 sport professionals, which include coaches, trainers, officials, and recreation coordinators. In addition, more than 90 percent of INDER professionals have completed a six-year bachelor's degree in sport, physical education, and recreation studies (Darnell and Huish 2015a). For a nation of 11.2 million people, this demonstrates an enormous capacity for publicly funded sport.

Of course, significant tensions exist as well. Many sport scholars have rightly criticized the negative effects of early-education recruitment for elite sport training (Hong 2004; Kidd 2011; Goellner et al. 2012). The practice was common in the Soviet Union, and continues in countries like China and Brazil (Green and Houlihan 2005) and there are questions regarding the agency and autonomy of children to pursue elite sport training, and whether such programs divert funds and expertise away from community-level participatory programs. There is also the question of whether public funds should be focused on elite athlete development while recreational and community programs are underfunded or privatized. These critiques are worth addressing in the Cuban case. First, while INDER and Cuba's Ministry of Education do recruit students for elite sport training, they also provide accommodation and facilities including social support, and opportunities to withdraw if need be. Recent fieldwork in Cuba, including discussions with officials, students, teachers, and coaches at the National Gymnastics School in Havana, suggests that students have some autonomy over their participation in elite training.

As for the critique that public monies aimed at elite training take away from any public sector commitments to community participation in sport and recreation (Lim 2008; de Almeida 2012), Cuba also provides an interesting counter. Since sport, in its entirety, is held within the public domain in Cuba, there is no real private sector competition or encroachment on INDER's jurisdiction. Without question, the costs of elite sport facilities, including accommodations, equipment, gym kit, meals, medical attention, and therapy place a financial burden on INDER, even though the general cost of services in Cuba is relatively low compared to other countries. However, even with significant material and human resources committed to elite training in Cuba, INDER continues to offer community-based sport programs across the country for no user fees. Material resources can be scant at the community level, hence a focus on Tai Chi, yoga, martial arts, and calisthenics, which require few material resources. Nevertheless, instruction and community-based coaching remains free to all Cubans.

Again, history is illustrative of Cuba's political commitment to sport. During the special period, both popular participation and elite performance in Cuban sport increased. In the 1992 Summer Olympics, Cuba ranked sixth overall with 14 gold medals, placing higher than Spain, the host country. In 1996, Cuba ranked an impressive eighth overall, and in 2000 the country placed ninth, ahead of Great Britain. In 2004, the last year for the 'Special Period' in Cuba, the Olympic team was still among the top 15 medal winners, outperforming many countries in the global North. Aside from the Olympic medal counts, Cuba's performance in the Pan American games is routinely in the top three, dating back to 1991. Such consistent elite sport performance is noteworthy for a country that was hobbled by economic chaos, and that boasts a populist and public sector approach to sport development (Huish, 2011). However, at the 2016 Olympic games in Rio de Janeiro, Cuba placed 18th, and at the 2012 London games Cuba placed 16th. Even though Cuban athletes still placed in the top tier of nations, there have been noticeable declines in the standings, which translate into rising frustrations within the Cuban sport community, and also pose new challenges to sport as a form of nation building for Cuba.

Making a profit in sport

In the same era of elite sport performance, popular participation in community-level sport expanded during the worst of the economic crisis from 1992–2004. With a lack of resources, constant blackouts, and serious dietary and food concerns, recreation and leisure was encouraged as a way to bolster health, improve community dynamics, and also to pass the hours (Carter 2008; Huish *et al.* 2013). In 1995, while continuing to expand participation and support for sport in Cuba, the Cuban National Assembly passed Act No. 77, which allowed many sectors of the Cuban economy to seek foreign investments in order to bolster domestic services (Huish *et al.* 2013). In 1993, INDER established Cubadeportes SA, a for-profit entity designed to acquire foreign remuneration. As Carter (2008) argues, the creation of a for-profit wing in Cuba's public sports provider generated enormous tensions within INDER, as it was the first time since 1961 where remuneration and sport would be reunited in Cuba.

Cubadeportes set up three principle areas. First, Cubadeportes would manage the import and export business of any sporting goods coming into Cuba, and also anything manufactured in Cuba for export. In the early 1990s, and just following the 1991 Pan American games, INDER created 'Batos' brand sport goods. Using domestic leather products, the brand produced baseball and boxing gloves for export (Carter 2008). However, with the resource crisis in full effect in the 1990s, the export of physical sporting equipment ceased, and Cubadeportes managed only to import limited sporting goods for national teams, even signing a deal with Adidas to supply official kit to the Cuban national teams (Campbell 2015). Adidas, a German multinational corporation with production facilities throughout Asia, was able to circumvent any US restrictions of trading with Cuba, including the infamous 1997 Helms-Burton Act and the 1963 Cuban Assets Control Act. More resource-intensive sports, like synchronized swimming, that require costly upkeep of pools, were neglected.

Second, while struggling to acquire long-standing trade agreements for material goods from abroad, Cubadeportes opened a new market in sport tourism (Carter 2008). The objective of this program is to acquire foreign capital from tourists who come to Cuba to either participate in sport activities with Cuban counterparts, watch Cuban sporting activities – notably baseball – and/or provide some training and coaching to foreign athletes. Professionalism ranges from elite athletes, such as when the Baltimore Orioles played a game in Havana, to high school students from the US traveling on short trips. Although various clauses of the US embargo against Cuba prohibit leisure tourism to Cuba, there are caveats for person-to-person diplomacy and outreach, and sport, in the eyes of the US government, is categorized along with music, religion, and art as a means of facilitating such diplomacy. This allows US citizens to come to Cuba to learn about sport by participating in organized tours of sports facilities and to watch games, such as Cuba's National Baseball Series.

Cuba's global cooperation in sport

Since the special period left Cuba struggling for material resources to export, INDER turned to human resources. As its third principle, Cubadeportes looked to develop working contracts with foreign national teams for coaching and training. Initially this was seen as a money-making opportunity so that affluent nations could hire Cuban expertise in order to advance their own national sport interests. Cuban coaches went to countries like Japan and Italy to coach baseball teams (Darnell and Huish 2015a). They also went to India, South Africa, and Russia as boxing coaches (CubaSí 2008; Borland 2011; Ministry of External Relations 2016). Under these agreements, the host nation would pay the Cuban trainer in local currency, often at a rate that would triple their salary earned in Cuban pesos. The host country would also pay a fee to Cubadeportes in hard currency. At the completion of the contract, the Cuban sport professional would return to Cuba to receive an additional salary bonus in Cuban convertible pesos. Only a few dozen coaches and trainers participated in these lucrative contracts, but the model grew in scope between 1995 and the present day.

Today Cuba has had working sport cooperation relations with some 100 nations, many of whom are not financially able to offer Cuba large cash sums for sport cooperation. Cubadeportes continues to assist in the arrangements, but the form of cooperation and remuneration varies widely from nation to nation, meaning that there is no standardized model for this form of sport cooperation. The expectations of the cooperation and the remuneration are negotiated based on need and capability, under what is referred to as 'the solidarity approach'. At its root, this approach sees two national partners sharing costs to achieve a common benefit (Featherstone 2012; Huish 2013). For Cuba, such cooperation through sport can be viewed as assisting other countries in overcoming underdevelopment, while also resisting hegemony from the global North.

Of course, Cuba is also willing to provide technical assistance to countries in the global South in exchange for various resources, services, or material goods. For example, during the Hugo Chavez years in Venezuela, Cuba offered a wide range of technical cooperation, including in sport, in exchange for preferred trade on oil exports (Brouwer 2011; Walker 2015). Cuban coaches in Venezuela delivered training in a variety of activities, from boxing to chess. Chess programs were also delivered by Cubans as part the Barrio Adentro program in Venezuela, a social program aimed at improving health, education, and social conditions in urban slums. Chess proved to be an important activity among 'barrio youth,' as it could be organized in small urban spaces, regardless of weather, and would occupy youths' time, limiting their chances of participating in gang-related activities (Cuba News Agency 2009).

Guatemala has also benefited from the technical assistance of Cuban coaches, who brought their pistol shooting team to train there; Guatemala went on to win three medals at the Pan American games in Toronto in 2015 (Rodríguez Sánchez 2016). In Campeche, a south-eastern Mexican state, Cuban coaches have worked with the state authority to establish a school for elite weightlifting, wrestling, and martial arts (MINREX 2015). In turn, Guatemala and Mexico both provide Cuba with preferential prices on material commodities including everything from clothes and beer, to automobile parts and medicine.

Cuban sport coaches have also worked in some of the world's poorest countries, like The Gambia, and Lesotho (Huish 2011; Darnell and Huish 2015b). In the case of Gambia, some financial remuneration was acquired through third-party donations from the government of Taiwan, but The Gambia's biggest contribution to Cuba was a preferred agricultural trade agreement on its largest export – peanuts – which are a popular commodity in Cuba. In Haiti, Cuban coaches arrived after the 2010 earthquake to work with displaced youth in rural areas. The Cuban delegation received nothing from Haiti for their services, but instead received some support for its sport and health-related activities from the government of Norway (Huish et al. 2013).

In sum, Cuba's sport-based cooperation with other nations is not simply a form of charity, nor is it entirely self-interested. At the same time, important benefits accrue to Cuba as a result. Thus, Cuba's international outreach and development activities through sport combine the provision of assistance with the expectation of receiving something in return.

The Latin American School of Sport and Physical Education

The preceding discussion shows that international outreach has been a key element for INDER since its inception. With so many sport professionals directly employed by INDER, there is, to an extent, a surplus of sport professionalism in Cuba and INDER capitalizes on this by offering coaches, trainers, and sport and recreation directors opportunities to travel to other countries in order to provide professional sport development training to Olympic and national teams. At the same time, the Cuban sport system has also welcomed foreign nationals into its own sport system as a form of cooperation. Indeed, amid INDER's attempts to use sport as a platform for development in Cuba, and to also attract resources from abroad, one further, and unique program operates to expand sport capacity building across the global South.

Cuba's Escuela Internacional de Educación Física y Deporte (EIEFD, International School of Sport and Physical Education) has trained students from more than 80 countries to receive a degree in physical education and to be qualified as coaches and trainers (Darnell and Huish 2015a). Founded in 1999, EIEFD targets students from low-resource countries to train in Cuba in sport and physical education sciences. There is no tuition for attending EIEFD; the only commitment is that students agree to return to their home countries in order to expand sport and recreation activities in marginalized communities. INDER converted a former army academy to make room for the school, and students are expected to complete the six-year curriculum, taught in Spanish, by first studying exclusively at the school, and then later working with other sport students at the community level across the country.

In order to send students to EIEFD, INDER conducts a 'social diagnostic' that analyzes a partner country's sport-related history (Darnell and Huish 2015a). If a country is deemed to have a track-record of using sport for coercive means, such as vote buying, bribing, or scandals involving doping, its citizens may not be welcomed to EIEFD. INDER also expects that the skills taught to EIEFD students will be made available to marginalized classes in their home country once they return. For EIEFD students, strong academic performance in high school or prep-school is expected. INDER does not ensure employment to the graduate, and there are no financial penalties to the student for not completing the program. The goal of EIEFD is to train students within the ethics of sport in Cuba in the hopes that the values will be received in other countries.

As Darnell and Huish (2015a) have demonstrated, the EIEFD training is recognized for its caliber, and compares well with four-year physical education degrees in the global North. The challenge with the program is in providing opportunities for graduates to secure meaningful employment in their home counties – especially in low-resource settings that do not have the infrastructure or organization ready to receive highly skilled sports professionals. This is a broader challenge of capacity building faced across the global South, and an ongoing struggle within policies and practices of South-South development cooperation (Darnell and Huish 2017). Still, for Cuba, EIEFD successfully fosters bilateral relations based on sport and education with partner countries in the global South. Such bilateral cooperation in both economics and politics is necessary for Cuba's national autonomy and survival. For some, this constitutes a form of 'soft power' through sport, in which Cuba attempts to exert its influence and secure resources through means other than economics or military action. At the same time, such actions can also be viewed primarily as a means of economic and political survival (Shearer 2014; Darnell and Huish 2017).

Concluding thoughts

In sum, Cuba's relationship with sport is unique on a global scale, essential for its own national interests, and also provides an interesting window into the use of sport to pursue national development outcomes amid particular political challenges. The post-1961 era witnessed the introduction of elite sport, albeit as a product of popular participation, while the post-1991 era positioned sport as a means of much-needed diplomacy and vital economic survival. At the same time, Cuba has maintained public support for sport, from elite training, to higher education, to community recreation.

Given this unique blend of social, historical, and political factors, the Cuban case leaves more questions than answers about some of the deeper geo-political elements of sport for development. To what extent is the nationalization of sport an important element of development? To what degree can sport be universally accessible, and what are the broader moral and normative values that come from this? By keeping sport in Cuba a public good, and by seeking cooperation abroad in order to fund and sustain it, has this served the greater good more than sport delivered through private or semi-private means? And finally, what does the future of sport hold for Cuba, as a tool of cooperation, a nationalist platform, and a means to foster economic and social development for its own people?

In 2016 US President Barack Obama attended a baseball game in Havana with Cuban President Raul Castro. The visit was monumental, as Mr Obama was the first US head of state to visit Cuba since Calvin Coolidge. While the meeting demonstrated a collegial sense of optimism for better diplomatic and cooperative efforts in areas such as trade, health, and even sport, the 45th US President Donald Trump, ruined any diplomatic gains with Cuba. Whereas serious discussions were underway between INDER and Major League Baseball to work out a deal for Cuban players, as of 2017 no certainty exists as to how sport relations between Cuba and the US will transpire, let alone the broader diplomatic relations between the two countries. Aside from a few person-to-person delegations of athletes, and philanthropists interested in Cuba, the waves of American tourists taking over Havana have simply not come. Likewise, no grand exodus of elite sport talent from Cuba to the US has occurred so far. What is clear is that sport remains central to Cuban identity and culture, and also serves a role beyond simply elite achievement or popular participation. Rather, sport has been a foundation of nationalism and independence for Cuba, and even an important part of its survival.

References

Bain, M. J. (2005). Cuba–Soviet relations in the Gorbachev era. *Journal of Latin American Studies*, *37*(04), 769–791.

Bain, M. J. (2007). *Soviet-Cuban Relations, 1985 to 1991: Changing Perceptions in Moscow and Havana.* Lanham, MD: Lexington Books.

Borland, K. (2011). Interview Boxing South Africans sent to Havana to learn Cuban secrets. *Reuters.* Available at: www.reuters.com/article/boxing-safrica-cuba-idUSB30064620110721.

Brouwer, S. B. (2011). *Revolutionary Doctors: How Venezuela and Cuba are Changing the World's Conception of Health Care.* New York: Monthly Press Review.

Bunck, J. M. (2010). *Fidel Castro and the Quest for a Revolutionary Culture in Cuba.* University Park, PA: Pennsylvania State University Press.

Campbell, M. (2015). Cuba's track federation allows athletes autonomy over sponsorships. *The Toronto Star.* 22 February. Available at: www.thestar.com/business/2015/02/22/cubas-track-federation-allows-athletes-autonomy-over-sponsorships.html.

Carter, T. (2001). Baseball arguments: Aficionismo and masculinity at the core of Cubanidad. *The International Journal of the History of Sport, 18*(3), 117–138.

Carter, T. (2008). New rules to the old game: Cuban sport and state legitimacy in the post-Soviet era. *Identities: Global Studies in Culture and Power, 15*(2), 194–215.

Cole, K. (2002). Cuba: The process of socialist development. *Latin American Perspectives, 29*(3), 40–56.

Cuba News Agency. (2009). Cuba's Chess Coaches to Work in Bolivia. Available at: www.chessdom.com/news-2009/cuba-chess-coaches-work-in-bolivia.

CubaSí. (2008). Cuban Boxing Coach Awarded in Russia. Available at: www.cubaheadlines.com/2008/12/13/14851/cuban_boxing_coach_awarded_russia.html.

Darnell, S. C. and Huish, R. (2015a). Cuban sport policy and South–South development cooperation: an overview and analysis of the Escuela Internacional de Educación Física y Deporte. *International journal of sport policy and politics, 7*(1), 123–140.

Darnell, S. C. and Huish, R. (2015b). Cuban sport and the challenges of South-South solidarity. In L. Hayhurst, T. Kay and M. Chawansky (eds), *Beyond Sport For Development and Peace: Transnational Perspectives on Theory, Policy and Practice.* London: Routledge, pp. 35–53.

Darnell, S. C. and Huish, R. (2017). Learning through South–South development: Cuban-African partnerships in sport and physical education. *Compare: A Journal of Comparative and International Education, 47*(2), 286–299.

de Almeida, B. S., Coakley, J., Marchi Júnior, W. and Starepravo, F. A. (2012). Federal government funding and sport: The case of Brazil, 2004–2009. *International Journal of Sport Policy and Politics, 4*(3), 411–426.

Echevarría, R. G. (2001). *The pride of Havana: A History of Cuban Baseball.* New York: Oxford University Press.

Eckstein, S. (1990). The rectification of errors or the errors of the rectification process in Cuba? *Cuban Studies, 20*, 67–85.

Featherstone, D. (2012). *Solidarity: Hidden histories and Geographies of Internationalism.* London: Zed.

Gems, G. R. (2006). *The Athletic Crusade: Sport and American Cultural Imperialism.* Lincoln, NE: The University of Nebraska Press.

Goellner, S. V., Votre, S. J. and Pinheiro, M. C. B. (2012). 'Strong mothers make strong children': Sports, eugenics and nationalism in Brazil at the beginning of the twentieth century. *Sport, Education and Society, 17*(4), 555–570.

Green, M. and Houlihan, B. (2005). *Elite Sport Development: Policy Learning and Political Priorities.* London: Psychology Press.

Hamilton, D. (2002). Whither Cuban socialism? The changing political economy of the Cuban revolution. *Latin American Perspectives, 29*(3), 18–39.

Henken, T. (2008). *Cuba: A Global Studies Handbook.* Santa Barbara, CA: ABC-CLIO.

Hong, F. (2004). Innocence lost: Child athletes in China. *Sport in Society, 7*(3), 338–354.

Huish, R. (2011). Punching above its weight: Cuba's use of sport for South–South co-operation. *Third World Quarterly, 32*(3), 417–433.

Huish, R. (2013). *Where no Doctor has Gone Before: Cuba's Place in the Global Health Landscape.* Waterloo, ON: Wilfrid Laurier Univ. Press.

Huish, R., Carter, T. F. and Darnell, S. C. (2013). The (soft) power of sport: The comprehensive and contradictory strategies of Cuba's sport-based internationalism. *International Journal of Cuban Studies, 5*(1), 26–40.

Kidd, B. (2011). Cautions, questions and opportunities in sport for development and peace. *Third World Quarterly, 32*(3), 603–609.

Lim, L. (2008). Boarding Schools Generate China's Sport Stars. *National Public Radio – Morning Edition.* Available at: www.npr.org/templates/story/story.php?storyId=92479526.

Ministry of External Relations. (2016). Foreign Relations with Cuba. Available at: www.mea.gov.in/Portal/ForeignRelation/Cuba_Jan_2016_en.pdf.

MINREX. (2015). Cuba y Campeche fortalecen relaciones. Sitio Oficial del Ministerio de Relaciones Exteriores de Cuba. Available at: www.minrex.gob.cu/es/cuba-y-campeche-fortalecen-relaciones.

Pachelli, N. (2017). A tennis Makeover in Cuba, With an American Assist. *The New York Times*. April 21. Available at: www.nytimes.com/2017/04/21/sports/tennis/cuba-national-tennis-center.html?_r=0.

Pérez, L. A. (1994). Between baseball and Bullfighting: the quest for nationality in Cuba, 1868–1898. *The Journal of American History*, *81*(2), 493–517.

Pérez, L. A. (1998). *The War of 1898: The United States and Cuba in History and Historiography*. Chapel Hill, NC: University of North Carolina Press.

Pérez, L. A. (1999). *On becoming Cuban: Identity, Nationality and Culture*. Chapel Hill, NC: University of North Carolina Press.

Pettavino, P. J. and Pye, G. (1994). *Sport in Cuba: The Diamond in the Rough*. Pittsburgh: University of Pittsburgh Press.

Pope, S. W. (1995). An army of athletes: Playing fields, battlefields, and the American military sporting experience, 1890–1920. *The Journal of Military History*, *59*(3), 435.

Rodríguez Sánchez, D. (2016). Cuban shooters looking to maintain historic achievements. *Granma*. 9 February. Available at: http://en.granma.cu/deportes/2016-02-09/cuban-shooters-looking-to-maintain-historic-achievements.

Ritter, A. R. and Rowe, N. (2002). Cuba: From 'dollarization' to 'euroization' or 'peso reconsolidation'? *Latin American Politics and Society*, 99–123.

Shearer, D. (2014). To play ball, not make war: Sports, diplomacy and soft power. *Harvard International Review*, *36*(1), 53.

Sotomayor, A. (2016). *The Sovereign Colony: Olympic Sport, National Identity, and International Politics*. Lincoln, NE: The University of Nebraska Press.

Thomas, H. (1971). *Cuba, or, the Pursuit of Freedom*. London: Eyre and Spottiswoode, p. 13.

Walker, C. (2015). *Venezuela's Health Care Revolution*. Toronto: Fernwood.

Zimbalist, A. (1993). Dateline Cuba: Hanging on in Havana. *Foreign Policy*, (*92*), 151–167.

42

Liberia

Tournaments and T-shirts

Gary Armstrong, James Rosbrook-Thompson and Holly Collison

Over the past 15 years the genre now referred to as Sport for Peace and Development (SPD) has seen various policy initiatives in many theatres of conflict. Those in this field include variously non-governmental organisations (NGOs), charities, world organisations, sporting governing bodies, national governments, commercial entities, individual foundations and academics. The opportunities for debate on this issue are endless and have provided platforms for the most earnest humanitarians as well as the self-aggrandising and delusional. In the elusive search for world peace and reconciliation in war-damaged societies people will understandably try various means of bringing about reconciliation. In such circumstances two objectives dominate the political process. The first is that armed combat is prevented and peace – however tenuous –is sustained. Second, future stability has to be sought and promoted both by those who seek to keep the peace and by those that began or participated in the conflict. There are various issues integral to such pursuits. The most obvious concerns the best way of achieving such desired outcomes and begs the supplementary question as to the people best placed to pursue them. What follows permits an ethnographic account to consider the promotion and delivery of specific SDP projects in post-conflict Liberia, West Africa, which provides for a micro-study SDP in action. Such delivery can be positioned variously as both the intentional use of sport – more specifically football – for rehabilitation and peacebuilding and as an everyday practice and national obsession that presented opportunities to intersect the game of football with moral, social and politically motivated interventions focused towards building a peaceful civil society. A challenge in a country like Liberia, that is scarcely visited by its funders and often instils fear among those academics tasked to monitor projects, is regulating practices and evaluating impact in a meaningful way. Liberia often presents a seductive narrative and image to the SDP *apparatachiks*. But, we might ask, at what consequence to the local populations whose primary focus is daily sustenance and survival? Do such interests do no harm?

The footballing Libero?

In the Liberian context the game and its proponents had a challenge on their hands. A nine-day research visit to Liberia in July 2004 (building on four previous visits beginning in 1997) and a separate four-year ethnographic study (2009–2012), forms the basis of this analysis. Two authors of this paper observed a number of initiatives funded and implemented from both national and international organisations. This includes what was then the largest global UN peacekeeping force struggling to contain a population that while war-weary was still prepared to murder under the nose of those tasked with peacekeeping. The other instance was the initiative of a global charity – let's call them *Kathlik*. Both entities were concomitantly attempting to implement sport for peace and development programmes. The UN tournament involved three days of activities in the capital city of Monrovia culminating in two games held at the former national stadium located in the city centre. The other took place on a Saturday afternoon in the centre of the city on wasteland 'requisitioned' for informal games of youth football.

Liberia perhaps presents a Ground zero scenario for many SDP *afficianados*. Host to a nihilistic civil conflict that traces its beginnings to the late 1980s, the years 1989–96 are colloquially referred to as the years of the First Liberian Civil War. In this time atrocities were carried out by no fewer than eight militia factions, many consisting of child soldiers. The destruction of the infrastructure saw some 250,000 people murdered and some 2.5 million people displaced. Integral to the mass murder was the figure of Charles Taylor who overthrew one regime in 1989 and introduced his own. He was eventually elected president of Liberia in 1997. Backed by his ever-loyal Small Boys Unit personal bodyguard (originally consisting of boys in their early to mid-teens) Taylor presided over successive reigns of terror which saw civil conflict re-emerge in the years 199–2003 it what is considered the Second Civil War. In this era, armed opposition arose from an entity called Liberians United for Revolution and Democracy which gained the military upper-hand. When closing in on Taylor and his forces Taylor resigned the presidency and sought exile in Nigeria. After various political and diplomatic negotiations and the interventions in Liberia of the US military, the West African forces of ECOMOG and the UN military and policing personnel (UNMIL and CIVPOL). Taylor was removed from Nigeria in 2012, arrested by UN forces and faced trial in the Netherlands on charges of crimes against humanity. Passing a 50-year custodial sentence, the judge opined that Taylor had committed some of the most heinous and brutal crimes ever recorded in human history. Among his many titles and capabilities when in power Charles Taylor was officially Chief Patron of Sport. The President saw the value of sport in both nation building and as a social practice beneficial to notions of personal development. He was not alone in his thinking.

Save the Children

Both *Kathlic* and UNMIL were relatively new to the SDP genre but were in Liberia by virtue of greater missions of respectively saving souls and peacekeeping. The UN was working in this arena as a consequence of sport being adopted as a Millennium Development Goal (see Armstrong and Collison 2011). Giving a modern twist to the biblical injunction to beat swords into ploughshares, the UN Sports for Peace programme urged Liberians to replace mortars with footballs. The latter was more complicated and resulted from a Catholic missionary's initiative to assist the rehabilitation of war-damaged and dispossessed children of Liberia (see Armstrong 2004; 2007; Armstrong and Rosbrook-Thompson 2012). The Bosco project was begun in the late 1990s by a Scottish-born Catholic priest involved in missionary work with the order of the Salesians of Don Bosco. This global Catholic missionary force had entered Liberia in more peaceful times and was renowned among Liberians for being the only Christian entity to remain throughout the years of conflict. The youth workers and other personnel who worked for the project sought to offer some form of shelter (both physical and moral) in both the conflict and post-conflict years were adherents to the pedagogic philosophy of their eponymous Italian patron saint. The promotion of football and football clubs was a by-product of the projects primary aims of sanctuary and pedagogy.

The two deliveries were thus driven by both secular and religious humanitarian impulses. In both instances the primary target of delivery was children and young people victims of the conflict that had plagued Liberia for the previous 15 years. Many of the children were orphaned; and a significant number were former combatants in the militias that had massacred looted and raped. All were in some way 'displaced persons' with no knowledge of their origin and families and without the means to return to whence they came should such details be known. Not that their parents would necessarily welcome them back even if presented with the children. The difficulties of survival had made children a commodity that in many instances was too expensive to keep, hence the hundreds abandoned annually and the thousands seen daily involved in labour practices ranging from street trading to labouring, to 'money love' prostitution. In this milieu one might understandably ask what football could do and how any football-related project might be delivered to good effect.

Fair and foul play

The game undoubtedly had a role to play in the post-conflict milieu. Informal football games and community matches had provided an initial contact point for the Bosco youth workers to do their work. Football organically evolved thus as a key engagement and access strategy. Having initially built night shelters to house the street children from danger, the project had promoted football as a way of occupying children in the day time, and via football games and teams as way of teaching the former perpetrators of nihilistic violence the value of cooperation and adherence to rules that are essential to building a new and civic society. The early signs were promising. Young men enjoyed the game and the hope was that when the call to arms announced by the various militia was next heard, those tempted to resume armed conflict might have too much of a stake in conformity to fight wars. By extension, they may have discovered via football that the stranger in their various football fixtures was a player – just like them – and not someone who needed to be killed. By 2001, the project had established 116 community football teams under its aegis, as it combined an enthusiasm for the game with the operation of a child protection scheme that was without parallel in the capital city of Monrovia.

Sadly, for those who consider football as a panacea to rehabilitation and reconstruction, some of the Bosco children in the initial post-conflict context of recovering ex-combatants were, on the resumption of hostilities, abducted by the forces of Charles Taylor (some ironically while participating in football training sessions) and forced to fight in battles against 'rebels' in the hinterland. Many of the girls in the Bosco football teams had been rape victims in the conflict years; 'sport' could offer no immunity from such violation nor necessarily was the football programme much of a consolation in the 2004 fragile post-conflict setting that informs this analysis. In that year, the Bosco scheme had just 16 neighbourhood football teams and no funding to donate footballs as an incentive to teams to visit the project's HQ and learn about the rights of the child. Significantly, in this moment of the post-conflict phase, the Bosco workers were not universally appreciated. Notices prohibiting 'Don Bosco Boys' entering were evident across city centre commercial premises. Those representing Bosco, however, had their work cut out. The very name of the organisation had become a byword for the youthful criminal ('rogue') networks that plagued the city through daily thefts and robberies. The presence of former combatants and even members of Charles Taylor's Anti-Terrorist Unit in the ranks of the visible drug dealers added no security to the multitude of traders trying to make an honest income in a society of scarcity (see Armstrong and Rosbrook-Thompson 2012). Many seeking to earn a living cared little for the street children and the football projects in their midst.

The peace was ever-fragile. All it needed was a spark. Two days before the 2004 tournaments began, a large-scale violent disorder involving local young and not so young men in the city centre was quelled after three hours by the forces of UNMIL.[1] The 15,000 strong UN peace-keeping response (consisting of soldiers drawn from 12 countries), took two hours to assemble.[2] The outcome of this altercation, which involved around 1,000 participants, was burned-out buildings, dozens injured, and three young men beaten to death. The origins of the disorder lay in a series of robberies involving groups of youths robbing small traders. The catalyst was an attempted theft from a market trader who in the ensuing struggle was stabbed in the eye. Armed with batons and knives, the mob attacked the area where 'rogues', 'hustlers' and 'drug dealers' gathered and burned down eight homes including two night shelters built by the Bosco projects. The UN and *Kathlik*s delivered their programmes to this back-drop.

The t-shirt and the speech

The first tournament attended in 2004 took place at the one-time national stadium one mile from where the three young men had laid dead 48 hours earlier. The event had strange parentage facilitated as it was by the evangelical Christian charity World Vision International and part sponsored by US sporting apparel giant Nike via the office of the US Ambassador to Liberia. Further support came from the Liberian Ministry of Youth and Sports and the Lone Star mobile phone company. Faith, commerce and government collectively put monies and trust in football. In stifling humidity, Sunday afternoon's final game was hosted by a structure whose walls displayed murals praising FIFA. Therein lies a story. The Liberian Football Association (LFA) had received significant funding from FIFA with the tacit proviso that it would vote for the (now disgraced) incumbent FIFA President, Sepp Blatter, in a future FIFA presidential election. It duly voted for Blatter, but the money earmarked for improving infrastructure and hosting youth tournaments was largely squandered or stolen. Given the conditions it attached to the funding, and the fact the LFA had made good on its election promise, FIFA didn't hold anyone at the LFA to account. New floodlights had been installed with the same monies. There was, however, no electric national grid to power them. The generator to power the lights bought with FIFA monies had long been removed – to power the home of a government minister. Despite the tournament's humanitarian *leitmotif*, the event came at a price; the cheapest admission was the equivalent to US$0.20, and the costliest ticket was US$2.

The fixture between the two local teams Shooz FC and Mighty Barrolle was played out on the poorly laid, FIFA-funded Astroturf surface. Shooz FC, which grew out of the demise of the Don Bosco-inspired football club called Busa. Shooz FC was a product of the former's club president whose monies came from haulage partnering a Ghanaian entrepreneur whose main business was shoe manufacturing. The former had sold the club's place in the Liberian Premier league to the new club and were now a new entity dedicated to producing players for selling on to European clubs, ideally for big money. The two sides were in part promoting a murky business world and sought to be part of an even murkier one that was the migration of athletic talent from the global South to the global North. For the club president, football was a source of income; the transfer of players held the possibilities of big earnings for them. The players were unlikely to see much of any monies.

A form of civil society was very evident. The two teams were presented in the centre circle to a UNICEF representative. The stadium's 200 seat VIP section was packed and animated. Before kick-off the men here delivered speeches. One criticised his predecessors in the administration of Liberian football. The other addressed the current schism – over power and money – between LFA President and the Minister of Youth and Sport. If football was a source of unity the philosophy had not got through to this cohort. The one female present sat – silently –in her role as the Chair of Finance of the LFA. The other female of note in the public eye was the referee's assistant, one of two Liberian women qualified for this role. The crowd of around 2,000 (95 per cent male) did not hear the big men's speeches or the monologue which followed delivered by the Canadian representative of UNICEF. He spoke on how football could bring reconciliation and how delighted he had been in the course of the week to see so many women involved in the game. He and his female UNICEF colleague – distinctive in white UNICEF t-shirts – were, however, unable to fully witness what they were promoting. The female worker left 15 minutes into the game, the man left shortly before half-time. Both teams received t-shirts adorned with the sponsor's logo. A football was the prize for the winners. The largesse came with no explicit curriculum or pedagogy. The event was undeniably joyous and 300 youths ran on to the pitch at the end to dance and cheer as the six-man brass band played anthemic tunes. The exhausted players did not receive food or drink for their efforts and the stadium did not have running water for showering.

The shirt and the response

The afternoon-long *Kathlik* tournament revealed four boys' teams, some resplendent in the shirts of the English Premier League team Everton all of which bore the name of 'Wayne Rooney' across the shoulders. The one-time teenage prodigy of the English game had a week previously been transferred from Everton to Manchester United for a fee of £27 million (around 10 per cent of the stated cost of the UN project in Liberia). Everton had publicly declared that Rooney merchandise worth an estimated £66,000 was now of no use to them. An enterprising teacher of religion and benefactor of the Catholic charity *Kathlik*, having contacted Everton, obtained the shirts for free. In the company of staff of the aforementioned charity he watched a game in honour of both *Kathlik* and-one assumed- Everton.

Football shirts had taken on a greater significance than apparel for performing. A similar gesture of goodwill was witnessed in 2010, when the son of former manager of Barcelona, Newcastle United and England, Sir Bobby Robson, accompanied representatives from the *Kathlik* organisation for a week-long Liberia visit. The Bosco staff in Monrovia learned that his father's death in 2009 led to thousands of Newcastle United football shirts being left at St James Park football stadium as a tribute. In 1999, his father had met the Bosco touring 'Millennium Stars' football team that travelled to the UK on a tour funded by *Kathliks*. The Robson family thought it would be a fitting tribute to their father to distribute the shirts to Liberian children. So, in a rare visit from the UK, *Kathlic* personnel pursued an intense and activity-packed football-themed promotional tour shadowed by a photographer, with a mandate to donate and propagandise the SDP work they funded within Liberia.

Some of those involved in the 2004 fixture were to wear the Rooney shirts days later. The children arrived at the venue in response to requests from their local adult friends running the Bosco project. The deal that the *Kathliks* representatives sought was that in return for attending they would receive the one shirt plus a backpack containing crayons and paper in an attempt to encourage literacy. They also had to attend a child protection workshop – run by the local Bosco project street workers – where they received a talk on what they must not tolerate from adults (regarding potential and actual abusive behaviours) and what they should avoid as young citizens playing their part in building a better society. In a society shorn of tradition and with 85 per cent illiteracy, the hook that was an enthusiasm for football was the best medium to cover the theoretical and practical notion of the 'civic'. One could talk through football. The problem was, however, knowing the extent of receptivity and indeed the relevance of the message.

In both cases, the reps from *Kathliks* were earnest, charming and aged under 30. They admitted that despite their organisation funding of the Bosco project no-one from their organisation had visited Liberia for some four years. The funding was sent annually on trust; there was no monitoring and evaluating nor indeed regulating of practices. During both visits children were observed being elected from the field of play to take part in short interviews conducted by one of the *Kathliks* visitors. The first question asked was: 'So, you're feeling confident for the future, yes?' Later in the day the reps would visit the main house of the Salesians. The four religious personnel residing there knew little of the football programme; the man who had begun it some seven years prior had left both the Order and Liberia two years previously. The 20-minute conversation the two *Kathliks* workers held with an octogenarian priest did not seek any evidence in the way of measurement and evaluation for the projects. The second rep of *Kathliks* was indicative perhaps of the genre of SDP – he was a professional photographer and the shot that the brochure needed and was later used was children in the replica shirts. In one sense all involved were winners. Poor children received a football shirt and crayons. Their world had been enhanced by foreign visitors facilitating teaching on child protection. The charity in return had got what it needed for donors and policy-makers, i.e. access to children and photographs of its football-related delivery for its brochures. A celebrity attending the event made for even better copy.

Proclamations and seductions

The aforementioned 2004 *Kathlik* tournament was graced in person by the most famous citizen and now president of Liberia – George Weah. The former World Footballer of the Year was contacted days previously by Bosco workers and asked to attend the occasion. On the day, he arrived from his nearby TV and radio station offices with a ten-man entourage, signed a few autographs, posed for a few photographs and left 15 minutes later. Referred to as 'The King' by the populace of the continent's oldest Republic (and in his own publicity), Weah's then newly founded Royal Communications broadcasting medium hinted at post-football political ambition. His carved throne, which featured the word 'King' above his head as people faced him in his office, carried magisterial pretensions. It was widely believed that Weah wanted the LFA presidency perhaps as a forerunner to becoming president of Liberia. His was a classic rags-to-riches story enabled by his footballing ability. In the eyes of many in SDP circles Weah was role model.

Not all people considered him as such a virtue. His presence in Liberia was at times advertent and inadvertently a source of political friction. Under Taylor's regime Weah's home was looted and his saloon car stolen by Taylor's Minister for Information. In 1997 his compound was surrounded by Taylor's Anti-Terrorist Unit armed militia (Armstrong and Rosbrook-Thompson 2012). However, a mob of hundreds living in the surrounding community gathered to both protect Weah and challenge the militia as to their intended actions. The man himself was well-versed in SDP-speak. The rhetoric of peace even from the mouth of a footballing hero was a risky business in a society that had a most precarious peace and not much to offer ex-combatants. In April 2005, a rally in the pre-election month following Weah's declaration stand as a presidential candidate turned violent when the free refreshments on offer ran out, thereby depriving hundreds of his supporters present any form of sustenance. While some vandalised the hosting premise, others stole the furniture. The same week saw the discovery of fraudulent electoral membership listings, somewhat embarrassing to a party campaigning on an anti-corruption ticket. Despite the violence that Weah and his supporters could incite, the task of peace was central to his image and mandate for acquiring future power.

Some may question the connection made here between Weah and the SDP sector and practices in Liberia, however, it is an impossible task to speak of the game in Liberia in any capacity without the mention of his name and his influence. In 1997 Weah was appointed as an UNICEF ambassador, a common practice within the promotion of the SDP agenda (Wheeler 2011). He also spoke explicitly about the connections to be made between football in Liberia and achieving sustained peace,

> Without peace civilization will not exist, with peace, there is stability, there is growth. Peace is an ongoing thing it is important for our generation and the generation to come. My part as a Liberian is to promote peace through football (taken from a campaign poster).

Another Liberian-specific context presents an issue for SDP policies. The target in Liberia for most development initiatives and NGO projects are children and youth. Youth in this context might best be considered as a socially constructed term and contextualised in Liberia as a social category for boys and men in a prolonged infantilised state (Collison 2016). With 50 per cent of its population under the age of 18, and with too much time on their hands in the absence of formal education or meaningful occupations, football was and remains the leisure activity of choice. In this regard, the achievements of Weah stand as the highest power and symbol of football as a vehicle for economic and social mobility. The evangelical rhetoric that Weah offers adds to the games' mystique (or possibly a deceit). This is what we will term the *seduction* the game provides for. Football at the global level can provide to its elite wealth beyond imagination, but few who dream of this in Liberia will ever have these dreams realised. Weah's achievement is one of the most remarkable stories in football's history,[3] but his iconic status might best be seen as a delusion. He is one in a 100 million or even more. One might sensibly argue that the youth of Liberia need to learn meaningful skills to bring gainful employment which will allow them to pursue football as the great triviality it should be. Football thus might not be the best vehicle for the reconciliation process in Liberian, manifesting as it does in many instances the fault-lines of Liberian politics. Its world-renowned footballing son might not be the appropriate candidate for a peaceful future either. Time will tell.

Contexts and contests

The case of Liberia then, highlights the various actors, networks, models and agendas of SDP. We should note, however, that the genre has long existed even if the delivery was less explicit in its rhetoric. Football as a source of inspiration for creating a more coherent and tolerant society was not new to the Liberian context. Football tournaments in pursuit of national unity had been promoted by Liberian governments since the mid-1960s. The regimes – both civil and military – that governed Liberia were not slow in recognising that the game might offer a general sense of civic happiness and shared endeavour. The game did not prevent 15 years of civil conflict and the football tournaments that appeared in the peace that followed the 1997 election and did not prevent the resumption of hostilities in 2002. The youths beaten to death on Monrovian streets could not call on the game to help them when vigilantes attacked. So, what learning might we take from the various football-related promotions established and witnessed?

Both tournaments were enlightening. The formal advocacy from the UN of SDP and its strategy for promoting the use of football for peace in Liberia was arguably style over substance. In the absence of a sustained SDP programme and prominent SDP organisations reluctant to work in Liberia, the game did have a use; namely, it became the vehicle for access and engagement for various initiatives. Its networks presented small windows of opportunity to present and preach SDP. In this regard, the onus was on the players and local populations to recognise and make the connections between football and peacebuilding. This situation demonstrates thus the need to consider SDP on a spectrum from formal established national programming schemes to ad hoc 'peace' tournaments, to football-related informal community practices. These initiatives present opportunities for individuals to advocate non-sporting ideals connected to the various peace promotions. Such a spectrum acknowledges SDP as a pursuit within both formal and informal practices and as an ideal that can be positioned as variously a primary or a secondary objective.

One learning outcome of all this might consider how any proclamation around the game has seemingly always to consider its role beyond the *ludic*. The emphasis instead focuses on the games policy potentials. The game is thus burdened with doing what politicians cannot – those who govern the game seem happy to assume this burden. Politicians are in league with them. Thus, In March 2007 Africa's first elected female President Ellen Johnson-Sirleaf (having defeated George Weah in an election run-off), performing the inaugural kick-off to launch a five-week UN-supported programme of football, kickball and volleyball to be held throughout Liberia's 15 counties declared: 'In sport, I learn to win without thinking I am the best; I learn to lose without thinking it is the end.' These are fine words, but not universally adhered to. Furthermore, she considered sport as an instrument for peace and social development and a practice that enhanced the efforts of the government in restoring hope and dignity. Alongside her stood Adolf Ogi, UN's Secretary-General Ban Ki-moon's Special Advisor on SDP. He was to stress how sport was an essential tool for peace and reconciliation adding – perhaps in tribute to the Bosco project – how via such practices: 'I learn to respect the opponent and the rules; I learn to accept the decision of the referee.' Seemingly there was thus no down-side around sport in its delivery or performance side to consider.

The football tournament captured on celluloid offers proof that reconciliation processes are evident. In such a discourse it is not incumbent on the UN officials to sit in the stifling heat to watch a mediocre game; having said the right words, they may retire to the office and dispatch their report. The UN tournament was not a product of any liaison with the Liberian Football Association or the Ministry of Youth and Sport. It was the UN and corporate interests imposing an event that was considered appropriate to the local context. The good intentions of *Kathlik* were a tribute to their organisation and promotion of humanity and compassion. Equally *Kathliks* bypassed local football structures and youth offices for the event to take place. While reliant on a Liberian organisation they part-funded the personnel involved on the day – both British and Liberian. They had never met before. For some, these considerations might not be considered problematic. We might best accept that in such a complex environment the SDP sector in some way mirrors the social norms and chaos of everyday life. Delivery is thus messy and in some instances carries more hope than substance.

As this setting shows all too clearly, any assumption that sport is politically neutral is correct at some but not all levels. State budgets in Liberia for SPD programmes were either a pittance or a figure proclaimed but never actually passed on to those attempting such infrastructural programmes. Regardless, the LFA continually promoted football as a tool for peacebuilding; and as the poster in its HQ proclaimed in 2010:

> Football the peacemaker, can heal the wounds, unites all groups of people, helps to reinforce peace, is the reconciliatory power, is quicker than politics, is the product we want to sell and publicise. All you need is a football.

Funding helps as well. But best not to ask too many questions as to whether the monies donated went to the specific SDP causes they were meant for. In truth the LFA had little capacity for SDP programming beyond facilitating and promoting opportunities presented by the competitive games, which was their primary remit. The semi-professional game they presided over and their high-status position within Liberia, while facilitating of SDP interventions and advocacy, could have been far more effective were they embedded in the structures in place. Those preaching the gospel of football in the needs for a post-conflict civil society might have better targeted their moral quest at the kleptomaniacs in both political and football office whose actions and deeds disgrace their proseletysing about the beautiful game.

The Liberian context offers a Janus-faced conclusion. We might question the SDP tokenism attached to the game in the aforementioned formats. We might question those that drift in and out for the purpose of personal or organisational representation and image. We might consider the paucity of evidence around SDP delivery and the efficacy of football (or sport) for the implementation of peace and development. The sports evangelists who populate this field have ever-available presentations for such efficacy and implicitly their advocacy. All that is required is an apt illustration of a priori held beliefs and a willingness to pretend that the illustrated difference did not happen. But we must not be churlish. The sight of children and young people happy and proud in football strips seeking recognition through the game hitherto absent in their lives is both enchanting and seductive. In this instance the NGOs and UN are right to tap into that which children seek and adults applaud. At its most simple such tournaments do no harm.

Such events thus do 'something', notably offer a semblance of post-conflict normality. The SDP exponents can defend such events using the ever-useful terminology of 'capacity building'. We accept that 'Football' carries much potential; what, we might ask could get so many disparate entities sharing the same space and enthusiasm? When would the people over the hill ever be able to meet their assumed enemies without the mediation that a football tournament offers? The various seductions the game of football carries, however, requires the SDP cheerleaders to think beyond good intentions and glossy brochures (Easterly 2006 and Third Age website). The charities and NGO's believe they are doing 'good work' when delivering SDP; sport is too often considered apolitical and thus non-conflictual, and questions are rarely asked of those seen to be so doing. Academics seeking research monies – not forgetting self-importance – don't inquire too deeply into what might challenge relationships with the SDP sector that suits them as much as anyone else. Those involved in the SDP genre need ideally to inquire more about what happens before the game kicks-off, as well as when the game ends and those both playing and cheering have gone home.

Notes

1 As stated by the United Nations,

> the United Nations Mission in Liberia (UNMIL) was established by Security Council resolution 1509 (2003) of 19 September 2003 to support the implementation of the ceasefire agreement and the peace process; protect United Nations staff, facilities and civilians; support humanitarian and human rights activities; as well as assist in national security reform, including national police training and formation of a new, restructured military.
>
> *United Nations 2003*

2 Europe had sent soldiers from Sweden and the Republic of Ireland. Africa was represented by troops from Nigeria, Ghana, Ethiopia and Namibia. The rest of the world consisted of military personnel from Ukraine, Jordan, Nepal, Pakistan and Bangladesh.

3 One had to admire the progress made by this humble child, one of nine siblings born to a technician father working in a furniture factory. Originating from Grand Kir, Weah belonged to a people who were stereotyped as fussy, learned, argumentative and good footballers. Approaching 40, he was a multimillionaire and cared for three children, one of which he had adopted. His radio and TV station had employed approximately 30 people. His entourage of drivers, bodyguards, cleaners and cooks saw him provide an income for another 20. He also paid the wages of his football club, named Junior Pro and he contributed to a community team and the coaches that they required. No-one knew for sure that estimates were that some 100 people in Liberia depended on him for an income and ultimately, a livelihood.

References

Armstrong, G. (2004). The lords of misrule: Football and the rights of the child in Liberia, West Africa. *Sport in Society*, 7(3), 473–502.

Armstrong, G. (2007). The global footballer and the local war-zone: George Weah and transnational networks in Liberia, West Africa. *Global Networks*, 7(2), 230–247.

Armstrong, G. and Collison, H. (2011). Design for living? Sporting policy and the United Nations. In A. C. Robias, S. Emmanuel and K. Black (eds), *Design for Sport*. Aldershot: Gower.

Armstrong, G. and Rosbrook-Thompson, J. (2012). Terrorizing defences: Sport in the Liberian civil conflict. *International Review for the Sociology of Sport*, 47(3), 358–378.

Collison, H. (2016). *Youth and Sport for Development: The Seduction of Football in Liberia*. Basingstoke, UK: Palgrave MacMillan.

Easterly, W. (2006). *The White Man's Burden: Why the West's Effort to Aid the Rest Have Done So Much Ill and So Little Good*. London: Penguin.

Jaye, T. (2009). International Justice and DDR: The case of Liberia. *International centre for Transitional Justice*.

Ogi, A. (2003). International Conference on Sport and Development. Press Release ORG/1374, 29/01/2003. 'Special Advisor to Secretary General on Sport for Development and Peace to hold a press conference on 30 January'. Available at: www.un.org/News/Press/docs/2003/org1374.doc.htm.

United Nations. (2003). Sport for Development and Peace – towards achieving the millennium development goals, Report from the United Nations Inter Agency Task Force on Sport for Development and Peace, New York: UN.

Wheeler, M. (2011). Celebrity diplomacy: United Nations' goodwill ambassadors and messengers of peace. *Celebrity Studies*, 2(1), 6–18.

Young, M. (2004). *Malinowski: Odyssey of an Anthropologist, 1884–1920*. New Haven, CT: Yale University Press.

43

Norway

Charity or development?

Hans K. Hognestad

Introduction

The notion of using sport as a means for social development is not new and exclusive to what has recently been defined as the 'SDP sector'. In order to embrace the entire history of sport for development we would need to study the very foundations of modern sport dating back to the days when diverse sports were facilitated as pedagogicial devices and 'rational recreation' for the growing working and middle classes in late nineteenth century Western societies (Kidd 2008). Authorized proselytization of 'the intrinsic positive values of sport' suggest rather that sport is intractable from broader social relations and political processes, as suggested by Darnell (2015: 430). This is a relevant framing of the history of modern sport also in a Scandinavian context, as sport from the early twentieth century became an integral part of social democratic policies focused on equality and the construction of egalitarian societies during times marked by political polarizations and conflict (Goksøyr 2008). As the Norwegian political scientist Svein Tuastad points out Scandinavian sports movements are based on a volunteer tradition. The history of organized sport in Norway is thus charged with an amateur ideology and operationalized in close conjunction with political authorities and in accordance with governmental legislation within the sport sector (Tuastad 2017: 3–4).

The rapidly growing field of SDP projects is almost exclusively run by field-specific NGOs, as well as sports clubs, sports organizations or international organizations such as Unicef or Save the Children, who support sports-related projects in various ways in order to promote their own development goals. Typically, sports projects in the South are run by the collaborative efforts of an operational local NGO in the South and a variety of donor organizations mostly from the global North (Hayhurst 2009). This arrangement creates challenges in which SDP projects run the risk of being subtly defined by a 'patronizing' financial source rather than by the democratically pursued interests of a relevant local community (Giulianotti *et al.* 2016; Hasselgård and Straume 2015).

In this chapter I shall analyse Norwegian strategies within the SDP sector. First, I shall dwell on how the participation in SDP by Norwegian partner organizations is shaped by the amateurist, volunteer tradition of organized Norwegian sport. Second, I will look specifically at how SDP projects in the South involving Norwegian partner organizations have changed since the modest start in the early 1980s with 'Sport for All' in Tanzania (Straume 2012). While

Norwegian policies on sport and development have never ignored the instrumental potentials of sport, a strong underlining of 'sport for sport's sake' permeates also the current SDP strategies of Norway's largest sports federation, The Norwegian Olympic and Paralympic Committee and Confederation of Sports (NIF). This point is evident at the very beginning of their current strategy document for SDP projects with the unreferred quote: 'I don't play sport to learn about HIV/AIDS. I play sport because it is fun.' (NIF 2015). This comment could be interpreted as a sobering reminder of what sport can and should do. However, the history of Norwegian involvement in SDP projects in the global South is also marked by cultural complexities and a sense of naivety regarding the social and psychological effects on the young individuals involved in such projects (Straume 2012). Later in this chapter I shall analyse how such North–South partnerships may be riddled with questions about *whose development* the respective partners are pursuing, based on field studies in Zambia with local and Norwegian partners.

Contextualizing Norwegian strategies on sport and development

Norwegian NGOs and government bodies were among the driving forces in early international sport, development and peace projects. Norwegian involvement in sports development cooperation started out in the early 1980s with a main focus on providing facilities and equipment in addition to the building of organizations, particularly local structures and sports clubs in Tanzania. NIF and the Norwegian Development Cooperation Agency (Norad) have worked since the start as key coordinators of this activity. The first projects started out in Tanzania in 1982 with Sports for All,[1] a project that lasted until 1990, when these activities were also launched in Zambia and Zimbabwe. South Africa was added to the list in 1996 and Namibia in 2003. These projects were facilitated largely as charity work and evolved, according to Hasselgård and Straume (2015), with certain strings attached which reflected the import of values typical of a Norwegian sports model, founded on social inclusion and sports for all. Following the arguments of Lorentzen (2007) the Norwegian sports movement should be understood as part of civil society organizations, often credited for its contributions to the construction of a Norwegian social democratic political system. However, the amateurist ideologies and voluntarism that continue to operate as orthodoxies of Norwegian sport also carry potentials for social exclusion and/or patronization. In a contemporary context this is a particularly critical issue for partner organizations in the global South which often lack the welfare structures of the global North. Such a critique of the Norwegian 'sports model' could be extended to the facilitation of sport also within local Norwegian communities, as has been brilliantly pointed out by Eduardo Archetti. He showed how this model is culturally coded and socially structured with a privileged participation for certain social groups (the ethnic Norwegian nuclear family), a model which appears less moulded to face new family structures of a more multicultural kind (Archetti 2003).

The idealism that has charged the unitary Norwegian sports movement ever since the founding of the first nationwide sports movement in 1861[2] has evidently influenced SDP projects with a Norwegian involvement. This is not to suggest that such involvement is a history of 'naivety' (Straume 2012). Following critique from researchers and others, the focus was gradually shifted from a 'charitable' approach in the 1980s and early 1990s, in the shape predominantly of donating footballs, boots and strips, towards developing local competence with a stress on the training of leaders, coaches and referees. Simultaneously it was argued that sport and development projects would contribute to a more general social development. The policies of the Norwegian government at the time demonstrated high ambitions and expectations regarding 'what sport can do'. Since Norad's Strategy Plan of 2005, sport has been included in the general intention of involvement, where it was stated that:

> Through the financing of efforts which the developing countries themselves define, Norad
> make investments within human rights, democracy, environment, economic growth, educa-
> tion, health, welfare and equality. These are considered investments for the future.
>
> *Norwegian Ministry of Foreign Affairs 2005. Translated from Norwegian by the author*

Hence, sport and culture was at this time defined within a broad umbrella of development work
grounded in the belief that sporting and cultural activities can contribute to more general development strategies. Importantly, sport was seen as a cheap form of development work compared
to previous assistance towards building local infrastructure; an approach which had been widely
criticized by leading Norwegian anthropologists such as Larsen (1989) who claimed development projects in African communities did not take local knowledge into consideration.

In recent decades the belief in sport as a universal language shared by people in both the
global North and the global South has added ammunition to SDP projects, not only in African
countries, but also in parts of Europe and Asia. From the late 1990s sport was seen globally as
a fruitful way of not only alleviating poverty and reconciling ethnic groups in post-conflict
contexts, but also for enhancing democratic practices to alter attitudes to HIV/AIDS. From
around the turn of the millennium the latter became *the* central issue of sports development
projects in Southern African countries where the HIV epidemic peaked in the early years of the
new millennium. In brief *sport as method* evolved as one of the most important elements in the
work for producing information on HIV/AIDS and in this way contribute to the fight against
the disease in African communities.

Simultaneously, the importance of developing sports for its own sake and the stress on the
values of sport in and of itself, have permeated the strategies of Norad and the Norwegian
Sports Association. Therefore equal importance has been attached to the development of both
sports organizations and particular sports. Since 1998, youth exchange has been a central part of
Norwegian SDP cooperation where students have been involved in 6 to 12 months' voluntarily
service in Southern African countries as part of their sports studies at the Norwegian School
of Sports Science in Oslo, Norway, and the University of Western Cape in Cape Town, South
Africa. This work has since the start been organized in cooperation with the Norwegian Peace
Corps and the Norwegian Sports Federation (NIF) and includes a preliminary course in sport,
development and cultural issues in addition to the practical challenges students may face in local
African communities. Similarly African students come to Norway as sports volunteers and there
is also an exchange between Southern African countries.

Different Norwegian governments have leaned heavily on strategies defined by the global
political community of the United Nations. In recent years, this connection has helped to shape
Norad's subsequent stress on the role of culture in development processes. Sport entered the
global political agenda at the start of the new millennium, which to a great extent drew inspiration from various UN-related work on culture and development, notably the report from the
World Commission on Culture and Development, *Our Creative Diversity*, published in 1996. This
report was intended as the cultural follow-up to the report on biological diversity produced by
the World Commission on Environment and Development in 1987, yet never received quite the
same attention as the latter. In a report from 2004 produced by the United Nations Development
Programme (UNDP) entitled *Cultural Liberty in Today's Diverse World*, development is defined as
an expansion of people's possibilities of choice while stressing the significance of bringing issues
of culture to the mainstream of development thinking and practice. In regard to the development emphasis here, the UNDP's goal was 'not to substitute more traditional priorities that will
remain our bread and butter – but to complement and strengthen them' (UNDP 2004). The
report concludes by stating that cultural freedom is not just a human right but also a decisive

precondition for development and stability. Even multilateral financial institutions such as the World Bank became more aware of the significance of culture in central development issues, particularly in relation to the alleviation of and fight against poverty.

In a Norwegian context sport was at the time included in a more general political strategy regarding North–South relations, defined in the *Action Plan for the Eradication of Poverty in the South 2015*, published by the Norwegian government (Norwegian Ministry of Foreign Affairs 2002). In that report the connections between poverty and cultural conditions were highlighted, and the significance of securing cultural rights as an important part of the fight against poverty was given a central position. Cultural rights were now regarded as a part of universal human rights in the way they are expressed in the UN Declaration of Human Rights and in the various legislative resolutions on civil, political, economic, social and cultural rights. From 1978, UNESCO's *Charter of Physical Education and Sport* defined sport as a fundamental human right for all, but was articulated in much more detail in the UN report *Sport for Development and Peace: Towards Achieving the Millennium Development Goals* (United Nations 2003). This report worked as a guiding document for the goals of the Norwegian Sports Association (NIF) and the Norwegian government from 2004. The greater focus on culture and sports within Norwegian development cooperation policy from the turn of the millennium must also be viewed in light of a modernization of Norwegian development management which evolved during the 1990s especially, which included a greater stress on wider development goals outside the world of sport. With this broader notion of cultural development in mind, the Norwegian Sports Association stated in their Strategy Plan 2004–2007 that their work should be focused on sport as a tool for enhancing human rights, democracy, environmental issues, economic growth, education, health, welfare and social equality. These are issues that could be identified as typical concerns for the construction and maintenance of societies modelled on a Scandinavian welfare state. In the introduction to Strategy Plan there is a much more general focus on the wider benefits of sport: evaluations of our work show that sport contributes to a general social development. Getting involved in sport effects for example democracy skills or improved attitudes to HIV/AIDS. Sport as a method evolves as an important element in this work. This has in recent years been developed further and constitutes a very central component in the work. One example of this is the development of Kicking Aids Out in which knowledge about HIV/AIDS is tied to organized sports activities (NIF 2004).

This universal, rather than culture specific, approach to sport and development, is reflected in a broad political consensus globally. To the extent we can locate disagreements about the positive outcomes of sport and development projects, it is often confined to a diverging focus on either development *of* sport or development *through* sport. While the former focus tends to address the intrinsic values of sport in itself, the latter focus highlights how sport can be applied instrumentally in order to achieve wider social and political goals. Significantly, the main message was that sport is a popular activity through which a lot of children and young people can be reached.

Cooperation with various local NGOs was encouraged in order to mobilize the local communities in projects and programmes. This included an 'internal' focus on the education of sports coaches, leaders and athletes in the local communities. However, in NIF's strategic document from 2004, there is a greater stress on forming partnerships that may promote wider social development goals (NIF 2004). In this document it was argued that sport is a universal language that can have positive influences on wider social and political tasks related precisely to the values of health, democracy, education, human rights and gender equality. Ongoing projects and activities supported are focused on mass sports rather than elite sports, which partly explains the general lack of support for developing sports facilities and structures provided for the development of sports talents on an elite level. The goals of 'Sport for All' were basic to strategies within sport and development projects while elite sports were, and still are, left out.

My own evaluations (Hognestad 2005; 2011) showed a gap between the possibilities, ambitions and dreams of children and young people involved in sports in developing countries and the vaguer and more general, civic ambitions of financial patronage in the North. The children who were selected for Norway Cup[3] participation had to attend courses in advance in which they and also their parents/guardians were informed about what this participation entailed. Among the main messages were that the Norway Cup is a mass sports tournament and not an elite tournament. This did not, however, prevent the players from nurturing a strong desire to win the tournament and also dream about being 'discovered' by potential scouts of glamorous European clubs watching their games. This competitive focus is quite possibly born out life in poverty, and football representing perhaps the only way out of the miseries and concerns of everyday life in the many poor compounds in Lusaka. These findings had strong continuities with an earlier study by Bjertnæs (2007) on a project involving a football team from Namibia which participated in the Norway Cup; this study showed that while signs of empowerment could be found in the individuals having taken part in the Norway Cup, it was difficult to document any longer-term effects on the wider community.

Again this raises the question about where the limits of sport should be drawn with regard to creating opportunities and reaching development goals defined by the local communities. Hence there are a fairly large variety of questions and concerns generated by the participation in SDP projects that involve partner organizations from the global South and the global North. The most obvious concern is: who benefits from such participation? Hanne Bjertnæs' findings above give an indication that while participation could benefit the individuals involved, it is much more difficult to measure changes within the wider local community. Second, on whose terms would participation take place? This is a particularly complex point as SDP projects involving clubs and organizations in the global South tend to depend on a donor or sponsor from the global North. This clearly gives the latter a moral hegemony regarding which values and ambitions should be pursued in the projects; 'money talks'. Third, in the words of Marcel Mauss (1966), equality is a prerequisite in a reciprocal partnership. Hence what, if any, are the mutual benefits between partners from the North and South? I shall explore these issues in discussing some of my own findings from studies in Lusaka, Zambia, in 2004 and 2011 respectively, based on interviews with leaders of Zambian teams and organizations which participated in the Norway Cup in the decade between 1999 and 2009.

From Kabwata Girls to Team Zambia: addressing gender issues

Edusport[4] became one of the pioneering sports organizations in Zambia from the late 1990s onwards. This local organization managed to get funding from both NIF and various private groups in Norway to send a girls' team to the Norway Cup. Kabwata Girls, from the township Kabwata in Lusaka, represented the start of initiatives aimed at getting girls in Zambia more involved in sports. They participated for three successive years between 1999 and 2001, winning the tournament (under 16 girls) twice and losing the other final. The team received media attention both in Norway during the tournament, but particularly in Zambia; as Chris Bwalya, a reporter and photographer at the Zambia National Broadcasting Corporation, remembered:

> I travelled with the team as a cameraman in 2000. The final against Alabama from the United States was shown live on Zambian television. We interviewed players and coaches during the tournament and produced daily news from *Ekebergsletta*[5] to Zambian TV.
>
> *Interview with author, 10 April 2011*

After the tournament the young girls became celebrities, and the president at the time, the late Frederick Chiluba, even gave a reception for the Kabwata Girls at the State House in Lusaka. Eleven years later I met one of the players from then, Rose Mwape, outside the offices of Edusport, in the Kabwata township. Now 26 years old and a mother of three, she told me about how, in her view, the Norway Cup had changed their opportunities and lives:

> I remember the first time. We won the qualifying tournament organized by Sports for All at the Zimco complex [sports facilities complex in Lusaka]. Suddenly we were going to Norway. It felt unreal. It changed our lives and initiated a grassroots movement which saw an incredible rise in the number of young girls playing football. In Norway we stayed with our host team Heggedal all three years and they even helped to raise money to cover school fees for some of the players.
>
> *Interview with author, 2 April 2011*

A few of the original Kabwata Girls' team continued to play football, including Annie Namukanga, who went on to captain the national team and finished her degree at Loughborough University in England, thanks to a scholarship obtained through her role as a leader for the 'Go Sisters' programme in Zambia.

A Lusaka-based programme, Go Sisters was founded in 2002 after a local sport NGO, Edusport, received a grant of NOK 200,000 (approximately US$25,000) from the board of Their Royal Highnesses Crown Prince Haakon and Crown Princess Mette-Marit's Humanitarian Fund. As said, Go Sisters was conceived by the former captain of Kabwata Girls, Annie Namukanga. The purpose of the organization is to strengthen girls' possibilities for education, control over their own bodies, and to get girls involved in organized sport. However, dominant gender roles in particular make it difficult for married women especially to play football. This was one of the backgrounds for the decision to select a girls' team from Zambia again for the 2009 tournament. As executive director of Sport in Action, Frank Mushindu, explained:

> After knowing we would have a Zambian team in the 2009 Norway Cup, we organized a tournament. It was a cooperative project between Edusport, Sport in Action and Score, and an equal number of players were recruited from these NGOs. The focus was on promoting girls and women in sports. But a focus was also on getting parents involved and making them aware that sport is good for a lot of things and sport can in fact also be one way of ensuring that children do not drop out of school. In a different way, the players who come back to Zambia become famous and not everyone has been able to handle that. This was especially the case with Kabwata Girls. They got more attention from the boys, and a few got pregnant while still being teenagers.
>
> *Interview with author, 12 April 2011*

The latter comment points to another, less obvious outcome of the celebrity status of participation in the Norway Cup and other international sport tournaments, and highlights the need for parents and local NGOs to make sure that they follow up with educational messages after the event.

The selection of players for the girls' team in 2009 was influenced by guidance from NIF who wished to highlight a combination of issues related to gender and poverty. The composition of girls with different backgrounds had an effect on how they experienced the trip according to Mushindu:

Obviously, travelling to Norway was for most of the girls a very big step. Negative effects were visible in the first few days. Some of them got home sick and felt lost in an alien environment. The weather was particularly bad that year with a lot of rain. The girls came from very disadvantaged backgrounds. Some of them were orphans. This was one of the requirements which were outlined by NIF. We had to recruit girls from deprived areas so you can imagine that also when they came back, they also came back to a more upsetting reality. We now have concrete plans in place to strengthen girls' activities in Zambia. After the tournament we did a debriefing with players and parents involved. It turned out that some parents had incredibly high expectations. They thought their children would come back with loads of money. But all in all, I would certainly say that the positives outweigh the negatives with regards to the trip to Norway. We focus on combining football with the teaching of life skills as a tool for reaching out to communities. Activities may not only include sports, arts and traditional dances are also on the agenda.

Interview with author, date 12 April 2011

These comments suggested that there were disagreements about the criteria for selecting players, between the local sports organizations and their Norwegian partner. Sport in Action and Edusport are sports organizations which at the time were asked to include girls from very deprived areas who had not played football before. This expectation highlighted a dilemma between whether they as a sport NGO should act as a group of social workers or as sports coaches and leaders. More significantly for the children involved, there are obvious social and psychological challenges of bringing children from a deprived area in the global South to take part in various activities wrapped up as 'cultural exchange' in the global North before transporting these children back to their original environments. However, my findings also showed how Norway Cup participation possibly helped to build sporting careers for a number of youth players. For example, there were four players in the Zambian team 'Kalingalinga boys', who won their class in the 2005 Norway Cup tournament, part of the 2012 Zambia national team who won the Africa Cup of Nations that year. According to a dismayed source in Zambia, NIF did not want to profile the longer-term sporting success of their support for this team back in 2005 because he believed this would be at odds with NIF's 'anti-elitism' and broader focus on sport and inclusion.[6] This issue points to some crucial dilemmas regarding how to identify a successful SDP project, in which, from a Norwegian point of view, current or subsequent sporting success are less relevant than mass sport participation.

Social workers or football coaches? Questioning the limits of sport and development

A common denominator for clubs in the global South involved in partnership-based development projects involves the extension of sport participation into teaching non-sporting life skills. This activity was a key criterion for selection of the 2009 Team Zambia which went to Norway, according to the General Secretary of NOWSPAR,[7] Llombe Mwambwa. She explained how the story of Team Zambia started with the foundation of NOWSPAR in 2006, with a different sport to football, namely judo:

There was an obvious need in Zambia to address both issues of gender equality and gender abuse. It started when I tried to be elected as president for the Zambian judo association. I ended up being the president for ten years. Judo is self-defence. It is very important to enable girls to defend themselves and to give them better self-confidence and a sense of control over their lives. I discovered how limited opportunities were for girls in sport. We felt that an NGO like Go Sisters had a competitive focus in their activities, while we wished to highlight human rights issues in relation to gender.

Interview with author, 13 April 2011

As the latter remark suggests, NOWSPAR differed from other sports organizations by focusing on human rights and other issues outside the sport itself. Having previously travelled with boys' teams in 2004 and 2006 to take part in the Norway Cup, Matilda Mwaba identified a few challenges regarding the selection for the team in 2009:

Having previously travelled with boys teams who came from the same district and played football together on a regular basis through organizations like Edusport, Sport in Action, Breakthrough Sports or SCORE, things were easier with them than with the girls' team who went in 2009. Team Zambia was a much more complex affair. Most girls had played football but not in a very organized way and with many of them coming from very challenging backgrounds it took a lot of effort to sort out all the birth certificates which were needed for them to get new passports.

Interview with author, 13 April 2011

Secretary-General of NOWSPAR, Llombe Mwambwa, viewed the most important benefits of participation in the Norway Cup in terms of networking and a closer cooperation with a variety of sport for development programmes and projects. Asked if she had to choose between spending a certain amount of money on travelling to the Norway Cup or on local projects, Mwambwa hesitated a bit before saying:

I would probably invest the money locally rather than send the girls to the Norway Cup. As an organization we see cultural exchange as secondary to local projects and activities. However, I would say that there is possibly a link here as the Norway Cup is important for motivation and possibly generates an increased local participation in sports.

Interview with author, 13 April 2011

This latter remark points to recent trends within SDP projects involving Norwegian partners; there is currently a greater focus on and distribution of resources to local communities in the South than on what previously was defined as 'cultural exchange'. This entails a greater stress on sport and social inclusion and what Fred Coalter defined as 'sport plus', that is, the development of sport for sport's own sake and less on sport and a variety of external development goals related to issues such as human rights, education, health, and so on. These external dimensions are not ignored, but are much less dominant in the current international development strategy of 2016–2019 (NIF 2015).

NIF currently focus their sport and development efforts more on supporting the facilitation of sporting activities in local communities in the South in recent years and have withdrawn from any direct involvement in sport and cultural exchange programmes after 2009, focusing their activities on local projects in communities in the global South. In their current strategic plan there is less prominence on issues such as health, education, democracy etc.; instead, this reads like a 'back to basics' strategy with a stress on improving the conditions for practising sport for everyone. Where there was previously a greater emphasis and indeed belief that sport contributes to a general social development, the less instrumental aspects of sport are currently highlighted more. Without ignoring the possible impacts on the wider community these effects are moderated to the current ambitions of facilitating sporting activities:

> Sport can change the world (a bit). Our vision for the development collaboration is: 'Enhance the opportunity of children and youth to bring about positive change through sport for themselves and others.'
>
> *NIF 2015, translation from Norwegian by author*

Examples of this more recent focus, which is on both individual and local development goals, are provided by support for the East Africa Cup in Moshi, Tanzania, and the Football for All programme in Vietnam. The latter project is run by the Norwegian Football Association (NFF) with a Norwegian project leader and received NOK14 million (approximately US$1.8 million) in public funding from Norad (The Norwegian development agency) between 2008 and 2015 (*Bistandsaktuelt* 2015).[8] This project has typically been hailed as successful by the Norwegian FA in terms of mass participation and contribution to an improvement of the local sporting infrastructure. While the project has been criticized by their funding partner Norad for a series of organizational issues in a country where the potential for corruption is rife (*Bistandsaktuelt* 2015), old challenges regarding on whose premises local involvement is decided seem to resurface with this latest turn.

Conclusion

In this chapter, I have highlighted some tendencies in North–South collaborations within the SDP sector, focusing on Norway–Zambia partnerships over the last 20 years. In simple terms, the story of SDP projects with Norwegian partners could be described as a move from 'charity work' in the 1980s and early 1990s, through donations of footballs, strips and other sports equipment via a focus on cultural exchange and mutuality between youth in the South and the North (financing participation of teams from the South at the annual Norway Cup), to a more recent trend of ploughing support into local SDP projects in the South. Always wrapped up with good intentions, it seems apparent that SDP projects run by Norwegian agencies, heavily influenced by the idealism of a socially inclusive sports model, have also struggled to incorporate the social and cultural complexities involved in collaborations with partners in the local communities in the global South. Attempts at addressing previous critiques concerning patronization (Giulianotti *et al.* 2016) seem to resurface in new guises. By attempting to focus on 'sport for sport's sake' and limiting their ambition to change the world through sport just 'a little', it seems that this rhetoric has, by and large, served to spin publicly funded Norwegian SDP projects full circle. Rather than keeping up a broader ambition of generating development and peace in and through sport, current publicly funded sport and development projects appear limited to various types of charity work in the shape of importing sporting equipment and facilitating local sports activities in the South.

Notes

1 Sports for All was established by the International Olympic Committee in 1983 in order to improve the levels of physical activity, underlining the social and health benefits of sports. See www.olympic.org/sport-for-all-commission.
2 Centralforeningen for legemsøvelse og våbenbrug ('The central union for physical exercise and the use of weapons') was the first nationwide sports organization, founded in 1861.

3   An annual international football tournament hosted by Bækkelaget sportsklubb in Oslo every year since 1972. With 1908 teams from 52 nations it ranks as the world's largest football tournament for children and youth (2017 figures, see Aftenposten, 2017). The Norwegian government have covered some of the costs of bringing youth teams from the global South to this tournament. Norad have supported up to 30 teams which all hail from countries with which the Norwegian government has a working agreement.

4   Edusport was founded in 1999 after an initiative by Oscar Mwaanga, currently an associate professor at Southampton Solent University. From the start Edusport tried to combine development of sport with education as a means for social development. This NGO cooperates with schools, churches and a wide range of national and international sports bodies and is still one of the leading organizations in Zambia on sport and development. See www.edusport.org.zm

5   A large park with football pitches just south of the Oslo city centre. Used as the main venue during the Norway Cup each year.

6   Interview with Bwalya Mwaamba, President of Edusport, 11 April 2011.

7   NOWSPAR (National Organization For Women in Sport Physical Activity and Recreation) was founded in the Zambian capital Lusaka in 2006 to promote greater involvement of girls in sport.

8   Periodical published in Norwegian by the Norwegian Agency for Development Cooperation (Norad).

References

Archetti, E. (2003). Den norske 'idrettsmodellen': Et kritisk blikk på sivilt samfunn i Norge [The Nowegian 'sport model': A critical look at civil society in Norway], *Norsk Antropologisk Tidsskrift*, 1: 8–15, Oslo: Universitetsforlaget.

Aftenposten. (2017). Norway Cup ER faktisk størst i verden [Norway Cup IS actually the world's largest], article by Stein Erik Kirkebøen. Available at: www.aftenposten.no/osloby/i/dV2mo/–Norway-Cup-ER-faktisk-storst-i-verden-Pa-en-mate (accessed 27 July 2017).

Bjertnæs, H. (2007). Playing to Win or Playing for Empowerment? An Analysis of a Namibian Team Participating in the Norway Cup Project. Unpublished Master's thesis, University of Tromsø.

Bistandsaktuelt. (2015). Krass kritikk av fotballprosjekt. [Crass critique of football project] article by T. A. Bolle. Available at: www.bistandsaktuelt.no/nyheter/2015/krass-kritikk-av-fotball-prosjekt/ (accessed 10 December 2015).

Coalter, F. (2010). The politics of sport for development: Limited focus programmes and broad gauge problems? *International Review for the Sociology of Sport*, 45(3), 295–314.

Darnell, S. (2015). Sport, International Development and Peace. In R. Giulianotti (ed.), *Routledge Handbook of the Sociology of Sport*. New York: Routledge.

Giulianotti, R. Hognestad, H. and Spaaij, R. (2016). Sport for Development and Peace: Power, Politics and Patronage. *Journal of Global Sport Management, 1*(3–4), 129–141.

Hasselgård, A. and Straume, S. (2015). Sport for development and peace policy discourse and local practice: Norwegian sport for development and peace to Zimbabwe. *International Journal of Sport Policy and Politics*, 7(1), 87–103.

Hayhurst, L. M. C. (2009). The power to shape policy: Charting sport for development and peace policy discourses. *International Journal of Sport Policy and Politics, 1*(2), 203–227.

Hognestad, H. (2005). 'Football is Survival Here': rapport fra pilotundersøkelse i Zambiaom erfaringer fra Norway Cup ['Football is survival here': Report from a pilot project in Zambia about experiences from Norway Cup participation]. Oslo: Norwegian School of Sport Sciences.

Kidd, B. (2008). A new social movement: Sport for development and peace. *Sport in Society, 11*(4), 370–80.

Larsen, T. (1989). Kultur og utvikling ['Culture and Development], in T. H. Eriksen (ed.), *Kulturdimensjonen i bistandsarbeidet: hvor mange hvite elefanter? [The Cultural Dimension in Development Assistance: How Many White Elephants?]*. Oslo: Ad Notam Gyldendal.

Lorentzen, H. (2007). *Moraldannende kretsløp: Stat, Samfunn og Sivilt Engasjement* [The formation of moral circuits – State, society and civil engagement]. Oslo: Abstrakt forlag.

Mauss, M. (1966). *The Gift: Forms and Functions of Exchange in Archaic Societies*. London: Cohen and West.

NIF. (2004). *Strategic Plan for Development Cooperation 2004–07*, Oslo: The Norwegian Olympic and Paralympic Committee and Federation of Sports (NIF).

NIF. (2015) *Strategic Document for Sport Development Cooperation 2015–19,* The Norwegian Olympic and Paralympic Committee and Federation of Sports (NIF).

Norwegian Ministry of Foreign Affairs. (2002). *Action Plan for the Eradication of Poverty in the South 2015*. Oslo: Norwegian Ministry of Foreign Affairs.

Norwegian Ministry of Foreign Affairs. (2005). *Strategy for Norway's Culture and Sport Cooperation with Countries in the South*. Oslo: Norwegian Ministry of Foreign Affairs.

Straume, S. (2012). Norwegian Naivety Meets Tanzanian Reality: The Case of the Norwegian Sports Development Aid Programme, Sport for All, in Dar es Salaam in the 1980s', *The International Journal of the History of Sport, 11*: 1577–99.

Tuastad, S. (2017). The Scandinavian Sport Model: Myths and Realities: Norwegian Football as a Case Study', *Soccer and Society*, doi:10.1080/14660970.2017.1323738 accessed 5 May 2017.

UNDP. (2004) *Human Development Report – Cultural Liberty in Today's Diverse World*, Geneva: UNDP.

UNESCO. (1978). *International Charter of Physical Education and Sport*, Paris: UNESCO.

United Nations. (2003). Sport for Development and Peace: Towards Achieving the Millennium Development Goals. Report from the United Nations Inter Agency Task Force on Sport for Development and Peace. New York: UN.

44

South Africa

Trends and scholarship

Cora Burnett

Introduction

In the aftermath of the Apartheid regime (1948–1994), the international agencies were eager to assist the South African sporting fraternity with development – first sport development (in the late 1990s) and then SDP initiatives when it became a novel export product legitimized by the United Nations as a tool for 'development' (Coalter 2013; Kidd 2008). These initiatives and national programmes focused on equalizing resource distribution to benefit the socio-economically disenfranchised populations (Sport and Recreation South Africa 2013).

Non-governmental agencies gained access to SDP Aid and benefited from the influx of donors associated with the 2010 FIFA World Cup in South Africa. Various legacy programmes attracted academic-led impact assessments and were criticized for neocolonial ideologically informed practices. The discourse of unequal power relations between donors (mostly from the global North) and implementing agencies in the global South, became a prominent discourse (Cornelissen 2010; 2011). The question of 'social or human legacy' remains a contentious issue.

Global inequality found expression in scholarly work produced by relatively few South-bound academics (Cronin 2011). Reporting took place on shifting trends, and the Indigenous knowledge production report on the trends, stakeholder dynamics and scholarly work in the field was published. The SDP field in South Africa is vibrant and offers a microcosmic mix of local realities and global influences having infiltrated many sectors. It will continue to be shaped by institutions and leaders at all levels of engagement.

SDP-related trends

Although SDP emerged as a relatively recent phenomenon that found explicit expression and traction in South African policy frameworks, public debates and scientific documentation, the phenomenon has also manifested in traditional African societies. In these societies, initiation schools were the institutions of instruction where boys and girls learnt life skills to ensure the survival of a society along highly stratified socio-political and gender lines (Hammond-Tooke 1980). Young boys and girls were taught by role models and peer educators through structured 'lessons' to equip them with the necessary knowledge and skills for daily living (Schapera 1966).

During colonial times, religious, political and educational influences shaped South African society in a unique way since the first white settlers set foot on the continent in the seventeenth century. Sport became a means of education since the emergence of a public school system with main influences from Europe directing sport and physical education practices. The differential access to resources impacted on the quality and type of activities offered at schools, yet over time, life skills were taught with content that was relatively similar to current SDP or Positive Youth Development practices (Coakley 2011; Holt 2016).

Within a globalized society, SDP emerged as a policy framework that directed multiple stakeholders and implementation practices. Since the United Nations initiated sport as a tool for 'development' and 'reconciliation', governments, transnational corporates, non-government bodies and sport powerhouses came on board to constitute a global social movement (Kidd 2008) and a philosophy (Coalter 2013), and serve as a vehicle for transformative social change carrying the blueprint of global targets (Sustainable Development Goals) (Schulenkorf and Adair 2014).

Within the South African academic environment, postgraduate studies since the 1940s addressed the transformative influence of play, games and sports with most studies focusing on causality between these movement phenomena and positive (societal) outcomes (Burnett and Katzenellenbogen 1993). Towards the end of Apartheid (1948–1994), sport was packaged for global and national markets of 'development'. By the end of Apartheid, the sporting world was eager to welcome South Africa in its fold, and 'sport' came as part of a shared development strategy. One of the first such initiatives was the United Kingdom–South Africa Sports Initiative (UKSASI) offered to the newly established Department of Sport and Recreation in 1994. This initiative followed the Vision for Sport conference offered jointly by the National Sports Council (South Africa) and British Sports Council (Burnett and Hollander 1999). President Mandela, the first democratically elected president, emphasized the national significance of the initiative by stating as having 'made a practical contribution to our efforts in reconstruction and development, reconciliation and nation-building' (National Sports Council 1997: 14).

Britain became an ally in addressing hegemonic relations within South Africa with 'sport as welfare' and the potential to create social cohesion, national identity, upward social mobility, empowerment and crime reduction within impoverished communities (National Sports Council 1996; Tyamzashe 1996). It soon became apparent that the initiative did not deliver on expected outcomes due to various systemic challenges which also caused other local initiatives to fail (Burnett and Hollander 1999).[1] Not only were such projects not sustainable, but they could not deliver on 'gender equity targets' (Boshoff 1997).

Other foreign sport aid was soon to follow. For instance, the Australian Sports Commission implemented various sport development (and sport-for-development) programmes such as the Australia–South Africa Sport Development Programme for junior sport development (late 1990s), the Active Community Clubs Programme and Australia Sport Outreach Programme (2005–2011) (Burnett 2001; 2006). Other first world countries offered such Sport Aid with the German Government, German Development Corporation and European Union partnering with Sport and Recreation South Africa in 2007 to deliver sport-for-development programmes. This occurred in the aftermath of the 2006 FIFA World Cup in Germany, and prior to the 2010 FIFA World Cup in South Africa. The GIZ/YDF (German Development Corporation's Youth Development through Football) programme was mainly delivered by non-governmental organizations (NGOs) in 10 African countries, culminating in sustainable initiatives through resource development and partnership with the South African Football Association as the main exit strategy (Burnett 2012). This project was possibly the most ambitious of its kind being implemented and monitored for seven years (2007 to 2013). The project leaders planned a pathway for sustainability from the onset, while facilitating and co-funding the delivery of sport-for-development activities to about 40,344 South Africans between the ages of seven and 25 years old. Robust research informed programme design and strategic implementation, while providing evidence of intended and unintended consequences (Burnett 2013).

Such mega-event-based sport-for-development initiatives attracted increased academic and public scrutiny due to unequal power configurations and the delivery of 'development' on donors' terms that directly influenced the identification of 'development outcomes' (Cornelissen 2011; Swart *et al.* 2012).[2] Exposing neocolonial structural arrangements and practices, underpins the emergence of a 'struggle and resistance' culture, rather than a blind acceptance of 'sport aid' (Darnell 2012). The IOC-funded Olympafrica and Sport for Hope centres are increasingly attracting critical scrutiny and offer reflective learning opportunities for developing nations hosting mega sport events in return for 'sport humanitarian aid' (Guest 2013).

Other eminent strategic thrusts within this field are the emergence of sport as an integrated initiative in mainstream development work, equal power sharing between implementing partners, and insitutionalization such as being integrated within physical education/life orientation school curricula (Burnett 2016). The structuring of the NGO sector, first through GIZ and Nike South Africa's intervention and funding, and then through the government-funded Sport for Social Change Network (SSCN) Southern Africa, is another recent development. The drive for sustainability thus translated in the insitutionalization and integration of SDP programmes with existing curricula and organizational culture.

International influences and national responses

Following the establishment of the United Nations Inter-Agency Task Force on Sport for Development and Peace (SDP), a group of UN organizations convened in 2002 under the auspices of the UN Secretary-General to reflect on sport-related activities within the US system and interrogate their contribution to the (then) Millennium Development Goals. In the wake of the 2004 Athens Summer Olympic Games, the Sport for Development and Peace International Working Group (SDP IWG) was established with South Africa's Deputy Sport Minister as Chair. Being hosted by the United Nations Office for Sport for Development and Peace (UNOSDP) since 2009 (as per the General Assembly's Resolution A/RES/63/135), the SDP IWG was mandated 'to promote and support the adoption of policies and programmes by national governments to harness the potential of sport to contribute to the achievements of development objectives.' The mandate includes the following, namely: (i) providing a forum for the exchange of knowledge, experience and best practice; (ii) supporting the implementation of policy recommendations; and (iii) sustaining awareness for governments' take-up of SDP initiatives (UNOSDP 2014).

The leadership position of South Africa's Deputy Minister of Sport and Recreation in the SDP IWG since 2004, has influenced national policy and strategy. The Ministry of Sport and Recreation focused on redressing the systemic disenfranchisement caused by the Apartheid dispensation, guided by a human rights framework. Social transformation became a key strategic thrust which significantly deviated from the nation-building ideology of President Nelson Mandela whose inspirational views are still held in high regard. As preface to the first National Sport and Recreation Plan drafted in 2011, a quote from his speech delivered at the Laureus World Sports Awards Ceremony in 2000, reads:

> Sport has the power to change the world. It has the power to inspire. It has the power to unite people in a way that little else can. Sport can awaken hope where there was previously only despair.

> *Sport and Recreation South Africa 2011, front page*

National development priorities frame the provision of access for optimal participation in structured school and community-based sport clubs as a foundation for delivering sport nation-wide (BauNews 2006). The first National Sport and Recreation Plan (drafted in 2011) adheres to the democratic principles enshrined in the Constitution that awards the minister with legislative powers, guided by various prominent Acts, which include:

- Occupational Health and Safety Act, 1993 (Act No. 85 of 1993);
- Public Service Act, 1994 as amended by Act 30 of 2007;
- Broad-based Black Economic Empowerment Act 2003 (Act No. 53 of 2003);
- Division of Revenue Act where Spot and Recreation South Africa (SRSA) coordinates financial allocations to provincial departments responsible for sport through the Mass Participation and Sport Development Grant.

With the Vision 2030 guiding elite sport development and sport for development ensuring 'An Active and Winning Nation', the National Sport and Recreation Plan identified 31 strategic objectives. Six of these objectives have a non-elite sport focus by referring to health, physical education, recreation and sport-for-development initiatives (Sport and Recreation South Africa 2013). For the latter strategic drive, SRSA implemented a community-based mass sport participation programme, known as *Siyadlala* (a Zulu word meaning, 'Let us play'). Four main categories of organized sports, games and physical activities were introduces, namely aerobics, ball games (e.g. handball, basketball and baseball), athletics (big walk/fun run) and Indigenous games. The latter entailed nine games associated with the cultural background and/or history of different racial groups in South Africa (Burnett and Hollander 2006).

In 2007, Sam Bopape, the then spokesperson of the National Department of Education promoted the slogan of *a child in sport is a child out of court* with reference to the School Sport Mass Participation Programme:

> some objectives were to foster pride and respect amongst the youth by enhancing social cohesion, nation-building and turning schools into functional learning institutions. We also aim to strategically link schools to national interventions such as HIV and AIDS awareness campaigns, crime prevention and substance abuse.
>
> *Visagie 2007: 5*

The challenge of providing an inclusive 'sport-for-all' framework necessitated a school-based delivery model. In 2008, the School Mass Participation Programme for sport was launched which provided additional sports such as rugby, cricket, netball and football at 'no-fee' schools. It presented a blend of competitive sport and addressing the various social ills of children living in relative conditions of chronic poverty. A baseline study reported high levels of teenage pregnancies, school-based violence, high rates of early school drop-out and gender-based inequalities (Burnett and Hollander 2008).

The challenge with the choice of physical activities was that most of these sports (e.g. rugby, football and cricket) were not attractive sports for girls' participation, which led to a relatively large drop-out rate. Also, the sport for social change philosophy was relatively new and most teachers and ex-players who coached the activities found it challenging not to promote the competitive element – especially in football (Burnett and Hollander 2008). In the 161 schools that formed part of the baseline study, it became clear that special interventions were to be developed to meaningfully address behavioural change which was not in the scope of the programme at that stage.

In 2011, SRSA and the Ministry of Basic Education signed an MOU to ensure that all learners in public schools would benefit from participation in school sports or structured physical activities as part of the subject – life orientation. As a school subject, life orientation fosters life skill development with the physical education component following mainly health and sport-for-development theoretical frameworks.[3]

The 2013 White Paper produced by SRSA, recognizes the UN stance on sport and recreation as a fundamental human right and as a tool for development and peacebuilding. This has special meaning to foster peaceful co-existence over deeply rooted racial, class and gender divides (Sport and Recreation South Africa 2013). The sport ministry's bilateral partnership with an international non-government organization, LoveLife,[4] demonstrated the emphasis on also promoting a health paradigm in the expectation that education would serve as a preventative measure for young people and in this way, combat the relatively high infection rate of HIV/AIDS. In 2015, national statistics indicated that 6.19 million people were HIV-positive which represents 11.2 per cent of the total population with a gender bias, as 19 per cent of the infected were females between the ages of 15 and 49 years of age (Moloi 2016: 602).

High rates of poverty and socio-economic inequality with the Gini coefficient of 0.64 indicated a relatively high level of income inequality, which may vary from 0 (complete equality) to 1 (complete inequality) (Van Heerden 2016: 314). Another significant indicator of widespread poverty relates to the fact that 84.5 per cent of all 24 060 public schools in South Africa are 'no-fee' schools with 35 per cent (8 419) falling in the poorest category (quintile 1) (Ndebele 2016: 468).[5]

The public school system in South Africa needs many more resources to be able to deliver quality educational programmes, including physical education in a school curriculum against competing subject areas. This contributed to the NGO sector's increasing involvement in delivering content in the life orientation curriculum, physical education (practical component of life orientation) and school sport. Most of these agencies were involved in sport for development initiatives, or still present such activities in their local communities. The private sector also entered into the currently 'crowded curriculum space' in lower quantile public schools to offer programmes. Nike South Africa's Soweto Active School Programme that is aligned with the global Designed to Move strategy, is such an initiative. Many other physical activity programmes are offered by relatively well established NGOs such as Grassrootsoccer, Altus Sport, Sportstec and other SSCN Southern Africa member organizations.

These developments resonate with an emerging phenomenon globally described by Bruce Kidd as follows:

> During the last two decades, national and international corporations, foundations, non-governmental organizations (NGOs), sports organizations and professional and Olympic athletes have responded to the inadequacy of public schools and recreation centres that once provided accessible opportunities for sport and physical activity by creating their own organizations and programmes.
>
> *Kidd 2011: 161*

A current initiative entails a partnership between SRSA, the Department of Basic Education (DBE), UNICEF and a newly established association (South Africa University Physical Education Association – SAUPEA) with membership from 14 out of the 26 South African public universities. SAUPEA members are currently conducting a nationwide research on the status of physical education and school sport to understand current delivery models and approaches. The research aims to inform policy development and strategic decision-making by the government sector. As an additional spin-off, the co-funding agency (UNICEF) has an interest in the field to refocus sport for development initiatives and partnerships in addressing children's rights and protection issues in view of their future anticipated partnership.[6]

The restructuring of the sport-for-development field possibly stems from various global and national-level influences. As a global force, the United Nations in partnership with international organizations such as the IOC (which has had observer status in the UN General Assembly since 2009) and the Commonwealth Games Federation have announced the sport-for-good philosophy to guide structural adaptations and practice. Both these influential international leading sport organizations identified several sustainable development goals which would be endorsed and proposed for delivery by prospective Olympic Games host countries.[7] The Olympic Movement's interest around SDP in developing countries seems to focus on an increase in opportunities for active participation and education by promoting sport for all and health as cornerstones for an improved quality of life for marginalized youth (Kidane 2001).

South Africa's sport fraternity as host of the 2022 Commonwealth Games would have attracted multiple partnerships to deliver on a collective mandate for various constituencies and for South African citizens at large. However, this did not materialize as South Africa pulled out as a host city although the sporting community continued to engage with various South African-based stakeholders by forming reciprocally beneficial partnerships. Within the thick of these relationships, academics from different academic backgrounds engage in knowledge production and advocacy within the SDP sphere.

Research and scholarship

It is a stark reality that although most of the SDP projects are offered in Africa, Asia and Latin America, 90 per cent of the authors publishing on them are based in North America, Europe and Australia (Schulenkorf *et al.* 2016). As academics from non-first world countries, Africa-based scholars are sometimes invited to contribute to international forums and debate, but often solely to deliver 'context'. It seems that scholars from the global North's insights are recognized first and foremost in advancing first world discourses through the production of (new) knowledge and theory generation.

Critical work and critical reflections on neoliberal philosophies and neocolonial stances of global northern donors and developing agencies undermine sustainable and community-driven development in impoverished communities (Darnell 2012; Levermore 2009). Even the knowledge production and interpretation of 'positive social transformation' bear the logic of neoliberalism, while ignoring systemic challenges, power structures and broader policy domains in which initiatives are operationalized (Hayhurst 2013; McKay 2015). Neoliberal ideology (re)constructs reality in such a way that by training local volunteers for the delivery of course material, the mediated version of 'reality' is negotiated (Forde 2014). It is not about including Indigenous 'voices', but rather about understanding them and utilizing local insights for interpretations, reflection and knowledge construction. Without theory generation to describe contextual sport-for-development manifestations and create conceptual clarity, the phenomenon will be constructed within the plurality of paradigms to serve the hegemonic discourses of scholars making the argument.

It is not an issue of locality alone, but of understanding local realities and producing scholarly work that would enrich the existing sport-for-development diverse bodies of knowledge. In 2015, Chris Bolsmann and Cora Burnett acted as guest editors for the *South African Review of Sociology* with the aim of promoting the study of sport-related issues to mainstream academics and postgraduate students in sociology. The argument was made that South African sport should be taken seriously. Of the six papers that were selected for publication after the peer-review process, two addressed sport-for-development related topics.

Laurenz Langer's (2015) article maps the field and subsequent discourses of SDP. He critically reflects on the depth of impact assessment SDP research and argues for scientific inquiry to reach beyond indicator-directed investigations. He argues for multiple layers of analysis, inclusive of Indigenous ways of interpreting data that articulates with real-life experiences and constructions. The other paper reported on a sport-for-development intervention framework of the mega-event legacies (2010 FIFA World Cup) and offered a critical stance, while proposing innovative frameworks for the conceptualization of legacy (Waardenburg et al. 2015). The latter criticism contributes to existing critical research where various researchers questioned the widely proclaimed social development outcomes of the 2010 FIFA World Cup.

Scarlett Cornelissen from the University of Stellenbosch questions the emerging power axis of hosting mega events such as the 2008 Olympic Games, the 2010 FIFA World Cup and the 2010 New Delhi Commonwealth Games and argues that such events are part of the 'imagineering of emerging powers', while societal benefits (including development) come at material and symbolic costs for the host nation (Cornelissen 2010). Another theme relates to the clarification of the concept of 'legacy' and the proposal that such events' legacies should integrate triple bottom-line principles in the planning, design and evaluation of mega-event impacts as they may find expression within a particular context (Cornelissen et al. 2011). The 2010 FIFA World Cup attracted multiple sectors to invest in sport-for-development projects which had the potential to shape the sector and broader sports environment in different ways (Cornelissen 2011).

Various South African universities engage in publishing within the field of SDP with the University of Johannesburg and the University of the Western Cape producing the majority of research papers in the field. At the latter university, the Interdisciplinary Centre of Excellence for Sport Science and Development (ICESSD) is one of its kind in South Africa and focuses on sport and development with dedicated research and agency within the fields of peacebuilding, social transformation, sport policy, governance, monitoring and evaluation, community development and health (Keim and De Coning 2014). In collaboration with Africa-based researchers, a baseline study on the status of policies in sport and country profiles of 10 selected African countries regarding sport and development was conducted between 2011 and 2014. This study provided informative data for policy status and development in answer to a UNESCO request for a continental sport and development index.

Many of the ICESSD's research was built on Keim's work within a human justice paradigm and building a case for sport as a tool for social integration in post-Apartheid South Africa (Keim 2003), community development and peaceful co-existence (Keim 2006). Other research is mostly descriptive and reflects on the role of the university in the production and transfer of knowledge with emphasis on the practical application of knowledge by practitioners and policy-makers within their spheres of engagement (Keim et al. 2011). In a more recent paper, Laattoe and Keim (2015) report on a 'sport for social change' interuniversity project between the University of the Western Cape, the University of Connecticut (USA) and their NGO partners. One of the postgraduate students, Ben Sanders produced several papers on the opportunities and challenges facing NGOs within the sport-for-development sector (Sanders et al. 2014). Similar evaluative research reports on programme effects as in the case of the Grassrootsoccer resiliency pilot programme (Peacock-Villada et al. 2007) and an interprofessional community-based participatory project (Frantz et al. 2016).

According to the Comic Relief review on the mapping of impact research in the field of sport-for-development (Cronin 2011), Burnett produced the majority of such research within the African context, including the relatively widely used research methodology

(Sport-in-Development Impact Assessment Tool or S·DIAT). Most of the research was conducted in South Africa, although larger-scaled (internationally funded) projects extended to other African countries (Burnett 2015a).

In post-Apartheid South Africa, international sporting bodies such as UK Sport and the Australian Sport Commission requested impact assessments for their respective sport development and sport-for-development outreach programmes in South Africa, Botswana and Swaziland (Burnett 2001). About 30 research outputs (reports, articles and conference proceedings) followed on the Australian Sport Commission's (ASC's) research. Some publications offer critical reflections and discourse development underpinned by neo-classical capital theory (Bourdieu), Coleman's rational choice theory, the network theory and Putnam's framework of civil engagement, integrated with the Marshallian concept of citizenship as to inform a conceptual framework for analysis of 'social capital' (Burnett 2006).

The ASC's research attracted other development agencies such as the GIZ/YDF's (German Development Corporation's Youth Development through Football) project which was implemented in 10 selected African countries from 2007 to 2013. The German Development Agency, co-funded by the European Union, ensured a reciprocally beneficial partnership and funding for supplementing 'impact assessments' with 'academic inquiry'. For instance, they provided additional funding for research on violence (gangs at the Cape Flats) and the publication of *Stories from the Field*.[8] In this way strategic research, praxis and academic objectives merged as a win-win scenario for all stakeholders involved.

In collaboration with a colleague in the field of sport management, various national scale impact assessments in the field of sport (and) development assisted with the refinement of methodology and research strategies. Such projects included the impact assessment of SRSA's Community Mass Sport Programme (2004–2006) and the School Sport Mass Participation Programme (2008) (Burnett and Hollander 2006; 2008).

From of the Chair of the Commonwealth Games Development Committee, Burnett received an invitation to do research at the 2014 Glasgow Commonwealth Games. The research aimed to investigate the perceptions, experiences and expectations relating to 'development work' of Commonwealth Games Associations.[9] This experience motivated a successful application of the IOC's Advanced Olympic Research Grant. Being Director of the University of Johannesburg's Olympic Studies Centre, the IOC-funded research on Olympic Movement Stakeholder Collaboration for Delivering on Sport Development in Eight African (SADC) Countries, led to the positioning of the Centre within the African context (Burnett 2015b). The research bridged into the sport management field, while also reflecting on sport education and sport-for-development initiatives implemented by Olympafrica centres in the different African countries. A recent publication explores the potential synergy between Olympism education and current physical education practices in the South African context (Burnett 2016).

The complexity and multidisciplinary work in the field of SDP drew researchers from different perspectives. Examples include studies from academics in the field of sport management reporting on issues of governance, consumer satisfaction and stakeholder engagement (Surujlal and Dhurup 2008). Gender issues are at the core of many discriminatory SDP practices and were vividly demonstrated by spectators at the 2010 Football for Hope Festival (Ogunniyi 2015). Therapeutic recreation is another applied study field at South African universities which addresses sport-related interventions for at-risk youth (Young *et al.* 2015). Inevitably, educational frameworks would be utilized for investigating the transfer of knowledge, socialization processes and behavioural change components (Burnett 2016).

As a South African researcher, the meaningfulness lies in knowledge production for positive societal change and strategic praxis – to have a voice in discourse development from the global

South may influence multiple stakeholders (from government, to NGOs and international sport agencies) through critical inquiry.

Notes

1   Burnett and Hollander (1999) did an evaluation on the United Kingdom–South Africa Sports Initiative, whereas Boshoff (1997) reported on an evaluation of the Western Cape Sports Administration's Forum – a local universities project to train community-based ('barefoot') sport administrators.
2   Most criticism from academics focused on the cost of hosting the 2010 FIFA World Cup in a developing nation in view of many competing development needs. Cornelissen (2011) is critical of meaningful structural changes of a FIFA legacy, while Swart *et al.* (2011) questions the sustainability of community-level changes.
3   Life Orientation is a school subject which comprises of various subject areas of which physical education is but one of such areas. From Grade 4 (intermediate phase) up to Grade 12, one hour per week is allocated for this learning area which makes it problematic to achieve meaningful health-related benefits and quality programmes focused on physical literacy.
4   loveLife is South Africa's largest youth leadership and HIV-prevention NGO with influential partnerships with the government sector, private foundations and the private sector. Sport is included in the offerings at the 22 loveLife centres country-wide servicing with programmes offering services to about 8,000 schools with 1,200 peer educators (groundBREAKERS) delivering programmes (see www.ngopulse/organisation/lovelife).
5   The quintile ranking system is a poverty index used by the DBE for funding purposes (school subsidies). The poorest schools fall under quintile 1, and the most well resourced fall under quintile 5.
6   During the 2014 Glasgow Commonwealth Games, an international partnership with UNICEF resulted in raising substantial funding (about £5 million) for the 'sport-for-good' cause and for charity.
7   In February 2015, the IOC brought out a position document stating The Contribution of Sport to the Sustainable Development Goals and the post-2015 Development Agenda, while identifying six goals to address through sport. In 2016, the Commonwealth Secretariat followed suit and announced a similar commitment for all Commonwealth countries.
8   Stories from the field: GIZ/YDF Footprint in Africa is a publication authored by Burnett in 2012 as a popular version of the research in addition to a CD with 45 case studies that could be used for academic purposes.
9   Cora Burnett and Wim Hollander were invited by the International Commonwealth Federation to conduct research at the 2014 Glasgow Games in order to construct a CGF Development Framework.

References

BauNews. (2006). Children must take part in sport. *Express*, 22 December, p. 18.
Boshoff, G. B. (1997). 'Barefoot' sports administrators: Laying the foundation for sports development in South Africa. *Journal of Sport Management, 11*(1), 69–79.
Burnett, C. (2001). Social impact assessment and sports development. Social spin-offs of the Australia – South Africa Junior Sport Programme. *International Review for the Sociology of Sport, 36*(1), 41–58.
Burnett, C. (2006). Building social capital through an 'Active Community Club'. *International Review for the Sociology of Sport, 41*(3–4), 283–294.
Burnett, C. (2012). GIZ/YDF as a driver of sport for development in Africa. *Journal of Sport and Development, 9*(1), 1–11.
Burnett, C. (2013). GIZ/YDF and youth as drivers for sport for development in the African context. *Journal of Sport for Development, 1*(1), 1–10.
Burnett, C. (2015a). Assessing the sociology of sport: On sport for development and peace. *International Review for the Sociology of Sport, 50*(4–5), 385–390.
Burnett, C. (2015b). Olympic Movement Stakeholder Collaboration for Delivering on Sport Development in Eight African (SADC) Countries. IOC Olympic Studies Centre.
Burnett, C. (2016). Relevance of Olympism education and sport-for-development programmes in South African schools. *South African Journal for Research in Sport, Physical Education and Recreation, 38*(3), 15–26.
Burnett, C. and Hollander, W. J. (1999). Sport development and the United Kingdom–South Africa Sports initiative: A pre-evaluation report. *Journal of Sport Management, 13*(3), 237–251.

Burnett, C. and Hollander, W. J. (2006). *The Impact of the Mass Participation Project of Sport and Recreation South Africa (Siyadlala) 2004/5*. Pretoria: Sport and Recreation South Africa.

Burnett, C. and Hollander, W. J. (2008). *The Pre-Impact Assessment of the School Sport Mass Participation Project*. Johannesburg: University of Johannesburg, Department of Sport and Movement Studies.

Burnett, C. and Katzenellenbogen, E. H. (1993). *Human Movement Studies. An annotated bibliography of theses and dissertations*. Johannesburg: Rand Afrikaans University.

Coakley, J. (2011). Youth sports: What counts as 'positive development?'. *Journal of Sport and Social Issues, 35*(3), 306–324.

Coalter, F. (2013). *Sport for Development: What Game are we Playing?* London: Routledge.

Cornelissen, S. (2010). The geopolitics of global aspiration: Sport mega-events and emerging powers. *The International Journal of the History of Sport, 27*(16–18), 3008–3025.

Cornelissen, S. (2011). More than a sporting chance? Appraising the sport for development legacy of the 2010 FIFA World Cup. *Third World Quarterly, 32*(3), 503–529.

Cornelissen, S., Bob, U. and Swart, K. (2011). Towards redefining the concept of legacy in relation to sport mega-events: Insights from the 2010 FIFA World Cup. *Development Southern Africa, 28*(3), 307–318.

Cronin, O. (2011) *Comic Relief Review: Mapping the Research on the Impact of Sport and Development Interventions*. Manchester: Orla Cronin Research.

Darnell, S. (2012). *Sport for Development and Peace: A Critical Sociology*. London: Bloomsbury Academic.

Forde, S. D. (2014). Look after yourself, or look after one another? An analysis of life skills in sport for development and peace HIV prevention curriculum. *Sociology of Sport Journal, 31*(3), 287–303.

Frantz, J. M., Filies, G., Jooste, K., Keim, M., Mlenzana, N., Laattoe, N. and Rhoda, A. (2016). Reflection on an interprofessional community-based participatory research project: research-interprofessional education, practice and research supplement. *African Journal of Health Professions Education, 8*(2), 234–237.

Guest, A. M. (2013). Sport psychology for development and peace? Critical reflections and constructive suggestions. *Journal of Sport Psychology in Action, 4*(3), 169–180.

Hayhurst, L. M. (2013). Girls as the 'new' agents of social change? Exploring the 'Girl Effect' through sport, gender and development programs in Uganda. *Sociological Research Online, 18*(2), 8.

Hammond-Tooke, W. D. (ed.) (1980). *The Bantu-Speaking Peoples of Southern Africa*. London: Taylor & Francis.

Holt, N. L. (ed.) (2016). *Positive Youth Development Through Sport*. London: Routledge.

Keim, M. (2003). *Nation Building at Play: Sport as a Tool for Social Integration in Post-Apartheid South Africa* (Vol. 4). Oxford: Meyer and Meyer Sport.

Keim, M. (2006). Sport as opportunity for community development and peace building in South Africa. *Sport and Development*. Leuven: Uitgeverij Lannoo Press, pp. 97–106.

Keim, M., and De Coning, C. (eds) (2014). *Sport and Policy Development Policy in Africa. Results of a Collaborative Study of Selected Country Cases*. Stellenbosch: Sun Media.

Keim, M., Jordaan, G., Rato Barrio, M., Chikwanda, C., Grover, T., Bouah, L., Asihel, S., Cabral, J. and Ley, C. (2011). Sport and development from the perspective of University. In K. Petry and M. Gross (eds), *Sport und Internationale Entwicklungszusammenarbeit*. Köln: Sportverlag Strauss.

Kidane, F. (2001). The Olympic movement in developing countries. *ICHPER-SD Journal, 37*(2), 16–22.

Kidd, B. (2008). A new social movement: Sport for development and peace. *Sport in Society, 11*(4), 370–380.

Kidd, B. (2011). Cautions, questions and opportunities in sport for development and peace. *Third World Quarterly, 32*(3), 603–609.

Laattoe, N. and Keim, M. (2015). Sport for social change: an inter-university collaboration between the University of the Western Cape, South Africa, and the University of Connecticut, USA, and their NGO partners: Sport education and community development. *African Journal for Physical Health Education, Recreation and Dance, 21*(Supplement 1), 251–262.

Langer, L. (2015). Sport for development–a systematic map of evidence from Africa. *South African Review of Sociology, 46*(1), 66–86.

Levermore, R. (2009). Sport-in-international development: Theoretical frameworks. In R. Levermore and A. Beacom (eds), *Sport and International Development*, Basingstoke, UK: Palgrave Macmillan.

McKay, J. (2015). Assessing the sociology of sport: On revisiting the sociological imagination. *International Review for the Sociology of Sport, 50*(4–5), 547–552.

Moloi, L. (2016). Health. In F. Cronje and J. Kane-Berman (eds), *South Africa Survey 2016*. Johannesburg: Institute of Race Relations.

National Sports Council. (1996). Youth Charter for Sport: Teaming up to tackle crime. Invitation to sponsors and supporters. Proceedings of the Vision for Sport Conference of the NSC. Johannesburg: NSC.

National Sports Council. (1997). The UK–SA Sports Initiative. *National Sports Council Bulletin*, 2(1), 1–14.

Ndebele, T. (2016). Education. In F. Cronje and J. Kane-Berman (eds), *South Africa Survey 2016*. Johannesburg: Institute of Race Relations.

Ogunniyi, C. (2015). A discourse of gender at the Football for Hope Festival 2010. *African Journal for Physical, Health Education, Recreation and Dance*, March Supplement, 67–79.

Peacock-Villada, P., DeCelles, J. and Banda, P. S. (2007). Grassroot soccer resiliency pilot program: Building resiliency through sport-based education in Zambia and South Africa. *New Directions for Student Leadership, 2007*(116), 141–154.

Sanders, B., Phillips, J. and Vanreusel, B. (2014). Opportunities and challenges facing NGOs using sport as a vehicle for development in post-apartheid South Africa. *Sport, Education and Society*, 19(6), 789–805.

Schapera, I. (ed.). (1966). *The Bantu-Speaking Tribes of South Africa: An Ethnographical Survey*. Cape Town: Maskew Miller.

Schulenkorf, N. and Adair, D. (2014). *Global Sport-for-Development. Critical Perspectives*. Basingstoke, UK: Palgrave Macmillan.

Schulenkorf, N., Sherry, E. and Rowe, K. (2016). Sport for development: An integrated literature review. *Journal of Sport Management*, 30(1), 22–39.

Sport and Recreation South Africa (SRSA). (2011). *Declaration and Resolutions of the National Sport and Recreation Indaba*. Pretoria: SRSA.

Sport and Recreation South Africa (SRSA). (2013). *National Sport and Recreation Plan*. Pretoria: SRSA.

Surujlal, J. and Dhurup, M. (2008). Volunteers' perceptions of benefits derived from volunteering: an empirical study. *South African Journal for Research in Sport, Physical Education and Recreation*, 30(1), 105–116.

Swart, K., Bob, U., Knott, B. and Salie, M. (2011). A sport and sociocultural legacy beyond 2010: A case study of the Football Foundation of South Africa. *Development Southern Africa*, 28(3), 415–428.

Tyamzashe, M. (1996). Message from Mtobi Tyamzashe, Director-General, Department of Sport and Recreation. (Guest editorial). *National Sports Council Bulletin*, April/May, 2–3.

UNOSDP. (2014). Sport for Development and Peace International Working Group. Available at: www.un.org/sport/content/un-players/me/ (accessed 20 January 2017).

Van Heerden, G. (2016). Assets and incomes. In F. Cronje and J. Kane-Berman (eds), *South Africa Survey 2016*. Johannesburg: Institute of Race Relations.

Visagie, N. (2007). Government departments unite to promote school sport participation. *Diamond Fields Advertiser*, 14 March, p. 5.

Waardenburg, M., Van den Bergh, M. and Van Eekeren, F. (2015). Local meanings of a sport mega-event's legacies: Stories from a South African urban neighbourhood. *South African Review of Sociology*, 46(1), 87–105.

Young, M. E. M., Titus, S. and Rampou, M. T. T. (2015). The effects of therapeutic recreation programmes on youth at risk. *African Journal for Physical, Health Education, Recreation and Dance*, March Supplement, 165–174.

45

South Pacific

Fostering healthy lifestyles

Nico Schulenkorf and Katja Siefken

Background

As a result of increasing political and institutional support, the number of sport-based development projects aimed at contributing to positive outcomes in the areas of economic development, social inclusion, cultural cohesion, healthy lifestyles, education, gender equity, as well as reconciliation and peacebuilding has grown exponentially over the past 15 years (Levermore and Beacom 2009; Schulenkorf and Adair 2014). Over this time, the term sport for development (SFD) has become commonplace in the context of international aid and development; in short, SFD represents the intentional 'use of sport to exert a positive influence on public health, the socialization of children, youths and adults, the social inclusion of the disadvantaged, the economic development of regions and states, and on fostering intercultural exchange and conflict resolution' (Lyras and Welty Peachey 2011: 311). As discussed throughout in this handbook, SFD goes beyond traditional forms of sport or talent development by focusing on wider development outcomes rather than sport as an end in itself.

In recent years, SFD programs have also been specifically linked to healthy lifestyle development. In addition to positive social impacts, sport and regular physical activity (PA) have shown to be associated with benefits to overall physical health, including reduced risk of cardiovascular diseases, diabetes and osteoporosis (Haskell *et al.* 2009; Lee *et al.* 2012). Epidemiological research further suggests that PA can also positively influence individuals' mental and socio-psychological status, including improvements in people's mood (Ströhle 2009), and a reduction of symptoms related to depression, anxiety and emotional stress (Prochaska *et al.* 1992; Steptoe and Butler 1996; Eyler *et al.* 2003; Rooney *et al.* 2003; Ströhle 2009; Rebar *et al.* 2015).

Taken together, health-related SFD programs can therefore be important for the health and well-being of individuals and their communities, particularly in the context of growing rates of overweight and obesity as well as associated lifestyle diseases for people around the world. These issues are particularly pressing for communities in the geographically remote and culturally diverse South Pacific region, where locals have been facing significant social and physical health challenges for several decades.

Pacific Island countries

The Pacific Island Countries (PICs) comprise 23 nations and territories[1] spread over more than 25,000 islands and islets in the Pacific Ocean. The PICs are home to approximately 10 million people and the population was expected to continue growing, reaching an estimated 15 million by 2035 (SPC 2012). At the same time, many of the smaller PICs are experiencing a steady outflow of their population to places like Australia and New Zealand.

People in the very remote and diverse Pacific region have been traditionally grouped along ethnic and cultural lines as Melanesian, Micronesian and Polynesian. The Melanesian islands include Papua New Guinea, New Caledonia, Vanuatu, Fiji and the Solomon Islands. The Micronesian islands include the Marianas, Guam, Palau, the Marshall Islands, Kiribati, Nauru and the Federated States of Micronesia. The Polynesian islands include Samoa, American Samoa, Pitcairn, Tokelau, Tonga, Tuvalu, Niue, the Cook Islands, French Polynesia, and Wallis and Futuna.

Historically, Pacific lifestyle was characterized by the consumption of fish and fresh local food and high levels of PA. Physical labour was essential for survival and no transport systems were available on the islands; if nearby villages were to be reached, the single modus of transport is walking or using an outrigger canoe. Motorized vehicles and electronic devices did not exist. While specific health information of Pacific societies prior to European contact is sparse (Taylor *et al.* 1989), anecdotal evidence suggests that non-communicable diseases (NCDs) were previously rather uncommon in the Pacific Islands (Zimmet *et al.* 1990) and Pacific islanders were traditionally strong and active (Coyne 1984; Taylor *et al.* 1989).

However, since the 1950s the average lifestyle of Pacific islanders has changed dramatically. Several studies have shown that across the Pacific, rapid changes in lifestyle behaviour have occurred due to the interrelated concepts of globalization, modernization and urbanization (Strong *et al.* 2005; Bauman *et al.* 2009; Hughes and Marks 2009; WHO 2010a). Here, two changes stand out as key contributors to Pacific people's adjusted daily routines and subsequent health risks:

1) Dietary change: root crops were mostly replaced by white rice and white bread. Fresh fish was largely replaced by tinned meat, the consumption of fruit and vegetables decreased, while the consumption of sugar, oil, salt, refined cereals, tobacco and alcohol increased.
   (Taylor *et al.* 1992; Snowdon *et al.* 2010; Thow *et al.* 2011)
2) Activity change: physical labour on the field or sea was largely replaced by the availability/use of electronic machines (e.g. motorized boats). A move to urban centres has led to an increase in sedentary occupations, the use of motorized transport and to a reduction in PA levels.
   Coyne 1984; Englberger et al. 1999; WPRO and SPC 2008

These lifestyle behaviour modifications have led to a shift in disease patterns: lifestyle diseases – also known as NCDs – have rapidly overtaken communicable diseases and they now contribute to 75 per cent of all deaths in PICs (WHO 2014). In particular, four types of NCDs are the leading contributors to this epidemic: cardiovascular diseases, cancers, chronic respiratory diseases, and diabetes (WHO 2010a). Sadly, the South Pacific is the most troubled region with the worst records of NCDs in the world: in just over a decade, NCD mortality rates have increased from 8.6 million in the year 2000 to a record 10.9 million in 2013 (WHO 2014; 2015).

The consequences of lifestyle changes and subsequent illnesses are presenting a significant development challenge for Pacific people's overall well-being, including issues related to health, social and economic status. For example, as people are increasingly dependent on medical treatment, they are unable to work and hence are ill-placed to support their families.

It comes as no surprise, then, that at the 2011 Pacific Island Forum in Fiji – convened by the Secretariat of the Pacific Community and the WHO Office of the South Pacific – Pacific delegates declared the region to be in a state of emergency, facing a human, social and economic crisis (SPC 2011). As a form of crisis response, the region has been in need for effective and cost-efficient initiatives that can address the social, economic and health-related issues in PICs (Kessaram et al. 2015). Part of the solution is specifically designed SFD programs that aim to make a positive difference by promoting healthy lifestyle behaviour in the region. We will now discuss some of the key lessons learnt from SFD projects that have recently been implemented in this part of the world.

SFD in the Pacific Islands

With the intention of combining the different areas that contribute to inclusive social and health-related development, we have previously presented the Healthy Lifestyle Quadrant (HLQ) (see Schulenkorf and Siefken, in press). In short, the HLQ provides a visual representation of key areas of concern that need to be addressed in order to be successful in achieving desired social and health-related benefits: the socio-cultural context, health promotion activities; policy interventions; and managerial considerations in the context of sport and PA.

Using the HLQ as our background framework, we now turn to an applied discussion of recent and ongoing SFD projects in the South Pacific. Here, we build on our own lived experiences as researchers, program implementers and consultants across the Pacific (see, e.g. Siefken et al. 2011; 2014; 2015; Misener and Schulenkorf 2016; Schulenkorf 2016; Schulenkorf and Schlenker 2017), as well as findings garnered from similar projects, studies and policies that have been realized in the region.

Health promotion

Health is a multidimensional concept; the WHO defined health in its broader sense in its 1948 constitution as 'a state of complete physical, mental, and social well-being and not merely the absence of disease or infirmity' (WHO 1948: 100). This definition highlights that health describes more than just one's physical capacity; it also relates to a person's mental well-being, the aptitude to interact with others and the ability cope in daily life. *Health promotion* is a core function of public health; in the Ottawa Charter for Health Promotion (1986), it is defined as a 'process of enabling people to increase control over, and to improve their health' (WHO 1986). In short, health promotion is about giving people the power to achieve positive health outcomes with respect to physical, mental and social health.

When considering the role of sport in the context of health promotion, the provision of opportunities to exercise and interact with others can be thought of as ways in which positive health outcomes can be achieved. Here, SFD projects provide an augmented opportunity for people, as active participation in sport or PA is purposely combined with non-sporting development aspects, including health education and social engagement (see Schulenkorf and Adair 2014). For example, since 2014 the Vanuatu-based Volley4Change project has aimed at helping adolescents to realize and reduce their chances of developing NCDs by encouraging them to play Volleyball. Volley4Change forms part of the Australian Government's Pacific Sports Partnership (PSP) initiative; in short, the PSP is the largest government-supported SFD initiative in the South Pacific and covers 11 sports (for more details, see Sherry and Schulenkorf 2016). Volley4Change is managed by the Vanuatu Volleyball Federation and one of the key project goals is to empower women to be agents of change; in short, through playing Volleyball, exercising regularly, and attending nutritional awareness classes, women are supposed to experience and subsequently promote a healthier lifestyle in their families and communities. To achieve these goals, Volley4Change has in some instances partnered with nutritionists from the Northern District Hospital (NDH) to provide training in nutritional awareness for the participants, while basic health checks are being provided by nurses from the NDH.

Similarly, the Oceania Football Confederation's Just Play program (2014) engages in health promotion activities directed at both children and their parents as part of an inclusive SFD program. For example, in the Cook Islands, health-related awareness and education sessions have in the past been co-organized by Just Play and local stakeholders, including partners from organizations such as the Ministry of Health, the Red Cross, local educators and social workers. Parents of school children were, for example, part of an NCD workshop that was facilitated by the Cook Islands Ministry of Health, while the children completed a 'station run' where community experts talked about gender-related social issues – including domestic violence (Police), child protection, and a safe environment (Ministry of Social Development) and the importance of respect for others (Ministry for Internal Affairs).

At the Wokabaot Jalens – a healthy lifestyle program for female civil servants in urban Vanuatu – a similar approach was taken. While the increase of PA levels was indeed the key purpose of the initiative, health education and health promotion materials (posters, pamphlets, t-shirts), workshops and electronic health newsletter accompanied the program. Herein, participants were provided with information on healthy lifestyle behaviour, on healthy eating strategies etc. In short, they were continuously encouraged to create a healthy home for themselves and their families. Numerous workshops around the program further led to newly designed posters on healthy lifestyle behaviour that were taken to churches and that were put on display for social groups in the surrounding communities. Such proactive communication is a particularly important strategic approach in a cultural context where communal engagement plays a key role in people's lives. Notably, churches are often the central meeting point of communities in the Pacific Islands; they are places where knowledge and experiences are shared and where social messages can reach the wider community. Hence, partnerships with religious centres can play a central role for profound health promotion activities.

Overall, studies around PA have shown that SFD interventions can provide physically engaging and emotionally liberating experiences for participants and they may even serve as an effective adjunct to usual care in people experiencing mental illness (Schulenkorf, in press; Stubbs *et al.* 2016; Vancampfort *et al.* 2016). However, it should be acknowledged that it is simply too much to expect SFD programs to single-handedly address more serious and/or sustained trauma or mental health issues that people may experience. Previous health-related SFD studies have, for example, shown that there is no immediate association between increased PA levels and positive mental health outcomes in highly traumatized children (see e.g. Richards and Foster 2013). Any claims on cause and effect should therefore be treated with caution.

Sport management

In contrast to traditional health education strategies that often include the provision of educational health information in form of pamphlets, posters and flyers as well as engagement via classroom teaching, community forums or group workshops, SFD activities have shown to be a potentially more active and exciting platform for health promotion directed at children, adolescents and adults (Siefken *et al.* 2011; Berg *et al.* 2015; Dalton *et al.* 2015; Edwards 2015). As targeted initiatives, they can be 'fresh spaces' for community engagement 'where people from different backgrounds get the chance to work, learn, and celebrate with each other' (Schulenkorf

2010: 127). The organizational aspects of SFD are what we refer to as sport management. Here, the combination of technical knowledge (provided by sport and health management experts) as well as the cultural knowledge (provided by local communities) plays a key role in achieving relevant, meaningful and sustainable project outcomes (see, e.g. Schulenkorf 2012; Sherry *et al.* 2015).

An example for this approach is provided by the Hoops for Health (HfH) program. HfH is the basketball version of the previously introduced PSP and is currently implemented by the respective national federations of Fiji, Vanuatu, Kiribati and the Solomon Islands. HfH uses basketball as a means to encourage healthy lifestyle choices and to reduce NCDs risks in the Pacific. From a management perspective, HfH partners with key stakeholders and seeks to enter schools and communities to increase PA and sport participation, while simultaneously educating people on the risk of NCDs in the Pacific. Moreover, the program is managed to focus specifically on women as their secondary target market. For example, the organizers in Fiji established the 'Mum's A Hero' initiative to equip mothers with the knowledge and tools to improve the health behaviour of their families. Delivered alongside an accessible and engaging 3x3 version of basketball, nutritionists and public health experts come in to speak to the mothers about healthy eating and physical exercise tips.

Meanwhile, in the context of education-based SFD, Sherry and Schulenkorf (2016) undertook a study of a rugby league program aimed at primary school-aged children in Papua New Guinea (PNG) with the overall aim of addressing low school attendance rates and anti-social behavior. Their research once more underscored the importance of understanding and managing local complexities within a SFD program. In particular, this related to the use of strategic parameters that would help facilitate future benefits, including meso-level organizational outcomes and macro-level education impacts. In short, the authors recommended that specific development activities be discussed, designed, managed and delivered in targeted, strategic, and culturally relevant ways to benefit communities.

Socio-cultural development

Previous research from the Pacific Islands confirms that sport and/or health management and socio-cultural awareness are inextricably bound together; in particular, it has been shown that different social and cultural aspects need to be considered when designing SFD and health promotion programs. For example, a study by Englberger and colleagues (1999) concluded that social obligations to attend traditional feasts and social gatherings such as weddings and funerals were considered a problem in diet control. Given the communal significance of these gatherings and the great value placed on consuming (a lot of) food and drinks, the management team of any health promotion program needs to accommodate such factors in its design and delivery to remain culturally inclusive. Moreover, research by Siefken *et al.* (2014) showed that group activities are a critical factor for health promotion and engagement in the Pacific Islands region, as community members – particularly women – prefer to exercise with others in a comfortable social environment. Supporting this argument, Spaaij and Schulenkorf (2014) highlighted the importance of establishing 'safe spaces' when designing SFD projects; spaces in which people are able and willing to participate without any physical, social, cultural, political or environmental constraints.

The request for managing culturally relevant and sustainable projects is also pertinent within the context of Hartmann and Kwauk's (2011) exploration of SFD programs in Samoa. The authors highlighted the efficacy of sport to engage or 'hook' individuals, but questioned whether externally funded and internationally designed interventions were in fact relevant or meaningful for participating local communities. Kwauk's (2014; 2015) wider ethnographic work in Samoa continues to be critical of the often prevailing Eurocentric values – particularly on issues such as health and education – which dominate the foundation of many SFD programs.

Policies

In addition to socio-cultural considerations, policy management can play a key role in health promotion and behaviour change. From a sport and PA perspective, the main aim of public policy initiatives is to create supportive environments, infrastructure and programs to enable people to lead active lives (Bellew *et al.* 2011). In short, supportive policy environments are essential to provide individuals with the opportunity to achieve lasting positive lifestyle change (Le Galès 2010). While policy-makers in the health disciplines continue to struggle in their search for holistic strategies to combat and reverse the growing epidemic of NCDs (Schultz *et al.* 2011), there is long-standing recognition that public policies can assist in improving diets and tackling the problem of obesity (WHO 2008). However, to address the growing NCD epidemic in the South Pacific region, policies in the health sector alone will not be able to produce the necessary gains in peoples' health status and overall community development. A population-based, multisectoral, multidisciplinary and culturally relevant approach is utterly needed.

As highlighted by former New Zealand Prime Minister Helen Clarke at the Pacific NCD Summit 2016 in Nukualofa, Tonga, the NCD crisis in the Pacific Islands region is strongly linked to 'patterns of trade, consumption, agricultural production, foreign direct investment, and unplanned urbanization'. In other words, to make a significant difference to the lamentable status quo, whole-of-government approaches are needed as NCDs are influenced by different sources and their impacts are felt across different sectors of society. Moreover, the conditions in which people are born, grow, live, work and play – the social determinants of health – shape patterns of disease distribution. Hence – and as discussed earlier – the socio-cultural context must be taken into account. The Health in All Policies approach is a response to addressing the social determinants of health that are the key drivers of health outcomes and health inequalities. Herein, diverse governmental partners and stakeholders are engaged to collaborate on a shared vision to improve health and simultaneously advance other goals, such as promoting job creation and economic stability, transportation access and mobility, a strong agricultural system, environmental sustainability, and educational attainment (WHO, Government of South Australia, 2010b). Political commitment is clear: the 2016 Shanghai Declaration on promoting health in the 2030 Agenda for Sustainable Development underlines the need to protect health and promote well-being through public policies (WHO 2016). Howse (2012) correctly calls for these policies and laws that are suited to the specific Pacific environments. Such targeted initiatives would guarantee more sensitivity to cultural norms, values and customs, as well as more specific and efficient management of public health risks.

Against this background, a number of PICs have also started to implement policy interventions in sectors *outside* of the health domain. For example, the Pacific Obesity Prevention in Communities' (POPC) food policy project looked at policy initiatives in different PICs that either increased the cost of soft drinks, or sought to control fatty meat imports through their trade associations. Early research on the POPC project demonstrated that the health-related policy approaches (a) improved diets in a cost-effective way, and (b) supported the prevention and control of NCDs in countries such as Fiji and Tonga (Snowdon *et al.* 2011; Thow and Snowdon *et al.* 2011a). The POPC policy project is in line with recent calls for a change in perspective regarding pricing and access of food items in the Pacific Islands region. For example, Siefken *et al.* (2011) have shown that local produce, including fresh fruits and vegetables, are often more expensive than imported goods – clearly a significant challenge for local people and any healthy lifestyle interventions that aim to promote healthy diets.

Meanwhile, an infrastructure policy from Tonga provides an example for an exciting approach towards promoting safe and active lifestyles on the island. Issued by the Ministry of Land, the policy requires safe footpaths to be constructed alongside every new road that is being built on the island. This policy links with other sport and PA initiatives that aim to create supportive environments, infrastructure and programs to enable people to lead safe and active lives (Bellew *et al.* 2011). Similarly, the Vanuatu government had previously implemented an exemplary PA policy in the capital Port Vila: Walk for Life was a policy to increase public service employees' PA levels, their well-being and productivity through weekly walking activities and beyond. The policy was unique in releasing public servants from official duties across the whole of government at 3.00 p.m. on Wednesdays. Walk for Life was implemented from 2007–2011 and process evaluation showed partial, although sustained, uptake of regular PA among the target population (Schofield and Siefken 2009). While policy initiatives such as this have shown first positive signs towards healthy lifestyle choices, their existence and sustainability is often challenged due to limited political support, funding or the focus on immediate return on investment – clearly, this contradicts with the need for long-term engagement as the most promising strategy towards sustained social and physical development (see Schulenkorf 2012). Finally, SFD projects navigate in between different policies and regulations that may facilitate or hinder the development of healthy lifestyle outcomes. It is therefore important to incorporate external policies into SFD planning and management, and to push for supportive health-related policies in different sectors of society.

Summary

When looking at the social and health-related problems in the South Pacific – the region with the highest rates of obesity and related NCDs in the world – the need for community development initiatives is critical. In this chapter, we have reflected on a number of different SFD programs and health-related development initiatives that have been staged in this diverse and remote area of our planet. We have discussed strategies, achievements and limitations against the Healthy Lifestyle Quadrant – an inclusive framework that combines sport, health, socio-cultural development and policy-making (see Schulenkorf and Siefken, in press).

Overall, the management of SFD projects represents a critically important aspect that cuts across the abovementioned areas of sport, health, culture and policy. Evidently, SFD managers and health experts rarely work in isolation when designing and implementing specific interventions. In fact, importance is laid on cooperating with different stakeholders or partners – both local and international – that can bring their knowledge and expertise to the overall program. Around the world, many SFD programs cooperate with a wide array of partners from sport and beyond, including sport associations, event organizers, government agencies, NGOs and the corporate sector to guarantee and potentially leverage a wide spectrum of social, cultural, political, economic and sport-related resources (see e.g. Schulenkorf 2012; 2016; Misener *et al.* 2015; Welty Peachey *et al.* 2015). In the South Pacific, strong partnerships with the health sector are of particular importance if crucial lifestyle and behaviour changes can be realized for individuals, families and communities.

Note

1   See www.hawaii.edu/cpis/psi/anthro/pac_dev/Pac_Dev6.html.

References

Bauman, A., Finegood, D. T. and Matsudo, V. (2009). International perspectives on the physical inactivity crisis: Structural solutions over evidence generation? *Preventive Medicine, 49*(4), 309–312.

Bellew, B., Bauman, A., Martin, B., Bull, F. and Matsudo, V. (2011). Public policy actions needed to promote physical activity. *Current Cardiovascular Risk Reports, 5*(4), 340, doi:10.1007/s12170-011-0180-6.

Berg, B. K., Warner, S. and Das, B. M. (2015). What about sport? A public health perspective on leisure-time physical activity. *Sport Management Review, 18*(1), 20–31, doi:http://dx.doi.org/10.1016/j.smr.2014.09.005.

Clarke, H. (2016). Keynote Address on 'Non-communicable Diseases – a Sustainable Development Priority for Pacific Island Countries'. Nukualofa, Tonga: Pacific Non-communicable Diseases Summit. Translating Global and Regional Commitments into Local Action. Available at: www.undp.org/content/undp/en/home/presscenter/speeches/2016/06/20/helen-clark-keynote-address-non-communicable-diseases-a-sustainable-development-priority-for-pacific-island-countries-.html.

Coyne, T. (1984). *The Effect of Urbanisation and Western Diet on the Health of Pacific Island Populations.* Noumea, New Caledonia: South Pacific Commission.

Dalton, B., Wilson, R., Evans, J. R. and Cochrane, S. (2015). Australian Indigenous youth's participation in sport and associated health outcomes: Empirical analysis and implications. *Sport Management Review, 18*(1), 57–68, doi:http://dx.doi.org/10.1016/j.smr.2014.04.001.

Edwards, M. B. (2015). The role of sport in community capacity building: An examination of sport for development research and practice. *Sport Management Review, 18*(1), 6–19, doi:http://dx.doi.org/10.1016/j.smr.2013.08.008.

Englberger, L., Halavatau, V., Yasuda, Y. and Yamazaki, R. (1999). The Tonga healthy weight loss program 1995–1997. *Asia Pacific Journal for Clinical Nutrition, 8*(2), 142–148.

Eyler, A. A., Brownson, R. C., Bacak, S. J. and Housemann, R. A. (2003). The epidemiology of walking for physical activity in the United States. *Medicine and Science in Sport and Exercise, 35*(9), 1529.

Hartmann, D. and Kwauk, C. (2011). Sport and development: An overview, critique, and reconstruction. *Journal of Sport and Social Issues, 35*(3), 284–305, doi:10.1177/0193723511416986.

Haskell, W. L., Blair, S. N., and Hill, J. O. (2009). Physical activity: health outcomes and importance for public health priority. *Preventive Medicine, 49*, 280–282.

Howse, G. (2012). Elements of Pacific Public Health Laws: An Analysis of the Public Health Acts of Papua New Guinea, Vanuatu, the Solomon Islands, and Fiji. *Asia-Pacific Journal of Public Health, 24*(5), 860–866.

Hughes, R. G. and Marks, G. C. (2009). Against the tide of change: Diet and health in the Pacific islands. *Journal of the American Dietetic Association, 109*(10), 1700–1703.

Kessaram, T., McKenzie, J., Girin, N., Roth, A., Vivili, P., Williams, G. and Hoy, D. (2015). Noncommunicable diseases and risk factors in adult populations of several Pacific Islands: Results from the WHO STEPwise approach to surveillance. *Australian and New Zealand Journal of Public Health, 39*(4), 336–343.

Kwauk, C. (2014). No longer just a past time: Sport for development in times of change. *The Contemporary Pacific, 26*(2), 202–223.

Kwauk, C. (2015). Let them see a different path: Social attitudes towards sport, education and development in Samoa. *Sport, Education and Society, 21*(4), 644–660, doi:10.1080/13573322.2015.1071250.

Lee, I.-M., Shiroma, E. J., Lobelo, F., Puska, P., Blair, S. N. and Katzmarzyk, P. T. (2012). Effect of physical inactivity on major non-communicable diseases worldwide: An analysis of burden of disease and life expectancy. *The Lancet, 380*(9838), 219–229.

Le Galès, C. (2010). Challenges in making broad healthy lifestyle plans: Revisiting the nature of health interventions. In L. Dube, A. Bechara, A. Dagher, A. Drewnowski, J. LeBel, P. James, and R. Yada (eds), *Obesity Prevention: The Role of Brain and Society on Individual Behavior* (1st edn). Oxford: Academic Press.

Levermore, R. and Beacom, A. (eds). (2009). *Sport and International Development.* Basingstoke, United Kingdom: Palgrave Macmillan.

Lyras, A. and Welty Peachey, J. (2011). Integrating sport-for-development theory and praxis. *Sport Management Review, 14*(4), 311–326.

Misener, L., McGillivray, D., Gayle, M. and Legg, D. (2015). Leveraging parasport events for sustainable community participation: The Glasgow 2014 Commonwealth Games. *Annals of Leisure Research, 18*, 450–469, doi:10.1080/11745398.2015.1045913.

Misener, L. and Schulenkorf, N. (2016). Rethinking the social value of sport events through an asset-based community development (ABCD) perspective. *Journal of Sport Management, 30*(3), 329–340, doi:http://dx.doi.org/10.1123/jsm.2015-0203.

Oceania Football Confederation. (2014). *Just Play Guide (Version 2)*. Auckland, New Zealand: OFC Social Development Programme.

Prochaska, J. O., DiClemente, C. C. and Norcross, J. C. (1992). In search of how people change: Applications to addictive behavior. *The American Psychologist, 47*(9), 1102–1114.

Rebar, A. L., Stanton, R., Geard, D., Short, C., Duncan, M. J. and Vandelanotte, C. (2015). A meta-meta-analysis of the effect of physical activity on depression and anxiety in non-clinical adult populations. *Health Psychology Review, 9*(3) 366–378.

Richards, J. and Foster, C. (2013). Sport-for-development interventions: Whom do they reach and what is their potential for impact on physical and mental health in low-income countries? *Journal of Physical Activity and Health, 10*(7), 929–931.

Rooney, B., Smalley, K., Larson, J. and Havens, S. (2003). Is knowing enough? Increasing physical activity by wearing a pedometer. *Wisconsin Medical Journal, 102*(4), 31–36.

Schofield, G. and Siefken, K. (2009). Assessment: Walk for Life Policy Vanuatu Government Public Service: Report for the World Health Organization South Pacific Office.

Schulenkorf, N. (2010). The roles and responsibilities of a change agent in sport event development projects. *Sport Management Review, 13*(2), 118–128, doi:10.1016/j.smr.2009.05.001.

Schulenkorf, N. (2012). Sustainable community development through sport and events: A conceptual framework for sport-for-development projects. *Sport Management Review, 15*(1), 1–12, doi:10.1016/j.smr.2011.06.001.

Schulenkorf, N. (2016). The contributions of special events to sport-for-development programs. *Journal of Sport Management, 30*(6), 629–642, doi:10.1123/JSM.2016-0066.

Schulenkorf, N. (2017). Managing sport-for-development: Reflections and outlook. *Sport Management Review, 20*(3), doi:http://dx.doi.org/10.1016/j.smr.2016.11.003.

Schulenkorf, N. and Adair, D. (2014). Sport-for-Development: The Emergence and Growth of a New Genre. In N. Schulenkorf and D. Adair (eds), *Global Sport-for-Development: Critical Perspectives* (pp. 3–11). Basingstoke: Palgrave Macmillan.

Schulenkorf, N. and Schlenker, K. (2017). Leveraging sport events to maximize community benefit in low- and middle-income countries. *Event Management, 21*(2), 217–231, doi:10.3727/152599517X14878772869766.

Schulenkorf, N. and Siefken, K. (in press). Sport-for-development and (partnerships with) the health sector: Reflections from the Pacific Islands. In J. Welty Peachey and C. Green (eds), *Forming Partnerships and Linkages in Sport for Development and Peace: Considerations, Tensions, and Strategies*. Urbana, IL: Sagamore.

Schultz, J. T., Moodie, M., Mavoa, H., Utter, J., Snowdon, W., McCabe, M. P. *et al.* (2011). Experiences and challenges in implementing complex community-based research project: The Pacific obesity prevention in communities project. *Obesity Reviews, 12*, 12–19, doi:10.1111/j.1467-789X.2011.00911.x.

Secretariat for the Pacific Community (SPC). (2011). Pacific in a Crisis, Leaders Declare. From Secretariat of the Pacific Community (SPC). Available at: www.spc.int/hpl/index.php?option=com_contentandtask=viewandid=124andItemid=1.

Secretariat for the Pacific Community (SPC). (2012). Statistics for Development: Statistique pour le Développement. From Secretariat of the Pacific Community (SPC). Available at: www.spc.int/sdp/index.php?option=com_contentandview=articleandid=74%3Apacific-islands-population-tops-10-millionandcatid=1andlang=en.

Sherry, E. and Schulenkorf, N. (2016). League Bilong Laif: Rugby, education and sport-for-development partnerships in Papua New Guinea. *Sport, Education and Society, 21*(4), 513–530, doi:10.1080/13573322.2015.1112780.

Sherry, E., Schulenkorf, N. and Chalip, L. (2015). Managing sport for social change: The state of play. *Sport Management Review, 18*(1), 1–5, doi:10.1016/j.smr.2014.12.001.

Siefken, K., Schofield, G. and Schulenkorf, N. (2011). Formative Investigation and Implementation of Healthy Work Programmes in Tuvalu, Kiribati and Tonga. Report for the World Health Organization. Auckland, New Zealand; 2011.

Siefken, K., Schofield, G. and Schulenkorf, N. (2014). Laefstael Jenses: An investigation of barriers and facilitators for healthy lifestyles of women in an urban Pacific island context. *Journal of Physical Activity and Health, 11*(1), 30–37.

Siefken, K., Schofield, G. and Schulenkorf, N. (2015). Process evaluation of a walking programme delivered through the workplace in the South Pacific island Vanuatu. *Global Health Promotion*, *22*(2), 53–64, doi:10.1177/1757975914539179.

Snowdon, W., Lawrence, M., Schultz, J., Vivili, P., and Swinburn, B. A. (2010). Evidence-informed process to identify policies that will promote a healthy food environment in the Pacific Islands. *Public Health Nutrition*, *13*(6), 886–892.

Snowdon, W., Moodie, M., Schultz, J. and Swinburn, B. (2011). Modelling of potential food policy interventions in Fiji and Tonga and their impacts on noncommunicable disease mortality. *Food Policy*, *36*(5), 597–605, doi:10.1016/j.foodpol.2011.06.001.

Spaaij, R. and Schulenkorf, N. (2014). Cultivating safe space: Lessons for sport-for-development projects and events. *Journal of Sport Management*, *28*(6), 633–645, doi:10.1123/jsm.2013-030.

Steptoe, A. and Butler, N. (1996). Sports participation and emotional wellbeing in adolescents. *The Lancet*, *347*(9018), 1789–1792.

Ströhle, A. (2009). Physical activity, exercise, depression and anxiety disorders. *Journal of Neural Transmission*, *116*(6), 777–784.

Strong, K., Mathers, C., Leeder, S. and Beaglehole, R. (2005). Preventing chronic diseases: How many lives can we save? *The Lancet*, *366*, 1578–1582.

Stubbs, B., Vancampfort, D., Rosenbaum, S., Ward, P. B., Richards, J., Ussher, M. and Schuch, F. B. (2016). Challenges establishing the efficacy of exercise as an antidepressant treatment: A systematic review and meta-analysis of Control group responses in exercise randomised controlled trials. *Sports Medicine*, *46*(5), 699–713, doi:10.1007/s40279-015-0441-5.

Taylor, R., Badcock, J., King, H., Pargeter, K., Zimmet, P., Fred, T. *et al.* (1992). Dietary intake, exercise, obesity and noncommunicable disease in rural and urban populations of three Pacific island countries. *Journal of the American College of Nutrition*, *11*(3), 283–293.

Taylor, R., Davis Lewis, N. and Levy, S. (1989). Societies in transition: mortality patterns in Pacific island populations. *International Journal of Epidemiology*, *18*(3), 634.

Thow, A. M., Heywood, P., Schultz, J., Quested, C., Jan, S. and Colagiuri, S. (2011). Trade and the nutrition transition: Strengthening policy for health in the Pacific. *Ecology of Food and Nutrition*, *50*(1), 18–42.

Thow, A. M., Snowdon, W., Schultz, J. T., Leeder, S., Vivili, P. and Swinburn, B. A. (2011a). The role of policy in improving diets: experiences from the Pacific Obesity Prevention in Communities food policy project. *Obesity Reviews*, *12*(2), 68–74, doi:10.1111/j.1467-789X.2011.00910.x.

Vancampfort, D., Rosenbaum, S., Schuch, F., Ward, P. B., Richards, J., Mugisha, J., … Stubbs, B. (2016). Cardiorespiratory fitness in severe mental illness: A Systematic review and meta-analysis. *Sports Medicine*, 1–10, doi:10.1007/s40279-016-0574-1.

Welty Peachey, J., Borland, J., Lobpries, J., and Cohen, A. (2015). Managing impact: Leveraging sacred spaces and community celebration to maximize social capital at a sport-for-development event. *Sport Management Review*, *18*(1), 86–98, doi:10.1016/j.smr.2014.05.00.

World Health Organization (WHO). (1948). *WHO Definition of Health*. Geneva. Available at: www.who.int/about/definition/en/print.html.

World Health Organization (WHO). (1986). *Ottawa Charter on Health Promotion: International Conference on Health Promotion*. Geneva: WHO. Available at: www.who.int/hpr/NPH/docs/ottawa_charter_hp.pdf.

World Health Organization Western Pacific Regional Office (WPRO), and Secretariat of the Pacific Community (SPC) (2008). Pacific Physical Activity Guidelines for Adults: Framework for accelerating the communication of physical activity guidelines. Manila: WPRO and Secretariat of the Pacific Community (SPC). Available at: www.wpro.who.int/NR/rdonlyres/…/PAG_layout2_22122008.pdf.

World Health Organization (WHO). (2008) *A Framework to Monitor and Evaluate Implementation: Global Strategy on Diet, Physical Activity and Health*. Geneva: WHO.

World Health Organization (WHO). (2010a). *Global Status Report on Noncommunicable Diseases 2010*. Geneva: WHO.

World Health Organization (WHO), Government of South Australia. (2010b). Adelaide Statement on Health in All Policies. Moving towards a shared governance for health and well-being. Report from the International Meeting on Health in All Policies, Adelaide 2010.

World Health Organization (WHO). (2014). *Global Status Report on Noncommunicable Diseases 2014*. Geneva. Available at: http://www.who.int/nmh/publications/ncd-status-report-2014/en/.

World Health Organization (WHO). (2015). *Noncommunicable Diseases: Fact Sheet*. Geneva: WHO. Available at: www.who.int/mediacentre/factsheets/fs355/en/.

World Health Organization (WHO). (2016). Shanghai Declaration on Promoting Health in the 2030 Agenda for Sustainable Development. Available at: www.who.int/healthpromotion/conferences/9gchp/shanghai-declaration/en/.

Zimmet, P., Dowse, G., Finch, C., Serjeantson, S. and King, H. (1990). The epidemiology and natural history of NIDDM: Lessons from the South Pacific. *Diabetes/Metabolism Reviews*, *6*(2), 91–124.

46

Zambia

The SDP ideal?

Davies Banda and Hikabwa Chipande

Introduction

This chapter addresses the impact of neoliberal approaches to sport provision in Zambia with particular focus on community sport provision. The rationale for focusing on community sport is twofold. First and foremost, the emergence of what has become a recognized Sport for Development and Peace (SDP) movement in Zambia occurred through a period of the rampant mushrooming of non-governmental organizations (NGOs) operating as community-based organizations (CBOs). And second, new sport policy trends in Zambia reflect a strong state recognition of SDP NGOs as key actors in community sport provision. The chapter discusses Zambia's immediate postcolonial era and its influence on community sport. It focuses on the social welfarist policies and the government's socialist ideology as having left its legacy on community sport provision. The intention is to provide a nuanced approach in mapping community sport in Zambia by highlighting community welfare halls and centres under a corporatist state.

Therefore, the chapter proceeds by first discussing the formation of Zambia's corporatist state and reasoning behind that approach by the first postcolonial government. The chapter then highlights how community welfare centres and halls were at the core of delivering social welfare policies under corporatism. It shows how employment obtained under such institutional structures served as social security for sportsmen and women during and beyond their active playing careers as elite athletes. The final section discusses the new trends trying to 'exhume' old programmes and resuscitate old welfarist provision of sport and recreation.

Political, social and economic history

SDP literature has utilized development studies to understand and take note of how colonial legacies and development theories in locations like Zambia have shaped the emergence of the SDP movement. Ferguson's (1999) *Expectations of Modernity* exposes the fallacies of development as modernization in Zambia's urban regions (see also McEwan 2009). He postulates how as a modern nation-state, Zambia's burst of industrial development had transformed the nation and given hope to the locals. With modernization seen as a linear path towards economic growth, the industrial transformation in Zambia looked set to enable wealth generated from copper production to trickle down to all segments of society. However, internal and external factors caused Zambia to fall into economic decline, which subsequently destabilized its rich social welfare provision. This section highlights those internal and external causes focusing specifically on postcolonial Zambia.

As a former British colony, Zambia's economy at the time of gaining political independence on 24 October 1964 was under the control of foreign investors. Simutanyi (2006) argues that the postcolonial government's socialist ideological orientation influenced Zambia's nationalist leaders to promote state-led development. Hence, Zambia became a corporatist state in the late sixties as a form of protectionism against economic imperialism. Soon after gaining political freedom, Kenneth Kaunda's United Nations Independence Party (UNIP) adopted a philosophy of Zambian Humanism (Mwaipaya, 1981). Humanism guided Zambia's early reforms as it was used to underpin UNIP's socialist approach for nationalizing the economy as a form of opposition against capitalism and Marxist ideologies. Kaunda, Zambia's pan-Africanist leader, being wary of foreign control of the economy, set up two major corporations namely: Zambia Industrial and Mining Corporation (ZIMCO) and the Industrial Development Corporation (INDECO). Indeed, it was through these major corporations that government would later gain state control and majority participation in the economy. Through boosting the state's control and ownership of key economic sectors, UNIP would in turn achieve its socialist ideals. This was not unique to Zambia; many other independent African states such as Ghana, Tanzania, Kenya and others adopted this ideology that came to be known as African socialism (Chipande 2015).

State control was gained through the Mulungushi Reforms of 1968 and Matero Reforms of 1969 (Potter 1971; Turok 1979), which enabled Kaunda's government to take over 51 per cent shares of foreign-owned companies. Upon gaining economic control, Kaunda and his government formed huge parastatals operating as state-owned corporations (SOCs). These corporations were the cockpit from which UNIP steered Zambia's developmentalist state and its modernization agenda. As Chairman of both INDECO and ZIMCO, President Kaunda not only enjoyed economic control but also ultimate political control after introducing one-party participatory democracy in 1972 (Gertzel *et al.* 1984; Phiri 2001). Such impositions upon the Zambian people enabled UNIP to centralize power, and manage to gain 80 per cent state control of the Zambian economy by 1980 (Simutanyi 2006; Mususa 2010). Furthermore, to gain full compliance of SOCs, state control was reinforced through political appointments of the composition of Boards of Directors and senior public servants to serve on SOC boards. Turok (1981: 424) highlights the manner of political influence cabinet ministers exercised over the governance and operations of SOCs in that 'each [was] managed by a board that [was] subject to the control of a particular minister who appoint[ed] the members as well as the general manager'.

State intervention in economic affairs assured Kaunda and UNIP a firm voice in controlling the country's major industries. By hand-picking the Board of Directors, UNIP was assured the compliance of SOC executives towards the party's wider policy objectives. Therefore, a majority of the sectors of the Zambian economy such as transport, finance, agricultural, tourism, manufacturing and trading were grouped under the control of politically appointed statutory boards. Such political appointments influenced board members acting in a regulatory capacity to do so in accordance to the desires of the state, the appointing officer (see Schmitter 1979; Williamson 1985). Hence, UNIP's socialist objectives were to be realized through the compliance of those appointed to manage or govern the operations of state apparatuses.

Backed by high copper prices on the world market, Zambia's developmentalist state reached its economic zenith during its first 10 years of gaining political freedom (McCulloc *et al.* 2000; Nugent 2004). Revenues generated from SOCs became a major source of investment in social welfare policies and implementation designed to benefit the nation as a whole (Noyoo 2007).

Such investment into social welfare also included development of sport and recreation physical infrastructure, maintenance, supply of sports and recreation equipment and employment of community sport and recreation personnel. However, this high economic growth started to stagnate when the impact in 1975 of the implications of a cyclical down-turn in the world price of copper halted and started to reverse Zambia's economic and social gains (Nugent 2004).

SOC community welfare centres

Then there is the detour I like.
It is to a place framed by memory; it reminds me of my
childhood summer afternoons at the public pool, of picnics and
fountains. It is the town's public pool. Amidst everything else, I
find it a truly beautiful place, an Olympic size pool and pared
down Grecian-like change rooms set on the shorter sides of the
pool, palm trees, fountains and more so, looking like yesterday,
like the Copperbelt I knew then! I have been to the pool on many
mornings, the guards there allowing me to walk around it. I have
not swam in it, though I have wanted to and planned to on many
occasions, because I am not sure it is cleaned. It looks clean and
one morning I found one person swimming in it. The thing is, I
have seen the overgrown tennis courts, rat-infested recreation
halls, the desolate but still beautiful golf course and wondered, can
the swimming pool have escaped their fate, is there something I
am missing?

Extract from Mususa 2014

Mususa's extract above provides familiar memories of early childhood post-independence under corporatism. Many urbanites in Zambia reflect back at a time when their participation in sport and recreation activities as a child was heavily influenced by the corporate social responsibility (CSR) programmes of SOCs. Though this extract focuses specifically on growing up on the Copperbelt and remembering the 'good old days', childhood memories of those in non-mining towns are also closely related to Mususa's cherished 'good old days'. Mususa paints two pictures in her extract. The first is that of a wealth social welfare provision supported by a vibrant copper mining economy. The second is a desolate one, of dilapidated facilities during economic decline. Both these paintings tend to be fresh in the memories of many urbanites in Zambia who witnessed the two periods.

Young people growing up in mining and non-mining urban communities in the late 1960s to mid-1980s were very accustomed to the role of community welfare centres. Youth development schemes, social casework and women's clubs were some of the main targeted activities delivered at community welfare centres (see Lungu and Mulenga 2005). As part of a state prescribed CSR model, SOCs had community and recreation departments responsible for social welfare policies under a corporatist state (Noyoo 2007; Banda 2010). The Zambia Consolidated Copper Mines (ZCCM), the largest SOC affiliated to ZIMCO, had continued the social welfare programmes introduced during the colonial era (Mususa 2012). Chipande (2016) traces these mining township welfare centres to pre-independence times under the colonial government as part of the community fabric of life on the Copperbelt in Northern Rhodesia (now Zambia). However, this time, though not racially structured, the provision of a range of social amenities were characterized by a social class divide (Lungu and Mulenga 2005; Noyoo 2007).

Mususa (2012) outlines the recreational provision as covering sports clubs, libraries, theatres, cinemas and ballroom dancing facilities (see also Central Native Welfare Advisory Committee cited in Chipande 2016). Social class dictated access and eligibility to some societies and facilities. Such class division dictating the eligibility of users to social amenities was based on the employment status of the head of a family employed by the SOC (Banda 2010). The eligibility criteria also influenced the type of sport and recreational activities young people adopted. For example, Banda argues that those whose guardian was classified as senior staff employees could access golf, squash and tennis facilities. Whereas, proletarian sports such as boxing and football previously offered to Africans during the colonial era continued as part of the welfare system among the working class in mining residential communities. Similarly, other SOCs located in non-mining towns tried to emulate the ZCCM's provision of sport and recreation. For example, in Kafue, two locally based SOCs, Nitrogen Chemicals of Zambia (NCZ) and Kafue Textiles of Zambia (KTZ), supported the provision of social welfare in Kafue which boasted of successful sporting teams in football, netball, volleyball and basketball.

Local government community welfare halls

Under local authority provision, community welfare halls were the hub of recreation, leisure and sporting facilities in urban and rural areas. Community welfare halls were popular places for youths to access organized community sport and other recreational activities. These activities comprised sports, boy scouts and girl guides, women's crafts, cookery and literacy classes for adults, libraries, outside or open air cinemas, and children or toddler's playgrounds. At local government level, local authority budgets covered the maintenance of community welfare halls, employment of delivery staff as well as financing of the provision of sport and recreation activities. Sustaining such state-led wider welfare provision later proved to be unsustainable despite the developmentalist state's redistribution of resources to support it. For example, in Livingstone, a non-mining, tourist town, the Maramba and Dambwa community welfare halls were places where youths participated in organized community sport and accessed coaching sessions. Positioned as community resources to meet wider social welfare needs, community welfare halls as well as SOC welfare centres hosted public health workshops, reproductive sexual health talks, under-five children's health programmes, nurseries and pre-schools (personal communication).

However, despite enjoying a buoyant economy soon after political independence (Nugent 2004; Situmbeko and Zulu 2004), disparities in provision between rural and urban areas were evident. Populations based in urban areas benefited from these facilities, programmes and access to competitive structures of sport. Rural areas were and have continued to be underserved and deprived of the economic and social benefits that urban areas have experienced. We will return to this urban versus rural skewed distribution when we address the geographical limitation of SDP NGOs.

Privatization and the demise of social welfare provision officers

Local scholars (Situmbeko and Zulu 2004; Lungu and Mulenga 2005: Simutanyi 2006; Noyoo 2007) have critiqued the demise of SOCs as emanating from both internal and external factors. It has been argued that a combination of internal decisions and external forces caused the Zambian economy to stagnate and later plunge into a steep decline as SOCs' revenue collection plummeted. The historical nationalization of the economy is fundamental to the internal causes of the economic downfall. It is argued that nationalization shielded SOCs from both internal and external competition having created a monopolistic environment which stifled innovation. It is further argued that such monopolistic conditions bred excessive complacency within various levels of management. Other internal causes indicate that corruption practices within SOCs had grown rampantly (Noyoo 2008) leading to inefficiencies in the provision of services.

Despite the operational inefficiencies of SOCs, Kaunda's government persistently continued to inject state subsidies into these firms in order to prolong their lifespan. Meanwhile, externally orchestrated neoliberal structural adjustment policies demanded otherwise, asking the state to cease such measures (Simutanyi 1996). Other external measures by the International Monetary Fund (IMF) included removal of food subsidies on agricultural products and public reforms which demanded downsizing of the public sector workforce and services to reduce state expenditure. Kaunda's socialist stance caused him to discontinue the IMF austerity measures soon after initial implementation was accompanied by civil arrest in 1986.

As the economic crisis deepened, and growing opposition against his policies, Kaunda succumbed to the call for constitutional review and returned to plural politics in 1990 (Phiri 2006). In 1991, after a landslide victory, the Movement for Multiparty Democracy (MMD) formed the next government. The MMD government discontinued Kaunda's welfarist policies, removed food subsidies and price controls, and embarked on an aggressive privatization of the economy. The state ceased to be the central actor in economic investment in a new democratic political dispensation (Lungu 2008). Under the MMD's political rule, its capitalist approaches had reduced the autonomy and discretion of government bureaucracies common under UNIP. In sport, notable ramifications of structural adjustment reforms started to manifest after privatization of SOCs. Though some major fissures pertaining to community sport delivery had already started to exhibit between 1983 and 1991, the straw that broke the camel's back was the privatization of SOCs by the MMD government. Before then, Kaunda's UNIP was still urging SOCs to continue their community welfare programmes despite the IMF demands to reconsider the government's funding of social welfare policies:

> the party and its government should continue to encourage sport and recreation especially among young people in order to get them off the streets […] parastatals and other working places should endeavour to provide these recreational facilities
>
> *Kaunda's speech at Third National Convention 1984*

Unfortunately, the privatization and liquidations of SOCs and implementation of public sector reforms meant a loss of the workforce stationed at community welfare centres and halls. Recreational facilities too, as painted in Mususa's extract, were left to dilapidate. Austerity measures in both central and local government spending and the privatization of loss-making SOCs resulted in a huge loss of jobs between 1993 and 1995. SOCs and public sector workforce redundancies (Simutanyi 1996; Noyoo 2007) resulted in severe implications on community sport provision (Banda 2010).

Implications of SAP on workforce redundancies and community sport provision

Traditionally, SOCs as well as local authorities, had developed practices of securing employment for their current or former sportsmen and women as community welfare officers. Only football players at the time within SOCs and athletes playing for the uniformed security wings (Banda 2010) enjoyed professional elite athlete status (see Chipande 2010; 2016 for football professionalism). Therefore, a majority of sportsmen and women without academic qualification for a desk job were employed within departments of community welfare. This formed their social security beyond their active competitive sports careers. But more importantly after their sporting careers, was the passing of knowledge and experience to young people:

> Footballers and sportsmen and women in general were taken care of by companies. We offered them jobs within welfare departments and they gave back to the community through coaching and mentoring.
>
> *Interview, Senior Sports Council Administrator, 3 Sept 2008*

The loss of jobs due to privatization demonstrates the impact that neoliberal approaches have had on community sport provision in Zambia. Since these developments contributed to the emergence of the SDP movement in Zambia, it reveals the loss of quality provision and magnitude that cannot be fulfilled by SDP NGOs. Pitcher (2012) reports that 61,000 jobs were lost in the formal sector between 1991 and 2000. Among those job losses were the vulnerable community sport and recreation jobs as the new foreign investors placed profit motives above social welfare programmes of former SOCs as articulated by a National Sports Council of Zambia (NSCZ) chairperson:

> The pendulum has kind of shifted, because the [new investors in the] mines after privatization … started saying we have come here not to be a charity but to make profits. So they ignored helping for about 15 years or so.
>
> *Personal interview, 3 Sept 2011*

Such profit motives consequently resulted in the closure of social welfare departments responsible for sport and recreation. Similarly, local authorities ceased their provision leaving behind gaps in public service provision country-wide. Meanwhile, the MMD's neoliberal approaches, compounded by the pluralist political environment, welcomed non-state actors as development partners helping fill up the gaps left behind by state inefficiencies in education and health.

However, non-state sports actors similar to those welcomed within the health and education sector were prohibited to operate within the sport policy environment. Despite the gaps in provision after the demise of SOCs, the government's bureaucratic tendencies restricted provision of sports services only to state actors and NSCZ affiliated members (see Lindsey *et al.* 2017). Contrary to the pluralistic and liberalized environment, sport sector state officials fell short of grasping the public demand for community sport and the role that emerging CBOs could play. Rather, the resentment of non-state actors were politically motivated, seen as competitors having caused the diversion of international donors' funds from the state towards two emerging SDP NGOs. Politically, the recognition of sport as a tool for addressing non-sporting outcomes among youths as advocated for in the 1984 National Convention Report were well known. Further emphasis regarding the power of sport as a tool for achieving non-sporting outcomes was demonstrated nationwide in 1993. This was by way of a televised HIV/AIDS prevention advertisement promoting condom usage by Kalusha Bwalya, Zambia's most celebrated football icon. Still, mixing sport and public health seemed incompatible for some government sports sector officials that they failed to appreciate and welcome the SDP movement.

Indeed, it was not until 1999, when restrictions on registration of the first two Indigenous SDP NGOs, Sport in Action (SIA) and EduSport Foundation were formally recognized (Mwaanga and Mwansa 2014). At the time of their formation the two SDP NGOs had forged partnerships with mainstream development partners addressing non-sporting outcomes. Their collaborative work with health-based NGOs and education institutions gave the two organizations both local and international recognition as part of the development sector NGOs. As local legitimization burgeoned, the community practices of both organizations in relation to sport started to address the gap created by the demise of community welfare sports programmes. For example, both SDP NGOs developed curriculums that addressed both sporting and non-sporting outcomes (Coalter 2007). Their focus on life skills training programmes, which previously were delivered via community welfare halls gave these Indigenous organizations impetus for growth. SDP NGOs were responding to community needs, which the local populace longed for since the demise of community sport provision under a corporatist state.

New trends: SDP NGOs and community sport delivery

We have demonstrated above through our post-independence analysis of how community sport provision was funded from local resources – mainly copper production. Still today, since their inception, SDP NGOs are heavily dependent on foreign resources. Development practices within the international donor community were those favouring partnerships with CBOs over state actors (Hulme and Edwards 1997). Hence, both EduSport and SIA received their financial support directly from international cooperating partners. Therefore, contrary to local resources and the central planning of the developmentalist state aimed at rectifying the evils of colonialism, SDP NGOs face limitations in their agency. Southern agency within SDP initiatives (Lindsey et al. 2017) has been questioned and at times found to be restrained due to the sector's over-dependency on foreign resources. Black (2010: 124) has warned of the dangers of 'reinforcing global hierarchies and limiting the imaginative possibilities for change'. This is not uncommon to Zambia where official development agencies are the main funders of SDP initiatives since inception. These being: the Norwegian Agency for Development Cooperation (NORAD) through Norwegian Olympic Committee and Confederation of Sports (NIF); the Department of International Development (DFID) through UK Sport; the Swedish International Development Cooperation through Save the Children; and UNICEF. Within the last decade, seven higher education institutions from the UK known as the Wallace Group, with offspring charities, have contributed to community sport in Zambia.

The preponderance of international agencies supporting the SDP movement in Zambia presents key challenges similar to those in mainstream international development. These challenges have included top-down strategic relationships (Black 2010); governance mainly dominated by higher-income countries (Levermore 2009); fragmentation and lack of integration into local area policy networks (Lindsey and Banda 2011); hegemonic relations lacking genuine dialogue (Darnell 2007); and dominance of external knowledge (development discourses) by western academics depicted as 'colonial residue' (Hayhurst 2009; Darnell and Hayhurst 2011; Hasselgård and Straume 2015). These issues of hegemony in SDP have proven to be problematic due to the top-down nature of the relationship between funders in the global North and recipients in the global South. Such that claims regarding the authenticity of empowerment of local organizations and ownership of programmes by locals tend to be difficult to substantiate as long as local organizations look up to their donors for resources. The donor and recipient relationship has contributed to the stifling of local agency or Southern agency (Fokwang 2009) for fear of alienating funds.

SDP legitimization, recognition and policy alignment

In the past, SDP projects have exhibited very weak links to meeting localized strategic policy outcomes such as the Poverty Reduction Strategic Plans (PRSP). Hence, some scholars (Darnell 2007; Hayhurst 2009; Lindsey and Banda 2011) have questioned the motives behind such programmes which depicted less local input and alignment to local policy outcomes. Previous research findings revealed that there was limited involvement of SDP NGOs in relevant national policies and communication between NGOs and government agencies in Zambia (Lindsey and Banda 2011). However, recent developments particularly coming from active voices within the Ministry for Sport, Youth and Child Development (MSYCD) suggest that there is a much wider recognition among government agencies regarding the role played by SDP NGOs.

While it was policy rhetoric in the past, practical integration of SDP activities into official government initiatives has improved over time. These involve consultative engagements in project planning and practical delivery. Such collaboration between SDP NGOs and government agencies has become a common feature of Zambian community sport. For example, the Director of Sport reiterated that:

> The government has provided an enabling environment for SDP NGOs to operate … and acknowledges that SDP provide vital opportunities for vulnerable young people and advance the participation of women in sport, particularly community sport.

This collaborative action signifies development in cordial relations within a community sport policy space that was before antagonistic between quasi-government or government agencies and SDP NGOs. Recent developments show clear alignment between government's community sport objectives and recognition of community actors to ensure substantial results and sustainability of programmes. The developments in sport policy are attributed to stability of two office bearers within the MYSCD who have had long terms of office free of reshuffles or transfers:

> The Permanent Secretary and I have had long spells in office and that has been vital for policy continuity and development of initiatives for sport. Though nothing much from government resources other than policy enactments has been done for sport.
>
> *Director of Sport, personal communication, 1 December 2016*

The sport policy space, particularly, in relation to SDP as attested by the Director of Sport, has evidenced progressive developments in favour of SDP NGOs and wider grassroots sport. In the past, government has lacked resources to support SDP NGOs as stated above. Recently, central government procured sports equipment specifically to support the delivery of community sport. SDP NGOs, SIA in particular, have been targeted as the main programme deliverer of the new scheme. The delivery format of the new scheme resonates with this chapter's historical coverage of community sport under a corporatist state. The MSYCD aims to rejuvenate sports within community welfare halls as suggested by the Director of Sport:

> The ministry has a procurement of sports equipment aimed at rehabilitating community welfare halls. The equipment is to be delivered throughout all constituents country-wide
>
> *Director of Sport, personal communication, 1 December 2016*

This recent development is indicative of government intention to play an active role in community sport. It also demonstrates a realization by both state actors and non-state actors of the failures of a fragmented approach to community sports delivery. Community welfare halls and school sports fields targeted for dual usage will play a key role in resource mobilization. However, unlike welfare halls, community sports fields have disappeared as local authorities have failed to protect the fields from councillors and political cadres selling them off for housing projects, churches and bars.

In regards to the recognition of SDP NGOs' work in communities, the impact of the Wallace Group composed of seven UK universities cannot be neglected. Despite some shortcomings, SIA and EduSport have earned legitimation in many schools and communities as a result of the Wallace Group partnership. Indeed, it is from the deployment of peer leaders and student volunteers into schools that the SDP movement in Zambia has gained government recognition. The partnership commonly known as IDEALS (International Development through Excellence and Leadership in Sport) has continued since its launch in 2006 supported by UK Sport. A combination of resources comprising local peer leaders (see Nicholls 2009), foreign student volunteer coaches, a variety of equipment, and access to schools or community facilities has enhanced the positive profile of the two organizations.

However, while IDEALS has helped legitimize the role of both SIA and EduSport, it has reinforced the geographical limitation of the two NGOs. The IDEALS programme mainly operated in the capital city Lusaka and its surrounding areas. Beyond the two largest local SDP NGOs, a plethora of CBOs exist at grassroots level serving community sport's needs. They include both local and foreign-based SDP organizations under an umbrella network: Sport for Social Change (SSCN). These too are concentrated in urban areas. However, apart from the two main local NGOs, other SDP agencies have not had much influence within government policy circles. This may be deliberate on the side of government as some local and foreign SDP NGOs have not withstood the test of time compared to SIA and EduSport. Both organizations have shown consistency in both leadership and programming.

Conclusion

We have shown how socialist ideologies influenced the planning, resourcing and deployment of welfare officers to fulfil UNIP's social welfare policies. In order to understand SDP in Zambia, one needs to understand the political, economic and social history of Zambia as a corporatist state. Despite the negative legacies of Kaunda's nationalization policies and his authoritarian rule, state intervention was seen as inevitable. It was seen as a solution to rectify colonial legacies and plan for development that would trickle down to all citizens. People still regard Kaunda's social welfare programme, in particular community welfare centres and halls, as vital for developing life skills and communal life. The state played a key role in early national development as it facilitated the building of infrastructure and supported establishment of community-level programmes.

As privatization of the economy and public sector reforms were being implemented, embracing these actions was not a panacea to Zambia's problems. Had the human development approach been the underlying development paradigm, then one would have expected preservation of the positive legacies of a corporatist state during the privatization negotiations of SOCs. The chapter identified the ZCCM as a jewel in Zambia's crown and that this SOC acted as a model to others in relation to its social welfare provision. Preserving some of the positive legacies of this social welfare policy such as community welfare halls and centres could have sustained the fabric of communal life, inclusive of sport and recreation. However, sport being a low priority for a nation undergoing steep economic decline, investors took advantage of the desperate economy. Privatization destabilized the model of community sport as the workforce that delivered social welfare were left vulnerable to redundancies since sport did not rank high on government priorities.

The new government initiatives look like 'new wine in old skins' approach. The new being the recognition of sport as a development tool by government coupled by new policy enactments confirming official government stance. Will the old infrastructure withstand the demands and be fit for purpose? Having been left to dilapidate, will these old facilities serve the community sport demands of a population growing at 3.2 per cent annually (WPR 2017)? There are, however, some positives from this approach as it seems to indicate that both parties, SDP NGOs and the MSYCD, have taken heed of SDP NGOs' geographical limitation. Rural areas are likely to benefit since government already has infrastructure, schools or community facilities. Despite the wasted opportunities during decades of antagonistic relationships, SDP NGOs and government are stronger together. The dawning of this realization will benefit the SDP movement as it consolidates it efforts at grassroots level and impacts sports in general across the nation.

References

Banda, D. (2010). Zambia: Government's role in colonial and modern times. *International Journal of Sport Policy, 2*(2), 237–252.

Black, D. R. (2010). The ambiguities of development: Implications for development through sport. *Sport in Society, 13*(1), 121–129.

Chipande, H. D. (2010). *Football in Zambia: Introduction and Development of Competitive Football in Zambia (1930–1969)*. Saarbrücken, Germany: VDM Verlag Dr Müller.

Chipande, H. D. (2015). Chipolopolo: A Political and Social History of Football (soccer) in Zambia 1940s – 1994. Unpublished PhD Thesis, Michigan State University.

Chipande, H. D. (2016). Mining for goals: Football and social change on the Zambian Copperbelt, 1940s–1960s. *Radical History Review, 125*: 55–73.

Coalter, F. (2007). *A Wider Role for Sport: Who's Keeping the Score?* London: Routledge.

Darnell, S. C. (2007). Playing with race: Right to play and the production of whiteness in 'development through sport'. *Sport in Society, 10*(4), 560–579.

Darnell, S. C. and Hayhurst, L. M. C. (2011). Sport for decolonization: Exploring a new praxis of sport for development. *Progress in Development Studies, 11*(3), 183–96.

Ferguson, J. (1999). *Expectations of Modernity. Myths and Meanings of Life on the Zambian Copperbelt*. Berkeley, CA: University of California Press.

Fokwang, J. (2009). Southern perspectives on sport in development: A case study of football in Bamenda, Cameroon. In R. Levermore and A. Beacom (eds), *Sport and International Development*. Basingstoke: Palgrave Macmillan.

Gertzel, C., Baylies, C. and Szeftel, M. (1984) *The Dynamics of the One-Party State in Zambia*. Manchester: Manchester University Press.

Hasselgård, A. and Straume, S. (2015). Sport for development and peace policy discourse and local practice: Norwegian sport for development and peace to Zimbabwe. *International Journal of Sport Policy and Politics, 7*(1), 87–103.

Hayhurst, L. (2009). The power to shape policy: Charting sport for development and peace policy discourses. *International Journal of Sports Policy and Politics, 1*(2), 203–227.

Hulme, D. and Edwards, M. (1997). NGOs, states and donors: An overview. *In* D. Hulme and M. Edwards (eds), *NGOs, States and Donors: Too Close for Comfort?* Basingstoke: MacMillan.

Lungu, J. (2008). Socio-economic change and natural resource exploitation: A case study of the Zambian copper mining industry. *Development Southern Africa, 25*(5), 543–560.

Lungu, J. and Mulenga, C. (2005). *Corporate Social Responsibility Practices in the Extractive Industries in Zambia*. Ndola: Mission Press.

Lindsey, I. and Banda, D. (2011). Sport and the Fight against HIV/AIDS in Zambia: A 'partnership' approach? *International Review of Sociology of Sport, 46*(1), 90–107.

Lindsey, I., Kay, T., Jeanes, R. and Banda, D. (2017), *Localizing Global Sport for Development*. Manchester: Manchester University Press.

McCulloch, N., Baulch, B. and Cherel-Robson, M. (2000). *Globalisation, Poverty and Inequality in Zambia during the 1990*. Brighton: Institute of Development Studies, University of Sussex, November 2000.

McEwan, C. (2009). *Postcolonialism and Development*. London: Routledge.

Mususa, P. (2010). 'Getting by': Life on the Copperbelt after the privatisation of the Zambia Consolidated Copper Mines. *Social Dynamics, 36*: 380–394.

Mususa, P. (2012) Mining, welfare and urbanisation: The wavering urban character of Zambia's Copperbelt. *Journal of Contemporary African Studies, 30*: 571–587.

Mususa, P. N. (2014). There used to be order: Life on the Copperbelt after the privatisation of the Zambia Consolidated Copper Mines. Unpublished PhD Thesis. University of Cape Town.

Mwaanga, O. and Mwansa, K. (2014). Indigenous discourses in sport for development and peace: A case study of the Ubuntu cultural philosophy in EduSport Foundation, Zambia. In N. Schulenkorf and D. Adair (eds), *Global Sport-for-development: Critical Perspectives.* Basingstoke: Palgrave Macmillan. 115–129.

Mwaipaya, P. (1981). *African Humanism and National Development. A Critical Analysis of Fundamental Theoretical Principles of Zambia Humanism.* Washington, DC: University Press of America Inc.

Nicholls, S. (2009). On the backs of peer educators: Using theory to interrogate the role of young people in the field of sport-for-development. In R. Levermore and A. Beacom (eds), *Sport and International Development.* Basingstoke: Macmillan, pp. 156–175.

Noyoo, N. (2007). Corporate Social Responsibility and Social Policy in Zambia. Presented at the Conference on Business, Social Policy and Corporate Political Influence in Developing Countries, 12–13 November 2007. Geneva.

Noyoo, N. (2008). *Social Policy and Human Development in Zambia.* Lusaka: UNZA Press.

Nugent, P. (2004) *Africa since Independence.* Basingstoke: Palgrave MacMillan.

Phiri, B. J. (2001) Colonial legacy and the role of society in the creation and demise of autocracy in Zambia, 1964–1991. *Nordic Journal of African Studies, 10*(2), 224–244.

Phiri, B. (2006). *A Political History of Zambia: From the Colonial Period to the 3rd Republic.* Trenton, NJ: Africa World Press.

Pitcher, A. (2012). *Party Politics and Economic Reform in Africa's Democracies.* New York: Cambridge University Press.

Potter, J. G. (1971). The 51 per cent nationalisation of the Zambian Copper Mines. In M. L. O. Faber and J. G. Potter (eds), *Towards Economic Independence: Papers on the Nationalisation of the Copper Industry in Zambia.* London: Cambridge University Press.

Schmitter, P. (1979). Still the century of corporatism. In P. Schmitter. and G. Lehmbruch (eds), *Trends Toward Corporatist Intermediation.* Beverly Hills, CA: SAGE.

Simutanyi, N. (1996) The politics of structural adjustment in Zambia. *Third World Quarterly, 17*(4), 825–839.

Simutanyi, N. (2006). Neo-Liberalism and the Relevance of Marxism to Africa: The Case of Zambia. Paper presented to the 3rd International Conference on 'The Works of Karl Marx and the Challenges of the 21st Century', Havana, Cuba, 3–6 May 2006.

Situmbeko, L. C. and Zulu, J. J. (2004). *Zambia: Condemned to Debt: How the IMF and World Bank have Undermined Development.* London: World Development Movement.

Turok, B. (1979). *Development in Zambia: a Reader.* London: Zed Books.

Turok, B. (1981). Control in the parastatal sector of Zambia. *The Journal of Modern African Studies, 19*(3), 421–445.

Williamson, P. (1985). *Varieties of Corporatism.* Cambridge: Cambridge University Press.

World Population Review. (2017). Zambia Population 2017'. Available at: http://worldpopulationreview.com/countries/zambia-population/ (accessed 27 February 2017).

Index

Note: Page numbers in *italics* refer to figures and in **bold** to tables.

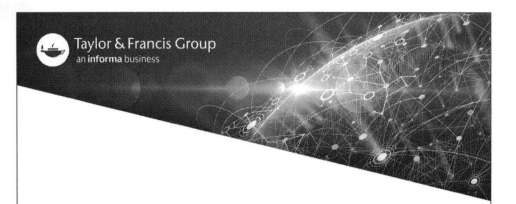